## Table B.5      *t* **Distribution***

The cumulative *t* distribution is defined by

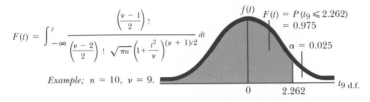

$$F(t) = \int_{-\infty}^{t} \frac{\left(\frac{\nu - 1}{2}\right)!}{\left(\frac{\nu - 2}{2}\right)! \; \sqrt{\pi n} \left(1 + \frac{t^2}{\nu}\right)^{(\nu + 1)/2}} \, dt$$

$F(t) = P(t_9 \leqslant 2.262)$
$= 0.975$

$\alpha = 0.025$

*Example; n = 10, ν = 9.*

$t_9$ d.f.

0    2.262

| F(t) | .75 | .90 | .95 | .975 | .99 | .995 | .9995 |
|---|---|---|---|---|---|---|---|
| ν (α) | (.25) | (.10) | (.05) | (.025) | (.01) | (.005) | (.0005) |
| 1 | 1.000 | 3.078 | 6.314 | 12.706 | 31.821 | 63.657 | 636.619 |
| 2 | .816 | 1.886 | 2.920 | 4.303 | 6.965 | 9.925 | 31.598 |
| 3 | .765 | 1.638 | 2.353 | 3.182 | 4.541 | 5.841 | 12.941 |
| 4 | .741 | 1.533 | 2.132 | 2.776 | 3.747 | 4.604 | 8.610 |
| 5 | .727 | 1.476 | 2.015 | 2.571 | 3.365 | 4.032 | 6.859 |
| 6 | .718 | 1.440 | 1.943 | 2.447 | 3.143 | 3.707 | 5.959 |
| 7 | .711 | 1.415 | 1.895 | 2.365 | 2.998 | 3.499 | 5.405 |
| 8 | .706 | 1.397 | 1.860 | 2.306 | 2.896 | 3.355 | 5.041 |
| 9 | .703 | 1.383 | 1.833 | 2.262 | 2.821 | 3.250 | 4.781 |
| 10 | .700 | 1.372 | 1.812 | 2.228 | 2.764 | 3.169 | 4.587 |
| 11 | .697 | 1.363 | 1.796 | 2.201 | 2.718 | 3.106 | 4.437 |
| 12 | .695 | 1.356 | 1.782 | 2.179 | 2.681 | 3.055 | 4.318 |
| 13 | .694 | 1.350 | 1.771 | 2.160 | 2.650 | 3.012 | 4.221 |
| 14 | .692 | 1.345 | 1.761 | 2.145 | 2.624 | 2.977 | 4.140 |
| 15 | .691 | 1.341 | 1.753 | 2.131 | 2.602 | 2.947 | 4.073 |
| 16 | .690 | 1.337 | 1.746 | 2.120 | 2.583 | 2.921 | 4.015 |
| 17 | .689 | 1.333 | 1.740 | 2.110 | 2.567 | 2.898 | 3.965 |
| 18 | .688 | 1.330 | 1.734 | 2.101 | 2.552 | 2.878 | 3.922 |
| 19 | .688 | 1.328 | 1.729 | 2.093 | 2.539 | 2.861 | 3.883 |
| 20 | .687 | 1.325 | 1.725 | 2.086 | 2.528 | 2.845 | 3.850 |
| 21 | .686 | 1.323 | 1.721 | 2.080 | 2.518 | 2.831 | 3.819 |
| 22 | .686 | 1.321 | 1.717 | 2.074 | 2.508 | 2.819 | 3.792 |
| 23 | .685 | 1.319 | 1.714 | 2.069 | 2.500 | 2.807 | 3.767 |
| 24 | .685 | 1.318 | 1.711 | 2.064 | 2.492 | 2.797 | 3.745 |
| 25 | .684 | 1.316 | 1.708 | 2.060 | 2.485 | 2.787 | 3.725 |
| 26 | .684 | 1.315 | 1.706 | 2.056 | 2.479 | 2.779 | 3.707 |
| 27 | .684 | 1.314 | 1.703 | 2.052 | 2.473 | 2.771 | 3.690 |
| 28 | .683 | 1.313 | 1.701 | 2.048 | 2.467 | 2.763 | 3.674 |
| 29 | .683 | 1.311 | 1.699 | 2.045 | 2.462 | 2.756 | 3.659 |
| 30 | .683 | 1.310 | 1.697 | 2.042 | 2.457 | 2.750 | 3.646 |
| 40 | .681 | 1.303 | 1.684 | 2.021 | 2.423 | 2.704 | 3.551 |
| 60 | .679 | 1.296 | 1.671 | 2.000 | 2.390 | 2.660 | 3.460 |
| 120 | .677 | 1.289 | 1.658 | 1.980 | 2.358 | 2.617 | 3.373 |
| ∞(z_α) | .674 | 1.282 | 1.645 | 1.960 | 2.326 | 2.576 | 3.291 |

* This table is abridged from the "Statistical Tables" of R. A. Fisher and Frank Yates published by Oliver & Boyd, Ltd., Edinburgh and London, 1938. It is here published with the kind permission of the authors and their publishers.

# BUSINESS AND ECONOMICS STATISTICS

## WITH COMPUTER APPLICATIONS

# WILLIAM E. BECKER
# DONALD L. HARNETT

Indiana University

# BUSINESS AND ECONOMICS STATISTICS
## WITH COMPUTER APPLICATIONS

**ADDISON-WESLEY PUBLISHING COMPANY**
Reading, Massachusetts • Menlo Park, California • Don Mills, Ontario
Wokingham, England • Amsterdam • Sydney • Singapore • Tokyo • Madrid
Bogotá • Santiago • San Juan

Sponsoring Editor: *Cindy Johnson*
Manufacturing Supervisor: *Hugh Crawford*
Copy Editor: *Helen Greenberg*
Cover concept: *William Becker* and *Donald Harnett*
Text Designer: *Rosedesign Associates*
Art Coordinator: *Marcia Strykowski*
Illustrator: *Textbook Art Associates*

**Library of Congress Cataloging in Publication Data**

Becker, William E.
    Business and economics statistics with computer applications.
    1. Statistics.   2. Commercial statistics.
I. Harnett, Donald L.   II. Title.
HA29.B3837 1987        519.5′024658        85-9025
ISBN 0-201-10956-5

To our families

# PREFACE

The primary objective of this book is to provide students with an introductory one-semester text that will assist them in applying statistical analysis to real-world business and economics problems. Since easy-to-use statistical computer packages are now readily available, our examples and case studies emphasize the use of micro or mainframe computers to perform cumbersome calculations. Computational procedures are presented and demonstrated only to the extent they assist students in understanding the statistical principles involved in the analysis.

No mathematical background beyond basic algebra is assumed for this text. It is our view that sophisticated and usable statistical analytical skills can be taught and learned without burdening the student with difficult and involved formulas. For computational purposes, we have been fortunate to have special access to the statistical package, Microstat. This package is a menu-driven program which has sold over 3000 copies and has been adopted by numerous large companies and government agencies. While most of the computer displays in this book were generated by Microstat, our approach to the use of computers in statistics remains generic. No prior exposure to or familiarity with any computer package is required.

Real-world problem-solving examples are used throughout the book. An attempt was made to associate these problems with actual situations described in publications (such as *Business Week,* the *Wall Street Journal,* and the *Journal of Economic Literature*), as well as popular press publications (such as *Newsweek* and *Time*). Since all the quantitative measures required for specific forms of statistical analysis are not typically provided in such publications, missing information is assumed as needed for pedagogical purposes. Short cases containing all the information for the analysis to be demonstrated introduce each major section. These cases typically end with specific action required on the part of the decision maker. Whenever it is appropriate, students are shown how to make their decisions on the basis of probability considerations—e.g., *p*-values are emphasized in hypothesis testing.

In addition to the case studies, all thirteen chapters contain glossaries, numerical graphical displays, and worked examples. Appendix A provides three data sets, using actual numerical values from business and economic data. For student assignments there are 575 exercises contained within the thirteen chapters. Detailed answers to the even-numbered exercises are provided in the back of the book. A student problem guide provides additional confidence-building exam type questions and several open-ended problems for each chapter. Also available to adopters are a solutions manual, transparency masters, and a test bank with over 450 multiple choice questions.

## FOR THE READER

Our intent has been to prepare a readable statistics text written in a nontechnical manner. Emphasis is on real-world applications with special attention to the use of the computer in statistics.

Before beginning Chapter 1, the reader might turn to the two appendixes and the Answer Section. Appendix A contains the following three data sets:

A.1 Cross-sectional data on Sales, Profits, Margins, and Performance for 294 companies (from *Business Week,* used by permission).

A.2 Time series data for 1948–1984 on the Consumer Price Index, Industrial Production, Unemployment Rates, Business Failures, and New Business Incorporation.

A.3 Income and Assets for Workingman's Federal Savings and Loan Association, Bloomington, Indiana (used by permission).

Appendix B contains eight statistical tables whose use is described throughout this text. Because Table B.4 and B.5 are frequently referenced, these two tables are reproduced on the end papers at the beginning of the book. The Answer Section contains answers to the even-numbered exercises in each chapter.

Each chapter begins with several examples of business and economics problems that can be solved with the techniques to be demonstrated in the chapter. Many of these examples are drawn from the authors' consulting experience. Case studies are used to introduce new topics within a chapter. These case studies describe an actual or hypothetical situation which is then used to show various forms of statistical analysis and decision making. Periodically **EXAMPLES** are used to illustrate a particular concept or a formula. **WORKED EXAMPLES** present a typical problem (such as might appear on an exam) and are followed by a concise **ANSWER** to that problem.

The exercises presented throughout each chapter are designed to represent a variety of realistic situations. Problems covering topics from an entire chapter (rather than a specific section) are called "Chapter Exercises." Whenever possible, an exercise is identified by the application it represents, using the following labels:

| | | | |
|---|---|---|---|
| ACT | Accounting | MFG | Manufacturing |
| ADM | Administration | MKT | Marketing |
| ECN | Economics | OPS | Operations |
| FIN | Finance | PUB | Public Service |
| LAW | Law | REL | Real Estate |

The reader is encouraged to work as many of the exercises as possible to aid the learning process.

## COMPUTER USE IN STATISTICS

Computers play an increasingly important role in almost all phases of statistical analysis. The modern manager typically has easy access to a computer and to one or more statistical packages. Knowledge of the use of statistical tools has become a vital asset in many decision-making situations requiring work with large data sets. There are many different statistical packages available for microcomputers as well as mainframes. Some of the most widely used packages include the following:

| | |
|---|---|
| BMD | Biomedical Package |
| MINITAB | |
| MICROSTAT | (Student version available with this text) |
| SAS | Statistical Analysis System |
| SPSS | Statistical Package for the Social Sciences |

While we use only Microstat and SPSS printouts to demonstrate the use of computers in statistics, most of the statistics packages now available can be used with this book. To illustrate the versatility and ease in use of menu-driven statistical package for microcomputers, we offer the following main menu display from the student version of Microstat.

```
A. DATA MANAGEMENT SUBSYSTEM    H. REGRESSION ANALYSIS
B. DESCRIPTIVE STATISTICS       I. NONPARAMETRIC STATISTICS
C. FREQUENCY DISTRIBUTIONS      J. CROSSTAB/CHI-SQUARE TESTS
D. HYPOTHESIS TESTS: MEAN       K. PROBABILITY DISTRIBUTIONS
E. ANALYSIS OF VARIANCE         L. HYPOTHESIS TEST: PROPORTION
F. SCATTERPLOT                  M. [Help]
G. CORRELATION MATRIX           N. [Terminate]
```

This menu gives the initial options available to the user. For example, entering the letter A at the computer keyboard brings up another menu that is used to enter data and perform arithmetic operations; entering a B brings up a menu that is used to calculate the measures described in Chapter 3 of this book, such as averages and standard deviations. The use of these menus is demonstrated in the student workbook by J. B. Orris accompanying this text. A student version of the Microstat floppy disk is available from Addison-Wesley at a very attractive price. Site licenses are also available from Addison-Wesley for this student version.

# ACKNOWLEDGMENTS

In the development of this book many people have assisted us. We are indebted to the Indiana University students who made comments and suggestions on our early drafts. Special thanks are due several of these students, in particular: Joe Ackerman, Susan Barr, Chryso Kyvernitou, Jim Nenni, Selim Oztalay, Jon Reichert, Kristine Schneider, and Sue Tornlison. The helpful suggestions of the following professors who reviewed our manuscript are also gratefully acknowledged: John Brode, University of Lowell; Roger Gledhill, Eastern Michigan University; Michael Hand, Willamette University; Virginia Knight, Duke University; Ronald Koot, Penn State University; Burt Madden, University of Arkansas; Carol Stamm, Western Michigan University; Jim Sullivan, Bowling Green State University; and Fike Zahroon, Moorhead State University.

We are grateful to the Literary Executor of the late Sir Ronald A. Fisher, R.F.S., to Dr. Frank Yates, F.R.S., and to Longman Group Ltd., London, for permission to reprint tables from their book *Statistical Tables for Biological, Agricultural and Medical Research* (6th Edition, 1974).

In the preparation of the final manuscript, Mary K. Welsh provided invaluable assistance in proofreading and word processing. Suzanne Becker's skills in statistics and editing, and patience as a spouse and friend, have helped us survive the years of preparation and certainly made this a better text.

*Bloomington, Indiana*                                      Bill Becker and Don Harnett
*August 1986*

# CONTENTS

## Chapter 4   PROBABILITY CONCEPTS AND RANDOM VARIABLES

## Chapter 5    THE BINOMIAL, HYPERGEOMETRIC, AND POISSON DISTRIBUTIONS

## Chapter 6    CONTINUOUS PROBABILITY DISTRIBUTIONS

## Chapter 7    ESTIMATION

## Chapter 8    HYPOTHESIS TESTING

## Chapter 9    SIMPLE LINEAR REGRESSION AND CORRELATION

## Chapter 10    MULTIPLE REGRESSION: CROSS-SECTION AND TIME-SERIES ANALYSIS

| Chapter 11 | ANALYSIS OF VARIANCE |
|---|---|

## Chapter 12    STATISTICAL DECISION THEORY

## Chapter 13    NONPARAMETRIC STATISTICS

# BUSINESS AND ECONOMICS STATISTICS
## WITH COMPUTER APPLICATIONS

# CHAPTER ONE

*"Statistical thinking will one day be as necessary for efficient citizenship as the ability to read and write."*
H.G. Wells

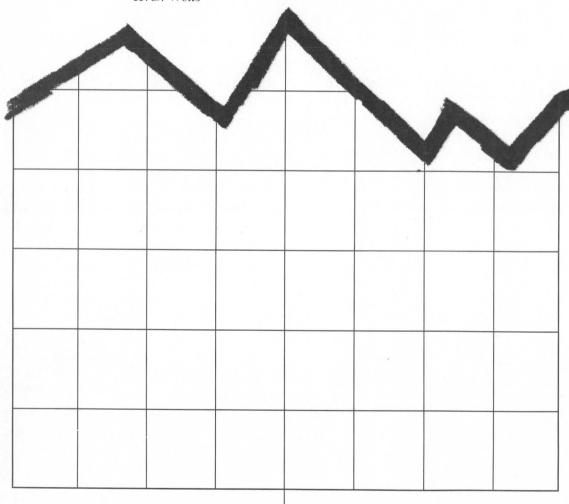

# DATA
# COLLECTION

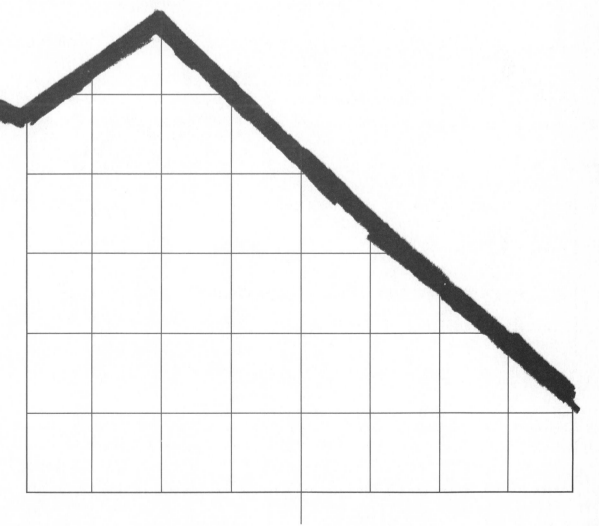

## 1.1 INTRODUCTION

Some knowledge of statistical techniques for use in decision making is essential for career success in almost all areas of business, industry, government, or public service. While the need for such knowledge was once essential only to those pursuing advanced training in economics, genetics, physics, and other sciences, today accountants, production managers, marketing executives, lawyers, and employment managers require knowledge of statistics. It is difficult to think of any higher-level management or profession that does not require some use of or ability to interpret statistical analysis. For example:

- In accounting, inventory auditing in large corporations is done by counting and pricing only a small sample of items in stock, comparing these totals with what is shown on the corporation's records, and then statistically estimating the total value of the inventory from the relationship established between this sample count and the actual record.

- In production and operations management, quality control is monitored by randomly selecting a few items from the line, checking their compliance with specifications, and then drawing a statistical conclusion about the quality of similar items.

- In marketing, a sample of customers is commonly used to assess the reaction of all potential customers to a new product.

- In personnel and legal proceedings, claims of sex or race discrimination in hiring or salary determination are assessed by statistically comparing the characteristics of an actual workforce to those of an ideal workforce (where there is no discrimination).

In all of these examples statistics are used because only a subset of information (sample data) is available. The statistical techniques discussed in this book include methods for collecting, presenting, and analyzing sample data for decision making. A large portion of this book focuses on statistical inference, which is the process of making statements about a population on the basis of sample information.

By the end of this chapter you should be able to (1) distinguish between sample and population information, (2) discuss alternative methods of data collection, and (3) recognize potential problems in trying to make statements based on sample information.

## Student Opinion About Careers in Small Business

You are the director of a small-business trade association. Your board of directors has asked you to find out why bright young college graduates from the most prestigious business schools are not taking jobs with small businesses. Your board wants you to support and document your findings but has not increased your small research budget to permit a large study. What are you going to do?

# 1.2 Sample and Population Information

In any analysis it is typically too expensive or physically impossible to obtain full information. By full information we mean all information of interest to a decision maker. For example, in auditing a large and diverse corporate inventory, it may be too costly to check each item in the production process. Similarly, one may not be able to check the durability of batteries, since such a check implies the destruction of each item tested. In the student opinion case previously described, the budget is too small to allow the director to contact all prestigious business school students in order to ask how they view jobs with small businesses. In these situations it is not possible to obtain all the information we would like.

| | |
|---|---|
| **DEFINITION**<br>**Population** | All the information of interest to a decision maker is called a population. |

Despite the fact that the population values are generally unknown to a decision maker, it is possible in these situations to make statements about the population (i.e., about the entire inventory, the reliability of every item produced, or the opinion of all students). We do this by looking at a subset of the population, called a **sample**.

---

| DEFINITION | A sample is a subset of all the information of interest to a decision |
|:--|:--|
| Sample | maker. |

---

The process of making statements about a population on the basis of a sample is called **statistical inference**. Figure 1.1 illustrates the relationship between a population, a sample, and statistical inference.

Statistical inference depends on having a representative sample on which to base a statement about the population. A representative sample can be thought of as a small-scale replica of the population. Typically, however, it is impossible to know exactly how well a specific sample represents the population.

---

# 1.3 Population Identification and Data Sources

As we have indicated, one objective of statistics is to make statements (inferences) about a population based on information contained in a sample. To do this it is important to define carefully the population of interest. Unless the desired population is well defined, making plans for drawing a representative sample is difficult, if not impossible. For example, if one wishes to study how consumers will react to a new product, the population of potential purchasers must be defined before a sample study can be designed. Similarly, if the objective is to analyze the opinions of students at prestigious business schools, a necessary first step is to define which schools are considered prestigious.

Once a relevant population is defined, the next step is to decide what type and how much sample data are needed, and how these data can best be gathered. The answers to these questions will greatly affect the cost of the

Figure 1.1

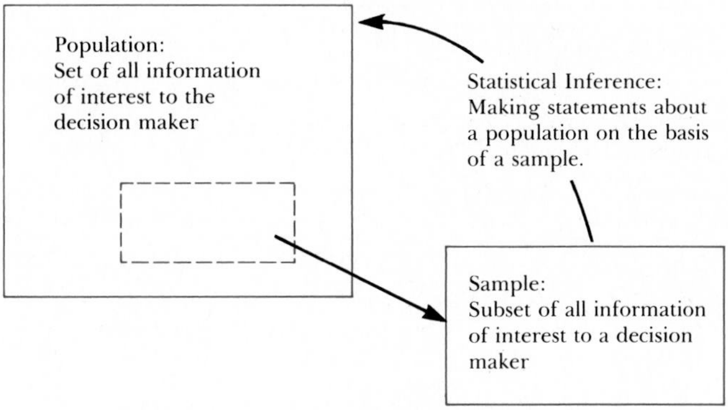

Population:
Set of all information
of interest to the
decision maker

Statistical Inference:
Making statements about
a population on the basis
of a sample.

Sample:
Subset of all information
of interest to a decision
maker

study. Usually, the least expensive way to gather data is to use existing information. The most expensive methods involve collecting new data, such as conducting surveys or running experiments. Let's first consider the less expensive methods for obtaining data and then discuss surveys and experiments.

# 1.4 Internal and External Data

In many businesses, some of the data required for a statistical analysis are obtained from internal sources (such as annual reports, technical manuals, personnel files, computer files of accounting data, and other routinely filed information). For example, *Business Week* uses internal corporate data when it puts together its annual "Corporate Scoreboard" issue. Some of these data are displayed in Appendix Table A.1 in the back of this book.

As more and more corporations establish centralized information systems and computerized information networks, internal data should become more easily and efficiently obtained. For instance, because Workingmans Federal Savings and Loan Association's data base is computer managed, it was relatively easy for its accounting department to provide us with the data in Appendix Table A.3.

Together with internal data, businesses often use data from external sources. For example, aggregate data on national economic activity are readily available from the U.S. Bureau of Labor Statistics, the U.S. Commerce Department, the Federal Reserve Board of Governors, and numerous other federal and state agencies. Appendix Table A.2 illustrates the type of data available from such agencies.

In addition to government agencies, trade associations such as the American Bankers Association and the U.S. Chamber of Commerce provide information related to their areas of interest. Similarly, union and professional organizations, such as the American Federation of Labor–Congress of Industrial Organizations (AFL-CIO) and the American Medical Association, provide information of interest to members. In our case study involving the opinion of students at the most prestigious business schools, ratings of business schools are available from the American Assembly of Collegiate Schools of Business (AACSB).

While internal and external data may be readily available, researchers should determine the methods by which the data sets were collected, recorded, and classified. For example, in an analysis that covers many years, it is essential to determine how important concepts are defined and how the data collection methods and the sample base may have changed over time (in order to determine how these changes might affect the data). Caution is needed in the use of any data set regardless of whether the data source is internal or external, manual or computer stored, or government or privately generated. *A statistical analysis is only as good as the data on which it is based.*

# 1.5 Surveys and Experiments

If existing sources do not contain the desired information, data are often generated through either a survey or an experiment.

Surveys often involve questioning people. For instance, a sample survey might involve stopping people in a shopping mall to ask them what brand of soft drink they prefer. In a study involving the opinion of prestigious business school students about small businesses, a survey questionnaire could be mailed to all existing students at one or two highly ranked business schools. Interestingly, according to a recent *Wall Street Journal* (*WSJ*) article, this is precisely what the Small Business and New Enterprise Club did at Harvard. (Of the 753 students who responded to the survey, 85% said they were interested in working for a small business at some point in their careers. Because of higher starting salaries, better training, and less employment risk at the larger corporations, however, only 37% wanted to join small companies immediately after graduation.)

Experiments differ from surveys in that in an experiment behavior is observed under controlled conditions. For example, when Coca-Cola's chemists discovered a new formula for its syrup, an experiment was conducted to determine if consumers preferred the new syrup to the old. A series of 190,000 blind taste tests of 13- to 59-year-olds in more than 13 cities convinced Coca-Cola executives that the new formula was preferred to the old. To remove or control for any influence the bottle or label might have on the person's judgment in this experiment, subjects were presented with identical containers. The order in which the syrup was presented to subjects was also mixed. These controls prevented subjects from knowing which syrup they were tasting, hence the term *blind* taste test. This Coca-Cola experiment controlled for age because researchers suspected that age might influence taste. It also controlled for geographical differences, since market shares differ from city to city.

Ideally, an experiment will control for any factors (other than chance) that might influence sample results. Thus, data from carefully designed experiments often provide more convincing evidence than survey data. Unfortunately, an experiment that controls perfectly for all factors is often impossible or too expensive. For instance, if time of day influences taste and if the Coca-Cola test took place at different times, the results of this experiment would be questionable. Furthermore if "broad image" is more important than taste, as suggested in Exercise 1.33, then a marketing executive might not wish to consider blind taste tests. In the case of Harvard's New Enterprise Club, the cost of conducting an experiment to control for all the factors that might influence job preference could not be financed by the club.

## 1.6 Sampling Errors in Data Collection

Regardless of whether data are collected using an experiment or a survey, the object is to get a sample that is representative of the population. Even if one could conduct a perfectly controlled experiment, however, a sample may not perfectly represent the population because drawing items from the population involves chance. The characteristics of a sample are determined by the characteristics of the population and by the chance factor involved in drawing a subset of information from it.

For example, suppose 60% of the population prefers Coke's new formula over the old one. Even a perfectly designed experiment will not yield a proportion of 60% in every sample. Because of the chance factor involved in selecting people to be in the experiment, some samples will yield a proportion above and some below 60%. While most samples could be expected to be representative of the population (a sample proportion close to 60%), it is possible to get a sample that is not representative.

In Coca-Cola's actual sample of 190,000 people, 61% preferred the new syrup. Remember, Coca-Cola executives had this experiment conducted because they didn't know the proportion in the population who would prefer the new syrup. On the basis of this sample, Coke executives may believe that the true population proportion is close to 0.61, but because of the chance factor inherent in sampling they will never know for sure if this particular sample was representative of the population. The difference caused by chance between population information and sample information is called **sampling error**.

---

**DEFINITION**
**Sampling Error**

Sampling error is the difference between the information in the sample and the information in the population that occurs because a sample is only a subset of the population.

---

Although sampling errors generally cannot be completely avoided, the decision maker would like to minimize them. Often, one way to do so is to increase the sample size; in general, the larger the sample, the less likely it is that serious sampling errors will occur. To avoid sampling error Coca-Cola used an extraordinarily large sample size of 190,000.

## 1.7 Nonsampling Errors in Data Collection

There are sources of error that have nothing to do with the chance factor inherent in sampling. These errors are called **nonsampling errors**.

| DEFINITION Nonsampling Error | Nonsampling error is the difference between sample information and the population information that occurs because of omitted or missing observations or incorrect measurements or because a sample was drawn incorrectly or from the wrong population. |
|---|---|

Nonsampling errors will be discussed at length. These types of error may cause serious problems that even sophisticated statistical techniques cannot easily overcome. In general, nonsampling errors can be minimized by careful planning and data collection.

## Measurement Error

Measurement error is one form of nonsampling error. Measurement errors often occur because a respondent is unclear about the question asked. For instance, questions aimed at establishing a person's work status might be misunderstood because of poor definitions; for example, retired people might mistakenly report themselves as "unemployed." Another source of measurement error may occur when the respondent does not know the desired information with certainty. In completing a dental questionnaire, for example, a respondent might not remember the exact date of the last checkup and thus record the wrong date.

Measurement errors may occur because of recording mistakes. For example, a researcher may make an inaccurate observation, or there may be a keypunching or typographical error in recording the data, or someone may merely add a column of numbers incorrectly.

Serious measurement error can destroy the value of an entire data set. For instance, an investor considering the development of a retirement housing community in a given location would want an estimate of the demand for such housing by retired persons in that area. The possibility that retired persons will respond "unemployed" rather than "retired" on a survey questionnaire could make the survey worthless. For such an important and costly investment decision, a considerable amount of time and money should be spent to ensure that respondents understand all questions. One way to do this would be to hire interviewers to meet personally with each respondent, rather than relying on mailed questionnaires or telephone surveys.

How much time, money, and care are used to avoid measurement errors depends on the chance of making the error and the cost involved. Typically, the least expensive methods of collecting data are also the most likely to have nonsampling errors. Table 1.1 provides a brief review of the costs and possible measurement errors that might develop as a result of using (1) direct measurement, (2) a personal interview, or (3) self-enumeration via a questionnaire.

**Table 1.1**

| Sampling Procedures |
| --- |

### Direct observation

Sampling may be by direct observation. For example:
1. In a time study, a researcher periodically checks on the activities of a manager (reading reports, giving dictation, talking on the telephone, etc.) and records this activity on a time sheet.
2. In a personnel training study, a researcher records the interaction between trainer and trainee on a hidden video recorder.
3. In a marketing study of automobile purchasing behavior, a researcher observes and records the exchange between the salesperson and potential customers.

Advantages
1. Data can be collected at various times, or even continuously.
2. There are no limitations on what is observed and recorded.
3. Distorted or incomplete recall by subjects is not a problem.

Disadvantages
1. Participants may be aware of the observer and may alter their behavior as a result.
2. Observers, because of personal biases or a lack of training, may not record precisely what they observe.
3. The method is expensive because of the cost of training and paying the observers.

### Personal Interview

In a personal interview predetermined questions are asked. These questions are written on a form and the responses are recorded by the interviewer. The actual questioning may be done either face to face or over the telephone. Telephone interviews, for example, are often used in political polls.

Advantages
1. People are more likely to respond when they are contacted directly. Thus, personal interviews tend to yield high response rates.
2. Direct contact enables the interviewer to clarify any questions or

**Table 1.1
(cont.)**

| Sampling Procedures |
|---|
| misunderstandings that the interviewee might have about questions asked. Thus, personal interviews are more likely to result in reliable and valid responses from those contacted. |
| 3. Supplemental information, such as a respondent's facial reaction to given questions, can be recorded in personal interviews. |
| Disadvantages |
| 1. The interviewer may not follow directions. In any study, it is essential that the sample be collected using a method that yields a good representation of the population. It is not uncommon, however, for interviewers to disregard the procedures specified. For example, suppose an interviewer is told to survey the father in each household. In some cases the father may not be available, so the interviewer decides (incorrectly) to interview the mother. |
| 2. Interviewers may influence respondents by the manner in which they ask a question or by the reaction they give to a response. |
| 3. Personal interviews are a relatively expensive method of data collection because it is usually necessary to pay for the time of the interviewers. |
| *Self-enumeration via questionnaires* |
| Possibly the most often used method of data collection is a questionnaire the participants fill out themselves. Such questionnaires may be distributed by mail, handed out in a shopping mall, stuffed in newspapers, or distributed by countless other methods. |
| Advantages |
| 1. This method is relatively inexpensive, since no observer or interviewer is required. |
| 2. The questionnaire can be put aside until it is convenient for the respondent to answer it. |
| Disadvantages |
| 1. There is no control over who completes the questionnaire. Thus, the data collected may not be representative of the population. |
| 2. Most people do not like to fill out questionnaires. Thus, a low response rate can be expected from self-enumeration. To increase the response rate, follow-up letters, telephone calls, and even personal interviews are often necessary. Such follow-up work adds to the cost of the study. |
| 3. The time period between the date the questionnaires are issued and the date they are returned may be relatively long. Thus, timely data may be difficult to collect by self-enumeration. |

## Omitted and Missing Observations

As indicated in Table 1.1, self-enumeration collection techniques (whereby questionnaires are distributed to and filled out by sample participants) typically do not lead to a high response rate. Many people do not like to take the time to fill out questionnaires. The people who do not respond to the questionnaire are a source of "missing observations." Such missing observations could lead to incorrect inferences about the population if those who do take the time to complete the questionnaire are not representative of the population under investigation.

Consider, for example, a local Ford dealer who is in the process of improving the service department. One question this dealer wants answered is whether or not the customer's car was finished when it was promised. As part of a survey, a representative sample of 100 recent customers are sent a questionnaire and asked to indicate if their service was finished on time or late. Thirty people respond to the questionnaire as follows:

Number of people responding "on time":    10

Number of people responding "late":        20

Since 20 of the 30 people responding said their service was late, the dealer might conclude that the vast majority of customers receive late service. This conclusion is not necessarily correct, however, since we have no way of knowing if the 30 people who responded are representative of the population. It may be that the people who report receiving late service are upset, and thus much more likely to respond to a survey. If the 70 people who didn't respond all had on-time service, and if they had responded, then the sample results would have been as follows:

Hypothetical response "on time":    80

Hypothetical response "late":        20

This hypothetical (but possible) result suggests that service is not all that bad. Unfortunately, on the basis of only a 30% response rate (30 out of 100), we are still very uncertain about the population, and hence may not wish to make any statement about the service at this dealership.

Numerous techniques can be used to increase response rates. For instance, the questionnaire and the accompanying letter of explanation must make it clear that the study will be of value to the respondent. If this letter and questionnaire are mailed to individuals, it is essential that a preaddressed, stamped envelope be provided for the return of the completed questionnaire.

Follow-up mailings to those who did not respond to the first mailing may be required. It may also be necessary to contact nonrespondents by telephone or in person. In the study by Harvard Business School students, offers of chances to win prizes of pizza and ice cream were used to induce students to respond to the questionnaire.

Entire books have been written on effective survey techniques. Before you attempt to carry out a survey yourself, you would be wise to visit a library and review some of the books cited in the card catalog under "Survey Techniques." Remember, without a sample designed to be representative of the population, your conclusions about the population will always be suspect.

## Exercises

**1.1** What is the difference between a sample and a population?

**1.2** Specify a situation in which a sample must be drawn because it is impossible to examine an entire population.

ADM **1.3** Is it possible for the employees of a company to be viewed as a sample for one type of analysis and as a population for another type? Give an example of both situations.

ECN **1.4** For each of the following, find a library source where data for the most recent time period can be obtained.

a) Total earnings of full-time and part-time workers in the United States by number of years of school completed, sex, and race.

b) The U.S. monthly unemployment rates by sex, age, and race.

c) The U.S. monthly consumer price index.

d) The number of business failures per year in the United States.

e) The sales and profits of U.S. corporations classified by major business type.

MKT **1.5** A company marketing a new beer ships it in cans to a sample of college town bars and ships it in bottles to bars and liquor stores in other cities. The company hopes to determine which type of container its customers prefer.

a) Do the resulting sales data represent a population, a survey, or experimental data? What (if any) difference does your answer make for analysis of the data?

b) If sales of the new beer are greater in the college town, is it reasonable to conclude that the cans are the preferred type of container? Explain.

1.6  Comment on the following statement: "In a perfectly controlled experiment, every subject is identical except for the fact that some are exposed to one set of circumstances (experimental group) while others are exposed to another set of circumstances (control group). Any differences between the two groups must be obvious, and there is no need for statistical analysis."

1.7  For each of the following types of data, state which method of collection (e.g., self-enumeration, personal interviews, etc.) is best. Define what you mean by best in terms of cost considerations, consistency or reliability of responses, validity or understanding on the part of respondent, and so on.

a) Data on the blood pressure of the chief executive officers (CEO) for large corporations.

b) Data on the family background, education, and income of migratory cherry pickers in northern Michigan.

c) Data from the National Academy of Science on members' field of specialization, current employment affiliation, academic training, and publications.

PUB  1.8  In trying to predict the outcome of a union election, what difference would it make if you talked to members whose names were chosen from the union directory versus members whose names were chosen from those voting in last year's union election?

ECN  1.9  As reported in *The American Economic Review* (May, 1979), a sample of 600 economists were surveyed by mail to assess their reaction to certain economic policies. One question was, "Should wage-price controls be used to control inflation?" Out of the 100 responding economists, 28 said yes and 72 said no.

a) If the response rate had been 100%, by how much could the results to this question have changed?

b) What factors might have caused economists not to respond?

PUB **1.10** Indicate whether the following represent (1) measurement error, (2) possible bias because of a low response rate, or (3) sampling error. (Hint: your answer may include more than one of the three categories).

a) On Monday morning a pollster interviews 50 voters and finds that 40% of them favor trade restrictions on imports from Japan. In the afternoon, the pollster interviews 60 voters and finds that only 30% favor such restrictions.

b) In a household survey an interviewer can find only 43 homes where the head of the household was willing to complete the survey. The interviewer contacted 128 homes.

c) In a marketing survey, an interviewer rewords two questions.

---

# 1.8 Random Samples

As already stated, we can never be sure that a particular sample is representative of a population. Even if we take care to ensure that there are no measurement errors or errors due to omitted observations, differences between the composition of a sample and a population may still exist because of the chance factor inherent in sampling. However, if we use a method of sampling that makes any element in the population equally likely to be selected, we can have some confidence that our sample composition is representative of the population composition. Such a selection method is known as **simple random sampling**.

| | |
|---|---|
| **DEFINITION**<br>**Simple Random**<br>**Sampling** | Simple random sampling refers to any technique designed to draw sample items from a population in such a way that each item (and every group of items) in the population is equally likely to be selected. |

As you will see in later chapters of this book, simple random sampling plays a critical part in statistical analysis. While any one sample obtained by simple random sampling may not give a perfect representation of the population, Chapter 7 will show that across many samples the average characteristics of these samples will represent the corresponding characteristics in the population. Chapters 4, 5, and 6 will provide the necessary concepts from probability theory to define when sample characteristics are close to those of the population. Based on these probability definitions, Chapter 8 will provide methods for testing hypotheses about certain population characteristics. Chapters 2 and 3 will introduce the sample and population characteristics considered in these later chapters.

Because of the critical role of random sampling in statistical analysis, we need to specify procedures by which random samples might be obtained. For simple random sampling, each element and each group of items in the population must have the same probability of being included in the sample. Blind draws and random number tables are the most frequently used methods for simple random sampling. Systematic selection, block sequence selection, and stratified and cluster sampling are random sampling methods, but they do not represent *simple* random sampling (because, as we will see, each *group* of items does not have the same probability of being in the sample).

## 1.9 Blind Draw

A simple and often used method of simple random sampling is called a **blind draw**. A few of the many common examples of blind drawing include picking names from a hat, selecting Bingo numbers from a revolving drum, or drawing cards from a shuffled deck. In blind draws an attempt is made to randomize the population items prior to selection in the hope that each item will have an equal likelihood of being selected.

Consider a market researcher who wishes to randomly select 100 state employees in a state where there are 5000 such employees. Using the blind draw approach, the researcher might place the names of each of the 5000 employees on separate cards and then mix the cards (by shuffling, shaking them in a box, or spinning them in a drum). Then 100 cards (employees) could be drawn with no reference to the information on them. If the mixing process is thorough, this procedure will provide a random sample of the 5000 state employees. We do not know if this procedure will result in a *representative* sample of state employees, for sampling errors may occur in even the most carefully designed random samples.

*There is no way to know for sure whether a particular sample result is representative of an unknown population.* We can review the method by which the sample results were obtained. Sometimes we can even review the results themselves to see if they are consistent with what we would expect from a random process. While we may have some confidence that a simple random sample is representative of the population, the chance factor in randomization makes it impossible to ever say with certainty that the sample is or is not representative of the unknown population.

Putting names or numbers in a revolving drum may appear to be a good method of randomizing, but the sample may not be representative. For instance, during the Vietnam War military draft status was determined by the order in which birthdays were drawn from a plastic drum. In one year in which this method was used (1970), the Selective Service placed 366 cards in a drum, each card representing one day of the year (a birthday), including leap years. The drum was turned several times and a Selective Service agent proceeded to select cards.

While this method looked impressive, many people questioned whether the results were really a random ordering of birthdays. Of the first 183 birthdays drawn, 46 were from November and December. On the average, we would expect only about 30 November and December birthday cards to be among the first 183 selected. These sample results suggest that this process may not have been random (a nonsampling error). It is also possible that the process *was* random, and that sampling error led to these results. This example is examined more closely in Exercise 4.8.

# 1.10 Computer-Generated Random Number Tables

The best method of obtaining a simple random sample is to use a table of random numbers. For most situations this approach is much easier and less expensive than the blind draw approach. Table 1.2 (which is also Appendix Table B.1) consists of columns and rows of the random digits 0 through 9. These digits are called **random numbers** because they have no particular order or pattern. Most statistical packages for computers will generate random numbers. In fact, Table 1.2 was generated on a microcomputer.

Random number tables are used by first assigning a number to each element in the population. For example, in our population of 5000 state employees each person can be thought of as having a number that is assigned on the basis of alphabetical order (i.e., the first employee in the alphabetical list is number 1, the second is number 2, and so forth, with the last person being number 5000).

After consecutive numbers are assigned to the 5000 alphabetically ordered employees, an arbitrary starting point is picked in a random number table. Note that in Table 1.2 the random numbers are in groups of five digits. This grouping is completely arbitrary. Because our population size (5000) has four digits, we need to pick four-digit numbers from Table 1.2. Any plan for picking four-digit numbers may be used as long as the plan is determined without first looking at specific values in the table.

Suppose we decide to take the first four digits of each five-digit number. To pick the starting point, close your eyes and place your pencil point on the table. Assume that your pencil lands in the first column of numbers, on the 10th number from the bottom. This number is 13862. The first four digits of this number are 1386, which means that the first employee selected for the sample is one who is 1386th on the alphabetical list.

The next number for our sample is selected by moving in some (predetermined) direction away from the starting point. Suppose we had decided beforehand to move down the column. Because the next four-digit number is 4654, the employee numbered 4654 is the second person in the sample. The third person would be the employee numbered 2662. Notice that the next four-digit number, 8717, cannot be used because it is larger than the population size (5000). This number is thrown out. Similarly, the next three numbers are larger than the population size and are also thrown out. Thus, the fourth number for the sample is 2597. This process of picking numbers continues until 100 numbers (the sample size) are selected.

If the same number occurs more than once in using a table of random numbers, the repeated numbers are typically ignored. This is because it would be illogical (if not difficult) to interview the same person twice or to test the same piece of material more than once. When repeated numbers are ignored, sampling is *without replacement*. If the same number can be used more than once, sampling is *with replacement*. As you will see in later chapters, statistical methods for making inferences from a sample to a population depend on whether sampling is with or without replacement.

As stated at the beginning of this section, random number tables are generated by computer programs. These programs can be used to generate random numbers to fit specific needs. For example, an accountant may wish to sample randomly just 10 of 500 consecutively numbered invoices for clerical errors. Instead of using an existing random number table, the accountant can use a microcomputer random number generator to identify the 10 invoices to be checked.

After bringing up a typical computer program, which requires information about the sample size (10) and the population size (500), the random

| Table 1.2 | | | Random Numbers | | | | |
|---|---|---|---|---|---|---|
| 46389 | 87437 | 23092 | 23988 | 11809 | 00826 | 97197 |
| 06218 | 69271 | 17918 | 06807 | 17834 | 10407 | 62125 |
| 21388 | 38052 | 48426 | 10275 | 93059 | 08944 | 06728 |
| 46159 | 62812 | 95214 | 99486 | 21683 | 13142 | 64595 |
| 72488 | 75788 | 58559 | 81198 | 51247 | 37079 | 86965 |
| | | | | | | |
| 55824 | 11156 | 84965 | 21592 | 80200 | 90622 | 03054 |
| 37080 | 83197 | 48692 | 84138 | 63048 | 33428 | 91568 |
| 82840 | 57952 | 82966 | 12036 | 41745 | 88006 | 11059 |
| 19838 | 11605 | 61116 | 82697 | 68569 | 00792 | 26999 |
| 20442 | 00620 | 90008 | 60867 | 19906 | 91433 | 68589 |
| | | | | | | |
| 79626 | 78430 | 52310 | 04791 | 22603 | 92953 | 22232 |
| 94405 | 24656 | 73998 | 16152 | 03246 | 29258 | 36207 |
| 28172 | 65833 | 49207 | 10259 | 53702 | 31945 | 85138 |
| 24593 | 55250 | 56568 | 29096 | 92112 | 01087 | 08006 |
| 01563 | 54844 | 82599 | 63547 | 97886 | 45001 | 78997 |
| | | | | | | |
| 03954 | 73168 | 06872 | 10690 | 77396 | 67933 | 79067 |
| 77964 | 26241 | 95040 | 37687 | 21382 | 14311 | 64713 |
| 61111 | 27603 | 17529 | 32020 | 67557 | 53208 | 87638 |
| 97861 | 27715 | 13045 | 20781 | 06147 | 63141 | 01961 |
| 23108 | 60807 | 50527 | 90977 | 22346 | 51612 | 36488 |
| | | | | | | |
| 57970 | 52760 | 90230 | 77747 | 32004 | 37867 | 89920 |
| 90262 | 05217 | 78527 | 82927 | 18339 | 59288 | 03588 |
| 75041 | 08560 | 56611 | 56132 | 59313 | 20722 | 24840 |
| 56872 | 25211 | 07823 | 27621 | 02037 | 00605 | 85640 |
| 93257 | 31809 | 75145 | 65364 | 21217 | 55078 | 64434 |
| | | | | | | |
| 13862 | 62672 | 83940 | 50451 | 53283 | 82739 | 77006 |
| 46547 | 67787 | 25828 | 71838 | 03498 | 56263 | 34533 |
| 26629 | 13913 | 37428 | 39222 | 20239 | 07280 | 38117 |
| 87171 | 54619 | 03367 | 89988 | 43139 | 72682 | 88761 |
| 89437 | 61905 | 57203 | 57077 | 97460 | 10392 | 64742 |
| | | | | | | |
| 61428 | 35260 | 21904 | 01420 | 15774 | 79443 | 40092 |
| 53336 | 77461 | 89279 | 70282 | 77159 | 70998 | 80642 |
| 25970 | 27319 | 63017 | 43080 | 24929 | 42378 | 22396 |
| 17897 | 77894 | 88788 | 61126 | 43599 | 81980 | 23070 |
| 17048 | 36505 | 48622 | 27170 | 60640 | 36701 | 10985 |

|  | Table 1.3 | Computer-Generated Random Numbers for a Sample of Size 10 and a Population of Size 500 |
|---|---|---|

| Order | Random Number |
|---|---|
| 1 | 219 |
| 2 | 316 |
| 3 | 408 |
| 4 | 406 |
| 5 | 2 |
| 6 | 233 |
| 7 | 350 |
| 8 | 148 |
| 9 | 382 |
| 10 | 75 |

generator will give a printout similar to that in Table 1.3. According to Table 1.3, the accountant should check invoices 219, 316, 408, 406, 2, 233, 350, 148, 382, and 75.

Unlike the user of a large random number table, the accountant in this example does not have to be concerned about getting numbers larger than 500 because the limiting population size was specified to be 500. Duplicate numbers, however, can occur. Thus, if sampling is to be without replacement, larger than necessary sample sizes may be specified so that the duplicate numbers can be discarded.

# 1.11 Systematic Selection

To obtain a sample of 100 people from a population of 5000 employees one might simply go to the alphabetical list and select every 50th name (starting randomly within the first 50 names). This approach is called **systematic sampling**. Systematic sampling is convenient whenever a population consists of lists, stacks of material, or chains of events. Systematic sampling is often used by accountants when checking entries in a ledger or by quality control analysts monitoring an assembly line.

Systematic samples have a number of desirable properties. For example, if one wanted to minimize the possibility that the sample contains adjacent items on an alphabetical population list (such as members of the same family), systematic sampling might be desirable. On the other hand, if one wanted to estimate average monthly accounts receivable for a small retail store, systematic selection of months could give misleading information. For instance, if every 12th month was selected, starting with December, then the result would not give a good representation of average monthly accounts receivable for the years under study because December is the busiest month of the year for most retailers. Systematic sampling is not *simple* random sampling because not every group of items has the same opportunity of being in the sample (e.g., no two adjacent items can be selected).

## 1.12 Block Sequence

Block sequence sampling is similar to systematic sampling in that observations are selected at fixed intervals. Unlike systematic sampling, however, block sequence sampling requires one to take a group of observations (a "block") that are adjacent to each other in a sequence. The blocks are usually a fixed interval apart. Like systematic sampling, block sequence sampling is random sampling but not *simple* random sampling.

If a researcher wants to maximize the likelihood of having family members contained in the sample of 5000 state employees, then block sequence sampling should be used. A sample of 100 employees might be obtained by selecting the 197th through 200th employees in the alphabetical list, then skipping the next 196 employees, picking the 397th through 400th employees, and so forth. Block sequence selection is used by quality control analysts when they suspect that errors or bad production techniques are accumulating. To spot such cumulative effects it is necessary to see more than one item from a given sequence or production lot.

## 1.13 Stratified Samples

In some situations the sampling process is more efficient if the population is divided into subgroups, each of which has a common characteristic. For example, the population of state employees might be divided into jobs types, such as clerical, manual labor, administrative, or professional. Employees might also be divided according to where they live, perhaps by county within the state. Many heterogeneous populations can be divided into subgroups that are more homogeneous. These smaller and more homogeneous subgroups are called **strata**. **Stratification** is the act of dividing a population into subgroups that share a given characteristic.

If a researcher can identify the elements in a given stratum and knows the proportion of the population contained in these strata, then small but highly representative samples can be chosen from each stratum. Such samples are called **proportional stratified random samples**. For example, suppose the list of state employees previously mentioned is divided into four job classifications, whereby 2500 employees are clerical, 1000 are labor, 750 are administrative, and 750 are professional. A proportional stratified random sample of 100 employees must reflect these same proportions—that is, 50 randomly selected clerical workers, 20 randomly selected laborers, 15 administrators, and 15 professional employees.

Stratified samples are typically used when a relatively small sample is to be drawn from an extremely large and diverse population (e.g., the U.S. population). For example, the Gallup Poll, the Harris Poll, and most other national surveys attempt to use stratification techniques to increase the similarity between the characteristics of the population and a sample. A stratified random sample will typically give a better representation of the population than will a simple random sample of the same size. Thus, stratified samples provide more information for a given dollar expenditure on the sample. However, to collect a stratified sample the population strata must be known in advance. Such knowledge may not always be available or economically feasible to obtain.

# 1.14 Cluster Sampling

If the members of a population are physically separated from one another and sampling requires personal contact, then the sampling procedures previously described may be impractical. For example, suppose General Mills wants potential customers to compare two new cereals. If the study involves many people, it would be very costly to visit randomly selected homes. Instead, the sampling plan might consist of visiting a specific neighborhood in some city and picking (say) every third house on every fifth street.

Sampling (randomly) from a specific group of items is called **cluster sampling**. Usually the items in the group are geographically close to each other, to make sampling less expensive. Ideally, the cluster selected for a sample is representative of the population.

# 1.15  Concluding Comments

An old saying in statistics regarding the importance of having good data is: "Garbage in, garbage out" (GIGO for short). Henceforth in this book we will assume that any data given are for a population or are a simple random sample from the relevant population. We will no longer raise questions about the origins of the data. It will be your job to remember that unless a sample is representative of the population under investigation, there is little that statistical analysis can do to counter the problem that the quality of the output depends on the quality of the input.

## Exercises

**1.11**  What are the advantages and disadvantages of the alternative methods of sampling (e.g., random, systematic, block sequence) in the following situations?

**a)** To check the daily attendance record of employees.

**b)** To audit weekly average balances in checking accounts.

**c)** To monitor insurance policy claims.

**d)** To assess the impact of unemployment in the United States.

PUB  **1.12**  How can stratification reduce the cost of conducting national polls while increasing the accuracy of predictions?

ACT  **1.13**  As an accountant you wish to select a sample of 20 accounts from among 1000 bank accounts for a sample audit. Assume that these accounts can be represented by three-digit numbers such as 000, 001,

. . . 998, 999. Use the random number table (Table 1.2) to select the accounts to be included in the audit. What account numbers will you audit? Would another accountant selecting accounts at random necessarily be auditing the same accounts? (Explain why or why not.)

**1.14** Explain why a sample of 20 names, drawn from among 200 cards in a hat, is really not a simple random sample if the name cards drawn are not replaced. Why would a researcher not want to replace the name cards?

**1.15** Explain why, in drawing 20 names from a population of 20,000, the consideration of replacement or nonreplacement is irrelevant in a discussion of randomization.

**1.16** Why do most problems in business and economics involve the collection and use of sample data as opposed to population data?

**1.17** A researcher was heard to say that a sample was "good." What do you think this person meant? What might be the difference between a "good" and a "bad" sample?

MKT **1.18** A marketing research firm has been hired to determine the age and certain likes and dislikes of the customers shopping at a local grocery store. The decision has been made to sample 150 customers. The store manager wants these customers to complete a short questionnaire.

   **a)** If no list of previous customers is available, describe a plan for selecting 150 customers.

   **b)** Assume that the store has a list of regular customers. Describe a sampling plan that uses random sampling.

MKT **1.19** The list in part (b) of Exercise 1.18 contains 4000 names. Find a computer program that will generate random numbers between 1 and 4000 and use this program to generate 30 numbers for a random sample.

**1.20** Give a business example for which each of the following types of sampling might be most appropriate (do not use the examples in the text).

   **a)** Systematic random sampling.

   **b)** Block sequence sampling.

   **c)** Stratified sampling.

   **d)** Cluster sampling.

**1.21** Describe the difference between sampling and nonsampling errors. In your description, indicate a specific sampling situation and illustrate how each type of error might occur in this situation.

## Chapter Exercises

**1.22** Suppose you determine the average age of the students in your statistics class. Is this a sample or a population value? If it is a sample, what is the population? What type of sampling plan does this represent? Why might such a sample not be representative of the population?

PUB **1.23** A recent *WSJ* article by J. M. Perry stated, "All the public poll-takers [e.g., Gallup, Harris and Roper] try to squeeze as much as they can out of each wave of interviews." Perry cites voter attitude cases in which pollsters have given the impression that their results were based on new surveys when in fact they were based on samples a week or two old. Why would pollsters be reluctant to carry out new surveys on a fixed-interval basis or every time there is a change in political climate?

ECN **1.24** An issue of *Business Week* stated: "Many observers claim they spy signs of an incipient recovery in the overall pattern of current economic statistics. Chief economist Jason Benderly of Prudential Insurance Co., however, contends that economists are 'really flying blind this time of year, because . . . the numbers could be off by up to that amount [8–15%] in either direction.'" According to Benderly, anyone who draws firm conclusions about the economy on the basis of data at this time of year is treading on thin ice.

a) Benderly is concerned about drawing inferences about a population (1983 events) based on a sample (December 1982 data). What is the basis of his warning about drawing conclusions (i.e., small-sample biases, sampling error, nonsampling error, random sampling differences in drawing one sample versus another, missing observation problems, etc.)?

b) If reported retail sales rose by 5% from November to December 1982, how high or low could the actual change have been?

**1.25** In each of the following problem-solving situations, specify the appropriate populations.

PUB     a) A city planning officer wants to know whether a bond referendum will be approved by the voters.

MKT     b) A market researcher wants to estimate the potential market share of a new brand of paper towel.

ACT     c) Concerned with cash flow, the president of a small corporation wants to know the magnitude of delinquent accounts receivable.

ADM     d) An industrial trainer wants to know whether her new self-paced, computer-based teaching system for new MBA (masters in business administration) trainees is effective across a wide cross section of industries.

**1.26** For the situations described in Exercise 1.25, indicate how an appropriate sample might be chosen. Specify the set of subjects, items, or events on which the sample measurements will be obtained. Discuss why given collection and sampling methods are or are not to be employed.

FIN  **1.27** Appendix A.1 contains the sales, profits, and related ratios for 296 corporations in key industries. If you were to draw a sample of 20 companies for the purpose of following future changes in margins and earnings per share, what method would you use to get a random selection of companies? (State the reasons for using your method.) Why wouldn't you want to use a block sequence sampling method?

FIN  **1.28** Use a random number table (e.g., Table 1.2) to select a sample of 20 companies from Appendix Table A.1. Begin by placing a number on each of the 296 companies in Appendix A.1—Allied Bancshares is 1, BancOne is 2, and so forth. Next, find the appropriate numbers to be in your sample using the random number table. Record the names of your 20 companies and report their individual 12-month earnings per share.

FIN  **1.29** Reconsider the 20 values representing 12 months' earnings per share obtained in Exercise 1.28.

    a) Calculate the sample average. (The sample average is calculated by adding the 20 earnings per share values together and then dividing by 20.)

    b) What is the population average? (Add all 296 values together and divide by 296.) How much does your sample average earnings per share differ from that of the population? Why does your sample average differ from the population average earnings per share?

LAW **1.30** In sex and race discrimination cases, considerable courtroom time is usually devoted to defining the preselection pool (population) from which potential employees might be hired. Typically, plaintiffs (those bringing suit against an employer) argue that the appropriate preselection pool should be the entire U.S. working-age population. Defendants (employers) argue for a much more restrictive preselection pool, for example, only those in the local community with a specific education level. Why do the plaintiffs and defendants argue in this way over the appropriate preselection pool?

**1.31** Go to a current issue of the *WSJ* or *Business Week* (or any similar business publication) and find an example of a sample used to represent a population. Determine as best you can the sampling method used. Was it a random sampling plan? What was the population under investigation? Why might this sample not represent the population?

**1.32** Design a sample for the main library at your college or university. Assume that the library wants to administer a questionnaire not only to users but to potential users as well. Be sure to specify the population. Use as many of the techniques discussed in this chapter as possible. Assume that the budget for this study is limited. Lists of students (by class), faculty, and staff are available from the university.

MKT **1.33** An article in *Newsweek* quotes William Meyers, author of *The Image-Makers: Power and Persuasion on Madison Avenue*, as saying that image is as important as taste in the soft-drink field. The article also quotes Faith Popcorn of Brainreserve as saying that Pepsi has the image for the youth market. If this is true, what problems do you see in trying to draw conclusions about the market success of Coca-Cola's new syrup from the taste test described in Section 1.5?

## Glossary

**blind draw:** A technique by which sample items are selected by procedures such as picking slips of paper from a hat, drawing Bingo balls from a drum, or taking cards from a deck.

**block sequence sampling:** A sampling technique in which observations are obtained by choosing blocks of items that are adjacent to each other in the listed sequence in the population.

**cluster sampling:** A method of collecting a sample that takes the sample data from a predetermined group of items (a cluster) that is expected to represent the population.

**experiment:** A method of collecting sample data by observation under specified conditions.

**nonsampling errors:** The discrepancy between a value for a sample and the comparable population value (if the population were known) that is caused by poor planning and care in conducting an experiment. Nonsampling errors include sampling from the wrong population, wording questions improperly, and adding a column of numbers incorrectly.

**population:** The entire set of information of interest to the decision maker.

**proportional stratified random sample:** A sample obtained from a population that has been stratified so that the proportion of subjects in the sample possessing the characteristic of the strata is the same as the proportion possessing the characteristic in the population.

**random number:** A number (often a digit between 0 and 9) whose value cannot be predicted in advance (each possible value is as likely to occur as any other number).

**sample:** A subset of the entire set of information of interest to the decision maker.

**sampling error:** The discrepancy between a value for a sample and the comparable population value caused by the fact that a sample is only a subset of a population.

**simple random sample:** A random sample chosen in such a way that every item and every group of items in the population has the same opportunity of being included in the sample.

**statistical inference:** The process of making statements about a population on the basis of a sample.

**strata:** subgroups of a population that share a given characteristic or are homogeneous in terms of some attribute.

**stratification:** The act of dividing a population into subgroups that share a given characteristic or attribute.

**survey:** Collecting sample data by observations, questionnaires, or interviews.

**systematic sampling:** A sampling technique whereby observations are obtained by choosing every $i$th item in the population when the population is arranged in a list.

# CHAPTER TWO

*Figures speak and when they do courts listen.*
Brooks v. Beto *(5th Circuit Court, 1966)*

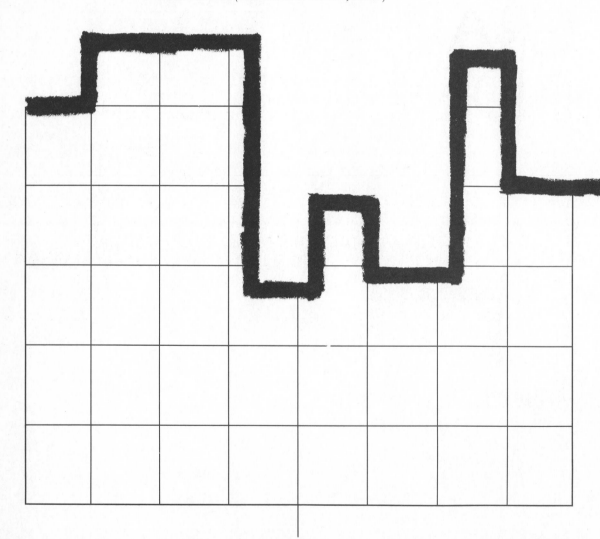

# DESCRIPTIVE STATISTICS: GRAPHS AND INDEX NUMBERS

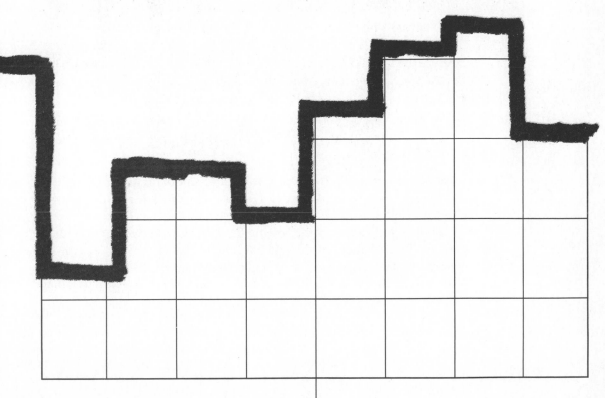

A main objective of statistics is to make inferences about a population based on information obtained from a sample. To make statements about a population based on a sample, it is often convenient to describe data in graphical and numerical ways that are conducive to the decision-making process. For example:

- A quality control engineer may need to determine whether batches of Z80 computer chips coming from an assembly line meet their specifications. One way to do this might involve determining the proportion of defective chips in a random sample and then recording the results on a graph. Such a graphical illustration may help identify changes in quality.

- Financial analysts often use graphical methods to compare the expected return and risk of various investments. These graphs make it easier to recognize possible trade-offs between return and risk.

- Market share data are typically presented graphically so that management has a visual reference in assessing trends.

- An economist describing inflationary trends must be able to measure the level of general prices and calculate the rate at which prices are changing.

Entire books are devoted to describing and summarizing data. Only a few methods are presented in this and the next chapter. This chapter emphasizes graphical and index methods used to describe data, while Chapter 3 emphasizes numerical methods to summarize data. By the end of this chapter, you should be able to construct and interpret histograms, bar and pie charts, and other graphs of relative and absolute frequency. You should also be able to construct and use index numbers to represent data that are collected over time.

## Mobile Managers and Their Pay

As a high-level business executive, you are concerned because your current salary of $89,999 per year has not kept pace with the increase in general prices. A *Wall Street Journal* (*WSJ*) article on the compensation of corporate managers of your caliber provides salary information for executives who have recently been transferred or have taken new jobs (see Table 2.1). You wish to relate this salary information to your own situation and to decide whether to ask for a raise or perhaps make inquiries about a new job.

# 2.2 Qualitative and Quantitative Data

The income information in Table 2.1 represents **quantitative data** (numerical values). Managers also might be classified by other quantitative data, such as

**Table 2.1**

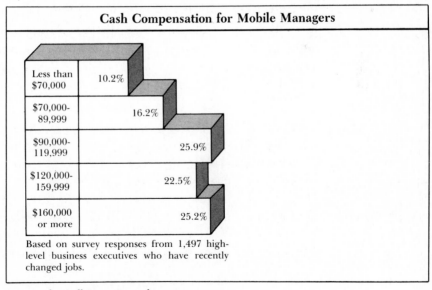

**Cash Compensation for Mobile Managers**

| | |
|---|---|
| Less than $70,000 | 10.2% |
| $70,000–89,999 | 16.2% |
| $90,000–119,999 | 25.9% |
| $120,000–159,999 | 22.5% |
| $160,000 or more | 25.2% |

Based on survey responses from 1,497 high-level business executives who have recently changed jobs.

Source: *The Wall Street Journal.*

Data: Heidrick & Struggles, Inc.   Reprinted by permission of *The Wall Street Journal*, © Dow Jones & Company, Inc., 1980. All rights reserved.

the number of years of schooling, the number of subordinates, or perhaps the size of the budget under their control. In contrast, **qualitative data** refer to categorical (nonnumerical) information, such as the sex, marital status, or title of an executive.

| | |
|---|---|
| **DEFINITIONS**<br>**Quantitative and**<br>**Qualitative Data** | Quantitative data are numerical values.<br><br>Qualitative data represent a cateogorical labeling of a characteristic. |

This chapter first discusses methods for representing quantitative data and then considers methods for presenting qualitative data.

# 2.3   Frequency Distributions and Their Graphic Representation

Quantitative data are often presented in a **frequency distribution**. A frequency distribution shows the number of times each value or each set of values is observed. For example, in Table 2.1 there are five sets of values. These sets of values were obtained from individual observations which were grouped into classes:

Class 1: less than $70,000

Class 2: $70,000–$89,999

Class 3: $90,000–$119,999

Class 4: $120,000–$159,999

Class 5: $160,000 or more

In this mobile manager case we do not know the actual number of observations falling into each of these classes. The number of observations per class is called the **absolute frequency** of the class. From Table 2.1 we do know the total number of observations (1497) and the relative frequency of each class (10.2%, 16.2%, 25.9%, 22.5%, and 25.2%). The **relative frequency** of a class is the proportion (or percentage) of observations in the class to the total number of observations in the data set. For example, the relative fre-

Table 2.2

| Absolute and Relative Frequency of Cash Compensation for Mobile Managers | | | |
|---|---|---|---|
| (1) | (2) | (3) | (4) |
| | | Absolute | Relative |
| Class | Income | Frequency | Frequency |
| ($i$) | (in dollars) | $f_i$ | $f_i/n$ |
| 1 | Less than 70,000 | $f_1 =$ 153 | 0.102 |
| 2 | 70,000–89,999 | $f_2 =$ 242 | 0.162 |
| 3 | 90,000–119,999 | $f_3 =$ 388 | 0.259 |
| 4 | 120,000–159,999 | $f_4 =$ 337 | 0.225 |
| 5 | 160,000 or more | $f_5 =$ 377 | 0.252 |
| Total | | 1497 | 1.000 |

quency of managers making less than $70,000 is 0.102, because 10.2% of the 1497 responding managers said that their compensation was less than $70,000.

Using the relative frequencies and the total number of observations, we can solve for the absolute frequencies. The absolute frequency (or number) of managers making less than $70,000 is 153, which is 10.2% of the 1497 respondents [152.9 = 0.102(1497)]. The relative frequency of managers making $70,000–$89,999 is 0.162. Thus, 242 [(242.5 = 0.162(1497)] managers said that their salary was in the $70,000–$89,999 class. As shown in the last two columns of Table 2.2, absolute frequencies for the other classes can be obtained in like manner. Table 2.1 shows only percentages, which are the same values shown in the last column of Table 2.2 multiplied by 100. Thus, Table 2.2 provides the same information as Table 2.1, but now both absolute and relative frequencies are presented.

In Table 2.2 the classes are labeled by the letter $i$, where $i$ is either 1, 2, 3, 4, or 5. The relative frequency of any particular class (called the $i$th class) is obtained by dividing the number of observations in this $i$th class ($f_i$) by the total number of observations ($n$). The total number of observations is designated by $N$ in a population and by $n$ in a sample. Thus the relationship between the absolute ($f_i$) and relative frequency ($f_i/N$ for a population or $f_i/n$ for a sample) can be defined algebraically.

Note that in Table 2.2 the sum of the relative frequencies is 1.00. Except for rounding errors, this will always be the case. For the managers in Table 2.2,

$$0.102 + 0.162 + \cdots + 0.252 = 1.000$$

Relative frequency $= f_i/N$ for a population of size $N$.

Relative frequency $= f_i/n$ for a sample of size $n$,

where $f_i$ is the frequency of the $i$th class.

Similarly, the sum of the absolute frequencies always equals the total number of observations. In Table 2.2,

$$153 + 242 + \cdots + 377 = 1497$$

Because the number of classes in Table 2.2 is small, all calculations can be performed using a calculator. When the number is large, such calculations are much easier using a computer. We used a computer spreadsheet program to check parts of Table 2.2. Our input to the program was columns 1, 2, and 4 of this table. This program makes it easy to convert absolute frequencies into relative frequencies and vice versa. To check that the relative frequencies added to 1.00, the spreadsheet command "SUM" was used for column 4. To create the absolute frequencies shown in column 3, we simply told the spreadsheet program (using multiplication and copy commands) to multiply each entry in column 4 by 1497. After we entered the original data (columns 1, 2, and 4), Table 2.2 was completed in a matter of seconds.

## Histograms

The *WSJ* diagram in Table 2.1 is misleading. Note that the *WSJ* drew all of the bars representing the relative frequencies using the same width. A properly drawn figure would have each width proportional to the income it represents. For example the width of the class $70,000–$89,999 ($20,000) should be two-thirds the width of the classs $90,000–$119,000 ($30,000). Numerous methods for distorting the image of data are reviewed in a delightful book by Darrell Huff, *How to Lie with Statistics*.

Histograms are the standard graphical method for presenting a frequency distribution. A histogram is a graph of a frequency distribution where class intervals are placed on the horizontal axis and absolute or relative frequencies are placed on the vertical axis. Figure 2.1 is the histogram for the frequency

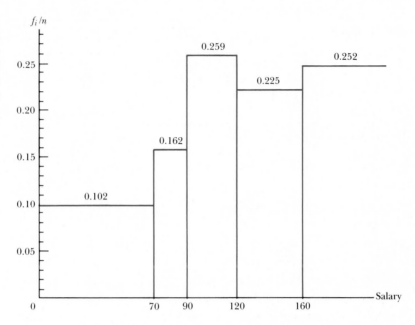

**Figure 2.1**
Relative frequency histogram: Compensation of mobile managers (from Table 2.2—in thousands of dollars).

distribution in Table 2.1. Because the scaling on the vertical and horizontal axes are clearly labeled, it is not easy to misrepresent or misinterpret the data. As we will show in the next section, however, Fig. 2.1 is far from ideal.

Figure 2.1 indicates that a manager making $89,999 per year has a salary in the lower half of the income distribution in Table 2.1. In fact, 73.6% (= 25.9% + 22.5% + 25.2%) of the high-level managers who took new jobs received more than $89,999. If you are in top management but are making only $89,999 per year, you might be wise to request a raise and begin inquiring about a new job. After all, 73.6% of the executives who took new jobs earned more than you do.

---

**WORKED EXAMPLE 2.1**

The following table presents the data on the length of unemployment (from the *Economic Report of the President*). These frequency data show, for instance, that 3,208,000 persons were unemployed for fewer than 5 weeks. Use these population data to construct a relative frequency distribution and draw the relative frequency histogram.

| Duration of Unemployment (weeks)* | | | | |
|---|---|---|---|---|
| Total | Fewer than 5 | 5–14 | 15–26 | 27 or more |
| 7449 | 3208 | 2411 | 1028 | 802 |

*Thousands of persons 16 years of age or older.

**ANSWER:**

Unemployment
relative frequency
distribution and
histogram

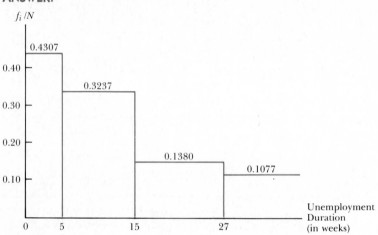

| Unemployment Duration (weeks) | $f_i/N$ Relative Frequency |
|---|---|
| Fewer than 5 | 0.4307 |
| 5–14 | 0.3237 |
| 15–26 | 0.1380 |
| 27 or more | 0.1077 |
| Sum = | 1.0000 |

## 2.4 Stem and Leaf Plot, Frequency Distribution, and Histogram Construction

Data are not always conveniently grouped into classes such as the *WSJ* information in Table 2.1. Rather, observations generally are collected as individual values, from which a frequency distribution is constructed.

## Charge Accounts

You are an accountant interested in determining last month's distribution of charge account balances for a large hardware store. It is too expensive to check all the accounts. Thus, you select a random sample of 40 customers who have charge accounts. The following values represent last month's balance for each of the 40 customers.

$71, $58, $66,  $119, $55, $46,  $22, $69, $84, $72,
$45, $61, $45,  $84,  $68, $107, $96, $58, $47, $61,
$91, $47, $102, $76,  $63, $55,  $52, $69, $75, $10,
$85, $32, $63,  $55,  $55, $65,  $66, $35, $70, $78.

From these sample data you wish to make an inference about characteristics of the population distribution of charge account balances.

As a first step in analyzing the charge account balances, you want a graphical description of the sample data from which to infer the shape of the population distribution. To construct a frequency distribution from the preceding data, however, it is not clear what class intervals best represent the data. Should you use a few wide class intervals (such as $10) or many narrow intervals ($5, for example)?

One method used to determine the classes for a frequency distribution is called a **stem and leaf plot**. In this approach each number in the data set is divided into two parts, a "stem" and a "leaf." The leaf is the last digit of the number and the stem is the rest of the digits. For example, the first number in the charge account data set ($71) has a stem of 7 and a leaf of 1, the second a stem of 5 and a leaf of 8, and the third a stem of 11 and a leaf of 9.

One advantage of the stem and leaf approach is that the data need not be in any particular order. It is necessary, however, to find the smallest and the largest stems in the data set. For the charge account data, the smallest stem is 1 (from $10) and the largest stem is 11 (from $119). After the smallest and largest stems are found, a vertical line is drawn and all possible stems are placed in order on the left-hand side of the line, with the smallest at the top and the largest at the bottom as in Fig. 2.2(a).

The leaves are placed on the right-hand side of the vertical line in the order in which they appear in the data. For example, the first observation in

Figure 2.2
Stem and leaf plots—
charge account data.

| Panel (a) | Panel (b) | | Panel (c) | | Panel (d) | |
|---|---|---|---|---|---|---|
| Stem | Stem | Leaf | Stem | Leaf | Stem | Leaf |
| 1 | 1 | 0 | 1L | 0 | 1L | * |
| 2 | 2 | 2 | 1U | | 1U | |
| 3 | 3 | 25 | 2L | 2 | 2L | * |
| 4 | 4 | 65577 | 2U | | 2U | |
| 5 | 5 | 8585255 | 3L | 2 | 3L | * |
| 6 | 6 | 6918139356 | 3U | 5 | 3U | * |
| 7 | 7 | 126508 | 4L | | 4L | |
| 8 | 8 | 445 | 4U | 65577 | 4U | ***** |
| 9 | 9 | 61 | 5L | 2 | 5L | * |
| 10 | 10 | 72 | 5U | 858555 | 5U | ****** |
| 11 | 11 | 9 | 6L | 1133 | 6L | **** |
| | | | 6U | 698956 | 6U | ****** |
| | | | 7L | 120 | 7L | *** |
| | | | 7U | 658 | 7U | *** |
| | | | 8L | 44 | 8L | ** |
| | | | 8U | 5 | 8U | * |
| | | | 9L | 1 | 9L | * |
| | | | 9U | 6 | 9U | * |
| | | | 10L | 2 | 10L | * |
| | | | 10U | 7 | 10U | * |
| | | | 11L | | 11L | |
| | | | 11U | 9 | 11U | * |

Original Data

$71, $58, $66,  $119, $55, $46,  $22, $69, $84, $72,
$45, $61, $45,  $84,  $68, $107, $96, $58, $47, $61,
$91, $47, $102, $76,  $63, $55,  $52, $69, $75, $10,
$85, $32, $63,  $55,  $55, $65,  $66, $35, $70, $78.

the data set is $71, which is a stem of 7 and a leaf of 1. The first leaf next to the stem of 7 in Fig. 2.2(b) is a 1. For the next number, $58, an 8 is the first leaf next to the stem of 5. Thus the number of times a stem occurs can be determined by counting the number of digits in the leaf. For instance, we know that a number in the 50s occurs seven times because there are 7 leaves (8, 5, 8, 5, 2, 5, 5) associated with the stem of 5.

From the stem and leaf plot in Fig. 2.2(b), the general shape of a histogram (with equal class widths of $10) can be seen. In particular, if a frequency distribution were constructed with $10 class widths, its histogram would look like Fig. 2.2(b) turned sideways.

Now suppose we want to see what the frequency distribution and histogram might look like if class widths of $5 were used. In this case the stems can be defined as "upper (U)" and "lower (L)" stems, where an upper stem is any number ending in 5, 6, 7, 8, or 9 and a lower stem is any number ending in 0, 1, 2, 3, or 4. For example, any number from $65 to $69 would be given the stem of 6U, representing the upper half of the $60's. Similarly, numbers between $60 and $64 would be given the stem 6L, representing the lower half of the $60's. Figure 2.2(c) indicates what the histogram would look like for a frequency distribution with classes of $5 width (again, turn the page sideways).

Stems can start and end at any value, and the widths of the stems can be adjusted to best represent the data. Often a computer program can be used to construct a stem and leaf plot. Figure 2.2(d) is the computer output using $5 class widths. Note that in this figure the actual leaves are not shown; rather, the number of leaves for each stem is indicated by the number of "*" symbols.

While it is easy to move from a stem and leaf plot to a frequency distribution, the question is which class widths give the best representation of the data? To answer this question, consider five rules of thumb for constructing frequency distributions.

## Five Rules for Constructing Frequency Distributions

1. An observation must fall into one and only one class—that is, classes cannot overlap.

2. Classes are generally chosen so that the widths of all classes are the same. This rule suggests that the income frequency distributions in Table 2.1 should have the same class width throughout the distribution. Instead, it begins with a $70,000 interval (less than $70,000), then goes to a $20,000 interval ($70,000–$89,999), and then moves to increasing interval widths up to the last one, which is infinitely wide ($160,000 and over). Although maintaining equal class widths may not be practical for a data set with a large range of values, unequal class intervals can cause problems when making certain calculations and can result in a misrepresentation of data.

3. The number of classes should be less than 15 but greater than 5. If possible, classes in the middle of the distribution should have at least one observation.

4. The midpoint (middle) of each class should be representative of the observations in that class. Ideally, observations should be evenly distributed around the class midpoint.

**5.** Open-ended intervals should be avoided if possible. Too much information is lost if categories such as "$160,000 or over" are used. If it is not possible to place several values conveniently in classes, those values should be listed separately.

Using these five rules of thumb, the stem and leaf plots in Fig. 2.2 suggest that a $5 class interval is too narrow, since it results in several classes with no observations. For instance, there are no observations between $110 and $115, as shown by the absence of leaves for the 11L stem (Fig. 2.2c). The $10 intervals provide a smooth and compact representation of the data. Each class's midpoint also tends to be representative of the data in the class. For example, the midpoint of the $50–$59 class (which is $55) is the approximate middle of the seven values in this class.

To construct a relative frequency histogram from a stem and leaf plot requires the absolute frequency for each stem to be divided by the total number of observations. For example, in Fig. 2.2 there are 40 observations, so each class frequency must be divided by 40. The first absolute frequency is 1 (for the one leaf associated with stem 1 in Fig. 2.2(b), so that the relative frequency is $1/40 = 0.025$. The third absolute frequency is 2 (for the two leaves associated with stem 3), resulting in a relative frequency of $2/40 = 0.050$. The entire relative frequency distribution and histogram are shown in Fig. 2.3.

To ensure that there is no overlap of classes in Fig. 2.3, we label class intervals as $10–$19.99, $20–$29.99, and so on. In the histogram, the height of the bar associated with each of these classes shows the relative frequency of the class. Finally, note that since this is a sample of charge accounts, the number of observations is $n = 40$ (not $N = 40$, which would indicate the population) and the $i$th class relative frequency is specified by $f_i/n$.

Although we are interested in describing the charge account sample data, in this case we are much more interested in the population from which the sample accounts were drawn. We really want to know the distribution of all the hardware store's charge account balances last month. As noted in the case, however, such information is too expensive to obtain. Since the 40 sample observations were randomly selected, and since they constitute a fairly large sample, we have some confidence that our sample values may be representative of the population. That is, with the exception of chance variations inherent in sampling, our sample should be an approximate small-scale image of the population from which it was drawn. From the sample's relative frequency distribution and histogram in Fig. 2.3, we can estimate that the most common charge account balance is between $60 and $69.99. Another estimate

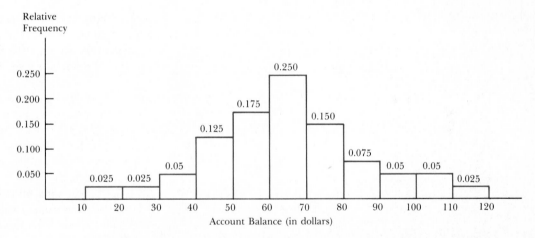

| Figure 2.3 Relative frequency distribution and histogram for charge account data. | Class (i) | Class Boundaries | Midpoint | Absolute Frequency ($f_i$) | Relative Frequency ($f_i/n$) |
|---|---|---|---|---|---|
| | 1 | $10–$19.99 | $15 | 1 | 0.025 |
| | 2 | $20–$29.99 | 25 | 1 | 0.025 |
| | 3 | $30–$39.99 | 35 | 2 | 0.050 |
| | 4 | $40–$49.99 | 45 | 5 | 0.125 |
| | 5 | $50–$59.99 | 55 | 7 | 0.175 |
| | 6 | $60–$69.99 | 65 | 10 | 0.250 |
| | 7 | $70–$79.99 | 75 | 6 | 0.150 |
| | 8 | $80–$89.99 | 85 | 3 | 0.075 |
| | 9 | $90–$99.99 | 95 | 2 | 0.050 |
| | 10 | $100–$109.99 | 105 | 2 | 0.050 |
| | 11 | $110–$119.99 | 115 | 1 | 0.025 |
| | | | | Sum=40 | 1.000 = sum |

would be that approximately 25% of all the hardware store's charge accounts are less than $70 but at least $60. Similarly, we can estimate that 2.5% of the accounts are greater than or equal to $110 but less than $120.

**WORKED EXAMPLE 2.2**

As the director of the motor vehicle pool at a large corporation, you are responsible for keeping track of the gas mileage of new cars in the pool. For a sample of 20 tanks of gasoline, the new cars have averaged 34, 36, 33, 23,

26, 37, 31, 28, 32, 28, 40, 35, 16, 21, 22, 24, 23, 34, 13, and 19 mpg. The purchasing department is interested in seeing a relative frequency distribution and histogram. Use the stem and leaf approach to develop an appropriate representation of these data.

**ANSWER:**

| Stem and Leaf Plots | | | |
|---|---|---|---|
| (10-mpg interval) | | (5-mpg interval) | |
| Stem | Leaf | Step | Leaf |
| 1 | 639 | 1L | 3 |
| 2 | 36881243 | 1U | 69 |
| 3 | 46371254 | 2L | 31243 |
| 4 | 0 | 2U | 688 |
| | | 3L | 43124 |
| | | 3U | 675 |
| | | 4L | 0 |
| | | 4U | |

| New-Car Miles Per Gallon Relative Frequency Distribution | |
|---|---|
| (5-mpg interval) | |
| MPG Interval | $f_i/n$ |
| 10–14 | 0.05 |
| 15–19 | 0.10 |
| 20–24 | 0.25 |
| 25–29 | 0.15 |
| 30–34 | 0.25 |
| 35–39 | 0.15 |
| 40–44 | 0.05 |
| | Sum = 1.00 |

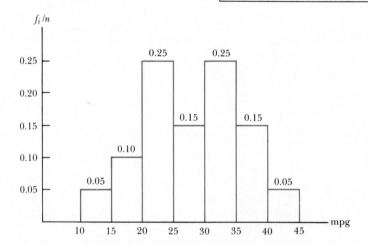

A 5-mpg interval is preferred over a 10-mpg interval because the latter has only four classes and does not provide as much information about the distribution of the data.

# 2.5 Cumulative Frequency

A **cumulative frequency** is the total number of observations that have values less than or equal to some specified amount. When data are in classes, as in Table 2.3, the specified number is usually one of the upper class boundaries ($19.99, $29,99, $39,99, . . . $119.99).

For example, the cumulative frequency of $29.99 for the charge accounts in Fig. 2.3 is 2, since there are two observations less than or equal to $29.99 (the one observation from the $10–$19.99 class plus the one observation from the $20–$29.99 class). Similarly, the cumulative frequency for $39.99 is 4 (there are four observations less than or equal to $39.99), and the cumulative frequency for $49.99 is 9 (there are nine observations less than $50). The cumulative frequency for the upper limit of the final class is 40, since $n =$ 40. A **cumulative relative frequency** is calculated by dividing a cumulative frequency by the total number of observations in the data set. Thus, column 3 in Table 2.3 is column 2 divided by 40.

Table 2.3

| Cumulative Distributions—Charge Account Data from Fig. 2.3 | | |
|---|---|---|
| Account Balances | Cumulative Frequency | Cumulative Relative Frequency |
| $10–$19.99 | 1 | 0.025 |
| $20–$29.99 | 2 | 0.050 |
| $30–$39.99 | 4 | 0.100 |
| $40–$49.99 | 9 | 0.225 |
| $50–$59.99 | 16 | 0.400 |
| $60–$69.99 | 26 | 0.650 |
| $70–$79.99 | 32 | 0.800 |
| $80–$89.99 | 35 | 0.875 |
| $90–$99.99 | 37 | 0.925 |
| $100–$109.99 | 39 | 0.975 |
| $110–$119.99 | 40 | 1.000 |

**WORKED EXAMPLE 2.3**

Dun and Bradstreet reports the following number of yearly business failures, by liabilities at the time of failure.

| Size of Liability | | | | |
|---|---|---|---|---|
| Under $5000 | $5000– $24,999 | $25,000– $99,999 | $100.000– $999,999 | $1,000,000– $8,999,999 |
| Number of business failures | | | | |
| 76 | 928 | 2708 | 2593 | 314 |

Calculate the cumulative relative frequency distribution for business failures by size of liabilities.

**ANSWER:**

| Business Failures by Liability | | | | |
|---|---|---|---|---|
| Under $5000 | $5000– $24,999 | $25,000– $99,999 | $100,000– $999,999 | $1,000,000– $8,999,999 |
| Cumulative relative frequency | | | | |
| 0.012 | 0.152 | 0.561 | 0.953 | 1.00 |

**Figure 2.4**
Cumulative relative frequency graph for charge account data.

Source: Table 2.3.

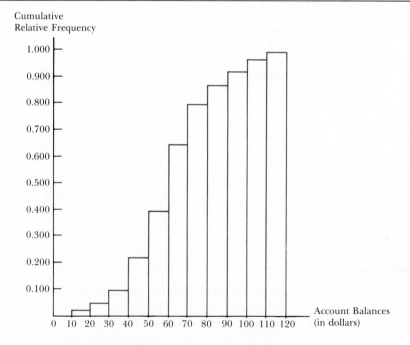

48    Chapter 2   Descriptive Statistics: Graphs and Index Numbers

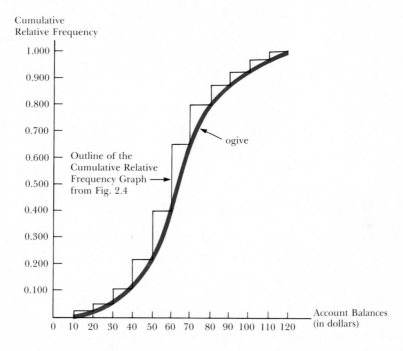

**Figure 2.5**
Ogive for charge
account data.

Source: Figure 2.4.

Cumulative
Relative Frequency

1.000

0.900

0.800

0.700

0.600

0.500

0.400

0.300

0.200

0.100

ogive

Outline of the
Cumulative Relative
Frequency Graph
from Fig. 2.4

Account Balances
(in dollars)

0   10   20   30   40   50   60   70   80   90   100  110  120

A graph of cumulative relative frequencies provides a good visual impression of the data. The cumulative relative frequency function shown in Fig. 2.4 was constructed from the charge account relative frequency distribution in Table 2.3. In Fig. 2.4, the height of each bar shows the percentage of data less than or equal to the upper limit of the class. Thus the bar for the class $60–$69.99 shows that 65% of the distribution is less than or equal to $69.99 or, alternatively, that 65% of the distribution is less than $70.

Sometimes an ogive is used to smooth the graph of a cumulative relative frequency. An **ogive** is a line connecting the lower-right corner points of a cumulative relative frequency graph. Thus, at each of these points, the ogive shows the amount of the distribution that is less than the value on the horizontal axis. For example, Fig. 2.5 is the ogive for the charge account data in Table 2.3. As in Fig. 2.4, it shows that 65% of the distribution is less than $70.

**WORKED EXAMPLE
2.4**

According to the U.S. Bureau of the Census, a recent *Current Population Report on Family Income* was based on information from 58,426,000 families in which the age of the head of the household was distributed as follows:

| Age of Householder | | | | | | |
|---|---|---|---|---|---|---|
| | 15–24 | 25–34 | 35–44 | 45–54 | 55–64 | 65–94 |
| *Percent* | 6.4 | 23.5 | 20.8 | 18.3 | 15.9 | 15.0 |

Graph the cumulative relative frequencies and the associated ogive for this age distribution. The majority of household heads are younger than what approximate age?

**ANSWER:**

Householder age cumulative frequency graph and ogive

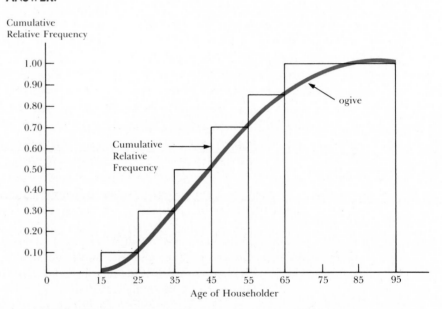

From this ogive we can see that about 51% (i.e., a majority) of the household heads are younger than 45.

As a closing note to our discussion of frequency and relative frequency, it is important to recognize that the accuracy of the cumulative relative frequency is determined by the precision of the individual relative frequencies. If relative frequencies are rounded or truncated (e.g., $f_i/n = 0.2349$ is reported as $f_i/n = 0.235$ if rounded or $0.234$ if truncated) then the cumulative relative frequency is accurate to fewer decimal places. Although rounding is preferred to truncation (because rounding errors should tend to cancel), one should never expect more accuracy after an arithmetic operation than was reported in the original values. Thus, in Worked Example 2.4, we should not be surprised that the sum of relative frequencies does not exactly equal 1.000 (or 100.0%). The fact that this sum is only 0.999 (or 99.9%) reflects rounding or truncation errors in one or all six of the reported relative frequencies.

## Exercises

**2.1** Explain the differences and similarities in the steps required to obtain absolute frequency, relative frequency, and cumulative frequency distributions.

**2.2** You have both absolute and relative frequencies for sample data. In order to make a statement about some population, why is it necessary to use the relative frequency?

**2.3** What is an ogive and why is it used with a distribution function?

ADM **2.4** Tuition for tutorial classes for the Graduate Management Aptitude Test is known to range from $400 in some midwestern college towns to as much as $4000 for classes in Manhattan. You have data on 90 such programs. Which of the following class widths would seem appropriate to classify the tuition distribution?

$100, $200, $300, $400, $500, $600, $900, and $1200

FIN **2.5** Following are three different ways of classifying the price-earnings ratios of some 900 corporations. Criticize each classification.

| Classification A | Classification B | Classification C |
|---|---|---|
| 1.00– 3.99 | 0– 4.00 | less than 10 |
| 4.00– 7.99 | 4.00– 8.00 | 11 less than 20 |
| 8.00– 9.99 | 8.00–12.00 | 21 less than 30 |
| 10.00–11.99 | 12.00–16.00 | 31 and over |
| 12.00–13.99 | 16.00–20.00 | |
| 14.00–16.99 | 20.00–24.00 | |
| 17.00–19.99 | 24.00–28.00 | |
| 20.00–22.99 | 28.00–32.00 | |
| 23.00–26.99 | 32.00 and over | |
| 27.00–31.99 | | |
| 32.00–99.99 | | |

ADM 2.6 As the office manager you are responsible for monitoring the typing skills of the clerical workers. The following distribution represents net typing speeds (words typed per minute less errors) for the 25 clerical workers in your typing pool.

| Typing Speed (wpm) | Frequency |
|---|---|
| 30–39 | 2 |
| 40–49 | 4 |
| 50–59 | 5 |
| 60–69 | 7 |
| 70–79 | 4 |
| 80–89 | 2 |
| 90–100 | 1 |

a) Develop the relative frequency distribution for these typing speed data.

b) Draw the relative frequency histogram.

c) Draw the cumulative relative frequency distribution and the associated ogive.

LAW 2.7 A small machine shop has just declared bankruptcy. As a bankruptcy lawyer you wish to classify the shop's accounts payable. The following are the major amounts owed by the machine shop (in thousands of dollars):

```
2.78   3.12   2.94   2.95   3.18   2.86   2.24   2.30   3.41   3.02
3.42   3.04   3.28   3.13   2.65   2.50   2.63   2.68   3.17   2.30
3.25   2.78   3.14   3.05   2.95   3.36   3.02   2.86   3.02   3.01
3.02   3.21   3.27   3.36   3.13   2.82   3.50   3.11   2.86   3.55
3.05   3.12   3.52   2.87   2.86   2.85   3.34   2.75   3.06   2.95
```

a) Use the stem and leaf approach to determine an appropriate frequency distribution. Convert this frequency distribution into a relative frequency distribution.

b) Draw the relative frequency histogram for these data.

c) Draw the cumulative relative frequency function and the associated ogive.

FIN 2.8 Use the information on book value per share in Appendix A.1 for banks and bank holding companies.

a) Use the stem and leaf approach to determine an appropriate frequency distribution. Convert this frequency distribution into a relative frequency distribution.

b) Draw the relative frequency histogram for these data.

c) Draw the cumulative relative frequency distribution and the associated ogive.

**2.9** What classes would you use for a relative frequency distribution for sample data on starting salaries (yearly) of business school graduates at your college or university? Would your class boundaries change if salaries were rounded to the nearest $100?

ADM  **2.10** *Business Week* publishes an annual list of "Executive Pay." The first 30 values for "Total Annual Compensation" for chief executive officers in 1984 were (in thousands of dollars):

$997, $238, $1019, $787, $658,  $1250, $391,  $425, $424, $626
$567, $279, $1195, $932, $678,  $950,  $1575, $744, $519, $629
$890, $678, $232,  $449, $1400, $523,  $905,  $629, $828, $512

a) Determine a frequency distribution for these salaries using appropriate classes.

b) Determine the relative frequency distribution and draw the histogram.

c) Draw the cumulative frequency distribution and the associated ogive.

# 2.6  Other Descriptive Graphs

While histograms and distributional functions are common graphical forms used in statistics, other pictorial forms are also widely used in the popular press. **Pie charts** are often used to present financial and marketing data. For example, Fig. 2.6 shows two *Newsweek* pie charts depicting actual energy sources in 1977 and those estimated by the World Coal Study for the year 2000. These pie charts indicate that 18.5% of our total energy needs were met by coal in 1977. The estimate for the year 2000 is that 34.6% of our energy needs will be met by coal.

Pie charts can be constructed using either qualitative or quantitative data. For data already in frequency form, a pie chart is constructed by converting

Figure 2.6
A changing
energy pie.

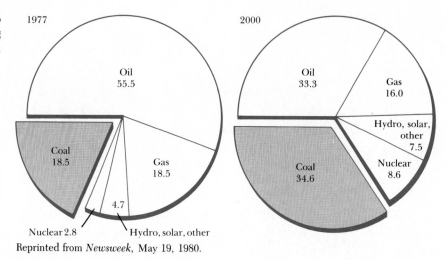

Reprinted from *Newsweek*, May 19, 1980.

the relative frequencies of each class into their respective degrees in a circle. The number of degrees required to represent the relative frequency of the *i*th class is obtained by multiplying 360° by the relative frequency of the *i*th class ($f_i/n$ or $f_i/N$).

As an example of pie chart construction, consider a public official who wishes to describe enrollments in the schools. Since the official's presentation will be televised, visual aids are essential. A pie chart is used to show the grade level share of students. Table 2.4 gives the enrollment of the schools. The degrees for each of the three slices in Fig. 2.7 were obtained by multiplying each relative frequency (for enrollment) by 360°. Computer programs are readily available to aid in constructing pie charts.

**Table 2.4**

| **Pie Chart Degree Calculation: Enrollment Data** | | | |
|---|---|---|---|
| **Students Enrolled in Grades:** | **Frequency** $(f_i)$ | **Relative Frequency** $(f_i/N)$ | **Degrees** $(f_i/N)(360°)$ |
| K–5th | 4,779 | 0.4352 | 156.7 |
| 6th–8th | 2,810 | 0.2559 | 92.1 |
| 9th–12th | 3,391 | 0.3089 | 111.2 |
| Total Enrollment (K–12th) | 10,980 | 1.0000 | 360.0 |

Figure 2.7
Enrollment pie chart.

Source: Table 2.4.

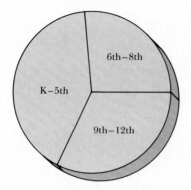

A **bar chart** is another useful method for representing qualitative data. Bar charts look like histograms (see Fig. 2.8); the difference is that bar charts need not show frequencies on the vertical axis. Rather, bar charts may present any quantitative value on this axis. In Fig. 2.8, for example, the vertical axis shows the extra tax dollars the U.S. Treasury expects to gain from a contro-

Figure 2.8
The extra taxes the U.S. Treasury expects from capital gains.

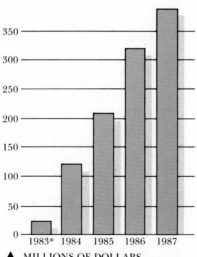

▲ MILLIONS OF DOLLARS

*SECOND HALF

Data: Joint Committee on Taxation. Reprinted from the April 23, 1983, issue of *Business Week* by special permission, © 1983 by McGraw-Hill, Inc.

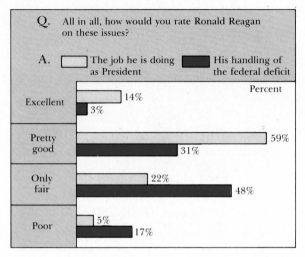

**Figure 2.9**
Opinion about the U.S. President Ronald Reagan.

Data: Louis Harris & Associates, Inc.   Reprinted from the February 21, 1983, issue of *Business Week* by special permission, © 1983 by McGraw-Hill, Inc.

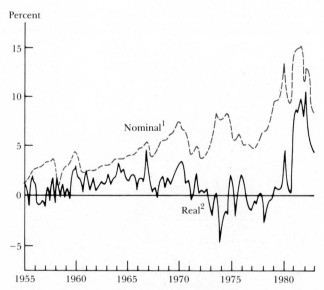

**Figure 2.10**
Nominal and real 3-month Treasury bill yield.

1. Converted to effective annual yield from discount base

2. Equals normal yield less actual rate of inflation, defined by personal consumption deflator, over the period to maturity. Deflator for first quarter 1983 forecast by Council of Economic Advisers

Sources: Department of Commerce, Board of Governors of the Federal Reserve System and Council of Economic Advisers

Chapter 2   Descriptive Statistics: Graphs and Index Numbers

versial law (requiring brokers to report all capital gains at the time of security sales). The classes in Fig. 2.8 (a *Business Week* chart) represent years.

Figure 2.9 is also a *Business Week* bar chart. This figure reports qualitative data from a Harris opinion survey on business executives' attitudes toward President Ronald Reagan. The horizontal axis indicates the percentage of times respondents answered "Excellent," "Pretty good," "Only fair," or "Poor" in rating the president. This bar chart is not a histogram because the responses on the vertical axis are not quantitative.

**Line charts** (see Fig. 2.10) are often used to present trends over time (called *time series*). For instance, Fig. 2.10 (from the *Economic Report of the President*) shows the trend in both the nominal and real rate of interest since 1955. The nominal rate is the observed Treasury bill rate, while the real rate is the observed Treasury bill rate less the rate of price inflation. Line charts are preferred to bar graphs for some time series because they can present the data as a continuous flow (whereby month-to-month or day-to-day changes are easily followed).

---

**WORKED EXAMPLE 2.5**

Consider the two following diagrams. What do they tell you about the trend in auto sales?

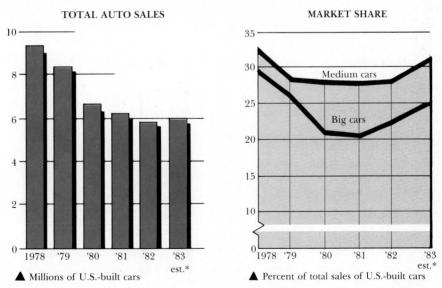

Data: Ward's Automotive Reports, BW Estimates.   Reprinted from the April 18, 1983, issue of *Business Week* by special permission, © 1983 by McGraw-Hill, Inc.

**ANSWER:**

The bar chart representing auto sales shows that 1983 sales were about 6 million units, up slightly from their 1982 low. The market share chart indicates that medium-sized cars still constitute a higher percentage of total sales than do big cars, although the percentage of big cars sold rose continuously since the beginning of 1981. Since the market share of medium-sized cars remained relatively fixed in 1981 but then also started rising in 1982, the percentage of small cars sold must have started falling in 1981.

## Exercises

**2.11**   Explain the differences and similarities between pie charts, bar charts, and line charts.

MKT   **2.12**   What does the following bar chart indicate regarding Volkswagen's market share of West German auto sales?

MARKET SHARES IN WEST GERMANY

☐ VOLKSWAGEN   ■ OPEL   ▨ FORD

Data: West German Federal Vehicle Office. Reprinted from the August 22, 1983, issue of *Business Week* by special permission, © 1983 by McGraw-Hill, Inc.

MKT **2.13** Draw two pie charts to represent the information on market shares in Exercise 2.12 for the years 1980 and 1983.

ADM **2.14** A well-known manufacturer conducted a telephone poll to assess how the public was responding to reports that 20 years ago the company was involved in toxic waste dumping. The following data reflect the responses to a question regarding the adequacy of the manufacturer's plans to assist in the cleanup.

Is the manufacturer's cleanup plan adequate?

| | |
|---|---|
| Yes | 485 |
| No | 73 |
| Don't know | 42 |

**a)** Draw a pie chart representing the responses.

**b)** Draw a bar chart representing the responses.

**c)** If the manufacturer wishes to include these results in its annual report, which chart should be used?

ECN **2.15** Interpret the following graph on retail sales from the *WSJ*.

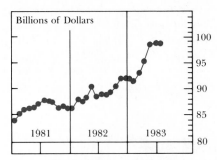

ECN **2.16** Why are economic quantities such as retail sales, gross national product, personal income, corporate sales, and other similar flows typically represented as line charts?

MKT **2.17** Draw a graph to show the sales (in billions of dollars) for the International Harvester Company in the following quarters.

| Year: | | 1981 | | | | 1982 | | | | 1983 | |
|---|---|---|---|---|---|---|---|---|---|---|---|
| Quarter: | I | II | III | IV | I | II | III | IV | I | II | |
| Sales: | 1.6 | 2.1 | 1.7 | 1.8 | 1.0 | 1.4 | 1.3 | 1.0 | 0.7 | 1.0 | |

**2.18** Determine if the placement office at your college or university provides summary data on starting salaries for last year. Are these data in a form discussed in this chapter? If not, explain why the form might have been selected.

ECN **2.19** Construct a line graph using the 1983–1984 monthly data on unemployment in Appendix Table A.2 (use the categories Male, Female, and Total).

# 2.7 Index Numbers

Index numbers are often used to measure changes in large sets of data over time. Although there are many different types of indexes in both the physical and social sciences, the most publicized indexes are used to measure economic activity over time, such as changes in prices, wages, and productivity.

Perhaps the best-known index is the Consumer Price Index (CPI). This index is used to set social security payments, make cost-of-living adjustments (COLAS) in wage contracts, and even determine changes in child support payments. The CPI is a series of numbers designed to represent the cost to consumers of a typical bundle of goods and services. Table 2.5 shows the CPI for selected years between 1947 and 1984.

What do the numbers in Table 2.5 mean? How do they illustrate the change in prices over time? These are the questions addressed in this section.

**Table 2.5**

| U.S. Consumer Price Index | | | |
|---|---|---|---|
| Year | Index | Year | Index |
| 1947 | 66.9 | 1975 | 161.2 |
| 1957 | 84.3 | 1976 | 170.5 |
| 1967 | 100.0 | 1977 | 181.5 |
| 1968 | 104.2 | 1978 | 195.4 |
| 1969 | 109.8 | 1979 | 217.4 |
| 1970 | 116.3 | 1980 | 246.8 |
| 1971 | 112.3 | 1981 | 272.4 |
| 1972 | 125.3 | 1982 | 289.1 |
| 1973 | 133.1 | 1983 | 298.4 |
| 1974 | 147.7 | 1984 | 311.1 |

Source: *Economic Report of the President.*

The CPI is not the only index reported by the U.S. government. Others include the Product Price Index (PPI), the Gross National Product (GNP) Deflator, the Index of Industrial Production (IIP), and the Export and Import Indexes. Even the CPI itself is not a single index; two U.S. consumer price indexes are compiled—the Consumer Price Index for All Urban Consumers (CPI-U) and the Consumer Price Index for Urban Wage Earners (CPI-W). Furthermore, at any given time there may be various forms of each of these indexes. For instance, two CPI-U's were computed in 1983—one based on 1967 dollars and the other based on 1977 dollars.

A price index involves a **bundle** of goods, that is, a set of goods and services purchased by a typical person. For example, in the case of the CPI-W the bundle is defined as purchases by a typical urban wage earner. These goods and services include (1) food and beverages, (2) housing, (3) apparel and upkeep, (4) transportation, (5) medical care, (6) entertainment, and (7) other goods and services. The total cost of the bundle is determined for each year in the series by multiplying the price of each item by the number of that item the consumer purchased. For example, suppose a typical consumer purchased 100 pounds of meat in 1967 at an average price of $1.00 per pound. The 1967 cost to this consumer for meat is thus 100($1.00) = $100. The total cost to a consumer is the sum of such costs for the various goods and services in the bundle.

One year of the series is designated as the base year. For the data in Table 2.5, 1967 is the base year. A price index is a ratio of the cost of the bundle of goods in any given year to the cost of that same bundle in the base year multiplied by 100. For example, the price index for 1977 using 1967 as the base year is defined as follows:

$$\text{1977 price index} = \frac{\text{total cost of bundle (1977)}}{\text{total cost of bundle (1967)}} \times 100$$

From Table 2.5, the 1977 price index is 181.5. This means that the total cost of the 1977 bundle is 81.5% higher than the cost of the 1967 bundle. In other words, between 1967 and 1977 prices increased by an average of 81.5% for the bundle purchased by this typical consumer in 1967.

To see how a price index is constructed, consider the bundle of goods shown in Table 2.6. We wish to construct a price index for food costs. The bundle of goods involves only three items: meat, eggs, and milk. As Table 2.6 indicates, in 1967 a typical person purchased 100 pounds of meat at an average price of $1.00 per pound. In 1977 this person bought meat at an average price per pound of $1.90. The price paid for eggs by our typical consumer was $0.42 per dozen in 1967 and $0.89 per dozen in 1977. This

| | | | Calculating a 1977 Price Index | | |
|---|---|---|---|---|---|
| (1) Bundle Item | (2) 1967 Quantity | (3) 1967 Price | (4) 1977 Price | (5) 1967 Total Cost | (6) 1977 Total Cost |
| Meat | 100 lb | $1.00/lb | $1.90/lb | $100.00 | $190.00 |
| Eggs | 25 doz | $0.42/doz | $0.89/doz | $ 10.50 | $ 22.25 |
| Milk | 70 gal | $0.54/gal | $0.79/gal | $ 37.80 | $ 55.30 |
| | | | Total cost of bundle = | $148.30 | $267.55 |

**Table 2.6**

consumer purchased 25 dozen eggs in 1967. Finally, 70 gallons of milk were purchased by this consumer in 1967 at $0.54 per gallon. In 1977 the price of milk was $0.79 per gallon.

To determine the total cost for any year, the price of each good is multiplied by the quantity purchased in the base year. Thus 100 pounds of meat multiplied by $1.00 per pound results in a total cost for meat in 1967 of $100 (shown in column 5 of Table 2.6). The total cost of the 1967 bundle is $148.30. Similarly, the total cost of the bundle in 1977 is $267.55. The 1977 price index for these three food items is:

$$1977 \text{ price index (base 1967)} = \frac{267.55}{148.30} \times 100 = 180.4$$

The price index for 1967 is 100.0, because 1967 is the base year. The index number 180.4 indicates that for this bundle of food items, 1977 prices were 80.4% higher than 1967 prices.

The index just calculated is an example of a **Laspeyres price index**. The CPI is also a Laspeyres index. In a Laspeyres index the *quantities* purchased in the base year are held constant. The index for any given year (19??) is defined as follows:

| | |
|---|---|
| **DEFINITION Laspeyres price index** | Laspeyres price index for 19?? $$= \frac{\text{total cost (base year quantity, 19?? prices)}}{\text{total cost (base year quantity, base year prices)}} \times 100$$ |

Chapter 2 Descriptive Statistics: Graphs and Index Numbers

If the typical 1967 consumer purchases 100 pounds of meat (as in the preceding example), then 100 pounds is used as the quantity of meat purchased per year throughout the series. The problem with this approach is that as the tastes of consumers change over time, the quantities used in the base year (i.e., the bundle) may become outdated. For example, suppose an index includes the price of black and white television sets. The quantity of black and white television sets purchased (per person) in 1967 was certainly greater than the quantity purchased in more recent years, which means that this particular purchase is given more consideration than it should be given in recent index numbers.

One way to avoid the problem of an outdated bundle of goods is to use a **Paasche price index**. In a Paasche index quantities are defined in terms of *current* purchases. That is, the most recent period is the base period.

---

**DEFINITION**
**Paasche price index**

Paasche price index for 19??

$$= \frac{\text{total cost (19?? quantity, 19?? prices)}}{\text{total cost (19?? quantity, base year prices)}} \times 100$$

---

The Gross National Product Deflator is an example of a Paasche index. A Paasche index tends to understate price increases and overstate price declines, while a Laspeyres index tends to overstate price increases and understate price declines. Paasche indexes are more difficult to update because the bundle changes each year, requiring recalculation of every number in the series. It is for this reason that Laspeyres indexes have come to dominate summary measures of economic data collected over time.

---

**WORKED EXAMPLE 2.6**

Determine a Paasche index for 1977 using the prices in Table 2.6 and assuming that the quantities for 1977 are as follows: meat, 120 pounds; eggs, 22 dozen; and milk, 65 gallons.

**ANSWER:**

Table 2.7

| | Calculating a 1977 Paasche Price Index | | | | |
|---|---|---|---|---|---|
| (1)<br>Bundle<br>Item | (2)<br>1977<br>Quantity | (3)<br>1967<br>Price | (4)<br>1977<br>Price | (5)<br>1967<br>Total Cost | (6)<br>1977<br>Total Cost |
| Meat | 120 lb | $1.00/lb | $1.90/lb | $120.00 | $228.00 |
| Eggs | 22 doz | $0.42/doz | $0.89/doz | $ 9.24 | $ 19.58 |
| Milk | 65 gal | $0.54/gal | $0.79/gal | $ 35.10 | $ 51.35 |
| | | | Total price of bundle = | $164.34 | $298.93 |

$$1977 \text{ Paasche Price Index (base 1967)} = \frac{298.93}{164.34} \times 100 = 181.9$$

---

Although price indexes are essential for representing changes in economic data, index numbers are also useful in representing changes in *any* series of numbers. For example, in legal cases of wrongful death, it is often necessary to project the potential earnings of the deceased (i.e., earnings the deceased would have been expected to earn). This requires the development of projections for workers with a background similar to that of the deceased. Table 2.8 (column 5) illustrates such an index, with a base (death) at age 21. The calculations in Table 2.8 show projected earnings for a full-time worker who has not completed high school for three diffferent earnings at age 21 ($13,850, $12,850, and $11,850). For example, column 2 in Table 2.8 shows that a 21-year-old earning $13,850 per year is projected to earn $20,024.62 (= $13,850 × 144.58/100) at age 61. Calculations for other earnings and ages are not difficult when one uses a spreadsheet, such as Lotus 1-2-3 or VisiCalc.

Price indexes are useful in determining how the price of any commodity has changed relative to general prices. For example, suppose an economist wishes to determine how the price of gasoline changed relative to prices in general between 1967 and 1983. The price for a gallon of gas was $0.35 in 1967, $0.75 in 1975, and $1.10 in 1983. Let's start by comparing 1967 and 1975. The CPI index is 100 for 1967 and 161.2 for 1975 (from Table 2.5). To compare 1967 and 1975, we "deflate" the 1975 price by dividing it by the CPI/100 = 1.612. The result is the real price of gasoline in 1975, based on

1967 prices.

$$\text{Real 1975 gas price} = \frac{\text{actual 1975 price}}{\text{CPI (1975)}} = \frac{0.75}{1.612} = 0.465$$

This result shows that the 1975 price of gasoline (based on 1967 prices) has increased by more than $0.11 ($0.465–$0.35) over the 1967 price after adjusting for the general increase in prices. If the price of gasoline had increased the same as the CPI, then the real price in 1975 would have been $0.35 per gallon.

This process of deflating a price is continued for each year of interest in the series. The price of gasoline in constant (1967) dollars is then $0.35 for 1967 (the base year), $0.465 for 1975, and $0.369 (= $1.10/2.984) for 1983. From these three observations, the real price of gasoline appears to have risen in the 1970s, but by 1983 it had declined to a level only slightly higher, in real terms, than it was in 1967.

Changing the base year of a price index will alter the level of the index but should not alter the rate of change in the series. For example, when the U.S. Bureau of Labor Statistics completes the rebasing of the CPI from the 1967 base of 100 to a 1977 base of 100, the percentage change from 1977 to 1978 will be the same for both series (with the exception of changes caused by altering the items included). In particular, the CPI was 181.5 in 1977 and

**Table 2.8**

| | Projected Earnings Based on an Index of Earnings for All Full-Time Workers without a High School Diploma | | | |
|---|---|---|---|---|
| (1) | (2) | (3) | (4) | (5) |
| Age | Earnings in year of death: $13,850 | Earnings in year of death: $12,850 | Earnings in year of death: $11,850 | Index of yearly earnings |
| 21 | 13,850.00 | 12,850.00 | 11,850.00 | 100.000 |
| 25 | 15,057.12 | 13,969.96 | 12,882.80 | 108.716 |
| 31 | 16,997.30 | 15,770.05 | 14,542.81 | 122.724 |
| 35 | 18,282.41 | 16,962.38 | 15,642.35 | 132.003 |
| 41 | 20,006.13 | 18,561.64 | 17,117.15 | 144.449 |
| 45 | 20,890.69 | 19,382.33 | 17,873.98 | 150.835 |
| 51 | 21,571.22 | 20,013.73 | 18,456.24 | 155.749 |
| 55 | 21,431.57 | 19,884.16 | 18,336.75 | 154.741 |
| 61 | 20,024.62 | 18,578.79 | 17,132.97 | 144.582 |
| 64 | 18,659.78 | 17,312.50 | 15,965.22 | 134.728 |

Source: W. E. Becker testimony in Ortiz V. Rudser (Indiana).

195.4 in 1978 (from Table 2.5). This is a 7.7% increase, since

$$\frac{195.4 - 181.5}{181.5} = 0.077$$

Thus, inflation between 1977 and 1978 was 7.7%. A new CPI with 1977 as the base will place the index for 1977 at 100. The new 1978 value will have to correspond to (or "splice" into) the old base. Thus the 1978 CPI value will be 107.7 using 1977 as a base. Because percentage changes are maintained when indexes are rebased, the researcher can always splice differently based indexes.

---

**WORKED EXAMPLE 2.7**

Determine a 1979 value for the CPI index in Table 2.5, assuming 1977 is used as the base rather than 1967.

**ANSWER:**

The price change between 1977 and 1979 was

$$\frac{217.4 - 181.5}{181.5} = 0.1978 \quad \text{(or 19.78\%)}$$

Thus the index for 1979 is 119.78 based on 1977 prices.

---

## Exercises

MKT **2.20** The price of an IBM personal computer in 1981 was approximately $3800. In 1983 it was $2500. What is the 1983 price relative to the 1981 price? What was the percentage change in price?

MKT **2.21** The price and quantity of four products sold by a small toy firm are as follows for the years 1982 and 1983:

| | 1982 | | 1983 | |
| --- | --- | --- | --- | --- |
| *Toy Description* | *Price* | *Quantity* | *Price* | *Quantity* |
| Plastic car | $ 1.50 | 150,000 | $ 1.55 | 150,000 |
| Wooden horse | $ 4.90 | 25,000 | $ 4.90 | 27,000 |
| Cloth doll | $15.35 | 10,000 | $16.00 | 9,000 |
| Tea set | $19.98 | 5,000 | $18.98 | 5,500 |

a) Compute a Laspeyres Price Index for these data.

b) Compute a Paasche Price Index for these data.

MKT **2.22** In Exercise 2.21 (a), what was the average change in prices for the toy firm? Why does the average change in prices for the toy firm differ in parts (a) and (b)?

ECN **2.23** If the CPI rises from 135 to 145, what is the percentage change in prices?

ECN **2.24** In the early 1970s, when the CPI was being rebased from 1957 = 100 to 1967 = 100, a newspaper reporter stated that the Nixon administration was rebasing the index to make it appear that inflation in the early 1970s was less than it really was. He said: "The 1967 based index will yield a lower index value than what was indicated by the 1957 based index. Thus Nixon appears to have reduced inflation by a statistical trick." Comment on this statement.

ECN **2.25** Your salary increases are tied to the CPI shown in Table 2.5. In 1976 you made $30,000. What was your salary in 1982?

FIN **2.26** Consider the data in Appendix Table A.3. Determine the net income for each year between 1970 and 1979 based on constant 1967 dollars (use Table 2.5).

FIN **2.27** Use the CPI values in Appendix Table A.2 to deflate the values from 1960 to 1980 for corporate profits tax liability (also shown in Appendix Table A.2). Display these results in both a bar chart and a line chart.

**2.28** What are the advantages and disadvantages of the Laspeyres and Paasche price indexes?

ECN

**2.29** You decide to construct a price index for men's clothing for 1985, using 1980 as the base year. Determine both a Laspeyres and a Paasche index using the following data for the purchases in one year by a typical consumer.

| | 1980 | | 1985 | |
|---|---|---|---|---|
| Clothing item | Price | Quantity | Price | Quantity |
| Shoes | $29.00 | 3.2 | $36.50 | 3.8 |
| Pants | $18.75 | 4.6 | $22.30 | 5.1 |
| Shirts | $13.95 | 6.2 | $15.95 | 5.8 |
| Underwear | $ 2.50 | 8.9 | $ 2.60 | 8.8 |

**2.30** Go to the library and find a data set reporting business or economic data over time, measured in dollars. Deflate these data for the years 1970–1984 using CPI in Appendix A.2. Summarize the deflated data in a bar chart or a line chart.

## Chapter Exercises

**2.31** What is the difference between a bar chart and a histogram?

ECN **2.32** U.S. population projections for 1990 and 2000 are as follows:

| Projected Number of Persons (in Billions) | | |
|---|---|---|
| Age (years) | 1990 | 2000 |
| Under 5 | 19 | 18 |
| 5–13 | 29 | 35 |
| 14–17 | 14 | 16 |
| 18–24 | 28 | 25 |
| 25–34 | 40 | 34 |
| 35–44 | 31 | 41 |
| 45–54 | 23 | 36 |
| 55–64 | 22 | 23 |
| 65 and over | 27 | 32 |

a) Determine the relative frequency distributions for each of the two years.

b) Draw on the same graph the relative frequency histograms for the two years.

c) What differences are being projected for the age distribution of the population between 1990 and 2000?

d) In answering part (c), why would you use the relative frequency information and not the absolute frequency data?

ADM **2.33** Shown here is a *Business Week* diagram that reports the reasons 600 high-level executives gave for the problems of "smokestack industries." Convert this information into a pie chart. Why is your pie chart not as appropriate as *Business Week's* diagram?

**The smokeless smokestack:**
**Whom does business blame?**

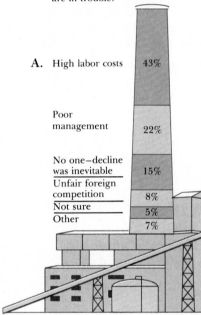

**Q.** What is the main reason U.S. smokestack industries are in trouble?

**A.** High labor costs — 43%

Poor management — 22%

No one—decline was inevitable — 15%

Unfair foreign competition — 8%

Not sure — 5%

Other — 7%

Data: Louis Harris & Associates, Inc. Reprinted from the April 18, 1983, issue of *Business Week* by special permission, © 1983 by McGraw-Hill, Inc.

LAW **2.34** Following are selected ages and the hypothetical projected income (in dollars) for an individual who died at age 42 while earning $35,622.

| Age | 47 | 52 | 57 | 62 | 67 | 72 |
|---|---|---|---|---|---|---|
| Projected Income | $37,310 | $38,518 | $39,035 | $38,624 | $37,030 | $33,974 |

**a)** Draw a bar chart to represent these data.

**b)** Draw a line chart to represent these data.

**c)** If you had to present these data in court and wished to give a visualization of the income this person could have expected if his work life had continued until age 72, which chart would you use and why?

**LAW**  **2.35**  You are asked to project the income of a person identical to the one described in Exercise 2.34 who also died at the age of 42. This person was earning $38,000. What is this person's projected income at age 72?

**FIN**  **2.36**  For the price-earnings ratios of the electrical industry represented in Appendix A.1, construct the frequency distribution for the price-earnings ratio column.

**FIN**  **2.37**  Prior to issuing a new bond, it is common to determine what similar bonds are yielding. A *Barron's* review of 30 of the most actively traded high-risk corporate 20-year bonds shows the following yields (in percentages):

15.7  16.1  13.0  18.5  15.2  11.1  12.7  14.9  16.7  13.8
15.9  14.4  11.7  13.6  15.3  17.2  12.2  14.4  16.3  13.8
14.3  16.4  13.9  15.5  16.2  15.1  14.8  12.6  17.3  18.2

a)  Use a stem and leaf method to develop a relative frequency distribution for these data. (Hint: use the first two digits as the stem.)

b)  What yield interval has the highest frequency?

**FIN**  **2.38**  What is the difference in the profit trend for the following two firms?

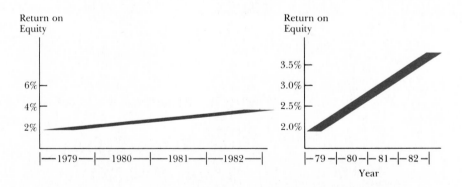

**FIN**  **2.39**  In 1973, when the PPI was 127.9, the Emerson Electronic Company had sales of $1.2 billion. In 1982, when the PPI was 280.6. Emerson had sales of $3.5 billion. In real terms have Emerson's sales increased or decreased? What were Emerson's 1982 sales in 1973 dollars?

**MKT**  **2.40**  Given the following distribution of Emerson's sales in 1973 and 1982,

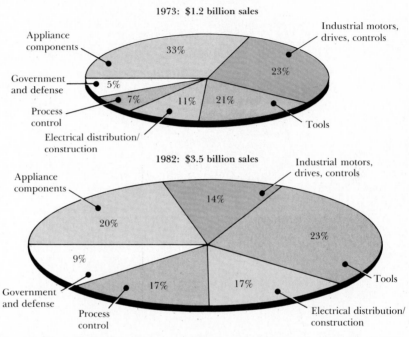

**Higher technology has
changed Emerson's product mix**

1973: $1.2 billion sales

Appliance
components

Industrial motors,
drives, controls

33%

23%

Government
and defense

5%

7%     11%     21%

Process
control

Tools

Electrical distribution/
construction

1982: $3.5 billion sales

Industrial motors,
drives, controls

Appliance
components

14%

20%

23%

9%

17%     17%

Tools

Government
and defense

Process
control

Electrical distribution/
construction

Reprinted from the April 4, 1983, issue of *Business Week* by special permission, © 1983
by McGraw-Hill, Inc.

by what percentage has the source of revenue coming from "Appliance
Components" decreased?

MKT  **2.41**  In the following *WSJ* pie chart (next page), how large is the market
for aspirin? What share of this aspirin market is held by Bayer? Draw
a pie chart showing the share of the aspirin market held by Bayer and
other companies.

FIN  **2.42**  The Dow Jones chart on page 72 appeared in the Bloomington, Indiana, *Sunday Herald Times* (August 21, 1983):

a)  Is this chart a histogram or just a bar chart? (Explain why.)

b)  What happened to stock prices between July 29, 1983, and August 8,
1983? (Give as much quantitative information as possible.)

**The Pain-Reliever Market**

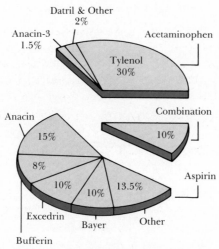

Total Market $1.3 Billion

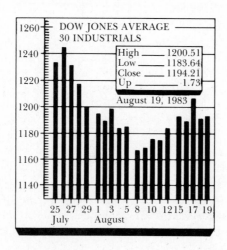

**c)** Cummins Engine closed on July 29, 1983 at $64.25 per share. If Cummins's price followed the Dow Jones Industrial Average, at what price would it have closed on August 19?

**d)** On August 19, 1983, Cummins actually closed at $64.75 per share. Why was your prediction in part (c) wrong?

ECN    **2.43**    Go to the library and find a microeconomics book that demonstrates, using indifference curve analysis, why the following statement (given in this chapter) is true: "A Paasche index tends to understate price increases and overstate price declines, while a Laspeyres index tends to overstate price increases and understate price declines." Demonstrate this statement graphically and give an intuitive explanation.

FIN    **2.44**    Graphs and charts can often be misleading unless one reads them very carefully. Consider, for example, the following line graphs on the decline of computer stocks, as reported in *Business Week*. Comment on the differences you see among the five stocks despite the fact that their charts look remarkably similar.

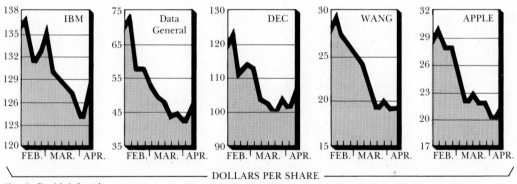

Chart by Derrick A. Langshaw

Reprinted from the April 25, 1985, issue of *Business Week* by special permission, © 1985 by McGraw-Hill, Inc.

MKT    **2.45**    The following pie charts (next page) from *Newsweek* describe the change in the beverage market share between 1976 and 1984. What has happened to the soft drink share of the market?

FIN    **2.46**    Draw a bar chart to represent the yearly assets of Workingmans Federal Savings and Loan in Appendix A.3. (Use the fourth-quarter assets as the 1980–1984 yearly totals.) What does this bar chart tell you about the change in Workingmans assets?

### BEVERAGE MARKET SHARE
In percent

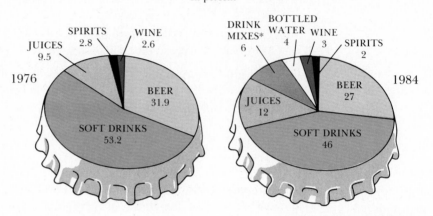

*Nonalcoholic powdered mixes

Data: Beverage World   Copyright 1985 by *Newsweek*, Inc. All rights reserved. Reprinted by permission.

| | |
|---|---|
| Under $4,999 | 5.7% |
| $5,000–$9,999 | 10.2% |
| $10,000–$14,999 | 11.6% |
| $15,000–$19,999 | 11.8% |
| $20,000–$24,999 | 11.5% |
| $25,000–$34,999 | 19.5% |
| $35,000–$49,999 | 17.0% |
| $50,000–$59,999 | 5.4% |
| $60,000 and up | 7.2% |

Reprinted by permission of Newspaper Enterprise Association.

FIN   **2.47**   Draw a line chart to represent the quarterly net income of Workingmans Federal Savings and Loan in Appendix A.3, for the first quarter of 1980 through the first quarter of 1985. What does this line chart tell you about the change in Workingmans net income?

FIN   **2.48**   Why is a bar chart used to represent assets in Exercise 2.46, while a line chart is used for income in Exercise 2.47?

ECN   **2.49**   The U.S. Family Income diagram on page 74 appeared in the Bloomington, Indiana, *Sunday Herald Times*:

    **a)** Draw a histogram to represent these data.

    **b)** Draw an ogive to represent these data.

    **c)** The majority of families make less than what approximate income?

    **d)** Why is this diagram less than a perfect presentation of a frequency distribution?

## Glossary

**absolute frequency:** The number of times an observation falls into a class.

**bar chart:** A graph in which the horizontal axis presents qualitative or quantitative information and the vertical axis shows associated information.

**bundle:** A set of goods and services purchased by a typical person.

**cumulative frequency:** The total number of observations that have values less than or equal to a specified amount.

**cumulative frequency distribution:** A presentation of an entire set of cumulative frequencies.

**cumulative relative frequency:** A cumulative frequency divided by the total number of observations.

**frequency distribution:** A presentation of the frequencies (absolute or relative) for each class in a data set.

**histogram:** A type of bar chart that represents a frequency distribution in which class intervals are represented on the horizontal axis and class relative or absolute frequencies are represented on the vertical axis.

**Laspeyres price index:** The ratio of the total cost of a bundle of goods in a given period to the cost of that bundle in a base period, where the bundle of goods is always of the base period.

**line chart:** A continuous graph showing the value of an index or series of numbers over time.

**midpoint:** The middle value of each class in a frequency distribution.

**ogive:** A series of straight lines connecting the lower boundaries of each class in a cumulative relative frequency distribution.

**Paasche price index:** The ratio of the cost of a bundle of goods in a given year to the base year cost for that bundle.

**pie chart:** A circle divided into sections to show the relative number of times a characteristic occurs.

**price index:** A ratio of the costs in any given period to the costs in a base period for a bundle of goods and services.

**qualitative data:** Information in the form of categorical labeling of a characteristic.

**quantitative data:** Information in the form of numerical values.

**relative frequency:** The proportion (or percent) of observations in a class of the total number of observations in the data set.

**stem and leaf plot:** A method of classifying quantitative data whereby the leaf is the last digit of a number and the stem is the preceding digit(s).

## Formulas

**Laspeyres Price Index for 19??**

$$= \frac{\text{total cost (base year quantity, 19?? prices)}}{\text{total cost (base year quantity, base year price)}} \times 100$$

**Paasche Price Index for 19??**

$$= \frac{\text{total cost (19?? quantities, 19?? prices)}}{\text{total cost (19?? quantities, base year prices)}} \times 100$$

**Percentage Change**

$$\begin{array}{l}\text{Percentage change}\\ \text{in a price index}\\ \text{between 1977 and 1978}\end{array} = \frac{\text{index(1978)} - \text{index(1977)}}{\text{index(1977)}} \times 100$$

**Relative Frequency**

$f_i/n$ for a sample and $f_i/N$ for a population

# CHAPTER THREE

*Figures do not lie but any liar can figure.*
*Anon.*

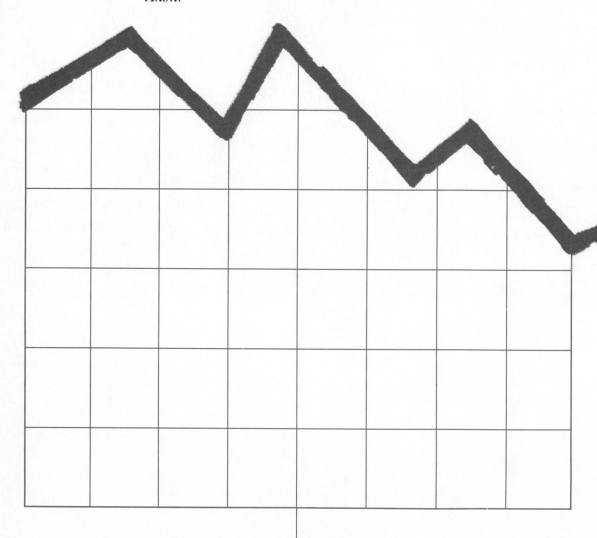

# DESCRIPTIVE STATISTICS: LOCATION AND DISPERSION

# 3.1  INTRODUCTION

In addition to describing frequency distributions graphically (as we did in Chapter 2), numerical measures are used to summarize quantitative information. Important numerical measures are presented in this chapter to describe (1) the location of data and (2) the spread or variability of a data set. These numerical measures form the basis for making inferences about population characteristics using sample data.

- A purchasing agent may decide whether to accept or reject a shipment of cloth rolls by determining the average number of flaws per year in a sample of the rolls. The sample provides the basis for a statement about the average number of flaws in the shipment (the population) and hence for accepting or rejecting the shipment.

- An instructional designer wishes to specify the length of the training time so that at least 50% of the participants will reach some level of competence. Competence is defined in terms of an average test score.

- A financial analyst wants to describe numerically the expected return on a certain type of investment, as well as the risk of this investment.

- A marketing researcher must be able to state the average price customers are willing to pay for a product and to estimate how many people will buy at that price.

These examples illustrate the need for measures indicating the central location and spread of a data set. This chapter introduces you to alternative measures of location and measures of dispersion. By the end of this chapter you should be able to calculate, and make use of, three measures of central location (the mean, the median, and the mode), other measures of location (percentages, percentiles, and quartiles), and three measures of dispersion (range, variance, and standard deviation). You will be able to calculate and interpret measures using the original data as well as frequency distributions, and also describe the characteristics of a distribution based on such measures. To illustrate these concepts, consider the following case.

## Consumer Doubt About an Insurance Firm

You are the state commissioner of insurance. An irate consumer group wants you to initiate a costly review process that it hopes will result in the fining of an insurance company for deceptive advertising. The insurance company is advertising that the average processing time to settle a household damage claim fully is only 8 days. The consumer group claims that the majority of such claims are not settled in even 13 days. Thus, the group asks, "How can the insurance company be guilty of anything short of fraud?" What action will you take before responding?

# 3.2 Measures of Central Location

Histograms, bar charts, and other graphical forms may not adequately summarize a data set. In the previous insurance case, a histogram would graph all of the data but would not provide any summary measures of, or method for comparing, the average time necessary to settle claims versus the time required to settle the majority of claims.

The insurance case requires answers to three questions: First, where is the middle of the data, that is, where is the central location of the distribution of processing time? Second, how spread out are the data, that is, how dispersed is the distribution? Third, are the central location and the dispersion of the distribution consistent with either, or both, the insurance company's or the consumer group's claims about processing time?

The first part of this chapter is devoted to answering the first of these questions, while the later parts will provide answers to the second and third questions. Thus, only at the end of this chapter will you be able to decide fully on the action to be taken in this case. Let's begin the analysis by considering the three measures of central location—mean, median and mode.

# 3.3 Mean

In statistics the average of a set of numbers is called the **mean**. Thus, in the insurance case, we know that the insurance company's claim is about the mean processing time.

| | |
|---|---|
| **DEFINITION**<br>**Mean** | The mean of a data set is the average of the values in that set. The mean is calculated by summing over all the values in the set and dividing this sum by the number of observations in the set. |

Since the insurance case does not provide any data, to illustrate the calculation of a mean, consider the data from the random sample of 40 charge accounts in the hardware store case in Chapter 2. The dollar amount owed by these 40 customers is repeated in Table 3.1. For these data the mean is calculated as follows:

$$(\tfrac{1}{40})(\$71 + \$58 + \$66 + \cdots + \$35 + \$70 + \$78) = \$64.45$$

(The notation $\$66 + \cdots + \$35$ means to add all the numbers from $\$66$ to $\$35$; to list all 40 observations is too cumbersome.)

A symbolic way to write the calculation of the mean of the 40 accounts values is as follows:

$$\text{Mean} = (\tfrac{1}{40})(x_1 + x_2 + x_3 + \cdots + x_{39} + x_{40})$$

where $x_1$ is the value of the first observation (i.e., $x_1 = \$71$), $x_2$ is the second

| Table 3.1 | Sample of Charge Account Data | | | | | | | | | |
|---|---|---|---|---|---|---|---|---|---|---|
| | $71, | $58, | $66, | $119, | $55, | $46, | $22, | $69, | $84, | $72, |
| | $45, | $61, | $45, | $84, | $68, | $107, | $96, | $58, | $47, | $61, |
| | $91, | $47, | $102, | $76, | $63, | $55, | $52, | $69, | $75, | $10, |
| | $85, | $32, | $63, | $55, | $55, | $65, | $66, | $35, | $70, | $78 |

Source: Figure 2.2.

Chapter 3  Descriptive Statistics: Location and Dispersion

($x_2 = \$58$), and so on, and $x_{40}$ is the final value ($x_{40} = \$78$). The ($\frac{1}{40}$) at the beginning indicates that the sum is divided by the number of observations.

As in Chapter 2, the symbol $x_i$ is used to indicate the $i$th value of the data set. For the accounts receivable, $i = 1$, or $i = 2$, or any number up to $i = 40$. Sigma notation provides a convenient way to write a formula for the mean of our data set. Capital sigma ($\Sigma$) is used to indicate a summation. The items to be summed always follow the sum sign ($\Sigma \ x_i$). The beginning and ending numbers of the summation are indicated by placing the starting number for $i$ below the sigma and the ending number above the sigma. Thus the notation

$$\sum_{i=1}^{40} x_i$$

indicates that the summation should begin with the first $x_i$ value (which is $x_1$) and should end with the 40th number (which is $x_{40}$). Thus

$$\sum_{i=1}^{40} x_i = x_1 + x_2 + \cdots + x_{40}$$

If we had wanted to sum the numbers starting with $x_{20}$ and ending with $x_{30}$, then the correct notation would be

$$\sum_{i=20}^{30} x_i = x_{20} + x_{21} + \cdots + x_{30}$$

Now we can define the mean of the charge account data, using sigma notation, as follows:

$$\text{Mean} = \left(\frac{1}{40}\right) \sum_{i=1}^{40} x_i = \left(\frac{1}{40}\right)(x_1 + x_2 + \cdots + x_{39} + x_{40})$$

When a set of $x$ values is a population, the average is called the **population mean** and is denoted by the Greek symbol $\mu_x$, which is read as "mu sub-ex." The subscript on $\mu$ indicates that this is a mean of $x$ values. (The mean of a population of $y$ values would be called $\mu_y$). The subscript on $\mu$ may be omitted when there is no confusion about the variable of interest. For populations, $N$ is used to indicate the number of observations.

When the set is a sample of $x$ values, the average is called the **sample mean** and is denoted by the symbol $\bar{x}$, which is read as "ex bar." (The mean of a sample of $y$ values would be denoted $\bar{y}$). For samples, $n$ indicates the number of observations.

The mean of a population of size $N$ is called $\mu_x$.

$$\mu_x = \frac{1}{N} \sum_{i=1}^{N} x_i = \left(\frac{1}{N}\right)(x_1 + x_2 + \cdots + x_N)$$

(3.1)

The mean of a sample of size $n$ is called $\bar{x}$.

$$\bar{x} = \frac{1}{n} \sum_{i=1}^{n} x_i = \left(\frac{1}{n}\right)(x_1 + x_2 + \cdots + x_n)$$

Generally we know whether a data set is a population or a sample. The charge account data, for example, represent a sample because the case indicated that these 40 values represent a random selection of all balances for the hardware store last month. Thus for these data $n = 40$ and $\bar{x} = 64.45$. (If the hardware store had only 40 charge account customers, then this data set would have been a population with $N = 40$ and the mean would be denoted $\mu_x$.)

In general, the characteristics of a population are called **parameters**. Thus $\mu_x$ is a population parameter. Characteristics of a sample are called **statistics**, so that $\bar{x}$ is a sample statistic. We will study other parameters and statistics in this chapter.

**WORKED EXAMPLE 3.1**

To assess the profit margin per dollar of sales at a convenience store, a random sample of five items is selected from the shelves. The profit margin per dollar on each item is given below. Calculate the average profit margin for this sample.

| Item | Profit Margin Per Dollar |
|------|--------------------------|
| 1 | 6.3¢ |
| 2 | 6.0¢ |
| 3 | 5.4¢ |
| 4 | 5.3¢ |
| 5 | 4.7¢ |

**ANSWER:**

For a sample of size $n = 5$,

$$\bar{x} = (\tfrac{1}{5})(6.3¢ + 6.0¢ + 5.4¢ + 5.3¢ + 4.7¢) = 5.54¢$$

## The Mean for Grouped Data

Data are often reported in the form of a frequency distribution, where class intervals are given but the actual values of the observations in the classes are not known. This is called **grouped data**.

For grouped data the mean cannot be calculated by summing the values in the frequency distribution (since the available information is not the original or raw data). However, a mean for the grouped data can be determined by making the assumption that the observations within a class fall evenly throughout that class. This assumption permits the use of the middle (or midpoint) of each class to represent all the values in that class. (This is a reasonable assumption if the rules for constructing frequency distributions described in Chapter 2 were followed.)

Using the midpoint of classes to calculate a mean for grouped data involves essentially the same steps used for ungrouped data. Instead of $x_i$, however, $m_i$ (for midpoint) is used to represent the values in the data set. As in Chapter 2, the frequency of each value in the data set is denoted by $f_i$. A grouped mean is calculated by multiplying each value of $m_i$ by the corresponding $f_i$ and then summing over the number of classes (which we call $c$). Thus the population and sample means for grouped data are as follows:

---

Population mean for grouped data

$$\mu_x = \frac{1}{N} \sum_{i=1}^{c} f_i m_i = \left(\frac{1}{N}\right)(f_1 m_1 + f_2 m_2 + \cdots + f_c m_c)$$

(3.2)

Sample mean for grouped data

$$\bar{x} = \frac{1}{n} \sum_{i=1}^{c} f_i m_i = \left(\frac{1}{n}\right)(f_1 m_1 + f_2 m_2 + \cdots + f_c m_c)$$

---

**Table 3.2**

| U.S. Unemployment by Weekly Duration (Thousands of Persons 16 Years of Age or Older) | | | | |
|---|---|---|---|---|
| | Year | | | |
| *Duration* | *1950* | *1960* | *1970* | *1980* |
| Less than 5 weeks | 1450 | 1719 | 2137 | 3208 |
| 5 less than 15 weeks | 1055 | 1176 | 1289 | 2411 |
| 15 less than 27 weeks | 425 | 503 | 427 | 1028 |
| 27 weeks or more | 357 | 454 | 235 | 802 |

Source: *Economic Report of the President.*

As an example of the calculation of a group mean, consider a labor economist who wishes to calculate the average length of unemployment for the years 1950, 1960, 1970, and 1980 (Table 3.2). Since actual unemployment periods are not reported in Table 3.2, the economist assumes that they are evenly distributed within each class. Thus the data in the four classes ($c = 4$) can be represented by the four midpoints:

$$m_1 = 2.5 \quad \text{(midpoint of class "less than 5 weeks")}$$
$$m_2 = 10.0 \quad \text{(midpoint of class "5 and less than 15 weeks")}$$
$$m_3 = 21.0 \quad \text{(midpoint of class "15 and less than 27 weeks")}$$
$$m_4 = 45.0 \quad \text{(arbitrary midpoint of class "27 weeks or more")}$$

The midpoint of 45 weeks for the class "27 weeks or more" was chosen arbitrarily. Without knowing the actual upper limit of this class, values other than 45 could be used. (As stated in Chapter 2, open-ended classes should be avoided because they may result in data distortions.) Table 3.3 presents the information necessary for calculating $\mu$.

Four means are shown in Table 3.3, one for each year. The numbers in columns 6 through 9 are the products of multiplying each midpoint ($m_i$) by its frequency ($f_i$). For example, the population mean for 1950 is

$$\mu = \left(\frac{1}{3287}\right) \sum_{i=1}^{4} f_i m_i = \left(\frac{1}{3287}\right)[1450(2.5) + 1055(10.0)$$
$$+ 425(21.0) + 357(45.0)] = 11.9$$

Another (equivalent) way of presenting the grouped means in Eq. (3.2) is to divide each value of $f_i$ by the number of observations (instead of dividing after summing). In this way, the formula for a population mean can be written as follows:

Table 3.3

| | | | | | | | | |
|---|---|---|---|---|---|---|---|---|
| **Mean of U.S. Unemployment Duration: Calculation of a** | | | | | | | | |
| **Population Mean Using the Midpoint Frequency Formulas** | | | | | | | | |
| **(from Table 3.2)** | | | | | | | | |
| (1) | (2) | (3) | (4) | (5) | (6) | (7) | (8) | (9) |
| **Weekly** | **Frequency of Duration ($f_i$) in:** | | | | | | | |
| **Duration** | | | | | $f_i m_i$ | $f_i m_i$ | $f_i m_i$ | $f_i m_i$ |
| **Midpoints** | 1950 | 1960 | 1970 | 1980 | 1950 | 1960 | 1970 | 1980 |
| 2.5 | 1,450 | 1,719 | 2,137 | 3,208 | 3,625.0 | 4,297.5 | 5,342.5 | 8,020.0 |
| 10.0 | 1,055 | 1,176 | 1,289 | 2,411 | 10,550.0 | 11,760.0 | 12,890.0 | 24,110.0 |
| 21.0 | 425 | 503 | 427 | 1,028 | 8,925.0 | 10,563.0 | 8,967.0 | 21,588.0 |
| 45.0 | 357 | 454 | 235 | 802 | 16,065.0 | 20,430.0 | 10,575.0 | 36,090.0 |
| sum = | 3,287 | 3,852 | 4,088 | 7,449 | 39,165.0 | 47,050.5 | 37,774.5 | 89,808.0 |
| | | | | μ | 11.9 | 12.2 | 9.2 | 12.1 |

$$\mu = \sum_{i=1}^{c} \left(\frac{f_i}{N}\right)(m_i) = \left(\frac{f_1}{N}\right)(m_1) + \left(\frac{f_2}{N}\right)(m_2) + \cdots \left(\frac{f_c}{N}\right)(m_c)$$

Each term in this equation contains the relative frequency ($f_i/N$). As an example of the use of this formula for a population mean, consider an instructor for an industrial training program who intends to give the top 15% of the trainees an A (= 4 points), the next 25% a B (= 3 points), and then 50% C (= 2 points), 6% D (= 1 point), and 4% F (= 0 points). Since it is impossible to know how many trainees will finish the program, N is unknown. Because

**Table 3.4**

| | | | |
|---|---|---|---|
| **Mean Grade Point Calculation** | | | |
| **Grade** | **(Midpoint = $m_i$)** | **$f_i/N$** | **$(f_i/N)m_i$** |
| A | 4 | 0.15 | 0.15(4) = 0.60 |
| B | 3 | 0.25 | 0.25(3) = 0.75 |
| C | 2 | 0.50 | 0.50(2) = 1.00 |
| D | 1 | 0.06 | 0.06(1) = 0.06 |
| E | 0 | 0.04 | 0.04(0) = 0.00 |
| | | | $\mu_x$ = 2.41 = mean grade |

$$\mu = \sum_{i=1}^{5} \left(\frac{f_i}{N}\right)(m_i)$$
$$= (0.15)(4) + (0.25)(3) + (0.50)(2) + (0.06)(1) + (0.04)(0) = 2.41$$

the relative frequency of grades is known, however, $\mu$ can be calculated as shown in Table 3.4.

**WORKED EXAMPLE 3.2**

In a small engineering consulting firm, 35% of the engineers have an average annual salary of $50,000, 40% average $58,500, and the remaining 25% average $57,700 per year. What is the average annual salary of all the engineers?

**ANSWER:**

Let $\mu$ be the average salary of the firm's engineers. Thus

$$\mu = \sum_{i=1}^{3} \left(\frac{f_i}{N}\right)(m_i) = (0.35)(\$50,000) + (0.40)(\$58,500) + (0.25)(\$57,700)$$
$$= \$17,500 + \$23,400 + \$14,425$$
$$= \$55,325$$

# 3.4 Median

So far in our insurance case introduced at the beginning of the chapter, we know only that the insurance company's ad is about the mean time required to process claims. In this section we will show that the consumer group's statement about the time required to process the majority of claims involves the **median** of the distribution of processing time and not the mean.

---

**DEFINITION Median**

The median of a data set is the value of the observation that divides the data set into two equal parts after the observations have been arranged in order from the lowest to the highest.

---

To find the median of a sample or population, the data must be arranged in order of magnitude. After the data have been ordered, the median is the value of the observation that splits the data into two parts so that half of the values are higher than this middle value and half are lower. As an example, suppose a data set has nine observations: $7, $2, $6, $5, $1, $2, $5, $3, and $2. To find the middle value, we first order the data from lowest to highest.

$1, $2, $2, $2, $3, $5, $5, $6, and $7

The fifth number in this series is $3. Thus the median = $3, since four observations are lower than $3 and four observations are higher.

If there are $N$ observations in a data set, the middle observation is given by the formula $(N + 1)/2$. For example, if $N = 9$ (as for the preceding data), then

$$\frac{N + 1}{2} = \frac{9 + 1}{2} = 5$$

indicates that the value of the fifth observation is the median.

If a data set consists of an *even* number of observations, then there is no unique middle value. For such data sets it is customary to define the median as the value halfway between the values of the two middle observations, assuming the data are arranged from lowest to highest. For example, the median for the set $2, $3, $4, and $5 is $3.50. Theoretically, any value between $3 and $4 could serve as the median, since any such number has half of the values above it and half below it.

---

**WORKED EXAMPLE 3.3**

Find the median for the data in Table 3.1.

**ANSWER:**

The dollar observations on charge accounts in Table 3.1, arranged in ascending order, are:

10, 22, 32, 35, 45, 45, 46, 47, 47, 52,
55, 55, 55, 55, 58, 58, 61, 61, 63, 63,
65, 66, 66, 68, 69, 69, 70, 71, 72, 75,
76, 78, 84, 84, 85, 91, 96, 102, 107, 119.

The two middle observations are $63 (the 20th observation) and $65 (the 21st observation). The median is defined to be halfway between these numbers, or $64.

---

If individual data values are not available (i.e., if we have only grouped data), it is easy to find the class that contains the median (called the **median** class). This is accomplished by using the cumulative relative frequency distribution. The first class with a cumulative relative frequency of 0.5000 or more is the median class.

**EXAMPLE** The data in Table 3.5 represent the income distribution for families in an economically depressed area. The median income class for these data is seen to be $2000–$2999, since this class (the third one) is the first one in which the cumulative relative frequency (in the final column) is 0.5000 or larger (55.55% of the distribution is below $2999). Alternatively, this is the class that contains the value of 1509th ordered observation $[(N + 1)/2 = (3017 + 1)/2 = 1509]$.

Table 3.5

| | | | | Frequencies | | |
|---|---|---|---|---|---|---|
| | Class (i) | Income by Class (in dollars) | Midpoint of Class | Absolute | Relative | Cumulative |
| | 1 | Without income | zero | 88 | 0.0292 | 0.0292 |
| Median | 2 | 1– 1,999 | $ 1,000 | 683 | 0.2264 | 0.2556 |
| Class ⟶ | 3 | 2,000– 2,999 | 2,500 | 905 | 0.3000 | 0.5555 |
| | 4 | 3,000– 3,999 | 3,500 | 586 | 0.1942 | 0.7498 |
| | 5 | 4,000– 4,999 | 4,500 | 327 | 0.1084 | 0.8581 |
| | 6 | 5,000– 5,999 | 5,500 | 138 | 0.0457 | 0.9039 |
| | 7 | 6,000– 6,999 | 6,500 | 131 | 0.0434 | 0.9473 |
| | 8 | 7,000– 8,499 | 7,750 | 70 | 0.0232 | 0.9705 |
| | 9 | 8,500– 9,999 | 9,250 | 32 | 0.0106 | 0.9811 |
| | 10 | 10,000–12,499 | 11,250 | 29 | 0.0096 | 0.9907 |
| | 11 | 12,500–14,999 | 13,750 | 14 | 0.0046 | 0.9954 |
| | 12 | 15,000–17,499 | 16,250 | 5 | 0.0017 | 0.9970 |
| | 13 | 17,500–19,999 | 18,750 | 6 | 0.0020 | 0.9990 |
| | 14 | 20,000–24,999 | 22,500 | 1 | 0.0003 | 0.9993 |
| | 15 | 25,000–29,999 | 27,500 | 0 | 0.0000 | 0.9993 |
| | 16 | 30,000–34,999 | 32,500 | 0 | 0.0000 | 0.9993 |
| | 17 | 35,000–49,999 | 42,500 | 1 | 0.0003 | 0.9997 |
| | 18 | 50,000–74,999 | 63,500 | 0 | 0.0000 | 0.9997 |
| | 19 | 75,000 or over | 100,000 | 1 | 0.0003 | 1.000 |
| | | | N = | 3,017 | 1.000 | |

Relative and Cumulative Frequencies of Family Income in a Depressed Area

While a median class can be found for grouped data, if individual data values are not available, then it may be impossible to determine the *exact* value of the median. However, we can approximate the median value within the median class by first assuming that the data fall equally throughout the class, and then interpolate to find the appropriate observation for the median. To illustrate this process for the data in Table 3.5, we will first show a mathematical procedure and then a graphical process to approximate the median.

As indicated previously, the median value for Table 3.5 falls between $2000 and $3000. To interpolate within this class notice that the previous classes had a cumulative frequency of 771 observations (= 88 + 683). Thus, to get the median value we must go 738 observations (= 1509 − 771) into the median class. That is, the median value is 81.5% of the way into the median class. This distance into the median class is given by the formula

$$\frac{\text{Number in the median class less than the median}}{\text{Total number in the median class}} = \frac{738}{905} = 0.815$$

Since the third class is $1000 wide (= $3000 − $2000), the distance to the median is 0.815($1000) = $815. Thus our approximation to the median is $2815 (= $2000 + $815).

An alternative method to approximate the median is to use the cumulative relative frequency distribution and its ogive. Starting at the point 0.5000 on the vertical axis, one merely moves horizontally to the ogive and then drops a line vertically to the horizontal axis. The value on the horizontal axis is the approximate median. This process is shown in Fig. 3.1, where the approximate median is $2815. It is important to note that this approximation for the median need not result in a median value identical to the value that is found by assuming that observations fall evenly throughout the classes. This is because the ogive uses a smoothed curve to fit the cumulative frequency distribution.

The *WSJ* article on mobile managers (see Chapter 2) stated that the mean mobile manager's salary was $134,500, while the median was $120,000. When the mean and median have different values, both should be reported, since knowledge about the magnitude of each tells something about the distribution. If the mean is greater than the median, as is the case for the mobile managers, then the distribution may be characterized by a small number of very high values that pull the mean up.

If the mean is less than the median, then the distribution may be characterized by a small number of very low values. This could be the situation in the insurance case, where the company advertised a mean settlement time

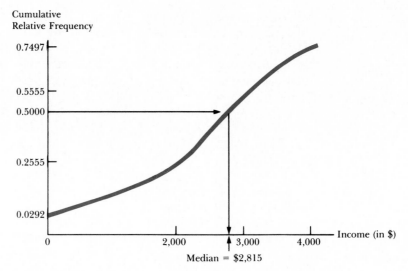

**Figure 3.1**
Ogive for the distribution in Table 3.5.

Cumulative Relative Frequency

0.7497

0.5555
0.5000

0.2555

0.0292

0        2,000        3,000        4,000        Income (in $)

Median = $2,815

of 8 days, while the consumer group claims that the majority of claims (50%) are not settled in 13 days. The consumer group may have overlooked the fact that although 50% of the claims were not settled in 13 days, a mean settlement time of 8 days may not be unreasonable if some claims were settled in a very short time (such as 1 day). The question we still have to answer, however, is whether it is possible to have a median above 13 days and a mean of 8 days. This question is answered in Section 3.12.

**WORKED EXAMPLE 3.4**

Following is the cost distribution for 12 software packages tested by *Byte* magazine. Calculate the population mean and median. Why do these two numbers differ?

| Software Cost | Frequency |
|---|---|
| $    0– 99.99 | 1 |
| $100–199.99 | 5 |
| $200–299.99 | 3 |
| $300–399.99 | 2 |
| $400–499.99 | 1 |

Chapter 3   Descriptive Statistics: Location and Dispersion

**ANSWER:**

Using Eq. (3.2), the mean is calculated as follows:

| Software Cost | $f_i$ | $m_i$ | $f_i m_i$ |
|---|---|---|---|
| $ 0– 99.99 | 1 | $ 50 | $ 50 |
| $100–199.99 | 5 | $150 | $ 750 |
| $200–299.99 | 3 | $250 | $ 750 |
| $300–399.99 | 2 | $350 | $ 700 |
| $400–499.99 | 1 | $450 | $ 450 |
| | 12 | | $2700 |

$$\mu = \left(\frac{1}{N}\right)(\Sigma\, f_i m_i) = \left(\frac{1}{12}\right)(\$2700)$$
$$= \$225$$

A visual inspection of these data indicates that the median value is $200, since there are six observations on either side of this value. The rule of thumb $[(N + 1)/2]$ does not give an intuitively appealing median for this example, illustrating the fact that the median is not always uniquely defined. The median ($200) is less than the mean ($225) because in this distribution the mean is pulled in the direction of the few high values.

# 3.5 Mode

Our final measure of central tendency is called the **mode**, which is the value (or class) that occurs with the greatest frequency. While the mode is not as widely used as the median or mean, it is useful in some business planning situations. For example, if one wishes to know what tire size is most often needed by consumers, or what is the most common loan request, then the mode is the value of interest.

| DEFINITION | The mode is the observation that occurs most frequently. For grouped |
|---|---|
| **Mode** | data, the modal class is the class with the highest frequency. |

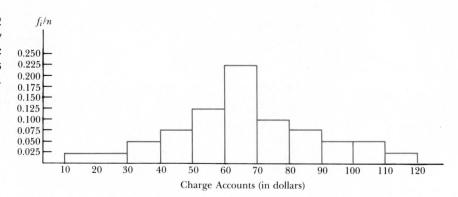

To find the mode for Worked Example 3.3, where the data set consisted of the 40 charge accounts, notice that $55 occurs more than any other number (four times). Thus the mode is $55. Note that $55 is not a particularly good indication of the middle of these data, since it does not take account of the value of the other observations. (The other values can be anything, but as long as $55 has the highest frequency, it is the mode.) In addition, a unique mode need not exist. For example, suppose we want to find the mode for the following data:

$2, $2, $2, $3, $4, $5, $5, $5, and $7

In this example there are two modes, $2 and $5. A data set with a single mode is called a **unimodal distribution**. A data set with two modes is said to be **bimodal** and a data set that has three modes is **trimodal**.

Finally, if data are grouped, the class with the highest frequency is called the **modal class**. For the charge account histogram from Chapter 2 (repeated in Fig. 3.2) the modal class is $60–$69, since this class has the highest relative frequency (0.25). The true modal value ($55) is not even contained in the modal class $60–$69.

**WORKED EXAMPLE 3.5**

From a Dun and Bradstreet report we know the following about the age of retail establishments and business failures.

| Age (in years): | 2 or less | 3 or 4 | 5 or 6 | 7 or 8 | 9 or 10 | Over 10 |
|---|---|---|---|---|---|---|
| Percentage of failures: | 14.0 | 34.9 | 18.0 | 11.5 | 6.2 | 14.4 |

In what age of the retailing business is failure most likely? Does this distribution have more than one modal class?

**ANSWER:**

The period in which most failures occur (the modal class) is the third or fourth year, where 34.9% of the failures take place. This distribution is unimodal.

# 3.6 Skewness

In addition to measures of central location for a distribution, the shape is also important. One indication of shape is called **skewness**. A distribution in which the mean value is greater than the median is said to be **positively skewed**. In a **negatively skewed** distribution, the mean is less than the median value. If the distribution is **symmetric**, the mean is the same value as the median.

There is a formula for measuring the skewness of a distribution, which is not of major importance for this text. Some knowledge about the skewness of a distribution is important, however, because inferences from a sample to a population often depend on assumptions about the symmetry (or lack of symmetry) present in the data. Many types of business and economic data are skewed.

In a negatively skewed unimodal distribution, such as Fig. 3.3(a), the mean is less than the median and the median is less than the mode. In a positively skewed distribution (Fig. 3.3b), the mean is greater than the median and the median is greater than the mode. Only for a symmetric unimodal distribution will all three measures of central tendency (mean, median, and mode) be equal (Fig. 3.3c).

In skewed distributions, the mean is pulled in the direction of the few extreme values. If these extreme values are on the right (or positive) side, the distribution is positively skewed. If the extreme values are on the left (or negative side), the distribution is negatively skewed. Thus, if the distribution of processing time is negatively skewed in the insurance case, the mean settlement time could be 8 days and the majority of claims could take 13 or more days to settle.

**Figure 3.3**
Skewness and the
measures of central
tendency.

(a) Negatively Skewed Distribution

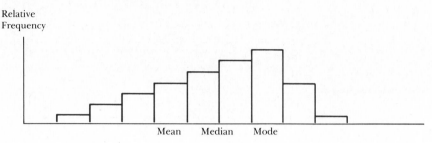

(b) Positively Skewed Distribution

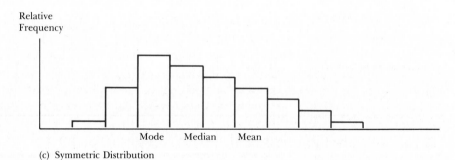

(c) Symmetric Distribution

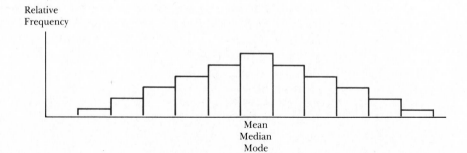

**WORKED EXAMPLE
3.6**

In 1979 the mean U.S. household income was $19,620, but only about 41% of U.S. households had an income of $19,620 or more. Using a histogram, explain how this is possible.

**ANSWER:**

U.S. household incomes are known to be positively skewed, so the mean exceeds the median. (The mean is pulled up by a few very high incomes.) Thus it is not surprising to find that less than 50% of the households have an income greater than the mean of $19,620. This positively skewed income distribution is as follows.

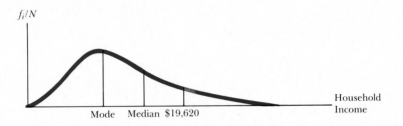

# 3.7 Proportions, Percentiles, and Quartiles

Another method of describing location in a data set is to indicate what proportion or percentage of the distribution has some characteristic. For example, labor economists monitor changes in the proportion of women who are in the U.S. workforce. Figure 3.4 is an illustration of this percentage between 1900 and 1985.

A population proportion is denoted by the Greek letter $\pi$ (pi), while a sample proportion is denoted by the letter $p$. If the proportions indicated in Fig. 3.4 represent population values, then

$$\pi_{1900} = 0.210, \ \pi_{1940} = 0.258, \ \pi_{1950} = 0.290$$
$$\pi_{1960} = 0.345, \ \pi_{1960} = 0.399, \ \pi_{1985} = 0.529$$

A proportion is the number of observations in the data set that have a certain characteristic (such as a woman in the workforce). As another example, an airline may wish to know what proportion of passengers on its flights prefer the nonsmoking section. Proportions are generally given as decimals (between 0 and 1). As we have seen, a decimal multiplied by 100 is a percentage (the values in Fig. 3.4 are given as percentages).

Figure 3.4

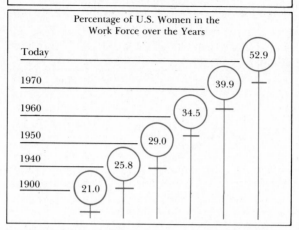

MONEYLIST *by Brendan Boyd*

Percentage of U.S. Women in the
Work Force over the Years

Today ———————————————— 52.9

1970 ——————————————— 39.9

1960 ——————————— 34.5

1950 —————— 29.0

1940 ——— 25.8

1900 —— 21.0

To illustrate a sample proportion, suppose we consider the data for the
Electrical, Electronics Industry in Appendix Table A.1 as a sample of all
companies. What proportion of companies in this industry had sales of over
$100 million? There are 59 companies in the Electrical, Electronics Industry,
of which 35 had sales of over $100 million. Thus the sample proportion with
sales of over $100 million is

$$p = \tfrac{35}{59} = 0.5932$$

**WORKED EXAMPLE
3.7**

What proportion of the charge accounts in Table 3.1 had a balance of $59.99
or less?

**ANSWER:**

We can determine this directly by looking for the class ending in $59.99 in
the cumulative relative frequency distribution in Table 3.6 (reproduced from
Table 2.3). These are sample data, so the answer is $p = 0.40$, which is the
cumulative relative frequency for the fifth class.

**Table 3.6**

| Class (i) | Class Boundaries | Midpoint | Absolute Frequency ($f_i$) | Relative Frequency ($f_i/n$) | Cumulative Relative Frequency |
|---|---|---|---|---|---|
| **Relative Frequency Distribution and Histogram for the Charge Account Data** | | | | | |
| 1 | $ 10–$ 19.99 | $15 | 1 | 0.025 | 0.025 |
| 2 | $ 20–$ 29.99 | 25 | 1 | 0.025 | 0.050 |
| 3 | $ 30–$ 39.99 | 35 | 2 | 0.050 | 0.100 |
| 4 | $ 40–$ 49.99 | 45 | 5 | 0.125 | 0.225 |
| → 5 | $ 50–$ 59.99 | 55 | 7 | 0.175 | 0.400 ← |
| 6 | $ 60–$ 69.99 | 65 | 10 | 0.250 | 0.650 |
| 7 | $ 70–$ 79.99 | 75 | 6 | 0.150 | 0.800 |
| 8 | $ 80–$ 89.99 | 85 | 3 | 0.075 | 0.875 |
| 9 | $ 90–$ 99.99 | 95 | 2 | 0.050 | 0.925 |
| 10 | $100–$109.99 | 105 | 2 | 0.050 | 0.975 |
| 11 | $110–$119.99 | 115 | 1 | 0.025 | 1.000 |
| | Sum = | | 40 | 1.000 | |

## Percentiles and Quartiles

Percentile and quartile values indicate locations within a data set. A **percentile** simply states how much of the distribution is less than or equal to some given value. For example, for the hardware charge accounts data given in Table 3.6, $59.99 represents the 40th percentile because 40% of the distribution is less than or equal to $59.99. Similarly, $79.99 represents the 80th percentile since 80% of the observations are less than or equal to $79.99. The 25th percentile is the upper bound of the **first quartile**. The **second quartile** has a lower bound equal to the 25th percentile and an upper bound of the 50th percentile (which for large samples is the median). The **third quartile**

---

| DEFINITION Percentile and Quartile | The *j*th percentile is the value of the observation that puts *j*% of the observations equal to or below it, where the data set has been ordered from smallest to largest. The 25th percentile is the upper bound of the first quartile, while the 75th percentile is the upper bound of the third quartile. The median is the 50th percentile and also equals the upper bound of the second quartile. |
|---|---|

is bounded by the 50th and 75th percentiles. The 75th percentile is also the lower bound of the **fourth quartile**.

As in our discussion of the median, for small or even-numbered data sets, percentile and quartile values may not be easily and uniquely obtained. For example, what value should be used for the first quartile for the charge account data in Table 3.1 after ordering as in Worked Example 3.3? Exactly 25% of the data (10 observations) are less than or equal to $52. The 11th observation is $55. Thus any value between $52 and $55 could be used to define the first quartile. Similarly, the third quartile could be any value between $55 and $56 (such as $55.50.)

## Exercises

**3.1** What is the difference between the population parameter $\mu$ and the sample statistic $\bar{x}$?

**3.2** What assumptions are necessary about the distribution of observations within a class to calculate a mean or median from grouped data?

**3.3** Under what conditions are the mean, median, and mode identical?

**3.4** When reporting income data, the business press typically emphasizes the median as the measure of central location. Why would the median be emphasized instead of the mean or mode? Give an example of situations in which the median might be inappropriate.

PUB **3.5** *The DeVoe Report* once quoted President Jimmy Carter as saying, "Half the people in this country are living below the median income—and this is intolerable." In this quotation, what cannot be refuted? What can be debated?

ADM **3.6** In the September 12, 1980, *WSJ* it was reported that average starting salary for MBA's with a nontechnical undergraduate degree was $21,500 and with a technical undergraduate degree $23,652. Can one conclude from this information that the average starting MBA salary was $22,576 [= ($23,652 + $21,500)/2]? Comment.

MKT **3.7** According to a May 1981 *United Press International* release, the average new house cost $76,300 but most houses cost less than $67,200. Draw a histogram depicting the distribution of new housing costs for 1981.

FIN **3.8** Following is a February 2, 1983, *WSJ* table that shows stock market behavior around the bottom of every major business slump since 1929.

It shows the change in the Dow Jones Industrial Average (DJIA) from its low point in each economic slump to its level when the economy starts to recover.

| Period | DJIA Change During Slump |
|--------|--------------------------|
| 1980 | + 18.6% |
| 1973–1975 | + 36.2 |
| 1969–1970 | + 25.8 |
| 1959–1961 | + 16.9 |
| 1957–1958 | + 8.5 |
| 1953–1954 | + 37.1 |
| 1948–1949 | + 17.7 |
| 1945 | + 22.8 |
| 1937–1938 | + 40.3 |
| 1929–1933 | + 52.7 |

a) What is the mean change in the DJIA given in the table?

b) What is the median change in the DJIA given in the table?

c) What does the information in parts (a) and (b) tell you about what might happen to the DJIA in future slumps?

ADM **3.9** The following distribution shows the net typing speed of the entire 41 clerks in a typing pool:

| Words Per Minute | Frequency |
|------------------|-----------|
| 30–39 | 1 |
| 40–49 | 7 |
| 50–59 | 12 |
| 60–69 | 11 |
| 70–79 | 6 |
| 80–89 | 0 |
| 90–99 | 3 |
| 100–109 | 1 |

a) What is the mean?

b) What is the median?

c) What is the mode?

d) What proportion of the clerks type 60 or more words per minute?

ACT 3.10 A small bank has loaned the following amounts of money at the indicated annual interest rates:

| Amount of Loan | Interest Rate (%) |
|---|---|
| $300,000 | 9.0 |
| 500,000 | 9.5 |
| 400,000 | 10.0 |
| 300,000 | 10.5 |
| 200,000 | 11.0 |
| 100,000 | 11.5 |
| 100,000 | 12.0 |

a) Find the mean and the median rate of interest received by the bank.

b) What is the shape of this distribution?

ACT 3.11 The security service for a large department store has been monitoring the value of goods it has retrieved from 200 shoplifters apprehended in the past year.

| Dollar Value | Relative Frequency |
|---|---|
| $ 1–$10 | 0.30 |
| $10–$20 | 0.20 |
| $20–$30 | 0.20 |
| $30–$40 | 0.15 |
| $40–$50 | 0.10 |
| $50 or more | 0.05 |

a) If the average for the over $50 category is $100, what is the mean value of goods shoplifted?

b) What is the median value of goods shoplifted?

c) What is the mode?

d) What is the shape?

e) How would your answers to parts (a), (b), and (c) change if the average for the over $50 category was $500?

ADM 3.12 In a sample of nine placement exams, job applicants scored 60, 50, 30, 20, 30, 70, 80, 90, and 80.

a) What is the mean score?

**b)** What is the median score?

**c)** What is (are) the mode(s)?

PUB  **3.13**  Go to the library and find an example of business or economic data that are positively skewed. Find an example of data that are negatively skewed.

PUB  **3.14**  Assume that the industrial training instructor described in Section 3.3 grades students on a relative scale: the top 15% receive an A and the next 25% B, followed by 50% C and 6% D. On the first exam a participant received a score of 66 and the mean was 50. On the second exam, this participant received a 70 and the mean was again 50. Is it necessarily true that this participant did better on the second exam? Comment.

ECN  **3.15**  Find the modal class for the data in Worked Example 3.4. What is the shape of this distribution?

**3.16**  Calculate a mean proportion for the data in Fig. 3.4, and then explain why this mean is of little value in representing the proportion of working women since 1900.

ECN  **3.17**  Go to Appendix Table A.3. In what proportion of the quarters since 1980 did Workingmens Federal show a positive net income? In what situations might this be viewed as population or sample data?

FIN  **3.18**  Select a random sample of 15 companies from among the 50 banks and bank holding companies listed in Appendix Table A.1. Determine the 1984 return on common equity for these 15 companies.

**a)** Find the sample mean, median, and mode.

**b)** Find the population mean, median, and mode. How well do your sample values approximate the population values?

**c)** Find the proportion in your sample with a return $\geq$ 10%. How well does this sample value approximate the population value?

# 3.8  Measures of Dispersion

In addition to determining the central location of quantitative information, it is important to determine the spread or variability of the data. For example, consider the door fender clearance on a new car. Because the assembly process is not perfect, some variation in the clearance can be expected. A small variability from the ideal is acceptable, but at some point the clearance will be too wide or too narrow to permit the door to operate properly. Information about the variability of door fender clearances is essential for quality control on the assembly line. Three measures of variability will be presented in this chapter, namely, the range, the variance, and the standard deviation.

# 3.9 Range

The range measures variability by determining the difference between the largest and smallest values in the data set.

---

**DEFINITION**
**Range**

The range is the difference between the maximum and the minimum values in the data set.

---

One easy way to determine the range is to order the data from the highest to the lowest observation. The range is then the difference between the first and last observations in the list. In quality control work, small samples (such as $n = 5$) are taken at regular intervals from the assembly line. For each sample the mean and range are calculated and plotted on a control chart so that a continuous check of mean length and tolerances can be performed. For example, one such sample of five measurements taken on an automobile assembly line might yield the following observations for door fender clearances:

0.430, 0.2511, 0.3124, 0.4375 and 0.2798 inches.

The sample mean is 0.3422 inches and the range is 0.1864 inches (0.4375–0.2511).

While the range is easy to calculate, outside of quality control work it is not used widely. For one thing, two distributions may have the same range but may be extremely different in terms of actual variability. For example, all three distributions in Fig. 3.5 have the same mean ($\mu = 2$) and the same range ($4 - 1 = 3$). Yet, distribution A appears to be more variable or spread out than distribution B, and B appears to be more variable than C.

Chapter 3   Descriptive Statistics: Location and Dispersion

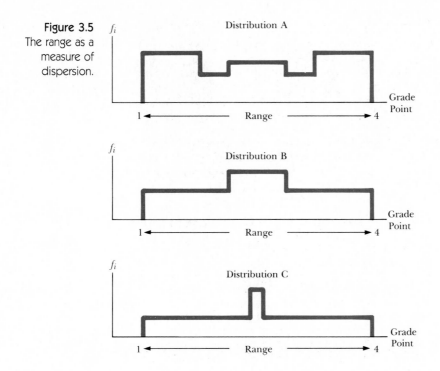

**Figure 3.5**
The range as a
measure of
dispersion.

## 3.10 Variance

The most common way to measure the spread of a distribution is to calculate its variance.

---

**DEFINITION**
**Variance**

The variance of a distribution is a measure of the average squared difference between observed values and their mean.

---

This definition of a variance holds for both a population and a sample. A population variance is denoted by the symbol $\sigma^2$, which is the square of the lowercase Greek letter sigma. A sample variance is denoted by $s^2$. While the definition of a variance is the same for populations and samples, there is a slight difference in the method for calculating a population versus a sample variance, as the following steps illustrate.

1. The first step in calculating a variance is to determine the mean of the data set. Recall that a population mean for $x$ is denoted by $\mu_x$ and a sample mean is denoted by $\bar{x}$.

2. The second step is to obtain the difference between observed values and the mean. These differences, called **deviations**, are calculated by subtracting the mean from each observed value. The notation used is:

Deviations for population data: $x_i - \mu_x$

   Deviations for sample data: $x_i - \bar{x}$.

For data with a great deal of variability, many of these deviations tend to be large. However, if the deviations are summed (over all values in the population or the sample), the sum will always equal zero. Let's find these deviations for the charge account customers in Table 3.1. Recall that the mean for these (sample) data is $\bar{x} = \$64.45$. The deviations around this mean are calculated as follows:

| $i$ | $(x_i - \bar{x})$ |
|-----|-------------------|
| 1 | ($71 - $64.45) |
| 2 | ($58 - $64.45) |
| 3 | ($66 - $64.45) |
| . | . |
| . | . |
| . | . |
| 38 | ($35 - $64.45) |
| 39 | ($70 - $64.45) |
| 40 | ($78 - $64.45) |

(These 40 deviations will sum to zero.)

3. The third step is to square each of the deviations and then sum all of these squared deviations. After squaring each of the deviations, the sum will no longer equal zero, since all negative signs have been eliminated by squaring. For the hardware store, this sum is:

Sum of squared deviations

$$= \sum_{i=1}^{40} (x_i - \bar{x})^2$$

$$= (\$71 - \$64.45)^2 + (\$58 - \$64.45)^2 + \cdots$$
$$+ (\$70 - \$64.45)^2 + (\$78 - \$64.45)^2$$
$$= 18{,}718 \text{ (dollars squared)}$$

4. The fourth and final step is to determine the average of the sum of the squared deviations. For a population, the sum of the squared deviations is divided by the population size, $N$. For a sample, the sum of squared deviations is divided by $n - 1$. (The reason for dividing by $n - 1$ will be discussed in Chapter 6.) Designating the population variance of $x$ as $\sigma_x^2$ and the sample variance as $s_x^2$, the formulas for a variance are:

---

Population variance

$$\sigma_x^2 = \frac{1}{N} \sum_{i=1}^{N} (x_i - \mu)^2$$

(3.3)

Sample variance

$$s_x^2 = \frac{1}{n-1} \sum_{i=1}^{n} (x_i - \bar{x})^2$$

---

The sample variance for the hardware store's sample of charge accounts is thus:

$$s_x^2 = \frac{1}{n-1} \sum_{i=1}^{40} (x_i - \bar{x})^2 = \left(\frac{1}{39}\right)(\$18{,}718)$$

$$= 480 \text{ (dollars squared)}$$

---

**WORKED EXAMPLE 3.8**

Calculate the variance for the sample data in Worked Example 3.1.

| Item | Cents Per Dollar |
|------|------------------|
| 1    | 6.3              |
| 2    | 6.0              |
| 3    | 5.4              |
| 4    | 5.3              |
| 5    | 4.7              |

ANSWER:

From Worked Example 3.1, the mean is $\bar{x} = 5.54$. Thus

| $x$ | $x - \bar{x}$ | $(x - \bar{x})^2$ |
|-----|---------------|-------------------|
| 6.3 | $6.3 - 5.54 = \phantom{-}0.76$ | 0.5776 |
| 6.0 | $6.0 - 5.54 = \phantom{-}0.46$ | 0.2116 |
| 5.4 | $5.4 - 5.54 = -0.14$ | 0.0196 |
| 5.3 | $5.3 - 5.54 = -0.24$ | 0.0576 |
| 4.7 | $4.7 - 5.54 = -0.84$ | 0.7056 |
|     | Sum $=$ | 1.5720 |

$$s_x^2 = \frac{1.5720}{4} = 0.393 = \text{the sample variance}$$

## Variance Formulas for Grouped Data

For grouped data we need to modify the formulas in Eq. (3.3). The formulas for grouped data are similar to those for ungrouped data, except that we use class midpoints ($m_i$) in place of $x_i$, and we must multiply the squared deviations by the frequencies ($f_i$). Equation 3.4 gives the variances for population and sample grouped data. As with $\mu$, subscripts on variances may be omitted when there is no confusion about the variable of interest.

Variances for grouped data

    Population variance

$$\sigma^2 = \frac{1}{N} \sum_{i=1}^{c} f_i(m_i - \mu)^2$$

(3.4)  where $m_i$ is the midpoint of the $i$th class, $f_i$ is the frequency of the $i$th class, and $c$ is the number of classes.

    Sample variance

$$s^2 = \frac{1}{n-1} \sum_{i=1}^{c} f_i(m_i - \bar{x})^2$$

Table 3.7 illustrates the calculation of a variance using the formula for the population and the 1980 unemployment duration data in Table 3.3. Table

Chapter 3   Descriptive Statistics: Location and Dispersion

**Table 3.7**

| | | | | | |
|---|---|---|---|---|---|
| **U.S. Unemployment Duration in 1980: Population Mean and Variance Calculations Using the Midpoint Frequency Formulas** | | | | | |
| **Weekly Duration Midpoints** $(m_i)$ | **Frequency of Duration** $(f_i)$ | $f_i m_i$ | $m_i - \mu_x$ | $(m_i - \mu_x)^2$ | $f_i(m_i - \mu_x)^2$ |
| 2.5 | 3,208 | 8,020.0 | $2.5 - 12.06 = -9.56$ | 91.3936 | 293,190.68 |
| 10.0 | 2,411 | 24,110.0 | $10.0 - 12.06 = -2.06$ | 4.2436 | 10,231.32 |
| 21.0 | 1,028 | 21,588.0 | $21.0 - 12.06 = \phantom{-}8.94$ | 79.9236 | 82,161.46 |
| 45.0 | 802 | 36,090.0 | $45.0 - 12.06 = \phantom{-}32.94$ | 1085.0436 | 870,204.96 |
| | 7,449 | 89,808.0 | | | 1,255,788.42 |

$$\mu = \frac{89,808}{7,449} = 12.06 \text{ (weeks)}$$

$$\sigma^2 = \frac{1}{N} \sum_{i=1}^{c} f_i(m_i - \mu_x)^2 = \frac{1}{7,449}(1,255,788.42) = 168.58$$

Thus the population variance for this duration of unemployment data is 168.58 (weeks squared).

Data Source: *Economic Report of the President.*

3.8 illustrates this calculation for the sample of salaries of mobile managers in Table 2.2, where the maximum salary is assumed to be $340,000. [Notice that even though we do not have the raw data on mobile managers' salaries, our approximation of the true mean using the group data formula ($138,199.70) is somewhat close to the true raw data mean of $134,500, as reported in the *WSJ* article.]

Other formulas for hand calculations of the variance are given in the appendix to this chapter. As demonstrated in Section 3.13, when data sets are large, computers are used to do computations.

# 3.11 Standard Deviation

The variance of any data set is always given in squared units of measurement, while the mean is given in the original unit of measurement. For instance,

**Table 3.8**

| Cash Compensation by Class | Midpoints in $1000 units $(m_i)$ | Fre-quency of Mid-points $(f_i)$ | $f_i m_i$ | $m_i - \bar{x}$ | $(m_i - \bar{x})^2$ | $f_i(m_i - \bar{x})^2$ |
|---|---|---|---|---|---|---|
| | | **Sample of Cash Compensation Received by Mobile Managers: Sample Mean and Variance Calculations Using the Midpoint Frequency Formulas** | | | | |
| Under $70,000 | 35 | 153 | 5,355 | −103.20 | 10,650.18 | 1,629,477.25 |
| $ 70,000– 89,999 | 80 | 242 | 19,360 | −58.20 | 3,387.21 | 819,703.63 |
| $ 90,000–119,999 | 105 | 388 | 40,740 | −33.20 | 1,102.22 | 427,661.39 |
| $120,000–159,999 | 140 | 337 | 47,180 | 1.80 | 3.24 | 1,092.24 |
| $160,000–340,000 | 250 | 377 | 94,250 | 111.80 | 12,499.31 | 4,712,238.77 |
| | | 1,497 | 206,885 | | | 7,590,173.28 |

$$\bar{x} = \frac{1}{n} \sum_{i=1}^{c} f_i m_i = \left(\frac{1}{1497}\right)(206,885) = 138.1997$$

(Since $m_i$ is in thousands of dollars, the sample mean is $138,199.70.)
Sample variance calculations:

$$s^2 = \frac{1}{n-1} \sum_{i=1}^{c} f_i(m_i - \bar{x})^2 = \frac{1}{1,496}(7,590,173.28)$$

$$= 5,073.645$$

The sample variance is $5073.645 \times 10^6$ (dollars squared), since $m_i$ is measured in thousands of dollars.

Data Source: *Wall Street Journal.*

in the U.S. unemployment duration data (Table 3.7), the unit of measurement for the mean is weeks and the variance is given in weeks squared. For the mobile manager salary data (Table 3.8), the mean is measured in dollars, while the variance is measured in dollars squared.

It is desirable to have the measure of dispersion in the same units of measurement as the measure of central location. By taking the positive square root of the variance, a type of average measure of dispersion can be obtained. This positive square root of the variance is called the **standard deviation**. It is measured in the same units as the mean and, as with the variance, the greater the dispersion of values around the mean, the larger the standard deviation.

Chapter 3 Descriptive Statistics: Location and Dispersion

| DEFINITION Standard Deviation | The standard deviation of a data set is a measure of dispersion. It is the positive square root of the variance. Since the standard deviation is based on the variance, it is a measure of the average deviation in the data set. For a population, the variance is given by $\sigma^2$. For a sample, the variance is denoted by the symbol $s^2$. |
|---|---|

For example, to find the standard deviation for the population data in Table 3.7, we simply take the square root of the variance, which was $\sigma^2 = 168.58$. Thus the standard deviation is $\sigma = \sqrt{168.58} = 12.98$ weeks. Similarly, for the sample salary data in Table 3.8, the standard deviation is $s = \sqrt{5,073,645,000} = \$71,229.52$.

**WORKED EXAMPLE 3.9**

There are three $10,000 investments available to a potential investor. They are expected to yield the following returns:

|  | Investment A | Investment B | Investment C |
|---|---|---|---|
| Mean return less principal of $10,000 | $1000 | $1000 | $1000 |
| Standard deviation | $500 | $750 | $1000 |

If the investor is risk averse (i.e., likes to avoid risky propositions), which investment should be made?

**ANSWER:**

A risk-averse investor should select investment A since it has the smallest standard deviation. The smaller the standard deviation, the less spread out the distribution. Investment A has the smallest standard deviation. Thus its possible returns are more tightly centered around the mean return. An investor selecting A does not face as big a gain or loss as an investor selecting B or C.

# 3.12 Dispersion and Data Location

The standard deviation is useful because it is directly related to the way values tend to be spread out around the mean. The Russian mathematician Tchebysheff discovered this relationship and stated it in a theorem that bears his name:

| | |
|---|---|
| **Tchebysheff's Theorem** | In any data set, the proportion of items within $\pm k$ standard deviations of the mean is at least $1 - (1/k)^2$, where $k$ is any number greater than 1.0. |

**Tchebysheff's theorem** applies to any data distribution regardless of its shape or variability. It can be used for population or sample data. The basic idea of Tchebysheff's theorem is presented in Fig. 3.6, where the population mean is $\mu$. It is important to note that $k$ in Tchebysheff's theorem indicates the number of standard deviations away from the mean. The letter $k$ is not the size of the standard deviation itself. The size of the population's standard deviation is represented by $\sigma$ (and for a sample by $s$).

As can be seen in Fig. 3.6, Tchebysheff's theorem states that if $k = 2$, then at least 75% $[1 - (1/2)^2]$ of the observations fall inside the interval $\mu$

**Figure 3.6**
Illustration of Tchebysheff's theorem for certain values of $k$.

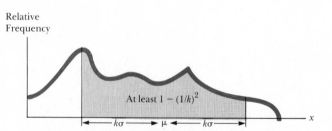

Tchebysheff's Theorem: Within $k$ standard deviations of the mean there will be at least $1 - (1/k)^2$ of the distribution. In particular,

| $k$ | 1.5 | 2.0 | 2.5 | 3.0 | 3.5 | 4.0 |
|---|---|---|---|---|---|---|
| $1 - (1/k)^2$ | 0.5556 | 0.7500 | 0.8400 | 0.8889 | 0.9184 | 0.9375 |

Chapter 3   Descriptive Statistics: Location and Dispersion

$\pm$ 2$\sigma$. If $k$ = 2.5, then the theorem states that at least 84% $[1 - (1/2.5)^2]$ is inside the interval $\mu \pm 2.5\sigma$. If $k$ = 3, then at least 88.9% $[1 - (1/3)^2]$ fall within the interval $\mu \pm 3\sigma$.

As an application of Tchebysheff's theorem, consider the insurance company case presented at the beginning of this chapter, where the company advertised that the mean processing time to settle a claim is 8 days. The consumer group claims that 50% of the claims filed with the insurance company take some 13 days to settle. Is this possible if the mean settlement time is 8 days?

To answer this question we need to know the standard deviation. If the standard deviation is 4 days, then between the company's claimed mean and the consumer group's implied median there are 1.25 $[=(13 - 8)/4]$ standard deviations. By Tchebysheff's theorem, at least 36% $[1 - (1/k)^2 = 1 - (1/1.25)^2 = 1 - 1/1.5625]$ of the distribution is between 3 and 13 days $[= \mu \pm k\sigma = 8 \pm 1.25(4)]$. Alternatively, at most 64% of the distribution is outside 3 and 13 days. Thus it is possible for 50% of the distribution (claims) to take more than 13 days to settle if 4% are settled in less than 3 days. This means that both the company and the consumer group could be correct. As the state insurance commissioner, your best course of action may be to explain this to the consumer group and not spend any more time on this case.

Tchebysheff's theorem applies to any distribution. If we know that the distribution is bell-shaped, as in Fig. 3.7, then a more precise statement can be made about the percentage of the distribution within any number of standard deviations of the mean. In Chapter 6 exact probability calculations associated with bell-shaped distributions will be introduced when the normal distribution is presented. For now, it is helpful just to state a rule of thumb about bell-shaped or normal distributions:

Between $\mu - 1\sigma$ and $\mu + 1\sigma$ there is about 68% of the distribution.

Between $\mu - 2\sigma$ and $\mu + 2\sigma$ there is about 95% of the distribution.

Between $\mu - 3\sigma$ and $\mu + 3\sigma$ there is almost 100% of the distribution.

This **rule of normality** is illustrated in Fig. 3.7.

Bell-shaped distributions such as that shown in Fig. 3.7 are completely symmetrical. This implies that 50% of the distribution falls on either side of the mean, and the mean = median = mode. From the rule of normality, we also know that about 34% (one-half of 68%) of a normal distribution is between $\mu$ and $\mu + 1\sigma$. If about 34% is between $\mu$ and $1\sigma$, then approximately 16% is above $\mu + 1\sigma$. Similar manipulations can be used to find other areas.

**Figure 3.7**
Rule of normality for a bell-shaped distribution.

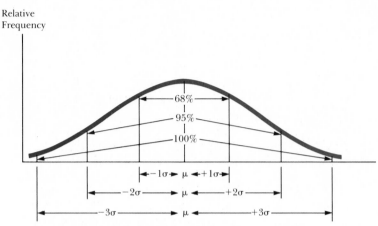

For a bell shaped distribution, the interval
$\mu \pm 1\sigma$ contains approximately 68% of the distribution, and
$\mu \pm 2\sigma$ contains approximately 95% of the distribution, and
$\mu \pm 3\sigma$ contains almost 100% of the distribution.

**WORKED EXAMPLE 3.10**

A new real estate broker wants to classify houses according to where the price falls relative to the distribution for the local housing market. From local records the broker knows the distribution of selling price is symmetrical, and that the mean selling price is $93,578, with a standard deviation of $15,500. What approximations can be made about the selling price distribution?

**ANSWER:**

Since the broker knows that the price distribution is symmetric, it may be reasonable to assume the distribution is also bell-shaped, in which case the rule of normality can be used:

$\mu \pm 1\sigma = $93,578 \pm 1($15,500) = [$78,078–$109,078].$
About 68% of the selling prices should be between $78,078 and $109,078.

$\mu \pm 2\sigma = $93,578 \pm 2($15,500) = [$62,578–$124,578].$
About 95% of the selling prices should be between $62,578 and $124,578.

$$\mu \pm 3\sigma = \$93{,}578 \pm 3(\$15{,}500) = [\$47{,}078\text{--}\$140{,}078].$$

Almost 100% of the selling prices should be between $47,078 and $140,078.

## 3.13 Computer Output for Descriptive Statistics

The calculations in this chapter are much easier if a statistical program for the computer is used. The output from one such program was used to generate Table 3.9, which presents statistics for the charge account data in Table 3.1. Notice that the computer will calculate a mean and a variance assuming the data are a sample or a population. Because the sum of squared deviations is divided by $n - 1$ for a sample variance ($s^2$) and by $N$ for a population ($\sigma^2$), the two variances (and standard deviations) are not the same number.

From Table 3.9 the range can also be calculated from the minimum and maximum, which are determined by the computer. As with our earlier hand calculations, the range is $109 (= 119 - 10). Using the computer program, we can also have the 40 observations on charge accounts ranked (Table 3.10). Thus an ordering (such as that in Worked Example 3.3) to obtain the median or a percentile is facilitated by the computer. Notice in Table 3.10 that the median is found by looking for the value of the observations ranked 20th and 21st. The median is a value that would fall between the 20th and 21st rankings, which is a value between $63 and $65.

| Table 3.9 | Computer Output for Charge Account Data |
|-----------|------------------------------------------|
| | ARITHMETIC MEAN = 64.45 N (or n) = 40 |
| | SAMPLE STD. DEV. = 21.90767341 |
| | SAMPLE VARIANCE = 479.9461541 |
| | POPULATION STD. DEV. = 21.63209422 |
| | POPULATION VARIANCE = 467.9475003 |
| | MINIMUM = 10 |
| | MAXIMUM = 119 |

**Table 3.10**

| | | | Computer Rank Ordering of Charge Account Data | | |
|---|---|---|---|---|---|
| OBSERVATION NUMBER | RANK | OBSERVATION VALUE | OBSERVATION NUMBER | RANK | OBSERVATION VALUE |
| 1 | 28 | 71 | 2 | 15 | 58 |
| 3 | 22 | 66 | 4 | 40 | 119 |
| 5 | 11 | 55 | 6 | 7 | 46 |
| 7 | 2 | 22 | 8 | 25 | 69 |
| 9 | 33 | 84 | 10 | 29 | 72 |
| 11 | 5 | 45 | 12 | 17 | 61 |
| 13 | 6 | 45 | 14 | 34 | 84 |
| 15 | 24 | 68 | 16 | 39 | 107 |
| 17 | 37 | 96 | 18 | 16 | 58 |
| 19 | 8 | 47 | 20 | 18 | 61 |
| 21 | 36 | 91 | 22 | 9 | 47 |
| 23 | 38 | 102 | 24 | 31 | 76 |
| 25 | 19 | 63 | 26 | 12 | 55 |
| 27 | 10 | 52 | 28 | 26 | 69 |
| 29 | 30 | 75 | 30 | 1 | 10 |
| 31 | 35 | 85 | 32 | 3 | 32 |
| 33 | → 20 | 63 | 34 | 13 | 55 |
| 35 | 14 | 55 | 36 | → 21 | 65 |
| 37 | 23 | 66 | 38 | 4 | 35 |
| 39 | 27 | 70 | 40 | 32 | 78 |

Source: Table 3.1.

## Exercises

**3.19** Calculate the sample mean $\bar{x}$ and the sample variance for the following data: 3, 2, 2, 0, $-1$, $-2$.

**3.20** Calculate the population mean and the population variance for the following data: $14, $10, $11, $13, $10, $12, $10.

FIN **3.21** The stock market data in Exercise 3.8 can be viewed as representing a sample of all possible business slumps from an infinite time horizon. Viewing the data in this way, calculate the variance of these DJIA changes.

ADM   **3.22**   Calculate the variance of typing speed for the entire clerical pool in Exercise 3.9.

MKT   **3.23**   In a study of new car prices, a sample of 10 dealerships in a large East Coast city showed a wide discrepancy in final sale prices. For cars of identical specifications, the following prices were recorded:

| Price | Relative Frequency |
|---|---|
| $9,800–$10,000 | 0.10 |
| $9,600–$ 9,799 | 0.30 |
| $9,400–$ 9,599 | 0.40 |
| $9,200–$ 9,399 | 0.20 |

Calculate the mean and the standard deviation for these sample data.

ACT   **3.24**   A study of the loss payment per insurance claim by automobile owners showed an average of $800, with a standard deviation of $90. If the distribution of lost payments is bell-shaped, then what percentage of payments is above $890? What percentage of payments is below $620?

      **3.25**   If the mean of a variable is measured in dollars, what is the unit of measurement for the variance? For the standard deviation?

MKT   **3.26**   A sample of five new Fords is selected and their mean gas mileage is recorded as 31.1, 31.2, 31.3, 31.2, and 31.3 miles per gallon.

    a) Calculate the mean, variance, and standard deviation.

    b) Subtract 31 from each observation and recalculate the mean, variance, and standard deviation.

    c) Why are your answers in parts(a) and (b) the same or different?

ADM   **3.27**   For the data in Worked Example 2.2, what are the mean, variance, and standard deviation?

ADM   **3.28**   Using your answers in Exercise 3.27, are the data in Worked Example 2.2 consistent with Tchebysheff's theorem?

MKT   **3.29**   While the nature of the waiting time in a fast food restaurant line is unknown, the mean waiting time is known to be 3 minutes, with a standard deviation of 0.5 minute.

    a) Approximate the ~~number~~ Percent of customers served within 1 to 5 minutes.

    b) From the information provided, is it possible to determine ~~how many~~ what percent customers have to wait more than 5 minutes?

**3.30** Why does the rule of normality specify that 95% of a distribution is within two standard deviations while Tchebysheff's theorem states that at least 75% of a distribution is within two standard deviations?

ADM **3.31** The local chamber of commerce surveyed its members to assess what they considered to be appropriate dues. The responding sample of 110 members yielded the following results:

| Dues Assessment (Percent of Gross Sales) | Frequency |
|---|---|
| 0.50–0.75 | 15 |
| 0.76–1.00 | 25 |
| 1.01–1.25 | 29 |
| 1.26–1.50 | 21 |
| 1.51 or more | 20 |

a) If the average of the "1.51% or more" class is 2.0%, what are the mean and variance for this distribution?

b) If the average for the "1.5% or more" class is 5.0%, what are the mean and variance of this distribution?

c) What effect do extreme values have on the mean and variance?

FIN **3.32** Using the data in Worked Example 2.3, what is the average size of liabilities of firms that fail? What are the variance and standard deviation? In what units are the variance and standard deviation measured?

FIN **3.33** Using your calculation in Exercise 3.32 and the information in Worked Example 2.3, is the distribution of liabilities of firms that fail consistent with the rule of normality? Why or why not?

## Chapter Exercises

PUB **3.34** According to an April 1, 1983, *WSJ* article, Americans have voluntarily contributed to reducing the $1.2 trillion public debt with checks totaling $135,575.15. "Nearly half of the contributions are for less than $10," says Internal Revenue Service spokesperson Ellen Murphy, but 'a very generous soul' forwarded $25,000." Draw a histogram showing the distribution of contributions. (Label all relevant points.)

**3.35**   A population consists of four observations: $1, $2, $3, and $4.

   **a)** Calculate the population mean.

   **b)** If a sample of size 3 was selected from the four population values, how many distinct samples could be drawn, ignoring the order in which values are selected? Calculate the mean of each of these samples.

   **c)** What is the overall mean of the sample means you calculated in part (b)? How does the mean of the sample means relate to the population mean?

ADM   **3.36**   The following trainee evaluation data were obtained for two business intern program instructors. The data were based on the trainees' response to the question: "The overall teaching ability of this instructor is———?"

| Factor | Instructor A* | Instructor B* |
|---|---|---|
| Number of trainees in intern program | 350 | 300 |
| Number of trainees responding | 50 | 250 |
| Mean response value | 3.0 | 4.0 |
| Standard deviation of responses | 1.5 | 1.0 |
| Median response value | 5.0 | 4.0 |

*Ratings range from 0 (lowest) to 8 (highest).

   **a)** What is the response rate for instructors A and B as a percentage of the students in the intern program?

   **b)** If there had been a 100% response rate, how high and how low could intructor A's and instructor B's average score have been?

   **c)** What proportion of the students who responded rated instructor A and instructor B at least 1 (or better) but 5 or less?

   **d)** A senior executive, in reviewing the preceding data, concluded that B is clearly the better instructor. This executive stated: "The majority of students gave instructor B an average score higher than that of A. The high variability in A's scores simply reflects the fact that the majority of students must have given A low scores, while the low variability in B's scores reflects only minor skewness in the opinion about B. The majority of students cannot be wrong. Therefore, instructor B must be the better teacher." Point out at least five errors or shortcomings in this executive's reasoning.

FIN   **3.37**   Calculate the median liability of firms that fail in Worked Example 2.3. Is the median or mean (which you calculated in Exercise 3.32) a better measure of the middle of this distribution? Explain.

PUB   **3.38**   Regarding the future growth of his state versus others, a governor of a western state said: "We do not want to have average growth. When one is average, one is simply the best of the worst. We want to be among the best."

    **a)** Under what distributional assumptions is the average "the best of the worst"?

    **b)** Is it ever possible to be average and be "among the best"?

    **c)** What doesn't this governor understand about the distributions?

FIN   **3.39**   For the bond yield data in Exercise 2.37, calculate the mean and standard deviation using a raw data formula. Why is it better to use a raw data formula than the frequency formulas?

ACT   **3.40**   During economic recessions, small businesses tend to be especially hard hit because their accounts receivable increase as the time period between billing and final payment increases. For a small haberdashery the number of days since billing for 20 sample accounts receivable is

58, 41, 20, 24, 30, 39, 78, 45, 69, 91, 55,
60, 47, 71, 66, 33, 51, 42, 37, and 82

    **a)** Calculate the mean and the standard deviation for this sample.

    **b)** Find the proportion of observations in the interval $\bar{x} \pm 1s$ and $\bar{x} \pm 2s$. Are these proportions consistent with Tchebysheff's theorem and the empirical rule of thumb?

ECN   **3.41**   Calculate the mean and the median for the age distribution in Worked Example 2.4. Is either one a better representation of the middle of the distribution? Explain.

ADM   **3.42**   Use a computer program to determine the rank of each observation in Exercise 2.10. What is the median of this distribution?

ADM   **3.43**   Use a computer program to calculate the mean, variance, and standard deviation for the executive pay data in Exercise 2.10. (Make sure to indicate the units of measurement.) Are these data consistent with Tchebysheff's theorem and with the rule of normality? Why or why not?

MKT **3.44** In buying microcomputers customers seldom purchase a system on the first visit to the showroom. In a sample of 20 customers who had just purchased microcomputers, the following number of visits prior to purchase were recorded:

| Visits | Relative Frequency |
|--------|--------------------|
| 1 or 2 | 0.05 |
| 3 or 4 | 0.25 |
| 5 or 6 | 0.30 |
| 7 or 8 | 0.30 |
| 9 or 10 | 0.10 |

a) Calculate the mean and the variance.

b) What did you have to assume about the distribution in order to calculate the mean and variance?

ADM **3.45** A corporate sales manager claims that the average yearly commission payments received by his staff equal $75,000, with a standard deviation of $10,000. A disgruntled salesman called the manager a liar and stated that the majority of the staff receive less than $65,000. Could both of these people be correct in the use of their figures? If so, how? If not, why not?

FIN **3.46** From corporation performance data in 1982/1983, the 10 companies with the highest earnings growth were the following:

| | Change in Profits from 1982 (%) | | Change in Profits from 1982 (%) |
|--------|-----|--------------|-----|
| Amdahl | 821 | Singer | 600 |
| Ryland Group | 706 | Hutton | 534 |
| K Mart | 656 | Chubb | 457 |
| Carson Pirie Scott | 655 | Allied Stores | 453 |
| Associated Dry Goods | 627 | RLC | 450 |

a) What are the mean and standard deviation for the change in profits between 1982 and 1983 for these top 10 earners?

b) Find the proportion of these observations in the interval $\bar{x} \pm 1s$ and $\bar{x} \pm 2s$. Are these proportions consistent with Tchebysheff's theorem and the empirical rule of thumb?

FIN   **3.47**   Using any of the random sampling methods discussed in Chapter 1, select 10 companies at random from Appendix A.1. Calculate the mean and standard deviation for the change in profits between 1983 and 1984. Is your mean change close to the "All-Industry Composite" mean of 19%? Using your sample standard deviation from the random sample as an approximation for the population's standard deviation of changes in profits, how many companies had changes outside of $\bar{x} \pm 3s$? Are these results consistent with Tchebysheff's theorem and the empirical rule of thumb? Why or why not?

ECN   **3.48**   For the two distributions in Exercise 2.32, is there any difference in the distributions in terms of their mean or median values? Why did or didn't a mean or median difference show up for these data?

PUB   **3.49**   According to a *WSJ* article the Federal Trade Commission stated that the average time to process claims in the General Motors arbitration procedure involving faulty cars is under 60 days. Mr. Johnson, of the Center for Auto Safety, is quoted as saying ". . . that in fact about 16% of the cases have taken longer than 60 days to settle." Could both the FTC and CAS be correct? Explain why or why not.

MFG   **3.50**   According to a *Popular Mechanics* article Gates Rubber Company has found that the average life of its V-belts is four years and 11 months, with a range of just over four years to just under six years. Assuming the life of V-belts is "bell shaped," with a standard deviation of 3.3 months, at what V-belt age should you replace belts so that you have only a 0.025 probability of breakage before replacement?

## Glossary

**bimodal distribution:** A distribution that has two values that occur the same number of times and occur more often than any other values.

**deviation:** The difference between an observed value and the mean of the distribution.

**first quartile:** The lowest one-quarter of a distribution, whose upper bound is the 25th percentile.

**fourth quartile:** the upper one-quarter of a distribution, whose lower bound is the 75th percentile.

**grouped data:** information presented in the form of a frequency distribution.

**mean:** A measure of central tendency that represents the arithmetic average of the values in a data set. It is calculated by summing over all the values in the set and dividing this sum by the total number of observations.

**median:** A measure of central tendency that is the value of the observation in the middle of a frequency distribution or otherwise ordered data set. It is the value that divides the data into two equal parts when the data are arranged in order from smallest to largest values.

**median class:** The frequency class that contains the median.

**modal class:** The frequency class with the highest frequency.

**mode:** For a population or sample, the value that occurs most frequently. It is the measure of central tendency that defines the highest frequency or peak of a frequency distribuiton.

**negatively skewed distribution:** A distribution in which the mean is less than the median.

**parameter:** A characteristic of a population (e.g., the mean $\mu_x$ is a parameter that characterizes the central location).

**percentile:** The $j$th percentile is the value of the observation for which $j$ percent of the observations are less than or equal to it, where the data set has been ordered from smallest to largest values.

**population mean:** The arithmetic average for a population. It is a parameter that is designated by the Greek letter mu ($\mu$).

**population standard deviation:** The positive square root of the variance, designated by the Greek letter sigma ($\sigma$).

**population variance:** The average squared deviations around the mean for a population. It is a parameter that is designated by the Greek letter sigma squared, ($\sigma^2$).

**positively skewed:** A distribution in which the mean is greater than the median.

**range:** For a population or sample data set, the measure of dispersion that is calculated as the difference between the maximum and minimum values in the set.

**rule of normality:** For any bell-shaped distribution, the interval $\mu \pm 1\sigma$ contains about 68% of the distribution, $\mu \pm 2\sigma$ contains about 95% of the distribution, and $\mu \pm 3\sigma$ contains almost 100% of the distribution.

**sample mean:** The arithmetic average for a sample. It is a statistic that is designated by the symbol ex bar, $\bar{x}$.

**sample standard deviation:** The positive square root of the variance, designated by the letter $s$.

**sample variance:** A type of average squared deviation around the sample mean. It is a statistic that is designated by the letter $s$ squared ($s^2$).

**second quartile:** The lower-middle portion of a distribution, whose bounds are the 25th and 50th percentiles.

**skewness:** A measure of the shape of a distribution.

**standard deviation:** The positive square root of the variance.

**statistic:** A characteristic of a sample (e.g., the mean $\bar{x}$ is a statistic because it is a measure of central tendency for a sample).

**symmetric distribution:** A distribution whose shape is identical on both sides of the median. For symmetrical distributions, the mean = median.

**Tchebysheff's theorem:** In any data set, the proportion of items within $\pm k$ standard deviations of the mean is at least $1 - (1/k)^2$.

**third quartile:** The upper-middle portion of a distribution, whose bounds are the 50th and 75th percentiles.

**trimodal distribution:** A distribution with three modes.

**unimodal distribution:** A distribution with one mode.

**variance:** A measure of the average squared difference between observed values and their mean.

## Formulas

**3.1—Mean (Raw Data)**
For a population of size $N$ and observations $x_1, x_2, \ldots, x_N$, the mean is

$$\mu_x = \frac{1}{N} \sum_{i=1}^{N} x_i = \frac{1}{N}(x_1 + x_2 + \cdots + x_N)$$

For a sample of size $n$ and observations $x_1, x_2, \ldots x_n$, the mean is

$$\bar{x} = \frac{1}{n} \sum_{i=1}^{n} x_i = \frac{1}{n}(x_1 + x_2 + \cdots + x_n)$$

### 3.2—Mean (Grouped Data)

For a population frequency distribution of size $N$, where there are $c$ classes and the midpoint of the $i$th class is $m_i$ (which occurs with frequency $f_i$), the mean is

$$\mu = \frac{1}{N} \sum_{i=1}^{c} f_i m_i = \sum_{i=1}^{c} \left(\frac{f_i}{N}\right) m_i$$

For a sample frequency distribution of size $n$, where there are $c$ classes, the mean is

$$\bar{x} = \frac{1}{n} \sum_{i=1}^{c} f_i m_i = \sum_{i=1}^{n} \left(\frac{f_i}{n}\right) m_i$$

where $m_i$ is the midpoint of the $i$th class and $f_i$ is its frequency.

### 3.3—Variance (Raw Data)

For a population of size $N$ with mean $\mu$, the variance of $x$ is calculated by either one of the following equivalent formulas:

$$\sigma_x^2 = \frac{1}{N} \sum_{i=1}^{N} (x_i - \mu)^2 = \frac{1}{N} \sum_{i=1}^{N} x_i^2 - \mu^2$$

For a sample of size $n$ with mean $\bar{x}$, the variance of $x$ is calculated by either one of the following equivalent formulas:

$$s_x^2 = \frac{1}{n-1} \sum_{i=1}^{n} (x_i - \bar{x})^2 = \frac{1}{n-1} \left[ \sum_{i=1}^{n} x_i^2 - n\bar{x}^2 \right]$$

### 3.4—Variance (Grouped Data)

For a population frequency distribution of size $N$, with $c$ classes and mean $\mu$, the variance of $x$ (or $m$) is calculated by either one of the following equivalent formulas:

$$\sigma^2 = \frac{1}{N} \sum_{i=1}^{c} f_i (m_i - \mu)^2 = \frac{1}{N} \sum_{i=1}^{c} f_i m_i^2 - \mu^2$$

where $m_i$ is the midpoint of the $i$th class and $f_i$ is its frequency. For a sample frequency distribution of size $n$ with $c$ classes and mean $\bar{x}$, the variance of $x$ (or $m$) is calculated by either one of the following equivalent formulas:

$$s^2 = \frac{1}{n-1} \sum_{i=1}^{c} f_i (m_i - \bar{x})^2 = \frac{1}{n-1} \left[ \sum_{i=1}^{c} f_i m_i^2 - n\bar{x}^2 \right]$$

where $m_i$ is the midpoint of the $i$th class and $f_i$ is its frequency.

# APPENDIX    Computational Formulas

The calculation of variances and standard deviations without the aid of a computer is tedious, at best. For anyone interested in calculating these measures by hand, there are several formulas that lessen the computational burden. These formulas for population or sample raw data are:

$$\sigma^2 = \frac{1}{N} \sum_{i=1}^{N} (x_i - \mu)^2 = \frac{1}{N} \sum_{i=1}^{N} x_i^2 - \mu^2$$

$$s^2 = \frac{1}{n-1} \sum_{i=1}^{n} (x_i - \bar{x})^2 = \frac{1}{n-1} \left[ \sum_{i=1}^{n} x_i^2 - n\bar{x}^2 \right]$$

For grouped data, alternative formulas for the variance of a population and a

**Table 3.11**

| U.S. Unemployment Duration in 1980: Population Mean, Variance, and Standard Deviation Calculations Using the Midpoint Frequency Formulas | | | | |
|---|---|---|---|---|
| Weekly Duration Midpoints $(m_i)$ | Frequency of Duration $(f_i)$ | $f_i m_i$ | $m_i^2$ | $f_i m_i^2$ |
| 2.5 | 3,208 | 8,020.0 | 6.25 | 20,050.00 |
| 10.0 | 2,411 | 24,110.0 | 100.00 | 241,100.00 |
| 21.0 | 1,028 | 21,588.0 | 441.00 | 453,348.00 |
| 45.0 | 802 | 36,090.0 | 2,025.00 | 1,624,050.00 |
| | 7,449 | 89,808.0 | | 2,338,548.00 |

$$\mu = \frac{1}{N} \sum_{i=1}^{c} f_i m_i = \frac{89,808}{7,449} = 12.06, \quad \frac{1}{N} \sum_{i=1}^{c} f_i m_i^2 = \frac{2,338,548}{7,449} = 313.94$$

$$\sigma^2 = \frac{1}{N} \sum_{i=1}^{c} f_i m_i^2 - \mu^2 = 313.94 - (12.06)^2 = 313.94 - 145.44$$

$$= 168.50 \text{ (weeks squared)}$$

Population standard deviation: $\sigma = 12.98$ weeks

Source: Table 3.3.

sample are:

$$\sigma^2 = \frac{1}{N} \sum_{i=1}^{c} f_i m_i^2 - \mu^2 \quad \text{and} \quad s^2 = \frac{1}{n-1} \left[ \sum_{i=1}^{c} f_i m_i^2 - n\bar{x}^2 \right]$$

Tables 3.11 and 3.12 provide examples of the calculation steps involved in the use of these formulas for group data. Note that these two tables use the same data as Tables 3.7 and 3.8. Thus the variances calculated here must be the same as those determined earlier (which they are, except for rounding errors).

**Table 3.12**

| Sample of Cash Compensation Received By Mobile Managers: Sample Mean, Variance, and Standard Deviation Calculations Using the Midpoint Frequency Formulas | | | | | |
|---|---|---|---|---|---|
| Cash Compensation by Class | Midpoints in $1,000 Units $(m_i)$ | Frequency of Midpoints $(f_i)$ | $f_i m_i$ | $m_i^2$ | $f_i m_i^2$ |
| Under $70,000 | 35 | 153 | 5,355 | 1,225 | 187,425 |
| $ 70,000– 89,999 | 80 | 242 | 19,360 | 6,400 | 1,548,800 |
| $ 90,000–119,999 | 105 | 388 | 40,740 | 11,025 | 4,277,700 |
| $120,000–159,999 | 140 | 337 | 47,180 | 19,600 | 6,605,200 |
| $160,000–340,000 | 250 | 377 | 94,250 | 62,500 | 23,562,500 |
| | | 1,497 | 206,885 | | 36,181,625 |

Calculation of quantities used in the variance formulas:

$$\bar{x} = \frac{1}{n} \sum_{i=1}^{c} f_i m_i = \left(\frac{1}{1,497}\right)(206,885) = 138.1997, \quad \sum_{i=1}^{c} f_i m_i^2 = 36,181,625$$

Since $m_i$ is in thousands of dollars the sample mean is $138,199.70

Sample variance and standard deviation calculations:

$$s^2 = \frac{1}{n-1} \left[ \sum_{i=1}^{c} f_i m_i^2 - n\bar{x}^2 \right] = \left(\frac{1}{1,496}\right)[36,181,625 - (1,497)(138.1997)^2] = 5073.645$$

The sample variance is $5073.645 \times 10^6$ (dollars squared), since $m_i$ is measured in thousands $(10^3)$ of dollars. The standard deviation is the square root of the variance. The sample standard deviation is thus $71,229.52.

Source: *Wall Street Journal*.

# CHAPTER FOUR

*It is remarkable that a science which began with the consideration of games of chance could have become the most important object of human knowledge.*
Pierre Laplace

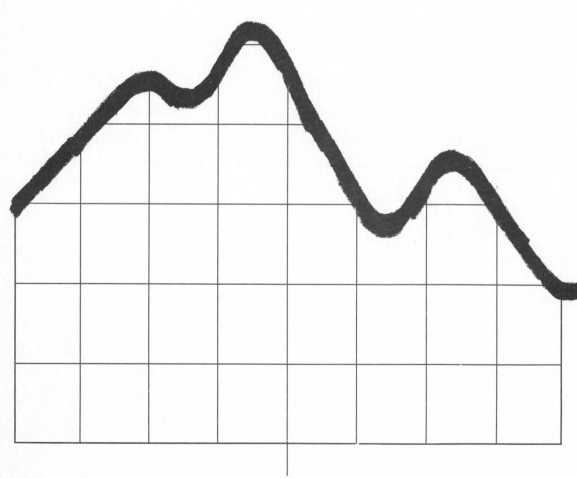

# PROBABILITY CONCEPTS AND RANDOM VARIABLES

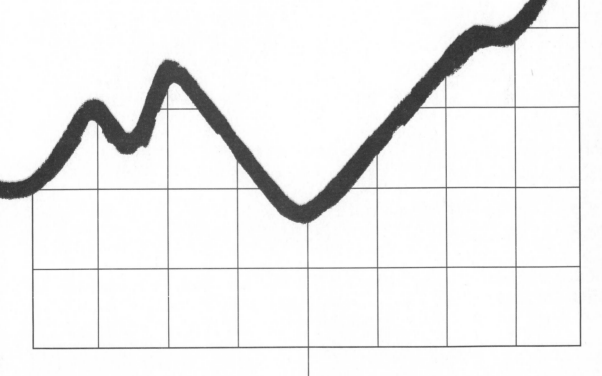

Probability provides the foundation for most statistical inferences. This is because sample evidence is used to make statements and decisions about a population. Probability theory provides a way to determine and express our uncertainty in making inferences about a population from sample information.

Although evidence of the use of probability concepts dates back to the Roman Empire, investigation into theoretical aspects began in the 1600s, when the mathematicians Blaise Pascal and Pierre Fermat corresponded about games of chance. The applications of probability theory were extended in the late 1700s to problems of astronomy, the social sciences, actuarial mathematics, and the spread of communicable diseases. Most advanced probability theories applied to economic issues were developed in the past 50 years, and today there are literally thousands of applications encompassing almost all walks of life. We illustrate a few.

■ A market research survey specifies that respondents must be selected at random from a given population, which means that the rules of probability must be used in selecting the sample.

■ Automobile manufacturers base the length and extent of their guarantees of new cars on the chances (probability) that various types of repairs will be needed.

■ Sales forecasts are often qualified by statements that reflect the chance that the forecast will be met.

■ The amount of inventory a retail store keeps on hand usually depends, to a great extent, on the probability (and cost) of being out of stock.

By the end of this chapter you should be able to identify random variables in economic and business situations. You should be able to differentiate between the implications of dependent and independent events. You should also be able to recognize the major types or rules of probability and be able to calculate relevant probabilities for use in decision-making situations.

## A Promotional Game

As the owner of an independent grocery store, you are considering running a promotional game in which each customer is given a small card upon entering your store. When a patch on the card is scratched off, the customer finds either a discount coupon for $1, $2, or $5 or simply a greeting saying "Thanks for shopping here." The company making the cards will print and randomly distribute them so that 10% of the cards have the $5 coupon, 20% have the $2 coupon, 30% have the $1 coupon, and the rest (40%) have the greeting. You are required by law to mark on the back of each card the chance that a customer will win a discount. For advertising purposes, you are also interested in various probabilities of a customer winning a discount. Finally, you are concerned about the likely cost of discounts.

# $4.2$ An Experiment

The starting point in probability is an experiment. As discussed in Chapter 1, an experiment controls for factors other than chance. Thus, at least in theory, an experiment represents a situation that can be replicated with only chance causing differences in results across replications.

---

**DEFINITION**
**Experiment**
An experiment is any situation capable (at least theoretically) of being replicated.

---

One experiment for the grocery store case might involve a customer receiving a coupon selected randomly from a stack of coupon cards. At least theoretically, this experiment could be replicated over and over with many different customers or with the same customer entering the store many times.

Another experiment might involve a mutual fund deciding which stock to purchase with $100,000. Still another one might involve selecting a new chief executive officer (CEO) for General Motors. While these experiments are not actually replicated, theoretically they could be.

In some cases the experiment involves actual replications. We might want to define the experiment as follows: "The customer receives a coupon on each of two visits." A *WSJ* sample of 780 managers can be thought of as a single experiment in which the process of sampling one person is repeated 780 times. When a process is repeated over and over it is important to specify whether the experiment is *with replacement* or *without replacement*. For example, suppose that in your grocery store each customer picks a card (called a *trial*), receives credit for the discount (if any), and then replaces the card. In this situation each customer picks one of the original 10,000 cards. If replacement does not occur, then the number of cards decreases by one on each successive trial and only 10,000 customers can receive coupon cards.

## 4.3 Outcomes and Events

Once an experiment has been defined, its **outcomes** need to be specified.

| DEFINITION Outcome | Outcomes are the result of an experiment. |
| --- | --- |

Specifying the outcomes of an experiment often depends on the interests of the decision maker. There are many ways to specify outcomes, but for one visit to the grocery store running the promotion, the outcomes are as follows:

| Outcome Set (S) |
| --- |
| Customer wins $0 |
| Customer wins $1 |
| Customer wins $2 |
| Customer wins $5 |

This list of four outcomes is called the **sample space** and is designated by the letter $S$.

---

**DEFINITION**
**Sample Space**

The sample space is the set of all outcomes.

---

In the grocery store promotion case we may be interested in a customer receiving any winning card ($1, $2 or $5 coupon) versus nothing ($0 coupon). The winning of $1, $2 or $5 is called an **event**, which is made up of three outcomes. Receiving a $0 coupon may also be called an event even though it consists of only one outcome.

---

**DEFINITION**
**Event**

An event is one or more outcomes treated as a group.

---

Events are designated by any letter other than $S$, since $S$ stands for the entire sample space. For example, the event "receive a winning coupon" may be represented by the letter $W$, while the event "receive $0 coupon" may be represented by the letter $N$. We express these events as follows:

$W$ = [$1, $2, $5]—receive a winning coupon

$N$ = [$0]—receive $0 coupon.

Using this notation, the entire sample space $S$ would be written as follows:

$S$ = [$0, $1, $2, $5] = [$W$, $N$]

---

**WORKED EXAMPLE 4.1**

A mutual fund is investing $100,000 in a single stock. The managers are interested in the price of the stock 6 months from now versus its price today. That is, will it rise, fall, or remain the same? Specify the sample space and the event "price changes."

**ANSWER:**

| Sample Space (S) |
| :--- |
| Price goes down |
| Price stays the same |
| Price goes up |

or alternatively, $S$ = [down, same, up]

Let $C$ be the event "price changes." Then $C$ = [down, up].

# 4.4 Probability of an Outcome

In any probability problem it is first necessary to determine the chance that an outcome (or set of outcomes) will occur. The chance that a single outcome will occur is the **probability of that outcome**.

| DEFINITION Probability of an Outcome | The probability of an outcome is a number between 0 and 1. It reflects the long-run relative frequency of the outcome. |
| :--- | :--- |

As this definition suggests, probability is similar to the concept of relative frequency introduced in Chapter 2. The difference is that relative frequencies represent outcomes that have actually been observed, while probability represents all possible outcomes that *could be* observed over a large (infinite) number of attempts. The idea of the long run is used here to indicate what could be observed if one repeated an experiment an infinite number of times.

A probability value reflects the chance that some outcome will occur. If the probability of an outcome is zero, then that outcome will never occur (e.g., the probability that a customer will win a $10 discount in your store is 0.00). A probability value of 1.00 indicates an outcome that is certain to occur (e.g., if the sample space $S$ has only one outcome, then the probability of that outcome is 1.00). Outcomes with a probability of 0.00 or 1.00 represent the extreme cases and are not encountered in most decision-making contexts. Most probabilities of outcomes fall between 0.00 and 1.00. The sum of all the probabilities of each of the outcomes in the sample space, however, must be 1.00.

To illustrate a long-run relative frequency interpretation of probability, suppose you are using a random number generator (as described in Chapter 1) to obtain random numbers. Each single digit generated (0, 1, 2, . . . 8, or 9) has a long-run relative frequency of $\frac{1}{10}$. This means that if we could count the number of times each 0 through 9 number occurs in an infinitely large set of digits, each would occur 10% of the time. Each digit, however, need not occur 10% of the time in any finite set of numbers. In the generation of the first 10 numbers, 3 may occur two times. In the next 10 numbers, 3 may occur zero times, and so on. The idea of probability as a long-run relative frequency shows that *on average* the number 3 will occur once in 10 times.

Suppose we let $P(0)$ denote the probability of the random digit 0, and let $P(1)$ be the probability of the digit 1, and so forth. From the preceding discussion,

$$P(0) = P(1) = P(2) = \cdots = P(9) = \tfrac{1}{10} = 0.10$$

and

$$P(0) + P(1) + P(2) + \cdots + P(8) + P(9) = 1.00$$

In our grocery store promotion case, the probabilities of alternative coupon outcomes can be determined by the relative frequency of the coupon denominations given in the case. In particular,

$$P(\$5) = 0.10, P(\$2) = 0.20, P(\$1) = 0.30, \text{ and } P(0) = 0.40$$

$$P(\$5) + P(\$2) + P(\$1) + P(0) = 1.00$$

Algebraically, the probability of any outcome can be expressed as follows:

(4.1)

Probability of a given outcome =

$$\frac{\text{Number of ways a given outcome may occur}}{\text{Total number of ways all outcomes may occur}}$$

For many years the National Basketball Association (NBA) flipped a coin (between the two worst teams) to see which received the first draft selection. What is the probability of heads and the probability of tails for a fair coin? How could heads dominate for several years if the NBA used a fair coin?

**ANSWER:**

With a fair coin, the long-run relative frequency should be the same for heads (H) and tails (T). Thus $P(H) = P(T) = \frac{1}{2} = 0.50$. In a finite number of trials, however, heads (or tails) could occur more than 50% of the time.

A new drug is being tested by Eli Lilly. A researcher estimates the odds against a drug user having any noticeable side effect to be 50 to 2. What is the probability that a randomly selected drug user will have a noticeable side effect?

**ANSWER:**

Odds of 50 to 2 imply that for every 50 users with no side effect there will be 2 with side effects, on average. Thus the probability of a side effect is the long-run relative frequency $2/(50 + 2) = 2/52$, or

$$P(\text{side effect}) = \tfrac{2}{52} = 0.03846$$

# 4.5 Probability of an Event

The **probability of an event** is the sum of the probabilities of the outcomes that make up the event. For example, the probability that a customer receives a winning coupon in one visit to the store is the sum of the probabilities that the customer receives a $1, $2, or $5 coupon card. Using our earlier notation, this probability is written

$$P(W) = P(\$5) + P(\$2) + P(\$1) = 0.10 + 0.20 + 0.30 = 0.60$$

The probability of an event is always calculated in the same manner. For example, if we ask "What is the probability of winning less than $5 (but more than zero)?" the event is [$1, $2]. Letting this event be represented by the letter $L$, the probability of $L$ is the sum of the probabilities of the outcomes win $1 and win $2:

$$P(L) = P(\$1) + P(\$2) = 0.30 + 0.20 = 0.50$$

The probability of $W$ can now be seen to be the probability of winning $5 plus the probability of $L$. Letting $H$ represent the event [$5], we can write

$$P(W) = P(L) + P(H) = 0.50 + 0.10 = 0.60$$

This calculation of the probability of receiving a winning coupon (event $W$) is special because event $H$ and event $L$ are **mutually exclusive**. That is, they cannot occur at the same time. A customer cannot receive a winning $5 coupon and a winning $2 or $1 coupon in one visit to the store.

If events are mutually exclusive, then the probability that one of them will occur is the sum of the probabilities of each event. As another example, consider the probability that a stock's price rises or falls. Because the event "price rises" and the event "price falls" are mutually exclusive, the probability of one or the other happening is the probability of the price rising plus the probability of its falling.

In the grocery store case, the events $W = $ [$1, $2, $5] and $N = $ [$0] are said to be **exhaustive** because together they constitute the entire sample space. No other event is possible in one visit to the store.

The events "stock price rises" and "stock price falls" are not exhaustive because the price could remain unchanged. The events $H$ and $L$ are not exhaustive because the customer could receive a $0 coupon, event $N$.

If events are mutually exclusive and exhaustive, then their probabilities must sum to 1. In the grocery store case, $P(W) + P(N) = 1$, because $W$ and $N$ are mutually exclusive and exhaustive, but $P(L) + P(H) \neq 1$, because $L$ and $H$ are not exhaustive.

**WORKED EXAMPLE 4.4**

Sunshine Chlorine has a list of the telephone numbers of 150,000 swimming pool owners in the United States. Sunshine has excellent delivery capability for pools in California and Arizona. A total of 10,000 of these owners live in Arizona and 15,000 live in California. How many outcomes are there in the experiment "call one owner"? That is, what is the size of the sample space? Describe a set of mutually exclusive and exhaustive events that might be of interest here. Show that the sum of these events is 1. What is the probability that a random call is to an owner in Arizona or California?

**ANSWER:**

The 150,000 phone numbers constitute the sample space. There are three mutually exclusive and exhaustive events:

1. The call is to Arizona

$$P(\text{Ariz.}) = \frac{10,000}{150,000} = 0.067$$

**2.** The call is to California

$$P(\text{Calif.}) = \frac{15{,}000}{150{,}000} = 0.100$$

**3.** The call is to some other state

$$P(\text{other}) = \frac{125{,}000}{150{,}000} = \underline{0.833}$$
$$\overline{1.000}$$

The probability of a call to Arizona or California is

$$P(\text{Arizona or California}) = 0.067 + 0.100 = 0.167$$

---

# 4.6 Probability Definitions for Multivariate Experiments

The discussion so far has involved experiments where there is only one variable, the outcome of which is determined by chance. For instance, in the grocery store promotion case the variable was the value of a coupon. This variable had four possible outcome values ($0, $1, $2, $5).

In some circumstances an experiment may involve more than one variable. For example, an insurance company recording automobile accidents may be interested in the age of the driver (one variable) as well as the gender of the driver (another variable). Similarly, voters may be classified by the state in which they live and by their gender, as well as their political preference. In multivariate experiments, factors other than the chance factors associated with the identified variables are controlled so that they cannot influence the outcome.

When more than one variable is involved, it is usually helpful to construct a **contingency table**, which shows the frequencies of the events for each variable. To illustrate, consider the following case:

## Auditing

You are auditing the accounts receivable for the credit card accounts of a bank. This bank has 8200 card holders who used their account within the last month. Some used it only to make direct purchases; others used it in a bank

**Table 4.1**

| | Number of Bank Accounts (Classified by Type of Advance and Dollar Amount) | | | | | |
|---|---|---|---|---|---|---|
| | **Balance Owed** | | | | | |
| | $B_1$ $0 < \$200$ | $B_2$ $\$200 < \$400$ | $B_3$ $\$400 < \$600$ | $B_4$ $\$600 < \$800$ | $B_5$ $\$800 < \$1000$ | *Totals* |
| $A_1$: *Cash Advance* | 531 | 761 | 738 | 450 | 340 | 2820 |
| $A_2$: *No Cash Advance* | 2421 | 1617 | 902 | 288 | 152 | 5380 |
| Totals | 2952 | 2378 | 1640 | 738 | 492 | 8200 |

machine to receive a cash advance. The bank gives the breakdown in Table 4.1 for the number of people in each of 10 different (joint) categories classified by type of advance and amount. You intend to audit a random sample of these accounts, but you first wish to know the probabilities that certain types of accounts and dollar amounts will show up in your sample.

The two variables of interest here are the balance owed (listed across the top of Table 4.1) and whether or not the card holder had a cash advance (listed down the left side). Because there are two variables of interest, Table 4.1 is called a *bivariate contingency table*. The values in the cells of this table show the number of combined outcomes that make up the events for these two variables. For instance, the value 531 in the upper-left cell shows there are 531 accounts that have a balance less than $200 and involve a cash advance. Similarly, the value in the lower-right cell indicates that there are 152 accounts with a balance of $800 but less than $1000 and no advance.

A number of probabilities can be calculated using Table 4.1. For example, the probability that a randomly selected customer had a cash advance is found by taking the ratio of the number of accounts with a cash advance (2820) to the total number of accounts (8200):

$$P(\text{cash advance}) = P(A_1) = \frac{2820}{8200} = 0.344$$

This value indicates that 34.4% of the accounts had a cash advance.

Because the two events $A_1$ (cash advance) and $A_2$ (no cash advance) are mutually exclusive (no overlap) and exhaustive (one or the other must occur), their probabilities must sum to 1.00. Thus we know that

$$P(\text{no cash advance}) = P(A_2) = \frac{5380}{8200} = 0.656$$

and

$$P(\text{no cash advance}) = 1 - P(\text{cash advance})$$

Probability calculations are easier if Table 4.1 is converted to a table of (long-run) relative frequencies by dividing the number in each cell by the total population size. The result is a joint probability table, Table 4.2.

## Joint Probabilities and Marginal Probabilities

The values associated with the A and B events in Table 4.2 are **joint probabilities**.

---

| | |
|---|---|
| **DEFINITION**<br>**Joint Probability** | A joint probability is the probability that an event will occur with another event. Joint probabilities typically involve a statement using the word *and*. |

---

**Table 4.2**

| | | | Probabilities of Bank Accounts<br>(Table 4.1 Values Divided by 8200) | | | |
|---|---|---|---|---|---|---|
| | | | **Balance Owed** | | | |
| | $B_1$<br>*$0 < $200* | $B_2$<br>*$200 < $400* | $B_3$<br>*$400 < $600* | $B_4$<br>*$600 < $800* | $B_5$<br>*$800 < $1000* | *Marginal Prob.* |
| *Cash Advance* $(A_1)$ | 0.065 | 0.093 | 0.090 | 0.055 | 0.041 | 0.344 |
| *No Cash Advance* $(A_2)$ | 0.295 | 0.197 | 0.110 | 0.035 | 0.019 | 0.656 |
| *Marginal Prob.* | 0.360 | 0.290 | 0.200 | 0.090 | 0.060 | 1.000 |

The number in the upper-left cell (0.065) represents the joint probability

$$P(A_1 \text{ and } B_1) = 0.065$$

This probability is the long-run relative frequency that both $A_1$ *and* $B_1$ will occur. In other words, if you select accounts randomly from the population of 8200 accounts, 6.5% of the time the account you draw will have a balance of less than \$200 and a cash advance. Similarly, 1.9% of the accounts drawn randomly will owe \$800 < \$1000 and will have no cash advance. The 10 joint probabilities in Table 4.2 are:

| | |
|---|---|
| $P(B_1 \text{ and } A_1) = 0.065$ | $P(B_1 \text{ and } A_2) = 0.295$ |
| $P(B_2 \text{ and } A_1) = 0.093$ | $P(B_2 \text{ and } A_2) = 0.197$ |
| $P(B_3 \text{ and } A_1) = 0.090$ | $P(B_3 \text{ and } A_2) = 0.110$ |
| $P(B_4 \text{ and } A_1) = 0.055$ | $P(B_4 \text{ and } A_2) = 0.035$ |
| $P(B_5 \text{ and } A_1) = 0.041$ | $P(B_5 \text{ and } A_2) = 0.019$ |

These 10 joint probabilities are for 10 mutually exclusive and exhaustive joint events. Hence, the sum of the 10 probabilities is 1.

Each value around the outside of Table 4.2 is called a **marginal probability** (because each one occurs in the margin or on the edge of the table).

---

| | |
|---|---|
| **DEFINITION** <br> **Marginal** <br> **Probability** | A marginal probability is the sum of joint probabilities down a column (or across a row) of a joint probability table. |

---

For example, the marginal probability we calculated earlier, $P(A_1) = 0.344$, is on the right margin of row $A_1$. The value $P(B_1) = 0.360$, shown at the bottom of the $B_1$ column, is another marginal probability that reflects the probability of drawing an account with a balance of less than \$200. There are seven marginal probabilities in Table 4.2. Note that the marginal probabilities across the bottom sum to 1.00, as do the marginal probabilities down the right-hand side. This has to be the case, since all five $B$ events are mutually exclusive and exhaustive, as are the two $A$ events.

## Conditional Probabilities

Numerous conditional probabilities can be calculated using the auditing data in Tables 4.1 and 4.2. First, suppose we want to determine the probability that a randomly selected account (person) had a cash advance, *given that* this person owes between $0 and $200. In symbols, this probability is written as follows:

$$P(\text{cash advance}|\text{owes } \$0 < \$200) = P(A_1|B_1)$$

To solve $P(A_1|B_1)$ we must recognize that our concern now is with only the 2952 customers who owe between $0 and $200. This is what the "given" notation means. No other customers are of interest. The probability $P(A_1|B_1)$ thus asks the question, "Assuming I have drawn one of the 2952 customers who owe $0 to $200, what is the probability that this person had a cash advance?" Table 4.1 shows that 531 of these 2952 customers had a cash advance. This means that there are 531 outcomes of interest in this problem and a total of 2952 equally likely outcomes. Hence, the probability $P(A_1|B_1)$ is

$$P(\text{cash advance}|\$0 < \$200) = P(A_1|B_1) = \frac{531}{2952} = 0.180$$

Thus 18% of the customers who owed less than $200 had a cash advance.

A conditional probability similar to the preceding one is

$$P(\text{no cash advance}|\$0 < \$200) = P(A_2|B_1) = \frac{2421}{2952} = 0.820$$

This result indicates that 82% of the customers who owed less than $200 did not have a cash advance. $P(A_1|B_1)$ and $P(A_2|B_1)$ must sum to 1.00 because customers owing less than $200 must have had either a cash advance or no cash advance (nothing else is possible). In other words, the events "$A_1|B_1$" and "$A_2|B_1$" are mutually exclusive and exhaustive. (Notice that the events "$A_1$ and $B_1$" and "$A_2$ and $B_1$" are not mutually exclusive and are not exhaustive.) There are 20 different conditional probabilities that can be calculated in this situation, 5 of which are as follows:

$$P(\$0 < \$200|\text{cash advance}) = P(B_1|A_1) = \frac{531}{2820} = 0.188$$

$$P(B_2|A_1) = \frac{761}{2820} = 0.270, \quad P(B_3|A_1) = \frac{738}{2820} = 0.262$$

$$P(B_4|A_1) = \frac{450}{2820} = 0.159, \quad P(B_5|A_1) = \frac{340}{2820} = 0.121$$

These five probabilities sum to 1 because the events $(B_1|A_1)$, $(B_2|A_1)$, $(B_3|A_1)$, $(B_4|A_1)$, and $(B_5|A_1)$ are mutually exclusive and exhaustive. A good but time-consuming exercise for the reader would be to determine the value of the 15 remaining conditional probabilities in this case.

---

**WORKED EXAMPLE 4.5**

Determine the conditional probability that a customer in the grocery store promotion described at the beginning of this chapter wins a $5 discount, given that this person has won some discount.

**ANSWER:**

Let the event "customer wins a discount" = $W$, and let the event "customer wins $5" = $H$. We need to determine $P(H|W)$ for 10,000 cards. There are 6000 coupons (60%) that lead to some discount, and 1000 (10%) of these lead to a $5 discount. Hence,

$$P(H/W) = \frac{1000}{6000} = \frac{1}{6} = 0.167$$

---

**WORKED EXAMPLE 4.6**

Determine from Worked Example 4.4 the probability that a random call is to Arizona, given that it goes to either Arizona or California.

**ANSWER:**

There are 25,000 numbers in Arizona and California combined, of which 10,000 are in Arizona.

$$P(\text{Arizona}|\text{Arizona or California}) = \frac{10,000}{25,000} = 0.40$$

---

## Additive Probability

The **additive probabilities** of two events, $E_1$, $E_2$, is the probability that *either* event $E_1$ *or* event $E_2$, *or both*, occur. Since for all statistical problems the word *or* implies that both events can occur, we will state additive probabilities from now on as "either $E_1$ or $E_2$," remembering that this also means *both*.

| | |
|---|---|
| **DEFINITION**<br>**Additive**<br>**Probability** | An additive probability is the probability that one event or another will occur. Additive probabilities always involve a statement using the word *or*. |

We have already calculated an additive probability for the grocery store case in Section 4.1:

P(customer wins $1 or $2)

To review, this probability was found by determining the total number of coupons (10,000) and then dividing by the number corresponding to win $1 (3000) plus the number corresponding to win $2 (2000). The result was

$$P(\text{customer wins \$1 or \$2}) = \frac{5,000}{10,000} = 0.50$$

Now let us determine a similar probability in our auditing problem for occurrence of the event "$B_1$ or $A_1$."

P($0 < $200 or cash advance) = $P(B_1 \text{ or } A_1)$

Remember, this is the probability of $B_1$ or $A_1$, or both $B_1$ and $A_1$. Referring to Table 4.1, there are 2952 accounts in $B_1$ and 2820 in $A_1$. Unlike the grocery store case, we can't just sum these two numbers because events $A_1$ and $B_1$ are not mutually exclusive. Events $A_1$ and $B_1$ share the 531 accounts that are in the category "both $B_1$ and $A_1$." That is, the 531 accounts are double counted if we merely add 2952 and 2820. The easy way to determine the total number of accounts in $B_1$ or $A_1$ is to add 2952 and 2820 and then subtract 531. This number divided by the total number of accounts, 8200, gives the probability $P(B_1 \text{ or } A_1)$.

$$P(B_1 \text{ or } A_1) = \frac{2952 + 2820 - 531}{8200} = 0.639$$

Thus 63.9% of the accounts had either a cash advance or a balance of $0 < $200, or both.

A committee is composed of two administrators (one male, one female), two faculty members (one female, one male), and one male student. A reporter picks one of the members to interview. What is the probability that the person selected will be a female or an administrator?

**ANSWER:**

There are five people who could be selected. Two are females and two are administrators, and one female is also an administrator. A sketch of this situation is

|        | Adm | Faculty | Student |   |
|--------|-----|---------|---------|---|
| *Male*   | 1   | 1       | 1       | 3 |
| *Female* | 1   | 1       | 0       | 2 |
|        | 2   | 2       | 1       | 5 |

We add the two administrators plus the two females, and subtract the overlap (the female administrator).

$$P(\text{female or adm.}) = \frac{2 + 2 - 1}{5} = \frac{3}{5} = 0.60$$

# 4.7 Replication of an Experiment

Recall that in some problems the events of interest involve replications of the experiment. For example, in the grocery store promotion case you may want to determine the probability that the second customer wins $5, given that the first customer has won $5. The experiment now involves two visits to the store. Notice that the events "first customer wins $5" and "second customer wins \$5" are not mutually exclusive, since both events can take place.

We have not specified whether this bivariate experiment is with replacement or without replacement. If it is with replacement, the value of $P$(second customer wins \$5) is the same as $P$(first customer wins \$5), since the probabilities $P(\$0) = 0.4$, $P(1) = 0.3$, $P(2) = 0.2$ and $P(5) = 0.1$ do not change from visit to visit (or from customer to customer).

When sampling is without replacement, the probabilities do change. For example, if the first customer wins \$5, then there are 9999 (of 10,000) cards remaining, of which 999 represent a \$5 discount. The probability that the second customer wins a \$5 discount is thus (using Eq. 4.1):

$P$(second customer wins \$5, given that first has won \$5)

$$= \frac{999}{9999} = 0.09991$$

The probability of winning \$5 is smaller for the second customer because the first customer has one of the 1000 cards giving a \$5 discount. In this example, the probability $P(\$5)$ changed from $P(\$5) = 0.10$ to $P(\$5) = 0.09991$ from the first to the second customer. This change is relatively small because the number of outcomes is relatively large (10,000). If the number of outcomes is small, the probabilities may change dramatically.

---

**WORKED EXAMPLE 4.8**

Two people are to be appointed to a committee. A list of eight candidates is prepared. Five of these people are females. If selection is random, are the events "first selection is a female" and "second selection is a female" mutually exclusive? Are they exhaustive? What is the probability that the first selection is a female and the second is a male? What is the probability of two females being selected? What is the probability of selecting at least one female? What is the probability that the second person selected is a female, given that the first one selected is a female?

**ANSWER:**

The two events are not mutually exclusive (both can occur) and they are not exhaustive (other events are possible). One way to determine the relevant probabilities is to first construct the contingency table, which shows the 56 outcomes classified by the events.

|  |  | First Selection | | |
|  |  | Male ($M_1$) | Female ($F_1$) | Total |
|---|---|---|---|---|
| **Second Selection** | Male ($M_2$) | 6 | 15 | 21 |
|  | Female ($F_2$) | <u>15</u> | <u>20</u> | <u>35</u> |
|  | Total | 21 | 35 | 56 |

This contingency table states that there are six ways a male could be selected first and a male second (male no. 1 then male no. 2, male no. 1 then male no. 3, male no. 2 then male no. 3, male no. 2 then male no. 1, male no. 3, then male no. 1, and male no. 3 then male no. 2). There are 15 ways a female could be selected first and a male second. Thus the probability that the first selection is female and the second is male is

$$P(F_1 \text{ and } M_2) = \tfrac{15}{56} = 0.268$$

The probability of selecting two females is

$$P(F_1 \text{ and } F_2) = \tfrac{20}{56} = 0.357$$

The probability of at least one female being selected is

$$P(F_1 \text{ or } F_2) = \frac{35 + 35 - 20}{56} = 0.893$$

The probability that the second is a female, given that the first is a female, is

$$P(F_2|F_1) = \tfrac{20}{35} = 0.571$$

# 4.8 Probability Formulas

Probabilities were calculated in Section 4.5 using relative frequencies, such as Table 4.1. In many problems a table of relative frequencies is not readily available. In such cases we need a formula for determining joint probabilities, conditional probabilities, and additive probabilities. The formulas now presented are merely formal rules for determining the same types of probabilities we have determined previously.

## Joint Probability Formulas

Joint probabilities have already been discussed; 10 were presented in Table 4.2. For example, we divided Table 4.1 by 8200 to get the following joint probability value (in Table 4.2):

$$P(\$0 < \$200 \text{ and cash advance}) = P(B_1 \text{ and } A_1) = \tfrac{531}{8200} = 0.065$$

$P(B_1 \text{ and } A_1) = 0.065$ is called a joint probability because it represents the probability that $B_1$ and $A_1$ occur together (i.e., jointly).

Suppose we let $E_1$ and $E_2$ be any two events (again, think of $E_1$ as the first of two events and $E_2$ as the second of two events). The joint probability $P(E_1 \text{ and } E_2)$ can be calculated by using either one of the following two formulas:

---

Joint probability formulas

(4.2)
$$P(E_1 \text{ and } E_2) = P(E_1)P(E_2|E_1)$$

or

$$P(E_1 \text{ and } E_2) = P(E_2)P(E_1|E_2)$$

---

A joint probability is thus the product of a marginal probability [either $P(E_1)$ or $P(E_2)$] and a conditional probability (either $P(E_2|E_1)$ or $P(E_1|E_2)$). It may be helpful to visualize Eq. (4.2) using what is called a **Venn diagram**. The entire rectangle in Fig. 4.1 represents all the outcomes that might occur in some experiment. The two circles in this figure represent two sets of outcomes of interest, $E_1$ and $E_2$. You might think of throwing a dart (randomly) at this

**Figure 4.1**
Venn diagram for a
joint probability.

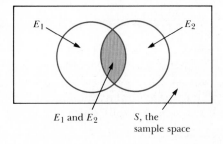

$E_1$ and $E_2$     $S$, the
sample space

rectangle and trying to determine the (joint) probability that it falls in *both* circles (the shaded area).

Think of the outcome that your dart falls in the circle as $E_1$; this happens with probability $P(E_1)$. Given that the dart falls in the $E_1$ circle, the probability that it also falls in the $E_2$ circle is the conditional probability $P(E_2|E_1)$. The product of $P(E_1)$ and $P(E_2|E_1)$ is the joint probability shown by the shaded (colored) area in Fig. 4.1. Let's use Eq. (4.2) to calculate

$$P(\text{cash advance and } \$0 < \$200) = P(B_1 \text{ and } A_1)$$

To do this let $E_1 = B_1$ (the first event) and $E_2 = A_1$ (the second event). Making these substitutions into Eq. (4.2) yields:

$$P(\$0 < \$200 \text{ and cash advance}) = P(B_1 \text{ and } A_1) = P(B_1)P(A_1|B_1)$$

or

$$P(\$0 < \$200 \text{ and cash advance}) = P(B_1 \text{ and } A_1) = P(A_1)P(B_1|A_1)$$

To calculate $P(B_1 \text{ and } A_1)$, we need to know the right-hand side of one (or both) of these two formulas. Suppose we know (from previous analysis) that $P(B_1) = 0.36$ and $P(A_1|B_1) = 0.18$. Using the first formula in Eq. (4.2),

$$P(B_1 \text{ and } A_1) = P(B_1)P(A_1|B_1) = (0.36)(0.18) = 0.065$$

which is the joint probability determined at the beginning of this section in Table 4.2. Had we recalled (from earlier analysis) that $P(A_1) = 0.344$ and $P(B_1|A_1) = 0.188$, we could have used the second formula and would get the same answer:

$$P(B_1 \text{ and } A_1) = P(A_1)P(B_1|A_1) = (0.344)(0.188) = 0.065$$

We can use Eq. (4.2) whenever a joint probability table like Table 4.2 is not available.

---

**WORKED EXAMPLE 4.9**

In electroplating chrome over plastic the flow of the current is critical in the adhesion of the chrome to the plastic. Seventy percent of the time the current is classified as uniform. When the current is uniform, the adhesion will be perfect in 90% of all cases. Determine the joint probability that the current will be uniform and the adhesion will be perfect.

**ANSWER:**

Let $P(U) = 0.70$ represent the probability of uniform current and $P(A|U) = 0.90$ represent the probability of a perfect adhesion, given that the current is uniform. Using Eq. (4.2),

$$P(U \text{ and } A) = P(U)P(A|U)$$
$$= (0.70)(0.90) = 0.63$$

## Conditional Probability Formula

If the first line of Eq. (4.2) is solved for the conditional probability $P(E_2|E_1)$, the result is the conditional probability formula shown in Eq. (4.3).

---

**(4.3)**

Conditional probability formula

$$P(E_2|E_1) = \frac{P(E_2 \text{ and } E_1)}{P(E_1)}$$

---

A **conditional probability** is thus a joint probability divided by a marginal probability. Using the Venn diagram in Fig. 4.1, this is the probability that a dart falls in circle $E_2$ *given that* we know it falls in circle $E_1$.

To illustrate Eq. (4.3), consider the previous auditing case where we calculated the probability of a cash advance, given a balance due of $0 < \$200$. Using Table 4.1, this probability was determined to be

$$P(\text{cash advance}|\$0 < \$200) = P(A_1|B_1) = \frac{531}{2952} = 0.180$$

Now using Eq. (4.3) and the probability data in Table 4.2 we have

$$P(A_1|B_1) = \frac{P(A_1 \text{ and } B_1)}{P(B_1)} = \frac{0.065}{0.360} = 0.180$$

(Notice that instead of using $E_1$ and $E_2$ in this formula we have used the original notation, $A_1$ and $B_1$. As long as one is consistent, any symbols may be used.)

**WORKED EXAMPLE 4.10**

A personnel director knows that 10% of the applicants for assembly line positions will be females and members of a minority race. Twenty-five percent of the applicants are female. If the next applicant is known to be a female, what is the probability that this person is a minority candidate?

**ANSWER:**

Let $E_2$ be the outcome that the candidate is a minority candidate and $E_1$ the outcome that the person is a female. The conditional probability that the person is a minority candidate, given that this person is a female, is

$$P(E_2|E_1) = \frac{P(E_2 \text{ and } E_1)}{P(E_1)} = \frac{0.10}{0.25} = 0.40$$

## Additive Probability Formulas

Recall that $P(E_1 \text{ or } E_2)$ is the additive probability that either $E_1$ or $E_2$ (or both) take place. This additive probability can be illustrated by the shaded (colored) area in Fig. 4.2.

If in Fig. 4.2 the area corresponding to the probability of $E_1$ is added to the area corresponding to the probability of $E_2$, the overlapping area (which is the joint probability of $E_1$ and $E_2$) is added twice. Thus, a formula for $P(E_1 \text{ and } E_2)$ must subtract this joint probability from the sum of $P(E_1)$ + $P(E_2)$.

**(4.4)**

Additive probability formula

$$P(E_1 \text{ or } E_2) = P(E_1) + P(E_2) - P(E_1 \text{ and } E_2)$$

**Figure 4.2**
Venn diagram for $P(E_1$ or $E_2)$.

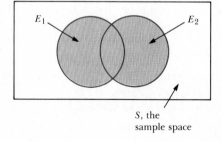

$S$, the
sample space

Recall that at the end of Section 4.4 we calculated the probability that $P(B_1 \text{ or } A_1) = 0.639$ using the frequencies in Table 4.1. This same probability can be calculated using Eq. (4.4) and Table 4.2.

$$P(B_1 \text{ or } A_1) = P(B_1) + P(A_1) - P(B_1 \text{ and } A_1)$$

$$= \frac{2952}{8200} + \frac{2820}{8200} - \frac{531}{8200}$$

$$= 0.36 + 0.344 - 0.065 = 0.639$$

**WORKED EXAMPLE 4.11**

Suppose you want to know the probability that a person considering buying a new Buick will either see a Buick ad on TV or read an ad in a local newspaper. From national survey data on consumer habits, the following probabilities are known:

$P(E_1) = P(\text{sees ad on TV}) = 0.26$
$P(E_2) = P(\text{reads ad in newspaper}) = 0.18$
$P(E_1 \text{ and } E_2) = P(\text{sees ad on TV and reads ad in paper}) = 0.13$

**ANSWER:**

Placing these values in Eq. (4.4) yields:

$P(\text{sees TV or reads newspaper ad})$
$\quad = P(\text{sees TV ad}) + P(\text{reads newspaper ad}) - P(\text{both})$
$\quad = 0.26 + 0.18 - 0.13$
$\quad = 0.31$

There is a 31% chance that a person will either see the TV ad or read an ad in the newspaper.

# 4.9 Independent Events

The formulas developed in Section 4.8 are general formulas in the sense that they apply whether the events are mutually exclusive, exhaustive, or independent. **Independent events** are events that have no influence on one another. When two (or more) events are independent, Eqs. (4.2) and (4.3) can be simplified. These two simplified formulas are given as Eq. (4.5).

---

For independent events $E_1$ and $E_2$,

(4.5)     $P(E_1 \text{ and } E_2) = P(E_1)P(E_2)$

$P(E_2|E_1) = P(E_2)$

---

Both formulas in Eq. (4.5) are based on the fact that $P(E_2)$ is unaffected by $E_1$. That is, the fact that $E_1$ is *given* does not influence the probability of outcome $E_2$. Nor does $E_2$ influence $E_1$. If either formula in Eq. (4.5) holds, then $E_1$ and $E_2$ are independent. If neither equation holds, then $E_1$ and $E_2$ are dependent.

---

**WORKED EXAMPLE 4.12**

Determine whether or not the events "cash advance" $(A_1)$ and "owes $0 < $200" $(B_1)$ are independent in the auditing case.

**ANSWER:**

It makes no difference if we let cash advance $= E_1$ or $E_2$ in Eq. (4.5); either formula will correctly indicate independence or dependence. Suppose we let

Cash advance $= E_2$     and     $0 < $200 = E_1$

The second formula in Eq. (4.5) then becomes

$P(\text{cash advance}|\$0 < \$200) = P(\text{cash advance})$

From previous calculations, we know that

$P(\text{cash advance}|\$0 < \$200) = \frac{531}{2952} = 0.180$

and

$P(\text{cash advance}) = \frac{2820}{8200} = 0.344$

Because 0.180 does not equal 0.344, these two events are dependent. In this problem 34.4% of the accounts had a cash advance, but only 18.8% of those with balances of $0 < $200 had a cash advance. Thus, in predicting whether or not an account has a cash balance, it is useful to know that the amount owed is $0 < $200 (i.e., these events are dependent).

---

**WORKED EXAMPLE 4.13**

A retailer for a large carpet outlet is trying to determine whether the brand of carpet a customer buys is independent of the way the different brands are displayed in the showroom. Two brands, Lee and Mohawk, are picked for an experiment. Each week over a 1-year period, Lee and Mohawk carpets were alternated between displays A and B. The number of customers who purchased each type from the indicated displays is shown in Table 4.3.

**Table 4.3**

| Carpet Displays | | |
|---|---|---|
| | Display A | Display B |
| Mohawk | 40 | 64 | 104 |
| Lee | 30 | 48 | 78 |
| | 70 | 112 | 182 |

**ANSWER:**

Using Table 4.3 and the second formula in Eq. (4.5):

$$P(\text{Mohawk}|\text{display A}) = \tfrac{40}{70} = 0.571 \qquad P(\text{Mohawk}) = \tfrac{104}{182} = 0.571$$

These probabilities are equal; hence the events are independent. The same conclusion should be reached using the first formula in Eq. (4.5):

$$P(\text{Mohawk and display A}) = \tfrac{40}{182} = 0.21978$$
$$P(\text{Mohawk})P(\text{display A}) = \tfrac{104}{182} \times \tfrac{70}{182} = 0.21978$$

These probabilities are equal, again confirming the independence of the events "Mohawk" and "display A."

---

## Exercises

**4.1** Explain the similarities and differences between absolute frequency, relative frequency, and probability.

**4.2**   Define the following terms and give an example of each one.

   **a)** experiment          **b)** outcome

   **c)** event               **d)** mutually exclusive events

   **e)** exhaustive events   **f)** independent events

**4.3**   Are the following statements true or false? If false, indicate why.

   **a)** Mutually exclusive events are always dependent.

   **b)** Dependent events are always mutually exclusive.

   **c)** Independent events are always mutually exclusive.

   **d)** Independent events are always exhaustive.

   **e)** Exhaustive events are always mutually exclusive.

MKT   **4.4**   Use the grocery store data to calculate the probability that a customer wins a discount of $1 or $5, on one visit to the store.

**4.5**   In each of the following cases, indicate whether the events are mutually exclusive and exhaustive. If not, indicate why.

   **a)** The two events

      1 = The next president of the United States will be a Republican.
      2 = The next president of the United States will be a Democrat.

   **b)** The two events

      1 = Unemployment will be high in the United States next month.
      2 = Interest rates will be high in the United States next month.

   **c)** The three events

      1 = The price of IBM stock will go up in the next month.
      2 = The price of IBM stock will stay the same in the next month.
      3 = The price of IBM stock will go down in the next month.

   **d)** The three events

      1 = There will be sunny weather tomorrow.
      2 = There will be cloudy weather tomorrow.
      3 = There will be rainy weather tomorrow.

MKT   **4.6**   You are planning to interview the managers of two of the five shoe stores in a shopping mall. Your plan is to pick two stores at random. You label the stores A, B, C, D, and E.

a) Make a list of 10 mutually exclusive and exhaustive events that could take place in this experiment. [Hint: one event is (A, B), another is (A, C), and so forth].

b) Consider the list in part (a) as the number of equally likely events in this experiment. What is the probability that store A will be one of the stores interviewed?

c) Use the list in part (a) to determine $P(A \text{ or } B)$.

**4.7** What does it mean when events are said to occur randomly? Do the events $0, $1, $2, and $5 occur randomly in the grocery store example? Does this mean that each customer has an equal chance of receiving a $1 discount as a $5 discount?

PUB **4.8** As discussed in Chapter 1, the U.S. Selective Service used a "fishbowl" approach for the draft lottery in 1970. Tokens for the 366 days of the year (to include leap years) were placed in a container, mixed together, and then drawn one at a time. Complaints were raised that days in November and December seemed to occur more often than if they were randomly drawn.

a) What is the probability that November 21 is the first day drawn if the selection is random?

b) If the draw is random, what is the probability that the first number drawn is in November?

c) Given that a November day is drawn first, what is the probability that the second day drawn is also in November?

ECN **4.9** You want to pick two companies at random from the list in Appendix A.1 without replacement.

a) What is the probability that the first company you pick is from the Service Industries category?

b) What is the probability that the second company you pick is from the Tobacco category, given that the first was from the Tobacco category?

c) Is the selection of the second company independent of the selection of the first company?

**4.10** Go to Appendix Table B.1, the table of random numbers.

a) If you pick a two-digit number at random, what is $P(50)$?

b) What proportion of the two-digit numbers in Appendix Table B.1 would you expect to be larger than 50 but smaller than 80?

**c)** Randomly select 25 two-digit numbers from Appendix Table B.1. Does the proportion of numbers between 50 and 80 correspond with your answer to part (b)? Did you expect it would?

**4.11** Indicate whether it appears that each pair of events is independent or dependent.

**a)** Interest rates increase, housing starts decrease.

**b)** The price of a new Chevrolet and a new Ford increases.

**c)** The weather in San Francisco and the Dow Jones Industrial Average.

**d)** Unemployment in Indiana and unemployment in California.

ACT **4.12** In recent years numerous articles have reported on the probability that a taxpayer will be audited. Use the following numbers to construct a frequency table (like Table 4.1) with two categories down the left side (audited or not audited) and six categories across the top (corresponding to the six income categories). Then construct a joint probability table (like Table 4.2). Use these tables to answer the following questions.

| Income | Chances of Being Audited (%) | No. of Filers (in Millions) |
|---|---|---|
| ≤ $10,000 (short form) | 0.3 | 27 |
| ≤ $10,000 (long form) | 1.0 | 9 |
| $10,000–25,000 (short form) | 0.6 | 21 |
| $10,000–25,000 (long form) | 2.5 | 11 |
| $25,000–50,000 | 2.9 | 18 |
| $50,000 or more | 5.7 | 4 |

**a)** Find the probability that a randomly selected taxpayer will be audited.

**b)** Find the probability that a person has an income of over $50,000, given that this person was selected for an audit.

**c)** What is the probability that a randomly selected taxpayer has an income of over $50,000 and is audited?

ECN **4.13** Consider the following information on the percentage share of the unemployed during the recession in early 1980.

| | |
|---|---|
| White adult males | 36% |
| White adult females | 25% |

| White teenage females | 8% |
| Nonwhite teenage females | 2% |
| Nonwhite adult females | 8% |
| Nonwhite teenage males | 2% |
| Nonwhite adult males | 10% |
| White teenage males | 9% |

a) Construct a joint probability table similar to Table 4.2 for the preceding data. Use two categories down the left: "Adult" and "Teenage." Use four categories across thee top: "White male," "White female," "Nonwhite male," and "Nonwhite female." Show that the eight joint probabilities in your table sum to 1.

b) What is the joint probability that an unemployed person is both a white male (WM) and a teenager (T), P(WM and T)?

c) Identify the six marginal probabilities. What is the probability that an unemployed person is a white male, P(WM)? What is the probability that an unemployed person is an adult, P(A)?

MKT     **4.14** Show that the events "Lee" and "display A" are independent in Worked Example 4.13.

FIN     **4.15** This problem is a simplified version of a probability problem reported in *Management Science* on the status of installment sales for a retail establishment. We will call this establishment Electro. A considerable portion of Electro's sales are on an installment basis, which means that the company has much of its current income tied up in accounts receivable. Although most of Electro's customers make their installment payments on time, a certain percentage of their accounts are always overdue, and some are never paid at all. Electro's experience with overdue accounts has been that when a customer falls two or more payments behind schedule, then this account is generally not going to be paid. Hence, Electro's policy in these cases is to discontinue credit to such customers and to write these accounts off as bad debts. At the beginning of each month, Electro reviews each account and classifies it as either paid up, current (meaning it is being paid on time), overdue (i.e., one payment past due), or a bad debt. The following table presents conditional probabilities for each dollar of accounts receivable at time $t$ relative to time $t + 1$ (1 month later).

|  | | State of Each Dollar at Month $t + 1$ | | | |
|---|---|---|---|---|---|
|  | | Paid | Current | Overdue | Bad Debt |
| State of | Paid | 1.00 | 0.00 | 0.00 | 0.00 |
| Each Dollar | Current | 0.30 | 0.50 | 0.20 | 0.00 |
| at Time $t$ | Overdue | 0.50 | 0.30 | 0.10 | 0.10 |
|  | Bad Debt | 0.00 | 0.00 | 0.00 | 1.00 |

a) Interpret, in words, the probability 0.30 in the first column.

b) How can you tell from this table that the four categories for time $t + 1$ are mutually exclusive and exhaustive?

c) Why do the probabilities sum to 1.00 across the columns but not down the rows?

d) What is the probability that a dollar can be classified at time $t + 1$ as either current or overdue if it is current at time $t$?

e) Find the value of $P$(paid at $t + 1$|current at $t$) and the value of $P$(paid at $t + 1$|overdue at $t$).

f) Are the events "paid at $t + 1$" and "current at $t$" independent or dependent if you know that $P$(paid at $t + 1$) = 0.44?

g) If $P$(current at $t$) = 0.70, find $P$(current at $t$ and current at $t + 1$).

ADM  **4.16** The Tousley-Bixler Construction Company, Inc., built the Indiana University Natatorium, the Little "500" Track and Soccer Stadium, and the IU Adult Hospital in Indianapolis, among others. Let's assume that Tousley-Bixler estimates the probability that they will be the winning bidder on each project, and they are continually concerned about the number of projects currently under construction. Obviously, they do not want too few projects, but they are also concerned with winning too many and thus overcommitting themselves. Currently, they are preparing bids on two projects (A and B), and they estimate the following probabilities:

| Win A | Win B | Win B|Win A |
|---|---|---|
| 0.40 | 0.24 | 0.09 |

a) Are the events "win A" and "win B" mutually exclusive and exhaustive? If not, what events would you include in a list of mutually exclusive and exhaustive events?

b) What is the probability that Tousley-Bixler will win both projects A and B?

c) What is the probability that Tousley-Bixler will win either A or B (or both)?

d) Are the events "win A" and "win B" independent or dependent?

ADM   **4.17**   As the administrator of a small hospital, you find that an automobile accident has created a critical need for types A and AB blood. Two visitors to the hospital have volunteered to give blood, but as yet their blood types are unknown. In general, 15% of the U.S. population have type A and 10% have type AB. The two visitors are not related to one another or to the patients.

a) What events are possible considering only the two volunteers and their types of blood?

b) Would you expect the blood type of the first volunteer to be independent of the blood type of the second volunteer? Explain.

c) What is the probability that, for the two volunteers, the first will have type A and the second type AB? What is the probability that both will have type A?

d) The patient needing type A is the more critical. What is the probability that either the first volunteer or the second will have type A? What is the probability that neither of the two volunteers will have type A?

ADM   **4.18**   The administrator for the hospital in Exercise 4.17 has found that one of the patients is RH negative ($RH^-$) and cannot be given RH positive ($RH^+$) blood. The proportion of people who are $RH^+$, $RH^-$, and either type A or type AB is as follows:

|        | Type A | Type AB |
|--------|--------|---------|
| $RH^+$ | 80%    | 60%     |
| $RH^-$ | 20%    | 40%     |

a) Is the event $RH^+$ independent of the event "type A"? Explain.

**b)** What is $P(RH^+|\text{type A})$? What is $P(RH^-|\text{type AB})$?

**c)** Suppose the first volunteer is known to have either type A or type AB. Can you determine the proportion of such people who have $RH^+$ blood?

MKT **4.19** Recall the example in Section 4.1 involving cards in which the customer receives either a greeting or a discount worth \$1, \$2, or \$5. The manager would like to place on the back of each card the following information:

**a)** The probability that a customer wins on both of two visits.

**b)** The probability that a customer wins \$10 in two visits.

**c)** The probability that a customer wins at least \$7 in two visits.

**4.20** Consider the following joint probability table:

|       | $A_1$ | $A_2$ | $A_3$ |
|-------|-------|-------|-------|
| $B_1$ | 0.10  | 0.05  | 0.10  |
| $B_2$ | 0.20  | 0.05  | 0.15  |
| $B_3$ | 0.10  | 0.10  | 0.15  |

**a)** Find the six marginal probabilities.

**b)** What is $P(A_1 \text{ and } B_1)$? Find $P(A_1|B_1)$.

**c)** Determine $P(A_1 \text{ or } B_2)$.

**d)** Are $A_1$ and $B_2$ independent or dependent?

**4.21** You are given the following probabilities: $P(A_1) = 0.60$, $P(A_2) = 0.10$, $P(A_3) = 0.30$, $P(A_1 \text{ and } A_2) = 0.24$.

**a)** Are $A_1$, $A_2$, and $A_3$ mutually exclusive and exhaustive?

**b)** Find $P(A_1|A_2)$.

**c)** Find $P(A_1 \text{ or } A_2)$.

**4.22** Indicate whether each of the following statements is true or false. If false, indicate why.

**a)** If $P(A_1|A_2) = 0$, then $A_1$ and $A_2$ are mutually exclusive.

**b)** If $P(A_1|A_2) = 0$, then $A_1$ and $A_2$ are independent.

**c)** If $P(A_1|A_2) = P(A_2|A_1)$, then $P(A_1) = P(A_2)$.

**d)** If $A_1$ and $A_2$ are independent, then $P(A_1) = P(A_2)$.

# 4.10 Random Variables

Thus far the outcomes of an experiment have been specified by using a list. In Section 4.5 we introduced the idea of a variable and its outcomes. Now we will define formally the concept of a **random variable** as the procedure for presenting the outcomes of an experiment.

---

**DEFINITION**
**Random Variable**

A random variable is a well-defined rule for assigning a number to each outcome in a probability problem.

---

To define a random variable we must make sure that each outcome of the experiment is assigned a specific number. Random variables are usually designated by a letter (such as $x$, $B$, or $y$). Thus the notation $x = 1$ corresponds to the value "1" associated with the random variable $x$. To illustrate, consider the following random variables:

$x$ = the random variable "amount of discount a grocery store customer can win in one visit." The assignment of numbers to the outcomes of this experiment indicates how much of a discount the customer wins: $x = 0$ (no discount), $x = 1$ ($1 discount), $x = 2$ ($2 discount), and $x = 5$ ($5 discount).

$B$ = the random variable "amount a credit card customer owes the bank at the end of the month." The values of this random variable are the dollar amounts owed, which are numbers between 0 and $1000.

$y$ = the random variable "your grade for this course," where the outcomes are $y = 4$ (an A), $y = 3$ (a B), $y = 2$ (a C), $y = 1$ (a D), or $y = 0$ (an F).

In some problems, one may have a choice as to how the numbers are assigned in defining a random variable. For example, suppose an Occupational Safety and Health Act (OSHA) inspector, checking a facility for safety, defines the following random variable:

$x$ = rate a facility.

There are several ways the inspector might assign a number to the results of this experiment. Each of the following examples represents a different way this random variable might be defined, depending on the circumstances.

1. The outcome of the experiment (the inspection) might be defined in terms of just two outcomes, as follows:
   $x = 1$ (the facility passes) or $x = 0$ (the facility fails).

2. The outcomes might be defined so as to permit the inspector more options:
   $x = 4$ (best rating), $x = 3$, $x = 2$, $x = 1$, and $x = 0$ (worst rating).

3. Even more variety might be permitted with the following model:
   $x = 100$ (best rating), $x = 99$, $x = 98$, . . . , $x = 0$ (where 0 is the worst rating).

The variables we have defined so far are all called *discrete* random variables because the numbers assigned to each outcome are restricted to certain values; in each preceding case, the numbers were all integers (i.e., no fractional values were used). Other examples of discrete random variables include the number of cars sold in a month or the number of people hired in an economic upturn.

---

| | |
|---|---|
| **DEFINITION**<br>**Discrete Random**<br>**Variable** | A discrete random variable is a rule for assigning separate values to each outcome in an experiment. |

---

# 4.11 Probability Mass Functions

After a discrete random variable is defined, we must specify the probability associated with each value of this variable. Such a specification is called a **probability mass function** (*p.m.f.*).

<table>
<tr><td>**DEFINITION**<br>**p.m.f.**</td><td>A probability mass function (p.m.f.) is a list, graph, table or formula that gives the probability for each possible value of a discrete random variable.</td></tr>
</table>

To illustrate a p.m.f., consider once again the grocery store promotion from the beginning of this chapter. The probabilities for this experiment were given in Section 4.3. Using the notation of this section, we define the p.m.f. as follows:

$$P(x = 0) = P(0) = 0.40$$
$$P(x = 1) = P(1) = 0.30$$
$$P(x = 2) = P(2) = 0.20$$
$$P(x = 5) = P(3) = 0.10$$

The probabilities in a p.m.f. must sum to 1.00. We will denote the probabilities in a probability mass function as $P(x)$.

**WORKED EXAMPLE 4.14**

Assume that the OSHA inspector mentioned earlier in this section decides to classify each facility on a five-point scale. From his experience over the past 10 years, this inspector knows that 20% of the facilities will be rated 4, 30% will be rated 3, 30% will be rated 2, 15% will be rated 1, and 5% will be rated 0. Formulate the p.m.f. represented by these percentages.

**ANSWER:**

$$P(x = 4) = 0.20$$
$$P(x = 3) = 0.30$$
$$P(x = 2) = 0.30$$
$$P(x = 1) = 0.15$$
$$P(x = 0) = 0.05$$

These values represent a p.m.f. because they give the probability $[P(x)]$ for each possible outcome of the experiment "rate a facility."

Worked Example 4.14 illustrates the specification of a p.m.f. by means of a list. Another way to specify it is to draw a graph, putting the random

**Figure 4.3**
Probability mass
function (p.m.f.) for
the OSHA rating.

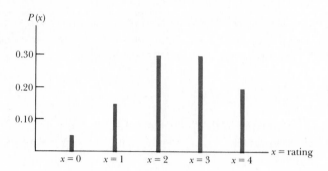

**Figure 4.4**
Probability mass
function (p.m.f.) for
discount coupons.

Probability List

$P(x = 0) = 0.40$
$P(x = 1) = 0.30$
$P(x = 2) = 0.20$
$P(x = 5) = 0.10$

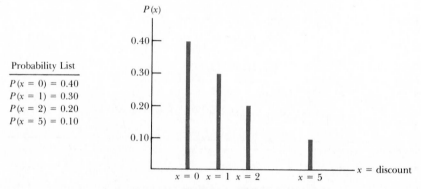

variable on the horizontal axis and the probabilities, $P(x)$, on the vertical axis. Such a p.m.f. is shown in Fig. 4.3. Note that a separate spike or bar is given for each value on the $x$ axis. Probability is shown by the height of the $x$ value.

We could also graph the p.m.f. for the grocery store promotion, as shown in Fig. 4.4.

# 4.12  The Expected Value of a Random Variable

As the owner of the grocery store in the example at the beginning of this chapter, you might want to determine the *average* discount a customer would earn in one visit to the store. Such an average is called an **expected value**, for it represents the amount one would expect an average customer to win; it is the average over all customers who receive a discount coupon. Expected values represent the same concept as the mean of a population from Chapter 3. Now, however, the population is described by the random variable and the p.m.f.

---

**DEFINITION**
**Expected Value**
The mean or average of a random variable $x$ is called the *expected value* of the distribution of $x$ and is written as $E(x)$ or $\mu_x$.

---

An expected value is calculated by multiplying each value of the random variable by its probability and then summing these products. Two different symbols are used to denote this mean, $E(x)$, and $\mu_x$.

---

**(4.6)**

Expected value of $x$

$$E(x) \; = \; \mu_x \; = \; \Sigma x P(x)$$

---

Equation (4.6) is equivalent to the one given in Chapter 3 for a mean, except that now each value of $x$ is weighted by probabilities instead of relative frequencies. The reader can think of Eq. (4.6) as a weighting of each value of $x$ by its long-run relative frequency.

To illustrate Eq. (4.6), suppose we calculate the mean discount to customers in the grocery store example. The first column in the following tabulation gives the values of $x$, the second column gives the probabilities, and the third column gives the product of $x$ times $P(x)$. The sum at the bottom of the third column is the mean (or expected value).

| $x$ | $P(x)$ | $xP(x)$ |
|-----|--------|---------|
| 0 | 0.40 | 0.00 |
| 1 | 0.30 | 0.30 |
| 2 | 0.20 | 0.40 |
| 5 | 0.10 | 0.50 |
| | | 1.20 $=$ $E(x)$ $=$ $\mu_x$ |

This result indicates that customers will earn a discount of $1.20, on the average, on each visit to the store. In other words, the amount a customer can expect to earn, on the average, is $1.20 per visit. Of course, no customer ever earns exactly $1.20 on one visit, since $1.20 is not one of the values of our random variable.

---

**WORKED EXAMPLE 4.15** Calculate the mean for the p.m.f. for the OSHA ratings given in Fig. 4.3.

**ANSWER:**

| $x$ | $P(x)$ | $xP(x)$ |
|-----|--------|---------|
| 4   | 0.20   | 0.80    |
| 3   | 0.30   | 0.90    |
| 2   | 0.30   | 0.60    |
| 1   | 0.15   | 0.15    |
| 0   | 0.05   | 0.00    |
|     |        | $2.45 = E(x) = \mu_x$ |

The average rating is thus 2.45. That is, on the average, this inspector gives ratings that average 2.45.

---

# 4.13 The Variance of a Random Variable

A probability distribution has a **variance** as well as a mean. As in Chapter 3, the variance is a measure of the spread of a population.

---

**DEFINITION**
**Variance of Distribution**

The variance of the distribution of the discrete random variable $x$ is the sum of the squared deviations of $x$ values around their mean, where each deviation is weighted by $P(x)$.

---

The variance of a p.m.f. for $x$ is denoted by the symbol $\sigma_x^2$. It is calculated using Eq. (4.7).

| (4.7) | The variance of $x$ |
|---|---|
| | $$\sigma_x^2 = \Sigma(x - \mu_x)^2 P(x)$$ |

To illustrate the calculation of a variance, suppose the Disabled American Veterans (DAV) mail printed return-address stickers to over 1 million U.S. homes. Each recipient is asked to donate either $1, $2, $5, $10, $15, or $20. Based on past experience, the amount a person donates is believed to follow the following p.m.f.:

$$x: \quad \$1 \quad \$2 \quad \$5 \quad \$10 \quad \$15 \quad \$20$$
$$P(x): \quad 0.10 \quad 0.20 \quad 0.30 \quad 0.20 \quad 0.15 \quad 0.05$$

Using Eq. (4.6), the mean of this p.m.f. is $\mu_x = \$7.25$. That is, the average donor can be expected to contribute $7.25.

To calculate a variance by Eq. (4.7), we first determine how far each value of $x$ deviates from the mean, which is $(x - \mu_x)$. These deviations are squared $[(x - \mu_x)^2]$, and then each squared deviation is weighted (i.e., multiplied) by the probability of its occurrence $[(x - \mu_x)^2 P(x)]$. Finally, these weighted squared deviations are summed.

The calculations for determining a variance for the DAV mass function shown in Table 4.4. The variance of the money received is $\sigma_x^2 = 29.585$ dollars squared.

Recall from Chapter 3 that a standard deviation is easier to interpret than a variance (e.g., it is hard to think in terms of squared dollars). As always, a standard deviation is the square root of the variance.

**Table 4.4**

| | Calculating the Variance for the DAV Donations | | | |
|---|---|---|---|---|
| $x$ | $P(x)$ | $(x - \mu_x)$ | $(x - \mu_x)^2$ | $(x - \mu_x)^2 P(x)$ |
| 1 | 0.10 | −6.25 | 39.06 | 3.906 |
| 2 | 0.20 | −5.25 | 27.56 | 5.512 |
| 5 | 0.30 | −2.25 | 5.06 | 1.518 |
| 10 | 0.20 | 2.75 | 7.56 | 1.512 |
| 15 | 0.15 | 7.75 | 60.06 | 9.009 |
| 20 | 0.05 | 12.75 | 162.56 | 8.128 |
| | | | | $29.585 = \sigma_x^2$ (dollars squared) |

$$\text{Standard deviation} = \sqrt{\sigma_x^2} = \sigma_x = \sqrt{\Sigma(x - \mu_x)^2 P(x)}$$

From Table 4.4, $\sigma_x = \sqrt{29.585} = 5.44$. This value will be interpreted in the next section.

---

**WORKED EXAMPLE 4.16**

Determine the variance and the standard deviation for the OSHA data given in Worked Example 4.15.

**ANSWER:**

| $x$ | $P(x)$ | $xP(x)$ | $(x - \mu_x)$ | $(x - \mu_x)^2$ | $(x - \mu_x)^2 P(x)$ |
|---|---|---|---|---|---|
| 4 | 0.20 | 0.80 | $+1.55$ | 2.4025 | 0.480500 |
| 3 | 0.30 | 0.90 | $+0.55$ | 0.3025 | 0.090750 |
| 2 | 0.30 | 0.60 | $-0.45$ | 0.2025 | 0.060750 |
| 1 | 0.15 | 0.15 | $-1.45$ | 2.1025 | 0.315375 |
| 0 | 0.05 | 0.00 | $-2.45$ | 6.0025 | 0.300125 |
| | $E(x) = u_x =$ | 2.45 | | | $1.247500 = \sigma_x^2$ |

$$\sigma_x = \sqrt{1.2475} = 1.1169$$

---

## Interpreting a Standard Deviation

We seldom try to interpret a variance. Rather, an indication of the spread of the population can be determined by calculating the standard deviation and then using the rules of thumb from Chapter 3. In the present context, these three rules state the following:

---

**RULES Standard Deviation**

The mean plus or minus one standard deviation ($\mu \pm 1\sigma$) will often contain about 68% of the probability.

The mean plus or minus two standard deviations ($\mu \pm 2\sigma$) will often contain about 95% of the probability.

The mean plus or minus three standard deviations ($\mu \pm 3\sigma$) will often contain almost 100% of the probability.

---

Chapter 4  Probability Concepts and Random Variables

Remember, these are just rough rules to help interpret a standard deviation. They may not work well if the number of outcomes in the p.m.f. is small or if the distribution is highly skewed. Let's use the DAV data to see how close these approximations are for that situation, where $\mu_x = 7.25$ and $\sigma_x = 5.44$.

$$\mu_x \pm 1\sigma_x = 7.25 \pm 5.44 = [1.81 \text{ to } 12.69]$$

Now we need to determine the probability that an $x$ value (for the DAV data) falls in the interval 1.81 to 12.69 (which are the integers 2 to 12). From Table 4.4, the probabilities between 2 and 12 are $0.20 + 0.30 + 0.20 = 0.70$. That is,

$$P(\mu_x - 1\sigma_x \le x \le \mu_x + 1\sigma_x) = 0.70$$

The first rule thus works quite well, since 70% is very close to 68%. Now let's try the second rule.

$$\mu_x \pm 2\sigma_x = 7.25 \pm 2(5.44) = [-3.63 \text{ to } 18.13]$$

Using Table 4.4, we see that only the value of $x = 20$ falls *outside* of the range of plus or minus two standard deviations. Since $P(x = 20) = 0.05$, the probability that $x$ falls *inside* the range is $1 - 0.05 = 0.95$, which is precisely the 95% value predicted by our rule of thumb.

For the third rule of thumb, the range is

$$\mu_x \pm 3\sigma_x = 7.25 \pm 3(5.44) = [-9.07 \text{ to } 23.57]$$

This range includes all the $x$ values in our problem; hence it contains 100% of the probability. The rule predicted that plus or minus three standard deviations will often contain almost 100% of the probability.

Thus the three rules work well in this example. In other problems they may not work as well.

---

**WORKED EXAMPLE 4.17**

Determine how well the three rules for interpreting a standard deviation work using the OSHA data in Worked Example 4.16.

ANSWER:

The mean is 2.45 and the standard deviation is 1.1169.

$$\mu_x \pm 1\sigma_x = 2.45 \pm 1.1169 = [1.3331 \text{ to } 3.5669]$$

This interval contains 60% of the probability, which is less than the 68% suggested by the rule.

$$\mu_x \pm 2\sigma_x = 2.45 \pm 2(1.1169) = [0.2162 \text{ to } 4.6838]$$

This interval contains 95% of the probability, which is exactly the percentage suggested by the rule.

$$\mu_x \pm 3\sigma_x = 2.45 \pm 3(1.1169) = [-.9007 \text{ to } 5.8007]$$

This interval contains 100% of the probability, which is exactly the percentage suggested by the rule.

## Exercises

**FIN**   **4.23**  The local Schwinn dealer has three models of men's 27-inch bicycles: a $200 model, a $220 model, and a $250 model. The dealer makes a profit of $30 on the first model, $40 on the second model, and $60 on the third model. For the coming year, the dealer estimates that for customers who buy the 27-inch size, 60% will want the lowest-priced model, 30% will purchase the $220 model, and 10% will buy the $250 model. Thus the probability of each profit is:

$P(\$30 \text{ profit}) = 0.60$
$P(\$40 \text{ profit}) = 0.30$
$P(\$60 \text{ profit}) = 0.10$

a) Define the random variable for this situation.
b) Graph the p.m.f.
c) Find the mean for the random variable.
d) Find the variance for the random variable.
e) If the dealer sells 100 of the 27-inch bikes, what profit can be expected?

**FIN**   **4.24**  The UCLA Credit Union is considering offering its share draft customers one of three different accounts, depending on the minimum balance kept in the account. The interest rate paid on these three accounts would be 6.0%, 7.0%, and 9.0%. The credit union expects

50% of its customers to opt for the account at 6.0%, 20% to opt for the account at 7.0%, and 30% to opt for the account at 9.0%.

a) Define the random variable for this p.m.f.

b) Graph this p.m.f.

c) Find the mean of the random variable.

d) Find the variance of the random variable.

MKT **4.25** Using the information in the grocery store coupon case to:

a) Calculate the variance for the distribution. What is the standard deviation?

b) Try the three rules for interpreting a standard deviation. Do they work well in this example? Why or why not?

**4.26** A professor gives 20% A grades, 40% B grades, 30% C grades, 5% D grades, and 5% F grades.

a) Graph the p.m.f.

b) Find the mean and variance of the grades.

c) What proportion of the grades are within one, two, and three standard deviations of the mean? Comment on how well the approximation rules hold for this problem.

ADM **4.27** The owner at Space Port has found that the repair record for the 15 video game machines at this location indicates the need for either minor repairs (which cost about $10), moderate repairs (which cost about $75), or major repairs (which cost about $200). The owner estimates the probability that during any given week a machine will need repairs to be $P(0 \text{ cost}) = 0.50$, $P(\$10 \text{ cost}) = 0.30$. $P(\$75 \text{ cost}) = 0.15$, or $P(\$200) = 0.05$.

a) Find the mean and variance in cost per machine per week.

b) Graph this p.m.f.

c) How well do the three rules for interpreting $\sigma$ work?

d) What cost should the owner expect over a year (52 weeks) at this location (15 machines)?

PUB **4.28** Return to Exercise 4.8, concerning the Selective Service lottery of 1970. Define a random variable assuming that interest is only in the month drawn (i.e., let January = 1, February = 2, etc.). Sketch this random variable. What is its mean?

**4.29** Define a random variable for the experiment "generate a one-digit random number." Sketch this random variable. Find its mean and variance. What proportion of this p.m.f. falls within one, two, and three standard deviations?

FIN  **4.30** A portfolio is known to contain U.S. Treasury notes as follows: 20% are 30-day, 50% are 90-day, and 30% are 120-day notes. Define a random variable for the experiment "select a note at random." Sketch this p.m.f. What are the mean and variance for this random variable?

## Chapter Exercises

**4.31** Probability is sometimes referred to as "long-run" relative frequency. What does this mean?

**4.32** Identify each of the following as either joint, conditional, or additive probabilities.

  **a)** The probability that either the stock market goes up this week or the prime interest rate declines.

  **b)** The probability a person earns an A in a statistics class, given that this person earned an A on the first exam.

  **c)** The probability that the next president of the United States is a female or a Republican.

  **d)** The probability that it rains today, given that it rained yesterday.

  **e)** The probability that an insurance agent is a member of the Million Dollar Club and is less than 30 years old.

**4.33** For two random variables A and B, under what conditions will

  **a)** The marginal probability of A equal the conditional probability of A given B?

  **b)** The probability of A or B equal the probability of A plus the probability of B?

ADM  **4.34** Numerous studies have reported on the hours worked by chief executive officers (CEOs). The following table reports on the proportion of executives of given size firms and their number of work hours.

|  | Less than 50 hr/wk | 50–59 hr/wk | 60–69 hr/wk | 70 or more hr/wk |
|---|---|---|---|---|
| CEOs from firms that are: | | | | |
| Large | 0.05 | 0.30 | 0.50 | 0.15 |
| Medium | 0.15 | 0.30 | 0.40 | 0.15 |
| Small | 0.20 | 0.25 | 0.30 | 0.25 |

a) Among large firms, what is the probability that a randomly selected CEO works more than 60 hours per week?

b) Suppose you interview a CEO randomly selected from a small firm. What is the probability that this person works less than 50 hours per week? Is this probability joint, conditional, or additive?

c) Describe sets of events for this situation that are:
1. Mutually exclusive and exhaustive.
2. Mutually exclusive but not exhaustive.
3. Exhaustive but not mutually exclusive.

d) If there were 200 CEOs from small firms, 300 from medium size firms and 500 from large firms what is the probability that a randomly selected CEO worked less than 50 hours and is from a small firm? What type of probability is this?

ADM    4.35    From the data in Exercise 4.34, as described in part d, construct two tables, similar to Tables 4.1 and 4.2, with only two categories on the left (small and large firms) and three categories across the top (less than 50 hours, 50–59 hours, and 60 or more hours). In the body of the first table place the number of CEOs in each cell. Place joint probabilities in the cells of the second table by dividing each number in the first table by the appropriate total. Note that the population now consists of only 700 CEOs, as we are omitting medium-sized firms.

a) State, in words, the interpretation of the probability in the upper left cell.

b) Write the five marginal probabilities. Which events are mutually exclusive and exhaustive? Show that the sum of the mutually exclusive and exhaustive events is 1.0.

c) Write the six joint probabilities. Show that the sum of three of these joint probabilities equals a marginal probability.

d) Write a conditional probability, but do not calculate its value.

MKT **4.36** *Reader's Digest* has announced a contest for which 2 million households will receive an entry form. They estimate that 10% of the forms will be returned to them. On each form the person must indicate "Yes" (they want to subscribe to the magazine) or "No." *Reader's Digest* estimates that four fifths of the entry forms returned will say "No." There will be 100 awards given to the "Yes" responses and 100 awards given to the "No" responses.

a) What is the probability that a form picked at random before it is mailed will be a winner?

b) What is the probability that a person who responds "Yes" will be a winner? Is this a joint, conditional, or additive probability?

c) What is the probability that a person who responds "No" will be a winner? Why is this answer different from the one in part (b)?

d) If we know that a person responded but do not know if this person said "Yes" or "No," what is the probability that this person is a winner?

FIN **4.37** One way of classifying the stock market's performance each day is to use only two events, "market goes up" or "market does not go up."

a) Make up your own method for classifying daily stock market performance using six mutually exclusive and exhaustive events.

b) Use the performance of the stock market over the past several weeks to make an educated guess about the probability of each of your six events in part (a). Do these probabilities sum to 1.0? Do they have to? Explain.

c) Write an additive probability but do not calculate it.

MKT **4.38** A *Business Week* article reports on a new insurance policy for violent crime that can be purchased for $210 and will pay $50,000 if you are a victim. According to police records, in your community the probability of your being victimized is 0.002. In terms of expected value, is the policy worth buying? What do you have to assume to use the 0.002 probability figure in your calculations?

FIN **4.39** In your role as consultant to United Airlines, you have decided to initiate a cost-benefit analysis on meal selection for the nonstop

Chicago–Hawaii flight. Each passenger on this flight is given a choice for the main meal of either chicken, steak, or mai-mai fish (a Hawaiian specialty). The catering service charges the airline $3 for each chicken meal served, $4 for each fish meal, and $6 for each steak meal. The p.m.f. for meal selection on this flight is:

$$P(3) = 0.20, \ P(4) = 0.50, \ P(6) = 0.30$$

a) Graph this p.m.f.

b) Find the average cost per meal.

c) How much will the airline save per flight if it serves only chicken? Assume that an average flight has 330 passengers.

d) Find the variance of the cost per meal.

**4.40** A dealer selling farm machinery estimates that monthly sales of a new grain harvester will follow this p.m.f.

| $x$: | 1 | 2 | 3 | 4 |
|------|---|---|---|---|
| $P(x)$: | $\frac{1}{10}$ | $\frac{2}{10}$ | $\frac{3}{10}$ | $\frac{4}{10}$ |

a) Graph this p.m.f.

b) Find the mean sales expected per month.

c) Find the standard deviation of sales per month.

ADM **4.41** Use the data in Exercise 4.34 to determine

a) the probability that a CEO worked more than 60 hours per week or is from a small firm.

b) if hours worked and the size of the firm are independent.

ECN **4.42** Use the data in Exercise 4.13 to determine

a) the probability of being either a teenager or nonwhite.

b) if being unemployed is unrelated to (independent of) whether or not one is a teenager.

MKT **4.43** In 1982 McDonald's had a game in which the customer received a card containing six spaces. Each space, hidden to the customer, contained either the picture of a prize or a "zap." Two of the prize pictures were identical. The customer had to uncover the spaces, one at a time. If a zap was uncovered, the game was over. If the customer uncovered two identical prize pictures, then the customer won the prize.

a) Assuming there were two zaps, what was the probability of winning if the pictures and zaps were randomly placed?

b) What was the probability of winning if there were three zaps?

**4.44** A p.m.f. is defined by the following formula:

$$P(x) = \frac{x}{6} \quad \text{for } x = 1, 2, 3$$

a) Sketch this p.m.f.

b) Find the mean and the variance of this p.m.f.

**4.45** Prove that if events $E_1$ and $E_2$ are independent, then $P(E_1 \text{ and } E_2) = P(E_1)P(E_2)$.

**4.46** Suppose you know $P(E_1|E_2)$ and $P(E_1)$, but do not know the value of $P(E_2|E_1)$. Create a formula that could be used to solve for $P(E_2|E_1)$, assuming $E_1$ and $E_2$ are exhaustive.

**4.47** A statistics class has 23 students. What is the probability that at least two students in this class have the same birthday (meaning the same day of the year, not necessarily the same year). (Hint: find the probability that no two birthdays are alike, using logarithms, and then subtract from 1.0.)

**4.48** In Chapter 3 we presented a theorem of the Russian statistician Tchebysheff that states that at least $(1 - 1/k^2)$ of any population will lie within $k$ standard deviations of the mean of that population, where $k$ is any number $\geq 0$. For example, if $k = 2$, this theorem says that at least $(1 - \frac{1}{4}) = \frac{3}{4}$ of any population will lie within $\mu \pm 2\sigma$. Similarly, if $k = 4$, then at least $(1 - \frac{1}{16}) = \frac{15}{16}$ of any population will lie within $\mu \pm 4\sigma$ of the mean. The value of $k$ does not have to be an integer.

a) Use the data in Table 4.1 to show that less than three-fourths of the Balance Owed population lies within plus or minus two standard deviations.

b) If $k = 3$, what percentage of a population will lie within $\mu \pm 3\sigma$? Show that the Balance Owed population in Table 4.1 satisfies this relationship.

**additive probability:** The probability that one event or another will occur. Additive probability always involves a statement using the word *or*.

**conditional probability:** The probability that one event will occur if another event has taken place (or will). Conditional probability typically involves a statement using the words *given that*.

**contingency table:** A table showing the frequencies of events associated with two random variables.

**dependent outcomes:** Events that have an influence on one another.

**discrete random variable:** A rule for assigning separate values to each outcome or event in a probability problem.

**event:** One or more outcomes treated as a group.

**exhaustive outcomes:** Outcomes that are the only possible result of an experiment.

**expected value:** The mean or average of the distribution of a random variable.

**experiment:** Any situation capable (at least theoretically) of being replicated.

**independent events:** Events that have no influence on one another.

**joint probability:** The probability that one event will occur with another outcome. Joint probability typically involves a statement using the word *and*.

**marginal probability:** The probability sum of joint probabilities, often occurring in the margin of a joint probability table.

**mutually exclusive events:** Events that cannot occur together.

**outcomes:** The result of an experiment.

**probability mass function (p.m.f.):** A list, graph, table, or formula that gives the probability for each possible value of a discrete random variable.

**probability of an event:** The sum of the probabilities of the outcomes that make up the event.

**probability of an outcome:** A number between 0 and 1 that reflects the long-run relative frequency with which the outcome occurs.

**random variable:** A well-defined rule for assigning a number to each outcome in a probability problem.

**rules of thumb:** Three rules that may help in interpreting $\sigma$ when the p.m.f. is not highly skewed. The three rules are:

$\mu \pm 1\sigma$ often contains about 68% of the population,

$\mu \pm 2\sigma$ often contains about 95% of the population,

$\mu \pm 3\sigma$ often contains almost 100% of the population.

**sample space:** The set of all outcomes.

**standard deviation:** The square root of the variance.

**variance:** A measure of average dispersion in a random variable that equals the sum of the squared deviations of the variable's values around their mean, with each deviation weighted by its probability.

**Venn diagram:** A graphic representation of the probability of two or more events.

## Formulas

**4.1—Probability of an Outcome**

$$\text{Probability of a given outcome} = \frac{\text{number of ways the given outcome may occur}}{\text{total number of ways all outcomes may occur}}.$$

**4.2—Joint Probability of $E_1$ and $E_2$**

$$P(E_1 \text{ and } E_2) = P(E_1)P(E_2|E_1)$$
$$P(E_1 \text{ and } E_2) = P(E_2)P(E_1|E_2)$$

**4.3—Conditional Probability of $E_2$, Given $E_1$**

$$P(E_2|E_1) = \frac{P(E_2 \text{ and } E_1)}{P(E_1)}$$

**4.4—Additive Probability of $E_1$ or $E_2$**

$$P(E_1 \text{ or } E_2) = P(E_1) + P(E_2) - P(E_1 \text{ and } E_2)$$

**4.5—Probabilities of Independent Events $E_1$ and $E_2$**

$$P(E_1 \text{ and } E_2) = P(E_1)P(E_2)$$
$$P(E_2|E_1) = P(E_2)$$

Chapter 4   Probability Concepts and Random Variables

**4.6—Mean or Expected Value of a Random Variable $x$**

$$E(x) = \mu_x = \Sigma\, xP(x)$$

**4.7—Variance of a Random Variable $x$**

$$\sigma_x^2 = \Sigma(x - \mu_x)^2\, P(x)$$

# CHAPTER FIVE

*There are three types of liars—liars, damned liars, and statisticians.*
Benjamin Disraeli

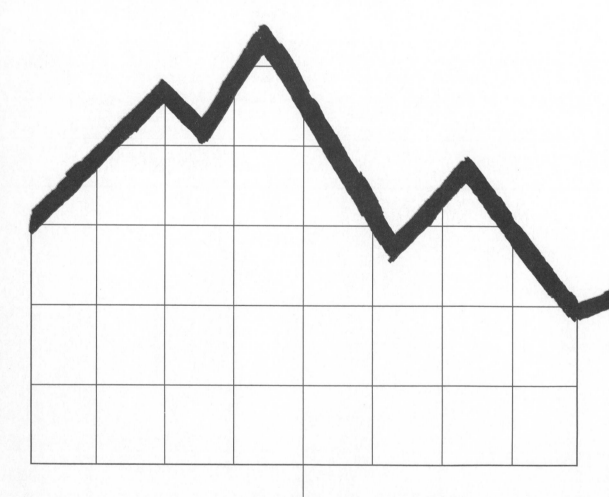

# THE BINOMIAL, HYPERGEOMETRIC, AND POISSON DISTRIBUTIONS

In this chapter we extend the discussion of probability mass functions (p.m.f.'s) presented in Chapter 4 by focusing on three special p.m.f.'s: the binomial, the hypergeometric, and the Poisson. These three distributions have been shown to apply to many different practical problems, as illustrated by the following examples.

- A production manager may use the binomial distribution to determine if a production process is working properly or if it is producing too many defectives.

- A corporate executive may use information from a sample of stockholders to estimate the number of proxy votes General Motors can expect to be returned by all stockholders.

- An affirmative action officer may use the hypergeometric distribution to determine the probability that the gender or racial composition of a workforce represents hiring practices that do not discriminate against minorities.

- An air traffic control director may use the Poisson distribution to determine the probability that a certain number of planes will request landing assistance in a fixed time period.

By the end of this chapter you should be able to recognize when the binomial, hypergeometric, and Poisson distributions are appropriate. Having made this decision, you should then be able to describe the appropriate p.m.f. using either a formula, a computer program, or a table in the back of the book (in the case of the binomial and the Poisson). You will also learn how to apply these three p.m.f.'s to tests about population parameters.

## Semiconductor Chips

You are a quality control manager for IBM in charge of the process producing random access memory (RAM) semiconductor chips. IBM, which uses its

**Figure 5.1**
A memory chip:
actual size and a
blow-up

Chips, smaller than the tip of a finger, form the core of computers, calculators, televisions, video games, missile control panels, telephone switching equipment and almost all other electronic products.

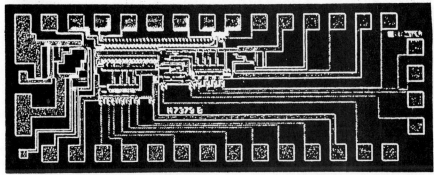

chips internally for its own products, makes more chips than all the world's semiconductor firms combined. The latest IBM product is a 288K RAM memory chip that can store 294,912 bits of information. The IBM process producing these chips normally results in defective chips 40% of the time (most Silicon Valley firms produce 50% defectives). However, you are convinced that a new process for the 288K chip will do even better and will yield only 30% defectives. To test the new process, you have taken a random sample of chips. Your interest now is in what p.m.f. should be expected if the new process does yield only 30% defectives.

# 5.2 The Binomial Distribution

The *binomial distribution* is a special type of p.m.f. designed for probability problems that have **trials**. Each trial always results in one of two outcomes. For example, we might think of a situation in which on each trial a different person is classified, and the outcome of this classification is either "male" or "female." Or we might identify the origin of cars, on each trial, with the outcome either "U.S. made" or "foreign made." Similarly, if the trials are day-by-day movements of the stock market, the outcomes might be either "market up" or "market not up." In the semiconductor chip case, a trial is the testing of each chip, with the outcome either "defective" or "not defective."

Several generations of the Bernoulli family, Swiss mathematicians of the 1700s, deserve credit as originators of much of the early research on binomial probability theory. The Bernoulli name is often associated with the identically repeated trials (**Bernoulli trials**) that make up a binomial problem. Identically repeated means that the classification process is replicated over and over in exactly the same manner. In a binomial problem we will be interested in the total number of identical outcomes in a fixed number of identical trials. Thus we may want to classify 100 cars (100 identical trials) to determine if 70 or more are U.S. made (70 identical outcomes). An airline may be interested in classifying passengers on certain flights as either smokers or nonsmokers to determine the expected number of smokers. And you, working for IBM, may want to classify each chip in a sample as either defective or not defective to determine the probability of a particular sample result given that there are 30% defectives.

For the binomial distribution, the outcomes of each trial must be independent of one another (one trial does not influence the outcome of any other trial). The existence of independent trials implies that the probability of each outcome does not change from trial to trial. Each trial must be an exact replication of every other trial. For example, suppose we are interviewing randomly selected people and classifying them by gender. If the fact that a male (or female) is being interviewed influences the probability that the next person interviewed will be a male (or a female), the assumption of independence is violated. The probability of interviewing a male and the probability of interviewing a female cannot change from one interview to the next. Similarly, for our semiconductor chips, the probability that a chip is defective must remain constant from trial to trial; whether one chip is classified as defective or not defective cannot influence the classification of any other chip. To summarize, the binomial distribution is used when

1. an experiment consists of $n$ identical trials,

2. each trial has only one of two possible outcomes,

3. the probability of each outcome does not change over the trials, and

4. the outcome of one trial does not influence the outcome of any other trial, that is, the trials are independent.

# 5.3 The Binomial Probability Mass Function

The number of trials, $n$, and the probability of one of the two outcomes (on each trial), $\pi$, are called the **binomial parameters**. The values of $n$ and $\pi$ must both be known in order to calculate binomial probabilities. For instance, in the semiconductor chip case we know that the probability of a defective chip in the new process is $\pi = 0.30$. If we now specify the number of identical and independent trials to be $n = 3$, we know from our discussion of independent events in Chapter 4 that the probability of all three chips being defective is the product of the three probabilities of a defect on each trial. Thus the probability of three defective chips in three trials is $0.027$ [$= P$(first defective) $\times$ $P$(second defective) $\times$ $P$(third defective) $= (0.3)(0.3)(0.3)$].

In general, the binomial probability of $x$ "successes" (i.e., outcomes of interest) occurring in $n$ trials is given by Eq. (5.1).

---

Formula for the binomial p.m.f.

**(5.1)**
$$P(x) = \frac{n!}{x!(n-x)!}\, \pi^x (1 - \pi)^{n-x}$$

---

Some readers may be unfamiliar with the symbols used here, such as $n!$, $x!$, and $(n-x)!$. The symbol "!" is read **factorial**. Thus $n!$ is read as "$n$ factorial," $x!$ is read as "$x$ factorial," and $(n-x)!$ is read as "$(n-x)$ factorial." To evaluate a factorial we multiply a series of numbers together, where each number is one less than the previous number. For example, if $x = 5$,

$$x! = 5! = (5)(4)(3)(2)(1) = 120$$

If $n = 7$,

$$n! \text{ is } 7! = (7)(6)(5)(4)(3)(2)(1) = 5040$$

If $n = 7$ and $x = 5$,

$$(n - x)! = (7 - 5)! = 2! = (2)(1) = 2$$

By definition, $0! = 1$.

The first part of Eq. (5.1), namely,

$$\frac{n!}{x!(n-x)!}$$

gives the number of ways that $x$ successes can be obtained in $n$ trials. Thus, in our semiconductor chip case, if $n = 3$ and we want to know how many different ways two defects could occur ($x = 2$), we would calculate

$$\frac{3!}{2!(3-2)!} = \frac{6}{2} = 3$$

The three different ways of obtaining two defects in three trials are shown by the circled 2's in Fig. 5.2. If the first chip is defective, $x_1$ equals 1, and if it is not defective, $x_1$ equals 0. Similarly, if the second chip is defective, then $x_2 = 1$, and if it is not, then $x_2 = 0$. If the third chip is defective, $x_3 = 1$ and 0 if it is not.

The second part of Eq. (5.1), namely, $\pi^x(1 - \pi)^{n-x}$, gives the probability of $x$ successes in $n$ trials. Each trial in a binomial problem can result in only one of two outcomes (success or failure), where $\pi$ is the probability of success and $(1 - \pi)$ is the probability of failure. The exponents $x$ and $n - x$ simply count how many times successes and failures occur. For example, the probability of a defect on each of the first two trials and no defect on the third is $(0.3)(0.3)(0.7) = (0.3)^2(0.7)^1 = 0.063$. But, as can be seen in Fig. 5.2, two defects in three trials can be obtained in two other orderings. Thus the probability of two defects (in any ordering) in three trials is $3(0.063) = 0.189$. Or by the binomial formula,

$$P(x = 2) = \frac{3!}{2!(3-2)!}(0.3)^2(1 - 0.3)^1$$

$$= 3(0.3)^2(0.7)^1 = 0.189$$

Similarly, for $x = 1$ we have

$$P(x = 1) = \frac{3!}{1!(3-1)!}(0.3)^1(0.7)^2$$

$$= 3(0.147) = 0.441$$

and for $x = 0$,

$$P(x = 0) = \frac{3!}{0!(3-0)!}(0.3)^0(0.7)^3 = 0.343$$

The reader should verify that $P(x = 3) = 0.027$.

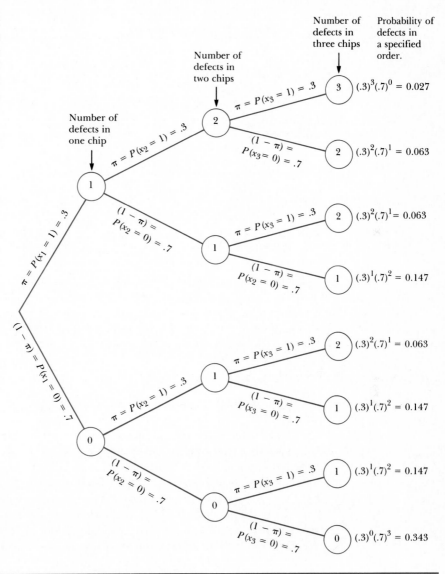

**Figure 5.2**
The possible
outcomes in a
binomial problem
where $n = 3$ and
$\pi = 0.30$.

Number of
defects in
one chip

Number of
defects in
two chips

Number of
defects in
three chips

Probability of
defects in
a specified
order.

$\pi = P(x_1 = 1) = .3$

$(1 - \pi) = P(x_1 = 0) = .7$

$\pi = P(x_2 = 1) = .3$

$(1 - \pi) = P(x_2 = 0) = .7$

$\pi = P(x_2 = 1) = .3$

$(1 - \pi) = P(x_2 = 0) = .7$

$\pi = P(x_3 = 1) = .3$

$(1 - \pi) = P(x_3 = 0) = .7$

$\pi = P(x_3 = 1) = .3$

$(1 - \pi) = P(x_3 = 0) = .7$

$\pi = P(x_3 = 1) = .3$

$(1 - \pi) = P(x_3 = 0) = .7$

$\pi = P(x_3 = 1) = .3$

$(1 - \pi) = P(x_3 = 0) = .7$

$3 \quad (.3)^3(.7)^0 = 0.027$

$2 \quad (.3)^2(.7)^1 = 0.063$

$2 \quad (.3)^2(.7)^1 = 0.063$

$1 \quad (.3)^1(.7)^2 = 0.147$

$2 \quad (.3)^2(.7)^1 = 0.063$

$1 \quad (.3)^1(.7)^2 = 0.147$

$1 \quad (.3)^1(.7)^2 = 0.147$

$0 \quad (.3)^0(.7)^3 = 0.343$

# 5.4 The Binomial Probability Tables

Recall from Chapter 4 that there are three ways to describe a p.m.f.—by a
formula, by a table listing, and by a graph. We will now illustrate how to

**Table 5.1**

| Selected Binomial Values for $n = 3$ from Appendix Table B.2 | | | | | | | | | | |
|---|---|---|---|---|---|---|---|---|---|---|
| $x \, \pi$   **21** | **22** | **23** | **24** | **25** | **26** | **27** | **28** | **29** | **30** | |
| 0   4930 | 4746 | 4565 | 4390 | 4219 | 4052 | 3890 | 3732 | 3579 | 3430 | **3** |
| 1   3932 | 4014 | 4091 | 4159 | 4219 | 4271 | 4316 | 4355 | 4386 | 4410 | **2** |
| 2   1045 | 1133 | 1222 | 1313 | 1406 | 1501 | 1597 | 1693 | 1791 | 1890 | **1** |
| 3   0093 | 0106 | 0122 | 0138 | 0156 | 0176 | 0197 | 0220 | 0244 | 0270 | **0** |
| **79** | **78** | **77** | **76** | **75** | **74** | **73** | **72** | **71** | **70** | $\pi \, x$ |

determine binomial probabilities by the binomial tables. Later, we will illustrate how binomial probabilities can be determined easily by a computer software package.

A table of the binomial p.m.f. for $n = 3$ is given in Appendix Table B.2. Part of this appendix table (specifically, page 637) is reproduced in Table 5.1. The numbers in Table 5.1 are from the middle of the binomial values for $n = 3$. The reader should find, on page 637, the numbers shown in Table 5.1.

The four-digit numbers in the body of Table 5.1 represent probabilities if we put a decimal point in front of each one. The two-digit numbers across the top and bottom (also lacking a decimal point) are the values of $\pi$, while the margins give the $x$ values.

## Interpreting the Binomial Tables When $\pi \leq 0.50$

To obtain probabilities when $\pi$ is less than or equal to 0.50, we read from the top of the table. In our semiconductor chip case $\pi = 0.30$. Hence, we first look for the column corresponding to $\pi = 0.30$. The correct column is the one with the heading 30. If we put a decimal point in front of each number in this column and use the $x$ values from the left margin, we have the p.m.f. for $n = 3$, $\pi = 0.30$. This p.m.f. is listed in Table 5.2 and shown in Fig. 5.3. (Cumulative binomial probabilities are also given in Table 5.2.)

The p.m.f. in Table 5.2 shows that when $n = 3$ and $\pi = 0.30$, we expect no defectives 34.3% of the time, one defective 44.10% of the time, two defectives 18.90% of the time, and three defectives 2.70% of the time. These are precisely the probabilities obtained with Eq. (5.1).

Binomial probabilities are often written in the following conditional form:

$$P(x = 2 | n = 3, \pi = 0.30) = 0.1890$$

This expression is read as "the probability that $x = 2$ when $n = 3$ and $\pi = 0.30$ is 0.1890." As another example, we might want to determine the prob-

| Table 5.2 | Binomial p.m.f. and Cumulative Probability for $n = 3$ and $\pi = 0.30$ | | |
|---|---|---|---|
| $x$ | $P(x)$ | Cumulative Probability | |
| 0 | 0.3430 | 0.3430 | |
| 1 | 0.4410 | 0.7840 | |
| 2 | 0.1890 | 0.9730 | |
| 3 | 0.0270 | 1.0000 | |

ability that $x$ is two or more when $n = 3$ and $\pi = 0.30$. This probability is calculated from the mass function in Table 5.2 by adding $P(x = 2)$ and $P(x = 3)$. The probability that $x$ is two or more is written as $P(x \geq 2)$ and is equal to 0.2160; that is,

$$P(x \geq 2 | n = 3, \pi = 0.30) = 0.1890 + 0.0270 = 0.2160$$

This result shows that there is a 21.60% chance that the number of defectives will be two or more. By the fact that probabilities must sum to 1.00, we also know the probability of less than two defectives:

$$P(x < 2) = 1 - 0.2160 = 0.7840$$

### Interpreting the Binomial Tables When $\pi > 0.50$

When $\pi$ is greater than 0.50, we must look across the *bottom* of the set of values given in a binomial table to find $\pi$ and then read the $x$ values on the

**Figure 5.3**
Graph of the p.m.f. in Table 5.2.

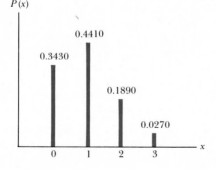

*right-hand* side of the table. For example, there are 10 $\pi$'s shown across the bottom of the 40 values in Table 5.1, namely, 0.79, 0.78, 0.77, . . . , 0.70. If $\pi = 0.75$, then the probability of $x = 2$ is found by reading across the bottom of the table until we get to 75 and then going up this column until we get to the row marked by $x = 2$ on the right-hand side. Thus $P(x = 2|n = 3, \pi = 0.75) = 0.4219$.

In using Appendix Table B.2, $x$ is found using the following rules:

If $\pi$ is found across the top of Table B.2 ($\pi \leq 0.50$), then $x$ must be read from the *left-hand* margin of the table.

If $\pi$ is found across the bottom of Table B.2 ($\pi > 0.50$), then $x$ must be read from the *right-hand* margin of the table.

---

**WORKED EXAMPLE 5.1**

In the final inspection of new Buicks on the assembly line in Detroit, a car is not certified for shipment unless it meets rigid standards. In the past, 75% of the new Buicks were certified on their first inspection. Describe the p.m.f. for three new Buicks undergoing their first inspection, letting $x$ be the random variable "new Buick passes on first inspection." What is the probability that at least two out of three randomly selected Buicks will pass?

**ANSWER:**

| $x$: | 0 | 1 | 2 | 3 |
|---|---|---|---|---|
| $P(x|n=3, \pi = 0.75)$: | 0.0156 | 0.1406 | 0.4219 | 0.4219 |

$$P(x \geq 2|n = 3, \pi = 0.75) = 0.4219 + 0.4219 = 0.8438$$

---

**WORKED EXAMPLE 5.2**

The personnel director at DuPont is designing a 10-question test to determine if employees who have finished a training course know about the company policies. The test is multiple choice. Each question has five possible choices, only one of which is correct. Thus a person who chooses randomly (i.e., completely guessing) has a chance of four in five, or 0.80, of being wrong on each question. Sketch the p.m.f. for this 10-question test, letting $x$ = "number of questions answered incorrectly" and assuming that the respondent answers by guessing. What is the probability that a person who guesses will miss five or fewer questions?

**ANSWER:**

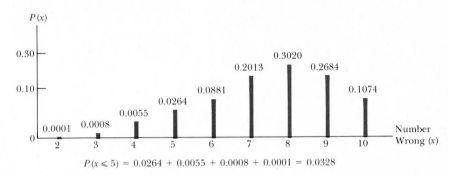

$$P(x \leqslant 5) = 0.0264 + 0.0055 + 0.0008 + 0.0001 = 0.0328$$

# 5.5 Determining the Binomial Mean and the Variance

Recall from Chapters 3 and 4 that one of the measures of central location is its mean (or average). In Chapter 4 we learned how to calculate the mean or expected value for a discrete p.m.f.; the formula presented there is

$$E(x) = \mu = \Sigma \, xP(x)$$

This formula can now be used to determine the mean (or average) for any binomial problem. For example, the mean of the p.m.f. for the Buick car problem in Worked Example 5.1 is:

$$E(x) = 0(0.0156) + 1(0.1406) + 2(0.4219) + 3(0.4219)$$
$$= 2.25 \quad \text{(Buicks passing)}$$

Thus, over the long run, 2.25 out of every 3 Buicks will pass.

A similar process, using Eq. (4.7) from Chapter 4, can be used to find the variance for this p.m.f. The interested reader may wish to practice the process by finding the variance for the Buick problem. (Hint: the answer is 0.5625.)

Fortunately, we do not have to use either Eq. (4.6) or (4.7) to find the mean and variance of the binomial distribution for different values of $\pi$ and

$n$. There is another formula for determining the mean and still another formula for determining the variance. These formulas, presented as Eq. (5.2), are easy to use.

**(5.2)**

Mean and variance for the binomial p.m.f.

$$\text{Mean:} \quad \mu = n\pi$$
$$\text{Variance:} \quad \sigma^2 = n\pi(1 - \pi)$$

Let's use these formulas to calculate the mean and variance for the DuPont problem (Worked Example 5.2). For that problem, $n = 10$ and $\pi = 0.80$. Substituting $n = 10$ and $\pi = 0.80$ into Eq. (5.2) yields:

$$\mu = n\pi = (10)(0.80) = 8.00 \quad \text{(wrong answers)}$$
$$\sigma^2 = n\pi(1 - \pi) = (10)(0.80)(0.20) = 1.60 \quad \text{(wrong answers squared)}$$

For people guessing on all 10 questions, the average number of wrong answers will be 8.00. The reader should verify that a mean of 8.00 is reasonable for the p.m.f. graphed in Worked Example 5.2.

Since the variance is 1.60, the standard deviation is 1.26 questions.

$$\sigma = \sqrt{1.60} = 1.26$$

Let's see if this standard deviation makes sense by using the $\mu \pm 2\sigma$ rule of thumb from Chapters 3 and 4. According to this rule, there should be approximately 95% of the probability within two standard deviations of the mean. Since $\mu = 8.00$ and $\sigma = 1.26$,

$$\mu \pm 2\sigma = 8.00 \pm (2)(1.26) = 8.00 \pm 2.52 = 5.48 \text{ to } 10.52$$

Notice that this interval contains values of $x$ larger than 5 but less than 11. The probability contained in the interval is (from Worked Example 5.2):

$$P(5 < x \leq 10) = 0.0881 + 0.2013 + 0.3020$$
$$+ 0.2684 + 0.1074 = 0.9672$$

The value 0.9672 (or 96.72%) corresponds well to the 95% rule.

**5.1** Under what conditions is the binomial distribution appropriate? What is a trial in a binomial situation? What is meant by the word *repeated* in describing binomial trials? What is meant by the word *independent* in repeated binomial trials?

**5.2** Give three examples of situations in the business world where the binomial distribution would be appropriate (do not use examples given in this book).

**5.3** Indicate why each of the following situations may not fit the conditions required for the binomial distribution.

a) Each of 100 randomly selected adults is asked if he or she is a Republican or a Democrat.

b) We note whether the next Supreme Court justice appointed is a male or a female.

c) Fifty business executives are asked if their salary exceeds $100,000. One-half of these executives are listed as vice presidents, while the other half are listed as managers.

ADM **5.4** A Chevrolet dealer recently sold six new customized vans. The dealer estimates a probability of 0.40 that a van will be returned at least once for work under the 12,000 miles or 12 month warranty. The dealer would like to know various probabilities for values of $x$, where $x$ is the random variable "van needs repair under warranty."

a) Use Appendix Table B.2 to sketch the binomial p.m.f. for $n = 6$, $\pi = 0.40$.

b) Calculate the mean and variance for this p.m.f. by using Eq. (4.6) and (4.7). Verify your result using Eq. (5.2).

c) Calculate $P(x \geq 3)$.

d) For this p.m.f., how often will $x$ be less than 2?

FIN **5.5** Twenty stocks on the New York Stock Exchange (NYSE) have been recommended by a broker who claims to have a new system for anticipating which stocks will increase in price. The price of the 20 stocks is observed over a 6-month period. For the NYSE in general, 65% of the stocks increase in price over the six months. You are interested in the probability distribution of price increases for the 20 stocks, assuming they represent merely a random sample of all stocks on the NYSE.

a) Sketch the binomial p.m.f. for $n = 20$, $\pi = 0.65$ using Appendix Table B.2.

b) Use Eq. (5.2) to determine the mean and variance of this p.m.f.

c) What percent of the probability is contained between plus and minus one standard deviation? What percent is contained between plus and minus two standard deviations? Are these percents fairly close to the rule of thumb given in Chapter 4?

d) If 13 of the stocks recommended by the broker increase in price, are you impressed by the new system? What is the lowest number that would impress you (e.g., 14, 15)? Calculate the probabilities to help explain your answer.

ACT   **5.6**   The Internal Revenue Service (IRS) is auditing a sample of last year's invoices of Anco, Inc., to determine if the correct excise tax was paid. They are auditing 100 randomly selected invoices. Based on similar situations, the IRS expects minor errors in about 2% of the invoices, even with an honest company.

a) How many errors should the IRS expect, on the average, in a sample of 100 invoices? What is the variance of the errors?

b) What is the probability that the IRS will find more than 5 errors in a random sample of 100, assuming the company is honest?

c) What percent of the probability is contained within plus or minus two standard deviations of the mean?

ADM   **5.7**   In a preselection application test there are 25 questions, and each question has four possible answers.

a) What is the probability that a respondent who is selecting answers randomly will circle the first answer to a question?

b) What is the expected number of correct answers for an applicant who selects randomly on all 25 questions?

c) How high would an applicant have to score before you would conclude that this person is not selecting randomly? Why is there no unique cutoff score as an indication that a person is not guessing?

LAW    **5.8**    A study of the population of workers available in the Detroit area for certain jobs in the automobile industry indicated that 20% are black, while 80% are nonblack. If one company hires 100 new workers for these jobs and 12% are black, would you conclude that the company is discriminating against blacks?

OPS    **5.9**    A geological survey for Mobil Oil indicated the probability of striking oil at each of 10 wells in a particular location to be 0.45. The fact that oil is found (or not found) at one well does not influence the probability of finding oil at any of the other wells.

     a) For the 10 wells, what is the expected number of strikes?

     b) What is the standard deviation of strikes? What percent of the probability lies within $\mu \pm 2\sigma$? Is this number close to the rule of thumb?

**5.10**    Go to Appendix Table B.2 for $n = 8$ and look at the binomial p.m.f. for several $\pi$'s that are less than 0.50 (such as $\pi = 0.20$ and $\pi = 0.30$). Are these p.m.f.'s skewed right or left? Answer the same question for several $\pi$'s greater than 0.50 (such as $\pi = 0.75$ and $\pi = 0.85$). Finally, look at the binomial p.m.f. for $n = 8$, $\pi = 0.50$. Is this distribution skewed right or left, or symmetrical? Based on your observations, make a general statement about the shape of the binomial p.m.f. when:

     a) $\pi$ is less than 0.50,

     b) $\pi$ is greater than 0.50, and

     c) $\pi$ equals 0.50.

FIN    **5.11**    For a random sample of $n = 10$ corporations from the Service Industry category in Appendix A.1, what is the expected number of corporations that should have sales that fell between 1983 and 1984? Draw a sample of 10 corporations from this category using the random number table in Appendix B.1. In your sample what is the number of corporations whose sales fell? Why does your number in this sample differ from the expected number?

LAW    **5.12**    Stanisfer, Inc., is being sued by six different people (in separate suits) for product liability. Stanisfer estimates that the company has a 90% chance of winning each suit.

     a) Use the binomial formula (Eq. 5.1) to calculate the probability that Stanisfer will win four out of the six suits. Does this probability agree with the $P(x = 4)$ value shown in Appendix Table B.2? From Table B.2, what is the probability that they will win all six suits?

b) Sketch the p.m.f. for these parameters. Use Eq. (5.2) to calculate the mean and variance, and place them on your sketch.

**5.13** Use Eqs. (4.6) and (4.7) to verify the mean and variance you calculated in Exercise 5.12(b).

---

## 5.6 Binomial Distribution and Large Sample Sizes

In our semiconductor example, $n = 3$ is too small to allow us to make major decisions about how well the new process is working. A small sample might be adequate for initial exploratory work, but for major and costly decisions large samples are generally warranted. Thus we will now consider a sample size of 50.

First, let's sketch the binomial p.m.f. for $n = 50$, $\pi = 0.70$ to demonstrate that one can define $\pi$ as the "defective rate" or the "perfect rate." If $\pi = 0.30$ is the defective rate, then $\pi = 0.70$ must be the perfect rate. In making this change in the definition of $\pi$ it is important to note that $x$ is no longer the number of defectives. If $\pi$ is now the probability of getting a perfect chip (i.e., $\pi = 0.70$), then $x$ is the number of perfect chips obtained. As long as $\pi$ and $x$ are defined on the same basis, it makes absolutely no difference whether $x$ is defined as success or failure. Figure 5.4 represents part of the binomial p.m.f. for $n = 50$, $\pi = 0.70$, taken from Appendix B, Table B.2.

The mean of the p.m.f. in Fig. 5.4 is

$$\mu = n\pi = 50(0.70) = 35 \quad \text{(perfect chips)}$$

The variance is

$$\sigma^2 = n(\pi)(1 - \pi) = 50(0.70)(0.30) = 10.5 \quad \text{(perfect chips squared)}$$

The standard deviation is the square root of the variance, or

$$\sigma = \sqrt{10.5} = 3.24 \quad \text{(perfect chips)}$$

Let's use our rule of thumb from Chapters 3 and 4 to see if our standard deviation value of 3.24 seems reasonable.

$$\mu \pm 1\sigma = 35 \pm 3.24 = 31.76 \text{ to } 38.24$$

**Figure 5.4** Binomial p.m.f. for $n = 50$, $\pi = 0.70$.

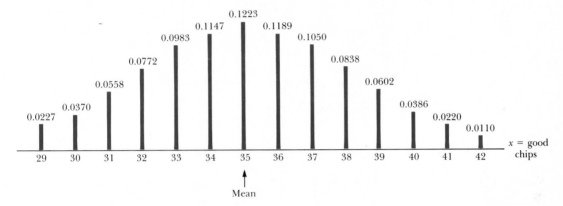

From Fig. 5.4, the sum of the probability values between 31.76 and 38.24 (which includes all whole numbers from 32 to 38) is $0.0772 + 0.0983 + 0.1147 + 0.1223 + 0.1187 + 0.1050 + 0.0838 = 0.7202$. This value is fairly close to our 68% rule of thumb for the probability between plus and minus one standard deviation. Now let's try plus or minus two standard deviations:

$$\mu \pm 2\sigma = 35 \pm 2(3.24) = 28.52 \text{ to } 41.48$$

The sum of the probability values in this interval (adding all probabilities from 29 to 41 in Fig. 5.4) is 0.9565, which again is very close to the rule of thumb (95%).

Now let's assume you have taken the sample of $n = 50$ chips and found 32 perfect chips. However, 32 perfect chips is only 64% ($\frac{32}{50} = 0.64$), which is less than the 70% you expected. How often, you wonder, will there be 32 or fewer perfect chips if the new process really does yield 70% perfect chips? In other words, what is the probability that

$$P(x \le 32 | n = 50, \pi = 0.70)?$$

The probability of getting 32 or fewer chips perfect can be determined from Table B.2 by adding $P(x = 22) + P(x = 23) + \cdots + P(x = 32)$. (Remember, any probability not shown, such as $P(x = 21)$, is small enough to ignore.) Thus, from Table B.2, for $n = 50$, $\pi = 0.70$,

$$P(x \le 32 | n = 50, \pi = 0.70)$$
$$= 0.0001 + 0.0002 + \cdots + 0.0772 = 0.2177$$

This result indicates that there is a 21.77% chance of obtaining 32 or fewer perfect chips when $\pi = 0.70$ and $n = 50$. In other words, more than one-fifth of the time there will be 32 or fewer perfect chips when $\pi = 0.70$ and $n = 50$. It is thus not unusual when $n = 50$ to have only 64% perfect chips when we expect 70%.

## 5.7 Using a Computer to Solve Binomial Problems

There are many statistical computer programs that calculate binomial probabilities. Such programs are convenient when a table (such as Appendix Table B.2) is not available or when the table does not have probabilities for particular values of $n$ or $\pi$. For example, Table B.2 does not have probabilities for $n$ between 10 and 20, between 20 and 50, between 50 and 100, or over 100. Similarly $\pi$ values are given in Table B.2 only to two decimal points. Thus we can find $\pi = 0.40$ and $\pi = 0.41$, but nothing between these two values (such as 0.405).

Computer programs generate probabilities using Eq. (5.1). An interactive computer program usually starts by asking the user for the sample size (designated as $n$ in Fig. 5.5; some programs will denote this parameter as N). Then it asks for the probability of success (designated by $\pi$ in Fig. 5.5 and by P in some programs) and the minimum and maximum value of $x$ for which probabilities are to be calculated (designated by X1 and X2 in Fig. 5.5). In Fig. 5.5 we see that the sample size is 12, the probability of success is 0.45, and all probabilities are to be calculated, since X1 is set at 0 and X2 is 12. Worked Examples 5.3 and 5.4 demonstrate the general procedures for generating and interpreting such computer-calculated binomial p.m.f.'s.

WORKED EXAMPLE
5.3

As a reporter for *Consumer Reports*, you test 12 new swing sets to determine how many break or bend when a load of 500 pounds is placed on the crossbar. Based on past reports, you estimate the probability that a set will break or bend to be 0.45. Your job now is to find the entire p.m.f. for $n = 12$, $\pi = 0.45$.

ANSWER:

To get the probabilities for $x = 0, 1, \ldots, 12$, you load an interactive program, bring up the binomial distribution, and enter the appropriate values of $n$ and

```
ENTER  n:12    ENTER  π: 0.45
ENTER X1:0     ENTER X2:12

   BINOMIAL DISTRIBUTION
     n = 12   π = 0.45

                        CUMULATIVE
     X        P(X)      PROBABILITY

     0      0.000766     0.000766
     1      0.007523     0.008289
     2      0.033853     0.042142
     3      0.092326     0.134468
     4      0.169964     0.304432
     5      0.222498     0.526930
     6      0.212385     0.739315
     7      0.148945     0.888260
     8      0.076165     0.964425
     9      0.027696     0.992121
    10      0.006798     0.998919
    11      0.001011     0.999931
    12      0.000069     1.000000
E(X) = 5.4000000, STD. DEV. = 1.7233688,
VARIANCE = 2.970000
```

$\pi$ as they are requested. Figure 5.5 demonstrates this process. The boldface values are the inputs you provide. The program provides both the cumulative and the individual probabilities. The probability of getting, say, six bent or broken swing sets is 0.212385 (shown in the second column in Fig. 5.5). The probability of getting five or fewer bent or broken sets is 0.526930 (shown in the third column).

---

**WORKED EXAMPLE 5.4**

The National Collegiate Athletic Association (NCAA) is concerned about the relatively small number of college athletes who receive their degree within 5 years after they enter college. One study found the precentage graduating in 5 years to be 54.8%. One small college under investigation graduated only 32 out of 78 athletes in the 5-year period. This college claims that 32 successes (out of 78, which is 41%) is not that much lower than 54.8%. To refute this claim, the NCAA wants to determine the probability of 32 or fewer successes when $\pi = 0.548$.

ANSWER:

Figure 5.6 gives the computer output. The value of $P(x \leq 32) = 0.010023$. Thus only about 1% of the time will there be 32 or fewer successes when $n = 78$ and $\pi = 0.548$.

Figure 5.6
Computer binomial calculations for $n = 78$ and $\pi = 0.548$.

BINOMIAL DISTRIBUTION
$n = 78 \qquad \pi = 0.548$

| x | P(x) | CUMULATIVE PROBABILITY |
|---|---|---|
| 24 | 0.000010 | 0.000016 |
| 25 | 0.000027 | 0.000042 |
| 26 | 0.000066 | 0.000108 |
| 27 | 0.000153 | 0.000261 |
| 28 | 0.000339 | 0.000600 |
| 29 | 0.000708 | 0.001307 |
| 30 | 0.001401 | 0.002708 |
| 31 | 0.002630 | 0.005339 |
| 32 | 0.004684 | 0.010023 |

## Exercises

MKT **5.14** A city manager trying to attract new businesses to the Chicago area reads in *WSJ* that the percentage of families in that city with incomes over $50,000 is 12% (based on the 1980 census). The manager takes a random sample of 100 Chicago families; 18 have incomes over $50,000. What is the probability that there will be 18 or more families with incomes over $50,000 if $\pi = 0.12$? What might the manager advertise based on this sample?

ACT **5.15** A school in Indianapolis provides coaching for people who are going to take the certified public accountant (CPA) exam. Nationally, the percentage of people who pass all portions of the exam at one sitting is 55%. In their most recent class of 50 students, 32 passed all portions in one sitting. If the students from this school are no better (or worse) prepared than students from other schools, what is the probability that 32 or more will pass? Do these results convince you that the school is doing better than the national average in terms of the number of their students who pass?

OPS **5.16** On the morning American Airlines flight from San Francisco to Chicago, each passenger is given a breakfast choice of pancakes or an omelet. Based on many such flights, American has determined that 60% of the passengers will select the omelet. To reduce expenses, the airline would like to stock a minimum number of meals. The food service manager would like to put only 50 pancake breakfasts on a flight with 100 passengers. Based on the historical data, what is the probability that more than 50 passengers will request a pancake breakfast?

MFG **5.17** A computer manufacturer purchases (from a supplier) electric fans to place in each machine to dissipate the heat generated. In the past, about 5% of the fans needed some adjustment before working properly. In the most recent shipment, of 100 fans, only 2 needed adjustment. How often will two or fewer need adjustment if $\pi = 0.05$? Does this latest shipment convince you that $\pi$ is now less than 0.05?

ADM **5.18** Twenty new assembly line workers are hired, supposedly at random, from a long list of applicants. Fifteen percent of the applicants are from minority groups. Only one of the new workers is from a minority group. What is the probability that one or fewer of the minority group is hired if $\pi = 0.15$? What conclusions might an impartial observer reach from these data?

FIN **5.19** Savings and loan associations and banks were permitted to offer their own money fund accounts beginning in December 1982. Of critical importance to these financial institutions is the number of their current accounts that switch to the new funds (they would prefer these accounts to remain at the old lower rate). A nationwide survey suggested that 50% of the eligible accounts would be switched. A local financial institution takes a random sample and 60 of 100 eligible customers indicate that they would switch their accounts. What is the probability that 60 or more (out of 100) will switch if $\pi = 0.50$? What does this suggest for the local financial institution?

ACT **5.20** The MasterCard records of the First National Bank are being audited by a CPA. Official records of the bank indicate that 60% of those card holders who have a balance due owe less than $200. Should the CPA be surprised if, in a random sample of $n = 50$ of those with a balance due, only 50% owe less than \$200? Hint: calculate

$$P(x \le 25 | n = 50, \pi = 0.60)$$

MKT    **5.21** An automobile company has an agreement with the Columbia Broadcasting System (CBS) to pay full price for six 1-minute TV commercials during a football game only if that game attracts 30% or more of the viewing market. The company takes a random sample of 100 people watching TV, and only 25 are watching the game. What is $P(x$ is 25 or less$|n = 100, \pi = 0.30)$? Would you consider this sufficient evidence for the company to refuse to pay full price?

MKT    **5.22** Schlitz beer received considerable attention several years ago by conducting, live on national TV, a taste test in which 50 beer drinkers were asked to taste and then indicate their preference between two unmarked bottles of beer. One bottle was always Schlitz, and the other was some other well-known brand. The person hosting the commercial then announced the results and declared Schlitz the winner if Schlitz received more than 50% of the votes (which was usually the case).

a) What is the probability that 26 or more of the beer drinkers picked Schlitz, assuming these people represented a random sample from a population that is indifferent between the two beers? (Hint: use $\pi = 0.50$.)

b) What minimum number of people (out of a sample of 50) would you want to pick Schlitz before you reject the assumption that $\pi = 0.50$?

FIN    **5.23** Consider the Service Industry category in Appendix A.1. Your theory is that 80% of the companies in this list had a return on common equity of more than 11%. Take a random sample of $n = 10$ of these companies and determine the proportion with a return of more than 11%. Do the data support your theory? Explain, using binomial probabilities for $n = 10$.

MKT    **5.24** A mail order firm specializing in expensive clothes is considering advertising in a magazine that claims that 75% of its 75,000 readers are college graduates. To test this claim, a sample of 200 readers is taken, and 128 (64%) are found to be college graduates. What is the probability of finding 128 or fewer college graduates if the percentage of college graduates is really 75%? Use a computer statistics package to solve this problem.

PUB **5.25** When Indiana passed legislation permitting local communities to pass a local income tax, the projection was that about 25% of the communities would adopt this option in the first year in order to raise taxes. In a random sample taken after 1 year, of 60 communities, only 10% had imposed this type of tax. What is the probability that 10% or less will adopt the tax in a sample of 60 if the true population proportion is 25%? Use a computer program.

LAW **5.26** Several years ago a bakery in Los Angeles was fined for distributing consistently underweight loaves of bread. Suppose that this bakery claims that the authorities just took a "bad sample" and that in reality 50% of their loaves are either of exactly the correct weight or slightly overweight.

**a)** If, in a random sample of 120 loaves, 65% are underweight, would you support the bakery's claim? Explain.

**b)** How many underweight loaves of bread in a sample of 120 would it take to convince you that the bakery is not telling the truth?

ADM **5.27** The Systems Department of Owens-Corning in Toledo, Ohio, prides itself on the fact that (on the average) only 5% of its 125 employees leave each year. This year 12 left, and Owens-Corning is interested in determining the probability that 12 or more will leave if the population value of $\pi$ is 0.05. Use the following computer output to solve the problem. Why do you think this computer output only lists values up to 19, when $x$ can be any number up to 125? Interpret the values at the bottom of the output.

```
        BINOMIAL DISTRIBUTION
         n = 125      π = 0.05

                             CUMULATIVE
         x        P(x)       PROBABILITY
         12     0.013071      0.013071
         13     0.005980      0.019051
         14     0.002518      0.021569
         15     0.000981      0.022549
         16     0.000355      0.022904
         17     0.000120      0.023024
         18     0.000038      0.023062
         19     0.000011      0.023073

   E(x) = 6.2500000, STD. DEV. = 2.4366984
   VARIANCE = 5.9375000
```

# 5.8 Hypergeometric Distribution

The hypergeometric distribution is used in problems that are similar to the binomial examples considered earlier except that now trials are not independent. To understand the distinction, consider the following case.

## USM Promotion Case

Since 1971, there have been numerous lawsuits claiming discrimination against a minority group in terms of promotions. You have been hired as a statistical consultant in one of these cases, a suit against United States Motors (USM) in Detroit. Last January, USM promoted six new assembly line workers at the plant making their new Alpha car. The position called for special skilled workers, and there were 10 qualified applicants for the job. The suit claims discrimination against the blacks because four of the qualified applicants were black, yet only one black was promoted. Your job is to determine the probability that one or fewer blacks is promoted by an unbiased process.

In this case there are just two outcomes (a person is promoted or not promoted), and there are repeated trials (each of the 10 people is either promoted or not promoted). However, this problem cannot be treated as a binomial because the probability of each outcome changes from trial to trial. For example, if the selection is random, the probability of promoting a black on trial 1 (the first promotion) is $\frac{4}{10} = 0.40$, since there are four blacks in 10 applicants. If a black is promoted on trial 1, then the probability that the person promoted on trial 2 is also black is $\frac{3}{9} = 0.33$, because there are 9 people left, 3 of whom are black). Thus, the probability of promoting a black changes from trial to trial, which means the binomial is inappropriate. The appropriate p.m.f. is called the *hypergeometric probability mass function*.

| RULES<br>Hypergeometric<br>and Binomial | The hypergeometric distribution assumes sampling from a finite population without replacement. The binomial distribution assumes sampling from an infinite population or sampling with replacement. |
| --- | --- |

Chapter 5   The Binomial, Hypergeometric, and Poisson Distributions

# 5.9 Calculating Hypergeometric Probabilities (Optional)

In all of our hypergeometric problems we will divide the population (such as all candidates for promotion in the USM job) into two categories. The two categories in this problem are the black candidates and the nonblack candidates. For a population of size $N$, let $N_1$ = the number in one subgroup who share a common attribute and let $N_2$ = the number in a second subgroup who do not possess this attribute. Because there were four blacks and six nonblacks,

$N_1$ = number in first group = four blacks

$N_2$ = number in second group = six nonblacks

$N = N_1 + N_2$ = total number in the population = 10 people

Now, for a sample of size $n$, let

$x_1$ = number of successes from the first group (blacks promoted)

$x_2$ = number of successes from the second group (nonblacks promoted)

$n = x_1 + x_2$

A typical hypergeometric problem involves calculating the probability of $x_1$ successes and $x_2$ successes in a sample of size $n$. Thus, in the USM promotion case, we are interested in the probability that $x_1 = 1$ (one black is promoted) and $x_2 = 5$ (five nonblacks are promoted). This probability is written as $P(x_1 = 1$ and $x_2 = 5)$. The formula for calculating a probability such as this one is given in Eq. (5.3).

Hypergeometric p.m.f.

(5.3)
$$P(x_1 \text{ successes and } x_2 \text{ successes}) = \frac{\dfrac{N_1!}{x_1!(N_1 - x_1)!} \dfrac{N_2!}{x_2!(N_2 - x_2)!}}{\dfrac{N!}{n!(N - n)!}}$$

Equation (5.3) is not hard to use for small populations, but calculating all the values of the factorials for larger $N$ values is time-consuming. Fortunately, as demonstrated in Section 5.10, such probabilities are easily determined using standard computer programs. For now, the reader should have a calculator ready to verify the calculations required in the USM promotion case. In this case $x_1 = 1$, $x_2 = 5$, $N_1 = 4$, and $N_2 = 6$. Substituting these values into Eq. (5.3) gives the following probability:

$$P(x_1 = 1 \text{ and } x_2 = 5) = \frac{\dfrac{4!}{1!(4-1)!}\dfrac{6!}{5!(6-5)!}}{\dfrac{10!}{6!(4!)}}$$

$$= \frac{\dfrac{24}{1(6)}\dfrac{720}{120(1)}}{\dfrac{3,628,800}{720(24)}} = \frac{(4)(6)}{210} = 0.1143$$

Thus, if being promoted has nothing to do with skin color, then the probability that exactly one black and five nonblacks will be promoted is 0.1143. Let's now use Eq. (5.3) to calculate $P(x_1 = 0 \text{ and } x_2 = 6)$.

$$P(x_1 = 0 \text{ and } x_2 = 6) = \frac{\dfrac{4!}{0!(4)!}\dfrac{6!}{6!(0)!}}{\dfrac{10!}{6!(4!)}} = \frac{\dfrac{24}{24(1)}\dfrac{720}{720(1)}}{\dfrac{3,628,800}{720(24)}} = \frac{1}{210} = 0.0048$$

The sum of the preceding two probabilities is the probability that one or fewer blacks will be promoted.

$$P(x_1 = 0 \text{ and } x_2 = 6) + P(x_1 = 1 \text{ and } x_2 = 5)$$

$$= 0.1143 + 0.0048 = 0.1191$$

This result shows that there is an 11.91% chance of one or fewer blacks being promoted if skin color is not related to the probability of being promoted. From a statistical point of view, this probability (0.1191) may not be low enough to support discrimination charges against the company; more evidence (perhaps in the form of a larger sample) may be necessary.

We have calculated the remaining probabilities for this problem, namely, $P(x_1 = 2 \text{ and } x_2 = 4) + P(x_1 = 3 \text{ and } x_2 = 3)$ and $P(x_1 = 4 \text{ and } x_2 = 2)$. The value of $x_1$ can't be any larger than 4 because there are only four black candidates. The entire p.m.f. is shown in Fig. 5.7. Notice that in Fig. 5.7

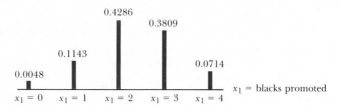

Figure 5.7
Hypergeometric
distribution for
$N_1 = 4$, $N_2 = 6$.

0.4286

0.3809

0.1143

0.0714

0.0048

$x_1 = 0$   $x_1 = 1$   $x_1 = 2$   $x_1 = 3$   $x_1 = 4$

$x_1$ = blacks promoted

the probabilities sum to 1.00, as must be the case for all p.m.f.'s. In addition, the mean of this hypergeometric p.m.f. can be calculated by Eq. (4.6) as follows:

$$\mu = \Sigma\, xP(x) = 0(0.0048) + 1(0.1143) + 2(0.4286)$$
$$+ 3(0.3809) + 4(0.0714) = 2.40$$

On the average, in this situation, we expect 2.4 blacks to be promoted. An equation for the mean of the hypergeometric p.m.f. is:

---

Mean of the hypergeometric p.m.f.

(5.4)
$$\mu_1 = \frac{nN_1}{N}$$

---

Recall that for the preceding problem $N_1 = 4$, $N = 10$, and $n = 6$. Using Eq. (5.4) to calculate the mean or expected number of blacks promoted $(x_1)$, we get the same result as we did previously: $\mu_1 = E(x_1) = 2.40$.

$$\mu_1 = 6(4)/10 = 2.40$$

Notice that Eq. (5.4) can be rewritten, by simply changing subscripts, to calculate the expected number of nonblacks $(x_2)$ in a sample of six. The expected number of nonblacks is $\mu_2 = nN_2/N = 6(6)/10 = 3.6$. Note that $\mu_2 = n - \mu_1$. Thus, once we know either mean, we can obtain the other by subtraction. Finally, as with all p.m.f.'s, a hypergeometric distribution has a variance and a standard deviation. However, we will not discuss these calculations here.

A CPA surveying checking account customers at a local bank sent out 20 questionnaires. Twelve were completed and returned. The CPA finds that 8 of the 20 questionnaires were sent to students and 12 to nonstudents. Only 2 of the returned questionnaires were from students, while the remaining 10 were from nonstudents. The CPA wants to know if this low response rate by the students can be attributed to something other than chance.

ANSWER:

This is a hypergeometric problem because it involves sampling without replacement from a finite population (the population is the 20 questionnaires, and the sample is the 12 responses). The CPA is concerned because the proportion of responses from students (2 out of 12, or 16.7%) is considerably less than the proportion of questionnaires sent to students (8 of 20, or 40%). The CPA wants to determine how often, by chance, there will be 2 or fewer student responses when there is a total of 12 responses.

In this case, $N_1 = 8$ students, $N_2 = 12$ nonstudents, $x_1 = 2$ student responses and $x_2 = 10$ nonstudent responses. Using Eq. (5.3), the probability of getting exactly two student responses, $P(x_1 = 2$ and $x_2 = 10)$, is:

$$P(x_1 = 2 \text{ and } x_2 = 10) = \frac{\dfrac{8!}{2!(6)!} \cdot \dfrac{12!}{10!(2)!}}{\dfrac{20!}{12!(8!)}} = \frac{28(66)}{125,970} = 0.0147$$

Similarly, the following calculations can be verified:

$$P(x_1 = 1 \text{ and } x_2 = 11) = \frac{96}{125,970} = 0.0008$$

and

$$P(x_1 = 0 \text{ and } x_2 = 12) = \frac{1}{125,970} = 0.0000$$

Thus, $P$(two or fewer students) $= 0.0147 + 0.0008 + 0.0000 = 0.0155$. This result shows that 1.55% of the time there will be two or fewer student responses by chance. In other words, it is very unlikely that two or fewer student responses will be received if the questionnaires are returned at random. Thus we suspect that the low response rate is caused by factors other than chance (e.g., we might conclude that students are less concerned or have less time to fill out questionnaires).

## 5.10 Using a Computer to Determine Hypergeometric Probabilities

It should be clear by now that calculating hypergeometric probabilities is tedious. Unfortunately, there is no table in Appendix B that presents hypergeometric probabilities, as there is for the binomial (it would take up a huge number of pages). The good news is that hypergeometric probabilities can readily be determined using any of the modern statistical computer programs. The following case illustrates the use of a typical program.

### Clock Pens

As the purchasing agent for Service Merchandise, you have purchased 300 clock pens (ballpoint pens with a built-in digital clock). If more than 10% of the clock pens are defective, you will return the entire shipment and cancel the order. But you cannot test all 300 pens. You have taken a random sample of 20 pens. Five of them are found to be defective. How often will a sample of 20 result in 5 or more defects if there are only 30 defectives in the shipment (30 is used because that is the largest number of defectives you will accept)? Should you accept or reject this shipment?

This is a hypergeometric problem because Service Merchandise is sampling without replacement from a finite population. In this situation the population size is $N = 300$, the sample size is $n = 20$, and the probability of interest is $P(x \geq 5)$. As can be seen in Fig. 5.8, an interactive computer program asks the user to input the population size, the sample size, and "No. of possible occurrences." The number of possible occurrences refers to the number of items in the population that possess the given attribute (number of defective pens in the population). The program also asks for the range of

**Figure 5.8**
Computer analysis of
a hypergeometric
distribution.

```
        ENTER POPULATION SIZE:300
         ENTER SAMPLE SIZE:20

   ENTER NO. OF POSSIBLE OCCURRENCES:30
     ENTER X1:0          ENTER X2:4

   HYPERGEOMETRIC DISTRIBUTION

   THE POPULATION OF SIZE 300 OBJECTS
    CONTAINS 30 POSSIBLE OCCURRENCES.

   THE SAMPLE SIZE IS 20

                        CUMULATIVE
     x       P(x)       PROBABILITY
     0     0.112932      0.112932
     1     0.269956      0.382887
     2     0.295130      0.678018
     3     0.195976      0.873994
     4     0.088536      0.962530
E(x) = 2.0000000 STD. DEV. = 1.2983137
VARIANCE = 1.6856186
```

$x$ values for which probabilities are to be calculated. These are shown in Fig. 5.8 as X1 and X2. We have requested probabilities for zero through four defective pens because when $P(x \le 4)$ is known, then $P(x \ge 5)$ can be calculated as $1 - P(x \le 4)$.

Since $P(x \le 4) = 0.962530$ (the last number in the "Cumulative Probability" column),

$$P(x \ge 5) = 1 - 0.962530 = 0.037470$$

Thus 5 or more defectives in a sample of 20 is quite rare when there are 30 defectives in the population (it will happen less than 4% of the time). As the purchasing agent for Service Merchandise, you might well be justified in sending the entire shipment back, or perhaps at least taking a larger sample.

## Exercises

MKT   **5.28**   A department store has identified nine employees who are eligible to win a free trip to Hawaii. Five of the nine are females and four are males. Five people are to be given the free trip.

**a)** What is the sample size in this problem? What is the population size? Find $P(x_1 = 3)$, where $x_1$ = female winners.

**b)** What is the probability that $x_1$ is three or more?

**c)** Why can't $x_1$ be less than one in this problem? Sketch the p.m.f. using $x_1 = 1, 2, 3, 4, 5$.

**d)** What is the mean of this p.m.f.?

ADM    **5.29** Four type O blood donors are needed for a hospital emergency. Ten people are available to have their blood typed to be possible donors; seven volunteer. Based on national statistics, the hospital suspects that 5 of the original 10 have type O blood. You are on the hospital staff and want to determine the probability that when $n = 7$ there will be four or more type O donors.

**a)** Describe $N_1$ and $N_2$ in this example and indicate the value of each one. Describe $x_1$ and $x_2$ and indicate what probability is of interest. Calculate this probability where $x_1$ equals the number of type O donors.

**b)** Sketch the p.m.f. for $x_1 = 2, 3, 4, 5$. Why can't $x_1$ be less than 2 or more than 5?

**c)** What is the mean of this p.m.f.?

MKT    **5.30** A shipment of 15 video cassette recorders to Sears arrived without markings to indicate whether each box contained a beta model or a VHS model. The order was for 5 betas and 10 VHS's. Two customers arrive and both want the beta model.

**a)** If two boxes are opened, what is the probability that both will be betas?

**b)** What is the probability of at least two betas if four boxes are opened?

**c)** What is the probability that the first three boxes you open will all be betas? If the first three are all betas, would you suspect that there may be more than five betas? Explain.

FIN    **5.31** Suppose E.F. Hutton has recommended five stocks for price appreciation over the next 6 months. For 6 months you follow these five stocks and five others recommended by another broker, and find that four of the E.F. Hutton stocks and two of the others have increased in price. Based on this sample, would you conclude that "When E.F. Huttton talks, people [should] listen"?

LAW    **5.32** A jury votes seven to five in favor of "guilty" in a case in which a man is accused of computer fraud. What is the probability that if six jurors are randomly selected, five or more have cast "guilty" votes?

OPS    **5.33**   An assembly line produces the Cadillac Seville, and each car is built to the customer's specifications. About half of the cars are ordered with a six-cylinder engine and the rest with an eight-cylinder engine. At the moment, the line has 10 engines available, five of which are 6 cylinder and five 8 cylinder. What is the probability that the supply of six-cylinder engines will be used up when the seventh car in line (waiting for an engine) gets its engine, assuming random orders for six- or eight-cylinder engines?

MKT    **5.34**   Out of 10 sales personnel, 7 (group A) make sales on 20% of their calls. The other three (group B) make sales on 50% of their calls.

     **a)**   What is the average ratio of sales to calls for all 10 sales personnel?

     **b)**   Suppose the sales manager selects three of these people at random to assign to a new territory. What is the probability that exactly two of them will be from group A?

     **c)**   Suppose we follow one salesperson in group A on the next five calls, each of which is considered independent of any of the others. What is the probability that this person makes more than one but fewer than four sales on these five calls?

PUB    **5.35**   For the Office Equipment and Computer category in Appendix A.1, assume that the 42 companies represent a random sample from all corporations. How many corporations in this sample had a price-earnings ratio of 10 or more? Determine the probability of observing this number by chance if $\pi$ is 0.50.

ADM    **5.36**   A bipartisan committee of 10 is being formed from among the 100 members of the U.S. Senate. Assume that 45 members are Democrats and 55 are Republicans. The committee selected has seven Republicans and three Democrats. What is the probability of this many (or more) Republicans if the selection is made randomly from the Senate?

MKT    **5.37**   A telephone survey is made of swimming pool owners to see if recent TV ads for a new chlorine have been seen. The telephone callers have a list of 150 households, one-third of which have pools. What is the probability that, among the first 10 calls to randomly selected numbers on this list, the callers will contact 8 or more of the households with pools?

OPS    **5.38**   A plastic gasket is being tested as a replacement for a rubber gasket used in automobile engines. Three hundred gaskets (180 plastic and 120 rubber) are subjected to considerable pressure. Of the 20 gaskets found to leak, 15 are plastic and 5 rubber. What is the probability of this many or more plastic gaskets leaking if the two types are equally effective?

MKT **5.39** IBM tested two types (A and B) of $5\frac{1}{4}$-inch floppy disks for reliability. One thousand owners of IBM personal computers were sent one floppy disk each, and asked to test it and report any problems. Five hundred of these people were sent type A and 500 were sent type B. Thirty users reported problems, 20 with type A and 10 with type B. What is the probability of 20 or more problems with type A if the two types are equally reliable?

PUB **5.40** A town of 42,500 registered voters is considering using bonds to pay for construction of a new city-county building. However, a local group called Save Our Taxes has collected 2500 signatures against the bonds. You take a random sample of 50 voters and none of these people has signed the remonstrance. Determine how likely this result is, using the following computer information.

HYPERGEOMETRIC DISTRIBUTION

THE POPULATION OF SIZE 42,500 OBJECTS CONTAINS 2500 POSSIBLE OCCURRENCES.

THE SAMPLE SIZE IS 50

| x | P(x) | CUMULATIVE PROBABILITY |
|---|---|---|
| 0 | 0.048169 | 0.048169 |
| 1 | 0.150713 | 0.198882 |
| 2 | 0.230964 | 0.429846 |
| 3 | 0.231051 | 0.660896 |
| 4 | 0.169669 | 0.830566 |
| 5 | 0.097514 | 0.928079 |
| 6 | 0.045668 | 0.973748 |
| 7 | 0.017917 | 0.991665 |
| 8 | 0.006009 | 0.997673 |
| 9 | 0.001749 | 0.999422 |
| 10 | 0.000447 | 0.999869 |
| 11 | 0.000101 | 0.999970 |
| 12 | 0.000020 | 0.999991 |

E(x) = 2.941800, STD. DEV. = 1.6628212,
VARIANCE = 2.7649744

FIN   **5.41**   Over a period of 200 trading days, the stock market was observed to advance on 110 days and not to advance on 90 days. You are wondering if a 20-day sequence of days in the middle of the 200 can be thought of as a random sample of the 200 days. During the 20 days, the stock market advanced on 15 and did not advance on 5. Using the hypergeometric distribution, calculate the probability that by chance there will be 15 or more advances in 20 days. What do you conclude about randomness?

**5.42**   In Exercises 5.11 and 5.23 you drew samples of $n = 10$ corporations from the Service Industry category in Appendix A.1. In both of these exercises you used the binomial distribution to make probability calculations. Under what conditions was it appropriate to use the binomial versus the hypergeometric distribution? Were these conditions actually fulfilled in these exercises? Redo Exercises 5.11 and 5.23 using the hypergeometric distribution and see if your probabilities change.

# 5.11   The Poisson Distribution

The **Poisson distribution** is used to determine the probability that there will be $x$ occurrences of some event (such as a malpractice suit) over a specified period of time (such as 1 year). Perhaps a bank is interested in the probability that $x$ customers make deposits during a half-hour period. Similarly, an airport may want to determine the probability that $x$ planes will request permission to land in a given 5-minute interval, or a company may wish to determine the probability that $x$ machines will break down on any one day. These are examples where the Poisson distribution may apply because such events may occur at random in a fixed period of time.

The Poisson distribution was developed by a French mathematician, S. D. Poisson (1781–1840). The first application of this distribution was by the Polish economist Ladislaus von Bortkiewicz (1868–1931), who studied the probability of deaths from the kick of a horse in the Prussian army and the number of deaths by suicide of women and children. More recently, this distribution has been extended to business problems in operations research and queuing theory. To illustrate the use of the Poisson distribution, consider the following case.

## Statesman Insurance

You are an actuary working on pricing policies for the Statesman Insurance Company. One of the policies provided by Statesman is malpractice insurance for physicians. Your company has policies covering over 4000 doctors throughout the United States. You have studied 20 years of malpractice claims from the doctors your company covers and found that the company has had an average of 6.4 claims per year. If you could determine the p.m.f. for the distribution of malpractice claims, it would help Statesman establish a pricing policy to protect itself from the random fluctuations in claims that occur from year to year.

---

The Poisson distribution is appropriate when the number of possible occurrences is very large but the number of actual occurrences is relatively small. For the Statesman case, the number of malpractice claims that could be filed in a year represents the possible occurrences and is very large, but the actual number of claims is relatively small (an average of 6.4 per year). In the same manner, the number of customers in a bank (per half hour), the number of planes wishing to land (in a 5-minute interval), and the number of machines needing repair (in a day) are small compared to the number of possible occurrences.

Suppose we let $x$ equal the number of occurrences that take place in some time interval. The value of $x$ can be 0 (no occurrences take place), or 1 (one occurrence takes place), or 2, or 3, and so forth, up to the largest number possible (which is the number of possible occurrences). Thus we need to be able to determine the probability of $P(x = 0)$, $P(x = 1)$, $P(x = 2)$, $P(x = 3)$, and so on. The formula for Poisson probability calculations is as follows:

---

Poisson p.m.f.

(5.5)
$$P(x) = \frac{e^{-\lambda}\lambda^x}{x!} \quad \text{for } x = 0, 1, 2, 3, \ldots, \text{ and } \lambda > 0$$

$$P(x) = 0 \quad \text{otherwise,}$$

where $e = 2.71828$, and $\lambda$ is the mean and variance.

---

Unless one has a calculator with an $e^\lambda$ key, hand calculations using Eq. (5.5) can be extremely tedious. Like the binomial p.m.f., Poisson probabilities can be determined by a table (Appendix Table B.3) or by a computer statistical package. We will illustrate the use of a table and a computer package but will not present hand calculator procedures using Eq. (5.5).

To determine a Poisson probability using a table or a computer program, it is first necessary to know the mean or expected number of occurrences in the time interval selected. As in the Statesman Insurance case, this mean is usually determined by looking at past data. The mean is designated by the Greek letter lambda ($\lambda$). Thus, for the Statesman case, $\lambda = 6.4$, indicating that the average number of claims is 6.4 per year. If past records for a bank indicate an average of 30.8 customers per half hour, then $\lambda = 30.8$. For an airport, perhaps $\lambda = 2.3$ (landings per 5 minutes). If in a machine shop an average of 0.5 machine need repair each day (or 1 every other day), then $\lambda = 0.5$. Notice in Eq. (5.5) that once the mean of the Poisson distribution has been determined the variance is also known, since the mean and the variance of a Poisson p.m.f. are the same numerical value.

## 5.12 Using Appendix Table B.3 to Determine Poisson Probability

Table B.3 gives the p.m.f. for many values of $\lambda$ (up to $\lambda = 20$). For example, the p.m.f. for $\lambda = 6.4$ shown on page 658 is reproduced in Table 5.3.

The value of $x$ could be larger than 18, but the probability of 18 (or more) occurrences when $\lambda = 6.4$ is so small that it cannot be represented by a reasonable number of decimal places and thus is not contained in Table B.3. As with any p.m.f., the probabilities must sum to 1.00. This is true of the probabilities in Table 5.3.

The Poisson p.m.f. is used in a manner similar to that of the binomial p.m.f. For example, the probability that Statesman will have exactly nine claims in any one year (assuming that $\lambda = 6.4$ and the Poisson distribution is appropriate) is 0.0825. The probability that they will have nine or more claims in one year is

$$P(x \geq 9) = P(9) + P(10) + \cdots + P(18)$$
$$= 0.0825 + 0.0528 + \cdots + 0.0001 = 0.1966$$

Thus there will be nine or more claims about 20% of the time.

| Table 5.3 | The Poisson Distribution (p.m.f.) for $\lambda = 6.4$ | | | |
|---|---|---|---|---|
| | $x$ | $P(x)$ | $x$ | $P(x)$ |
| | 0 | 0.0017 | 10 | 0.0528 |
| | 1 | 0.0106 | 11 | 0.0307 |
| | 2 | 0.0340 | 12 | 0.0164 |
| | 3 | 0.0726 | 13 | 0.0081 |
| | 4 | 0.1162 | 14 | 0.0037 |
| | 5 | 0.1487 | 15 | 0.0016 |
| | 6 | 0.1586 | 16 | 0.0006 |
| | 7 | 0.1450 | 17 | 0.0001 |
| | 8 | 0.1160 | 18 | 0.0001 |
| | 9 | 0.0825 | | |

The Poisson p.m.f. is always skewed to the right, and this skewness is more pronounced the closer $\lambda$ is to zero. Figure 5.9 illustrates the shape of the Poisson p.m.f. for the Statesman Insurance case where $\lambda = 6.4$. The probabilities were given in Table 5.3. Notice in Fig. 5.9 that the distribution is only slightly skewed (i.e., is fairly symmetrical) because $\lambda$ is not close to zero.

The interested reader can verify that the mean of the distribution in Fig. 5.9 is 6.4 by using the equation for calculating a mean from Chapter 4 (Eq. 4.6). We can verify that a variance of 6.4 is reasonable by using the rule of thumb from Chapter 3 and calculating the amount of probability within two standard deviations of the mean. Since the standard deviation is the square root of the variance, one standard deviation is the square root of 6.4, or 2.53.

$$\mu \pm 2\sigma = 6.4 \pm 2(2.53) = [1.34 \text{ to } 11.46]$$

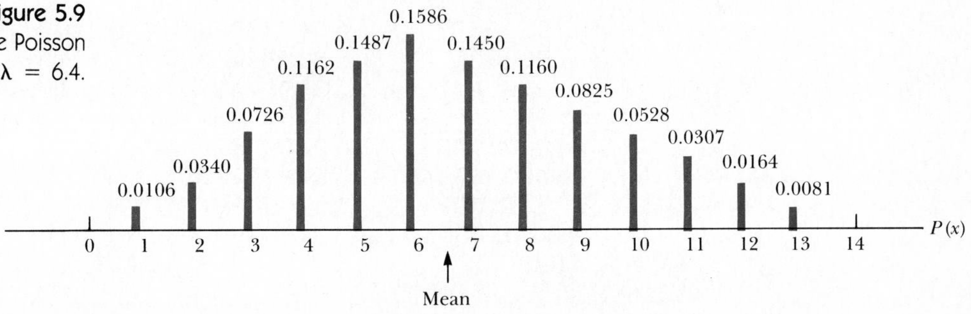

**Figure 5.9**
Sketch of the Poisson p.m.f. for $\lambda = 6.4$.

The sum of the probabilities starting with 2 and ending with 11 is 0.9571. This value is very close to the 95% rule of thumb.

## 5.13 Using a Computer to Solve Poisson Problems

There are a variety of statistical computer programs to solve Poisson problems. Once an interactive Poisson program has been loaded, it will ask for the "mean rate of occurrence," which is the value of $\lambda$. The program will also ask for X1 (the minimum value of $x$ for which probability is to be calculated) and X2 (the maximum value). Figure 5.10 presents this process for $\lambda = 2.3$, which is the mean number of airplanes wishing to land in a 5-minute interval.

Notice in Fig. 5.10 that the computer program provides the mean (which we knew to be 2.3), the variance (which is also 2.3), and the standard deviation (the square root of 2.3). From the "Cumulative Probability" column we see that the probability of, say, two or fewer planes landing is 0.596039. In

Figure 5.10
Computer
determination of
Poisson probabilities
for $\lambda = 2.3$.

```
           POISSON DISTRIBUTION
      MEAN RATE OF OCCURRENCE = 2.3
        ENTER X1: 0    ENTER X2:12
                          CUMULATIVE
      X        P(X)      PROBABILITY
      0       0.100259    0.100259
      1       0.230595    0.330854
      2       0.265185    0.596039
      3       0.203308    0.799347
      4       0.116902    0.916249
      5       0.053775    0.970024
      6       0.020614    0.990638
      7       0.006773    0.997411
      8       0.001947    0.999358
      9       0.000498    0.999856
     10       0.000114    0.999970
     11       0.000024    0.999994
     12       0.000005    0.999999
   E(X) = 2.3000000 STD. DEV. = 1.5165750
   VARIANCE = 2.3000000
```

Chapter 5  The Binomial, Hypergeometric, and Poisson Distributions

addition, we see that this p.m.f. is not nearly as symmetrical as the distribution in Fig. 5.10, since the value of $\lambda$ is now much closer to zero.

---

WORKED EXAMPLE
5.6

The Clark Company has one repairman who services the 200 machines in their shop and repairs machines that break down. The average breakdown rate is $\lambda = 0.5$ machine per day (or one breakdown every two days). The repairman can fix two machines a day. Clark is interested in determining the probability that there will be more than two breakdowns in a day, assuming a Poisson distribution.

ANSWER:

Either Appendix Table B.3 or a computer program can be used to determine the Poisson probability for $\lambda = 0.5$. The following output is from a computer program. From this output we can calculate the following:

$$P(x > 2) = 1 - P(x \le 2) = 1 - 0.985612 = 0.014388$$

Thus about 1.5% of the time there will be more than two breakdowns in a day.

```
           POISSON DISTRIBUTION

MEAN RATE OF OCCURRENCE = 0.5

                          CUMULATIVE
  X        P(X)          PROBABILITY
  0      0.606531         0.606531
  1      0.303265         0.909796
  2      0.075816         0.985612
  3      0.012636         0.998248
  4      0.001580         0.999828
  5      0.000158         0.999986
  6      0.000013         0.999999
```

## Exercises

ADM    **5.43** The manager of a new Kroger store has been studying the service time provided at checkout counters using the new automated price-reading system. The manager has determined that the number of customers that can be served in a half-hour period follows a Poisson distribution, with $\lambda = 6.4$. The manager would like to determine:

a) The probability that exactly six customers will be served in a half-hour period.

b) The probability that fewer than four customers will be served.

c) How much of the probability lies within two standard deviations of the mean.

OPS **5.44** The administrator of a tollbooth on the Pennsylvania Turnpike has studied the booth during weekdays over the past year and determined that arrivals (per minute) are Poisson distributed. The administrator generated the following computer output:

| X | P(X) | CUMULATIVE PROBABILITY |
|---|---|---|
| 0 | 0.7408 | 0.7408 |
| 1 | 0.2222 | 0.9630 |
| 2 | 0.0333 | 0.9963 |
| 3 | 0.0033 | 0.9996 |
| 4 | 0.0003 | 0.9999 |
| 5 | 0.0001 | 1.0000 |

a) What mean rate of occurrence did the administrator use?

b) What is the probability of more than three arrivals within 1 minute?

c) Is this distribution fairly symmetrical? What percent of the distribution lies within two standard deviations of the mean?

FIN **5.45** A study of the stock market over the past 10 years indicates that the number of times (per year) the Dow Jones Industrial Average (DJIA) has risen over 25 points can be considered to be a Poisson distribution with $\lambda = 2.7$.

a) What is the probability that the DJIA will rise over 25 points four or more times in a given year?

b) What is the probability that the DJIA will have no increases over 25 points in 1 year?

c) Sketch this p.m.f., indicating its mean and standard deviation.

**5.46** In each of the following, state why and under what conditions the binomial, hypergeometric, or Poisson is the most appropriate distribution to use.

a) A quality control engineer wants to know the probability of 4 or fewer misdialed long-distance telephone calls in a 1-minute time period if the expected number of calls is 10.

b) A teacher wants to know the number of questions a student can be expected to guess correctly on a 25-question multiple-choice exam where each question has five alternatives and only one correct answer.

c) A car dealer received a shipment of 10 cars, and the 3 red ones sold immediately. The manager asks, what is the probability of this happening by chance?

FIN **5.47** Consider the Service Industries category in Appendix A.1. For a random sample of 20 corporations from this category, let $x$ = the number of companies with a negative return on equity. What is the probability that your sample will yield $x$ or fewer successes for all possible values of $x$?

ADM **5.48** The Red Cross bloodmobile has scheduled a visit to a college campus and has asked donors to reserve, in advance, a time to give blood. Last year the percentage of no-shows was 26.4. This year 88 people have made advance reservations.

a) What is the mean number of people expected to show up based on last year's figures?

b) If you are asked the maximum and the minimum number of people who could reasonably be expected to show up for their appointments, what values would you give?

c) Use a computer program to calculate the probability of $x$ show-ups for $x = 50$ to $x = 79$. Assume that the binomial distribution is appropriate.

PUB **5.49** The U.S. Department of Transportation (DOT) has announced that it will award a grant for the study of traffic accidents to each of four different universities. Twenty universities have applied for a grant. If Stanford, Indiana University, and the University of North Carolina are among the 20 applicants, what is the probability that they will all be winners, assuming that the selection process is random?

**5.50** For the binomial distribution, the mean number of successes is $E(x) = n\pi$ and the variance is $n\pi(1 - \pi)$.

a) Suppose we are interested in the *proportion* of successes in a binomial situation, rather than the number of successes. If we designate the proportion of successes as $x/n$, then what is the expected value of $x/n$ or $E(x/n)$? What is the variance of $x/n$?

b) What differences are there between the p.m.f. for the number of successes and the proportion of successes in $n$ trials?

**5.51** Go to the library and find a statistics text that discusses the relationship between the binomial and Poisson distributions. Describe this relationship.

MKT **5.52** The negative binomial p.m.f. is appropriate when one is interested in determining the probability that $n$ binomial trials will be required to produce $r$ successes. This probability is

$$P(n) = \frac{(n - 1)!}{(r - 1)!(n - r!)} \pi^r(1 - \pi)^{n-r} \qquad \text{for } n > r + 1$$

Suppose an advertising agency is trying to evaluate the effects of a national commercial advertising a new brand of cat food. A caller is assigned to randomly contact residential dwellings in Columbus, Ohio, where 40% of the homes have cats.

a) What is the probability that it will take 10 calls to find exactly five homes with cats (assume that all calls are answered politely)?

b) What is the average number of calls required to have five successes if $E(n) = r/\pi$?

c) What is the variance of the number of calls if $\sigma^2 = r(1 - p)^2/\pi$?

MKT **5.53** The Anvoco Oil Company recently mailed 6500 letters to people in the state of Indiana who have a good credit rating (Anvoco bought a list of such people). The letter offered each person a free Anvoco credit card. Those people who sent for the card also received either $3, $5, or $10 in free gasoline. The amount of gasoline each person was to receive was randomly determined, and the amount was stated in the letter. For Indiana, 500 letters were sent offering $5 in free gas, 500 letters offering $10 in free gas, and all the remainder offering $3 in free gas. Anvoco had 5283 people take advantage of their offer, and they are now wondering if the amount of free gas offered had an influence on whether or not a person sent for the free credit card. They had requests for a credit card from 833 of the people offered either \$5 or \$10 in free gas. All the remaining requests were from people offered \$3 in free gas. What is the probability of 833 or more requests from the 1000 people offered \$5 or \$10 if requests do not depend on the amount of free gas?

ADM **5.54** The binomial distribution is appropriate when each trial of the experiment has only two possible outcomes. When there are more than two outcomes, the *multinomial distribution* can be used. In this p.m.f., we assume that the population is divided into $k$ different types of items. The probability in question is that of receiving a sample of $x_1$ of type 1, $x_2$ of type 2, $x_3$ of type 3, and so forth, where the population contains $N_1$ of the first type, $N_2$ of the second type, and so on. The probability of the first type is $\pi_1$, of the second type is $\pi_2$, and so on.

Multinomial distribution:

$$P(x_1 \text{ of } N_1, x_2 \text{ of } N_2, \ldots, x_k \text{ of } N_k)$$
$$= \frac{n!}{n_1! \, n_2! \, \cdots \, n_k!} (\pi_1^{x_1})(\pi_2^{x_2}) \cdots (\pi_k^{x_k})$$

where $n = n_1 + n_2 + n_3 + \cdots + n_k$

Suppose we know that 10 blood donors will be giving blood in the next hour. The probability of giving type O is 0.50, of type A is 0.20, of type AB is 0.15, and of type B is 0.15. What is the probability the $n = 10$ donors will be made up of $n_1 = 5$ of type O, $n_2 = 3$ of type A, $n_3 = 2$ of type AB, and $n_4 = 0$ of type B?

## Glossary

**Bernoulli trials:** Repeated trials that are identical and independent of each other and can have one of two outcomes.

**binomial parameters:** The number of trials, $n$, and the probability of success on each trial, $\pi$, are the parameters of the binomial distribution.

**binomial probability mass function:** A discrete probability formerly based on repeated, identical, and independent trials. Each trial can have one of two outcomes, and the probability of success remains constant from trial to trial.

**factorial:** The product of a series of declining whole numbers.

**hypergeometric probability mass function:** A discrete probability formula based on sampling from a finite population without replacement. Each trial can have one of two outcomes, and the probability of success changes from trial to trial.

**Poisson distribution:** Used to determine the probability that there will be $x$ occurrences of some event.

**Poisson probability mass function:** A discrete probability formula based on sampling in which the number of possible occurrences is large relative to the usual number of actual occurrences observed.

**trial:** An event or occurrence in which the outcome is determined by chance. (The trials discussed in this chapter can have one of two outcomes.)

## Formulas

**5.1—Binomial Mass Function**

$$P(x) = \frac{n!}{x!(n - x)!} \, \pi^x(1 - \pi)^{n-x}$$

where $n$ Factorial ($n!$)

$$n! = (n)(n - 1)(n - 2) \ldots (1)$$

**5.2—Binomial Mean ($\mu$) and Variance ($\sigma^2$)**

$$\mu = n\pi \qquad \sigma^2 = n(\pi)(1 - \pi)$$

**5.3—Hypergeometric Mass Function**

$$P(x_1 \text{ successes and } x_2 \text{ succeses}) = \frac{\dfrac{N_1!}{x_1!(N_1 - x_1)!} \dfrac{N_2!}{x_2!(N_2 - x_2)!}}{\dfrac{N!}{n!(N - n)!}}$$

### 5.4—Hypergeometric Mean

$$\mu_1 = \frac{nN_1}{N}$$

### 5.5—Poisson Mass Function

$$P(x) = \frac{e^{-\lambda}\lambda^x}{x!} \quad \text{for } x = 0, 1, 2, 3, \ldots, \text{ and } \lambda > 0$$

$$P(x) = 0 \quad \text{otherwise,}$$

where $e = 2.71828$, and $\lambda$ is the mean and variance.

# CHAPTER SIX

*In graphing the data they fell,*
*In line with a swoop and a swell.*
*Experimentally normal,*
*Their pattern was formal,*
*Their shape emulating a bell.*
Robert Lamborn

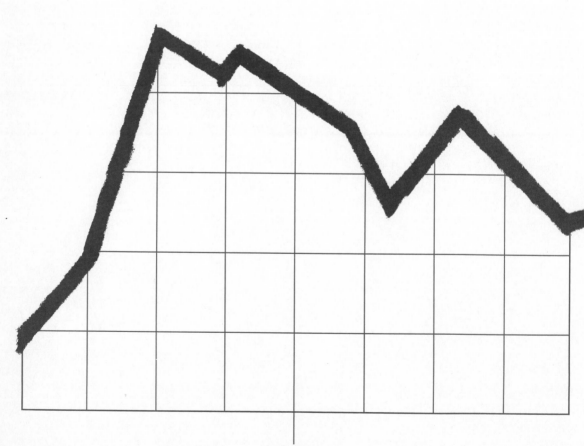

# CONTINUOUS PROBABILITY DISTRIBUTIONS

# 6.1 INTRODUCTION

Many business and economic problems involve measurements of time, weight, distance, or other infinitely divisible quantities. The solution of these problems typically involves probability statements. For example:

- In a dispute with the union steward, a production manager may wish to know the probability that a worker will be observed taking at least 3.5 minutes to complete a task if a time study report says that the task should be finished in an average of 2.1 minutes.

- A transportation authority is concerned that the average speed of trucks may exceed the 55 mph speed limit, since a random sample of 100 trucks shows a mean speed of 60.9 mph. The authority asks, "What is the probability of observing 60.9 mph if the true average speed is 55 mph?"

- On average, a car rental agency sells its cars when they are 1.08 years old, with 38,000 miles on the odometer. The sales director has decided to write the warranty given to the new owners, so that only 1% of the cars sold qualify for major warranty work. If major repairs are not expected until after 60,000 miles, what is the desired warranty length (in miles)?

- In Leading Edge personal computer ads, a competitor's PC is implied to have disk drives with a mean time between failure (MTBF) of only 8000 hours. A purchasing agent knows that the 17 PC's that his firm owns have an average time between failure of 9678 hours. The agent wants to know whether Leading Edge's claim relative to these PC's is reasonable.

These examples illustrate business problems that involve sampling and probability calculations on continuous random variables. This chapter describes probability calculations with continuous random variables. These calculations require the use of probability density functions (p.d.f.).

By the end of this chapter you will be able to state when the use of a p.d.f. is appropriate. In doing probability calculations you will learn to distinguish between samples with one observation and samples with more than one observation. You will also be able to make probability calculations with two p.d.f.'s (the "z" and the "t") and to recognize the conditions required for the use of each.

## Toro's Snow Thrower Rebate Program

You are the owner of a small lawn and garden service in Minneapolis. You are going to buy a new snow thrower and wish to assess the chance of receiving a complete purchase price rebate from the Toro Company. Toro's advertisements state that the company will refund the entire price of a machine if this winter's snowfall is less than 20% of the local average snowfall. The weather service reports that the average snowfall in your area is 46.0 inches, with a standard deviation of 15.2 inches. How likely is it that less than 9.2 inches of snow will fall this coming winter?

# 6.2 Continuous Random Variables

For most purposes, we can define as continuous any variable whose values do *not* have to be integers. Values that a **continuous random variable** can take are (at least theoretically) infinitely divisible. Thus, since time can be expressed as a decimal (e.g., 3.5 seconds or 4.85 minutes), it can be treated as continuous. We may also treat income as continuous because monetary units do not have to be integer values (e.g., $3.50 is possible, as is $0.15). Similarly, in the Toro case, we will consider snowfall as a continuous random variable because snowfall can be measured in any fractional unit from zero inches to several feet.

| | |
|---|---|
| **DEFINITION**<br>**Continuous**<br>**Random Variable** | A continuous random variable is a variable that can take any value within an interval. |

Because there is an infinite number of values that a continuous random variable can assume within an interval, the probability of any one of these values occurring can be considered to be zero. Thus, for a continuous random variable, we are not interested in the probability of a single value. We are interested in the probability that a range of values will occur. For a continuous random variable $x$, the probability that $x$ has a value between $a$ and $b$ is written as $P(a < x < b)$. This probability is equal to $P(a \leq x \leq b)$, since the probability at a point is considered to be zero; that is, $P(x = a) = 0$ and $P(x = b) = 0$.

---

**RULE**
**Probability**

For a continuous random variable, probability is calculated over an interval, never at a point. Thus

$$P(x < a) = P(x \leq a), \ P(x > a) = P(x \geq a)$$
$$\text{and } P(a < x < b) = P(a \leq x \leq b)$$

---

Graphs are usually the most convenient method for describing a continuous random variable and associated probabilities. The curve that describes the probability associated with the range of values that a continuous random variable can assume is called a **probability density function (p.d.f.)**. The area under the density function curve is the probability that any range of values will occur.

---

**DEFINITION**
**p.d.f.**

A probability density function (p.d.f.) for a continuous random variable is a curve that shows the probability of a range of values as the area under the curve.

---

For instance, in Fig. 6.1 three different density functions are shown. In each of these situations the probability of an $x$ value between $a$ and $b$ is the shaded area.

In the Toro case we want the probability that less than 9.2 inches of snow will fall this winter. Defining $x$ as inches of snowfall, we can now write this

Figure 6.1
Three p.d.f.'s where
area equals
probability.

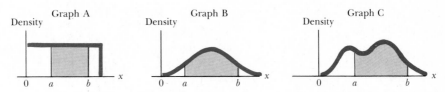

Note: For a continous random variable $x$, $P(a < x < b)$ is the shaded area under the density function in all three graphs.

Figure 6.2
Probability of less
than 9.2 inches of
snowfall.

Note: Because the area under the curve = probability, the shaded area is $P(0 < x < 9.2)$ in all three graphs.

probability as $P(0 < x < 9.2)$. Because snowfall can be treated as a continuous random variable, at least between zero and positive infinity, to calculate this probability we must find the area under the density function (curve) that best represents the probable occurrence of measured snowfall. For the three p.d.f.'s in Fig. 6.1, the probability of less than 9.2 inches of snowfall is shown by the shaded area in Fig. 6.2. The question is, which density function can be used to calculate the probability that less than 9.2 inches of snow will fall this coming winter?

## 6.3 The Normal Distribution

The normal distribution is the most widely used density function in statistics. This is because so many random variables have been found to be normally distributed. An early researcher, Karl Gauss (1777–1855), discovered that the measurement of errors often follows a normal distribution. Gauss's work has been extended to almost all fields; examples include measurement of the distance to the stars, sheets of metal, time standards for workers, the weight of packaged materials, the growth of plants, and even the measurement of snowfall.

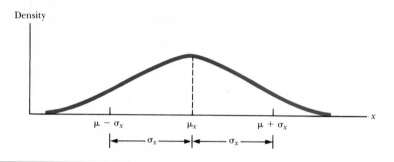

| DEFINITION | The normal p.d.f. for a random variable $x$ is a unimodal, symmetric, |
| Normal p.d.f. | and continuous probability function that has the shape of a bell. It has |
| | a mean of $\mu_x$ and a standard deviation of $\sigma_x$. |

All normal distributions have the distinctive bell shape shown previously, but not all bell-shaped density functions are normal. All the information necessary for describing a normal distribution is given by its mean $\mu$ and its standard deviation $\sigma$. If the variable $x$ is of interest, then we designate its mean as $\mu_x$ and its standard deviation as $\sigma_x$. If another variable $y$ is introduced, then its mean and standard deviation are designated as $\mu_y$ and $\sigma_y$, respectively. It is helpful to use such subscripts when several different variables are under study.

For any normally distributed variable, the mean represents the center of the distribution. Because the normal distribution is symmetric, the mean (and median and mode) must lie exactly in the middle of the density function. Figure 6.3 shows three different normal p.d.f.'s, each having a different mean.

For any normal distribution, the standard deviation indicates variability. Figure 6.4 shows three different normal density functions with the same mean of 0 but different standard deviations. Notice that as the size of a standard deviation increases from $\sigma_w = 2$ to $\sigma_v = 4$ to $\sigma_u = 6$, the area within one

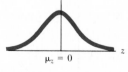
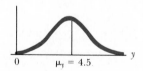

**Figure 6.3** Three different normal distributions (with means $\mu_z$, $\mu_y$, and $\mu_x$).

Chapter 6  Continuous Probability Distributions

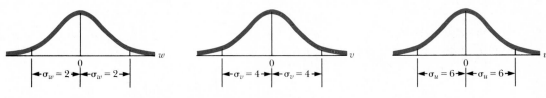

**Figure 6.4** Three different normal distributions (with standard deviations $\sigma_w$, $\sigma_v$, and $\sigma_u$).

standard deviation of the mean remains fixed; only the horizontal scaling changes.

Recall from Chapter 3 that the mean and the standard deviation of a symmetric unimodal distribution can be used to derive approximate probabilities for a probability distribution. The rule of thumb presented can be shown to be based on the normal distribution. In particular, we can state the following:

> Approximately 68% of the area (probability) under the normal curve falls between $\mu_x - 1\sigma_x$ and $\mu_x + 1\sigma_x$.
>
> Approximately 95% of the area (probability) under the normal curve falls between $\mu_x - 2\sigma_x$ and $\mu_x + 2\sigma_x$.
>
> Approximately 100% of the area (probability) under the normal curve falls between $\mu_x - 3\sigma_x$ and $\mu_x + 3\sigma_x$.

To use this rule of thumb in the Toro case, we must establish that assuming a normal distribution of snowfall is not unreasonable. Because snowfall does not have to be measured in integers, it may be treated as a continuous variable. The fact that normal distributions are defined down to a negative infinity, while snowfall cannot be less than zero, does not bother us here because the snowfall levels under consideration are not near zero [i.e., $P(x < 9.2) = P(0 < x < 9.2)$]. Finally, it seems reasonable that yearly snowfall will vary symmetrically around its mean. Thus, for our purposes it may be appropriate to assume that the underlying distribution of snowfall $(x)$ is a normal density function. Note that these steps do not *prove* that snowfall is normally distributed, but only that this assumption is reasonable.

From the rule of thumb, we know that if snowfall is normally distributed and if $\mu_x = 46.0$ inches with $\sigma_x = 15.2$ inches (as stated in the Toro case study), then approximately 95% of the yearly snowfall will be between $\mu_x$ plus or minus two standard deviations. That is,

$$\mu_x \pm 2\sigma_x = 46.0 \pm 2(15.2) = 15.6 \text{ to } 76.4 \text{ inches}$$

Thus we expect snowfall between 15.6 and 76.4 inches 95% of the time.

**Figure 6.5**
The normal
distribution for yearly
snowfall in
Minneapolis.

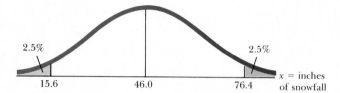

If 5% of the time snowfall is *not* between 15.6 and 76.4 inches, then we expect snowfall to be less than 15.6 inches 2.5% of the time. This is because the normal distribution is symmetric, and any area not contained in $\mu_x \pm 2\sigma_x$ must be equally divided between the upper and lower tails of the distribution. As Fig. 6.5 indicates, the probability that any given winter will have a snowfall of less than 15.6 inches is approximately 0.025.

Because the rule of thumb does not provide information about probabilities other than those involving $\mu \pm 1\sigma_x$, $\mu \pm 2\sigma_x$, or $\mu \pm 3\sigma_x$, we still cannot obtain the probability of concern, that of less than 9.2 inches of snowfall. All we know now is that this probability is less than 0.025 (because 9.2 is less than 15.6 inches).

---

**WORKED EXAMPLE
6.1**

General Electric (GE) makes 40-watt fluorescent lights that are guaranteed for 3 years. It is known that the life of these lights follows a normal distribution, with a mean of $\mu_x = 4.20$ years and a standard deviation of $\sigma_x = 0.60$ years. Determine the approximate probability that a light will last (1) more than 4.2 years, (2) between 3 and 4.2 years, and (3) less than 3 years. Sketch this p.d.f.

**ANSWER:**

1. Since the normal distribution is symmetric, 50% of the distribution lies on either side of $\mu_x$. Thus the proportion of GE lights that last more than $\mu_x = 4.2$ years is 0.50 (see Fig. 6.6).

2. The time interval between plus and minus two standard deviations is

$$\mu_x \pm 2\sigma_x = 4.2 \pm 2(0.6) \quad \text{or} \quad [3.0 \text{ to } 5.4 \text{ years}]$$

From the rule of thumb, the probability that a light lasts between 3 and 5.4 years is approximately 0.95. The approximate probability that it lasts for 3.0 to 4.2 years is one-half of this value, or 0.475 (Fig. 6.6).

3. Because the approximate probability is 0.50 that a light lasts less than the mean (of 4.2 years), the approximate probability that it lasts between

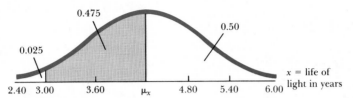

Note: 0.475 represents one-half of the probability in the second rule
of thumb [0.95].

3 and 4.2 years is 0.475. The approximate probability that it does not last
for 3 years is $0.500 - 0.475 = 0.025$ (Fig. 6.6).

## 6.4 Probability Calculations with the Standard Normal Table

In the Toro snow thrower case, we need to know the probability that this
winter's snowfall is less than a value that is not exactly one, two, or three
standard deviations away from the mean. In fact, the $x$ value of 9.2 inches
will be shown to be 2.42 standard deviations below the mean of $\mu_x = 46$
inches. To solve problems such as $P(x < 9.2)$, we use a probability distribution
that is formed by the **standard normal density function**.

The distance from any $x$ value to $\mu_x$, measured in standard deviations, is
denoted by the letter $z$. Values of $z$ are called *standard normal values* and
are calculated by using Eq. (6.1).

Standard normal value

**(6.1)**
$$z = \frac{x - \mu_x}{\sigma_x}$$

If the random variable $x$ is normally distributed, and if the infinite values
of $x$ are transformed using Eq. (6.1), the result is a new normal p.d.f. The
random variable for this new p.d.f. is denoted by the letter $z$ and the area
under this p.d.f. is called the **standard normal distribution**. All standard

**Figure 6.7**
The standard normal
density function ($z$).

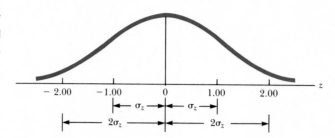

normal distributions are exactly as shown in Fig. 6.7, that is, the distribution (the random variable $z$) always has a mean of 0 ($\mu_z = 0$) and a standard deviation of 1.0 ($\sigma_z = 1.0$).

In solving a problem such as $P(x < 9.2)$ we transform (using Eq. 6.1) this problem into an equivalent problem using the standard normal distribution. The advantage of the standard normal distribution is that tables of cumulative values for $z$ are readily available. Appendix Table B.4 is one such table. Before demonstrating the use of Table B.4, let us transform the value $x = 9.2$ into its comparable $z$ value.

$$z = \frac{x - \mu_x}{\sigma_x} = \frac{9.2 - 46}{15.2} = -2.42$$

The value $z = -2.42$ shows that $x = 9.2$ is 2.42 standard deviations below the mean of $\mu_x = 46$ when $\sigma_x = 15.2$. The comparability between $x = 9.2$ and $z = -2.42$ is shown in Fig. 6.8.

In Fig. 6.8, the $z$ value of $-2.42$ is the same distance away from its mean (of 0) as the $x$ value of 9.2 inches is away from its mean (of 46.0 inches). Since both $x$ and $z$ are normal, the probability of being below 9.2 on the $x$ scale is identical to that of being below $-2.42$ on the $z$ scale. Thus we can write

$$P(x < 9.2) = P(z < -2.42)$$

The probability $P(z < -2.42)$ is a *cumulative probability*. Cumulative probabilities for $z$ are presented in Appendix Table B.4.

## Probability Calculations with Appendix Table B.4

Since the normal distribution is symmetric, Table B.4 shows cumulative probabilities only for positive $z$ values. Before considering the negative $z$ value in our Toro case, we first illustrate the use of Table B.4 by finding the cumulative

Figure 6.8
Relationship of a
normal random
variable x to the
standard normal z.

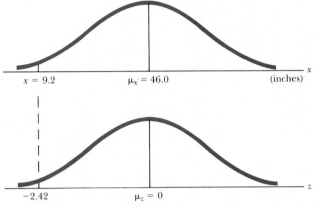

Note: The z value of −2.42 was determined from the x value 9.2 using

$$z = \frac{x - \mu_x}{\sigma_x} = \frac{9.2 - 46}{15.2} = -2.42$$

probability up to a positive $z$ value. For example, the probability of $z$ less than 1.43, $P(z < 1.43)$, is illustrated by the shaded area in Fig. 6.9.

The relevant portion of Table B.4 is shown in Table 6.1 (page 240). To find the cumulative probability for $z = 1.43$, look down the left-hand margin of the standard normal table for the first two digits in 1.43, namely, 1.4 (see step I, Table 6.1). For step II, move to the column corresponding to the third digit in 1.43, namely, the fifth column, labeled 0.03. We use 0.03 because $1.4 + 0.03 = 1.43$. The value at the intersection of 1.4 and 0.03 is 0.9236, which is the cumulative probability $P(z < 1.43)$. This cumulative probability is the shaded area in Fig. 6.9.

Figure 6.9 also illustrates the probability of a $z$ value greater than 1.43, $P(z > 1.43)$. Since the area under any p.d.f. must be 1.00, the probability $P(z > 1.43)$ is obtained by subtracting $P(z < 1.43) = 0.9236$ from 1.00.

Figure 6.9
The cumulative
probability (area)
$P(z < 1.43)$.

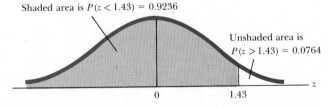

[Remember, $P(z > 1.43)$ is identical to $P(z \geq 1.43)$ because the probability of $z$ equaling a single value of 1.43 is zero.]

$$P(z > 1.43) = 1 - P(z < 1.43)$$
$$= 1 - 0.9236 = 0.0764$$

**Table 6.1**

| | | | | | Reading the Standard Normal Table | | | | | |
|---|---|---|---|---|---|---|---|---|---|---|
| Step I: To find the cumulative probability associated with any $z$ value between 1.40 and 1.49, go down the left column of Table B.4 to 1.4. | | | | | | | | | | |
| $z$ | 0.00 | 0.01 | 0.02 | 0.03 | 0.04 | 0.05 | 0.06 | 0.07 | 0.08 | 0.09 |
| 1.0 | | | | | | | | | | |
| 1.1 | | | | | | | | | | |
| 1.2 | | | | | | | | | | |
| 1.3 | | | | | | | | | | |
| 1.4 | 0.9192 | 0.9207 | 0.9222 | 0.9236 | 0.9251 | 0.9265 | 0.9279 | 0.9292 | 0.9306 | 0.9319 |
| 1.5 | | | | | | | | | | |
| . | | | | | | | | | | |
| . | | | | | | | | | | |
| . | | | | | | | | | | |
| 2.9 | | | | | | | | | | |
| 3.0 | | | | | | | | | | |
| Step II: To find the probability $P(z < 1.43)$, go across the 1.4 row to the column headed by 0.03. Find $P(z < 1.43) = 0.9236$. | | | | | | | | | | |
| $z$ | 0.00 | 0.01 | 0.02 | **0.03** | 0.04 | 0.05 | 0.06 | 0.07 | 0.08 | 0.09 |
| 1.0 | | | | | | | | | | |
| 1.1 | | | | | | | | | | |
| 1.2 | | | | | | | | | | |
| 1.3 | | | | | | | | | | |
| 1.4 | 0.9192 | 0.9207 | 0.9222 | **0.9236** | 0.9251 | 0.9265 | 0.9279 | 0.9292 | 0.9306 | 0.9319 |
| 1.5 | | | | | | | | | | |
| . | | | $P(z < 1.43)$ | | | | | | | | |
| . | | | | | | | | | | |
| 2.9 | | | | | | | | | | |
| 3.0 | | | | | | | | | | |

## Calculating Probabilities When z Is Negative

Equation 6.1 can yield negative as well as positive $z$ values. In fact, the $z$ that corresponds to a snowfall of $x = 9.2$ inches was calculated to be $-2.42$.

Cumulative probabilities for negative $z$ values are not given directly in Appendix Table B.4 but can be determined using the symmetry of the normal p.d.f. To illustrate this process, consider $P(z < -1.43)$. The first step in determining this probability is to graph the appropriate area (see step I in Fig. 6.10). Step II shows that the area to the left of $-1.43$ is exactly the same as the area to the right of $+1.43$. That is,

$$P(z < 1.43) = P(z > 1.43)$$

**Figure 6.10**
Calculating probabilities for negative $z$ values.

Step I: Shade the area being determined.

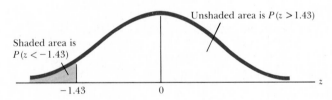

Step II: Recognize that $P(z < -1.43) = P(z > 1.43)$

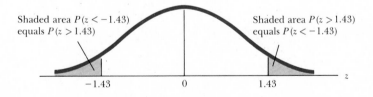

Step III: From Appendix Table B.4 find $P(z < 1.43)$.
Subtract $P(z < 1.43)$ from 1.0 to get $P(z > 1.43)$.

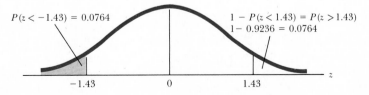

Step III in Fig. 6.10 determines the probability $P(z > 1.43)$ by using Table B.4 to find the cumulative value $P(z < 1.43)$ and then subtracting this cumulative value from 1.00.

$$P(z < -1.43) = 1 - P(z < 1.43)$$
$$= 1 - 0.9236$$
$$= 0.0764$$

We now have a procedure to determine the probability that it will snow less than 9.2 inches. If both $x$ and $z$ are normal, the probability that $x$ is less than 9.2 inches is identical to the probability that $z$ is less than $-2.42$ (go back and look at Fig. 6.8). Thus, if we determine the probability $P(z < -2.42)$, we will also have $P(x < 9.2)$. Figure 6.11 illustrates the calculations (steps) used to determine $P(x < 9.2)$.

$$P(x < 9.2) = P(z < -2.42) = 1 - P(z < 2.42)$$
$$= 1 - 0.9922 \qquad \text{(from Table B.4)}$$
$$= 0.0078$$

Because the probability of less than 9.2 inches of snowfall is only 0.0078, the 100% rebate advertised by Toro will occur less than 1% of the time (it will occur 0.78% of the time).

---

**WORKED EXAMPLE 6.2**

The 40-watt fluorescent lights in Worked Example 6.1 are guaranteed for 3 years. The life of these GE lights is known to follow a normal distribution with a mean of $\mu_x = 4.20$ years and a standard deviation of $\sigma_x = 0.60$ years. Determine the exact proportion of lights that will last for less than 3 years, $P(x < 3.0)$. Sketch this area. Why does this area differ slightly from that in Worked Example 6.1?

**ANSWER:**

First determine the value of $z$ that is comparable to $x = 3$ when the mean is $\mu_x = 4.20$ and the standard deviation is $\sigma_x = 0.60$.

$$z = \frac{x - \mu_x}{\sigma_x} = \frac{3 - 4.2}{0.60} = -2.00$$

Now we need to determine $P(z < -2.00)$. Using Appendix Table B.4,

$$P(z < -2.00) = 1 - P(z < 2.00)$$
$$= 1 - 0.9772 = 0.0228$$

**Figure 6.11**
Calculating probabilities in the Toro snow thrower case.

Step I: Shade the area being determined.

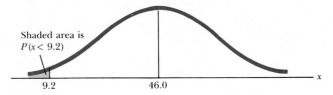

Shaded area is $P(x < 9.2)$

9.2    46.0    x

Step II: Transform the $x$ value to a $z$ value, via Formula 6.1. and shade the desired area.

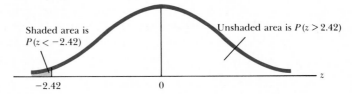

Shaded area is $P(z < -2.42)$

Unshaded area is $P(z > 2.42)$

$-2.42$    0    z

Step III: Recognize that $P(z < -2.42) = P(z > 2.42)$. Use Table B.4 to determine $P(z > 2.42) = 1 - P(z < 2.42) = 1 - 0.9922$

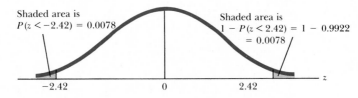

Shaded area is $P(z < -2.42) = 0.0078$

Shaded area is $1 - P(z < 2.42) = 1 - 0.9922 = 0.0078$

$-2.42$    0    2.42    z

Step IV: Solve the original problem, using Step III results.

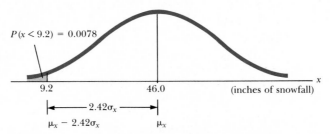

$P(x < 9.2) = 0.0078$

9.2    46.0    (inches of snowfall)    x

$2.42\sigma_x$

$\mu_x - 2.42\sigma_x$    $\mu_x$

Note: 9.2 inches is 2.42 standard deviations below the mean of 46 inches. From the $z$ distribution we find that the probability of being more than 2.42 standard deviations below the mean is 0.0078.

Figure 6.12
GE fluorescent lights.

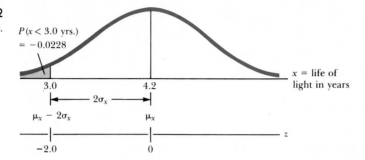

This result shows that 2.28% of GE's fluorescent lights will last for less than 3 years. This area is represented in Fig. 6.12. In Worked Example 6.1 we *approximated* the proportion of lights that would not last 3 years to be 0.025 (using the rule of thumb). Now we know that the exact proportion is 0.0228.

In many probability problems the area of interest involves two $z$ values on opposite sides (or the same side) of the mean. For example, suppose we want to determine the probability

$$P(-1.65 < z < 1.96)$$

This probability is shown as the shaded area in Fig. 6.13. The easiest way to handle this type of problem is to break it into two separate cumulative problems, namely, $P(z < 1.96)$ and $P(z < -1.65)$. If $P(z < -1.65)$ is subtracted from $P(z < 1.96)$, the resulting area is the probability that $z$ falls *between* $-1.65$ and $1.96$. This probability is determined by the following calculation and illustrated by the shaded area in Fig. 6.14.

$$P(z < 1.96) = 0.9750 \quad \text{(using Table B.4)}$$

$$P(z < -1.65) = 1 - 0.9505 = 0.0495 \quad \text{(using Table B.4 and the steps outlined in Fig. 6.10)}$$

$$P(-1.65 < z < 1.96) = P(z < 1.96) - P(z < -1.65)$$
$$= 0.9750 - 0.0495 = 0.9255$$

Figure 6.13
Area between $-1.65$
and $+1.96$.

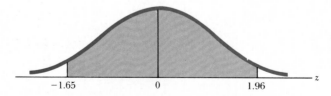

Chapter 6   Continuous Probability Distributions

Figure 6.14
Determining
$P(-1.65 < x < 1.96)$.

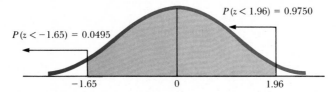

$P(z < -1.65) = 0.0495$

$P(z < 1.96) = 0.9750$

$-1.65$      $0$      $1.96$

Note: Shaded area is $P(-1.65 < x < 1.96) = 0.9255$

**WORKED EXAMPLE 6.3**

A time study report indicates that an assembly line task should be finished in an average of 2.10 minutes, with a standard deviation of 0.50 minute. What is the probability that an employee will take between 1.50 and 3.00 minutes? Sketch the area being determined. (Assume that the completion time is normally distributed.)

**ANSWER:**

When $x = 3.0$,

$$z = \frac{x - \mu_x}{\sigma_x} = \frac{3.0 - 2.1}{0.50} = 1.80$$

Similarly, when $x = 1.5$,

$$z = \frac{x - \mu_x}{\sigma_x} = \frac{1.5 - 2.1}{0.50} = -1.20$$

The probability we want to determine is thus

$$P(1.50 < x < 3.00) = P(-1.20 < z < 1.80)$$

This area is sketched in Fig. 6.15.

From Appendix Table B.4,

$$P(z < 1.80) = 0.9641$$

**Figure 6.15**
The area
$P(1.50 < x < 3.00) = P(-1.20 < z < 1.80)$.

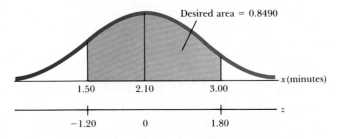

Desired area = 0.8490

$1.50$    $2.10$    $3.00$    $x$ (minutes)

$-1.20$    $0$    $1.80$    $z$

and

$$P(z < -1.20) = 1 - P(z < 1.20) = 1 - 0.8849 = 0.1151$$

Thus

$$P(-1.20 < z < 1.80) = P(z < 1.80) - P(z < -1.20)$$
$$= 0.9641 - 0.1151 = 0.8490$$

This result shows that 84.90% of the people who attempt this task are expected to take between 1.50 and 3.00 minutes to complete it.

---

**WORKED EXAMPLE 6.4**

Use the time study data in Worked Example 6.3 to find the probability that an employee will take between 2.50 and 3.50 minutes to finish the assembly line task. Sketch the area being determined.

**ANSWER:**

When $x = 3.5$,

$$z = \frac{x - \mu_x}{\sigma_x} = \frac{3.5 - 2.1}{0.50} = 2.80$$

Similarly, when $x = 2.5$,

$$z = \frac{x - \mu_x}{\sigma_x} = \frac{2.5 - 2.1}{0.50} = 0.80$$

Thus the probability we want to determine is

$$P(2.50 < x < 3.50) = P(0.80 < z < 2.80)$$

This area is sketched in Fig. 6.16.

From Appendix Table B.4,

$$P(z < 2.80) = 0.9974$$

**Figure 6.16**
The area
$P(2.50 < x < 3.50) =$
$P(0.80 < z < 2.80)$.

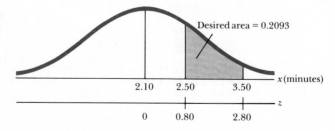

and

$$P(z < 0.80) = 0.7881$$

Thus

$$P(0.80 < z < 2.80) = P(z < 2.80) - P(z < 0.80)$$
$$= 0.9974 - 0.7881 = 0.2093$$

This result shows that 20.93% of the employees who attempt this task are expected to take between 2.50 and 3.50 minutes to complete it.

## Calculating *x* Values for a Stated Probability

The problems we have had so far have involved determining a probability when an $x$ value is given. Some probability problems, such as the following food stamps case, involve the reverse process—determining an $x$ value when a probability has already been given.

## Food Stamps

You are the director of an experimental regional welfare agency that is to provide food stamps to the needy in a new manner. Your experimental agency will provide food stamps only to those households whose income falls in the lowest 10% of all incomes in your region. Economic data for your region indicate that household incomes have a mean of $\mu_x = \$19{,}250$, with a standard deviation of $\sigma_x = \$5100$. Although most income distributions are highly skewed, your region's income distribution is approximately normal. For what income levels should your agency give out food stamps?

The process of determining $x$ values follows the same pattern used in the past section. Now, however, we want to solve for an $x$ value in Eq. (6.1) rather than for a $z$ value. Suppose we let the letter $b$ represent the particular $x$ value we are trying to find. Our modified Eq. (6.1) is now Eq. (6.2):

Formula for finding $b$ when $z$ is known

(6.2)   $$z = \frac{b - \mu_x}{\sigma_x}$$

The first step in using Eq. (6.2) is to find the appropriate value of $z$. Figure 6.17 shows the $x$ and $z$ values for the food stamp problem. To find the value of $z = -?$ in Fig. 6.17, we must first recognize that this $z$ value is negative, and negative values are not found in Appendix Table B.4.

Using the symmetry property of the normal distribution, a negative $z$ value can be found by locating its absolute or mirror value on the positive side of the $z$ distribution. The comparable positive $z$ value in Fig. 6.17 (denoted by $z = +?$) cuts off 10% of the *upper* tail of the normal distribution. This $z$ value in Table B.4 is found by searching the body of the table for a cumulative probability of 0.90. None of the probabilities in Table B.4 cuts off exactly 0.90; hence, we look for the closest probability. The closest probability is 0.8997, which corresponds to $z = 1.28$. The $z$ value for Eq. (6.2) is the negative of this number, or $z = -1.28$. (Note that $z = -1.28$ indicates that $b$ is to the left of $\mu_x = \$19,250$.) The mean and standard deviation of incomes were given in the problem as $\mu_x = \$19,250$ and $\sigma_x = \$5100$, respectively. Substituting these values into Eq. (6.2) yields

$$-1.28 = \frac{b - 19,250}{5100}$$

or

$$b = -1.28(5100) + 19,250 = 12,722$$

This results shows that food stamps should be given only to households with incomes less than $12,722.

**Figure 6.17**
Calculating $b$ when the probability is given.

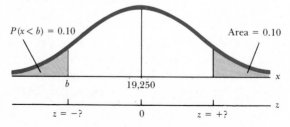

*Summary:* Probabilities associated with any normal random variable $x$ can always be found in Appendix Table B.4 by converting the $x$ value of interest into its corresponding standard normal $z$ value. Cumulative probabilities associated with positive $z$ values are read directly from Table B.4. If the calculated $z$ value is negative, the probability is determined by taking the complement of the cumulative $z$ value using the same $z$ value with a positive sign. The formula for standardizing an $x$ value is

$$z = \frac{x - \mu_x}{\sigma_x}$$

where

$x$ = the value of the random variable of interest,
$\mu_x$ = the mean of the $x$ variable,
$\sigma_x$ = the standard deviation of the $x$ variable,
$z$ = the number of standard deviations between $x$ and $\mu_x$.

When the problem calls for finding a value $(b)$ of the random variable $x$ that cuts off a given area (probability), the formula is:

$$z = \frac{b - \mu_x}{\sigma_x}.$$

## Exercises

**6.1** Indicate whether each of the following random variables is continuous or discrete.

a) The time it takes a mechanic to service a machine.

b) The number of new housing starts in the United States this month.

c) The age of an applicant for an assembly line position.

d) The sex of a new company vice president.

**6.2** List the important features and characteristics of a normal probability distribution. Sketch the normal p.d.f. distribution with a mean of 50 and a standard deviation of 12.

**6.3** Draw two graphs to show the differences and similarities between the standard normal probability distribution and all other normal distributions.

**6.4** Determine the extent to which each of the three statements in the rule of thumb differs from the exact probability based on the normal distribution.

**6.5** The random variable $z$ is normally distributed with a mean of $\mu_z = 0$ and a standard deviation of $\sigma_z = 1$. Find the following probabilities:

a) $P(z < 1.63) =$ _____

b) $P(z > -2.34) =$ _____

c) $P(z > 3.02) =$ _____

d) $P(z < -1.03) =$ _____

e) $P(1.02 < z < 2.01) =$ _____

f) $P(-2.31 < z < 1.37) =$ _____

**6.6** The random variable $z$ is normally distributed with $\mu_z = 0$ and $\sigma_z = 1$. Find the following values of $b$:

a) $P(z < b) = 0.9370$

b) $P(z > b) = 0.9929$

c) $P(z > b) = 0.0089$

d) $P(z < b) = 0.0170$

e) $P(-b < z < b) = 0.6680$

f) $P(0 < z < b) = 0.1950$

**6.7** A random variable $x$ is normally distributed with a mean of $\mu_x = 6$ and a standard deviation of $\sigma_x = 3$. Find the following probabilities:

a) $P(x < 7.50) =$ _____

b) $P(x > -1.00) =$ _____

c) $P(x > 8.43) =$ _____

d) $P(x < 1.00) =$ _____

e) $P(2.00 < x < 7.00) =$ _____

f) $P(-3.00 < x < 0) =$ _____

**6.8** The random variable $y$ is normally distributed with $\mu_y = 30.00$ and $\sigma_y = 10.00$. Find the following values of $b$:

a) $P(y < b) = 0.9846$

b) $P(y > b) = 0.9099$

c) $P(y > b) = 0.0110$

d) $P(y < b) = 0.4300$

e) $P(b < y < 30) = 0.0320$

f) $P(b < y < 30) = 0.4901$

OPS **6.9** A purchasing agent specifies that she can only accept number 8 bolts that exceed 2 inches. Your automatic bolt cutter can be set for mean length with a standard deviation of 0.001 inch. At what mean setting should your bolt cutter be set so that only 5% of the bolts are less than 2 inches in length? (Assume that bolt length is normally distributed.)

ADM **6.10** A personnel manager claims to have just hired someone with an IQ in the top 1% of all recent business school graduates. The relevant distribution of IQ's is known to be normal, with a mean of 120 points and a standard deviation of 10 points. What is the lowest IQ this person could have and still be in the top 1%?

FIN  **6.11**  A bank has completed a census of the interest rates charged for new residential mortgages in Chicago during a five-year period. The rates are normally distributed with a mean of 13.3% and a standard deviation of 1.8. What is the probability that a person selected at random from this population will have

a) paid more than 15%?

b) paid less than 10%?

c) paid between 12 and 14%?

ADM  **6.12**  According to a recent report, the average cost of operating a company car is 25 cents per mile, with a standard deviation of 3 cents per mile. If this cost is normally distributed, what is the probability of randomly drawing an employee whose cost per mile is less than 20 cents?

FIN  **6.13**  It is known that the average time required to process invoices for the Baldwin Company is 7 days, with a standard deviation of 1.3 days. If processing time is normally distributed, what proportion of invoices is processed between 5 and 11 days?

# 6.5  The Normal Sampling Distribution of $\bar{x}$

In the Toro snow thrower case our interest was in the snowfall in *one* randomly selected winter. For the GE example we focused on the life of *one* randomly drawn light. That is, we calculated probabilities for a sample of size $n = 1$. Now we extend our analysis to samples of any size. We first concentrate on large samples (that is, samples of more than 30 observations, $n > 30$) drawn from extremely large (or infinite) populations.

Samples almost always include more than one observation. For example, in sampling GE fluorescent lights you might decide on a sample of $n = 70$. You are told (and are willing to believe) that the population mean life of all such lights is $\mu = 4.20$ years, with a standard deviation of $\sigma_x = 0.60$. You know, however, that because of sampling error the mean life of your single sample of 70 lights may not equal exactly 4.20. The randomness inherent in sampling implies that for any given sample the $\bar{x}$ value may be above or below the actual population mean, where

$$\bar{x} = \sum_{i=1}^{n} x_i/n$$

But how large a sampling error can you expect? That is, how far away might the sample's $\bar{x}$ value be from 4.20 merely because of sampling error? To answer this question we need to look at all the values of $\bar{x}$ that could occur if many samples of size $n = 70$ were drawn.

Imagine that a great many people (actually, we want an infinite number) have each decided to sample $n = 70$ GE 40-watt fluorescent lights. Each of these people takes a random sample from the GE fluorescent light assembly line. The population is all the lights that could be produced on this assembly line, where the mean life of a light is $\mu_x = 4.20$ years and the standard deviation is $\sigma_x = 0.60$. All of the people who draw one sample from this population calculate the $\bar{x}$ value for their sample of size 70. Each person then reports his or her value of $\bar{x}$ to you, and you use these values to construct a relative frequency distribution.

If there were an infinite number of people reporting $\bar{x}$ values to you, your relative frequency distribution would really be a probability distribution because it would contain all possible values of $\bar{x}$. This probability distribution is called the **sampling distribution of $\bar{x}$**.

---

**DEFINITION**
**Sampling Distribution of $\bar{x}$**

The sampling distribution of $\bar{x}$ is the probability distribution of all possible sample means.

---

In working with the sampling distribution of $\bar{x}$, three characteristics of the probability distribution are most important—the mean, the standard deviation, and the shape. Each characteristic will now be discussed.

## The Mean of the Sampling Distribution of $\bar{x}$

The expected value or mean of the sampling distribution of $\bar{x}$ equals the mean of the population from which the samples are drawn. Letting $\mu_{\bar{x}}$ denote the mean of the sampling distribution of $\bar{x}$, this expected value is written as

$$E(\bar{x}) = \mu_{\bar{x}} = \mu_x$$

**EXAMPLE** The mean life of all fluorescent lights produced at GE was given as 4.20 years. Thus, if the overall mean of all the possible sample means were calculated, it would also be 4.20 years. The sampling distri-

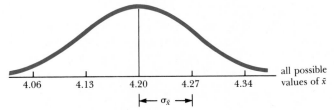

Figure 6.18
Sampling distribution
of $\bar{x}$ for GE lights.

all possible
values of $\bar{x}$

$\longleftarrow \sigma_{\bar{x}} \longrightarrow$

Note: This sampling distribution of $\bar{x}$ was obtained by assuming that an
infinite number of samples, each of size $n = 70$, could be drawn
from a population where $\mu_x = 4.20$ and $\sigma_x = 0.60$. Thus, $\mu_{\bar{x}} =$
4.2 and $\sigma_{\bar{x}} = \sigma_x/\sqrt{n} = 0.60/\sqrt{70} = 0.07$.

bution of $\bar{x}$ for this example is shown in Fig. 6.18. The standard deviation
of this distribution, denoted by $\sigma_{\bar{x}}$, is discussed in the next section.

## The Standard Deviation of the Sampling Distribution of $\bar{x}$

When samples are drawn from a large (infinite) population, the standard
deviation of the sampling distribution of $\bar{x}$ equals the standard deviation of
the population ($\sigma_x$) divided by the square root of the sample size. That is,

$$\sigma_{\bar{x}} = \sigma_x/\sqrt{n}$$

Note the result of this formula when $n = 1$ and $n = \infty$.

When $n = 1$, $\sigma_{\bar{x}} = \sigma_x$

When $n = \infty$, $\sigma_{\bar{x}} = 0$

When $n = 1$ the single observation in each sample is also the mean of
that sample—that is, $\bar{x} = x$. In other words, if $n = 1$ the distribution of $\bar{x}$ is
identical to the original distribution (of $x$), so $\sigma_{\bar{x}} = \sigma_x$. When $n = \infty$, each
sample consists of an infinite number of observations, which would include
all items in the population. In this case, all the sample means would be equal
to one another, and there would be no variability among them. Hence,
$\sigma_{\bar{x}} = 0$.

For all practical problems, the sample size is typically greater than one
and certainly less than infinity. An understanding of these extremes, however,
will help you in working with the $\bar{x}$ distribution.

**EXAMPLE** The standard deviation of the population of GE fluorescent
lights is $\sigma_x = 0.60$ years. Dividing 0.60 by the square root of the sample
size, $n = 70$, yields $\sigma_{\bar{x}} = 0.6/\sqrt{70} = 0.6/8.367 = 0.07$, which is the

standard deviation of the $\bar{x}$ sampling distribution shown in Fig. 6.18. (Note: If the sample size had been larger than 70, the standard deviation of the $\bar{x}$ distribution would be smaller than 0.07. Conversely, if $n$ is smaller than 70, $\sigma_{\bar{x}}$ would be larger.)

## The Shape of the Sampling Distribution of $\bar{x}$

The shape of the sampling distribution of $\bar{x}$ will be normal when either (1) the population of all $x$ values is normal or (2) the sample size is fairly large (usually $n > 30$ is sufficient). If neither criterion (1) nor (2) is met, the shape of the sampling distribution of $\bar{x}$ is not easily determined.

Part (1) of this statement says that when sampling from a population that is normally distributed, the shape of the sampling distribution of $\bar{x}$ will always be normally distributed as well. Part (2) of this statement is associated with the most important theorem in statistics, namely, the **central limit theorem**.

---

**DEFINITION**
**Central Limit Theorem**

The central limit theorem states that the shape of the sampling distribution of $\bar{x}$ approaches a normal p.d.f. as $n$ becomes larger.

---

In the GE light example, the sampling distribution of $\bar{x}$ as shown in Fig. 6.18 is normal because the central limit theorem implies that for a relatively large sample size ($n = 70 > 30$), the $\bar{x}$ distribution can be considered to be normal.

Whenever the sampling distribution of $\bar{x}$ can be accepted as being normal and the population's standard deviation is known, the formula for "standardizing $\bar{x}$" is as follows:

---

The $z$ formula for standardizing $\bar{x}$ is

(6.3)
$$z = \frac{\bar{x} - \mu_{\bar{x}}}{\sigma_{\bar{x}}} \quad \text{or equivalently} \quad z = \frac{\bar{x} - \mu_x}{\sigma_x / \sqrt{n}}$$

---

Chapter 6   Continuous Probability Distributions

It is important to note that the $z$ formula for standardizing $x$ (Eq. 6.1) is a special case of the more general $z$ formula for standardizing $\bar{x}$ (Eq. 6.3). That is, when $n = 1$, then either formula can be used. This equivalence is as follows:

$$z = \frac{\bar{x} - \mu_{\bar{x}}}{\sigma_{\bar{x}}} = \frac{\bar{x} - \mu_x}{\sigma_x / \sqrt{n}} = \frac{\bar{x} - \mu_x}{\sigma_x / \sqrt{1}} = \frac{x - \mu_x}{\sigma_x}$$

$\uparrow$ $\uparrow$

If $n = 1$, then the mean of the sample is the value of the one observation drawn, that is, $x = \bar{x}$.

*Summary*: The sampling distribution of $\bar{x}$ is always normally distributed (regardless of sample size) *if* the population is normally distributed. Even when the actual distribution of the population is unknown, the sampling distribution of $\bar{x}$ is close to being normally distributed *if* the sample size is large ($n > 30$). To use the standard normal distribution (Appendix Table B.4) to find the probabilities involving $\bar{x}$ values, the population mean, standard deviation, and sample size must be known, and either the population of $x$ values must be normal or the sample size must be large ($n > 30$).

# 6.6 Probability Calculations for the Sampling Distribution of $\bar{x}$

## Highway Truck Speeds

You are the director of transportation safety for the state. You are concerned because the average highway speed of all trucks may exceed the 55 mph speed limit. A random sample of 100 trucks shows a mean speed of 60.9 mph. At this point, you need to know the probability of observing a sample average speed of 60.9 mph if the population's average speed is 55 mph. The population's standard deviation is 5.5 mph.

The first thing to note in this case is that we are interested in the results from a large sample, $n = 100$. Even if the population (all possible truck speeds) from which these 100 observations are drawn is not normal, from the central limit theorem we know that the $\bar{x}$ distribution is normal because $n$ is large. That is, $z$ in the following "standardizing equation" has a normal p.d.f.

$$z = \frac{\bar{x} - \mu_{\bar{x}}}{\sigma_{\bar{x}}} = \frac{\bar{x} - \mu_x}{\sigma_x/\sqrt{n}}$$

From the $\bar{x}$ sampling characteristics, the mean of this $\bar{x}$ distribution is the same as the mean of the $x$ distribution. This implies that if the $x$ population has a mean of 55 mph, then the mean of all possible samples must also equal 55 mph, or $\mu_x = 55$ mph. Finally, the standard deviation of the sampling distribution of all the possible $\bar{x}$ values is

$$\sigma_{\bar{x}} = \sigma/\sqrt{n} = 5.5/\sqrt{100} = 0.55$$

Now we can convert the sample value of $\bar{x} = 60.9$ to its comparable $z$ value. Since $\mu_x = 55$ and $\sigma_{\bar{x}} = 5.5/\sqrt{100}$,

$$z = \frac{\bar{x} - \mu_x}{\sigma_{\bar{x}}} = \frac{60.9 - 55}{5.5/\sqrt{100}} = \frac{5.90}{0.55} = 10.73$$

As portrayed in Fig. 6.19, the $z$ value of 10.73 indicates that the sample average speed of 60.9 mph is 10.73 standard deviations above the expected sample average of 55 mph. From Appendix Table B.4 the highest $x$ value given is for 3.49. Only 0.0002 of the values in any normal distribution lie

**Figure 6.19**
Calculating
probabilities in the
highway truck speed
example.

Step I: Indicate on a graph the desired probability.

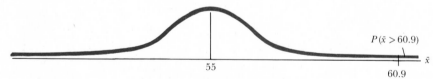

Step II: From Appendix Table B.4 the following areas are obtained.

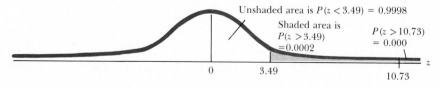

Chapter 6  Continuous Probability Distributions

beyond 3.49 standard deviations of their mean. Thus the probability of observing a value 10.73 standard deviations beyond the mean is so small that we assume it is zero for all practical purposes. That is, if trucks are averaging 55 mph, it is highly unlikely that we would observe the sample mean of 60.9 mph. But we did! Thus we conclude that the average speed of trucks is above 55 mph.

---

**WORKED EXAMPLE 6.5**

A company using part-time salespeople to sell cosmetics and jewelry door-to-door estimates that over the past year the average salesperson working in the suburbs should have earned $9000, if the sales techniques used were appropriate for the socioeconomic characteristics of these areas. The distribution of earnings is believed to be normal, with a standard deviation of $2000. A random sample of five of these salespeople resulted in $\bar{x} = \$8231$. What is the probability that $\bar{x}$ is this low (or lower) if a sample of five is drawn from a population where $\mu_x = \$9000$ and $\sigma_x = \$2000$? That is, what is

$$P(\bar{x} < 8231 | \mu_x = 9000, \sigma_x = 2000)?$$

Based on this probability, would it be unusual to observe a sample average of $8231 or less if the population mean is $9000?

**ANSWER:**

The first step in solving this problem is to determine if the distribution of $\bar{x}$ is normal. It is, because the parent population ($x$) was assumed to be normal. Next, let's transform the value $\bar{x} = 8231$ into its equivalent $z$ value.

$$z = \frac{\bar{x} - \mu_x}{\sigma_x/\sqrt{n}} = \frac{8231 - 9000}{2000/\sqrt{5}} = \frac{-769}{894.43} = -0.86$$

The probability that $\bar{x}$ is less than or equal to $8231 is identical to $P(z < -0.86)$. From the symmetry of the normal distribution, as illustrated in Fig. 6.20 (page 258), the probability that $z$ is less than $-0.86$ is the same as the probability that $z$ is greater than 0.86. The probabilities in Fig. 6.20 were determined by first finding the cumulative probability for $z = 0.86$ in Table B.4 (in the 0.8 row and the 0.06 column), which is 0.8051, and then taking the complement of this probability.

$$P(z < -0.86) = 1 - P(z < 0.86) = 1 - 0.8051 = 0.1949$$

Thus 19.49% of the time, a sample of size $n = 5$ will result in a sample average below $8321 when $\mu_x = \$9000$ and $\sigma_x = \$2000$. An event that occurs

Figure 6.20
Probability of average
salesperson's earnings
(the symmetry of the
normal distribution).

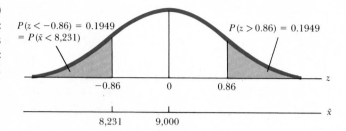

$P(z < -0.86) = 0.1949$
$= P(\bar{x} < 8,231)$

$P(z > 0.86) = 0.1949$

−0.86        0        0.86        z

8,231        9,000        $\bar{x}$

19.49% of the time is not very unusual, hence its occurrence should not cause us to doubt the population mean of $9000.

**WORKED EXAMPLE 6.6**

The company in Worked Example 6.5 would like to give one new salesperson some estimate of the upper and lower limits on earnings. The company decides to present a 95% range, that is, a range of earnings that would include 95% of all their salespeople. The upper limit will exclude 2.5% of the best salespeople, and the lower limit will exclude 2.5% of the worst. Since 5% of the sales force is excluded, 95% will be included.

**ANSWER:**

This problem requires the reverse of the process presented earlier in this chapter—determining an $\bar{x}$ value when the probability is known. Figure 6.21 illustrates this situation where $a$ is the lower limit and $b$ is the upper limit for a sample of size one.

Figure 6.21
Finding the upper and
lower limits for a
normal p.d.f. (where
$\mu_x = \$9000$ and
$\sigma_x = \$2000$).

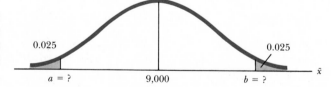

0.025        0.025

$a = ?$        9,000        $b = ?$        $\bar{x}$

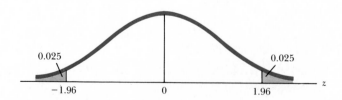

0.025        0.025

−1.96        0        1.96        z

Notice in Fig. 6.21 that because the normal distribution is symmetric, once we know the value of $b$ we also know the value of $a$. This is because both $a$ and $b$ cut off 0.025 of the normal distribution in their respective tails of the distribution. Thus the value of $a$ will be the same distance below 9000 as $b$ is above 9000.

We will first find the value of $b$. As shown in Fig. 6.21, the area beyond $b$ is 0.0250. This means that the cumulative area up to $b$ is 0.9750. To find $b$ we go to Table B.4 and find the $z$ value that excludes 2.5% of the upper tail of the normal distribution. This means looking for the $z$ value that corresponds to a cumulative probability of 0.9750. The probability 0.9750 is found almost in the center of Table B.4, in the 1.9 row and the 0.06 column. Thus

$$P(z > 1.96) = 0.025$$

Next, we use the $z$ standardizing formula to find $b$. This is done by replacing the symbol $\bar{x}$ by $b$. That is,

$$z = \frac{b - \mu_x}{\sigma_x / \sqrt{n}}.$$

The sample size in this case is $n = 1$, because we want earning limits for only one salesperson. Substituting $z = 1.96$, $\mu_x = 9000$, $\sigma_x = 2000$, and $n = 1$ into this formula yields

$$1.96 = \frac{b - 9000}{2000 / \sqrt{1}}$$

Solving for $b$,

$$b = 9000 + 1.96(2000/\sqrt{1}) = 9000 + 3920 = 12{,}920.$$

Because $b$ is \$3920 *greater* than \$9000, the value of $a$ is \$3920 *less* than \$9000. Thus $a = \$9000 - \$3920 = \$5080$. Alternatively, substituting these values into Eq. (6.3) yields

$$-1.96 = \frac{b - 9000}{2000 / \sqrt{1}}$$

so

$$b = 9000 - 1.96(2000/\sqrt{1}) = 9000 - 3920 = 5080$$

The 95% range on earnings for a salesperson at the cosmetics company is \$5080 to \$12,920.

If the company in the preceding example would like to estimate the 2.5% upper limit and the 2.5% lower limit on the average earnings for *four* of the new salespeople, what are the appropriate limits?

**ANSWER:**

Again, the appropriate $z$ value limits are 1.96 and $-1.96$. Now we have $\sqrt{4}$ in the denominator of the standardizing $z$ formula (Eq. 6.3) rather than $\sqrt{1}$. Substituting into Eq. (6.3) yields

$$z = \frac{b - \mu_x}{\sigma_x/\sqrt{n}} \quad \text{or} \quad 1.96 = \frac{b - 9000}{2000/\sqrt{4}}$$

Solving for $b$,

$$b = 9000 + 1.96(2000/\sqrt{4}) = 9000 + 1960 = 10{,}960$$

Because $b$ is \$1960 *greater* than \$9000, the value of $a$ is \$1960 *less* than \$9000. Thus $a = \$9000 - \$1960 = \$7040$. Alternatively,

$$z = \frac{a - \mu_x}{\sigma_x/\sqrt{n}} \quad \text{or} \quad -1.96 = \frac{a - 9000}{2000/\sqrt{4}}$$

so

$$a = 9000 - 1.96(2000/\sqrt{4}) = 9000 - 1960 = 7040$$

The 95% range on earnings for four of the cosmetics company salespersons is \$7040 to \$10,960.

## Exercises

MKT **6.14** The cosmetics firm in Worked Example 6.4 has determined that their salespeople work an average of $\mu_x = 17.3$ hours per week, with a standard deviation of $\sigma_x = 3.8$. The distribution of hours worked is normal.

a) Sketch the distribution of this parent population.

**b)** A random sample of size $n = 10$ salespeople is to be taken, and each one will be asked the hours worked during the last week. Sketch the sampling distribution of $\bar{x}$.

**c)** The random sample of size $n = 10$ yields the following hours: $x$: 15.5, 24.0, 18.0, 22.5, 13.25, 23.0, 21.5, 18.25, 16.0, 17.5. Find the mean of the sample. Then determine the probability that a random sample of 10 will yield a mean this large or larger, assuming $\mu_x = 17.3$ and $\sigma_x = 3.8$.

**d)** Form a 95% probability range for the hours worked by one salesperson.

**e)** Form a 95% probability range for the average hours worked by 16 randomly selected salespeople.

**6.15** Indicate whether the following statements are true or false. Explain why in each case.

**a)** The population mean is equal to a sample mean if the sample size exceeds 30.

**b)** The population mean is equal to the mean of all sample means.

**c)** The variance of the sampling distribution of $\bar{x}$ is the population variance.

**d)** The variance of the sampling distribution of $\bar{x}$ is

$$s^2 = \sum_{i=1}^{n} (x_i - \bar{x})^2/(n - 1)$$

**e)** The variance of the $\bar{x}$ distribution is $\sigma_x^2/n$.

**f)** The value of $\bar{x}$ has only one value in a given sample but takes on different values in different samples.

**6.16** Under what alternative conditions is the sampling distribution of the sample mean normally distributed?

MKT    **6.17** A grocery store sells an average of 478 loaves of bread each week. Sales ($x$) are normally distributed, with a standard deviation of 17.

**a)** If a random sample of size $n = 1$ (week) is drawn, what is the probability that this $x$ value will exceed 495?

**b)** If a random sample of size $n = 4$ (weeks) is drawn, what is the probability that the $\bar{x}$ value will exceed 495?

**c)** Why does your response in part (a) differ from that in part (b)?

**FIN** **6.18** A random variable $c$ measures the daily balances in customers' savings accounts. It is normally distributed, with a mean of $\mu_c = \$103$ and a standard deviation of $12.

a) If a random sample of size $n = 4$ is drawn, what is the probability that the $\bar{c}$ value exceeds $115?

b) If a random sample of size $n = 16$ is drawn, what is the probability that the $\bar{c}$ value exceeds $115?

c) What happened to the standard deviation of the $\bar{c}$ distribution when the sample size increased from $n = 4$ to $n = 16$?

d) What happened to the probability of observing $\bar{c} \geq \$115$ as the sample size increased from $n = 4$ to $n = 16$?

**OPS** **6.19** At a small publishing house average orders have been 100 books per day, with a standard deviation of 10. If daily orders are normally distributed, what is the probability that a weekly (5-day) average will be between 80 and 120 books?

**ACT** **6.20** Accounts receivable for a large corporation are normally distributed, with a mean of $43,000 and a standard deviation of $12,000.

a) If one account is drawn, what is the probability that its balance exceeds $70,000?

b) If 49 accounts are drawn, what is the probability that this sample's average balance exceeds $70,000?

c) Why are your answers different in (a) and (b)?

**MFG** **6.21** You are responsible for quality control at a plant that produces precision washers. The specification for the inside diameter is 0.5 inch. Over the years you have observed that the standard deviation ($\sigma$) of the inside diameter is 0.001 inch. To check for adherence to specifications, you draw a sample of 16 washers every hour. Your latest sample had a mean of 0.506 inch. How likely are you to observe this sample mean or a larger one if the population's average diameter is currently 0.5 inch? Based on this sample information would you be wise to stop production and inspect the machinery? Why or why not?

**6.22** In order to calculate the probability in Exercise 6.21, what did you have to assume and why?

# 6.7 The $t$ Distribution

In all the previous examples, the population standard deviation $\sigma_x$ was given or could be calculated from knowledge of the population values and their probability of occurrence. In the standardizing formula for $z$, the values of $n$, $\mu$, and $\sigma$ must be known before the sample is taken. Unfortunately, in most practical business problems it is unreasonable to assume that $\sigma$ is known. This section deals with situations where the population standard deviation is not known. To understand how to work with the sampling distribution of $\bar{x}$ when the population's standard deviation is not known, consider the following case:

## Automobile Steel

A steel mill produces sheet steel that is used in automobiles. Specifications from the auto companies require an average thickness of 0.20 inch. Your auto company recently received a shipment of the steel. You take a random sample of widths at 25 different locations on a roll of steel and find that the mean width of this sample is 0.190 inch, with a sample standard deviation of 0.020 inch. Past steel shipments have had normally distributed thicknesses. To determine if the entire roll could average 0.20 inch, you ask how likely is a sample average of 0.19 or less if the average roll thickness is in fact 0.20?

This case is similar to earlier ones, since we want to determine the probability of a sample result ($\bar{x}$) given certain population characteristics. In this case we want to determine the probability that $\bar{x}$ is 0.19 or less, given that $\mu_x = 0.20$ and $n = 25$.

$$P(\bar{x} \leq 0.19 | \mu_x = 0.20, n = 25)$$

The difference between this problem and earlier ones is that now we do not know the value of the population standard deviation, $\sigma_x$. When $\sigma_x$ is unknown, the appropriate p.d.f. is called the $t$ *distribution*.

Much of the early research on the $t$ distribution was by an Irish statistician, W. S. Gossett. Gossett worked for a Dublin brewery that did not permit its employees to publish their research; hence, he published under the pen name Student. In honor of his work, published in 1908, the $t$ distribution is often referred to as the *Student's t distribution.*

The formula for the $t$ distribution differs from the formula for the $z$ distribution in that the sample standard deviation $(s)$ is used in the denominator, replacing the population standard deviation $(\sigma)$. The $t$ formula for standardizing the random variable $\bar{x}$ is:

---

**(6.4)**

Formula for standardizing $\bar{x}$ when $\sigma_x$ is unknown

$$t = \frac{\bar{x} - \mu_x}{s_x / \sqrt{n}}$$

where $s_x = \sqrt{\dfrac{\Sigma(x - \bar{x})^2}{n - 1}}$ and $\bar{x} = \dfrac{1}{n} \Sigma x_i$

---

Like the variable $z$, the variable $t$ is a continuous random variable. Both the $t$ and the $z$ ratios are used to "standardize" $\bar{x}$ values. The $t$ distribution, however, is more spread out than the $z$ because the sample value $s_x$ is used in place of (as an estimator of) the population parameter $\sigma_x$. Unlike $\sigma_x$, values of $s_x$ vary from sample to sample. Although the average value of $s_x^2$ is $\sigma_x^2$, the probability that an individual $s_x$ value will be close to $\sigma_x$ depends on the sample size $(n)$; the larger the sample size, the more likely it is that an individual $s_x$ value will be close to $\sigma_x$.

## Degrees of Freedom

As Eq. (6.4) indicates, the $t$ distribution depends on both $\bar{x}$ and $s_x$. The denominator in the formula for $s_x$, $n - 1$, is usually referred to as the *degrees of freedom* and abbreviated *d.f.* The degrees of freedom represent the number of observations in the sample that are free to vary around the mean of the sample. For example, if the sample size is $n = 1$, then there are no values free to vary around the mean (since the value of this single observation is also the mean of the sample). If the sample size is $n = 2$, then only one value is free to vary about the sample mean. Once either one of the sample values is specified, the other value is simultaneously determined; that is, the second value is not freely determined. To illustrate this relationship let $a$ be the first value and let $b$ be the second value. For any $\bar{x}$ value, $b$ depends on the value of $a$ and hence is not free to vary. For example, if $\bar{x} = 10$ and $a$ is 15, then $b$ must be 5.

Similarly, when $n = 3$, any two values are free to vary, but once two are selected, then the third is fixed. In general, given an $\bar{x}$ value and $n$ sample observations, once $n - 1$ values are determined, the final value is no longer free to vary. This means that the d.f. for Eq. (6.4) equals $n - 1$.

---

**DEFINITION**
**d.f.**  For a random variable $\bar{x}$, the degrees of freedom for the $t$ distribution is d.f. $= n - 1$.

---

The $t$ distribution is a family of distributions—a separate one for each d.f. This family is shown in Fig. 6.22. Note that each $t$ distribution is symmetric, with a mean of zero. The $t$ distribution looks very similar to a normal distribution, but for any d.f. less than infinity the $t$ distribution is more spread out than the $z$. Because $s_x$ more closely approximates $\sigma_x$ as $n - 1$ increases, the $t$ distribution approaches the $z$ distribution as the sample size gets larger. While $t$ and $z$ distributions are identical only for d.f. $=$ infinity, for as few as 30 d.f. the $t$ distribution is similar to the $z$.

The characteristics of the $t$ distribution can be summarized as follows:

1. The $t$ distribution has a unimodal symmetric p.d.f.

2. Each $t$ distribution has a mean of zero.

3. The standard deviation of the $t$ distribution is greater than or equal to one. As the d.f. increase, the standard deviation approaches one.

**Figure 6.22**
The family of $t$ distributions.

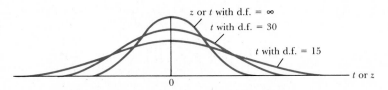

Note: As the sample size $n$ is increased the variability in $t$ is reduced and the $t$ distribution approaches the $z$ distribution.

Recall that the $t$ distribution is used to solve problems involving $\bar{x}$ when $\sigma_x$ is unknown. As with the normal distribution, the $t$-distribution cannot be used to solve such problems unless (1) the population $(x)$ is normally distributed or (2) the sample size is large $(n > 30)$. When either (1) or (2) holds, the first step is to transform a problem that is stated in terms of $\bar{x}$ into a problem that is stated in terms of $t$. For instance, in the steel thickness case presented at the beginning of the previous section, we want to find

$$P(\bar{x} \le 0.19)$$

where $\mu_x = 0.20$, $\sigma_x$ is unknown but $s_x = 0.02$, and thicknesses are assumed to be normally distributed. Using Eq. (6.4), the value of $t$ comparable to $\bar{x} = 0.19$ is

$$t = \frac{\bar{x} - \mu_x}{s_x/\sqrt{n}} = \frac{0.19 - 0.20}{0.02/\sqrt{25}} = -2.50$$

Thus $P(\bar{x} \le 0.19)$ is approximated by $P(t < -2.50)$ when $n = 25$ and $s_x = 0.02$. This relationship is shown in Fig. 6.23. Because the $t$ distribution is continuous, $P(t \le -2.50) = P(t < -2.50)$.

Notice in Fig. 6.23 that we placed a subscript on $t$, namely d.f. $= 24$, to remind us that this is the $t$ distribution for d.f. $= 24$. Now we want to find the probability (area) that the random variable $t$ is less than or equal to

**Figure 6.23**
Solving an $\bar{x}$ problem using the $t$ distribution.

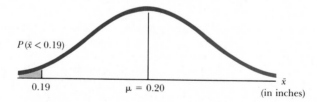

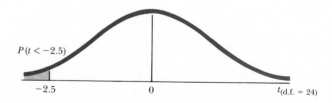

Figure 6.24
The symmetry of the *t*
distribution.

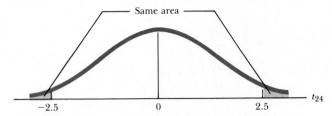

−2.50. Because the *t* distribution is completely symmetric, $P(t < -2.50) = P(t > 2.50)$, as shown in Fig. 6.24. The probability $P(t > 2.50)$ can be determined using either Appendix Table B.5 or a computer statistical package. Table B.5 is arranged differently from Appendix Table B.4 (the normal table), so we will explain its use.

Appendix Table B.5 presents cumulative probabilities for only a limited number of *t* distributions. Cumulative probabilities for 34 different *t* distributions are presented in Table B.5. These 34 *t* distributions differ because their d.f. $(n - 1)$ differ. The d.f. are listed down the left-hand column of the table. The *t* distribution of concern in Fig. 6.24 is about two-thirds of the way down the table, in the row labeled d.f. = 24 (remember, our sample was $n = 25$). This row (reproduced from row $n - 1 = 24$ in Table B.5) is shown in Table 6.2.

The numerical column headings in Table 6.2 are cumulative probabilities, and the numbers in the body of the table are the corresponding *t* values. For example, the first cumulative probability in Table 6.2 is 0.75, and the corresponding *t* value is 0.685. This indicates that with 24 d.f.,

$$P(t_{24} < 0.685) = 0.75$$

Imagine that many, many (an infinite number of) samples of size $n = 25$ are

**Table 6.2**

| **Finding Probabilities with the *t* Distribution, d.f. = 24** | | | | | | | |
|---|---|---|---|---|---|---|---|
| d.f. | 0.75 | 0.90 | 0.95 | 0.975 | 0.99 | 0.995 | 0.999 |
| . | | | | | | | |
| . | | | | | | | |
| . | | | | | | | |
| 24 | 0.685 | 1.318 | 1.711 | 2.064 | 2.492 | 2.797 | 3.467 |
| . | | | | | | | |
| . | | | | | | | |
| . | | | | | | | |

Figure 6.25
Probabilities for the
t distribution with
d.f. = 24.

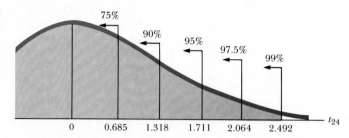

collected from some population where $\mu_x$ is known and $\sigma_x$ is unknown. For each sample $\bar{x}$ and $s_x$ are calculated, and then a $t$ value is determined, using

$$t = \frac{\bar{x} - \mu_x}{s_x/\sqrt{n}}$$

This process yields an infinite number of $t$ values. The statement $P(t_{24} < 0.685) = 0.75$ indicates that 75% of these $t$ values will be less than or equal to 0.685. Similarly, from Table 6.2, 90% of the $t$ values will be less than or equal to 1.318, 95% will be less than or equal to 1.711, and so forth. These probabilities are shown in Fig. 6.25.

The probability of steel roll thickness we set out to determine is

$$P(\bar{x} \leq 0.19 | \mu_x = 0.20)$$

This probability is approximated by

$$P(t > 2.50 | d.f. = 24)$$

The number 2.50 is very close to 2.492. Since the area to the right of 2.492 is 0.01, with d.f. = 24, we can write the following approximation:

$$P(\bar{x} \leq 0.19) = P(t < -2.50) = 0.01$$

This result indicates that only once in 100 times, on the average, should we observe a sample average of 0.19 inch or less if the mean thickness of the entire roll of steel is 0.20 inch. Such an observation is not very likely. Since 0.19 inch did occur, our assumption about the mean thickness of 0.20 inch appears to be incorrect.

---

**WORKED EXAMPLE 6.8**

Suppose an ad appearing in newspapers across the country suggests that the long-distance telephone service MCI saves subscribers an average of 33% on their long-distance calls. Because you are interested in purchasing this service, you take a random sample of eight calls and find the following savings.

| Long-Distance Call | Savings (%) |
|---|---|
| Boston to Providence | 50.0 |
| Milwaukee to Dallas | 34.2 |
| Evanston, Ill., to Reno | 32.1 |
| Lexington, Ky., to Houston | 28.9 |
| Los Angeles to Cleveland | 32.0 |
| Austin, Tex., to San Francisco | 30.2 |
| Washington, D.C., to St. Louis | 33.6 |
| New York, N.Y. to Miami | 40.6 |

The mean savings is $\bar{x} = 35.2$, which is larger than the 33 percent in the ad. You are curious about whether the ad might be understating the savings. The statistical question is; how often in a sample of $n = 8$ will $\bar{x}$ be 35.2 or larger, by chance, when $\mu_x = 33.0$? You assume that the population is normally distributed, but you have no idea of the population's standard deviation.

ANSWER:

The $t$ distribution is appropriate here since $x$ is assumed to be normal and the population's standard deviation is unknown. The sample standard deviation is determined using the following formula:

$$s_x = \sqrt{\frac{1}{n-1} \Sigma(x - \bar{x})^2}$$

where $\bar{x} = 35.2$ and $n = 8$. The calculation of $s_x$ is as follows:

| $x$ | $x - \bar{x}$ | $(x - \bar{x})^2$ |
|---|---|---|
| 50.0 | 14.8 | 219.04 |
| 34.2 | −1.0 | 1.00 |
| 32.1 | −3.1 | 9.61 |
| 28.9 | −6.3 | 39.69 |
| 32.0 | −3.2 | 10.24 |
| 30.2 | −5.0 | 25.00 |
| 33.6 | −1.6 | 2.56 |
| 40.6 | 5.4 | 29.16 |
| | Sum = | 336.30 |

Sample standard deviation:

$$s_x = \sqrt{\frac{1}{7}(336.30)} = \sqrt{48.043} = 6.93$$

Now that $s_x = 6.93$ has been determined, the value of $\bar{x} = 35.2$ can be transformed to its equivalent $t$ value:

$$t = \frac{\bar{x} - \mu_x}{s_x/\sqrt{n}}$$

$$= \frac{35.2 - 33.0}{6.93/\sqrt{8}} = \frac{2.2}{2.45} = 0.90$$

Thus the probability $P(\bar{x} > 35.2)$ can be approximated by determining $P(t_7 > 0.90)$, where d.f. $= 8 - 1 = 7$. Unfortunately, none of the values in the 7 d.f. row in Appendix Table B.5 gives the exact probability $P(t_7 > 0.90)$. It is possible, however, to specify a *range* of values for this probability by looking for the closest $t$ values above and below 0.90. The $t$ values in Table B.5 for d.f. $= 7$ are shown in Fig. 6.26. The probabilities given in this figure were derived by taking the complement of the probabilities at the top of Table B.5.

As we indicated earlier, the $t$ values in Fig. 6.26 do not provide enough information to allow us to determine the exact value of the probability $P(t_7 > 0.90)$, represented by the shaded area. By looking carefully at this figure, however, we can see that the shaded area must be greater than 0.10, because the area beyond $t = 1.415$ is 0.10. Similarly, the area beyond 0.90 must be less than 0.25, since this is the area to the right of 0.711. Thus the best we can do using Fig. 6.26 (or Table B.5) is to say that the probability that $t$ is greater than 0.90 lies between 0.25 and 0.10, or

$$0.25 > P(t_7 > 0.90) > 0.10$$

**Figure 6.26**
Right-tail probabilities for a $t$ distribution with d.f. $= 7$.

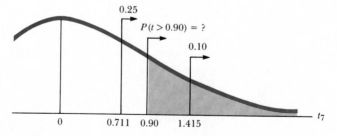

Chapter 6   Continuous Probability Distributions

To be more precise, either a much larger table of $t$ values is needed, or a computer program can be used. Section 6.8 shows how to determine $P(t_7 > 0.90)$ using a computer program.

**WORKED EXAMPLE 6.9**

Consider once again the last example, where you are thinking about purchasing MCI long-distance telephone service. Now you take a random sample of 100 calls and find that the mean savings by using MCI is $\bar{x} = 31.7$ and $s = 5.86$. What is the probability that $\bar{x}$ will be as small as 31.7 when $\mu_x = 33.0$, $s_x = 5.86$, and $n = 100$?

**ANSWER:**

While an argument could be made for using the $z$ distribution in this situation, because $n$ is so large and the population is normal, the $t$ distribution is still more appropriate because the population's standard deviation is unknown. The equivalent $t$ value for $\bar{x} = 31.7$ is

$$t = \frac{\bar{x} - \mu_x}{s_x/\sqrt{n}}$$

$$= \frac{31.7 - 33.0}{5.86/\sqrt{100}} = \frac{-1.3}{0.586} = -2.218$$

The probability $P(t < -2.218) = P(t > 2.218)$. To find this probability, we look in Appendix Table B.5 for d.f. $= 100 - 1 = 99$. Unfortunately, there is no row for d.f. $= 99$, so we move to the closest row, which is for d.f. $= 120$. Notice in Table B.5 that the $t$ values for d.f. $= 60$ and d.f. $= 120$ differ by only a small amount; hence, we could have moved in either direction. It is common to move to the closer numerical value. Some of the $t$ values and their associated probabilities from Table B.5 and d.f. $= 120$ are given in Fig. 6.27.

**Figure 6.27**
The $t$ distribution for d.f. $= 120$.

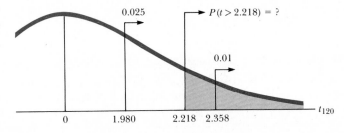

In Fig. 6.27 the shaded area is $P(t > 2.218)$, and we see that

$$0.025 > P(t > 2.218) > 0.01.$$

In the absence of a more complete $t$ table or a computer program, one might approximate the $t$ distribution probability by the probability associated with $z \geq 2.218$. From Appendix Table B.4, we find the $P(z < 2.22) = 0.9868$, so $P(z > 2.22) = 0.0132$. Because $n$ is large, $P(t > 2.218 | \text{d.f.} = 99) \approx P(z > 2.22) = 0.0132$. This result indicates that it is very unlikely to find a sample mean as low as 31.7 by chance when $\mu_x = 33$, $s_x = 5.86$, and $n = 100$.

## Exercises

**6.23** What are the major characteristics of the $t$ distribution?

**6.24** Find the following probabilities for the Student's $t$ distribution:

a) $P(t < 1.721 | \text{d.f.} = 21) = $ _____

b) $P(t < -9.925 | \text{d.f.} = 2) = $ _____

c) $P(t > -2.306 | \text{d.f.} = 8) = $ _____

d) $P(1.86 < t_8 < 2.90) = $ _____

e) $P(t_6 > 3.707) = $ _____

f) $P(-2.11 < t < 1.74 | \text{d.f.} = 17) = $ _____

**6.25** Find the following values of $b$ for the Student's $t$ distribution:

a) $P(t < b | \text{d.f.} = 3) = 0.9995$

b) $P(t < b | \text{d.f.} = 16) = 0.025$

c) $P(t_{13} > b) = 0.995$

d) $P(-b < t < b | \text{d.f.} = 19) = 0.95$

e) $P(t > b | \text{d.f.} = 23) = 0.005$

f) $P(0 < t_{21} < b) = 0.40$

ACT **6.26** A random variable $w$ measures the hourly wage of rod pushers. These workers are paid on a piece rate. The pay for all rod pushers in the Genborn Factory is normally distributed, with a mean of $\mu_w = \$17.98$.

a) If a random sample of size $n = 4$ is drawn and $s_w = \$6$, find the probability that $\bar{w}$ is greater than $\$22.90$.

b) If a random sample of size $n = 9$ is drawn and $s_w = \$6$, find the probability that $\bar{w}$ is greater than $\$20.77$.

c) What happens to the $t$ distribution as the sample size is increased from $n = 4$ to $n = 9$?

MKT  **6.27** A recent article in a leading magazine claimed that homemakers spend an average of 21 hours per week preparing meals. A director of marketing at a large food-processing company knows that a recent sample of 25 homemakers resulted in an average time for preparation of meals of 16 hours per week, with a standard deviation of 4 hours. The director asks, "What is the probability of observing a sample average of 16 hours or less if the true population average is 21 hours?"

a) To answer this question, what do you have to assume about the population of time preparing meals and the sampling distribution of sample mean time?

b) Given your assumptions in (a), answer the marketing director's question.

# 6.9 Using a Computer Program to Calculate Probabilities for $z$ and $t$

A number of different statistical programs for computers are useful in determining probabilities for the $z$ and $t$ distributions. The following illustrations demonstrate one such package.

## Using a Computer Program for the $z$ Distribution

A computer program can essentially duplicate the cumulative probabilities given in Appendix Table B.4 for the standard normal distribution. Typically, a program will determine either a cumulative probability based on a given $z$ value or the $z$ value given a probability. Both cases will now be illustrated, using examples from Sections 6.4 and 6.6.

For the GE example in Section 6.4 (see Fig. 6.10), we wanted to determine the cumulative probability for $z = -1.43$, $P(z < -1.43)$. Using Table B.4, the following value was determined:

$$P(z < -1.43) = 0.0764$$

To use a typical menu-driven computer program to do this calculation, one must first get to the "PROBABILITY DISTRIBUTIONS" menu. Next, the "z DISTRIBUTION" is brought up. The usual process to follow at this point is presented in Table 6.3 (user input is in boldface).

Table 6.4 presents a computer program process for the cosmetics example in Worked Examples 6.5 and 6.6 (see Fig. 6.20), where the $z$ value to be determined cuts off 0.025 in the upper tail. Since cutting off 0.025 in the upper tail is equivalent to a cumulative probability of 0.975, the problem is to find the value of $z$ with this cumulative probability. Our answer from

**Table 6.3**

| A Computer Process for a Normal Problem (Calculating Probabilities for Given $z$ Values) |
|---|
| After you have brought up the program, loaded the probability module, and accessed the $z$ distribution, your terminal screen may look similar to the following, where your responses are in boldface type and $\langle CR \rangle$ indicates the return key. |

```
              NORMAL DISTRIBUTION
    OPTIONS: A. CALCULATE PROBABILITY GIVEN Z
             B. CALCULATE Z GIVEN PROBABILITY
    ENTER: OPTION: A ⟨CR⟩
    ENTER: OBSERVED Z VALUE: -1.43 ⟨CR⟩
    ENTER: OPTION: A ⟨CR⟩ (for screen display)

        ┌──────────────────────────────────────┐
        │  NORMAL DISTRIBUTION                   │
        │  Z = -1.43                             │
        │  P = 0.0764,   1 - P = 0.9236          │
        │  PRESS ANY KEY TO CONTINUE             │
        └──────────────────────────────────────┘
```

| Table 6.4 | **A Computer Process for a Normal Distribution** |
|---|---|
| | **(Calculating z Values for Given Probabilities)** |

After you have brought up the program, loaded the probability module, and accessed the z distribution, your terminal screen may look similar to the following, where your responses are in boldface type and ⟨CR⟩ indicates the return key.

```
              NORMAL DISTRIBUTION
    OPTIONS: A. CALCULATE PROBABILITY GIVEN Z
             B. CALCULATE Z GIVEN PROBABILITY
    ENTER: OPTION: B ⟨CR⟩
    ENTER: CUMULATIVE PROBABILITY, P: 0.9750
    ⟨CR⟩
    ENTER: OPTION: A ⟨CR⟩ (for screen display)
```

```
         NORMAL DISTRIBUTION
    Z = 1.959963964
    P = 0.9750    1 - P = 0.0250
     PRESS ANY KEY TO CONTINUE
```

Section 6.6, $z = 1.96$, is the same as this computer answer after rounding off. (Note that a computer program will provide more digits to the right of the decimal point than are warranted.)

## Using a Computer Program for the *t* Distribution

In Worked Example 6.8, Fig. 6.26, the exact probability $P(t_7 > 0.90)$ could not be determined. Using Table B.5 only led to the fact that $P(t_7 > 0.90)$ is between 0.25 and 0.10; that is,

$$0.25 > P(t_7 > 0.90) > 0.10$$

A computer program can be used to determine the exact probability for any *t* value. This process is illustrated in Table 6.5 for $t = 0.90$. From this table, we see that after the information in boldface print has been entered, the computer calculates the probability that *t* is greater than 0.90; it is actually 0.1990.

| Table 6.5 | A Computer Process for the Student's *t* Distribution (Calculating Probabilities for Given *t* Values) |
|---|---|

After you have brought up the program, loaded the probability module, and accessed the *t* distribution, your terminal screen may look similar to the following, where your responses are in boldface type and ⟨CR⟩ indicates the return key.

```
               STUDENT'S t DISTRIBUTION
ENTER: D.F.: 7 ⟨CR⟩
ENTER: T: 0.90 ⟨CR⟩
ENTER OPTION: A ⟨CR⟩ (for screen output)

         ┌─────────────────────────────────────────────┐
         │     STUDENT'S t DISTRIBUTION                 │
         │  D.F. = 7                                    │
         │     T  = 0.90                                │
         │     P  = 0.8010,   1 - P = 0.1990            │
         │  PRESS ANY KEY TO CONTINUE                   │
         └─────────────────────────────────────────────┘
```

## Chapter Exercises

FIN  **6.28** An IRS agent questions the daily receipts being reported by Hinkle's House of Hosiery. Hinkle's claims that daily receipts average $375. An IRS random sample of receipts for 5 days results in receipts of $357, $456, $523, $467, and $392.

a) What is the approximate probability of getting the IRS sample average, or a larger value, if Hinkle's claim is true?

b) What did you have to assume in part (a) to calculate the requested probability?

c) Do you believe Hinkle's claim, based on the IRS sample information? (Give your reasons.)

**6.29** The random variable $z$ is normally distributed, with mean $\mu_z = 0$ and standard deviation $\sigma_z = 1$. Find the following probabilities using a computer program:

a) $P(z < 1.534) =$ _____

b) $P(z > -1.237) =$ _____

c) $P(z > 3.123) =$ _____

d) $P(z < -2.103) =$ _____

e) $P(1.021 < z < 2.901) =$ _____

f) $P(1.310 < z < 1.337) =$ _____

**6.30** The random variable $z$ is normally distributed with mean $\mu_z = 0$ and standard deviation $\sigma_z = 1$. Find the following values of $b$ using a computer program:

a) $P(z < b) = 0.9375$

b) $P(z > b) = 0.8490$

c) $P(z > b) = 0.07$

d) $P(z < b) = 0.15$

e) $P(-b < z < b) = 0.6666$

f) $P(0 < z < b) = 0.1952$

**6.31** Find the following probabilities for the Student's $t$ distribution using a computer program.

a) $P(t < 1.872 | \text{d.f.} = 23) =$ _____

b) $P(t < -7.348 | \text{d.f.} = 2) =$ _____

c) $P(t_9 > -2.675) =$ _____

d) $P(1.04 < t_7 < 3.23) =$ _____

e) $P(t_3 > 3.679) =$ _____

f) $P(-2.44 < t < 1.65 | \text{d.f.} = 16) =$ _____

OPS **6.32** A machine producing 3-inch bolts has, in the past, produced bolts that are normally distributed with a mean of exactly 3 inches in length $(\mu_x = 3)$. Ten bolts are selected at random from the machine's current output. The length of these bolts is as follows:

| Sample | Length (in.) | Sample | Length (in.) |
|--------|-------------|--------|-------------|
| 1 | 3.00022 | 6 | 2.99991 |
| 2 | 3.00008 | 7 | 3.00015 |
| 3 | 3.00013 | 8 | 3.00001 |
| 4 | 2.99997 | 9 | 3.00011 |
| 5 | 3.00041 | 10 | 2.99999 |

**a)** Determine the mean and standard deviation of this sample. (These computations are best performed on a computer.)

**b)** Determine the probability of obtaining a mean as large or larger than the one calculated in part (a), assuming $\mu_x = 3.00$.

**c)** Based on your answer to part (a), does it appear that the machine is working properly?

**6.33** If the sample size is doubled, then what happens to the magnitude of the variance and the standard deviation of the sampling distribution of the sample mean?

**6.34** What are the similarities and differences between the $z$ and $t$ distributions?

**6.35** Does the $t$ or $z$ distribution have more area beyond the value of 2? What causes this difference in the size of the area beyond the value of 2?

**6.36** In each of the following, state whether the $t$ distribution or the $z$ distribution is more appropriate for calculating the probabilities associated with the $\bar{x}$ distribution.

**a)** A small sample from a normal population with a known standard deviation.

**b)** A small sample from a normal population with an unknown standard deviation.

**c)** A small sample from a skewed population with a known standard deviation.

**d)** A large sample from a skewed population with a known standard deviation.

**e)** A large sample from a skewed population with an unknown standard deviation.

MKT    **6.37** Following Toro's lead, a manufacturer of farm equipment advertises that it will refund 100% of the purchase price of irrigation equipment if the local rainfall this year is more than 50% above the average (local) rainfall over the past 10 years. In your area the average rainfall has been 36 inches, with a standard deviation of 10 inches. If you purchase this equipment what is the probability of getting a 100% refund? What did you have to assume about the distribution of rainfall in your area?

MFG    **6.38**   Using the information on the life of Gates Rubber Company V-belts in Exercise 3.50, what proportion of V-belts break before they are 4.5 years old?

MFG    **6.39**   Use the information on the life of Gates Rubber Company V-belts in Exercise 3.50. Your small manufacturing plant has four machines that each require one V-belt. If you put new V-belts on each of these machines and then run them until each belt breaks, what is the probability that the average life of the four belts exceeds 4.5 years?

      **6.40**   Why does your answer in 6.38 differ from that in 6.39?

## Glossary

**central limit theorem:** A fundamental result in sampling theory stating that the sampling distribution of $\bar{x}$ approaches a normal p.d.f. as the sample size $n$ is increased.

**continuous random variables:** A variable that can take any value within an interval.

**degrees of freedom (d.f.):** The number of observations in the sample that are free to vary around the mean of the sample. For the random variable $\bar{x}$, d.f. $= n - 1$.

**expected value of $\bar{x}$:** The mean of the sampling distribution of $\bar{x}$ [designated by $E(\bar{x})$]. Note: $E(\bar{x}) = \mu_{\bar{x}} = \mu_x$.

**mean of the $\bar{x}$ p.d.f.:** The expected value or average of the sampling distribution of $\bar{x}$ (designated by $\mu_{\bar{x}}$). Note: $\mu_{\bar{x}} = E(\bar{x}) = \mu_x$.

**normal probability density function:** A p.d.f. which is unimodal, symmetric, and continuous, forming a bell-shaped curve. It has a mean of $\mu$ and a standard deviation of $\sigma$.

**probability density function (p.d.f.):** A curve for a continuous random variable that shows the probability of a range of values as the area under the curve.

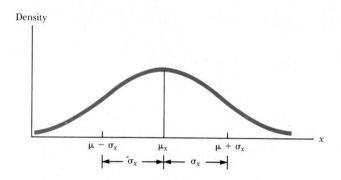

**sampling distribution of $\bar{x}$:** The probability distribution of all possible sample means. The mean (i.e., expected value) of the sampling distribution of $\bar{x}$ equals the mean of the population [i.e., $E(\bar{x}) = \mu_{\bar{x}} = \mu_x$] and its standard deviation is the population standard deviation divided by the square root of the sample size (i.e., $\sigma_{\bar{x}} = \sigma_x / \sqrt{n}$).

**standard deviation of the sampling distribution of $\bar{x}$:** A measure of dispersion of $\bar{x}$ values around their mean $\mu_{\bar{x}}$. It is calculated by dividing the standard deviation of the population ($\sigma_x$) by the square root of the sample size. That is, $\sigma_{\bar{x}} = \sigma_x / \sqrt{n}$.

**standard normal density function:** The curve or formula which defines the standard normal distribution. It is continuous, symmetric, unimodal with a bell shape and has a mean of zero and variance of one.

**standard normal distribution:** The distribution for a normal random variable (usually designated by the letter $z$) that has a p.d.f. with a mean of zero and standard deviation of one.

**Student's $t$ probability density function:** A p.d.f. that is based on two random variables—the sample mean $\bar{x}$ and the sample standard deviation $s_x$. Like the normal p.d.f., it is continuous, symmetric, unimodal with a bell shape, and has a mean of zero. Its variance is greater than one (except when $n = $ infinity).

Chapter 6   Continuous Probability Distributions

**6.1—Standard Normal Value:**

$$z = \frac{x - \mu_x}{\sigma_x}$$

**6.2—Formula for finding $b$ when $z$ is Known:**

$$z = \frac{b - \mu_x}{\sigma_x}$$

**6.3—The $z$ formula for Standardizing $\bar{x}$:**

$$z = \frac{\bar{x} - \mu_{\bar{x}}}{\sigma_{\bar{x}}} \quad \text{or equivalently} \quad z = \frac{\bar{x} - \mu_x}{\sigma_x/\sqrt{n}}$$

**6.4—Formula for Standardizing $\bar{x}$ when $\sigma_x$ is Unknown:**

$$t = \frac{\bar{x} - \mu_x}{s_x/\sqrt{n}}$$

$$\text{where } s_x = \sqrt{\frac{\Sigma\,(x - \bar{x})^2}{n - 1}} \quad \text{and} \quad \bar{x} = \frac{1}{n}\Sigma x_i$$

# CHAPTER SEVEN

*If the polls are so accurate, why are there so many polling companies?*
*Bill Foster*

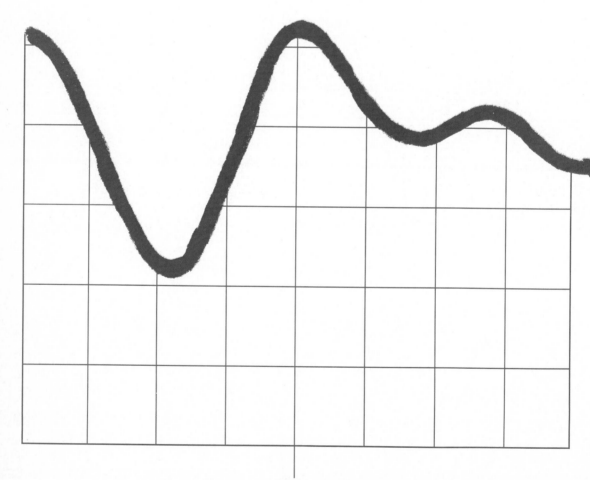

# ESTIMATION

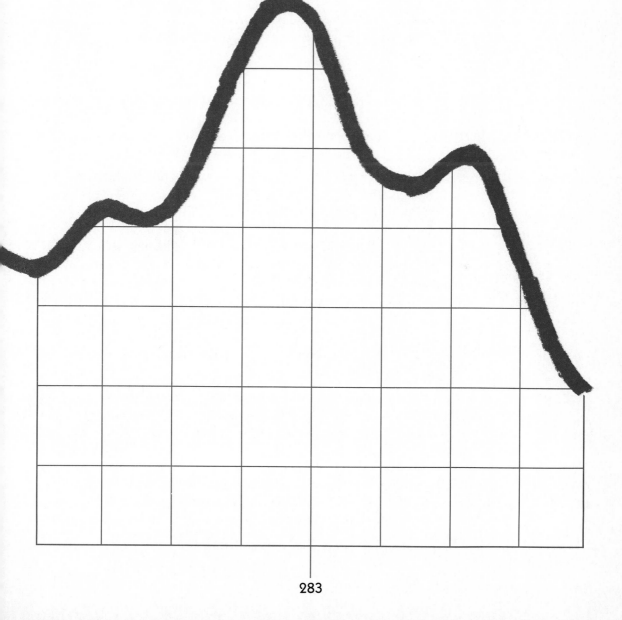

# INTRODUCTION

**Sample statistics** (such as the sample mean $\bar{x}$ and the sample variance $s^2$) are used to summarize sample data. Besides their use in describing sample data, statistics provide estimates of their population parameter counterparts ($\mu$ and $\sigma^2$). The use of sample statistics to estimate population parameters is important in scientific inquiry and business decision making. For instance:

- In conducting a workload study, a human resource manager audits the number of trucks unloaded on a sample of 18 days. The sample average number of trucks unloaded per day could then be used to estimate the average number of trucks unloaded over all days.

- In auditing the value of inventory in a warehouse, an accountant selects a sample of items and determines their average value. This sample average value is then used to estimate the total inventory value of all items in the warehouse.

- In a marketing study, a production manager attempts to establish the target audience for an advertising campaign by estimating the mean income of the typical purchaser.

- In trying to estimate the percentage of people who will vote for a presidential candidate, a political pollster surveys voters as they leave the voting booths. This sample information is then used to estimate the proportion of voters in the population who voted for a presidential candidate.

In these examples, sample statistics are used to make statements about possible values of population parameters. The sample statistic is the value determined from the sample and used to estimate the population parameter.

In the first three examples, the sample mean ($\bar{x}$) is used to estimate the population mean ($\mu_x$). In the last example, the sample proportion (designated by $p = x/n$, where $x$ is the number of voters in a sample of size $n$ who would vote for the candidate) is used to estimate the population proportion who would vote for the candidate (designated by the Greek letter pi, $\pi$). These estimates are called **point estimates** because they consist of a *single* value. Throughout this chapter we will assume that point estimates are made using the simple random sampling procedures discussed in previous chapters. In each case we will assume that the population is very large, if not infinite.

It is unlikely that any point estimate is exactly correct. For example, it would be unlikely for actual sales to exactly match forecasted sales of 100,000 units. To reflect the uncertainty in a point estimate, most analysts prefer to specify an *interval* of values for the population parameter. Such a set of values is called an **interval estimate**. The analyst who predicts that sales will fall between 90,000 and 110,000 units is making an interval estimate. By the end of this chapter you will have learned to determine the appropriate point and interval estimates for the population parameters $\mu$ and $\pi$, and you will be able to construct an interval around each of these estimates. From your knowledge of interval estimates, you will also be able to determine the appropriate or desired sample size to use in certain circumstances.

## Marketing Briefcases

You are a marketing analyst for a company selling high-quality leather goods by mail. One of your best-selling items is a leather briefcase. Your company attracts orders from business executives by placing ads in periodicals such as the *Wall Street Journal* (*WSJ*). One of your current projects is a random sample (a survey) to determine certain personal characteristics (such as the average age) of customers who recently purchased a leather briefcase. You are also interested in what proportion of these customers have seen the company's advertisement in the *WSJ* announcing a special sale on leather briefcases. The survey, consisting of 89 randomly selected customers who had purchased a briefcase, provides the following sample information:

$$\text{Average age: } \bar{x} = 38.6 \text{ years}$$
$$\text{Variance of age: } s_x^2 = 52.1 \text{ (years squared)}$$

Number of executives who read
about the sale in the *WSJ*: $= 34$

# 7.2 Point Estimates and Point Estimators

Although we have talked about estimating population parameters with sample information, we have not formally introduced the idea of an estimate or an estimator. **Estimates** are the numerical values that we calculate from sample data to make inferences about a population parameter. When a single value is used, it is called a point estimate. For instance, in the briefcase marketing example the sample average of 38.6 years is a point estimate of the population's mean age. Similarly, $34/89 = 0.382$ is a point estimate of the proportion of executives who read about the sale of briefcases in the *WSJ*.

---

**DEFINITION**
**Point Estimate**

A point estimate is a single value that is used to estimate a population parameter.

---

A point estimate is a single value that is calculated from only one sample. Different samples will produce different point estimates. Estimates are thus the outcome of a random process. The random variable that represents all point estimates that could be obtained is called the **point estimator**.

---

**DEFINITION**
**Point Estimator**

A point estimator is a random variable whose values are point estimates.

---

You should think of point estimation as a process that generates specific numbers, each of which is a point estimate. The following three point estimators are used frequently in business and economic problems.

$\bar{x}$ (the sample mean) is the best point estimator of the population parameter $\mu_x$ (the population mean).

$s_x^2$ (the sample variance) is the best point estimator of the population parameter $\sigma_x^2$ (the population variance).

$p$ (the sample proportion) is the best point estimator of the population parameter $\pi$ (the population proportion).

[As noted earlier, to associate a point estimator with its population parameter, it is common to place a subscript on both the estimator and the population parameter in order to identify the random variable. Thus $s_x^2$ is the sample variance estimating the population variance $(\sigma_x^2)$ when the random variable is $x$.]

There are a number of reasons why these estimators are considered the best. One important reason is that they are unbiased.

---

| DEFINITION | A point estimator is unbiased if its expected value (i.e., the average of |
|---|---|
| **Unbiased Point** | all its values) equals the population parameter. |
| **Estimator** | |

---

An **unbiased point estimator** does not mean that any *one* estimate will equal the population parameter being estimated. Rather, it means that the *average* of all possible point estimates will equal the population parameter. The point estimators $\bar{x}$, $s_x^2$, and $p$ are all unbiased estimators of their respective population parameters, $\mu_x$, $\sigma_x^2$, and $\pi$.

The sample mean $(\bar{x})$ is unbiased in estimating the population mean $(\mu_x)$. This means that the average of all possible values of $\bar{x}$ equals $\mu_x$. (Recall from Chapter 6 that from an infinite population there is an infinite number of samples of size $n$ that can be drawn. Thus there is an infinite number of $\bar{x}$ values, the average of which is the population mean.) For the briefcase survey, $\bar{x} = 38.6$ is our point estimate of $\mu_x$, the population mean of all customers purchasing briefcases. If we could take many (or infinite) different samples, where each sample is of size $n = 89$, and calculate each sample mean, then the average of all these sample means would equal the population mean. The single value of 38.6 need not equal the (unknown) population mean. Single values of $\bar{x}$, in fact, typically do *not* exactly equal $\mu_x$.

The sample variance $(s_x^2)$ is unbiased in estimating the population variance $(\sigma_x^2)$. Intuitively, this implies that the average of all possible values of $s_x^2$ equals $\sigma_x^2$. The sample variance for the briefcase survey, $s_x^2 = 52.1$, is our estimate of the variance of the population of ages. The average of *all* values of $s_x^2$'s, each calculated from samples of size $n = 89$, would equal $\sigma_x^2$. Our value of $s_x^2 = 52.1$ probably does not equal $\sigma_x^2$, as single values of $s_x^2$ typically do not equal $\sigma_x^2$.

The sample proportion $(p = x/n$, where $x$ is the number of successes in $n$ trials) is unbiased in estimating the population proportion $(\pi)$. In other words, the average of all values of $p$ equals $\pi$. In the briefcase survey, $x = 34$ and $n = 89$, so that $p = x/n = 34/89 = 0.382$ represents our estimate of the population proportion. This single value of $p$ does not necessarily equal $\pi$, however, since unbiasedness only implies that on average $p$ equals the population proportion $\pi$.

# 7.3 Confidence Intervals

An interval estimate is a range of values for the population parameter. Interval estimates can be constructed for each of the point estimates previously presented. We will focus on interval estimates for $\mu_x$ in Section 7.4 and 7.5 and on interval estimates for $\pi$ in Section 7.6. First, the concept of a confidence interval is presented.

The set of all numbers between the highest and lowest values that makes up an interval estimate is called a **confidence interval**. If $L$ represents the lowest value and $H$ the highest value, then we can represent a confidence interval as shown in Fig. 7.1. Note that the point estimate falls in the *middle* of the confidence interval shown in this figure. For most real-world applications, the point estimate is the center of a confidence interval. In this book we will restrict our discussion of confidence intervals to these cases.

Associated with every confidence interval is a number that indicates how much "faith" (or confidence) we have that the population parameter lies between the lower bound ($L$) and the upper bound ($H$). Four frequently used confidence levels are: 90% confidence, 95% confidence, 99% confidence, and 99.5% confidence. As will be seen in the next several pages, these levels of confidence are used to identify the confidence interval being calculated.

## The Meaning of a Confidence Interval

Confidence intervals are always associated with a specific level of confidence. For example, if we say that we are 90% confident that the $L$-$H$ interval in Fig. 7.1 contains the true population parameter, then this interval is called a 90% confidence interval for the population parameter. This means that if

**Figure 7.1**
A confidence interval.

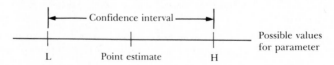

100 samples are taken, and for each sample a value of L and a value of H are determined, then the population parameter will be between the L and H values for 90 of the 100 intervals (on the average).

L and H are random variables that take on different values from sample to sample. Thus the 90% confidence interval for the population parameter being estimated can be written in the form of a probability statement.

$$P(L < \text{population parameter} < H) = 0.90$$

This statement does not say that there is a probability of 0.90 that the population parameter is between *specific* values of L and H. Again, the interpretation is that if we were to collect many different samples, these samples would yield many different values of L and H. Ninety percent of all possible L-H intervals would contain the population parameter. Ten percent of the intervals would not contain the population parameter.

Figure 7.2 illustrates the construction of 11 different confidence intervals, based on 11 different samples out of an infinite number of samples that could be drawn. The vertical line is the known value of the population parameter being estimated. Note in Fig. 7.2 that one of the L-H intervals (sample 6) does not cross the population line. In this interval the population parameter is not between specific L and H values. In general, we do not know the value of the population parameter being estimated and only a single sample is taken. When sampling, one never knows if the population parameter is between L and H.

For a 90% confidence interval, the probability that the lower bound L and the upper bound H will *not* contain the population parameter is 1 − 0.90 = 0.10. This probability of being incorrect is designated by the Greek letter alpha ($\alpha$).

**Figure 7.2**
Illustrating the calculation of many confidence intervals.

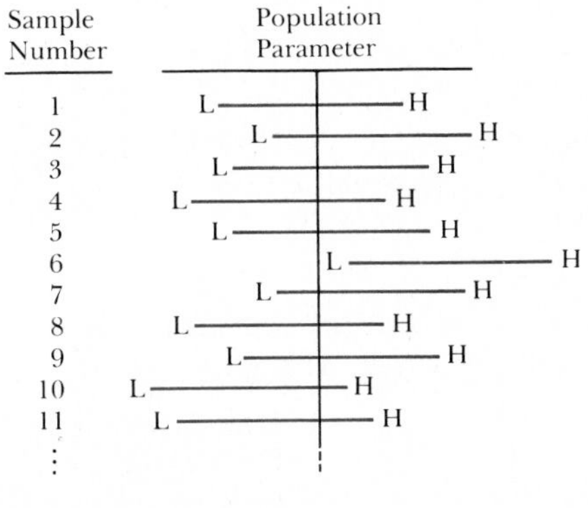

For a 90% confidence interval, $\alpha = 0.10$.

For a 95% confidence interval, $\alpha = 0.05$.

For a 99% confidence interval, $\alpha = 0.01$.

For a 99.5% confidence interval, $\alpha = 0.005$.

For any given value of $\alpha$, one can always determine the level of the confidence interval by calculating $(1 - \alpha)100\%$. For instance, if $\alpha = 0.05$, then the confidence interval is of size 95%:

$$(1 - \alpha)100\% = (1 - 0.05)100\% = 95\%$$

The decision maker usually sets $\alpha$ before collecting any sample data by considering the trade-off between the desired level of the confidence interval and the consequences of being incorrect. If $\alpha$ is set very low (e.g., $\alpha = 0.001$), then the confidence interval will be very wide and the decision maker can be highly confident that any *L-H* interval will contain the population parameter being estimated. But such an interval may be too wide to be useful; that is, it may not be informative because it is so wide. (Later in the chapter we will see that the width of an interval may be decreased by increasing the sample size.)

The marketing analyst concerned with briefcase sales may run very little risk of getting a wrong *L-H* interval (i.e., $\alpha$ would be very small) in stating that the population's mean age is between 20 and 50 years. But what is the use of such a wide interval? We could have guessed that $20 < \mu_x < 50$ without a sample. On the other hand, this person may run a considerable risk of being wrong ($\alpha$ would be very large) by specifying a small confidence interval (such as saying that the mean age is $34.5 < \mu_x < 35.5$). This relationship is pictured in Fig. 7.3.

**Figure 7.3**
The size of $\alpha$ and the size of the confidence interval.

(a) This narrow confidence interval will have a large $\alpha$.

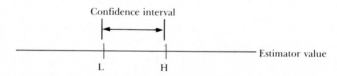

(b) This wide confidence interval will have a small $\alpha$.

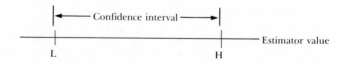

Chapter 7   Estimation

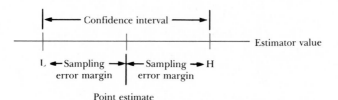

Figure 7.4
The margin for
sampling error in a
confidence interval.

In social science and business applications, $\alpha$ is frequently set at 0.01 or 0.05. Rarely is $\alpha$ set at any number larger than 0.10.

Once $\alpha$ is set by the decision maker and the sample has been taken, the values of $L$ and $H$ can be calculated. These values are determined by taking the point estimate, adding an amount to it to get $H$, and then subtracting the same amount from the point estimate to get $L$. Remember (from Fig. 7.1) that the point estimate is at the center of a confidence interval. The distance from the point estimate to $L$ (which is the same as the distance from the point estimate to $H$) represents the uncertainty of the point estimate because of sampling error. Think of this *sampling error* as the amount of margin (or leeway) you are allowing yourself in your estimate of the population parameter. Figure 7.4 illustrates this margin for sampling error.

From Fig. 7.4, we see that

$L$ = point estimate minus the margin for sampling error

and

$H$ = point estimate plus the margin for sampling error.

(Sections 7.4 through 7.6 explain how to determine the sampling error margin under various conditions.)

## The Probability of an Error

We will assume that the decision maker considers overestimation and underestimation errors to be equally serious. That is, to have the population parameter lower than $L$ is as serious an error as it is to have the population parameter higher than $H$. For example, as a marketing analyst estimating the number of customers who saw an ad in the *WSJ*, you are just as concerned with overestimating the value of the population parameter $\pi$ as you are with underestimating this population proportion.

To weigh overestimation and underestimation equally, $\alpha$ is divided into two equal parts. Each part is thus $\alpha/2$. This implies that the probability of an error (i.e., the population parameter is less than $L$) is set at $\alpha/2$. Similarly,

**Figure 7.5**
The division of α into
two equal parts.

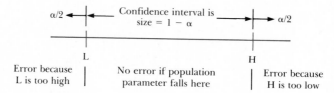

the probability of an error (i.e., the population parameter is greater than $H$) is set at $\alpha/2$. These probabilities are illustrated in Fig. 7.5.

As a marketing analyst estimating the proportion of customers who saw an ad in the *WSJ*, suppose you decide to form a 95% confidence interval. This means that you would set $\alpha = 0.05$. Dividing $\alpha = 0.05$ by 2 yields a probability of $\alpha/2 = 0.025$ that the population parameter will be less than $L$ and a probability of $\alpha/2 = 0.025$ that the population parameter will be greater than $H$.

For many confidence intervals we want to determine $z$ values that result in a probability of $\alpha/2$ in the upper tail of the standardized normal. The symbol used to denote such a $z$ value is $z_{\alpha/2}$. The subscript indicates how much probability is in the tail of the distribution. Because the normal distribution is symmetrical, the symbol $-z_{\alpha/2}$ is used to denote the $z$ value resulting in $\alpha/2$ in the *lower* tail of the $z$ distribution.

For example, if $\alpha = 0.05$, then $\alpha/2 = 0.025$ and $z_{\alpha/2} = z_{0.025}$. The value $z_{0.025}$ is the number that cuts off a probability of 0.025 in the *upper* tail of the standard normal. Since 0.025 in the upper tail is equivalent to a cumulative frequency of 0.975, we consult Appendix Table B.4 for a cumulative probability of 0.975. The $z$ value corresponding to 0.975 is $z_{0.025} = 1.96$. The value of $z$ cutting off 0.025 in the *lower* tail of the $z$ distribution is $-z_{0.025} = -1.96$. These $z$ values are pictured in Fig. 7.6.

As a second example, let us calculate the value of $z_{\alpha/2}$ when $\alpha$ is 0.02. In this case $\alpha/2 = 0.01$ is cut off in each tail of the $z$ distribution. First we look in Appendix Table B.4 for the $z$ value corresponding to a cumulative probability of $1 - \alpha/2 = 0.99$. There is no cumulative probability of 0.99,

**Figure 7.6**
Cutting off 0.025 in
the upper and lower
tails of z.

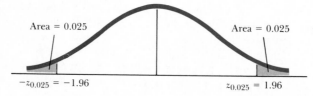

so we move to the next closest value, which is 0.9901. The $z$ value corresponding to 0.9901 is 2.33. Thus $z_{0.01} = 2.33$ (approximately) and $-z_{0.01} = -2.33$. (Recall from Chapter 6 that $z = -2.33$ gives the number of standard deviations that the lower cutoff point is away from the center of the distribution.)

---

# 7.4 Confidence Intervals for $\mu_x$ ($x$ Normal or $n$ Large, $\sigma_x$ Known)

In constructing a confidence interval for $\mu_x$, the point estimate is $\bar{x}$. From the discussion in Chapter 6 of the sampling distribution of $\bar{x}$, we know that the standard deviation of the $\bar{x}$ distribution is $\sigma_x/\sqrt{n}$, where $\sigma_x$ is the population standard deviation of the $x$ distribution. Also, if the population is normal or $n$ is large, then the distribution of $\bar{x}$ is also normal. Putting this information together results in the following equations for finding $L$ and $H$ when $\sigma$ is known:

$$L = \bar{x} - z_{\alpha/2}(\sigma_x/\sqrt{n}) \quad \text{and} \quad H = \bar{x} + z_{\alpha/2}(\sigma_x/\sqrt{n})$$

A $(1 - \alpha)100\%$ confidence interval for $\mu$ is typically written as follows:

**(7.1)**

$(1 - \alpha)100\%$ confidence interval for $\mu_x$ ($\sigma_x$ is known and $x$ is normal or $n$ is large)

$$\bar{x} - z_{\alpha/2}(\sigma_x/\sqrt{n}) < \mu_x < \bar{x} + z_{\alpha/2}(\sigma_x/\sqrt{n})$$

A large automobile company routinely administers a manual dexterity test to applicants for production line positions. While this test has remained the same (over the past 10 years), 2341 applicants have taken it. The population standard deviation of test scores is known to be 3.0. You decide to take a sample of the scores of $n = 36$ applicants in order to

1. find a point estimate of the mean score over all 2341 applicants ($\mu_x$).

2. construct a 90% confidence interval for the population mean. The sample mean score of the $n = 36$ applicants is $\bar{x} = 109.5050$.

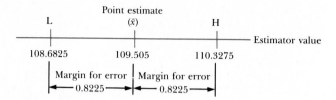

## ANSWER:

Your point estimate of $\mu_x$ is $\bar{x} = 109.5050$. The problem does not indicate whether $x$ is normally distributed. However, because $n$ is large and $\sigma_x$ is known, the $z$ distribution is appropriate. In this case $\alpha = 0.10$ since the desired confidence interval is 90%. Thus $\alpha/2 = 0.05$. To find $z_{0.05}$, we look in Appendix Table B.4 for a cumulative probability of $1 - \alpha/2 = 1 - 0.10/2 = 0.95$. The closest values are 0.9495 ($z = 1.64$) and 0.9505 ($z = 1.65$). Interpolation between these two numbers yields $z_{0.05} = 1.645$, which means that $-z_{0.05} = -1.645$. Remember that $\sigma_x = 3.0$, $n = 36$, and $\bar{x} = 109.5050$. Substituting these values into Eq. (7.1) results in the following 90% confidence interval:

$$\bar{x} - z_{\alpha/2}(\sigma_x/\sqrt{n}) < \mu_x < \bar{x} + z_{\alpha/2}(\sigma_x/\sqrt{n})$$

$$109.5050 - 1.645(3.0/\sqrt{36}) < \mu_x < 109.5050 + 1.645(3.0/\sqrt{36})$$

$$109.5050 - 0.8225 < \mu_x < 109.5050 + 0.8225$$

$$108.6825 < \mu_x < 110.3275$$

The margin for sampling error in this 90% confidence interval is $z_{\alpha/2}(\sigma/\sqrt{n}) = 0.8225$. Although we are 90% confident that the population mean ($\mu_x$) falls between 108.6825 and 110.3275, we do not know if $\mu_x$ falls in this interval or not. Figure 7.7 illustrates this confidence interval.

To understand the interpretation of a confidence interval, suppose the automobile company in Worked Example 7.1 knows that the population mean for all 2341 applicants is $\mu_x = 110.0$ and the population standard deviation is $\sigma_x = 3.0$. Imagine many different persons, each of whom takes a random sample of $n = 36$ applicants. Each person calculates a sample mean and a 90% confidence interval. To illustrate the concept of many different persons each collecting a single sample, we used a computer program to generate 2000 random samples, each of size $n = 36$, from a population that has a mean of $\mu_x = 110$ and a standard deviation of 3.0. Table 7.1 presents 11 of these random samples and the corresponding confidence intervals (the samples shown are 1, 2, 3, 49, 50, 111, 112, 789, 790, 1978, and 2000).

Note in Table 7.1 that sample 1 is the one used in Worked Example 7.1. (Remember, in most real-world cases only one sample is taken.) Also note that all the samples in Table 7.1 have the same margin for sampling error, namely, $z_{\alpha/2}\sigma/\sqrt{36} = 0.8225$. For these 11 samples, only one (111) does not contain the population mean of $\mu_x = 110$. Over an essentially infinite number of such confidence intervals, the probability of deriving an incorrect interval is $\alpha = 0.10$. The probability of a correct interval is 0.90. That is, an average of 9 out of 10 intervals will include (cover) the population mean.

**Table 7.1**

| | Eleven Samples and Confidence Intervals from a Population with $\mu_x = 110$, $\sigma_x = 3.0$ | |
|---|---|---|
| Sample Number | Point Estimates: $\bar{x}$ Values | Interval Estimates: 90% Confidence Interval |
| 1 | 109.5050 | $108.6825 < \mu_x < 110.3275$ |
| 2 | 109.6700 | $108.8475 < \mu_x < 110.4925$ |
| 3 | 110.0050 | $109.1825 < \mu_x < 110.8275$ |
| . | . | . |
| . | . | . |
| . | . | . |
| 49 | 110.5960 | $109.7735 < \mu_x < 111.4185$ |
| 50 | 109.8860 | $109.0635 < \mu_x < 110.7085$ |
| . | . | . |
| . | . | . |
| . | . | . |
| 111 | 108.9780 | $108.1555 < \mu_x < 109.8005$ |
| 112 | 110.4620 | $109.6395 < \mu_x < 111.2845$ |
| . | . | . |
| . | . | . |
| . | . | . |
| 789 | 109.6430 | $108.8205 < \mu_x < 110.4655$ |
| 790 | 110.2330 | $109.4105 < \mu_x < 111.0555$ |
| . | . | . |
| . | . | . |
| . | . | . |
| 1978 | 110.1240 | $109.3015 < \mu_x < 110.9465$ |
| . | . | . |
| . | . | . |
| 2000 | 110.7790 | $109.9565 < \mu_x < 111.6015$ |

**WORKED EXAMPLE
7.2**

A computer manufacturer wants to estimate the mean time needed for the cooling fan in its microcomputer to wear out. The time to failure ($x$) of this fan is assumed to be normally distributed, with a known variance of $\sigma_x^2 = 96{,}100$ (hours squared). A random sample of 18 fans resulted in an average time to failure of $\bar{x} = 4438$ hours. Use this information to construct a 99% confidence interval for $\mu_x$.

**ANSWER:**

The point estimate for $\mu_x$ is $\bar{x} = 4438$ hours. For a 99% confidence interval, $\alpha = 0.01$ and $\alpha/2 = 0.01/2 = 0.005$. Although $n$ is not large, $x$ is normally distributed, and $\sigma_x$ is known, so the $z$ distribution is appropriate. From Appendix Table B.4 we need the $z$ value corresponding to a cumulative probability of $1 - \alpha/2 = 0.995$. The closest cumulative probabilities in Table B.4 are 0.9949 ($z = 2.57$) and 0.9951 ($z = 2.58$). Although a linear approximation between 2.57 and 2.58 gives 2.575, you can verify by using a computer program that the correct value is 2.576. We will use the values $z_{0.005} = 2.576$ and $-z_{0.005} = -2.576$.

Since the population variance is $\sigma_x^2 = 96{,}100$, the population standard deviation is $\sigma_x = \sqrt{96{,}100} = 310$ hours. Substituting this value plus $n = 18$ and $\pm z_{0.005} = \pm 2.576$ into Eq. (7.1) results in the following 99% confidence interval:

$$\bar{x} - z_{\alpha/2}(\sigma_x/\sqrt{n}) < \mu_x < \bar{x} + z_{\alpha/2}(\sigma_x/\sqrt{n})$$
$$4438 - 2.576(310/\sqrt{18}) < \mu_x < 4438 + 2.576(310/\sqrt{18})$$
$$4438 - 188.22 < \mu_x < 4438 + 188.22$$
$$4249.78 < \mu_x < 4626.22$$

The margin for sampling error is 188.22. This confidence interval may be stated as follows: We have 99% confidence that the population mean $\mu_x$ lies between 4249.78 and 4626.22. Recall that we do not know if the population mean actually lies between these two values, nor can any probability statement be made about $\mu_x$ and these specific values of $L$ and $H$. All we know is that the methods we followed to find this confidence interval will yield a value of $L$ and a value of $H$ that contain $\mu_x$ 99% of the time. [As stated in Chapter 6, the $z$ distribution requires either the parent population to be normal or $n$ to be large ($n > 30$).]

# 7.5 Confidence Intervals for $\mu_x$ ($x$ Normal, $\sigma_x$ Unknown)

The assumption was made in Section 7.4 that the population standard deviation $\sigma_x$ is known. In most estimation problems it is not reasonable to make this assumption. When $\sigma_x$ is unknown, the sample standard deviation $s_x$ can be used to estimate $\sigma_x$. However, when $s_x$ is used to estimate $\sigma_x$, then the $t$ distribution must be used to determine the margin of sampling error (rather than the $z$ distribution).

As with the $z$ distribution, we need to find values of the $t$ distribution that cut off $\alpha/2$ in each tail of the distribution. The symbol

$$t_{\alpha/2, n-1}$$

is used to denote the $t$ value that cuts off $\alpha/2$ in the *upper* tail with $n - 1$ degrees of freedom (d.f.). Similarly, $-t_{\alpha/2, n-1}$ denotes the $t$ value cutting off $\alpha/2$ in the *lower* tail, with $n - 1$ d.f. For example, if $n = 20$ and $\alpha = 0.05$, then $n - 1 = 20 - 1 = 19$ and $\alpha/2 = 0.025$, and we need the $t$ values $\pm t_{0.025, 19}$. This means that we look for the $t$ value corresponding to a cumulative probability of 0.975 in Appendix Table B.5 for $n - 1 = 19$ d.f. and find

$$\pm t_{0.025, 19} = \pm 2.093$$

A confidence interval for $\mu_x$ assumes that the population ($x$) is normally distributed and the variance is unknown. In constructing a $(1 - \alpha)100\%$ confidence interval for $\mu_x$, the following formula is used:

---

(7.2)

$(1 - \alpha)100\%$ confidence interval for $\mu_x$ ($x$ normal, $\sigma_x$ unknown)

$$\bar{x} - t_{\alpha/2, n-1}(s_x/\sqrt{n}) < \mu_x < \bar{x} + t_{\alpha/2, n-1}(s_x/\sqrt{n})$$

---

The reader should compare this formula with Eq. (7.1) and note that the only difference is that Eq. (7.2) has $s_x$ substituted for $\sigma_x$ and uses the $t$ distribution rather than the $z$.

An accountant wishes to estimate the average level of accounts receivable for a certain Sears store. The population of accounts receivable $(x)$ is quite large and can be considered to be normally distributed. Construct a 90% confidence interval for $\mu_x$ using the random sample in Table 7.2.

**Table 7.2**

| Sears Accounts Receivable Sample | | | |
|---|---|---|---|
| **Account No.** | **Amount** | **Account No.** | **Amount** |
| 1 | $77.51 | 11 | $111.69 |
| 2 | 13.93 | 12 | 48.09 |
| 3 | 65.48 | 13 | 5.41 |
| 4 | 25.26 | 14 | 17.00 |
| 5 | 34.73 | 15 | 55.74 |
| 6 | 54.11 | 16 | 72.33 |
| 7 | 61.59 | 17 | 36.51 |
| 8 | 45.66 | 18 | 29.03 |
| 9 | 19.99 | 19 | 65.72 |
| 10 | 52.83 | 20 | 41.94 |

**ANSWER:**

A computer program was used to determine sample statistics from Table 7.2. This process is illustrated in Table 7.3. From this display, a point estimate of the mean of all accounts receivable is $\bar{x} = \$46.7275$. The $t$ distribution is appropriate for constructing an interval estimate because the population $(x)$ is normal and $\sigma_x$ is unknown. Since a 90% confidence interval is desired, $\alpha = 0.10$, $\alpha/2 = 0.05$. The degrees of freedom are $20 - 1 = 19$. The value of $t_{0.05,19}$ can be determined by looking in Appendix Table B.5 in the row for 19 d.f. and in the 0.950 column (representing a cumulative probability of $1 - \alpha/2 = 0.95$). From Table B.5, $\pm t_{0.05,19} = \pm 1.729$. From the computer printout, the accountant knows that the sample standard deviation is $s_x = 25.5045$. Substituting these values into Eq. (7.2) gives

$$\bar{x} - t_{\alpha/2,n-1}(s_x/\sqrt{n}) < \mu_x < \bar{x} + t_{\alpha/2,n-1}(s_x/\sqrt{n})$$

$$46.7275 - 1.729(25.5045/\sqrt{20}) < \mu_x < 46.7275 + 1.729(25.5045/\sqrt{20})$$

$$46.7275 - 9.8605 < \mu_x < 46.7275 + 9.8605$$

$$36.8670 < \mu_x < 56.5880$$

**Table 7.3**

| A Computer Printout for Descriptive Statistics |
|---|

First we bring up a statistical program, create a file called ACCOUNTS, and enter the data in Table 7.2. Next, we load the descriptive statistics module. The terminal will look as follows, where the entries are in bold type.

```
ENTER FILE NAME: ACCOUNTS

OPTIONS: A. INPUT ALL CASES
         B. INPUT SUBSET OF CASES

ENTER: OPTION: A

OPTIONS: A. SHORT FORM OUTPUT (MEAN, STD. DEV., MIN, MAX)
         B. EXTENDED OUTPUT OF SELECTED VARIABLES
         C. [TERMINATE]

ENTER: OPTION: A

OPTIONS: A. SCREEN OUTPUT
         B. PRINTER OUTPUT

ENTER: OPTION: A

ENTER JOB TITLE:

ACCOUNTS RECEIVABLE STATISTICS
```

```
              ACCOUNTS RECEIVABLE STATISTICS
NO.    NAME     N     MEAN    STD. DEV.   MINIMUM    MAXIMUM
 1   ACCOUNTS   20   46.7275    25.5045    5.4100    111.6900
     PRESS ANY KEY TO CONTINUE
```

The accountant can be 90% confident that the mean of all accounts receivable falls between $36.87 and $56.59, because on average 90% of similarly constructed intervals will contain $\mu_x$.

---

**WORKED EXAMPLE 7.4**

An article in the *WSJ* on June 10, 1984, reported that a Baltimore directory assistance operator was suspended because she averaged three seconds more than the 30-second standard. Suppose in this situation the suspension had been based on a random sample of the length of 10 different calls. Using the

10 calls in the following list, would a 95% confidence interval indicate that this operator had exceeded the 30-second standard?

| Call | Time (Seconds) | Call | Time (Seconds) |
|------|----------------|------|----------------|
| 1 | 28 | 6 | 36 |
| 2 | 29 | 7 | 27 |
| 3 | 31 | 8 | 37 |
| 4 | 38 | 9 | 29 |
| 5 | 45 | 10 | 30 |

ANSWER:

The sample average for the 10 calls is

$$\bar{x} = \tfrac{1}{10}(28 + 29 + \cdots + 30) = 33.0$$

The sample variance for the 10 calls is

$$s_x^2 = \tfrac{1}{9}[(28-33)^2 + (29-33)^2 + \cdots + (30-33)^2]$$
$$= \tfrac{1}{9}(300) = 33.33 \text{ (seconds squared)}$$

The sample standard deviation is

$$s_x = \sqrt{33.33} = 5.7735 \text{ seconds}$$

For $\alpha/2 = 0.025$ and d.f. $= 9$, $t_{0.025,9} = 2.262$. Substituting these values into Eq. (7.2) yields

$$\bar{x} - t_{\alpha/2,n-1}(s_x/\sqrt{n}) < \mu_x < \bar{x} + t_{\alpha/2,n-1}(s_x/\sqrt{n})$$
$$33 - 2.262(5.7735/\sqrt{10}) < \mu_x < 33 + 2.262(5.7735/\sqrt{10})$$
$$33 - 4.13 < \mu_x < 33 + 4.13$$
$$28.87 < \mu_x < 37.13$$

The time standard of 30 seconds falls within this 95% confidence interval. Hence this sample of 10 would not be sufficient statistical evidence to conclude that the population mean for this operator exceeded the time standard.

**7.1** Distinguish between a point estimate and a point estimator. Give an example of each.

ACT **7.2** A CPA takes a random sample of 75 of the checking accounts of a local bank. The mean balance is $438.12. Indicate whether each of the following statements is true or false. If the statement is false, explain why.

a) The population mean is $438.12 because $\bar{x}$ is unbiased when $\mu_x$ is estimated.

b) If an infinite number of samples were taken, the mean of all the sample means would be $438.12.

c) The population mean is close to $438.12 because $\bar{x}$ is unbiased.

d) We do not know how close $438.12 is to the population mean.

ECN **7.3** Income data are typically skewed to the right. You are working with these data and have been asked to make a point estimate of the center of the data.

a) What would be the center of the data in this situation?

b) Would you suggest using the mean or the median? Explain.

c) Suppose you decide to use the median. Do you think the median is an unbiased estimator? If so, what population parameter is the median estimating?

**7.4** Find the value of $z_{\alpha/2}$ for the following values of $\alpha$.

a) $\alpha = 0.06$,     b) $\alpha = 0.001$

c) $\alpha = 0.03$,     d) $\alpha = 0.01$

MKT **7.5** Based on a survey of 100 new Buick owners, a marketing analyst for General Motors has established a 98% confidence interval for the mean income for all new Buick owners to be:

$30,388 < \mu_x < $42,162.

a) The $\alpha$ used by this analyst was _____.

b) The analyst's point estimate of $\mu_x$ is _____.

c) The lower limit ($L$) is _____, the upper limit ($H$) is _____.

d) The value of $z_{\alpha/2}$ used in constructing this confidence interval was _____.

e) The margin for sampling error is _____.

MKT **7.6** Use the information and the confidence interval in Exercise 7.5 to determine whether the following statements are true or false. If a statement is false, explain why it is false.

a) Based on this confidence interval, General Motors can state that 98% of all new Buick owners have an income between $30,388 and $42,162.

b) If an infinite number of such confidence intervals were constructed, General Motors would find that 98% of the $\bar{x}$ would fall between $30,388 and $42,162.

c) Ninety-eight percent of all new-car owners with an income between $30,388 and $42,162 bought a Buick.

d) If an infinite number of such intervals were constructed, General Motors would find that 98% of the intervals would contain the population mean income of new Buick owners.

FIN **7.7** A stock broker has taken a random sample of four stocks from a large population of low-priced stocks. Stock prices for this population are normally distributed. The sample prices of the four stocks are $5, $12, $17, and $10.

a) Calculate a point estimate of the population mean.

b) Calculate a point estimate of the population variance. What is your estimate for a population standard deviation?

c) Calculate a point estimate of the proportion of stocks in this population with a price of $10 or more.

ADM **7.8** A revised company policy gives employees vacation days for unused sick days at the end of each year. In a random sample of six employees, the number of sick days used as vacation days was 7, 4, 9, 2, 8, and 7. Assume that the parent population ($x$) is normally distributed.

a) Determine a point estimate of the population mean, $\mu_x$.

b) Construct a 90% confidence interval for $\mu_x$, assuming the population standard deviation is known to equal 1.4. What is the margin for sampling error?

**c)** Calculate a point estimate for the population variance, $\sigma_x^2$. What is your estimate of $\sigma_x$?

**7.9** What assumptions about the parent population are necessary

   **a)** when making a point estimate of either $\mu_x$, $\sigma_x^2$, or $\pi$?

   **b)** when making an interval estimate of $\mu_x$?

MFG   **7.10** A 95% confidence interval for the population mean time (in seconds) needed to finish a specific production task is

$$150 < \mu_x < 176$$

   **a)** Sketch this interval, indicating the margin for sampling error.

   **b)** If the sample size had been $n = 52$, what was the (known) population standard deviation?

PUB   **7.11** A consumer interest group has compared the prices of a loaf of whole wheat sandwich bread at a random sample of $n = 6$ grocery stores from many stores in a large city. The prices in the sample were $0.89, $0.73, $0.91, $0.82, $0.99, and $0.87. The population of prices is normally distributed, with a known standard deviation of $0.05.

   **a)** Determine a point estimate of the population mean.

   **b)** Determine a 98% confidence interval for $\mu_x$. Explain why your interval is fairly wide.

   **c)** Calculate a point estimate of the population variance and standard deviation.

ACT   **7.12** Return to the hardware store case at the beginning of Section 2.3 (Chapter 2). Find a point estimate of $\mu_x$ and construct a 95% confidence interval for your estimate. Assume that $x$ is normally distributed, with a standard deviation of $\sigma_x = 20$.

**7.13** Comment on the validity of the following statements:

   **a)** "A 99% confidence is always better than a 95% confidence interval because one can be more confident about the population parameter."

   **b)** "A 90% confidence interval means that 90% of the time the population parameter will fall between the specified values of $L$ and $H$."

   **c)** "If the margin for sampling error is small, then the value of $\alpha$ must be large."

FIN    **7.14** Take a random sample of size $n = 25$ from all of the corporations
listed in Appendix A.1. Assume that the population of interest, "12
months' earnings per share," is normally distributed.

   a) Find a point estimate for the population mean.
   b) Find a point estimate for the population variance.
   c) Find a point estimate for the population proportion of companies with
   earnings per share of $3 or more.

MFG    **7.15** A 90% confidence interval for the population mean time (in minutes)
needed to finish a certain assembly process is

$$90 < \mu_x < 130$$

   a) Sketch this interval, indicating the margin for sampling error.
   b) If the sample size was $n = 25$, what was the sample standard deviation?
   c) To interpret this confidence interval, what did you have to assume
   about the population and why?

ACT    **7.16** An accountant determined a 95% confidence interval for the average
monthly losses from damaged goods at a store of $2300 < \mu_x < \$5500$
and concluded that there was a 0.025 probability that losses from
damaged goods would exceed $5500 in any given month. Is this in-
terpretation correct?

# 7.6  Confidence Intervals for $\pi$ (*n* Large)

In many situations the business analyst would like to estimate a population
proportion. Cigarette manufacturers want to know what proportion of the
population are smokers, automobile executives want to know what proportion
of adults are planning to purchase a new car this year, and a production
manager might like to determine the proportion of defectives in a production
lot. A population proportion is designated by the Greek letter pi ($\pi$). The
sample estimate of such a proportion is the sample proportion $p$, which is
the ratio of the number of successes in a sample to the sample size, $x/n$.

As indicated earlier in this chapter, $p$ is an unbiased estimator of the
population proportion $\pi$. When $n$ is large (usually $n > 30$ is sufficient) and

the expected value of $\pi$ is not close to 0 or 1, the normal distribution can be used to approximate an interval estimate for $\pi$ in much the same fashion as we did for $\mu_x$. In fact, we still use $\pm z_{\alpha/2}$, as we did then. Now the point estimate is $p = x/n$, and the margin for error is defined as follows:

Margin for error in estimating $\pi$:   $z_{\alpha/2}\sqrt{p(1-p)/n}$

The resulting confidence interval for $\pi$ is given in Eq. (7.3).

---

Approximate $(1-\alpha)100\%$ confidence interval for estimating $\pi$

(7.3)   $$p - z_{\alpha/2}\sqrt{p(1-p)/n} < \pi < p + z_{\alpha/2}\sqrt{p(1-p)/n}$$

where $p = x/n$

---

If $n$ is sufficiently large and $p$ is sufficiently close to 0.5, this confidence interval for $\pi$ will never result in endpoints ($L$ and $H$) less than 0 or greater than 1. Endpoints outside these limits are one indication that the normal approximation (the use of $z$) is inappropriate.

---

**WORKED EXAMPLE 7.5**

A *WSJ* article reported that 105 people in a Gallup survey of 202 small-company heads said that the size of the federal budget deficit is their greatest worry about the current economy. What point and interval values should be used to estimate the population proportion of small-company heads who worry most about the federal budget deficit? A 95% confidence is desired.

**ANSWER:**

The sample proportion, $105/202 = 0.52$, is used as the point estimate of the population parameter $\pi$. Equation (7.3) can be used to determine a 95% confidence interval where

$$\pm z_{\alpha/2} = \pm z_{0.025} = \pm 1.96$$

Substituting $p = x/n$, $x = 105$, $n = 202$, $z_{\alpha/2} = 1.96$ into Eq. (7.3) yields

$$p - z_{\alpha/2}\sqrt{p(1-p)/n} < \pi < p + z_{\alpha/2}\sqrt{p(1-p)/n}$$

$$\frac{x}{n} - z_{\alpha/2} \sqrt{\frac{\dfrac{x}{n}\left(1 - \dfrac{x}{n}\right)}{n}} < \pi < \frac{x}{n} + z_{\alpha/2} \sqrt{\frac{\dfrac{x}{n}\left(1 - \dfrac{x}{n}\right)}{n}}$$

$$\frac{105}{202} - 1.96 \sqrt{\frac{\dfrac{105}{202}\left(1 - \dfrac{105}{202}\right)}{202}} < \pi < \frac{105}{202} + 1.96 \sqrt{\frac{\dfrac{105}{202}\left(1 - \dfrac{105}{202}\right)}{202}}$$

$$0.5198 - 1.96(0.035) < \pi < 0.5198 + 1.96(0.035)$$

$$0.5198 - 0.0686 < \pi < 0.5198 + 0.0686$$

$$0.4512 < \pi < 0.5884$$

In this problem, the margin for sampling error is 0.0686. The *WSJ* can be 95% confident that the population proportion $\pi$ lies between 0.4512 and 0.5884, since on the average approximately 95% of the intervals constructed in this manner will contain $\pi$ and only 5% will not contain $\pi$. We do not know, however, whether the interval 0.4512 to 0.5884 is one of the 95% correct intervals or one of the 5% incorrect intervals. Figure 7.8 illustrates these values.

**Figure 7.8**
The confidence interval for executive economic opinion.

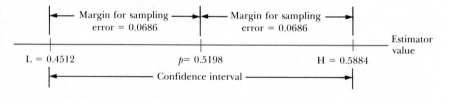

## 7.7 Replacing *t* with *z* in Large-Sample Estimation of $\mu_x$ when $\sigma_x$ is Unknown

As we indicated in Section 7.5, for most estimation problems the assumption that the population standard deviation ($\sigma_x$) is known is unrealistic. At that time we introduced the *t* distribution as the correct distribution to use when the population standard deviation is unknown. Unfortunately, when *n* is large ($n > 30$) the *t* distribution can be inconvenient to use because most *t* tables provide only a limited number of critical values and include values for only a small set of degrees of freedom. In such cases the $z$ distribution, which can be used to approximate the $t$ distribution, is generally easier to use. (If one has access to a computer program for the $t$ distribution, there is no reason to approximate the $t$ distribution with the $z$.)

Recall from Chapter 6 that when the degrees of freedom are infinite, the $t$ distribution is the same as the normal distribution. For this reason, the $t$ and $z$ values cutting off 0.025 in the upper tail are the same number (1.645) when $n$ is infinitely large. Of course, $n$ is never infinitely large, but even when it is reasonably large, the values in Appendix Table B.5 for $t$ are quite close to the comparable $z$ values. By custom, $n > 30$ is considered sufficient to substitute $z$ for $t$ in the confidence interval formula for $\mu_x$ when $\sigma_x$ is unknown (Eq. 7.2). Thus, Eq. (7.4) is a special case of Eq. (7.2) to be used only when $n > 30$ and a computer program for the $t$ distribution is not available.

---

(7.4)  Approximate $(1 - \alpha)$ 100% confidence interval for $\mu_x$ when $\sigma_x$ is unknown but $n > 30$

$$\bar{x} - z_{\alpha/2}(s_x/\sqrt{n}) < \mu_x < \bar{x} + z_{\alpha/2}(s_x/\sqrt{n})$$

---

The following case illustrates this formula.

## Excise Taxes

You are an accountant for Thorp, Inc., a company that makes small parts for truck engines. Based on letters from the Internal Revenue Service (IRS) in 1980 and 1982 you did not charge your customers excise tax on any of the parts sold after 1980. The IRS now says that you should have charged the excise tax for the period 1984–1986. The IRS did not examine all of Thorp's 22,974 sales invoices for this period. Instead, they took a random sample of 160 invoices and mailed you a summary of their calculations (shown in Table 7.4). You wish to check the process and the calculations used by the IRS in determining the amount of excise tax owed. The bill sent to Thorp for uncollected excise taxes was for $194,437.38.

You cooperated with the IRS in collecting the sample, and agree that the procedures used by the IRS were consistent with random sampling methods. Because you and your staff do not agree that the IRS should have imposed this tax retroactively, Thorp is determined to fight the assessment in court. In the meantime, your task is to study the calculations used by the IRS in determining the $194,437.38 assessment. The only information provided by the IRS to Thorp is the summary in Table 7.4.

In this problem the population standard deviation is unknown. Hence, the $t$ distribution is appropriate for constructing a confidence interval. Because the sample size is $n = 160$, there is a problem in using Appendix Table B.5, for the degrees of freedom in that table skip from 120 to infinity. The problem can be seen to be a minor one, however, by looking carefully at the entries in the rows for 120 and infinity. For example, in the column headed 0.950, the entry for 120 d.f. is $t = 1.658$, while the entry for infinity is $t = 1.645$. Because there is little difference between these two $t$ values, they will yield approximately the same value of $L$ and $H$ in constructing a confidence interval. Thus, in constructing a confidence interval when $\alpha = 0.10$ and $n = 160$, we could approximate the correct $t$ value by using $\pm t = \pm 1.645$.

The IRS used Eq. (7.4) in determining the Thorp tax assessment. First, from line 1 in Table 7.4, we see that they selected a 90% confidence interval (i.e., $\alpha = 0.10$). They took a random sample of $n = 160$ invoices (line 3),

**Table 7.4**

| Thorp Tax Assessment | |
|---|---|
| 1. Select confidence interval | 90% |
| 2. Average of audited sample values $(\bar{x})$ | $11.2078 |
| 3. Sample size used $(n)$ | 160 |
| 4. Population size $(N)$ | 22,794 |
| 5. Point estimate of total $(N\bar{x})$ | $255,470.59 |
| 6. Standard deviation of sample audit values $(s_x)$ | 20.5895 |
| 7. $z$ statistic | 1.645 |
| 8. Margin for sampling error $(zs/\sqrt{n})$ | 2.6776 |
| 9. Lower limit for average $(\bar{x} - zs/\sqrt{n})$ | $8.5302 |
| 10. Upper limit for average $(\bar{x} + zs/\sqrt{n})$ | $13.8854 |
| 11. Total margin for sampling error $(Nzs/\sqrt{n})$ | $61,033.21 |
| 12. Lower limit for total $(N\bar{x} - Nzs/\sqrt{n})$ | $194,437.38 |
| 13. Upper limit for total $(N\bar{x} + Nzs/\sqrt{n})$ | $316,503.80 |

and the point estimate of the amount of excise tax owed by Thorp (per invoice) was $\bar{x} = \$11.2078$ (line 2). The IRS point estimate of the total amount owed by Thorp for uncollected excise taxes is the average per invoice (11.2078) times the number of invoices (22,794), or

$$N\bar{x} = \$255,470.59 \qquad \text{(line 5)}$$

The sample standard deviation of the excise tax owed was $s_x = 20.5895$ (line 6). For a 90% confidence interval the z value is $\pm z_{0.05} = \pm 1.645$ (line 7). Substituting these values into Eq. (7.4) results in the following confidence interval for the mean amount owed per invoice:

$$\bar{x} - z_{\alpha/2}(s_x/\sqrt{n}) < \mu_x < \bar{x} + z_{\alpha/2}(s_x/\sqrt{n})$$
$$11.2078 - 1.645(20.5895/\sqrt{160}) < \mu_x < 11.2078 + 1.645(20.5895/\sqrt{160})$$
$$11.2078 - 2.6776 < \mu_x < 11.2078 + 2.6776$$
$$8.5302 < \mu_x < 13.8854$$

This lower limit ($L = 8.5302$) is found on line 9, while the upper limit ($H = 13.8854$) is found on line 10. Since this confidence interval is for each invoice, the IRS multiplied $L$ and $H$ by the population size to construct a confidence interval for the total amount of excise tax owed (which we call $\mu_T$). This 90% confidence interval, shown in lines 12 and 13, is

$$194,437.38 < \mu_T < 316,503.80$$

Thus the IRS is 90% confident that Thorp owes between \$194,437.38 and \$316,503.80. To be on the conservative side (and perhaps avoid legal problems), the IRS bill to Thorp for back taxes was for the lower limit, \$194,437.38.

## 7.8 Selecting the Sample Size

In all the examples thus far the sample size has been given. However, for some problems the sample size is unknown and we would like to determine the *desired sample size*. In general, in order to determine the appropriate sample size, decisions must be made about

1. the size of the confidence interval to be constructed once the sample is taken. This means that $\alpha$ must be known.

**2.** the desired *margin for sampling error* in the confidence interval. We will call this margin $D$.

There are two formulas for determining the sample size, one when the population mean $\mu_x$ is being estimated and $\sigma_x$ is known, and another when the population proportion $\pi$ is being estimated.

## Determining the Sample Size When $\mu_x$ is Being Estimated

Recall from Eq. (7.1) that the margin for error in estimating $\mu_x$ when $\sigma_x$ is known is $z_{\alpha/2}(\sigma_x/\sqrt{n})$. This margin is what we call $D$; that is,

$$D = z_{\alpha/2}(\sigma_x/\sqrt{n})$$

Solving this equation for $n$ yields Eq. (7.5) for determining the desired sample size.

---

Desired sample size for $\mu_x$ ($\sigma_x$ known)

**(7.5)**
$$n = \left[\frac{z_{\alpha/2}\sigma_x}{D}\right]^2$$

---

As we indicated earlier, in most problems it is unrealistic to assume that the population standard deviation is known. In some situations, the analyst may make a reasonable guess for the value of $\sigma_x$ based on past experience or using a rule of thumb based on the normal distribution. This rule says that when the population is normally distributed, then there should be four to six standard deviations between the highest and lowest observable values. A reasonable guess thus might be that there are five standard deviations between the highest and lowest observed values.

---

Rough guess for $\sigma_x$

**(7.6)**
$$\sigma_x^* = \frac{\text{highest} - \text{lowest}}{5}$$

---

Chapter 7   Estimation

**WORKED EXAMPLE 7.6**

A cash management analyst wishes to estimate the average elapsed time between the issuing of a billing statement by a large retailer and the receipt of payment. From past experience the analyst knows that the elapsed time tends to be normally distributed, with a standard deviation of 6.2 days. Find the appropriate sample size if the analyst wishes to estimate the mean elapsed time within one day (i.e., $D = 1.0$) with 95% confidence.

**ANSWER:**

In this case $z_{\alpha/2} = z_{0.025} = 1.96$ and $\sigma_x = 6.2$. The desired sample size is

$$n = \left[\frac{z_{\alpha/2}\sigma_x}{D}\right]^2 = \left[\frac{1.96(6.2)}{1.0}\right]^2 = 147.67$$

The desired sample size is found by rounding this number to the next highest integer. Thus the analyst should sample $n = 148$.

---

**WORKED EXAMPLE 7.7**

In Worked Example 7.6 the analyst knew that $\sigma_x = 6.2$. It is possible that the analyst did not know $\sigma_x$, but instead only knew that some bills are paid in 1 day and others take as long as 31 days (company policy is to extend credit for only a month). Under these conditions, what is the appropriate sample size?

**ANSWER:**

A guess for $\sigma_x$ would be

$$\sigma_x^* = \frac{\text{highest} - \text{lowest}}{5} = \frac{31 - 1}{5} = 6.0 \text{ days}$$

Using a guess of 6.0 for $\sigma_x$ in Eq. (7.5) results in a desired sample size of $n = 139$, which is not much different from the value of $n = 148$ in Worked Example 7.6, where $\sigma_x$ was known.

---

## Determining the Sample Size When Estimating $\pi$

In Eq. (7.3) the margin for sampling error in a confidence interval for the population proportion was

$$D = z_{\alpha/2}\sqrt{p(1 - p)/n}$$

Unfortunately, we cannot solve this equation for $n$, because we do not know the value of $p = x/n$ (remember, $x$ is a sample result). If, however, the analyst can make a reasonable guess about the value of $p$, then this guess (which we designate as $p^*$) can be substituted for $p$ in the preceding equation. In this case the desired sample size can be approximated by using Eq. (7.7).

Desired sample size when estimating $\pi$

(7.7)
$$n = \left[\frac{z_{\alpha/2}}{D}\right]^2 p^*(1 - p^*)$$

where $p^*$ denotes a guess about the value of $p$.

If the analyst has an intuitive idea about the possible value of $p$, this value should be labeled $p^*$ and then substituted into Eq. (7.7). If the analyst has no intuitive idea about $p$, then $p^* = 1/2$ should be substituted into Eq. (7.7). A value of $p^* = 1/2$ will result in a *larger* value of $n$ than will any other value of $p^*$ (try several values of $p^*$ if you do not believe this).

**WORKED EXAMPLE 7.8**

A manufacturer of computer microchips has been producing large quantities of 288K random access memory (RAM) chips. In the past, the production process resulted in about 40% defective chips. To determine whether a new process is producing fewer defectives chips, the manufacturer wants to take a random sample of chips and then construct a 99% confidence interval with an error of 0.10.

**ANSWER:**

Since $\alpha = 0.01$, $z_{0.005} = 2.576$. Using $p^* = 0.40$ and $D = 0.10$, the best guess about the optimal sample size is

$$n = \left[\frac{z_{\alpha/2}}{D}\right]^2 p^*(1 - p^*) = \left[\frac{2.576}{0.10}\right]^2 (0.40)(0.60) = 159.259$$

The analyst should thus sample 160 chips.

Chapter 7   Estimation

## Relating the Sample Size to $D$, $\alpha$, and $\sigma$

In a number of areas in business, particularly accounting and marketing, the statistical analyst may need to consider the effect on sample size of various levels of $D$, $\alpha$, and $\sigma$. Often the budget for conducting a sample survey is not adequate to support the desired sample size. In this circumstance, the analyst may be able to reduce $n$ by permitting a larger $D$ or using a larger $\alpha$.

---

## Marketing Survey Estimation

You are vice president for new development for Noble Pizza, a large midwestern chain. You are currently considering locating a franchise in a town of 35,000 people. Before doing so, you decide to estimate the mean household income for this city, where the population standard deviation of incomes is known to be $\sigma = 3000$. You decide to use $\alpha = 0.05$ and $D = \$100$. To find the sample size you substitute $z_{\alpha/2} = 1.96$, $D = \$100$, and $\sigma_x = 3000$ into Eq. (7.5). The desired sample size is

$$n = \left[ \frac{z_{\alpha/2}\sigma_x}{D} \right]^2 = \left[ \frac{1.96(3000)}{100} \right]^2 = 3457.44$$

Since $n = 3458$ is too large for your budget, you must find ways to reduce the sample size.

---

Any change in the right-hand side of Eqs. (7.5) or (7.7) (when calculating the optimal sample size in a proportions problem) will change the optimal sample size. Some possible changes will now be described.

*Changing D*    An increase in $D$ will decrease $n$, while a decrease in $D$ will increase $n$. The change in the optimal sample size when estimating $\mu_x$ can be determined by comparing Eq. (7.5) with the initial $D$ value [which we denote as $D(\text{old})$] with the new $D$ value [denoted as $D(\text{new})$]. The old $n$ is denoted as $n(\text{old})$, and the more recent one is $n(\text{new})$. Equation (7.5) with $D(\text{old})$ and $D(\text{new})$ is now presented:

$$n(\text{old}) = \left[ \frac{z_{\alpha/2}\sigma_x}{D(\text{old})} \right]^2 \qquad n(\text{new}) = \left[ \frac{z_{\alpha/2}\sigma_x}{D(\text{new})} \right]^2$$

If we take the ratio of $D$(old) to $D$(new) we get Eq. (7.8), which can be used to determine how a change in $D$ will influence the desired or appropriate sample size.

Ratio for changing $n$ when $D$ changes

(7.8)
$$\frac{n(\text{new})}{n(\text{old})} = \left[\frac{D(\text{old})}{D(\text{new})}\right]^2$$

**WORKED EXAMPLE 7.9**

Suppose in the Nobel Pizza case $D$ is doubled from \$100 to \$200. What is the effect on the desired sample size?

**ANSWER:**

The ratio of the new $n$ [denoted $n$(new)] to the old $n$ [denoted $n$(old)] is

$$\frac{n(\text{new})}{n(\text{old})} = \left[\frac{D(\text{old})}{D(\text{new})}\right]^2 = \left[\frac{100}{200}\right]^2 = \frac{1}{4}$$

This means that the new desired sample size is one-fourth the old sample size. Since the previously desired sample size was 3458, the new desired sample size is

$$n(\text{new}) = \tfrac{1}{4}(3458) = 864.5 \text{ (or 865)}$$

*Changing* $\alpha$    An increase in $\alpha$ will decrease the desired $n$, while a decrease in $\alpha$ will increase it. The change in the sample size can be determined by using the same process previously used. In this case the comparison is between $z$ values (from Appendix Table B.4), using $z_{\alpha/2}$(new) and $z_{\alpha/2}$(old).

Ratio for changing $n$ when $\alpha$ changes

(7.9)
$$\frac{n(\text{new})}{n(\text{old})} = \left[\frac{z_{\alpha/2}(\text{new})}{z_{\alpha/2}(\text{old})}\right]^2$$

Suppose that as the analyst for Noble Pizza, you decide to increase $\alpha$ from 0.05 to 0.10. What will be the effect on $n$?

**ANSWER:**

The old $z$ value was $z_{0.025} = 1.96$ and the new $z$ value is $z_{0.05} = 1.645$. The change in the optimal sample size is

$$\frac{n(\text{new})}{n(\text{old})} = \left[\frac{z_{\alpha/2}(\text{new})}{z_{\alpha/2}(\text{old})}\right]^2 = \left[\frac{1.645}{1.96}\right]^2 = (0.839)^2 = 0.704$$

This result shows that the new sample size is 70.4% of the old one. Since the previous sample size was 3458, the new desired size is

$$0.704(3458) = 2434.43 \text{ or } 2435.$$

From these examples, we see that doubling the value of $D$ will reduce the appropriate sample size more than will doubling the value of $\alpha$. The sample size can be reduced even more if *both* D and $\alpha$ are increased simultaneously. Also, note from Eq. (7.5) that if there is a new estimate of the population standard deviation ($\sigma_x$) that is lower than the previous estimate, the new sample size will be smaller than the old one.

Finally, we need to point out that if $D$ and $\sigma_x$ are held constant, then any increase in $n$ must necessarily decrease $\alpha$. This point was mentioned earlier in this chapter—namely, that the risk of being wrong in constructing a confidence interval can be reduced by increasing the sample size. To illustrate this process, suppose that as the Noble Pizza analyst you decide to increase the sample size from 3458 to 4000 while holding $D = 100$. The effect on $\alpha$ can be determined by substituting $n = 4000$, $D = 100$, and $\sigma_x = 3000$ into Eq. (7.5) and solving for $z_{\alpha/2}$ as follows:

$$4000 = \left[\frac{z_{\alpha/2}\sigma_x}{D}\right]^2 = \left[\frac{z_{\alpha/2}(3000)}{100}\right]^2$$

Solving yields

$$z_{\alpha/2} = \sqrt{\frac{4000(100)}{3000}} = \sqrt{4.44} = 2.11$$

From Appendix Table B.4, the $\alpha/2$ value corresponding to $z = 2.11$ is $1 - 0.9826 = 0.0174$. Doubling this value yields $\alpha = 0.0348$. Thus $\alpha$ is reduced from 0.05 to 0.0346 with the increase in $n$ from 3458 to 4000.

MKT    **7.17**   A manager of a large car dealership claims that the majority of customers feel that the dealership's mechanics do an excellent job. You wish to estimate the proportion of customers who actually hold this belief to within 0.10, with 95% confidence. How large a sample should you draw for this estimation?

FIN    **7.18**   As a financial analyst you want to estimate the return on sales of grocery stores. You have drawn a sample of 41 companies and have calculated $\bar{x} = \$0.04$ per dollar of sales, with a sample standard deviation of $s_x = \$0.005$.

    **a)** Use the $t$ distribution to calculate a 95% confidence interval for $\mu_x$.

    **b)** Use the $z$ distribution to calculate a 95% confidence interval for $\mu_x$.

    **c)** Why is your answer in (a) more appropriate than that in (b)?

    **7.19**   Using Eq. (7.3), the following 99% confidence interval was obtained for $\pi$: $-0.15 < \pi < 0.25$.

    **a)** What was the point estimate of $\pi$?

    **b)** Why is this confidence interval inappropriate?

ACT    **7.20**   You want to estimate the average daily withdrawals from new experimental savings accounts that were designed for customers at a local bank. You know that the maximum withdrawal from these accounts is $1000 and the minimum is $0. You want your estimate to be accurate to within $50, with 90% confidence. How many accounts should you sample?

PUB    **7.21**   A Harris Poll appearing on June 11, 1984, in *Business Week* reported that 48% of probable voters seem determined to vote against Reagan. Assume that this sample was based on a random selection of 789 probable voters. Construct a 99% confidence interval for the probable voters who seem determined to vote against Reagan.

MKT    **7.22**   A marketing research analyst wishes to estimate the proportion of the market captured by the company's leading shampoo. A random survey of 200 hair shampoo purchasers found that 21% purchased this brand. Form a 99% confidence interval for the population parameter $\pi$.

ECN    **7.23**   A survey of low-income families in Minnesota was designed to determine the average heating costs for a family of four during January and

February. Heating costs are known to have a standard deviation of $25.14. The economists conducting the study wish to construct a 95% confidence interval, with a margin for sampling error of no more than $4. Find the appropriate sample size.

ADM  **7.24** Based on a random sample of students, the personnel director for a large firm has estimated that the mean starting salary next year for masters in business administration (MBA) students with a technical background will be $32,000. This director calculates that for a 95% confidence interval, the margin of error should be $378.09. The population standard deviation is known to be $3980.

a) What sample size did the personnel director use?

b) If the personnel director had wanted a confidence interval with $\alpha = 0.10$, what sample size would have been appropriate?

c) How will the sample size change if the personnel director wants to reduce the margin of error by one-half?

MFG  **7.25** Following is a computer output of descriptive statistics on cost per unit of output. (The numbers under the MINIMUM and MAXIMUM headings are the lowest and highest cost values in the sample.)

| NAME | n | MEAN | STD. DEV. | MINIMUM | MAXIMUM |
|------|-----|---------|-----------|---------|---------|
| cost | 40 | 61.0700 | 12.0726 | 41.5000 | 80.0000 |

a) What is the point estimate of average cost?

b) Construct a 95% confidence interval for $\mu_x$ using Eq. (7.4).

MFG  **7.26** Using the information in Exercise 7.25, you now want to take another sample in order to estimate the plan cost. You want your estimate of average cost per unit to be within $2.00, with 90% confidence.

a) As an estimate of the population standard deviation, should you use the sample standard deviation or the minimum and maximum values to make a guess using Eq. (7.6)? Why?

b) How large a sample should you now select?

## Chapter Exercises

**7.27** How does the concept of probability apply to the interpretation of a 95% confidence interval for a population parameter?

**7.28** Use a table of random numbers to select a random sample of $n = 6$ corporations from the Office Equipment and Computer Industry category in Appendix A.1.

   a) Determine a point estimate of the mean fourth-quarter sales for the six companies.

   b) Determine a point estimate of the population variance for the fourth-quarter sales. Assume that the population is normal. Construct a 95% confidence interval for $\mu_x$ based on your answer to parts (a) and (b).

   c) Use all of the office and computer corporations in Appendix A.1 to determine the value of $\mu_x$ and $\sigma_x^2$. Were your point estimates in parts (a) and (b) reasonably close? Did the confidence interval in part (c) contain $\mu_x$?

**7.29** What assumptions are necessary for using the $t$ distribution to form a confidence interval for $\mu_x$? When is the $z$ distribution appropriate for forming confidence intervals? Under what circumstances should one *not* attempt to construct a confidence interval around a point estimate?

**7.30** Assume that two economists each independently take a random sample of size $n = 100$ in order to estimate the mean income for a geographical region. Both economists decide to construct a 95% confidence interval.

   a) Would you expect both economists to determine the same point estimate for $\mu_x$?

   b) If $\sigma_x$ is known, would you expect the margin for sampling error for the two economists to be identical? Explain.

   c) If $\sigma_x$ is unknown, would you expect the margin for sampling error to be identical? Explain.

**7.31** Repeat Exercise 7.8 (b), assuming that the population standard deviation is unknown. How does the margin for sampling error in this problem compare with the margin in Exercise 7.8(b)? Explain why you could have predicted the relationship between the two margins.

**7.32** A 1984 survey of 300 school district presidents by the National Institute of Education found that 135 had some computers available for student use after regular school hours.

   a) Find a point estimate for the population of school districts with computers available after school.

**b)** Construct a 95% confidence interval for the proportion of school districts with computers available.

FIN    **7.33** A 1984 survey by Dun and Bradstreet indicated that companies with fewer than 1000 employees expected to increase their spending by 20.4%. Form a 99% confidence interval, assuming that the sample standard deviation is 6.8% and the sample size is 346.

ACT    **7.34** An accountant has determined that the appropriate sample size to estimate a population mean is 400.

     **a)** If the accountant had previously set $\alpha = 0.10$ and now decides that $\alpha = 0.05$ is more appropriate, what is the new optimal sample size?

     **b)** If the accountant wants to change $D$ from 100 to 200, what will be the new optimal sample size? [Ignore the change in part (a).]

     **c)** If the accountant decides that the value of $\sigma_x$ is half of what it was orginally thought to be, what is the new optimal sample size? [Ignore the changes in parts (a) and (b).]

**7.35** Use a computer program to determine the mean and the variance for the variable "12-month earnings per share" for all of the service industry companies in Appendix A.1. Using a random number generator, select 10 service companies and compute the sample average "12-month earnings per share" and a 95% confidence interval.

     **a)** How close was your $\bar{x}$ value to $\mu_x$?

     **b)** Did your confidence interval include $\mu_x$? Why or why not?

**7.36** Use a computer to generate 10 random samples, each of size $n = 10$, for the variable "12-months earnings per share," using all the service industry companies in Appendix A.1.

     **a)** Construct a 90% confidence interval using the results of each of the 10 samples, assuming $\sigma_x$ is unknown. How many of these confidence intervals contain the population mean? (The answer to Exercise 7.35 gives the population mean.)

     **b)** Construct a 90% confidence interval using the results of each of the 10 samples, assuming $\sigma_x$ is known.

FIN    **7.37** A data file called **BANKS** was created using a computer program. This data file contains the price-earnings ratios of banks and bank holding companies. The descriptive statistics module of the computer program was then used to generate the following output:

```
              DESCRIPTIVE STATISTICS

    HEADER DATA FOR: A:BANKS
    LABEL: PRICE-EARNINGS RATIO
    NUMBER OF CASES: 50    NUMBER OF VARIABLES: 1

          PRICE-EARNINGS RATIO FOR BANKS
            AND BANK HOLDING COMPANIES

        VARIABLE NAME: PE RATIO    N = 50

            ARITHMETIC MEAN = 7.52

          SAMPLE STD. DEV. = 2.771870363
          SAMPLE VARIANCE = 7.683265306

      POPULATION STD. DEV. = 2.744011662
      POPULATION VARIANCE = 7.5296

  STANDARD ERROR OF THE MEAN = 0.392001666
                   MINIMUM = 5
                   MAXIMUM = 24

                       SUM = 376
            SUM OF SQUARES = 3204
             DEVIATION SS = 376.48
```

a) Interpret each line of this output by giving an explanation or a formula indicating how the measure was calculated.

b) This output gives two variances and two standard deviations. Explain why and how they differ. Which one is appropriate for these data?

LAW  **7.38** A large machine shop has just declared bankruptcy. As a bankruptcy lawyer you wish to estimate the shop's accounts payable. The following values represent a random sample of 50 accounts owed by the machine shop (in thousands of dollars):

| | | | | | | | | | |
|---|---|---|---|---|---|---|---|---|---|
| 2.78 | 3.12 | 2.94 | 2.95 | 3.18 | 2.86 | 2.24 | 2.30 | 3.41 | 3.02 |
| 3.42 | 3.04 | 3.28 | 3.13 | 2.65 | 2.50 | 2.63 | 2.68 | 3.17 | 2.30 |
| 3.25 | 2.78 | 3.14 | 3.05 | 2.95 | 3.36 | 3.02 | 2.86 | 3.02 | 3.01 |
| 3.02 | 3.21 | 3.27 | 3.36 | 3.13 | 2.82 | 3.50 | 3.11 | 2.86 | 3.55 |
| 3.05 | 3.12 | 3.52 | 2.87 | 2.86 | 2.85 | 3.34 | 2.75 | 3.06 | 2.95 |

a) Use a computer to provide descriptive statistics for these data.

b) Construct a 99% confidence interval for $\mu_x$.

c) Construct a 95% confidence interval for the proportion of accounts that are larger than $3000.

d) If you had desired a 95% confidence interval for $\mu_x$ that had a margin for sampling error of 0.25, what sample size would have been appropriate? (Use the sample variance from these data to estimate $\sigma_x$. Assume that the population is very large and that the accounts are normally distributed.)

**7.39** In Section 7.2 the estimator $s_x^2$ (sample variance) was presented as an unbiased estimator of the population variance. The estimator $s_x$ (sample standard deviation) is *not* an unbiased estimator of the population standard deviation. Explain (logically or mathematically) why $s_x$ is not an unbiased estimator of $\sigma_x$.

ECN **7.40** An informal study in the June 10, 1984, isssue of *Parade* magazine reported that the median pay in the United States is $18,700. What difficulties do you see in this type of study for assessing incomes? Would you be willing to use $18,700 as a point estimate of the central location of U.S. incomes?

PUB **7.41** According to an article in *The Herald Telephone*, in a survey of 811 Indiana residents at least 18 years of age, 75% said that they support a state-controlled lottery. The sampling error for this survey was reported to be ±4% at the 95% confidence level. The article quoted a spokesperson as saying, "This means we are 95 percent confident that we would have gotten results within 4 percent either way of these results (0.75 ± 0.04) if we had interviewed every adult Indiana resident who has a telephone." Comment on this interpretation of a confidence interval.

ECN **7.42** According to an article in *The Chronicle of Higher Education* (December 1984), a survey of faculty showed that the average yearly salary of faculty members was $29,700. The article stated "the 'confidence interval' for that figure is $410, meaning that there is a 95 percent probability that the estimated average varies from the true average of the sample population by no more than plus or minus $410." Comment on this interpretation of a confidence interval.

**7.43** Assume that a population has only the following four values:

$$x = [1, 2, 5, 7]$$

a) Make a list of all the *different* samples that are possible if $n = 2$ and sampling occurs with replacement. Construct a 90% confidence interval for each of these samples using the $t$ distribution. What proportion of these confidence intervals contain the population mean? (Are the assumptions of the $t$ distribution met in this example?)

b) Repeat part (a) assuming that sampling occurs *without* replacement.

## Glossary

**confidence interval:** The set of values between the lower bound ($L$) and the upper bound ($H$) of an interval estimate.

**$(1 - \alpha)100\%$ confidence interval:** The level of the confidence interval expressed as a percent, where $(1 - \alpha)$ indicates the proportion of time that the $L$-$H$ bounds will contain the population parameter.

**desired sample size:** A determination before a sample is taken of the best value of $n$ considering the values of $D$, $\alpha$, and $\sigma$.

**estimate:** A numerical value from a sample used to estimate a population parameter.

**interval estimate:** A range of values used to estimate a population parameter.

**margin for sampling error ($D$):** The distance between the point estimate and either $L$ or $H$ in a confidence interval.

**$p^*$:** A guess about the value of a population proportion.

**point estimate:** A specific value of a point estimator.

**point estimator:** A sample statistic used to estimate a population parameter.

**sampling-error margin:** The amount of leeway around a point estimate used to make an interval estimate.

**sample statistic:** A value determined from the sample and used to estimate a population parameter.

**$\sigma_x^*$:** A guess about the value of the population standard deviation.

**$t_{\alpha/2,n-1}$:** The value cutting off an area of $\alpha/2$ in the upper tail of the $t$ distribution with $n - 1$ degrees of freedom.

**unbiased point estimator:** A point estimator whose average value equals the population parameter being estimated.

**$z_{\alpha/2}$:** The value cutting off an area of $\alpha/2$ in the upper tail of the standardized normal distribution ($z$).

**7.1—A $(1 - \alpha)100\%$ Confidence Interval for $\mu_x$**
**($\sigma_x$ is Known and $x$ is Normal or $n$ is Large):**

$$\bar{x} - z_{\alpha/2}(\sigma_x/\sqrt{n}) < \mu_x < \bar{x} + z_{\alpha/2}(\sigma_x/\sqrt{n})$$

**7.2—A $(1 - \alpha)100\%$ Confidence Interval for $\mu_x$**
**($x$ Normal, $\sigma_x$ Unknown):**

$$\bar{x} - t_{\alpha/2,n-1}(s_x/\sqrt{n}) < \mu_x < \bar{x} + t_{\alpha/2,n-1}(s_x/\sqrt{n})$$

**7.3—A $(1 - \alpha)100\%$ Confidence Interval for Estimating $\pi$:**

$$p - z_{\alpha/2}\sqrt{p(1 - p)/n} < \pi < p + z_{\alpha/2}\sqrt{p(1 - p)/n}$$

where $p = x/n$

**7.4—Approximate $(1 - \alpha)100\%$ Confidence Interval for $\mu_x$**
**($\sigma_x$ is Unknown and $n > 30$):**

$$\bar{x} - z_{\alpha/2}(s_x/\sqrt{n}) < \mu_x < \bar{x} + z_{\alpha/2}(s_x/\sqrt{n})$$

**7.5—Desired Sample Size for $\mu_x$ ($\sigma_x$ Known):**

$$n = \left[\frac{z_{\alpha/2}\sigma_x}{D}\right]^2$$

**7.6—Rough Guess at the Value of $\sigma_x$:**

$$\sigma_x^* = \frac{\text{highest value observed} - \text{lowest value observed}}{5}$$

**7.7—Desired Sample Size When Estimating $\pi$:**

$$n = \left[\frac{z_{\alpha/2}}{D}\right]^2 p^*(1 - p^*)$$

where $p^*$ is a guess at the value of $p$.

**7.8—Ratio for Changing $n$ as $D$ Changes:**

$$\frac{n(\text{new})}{n(\text{old})} = \left[\frac{D(\text{old})}{D(\text{new})}\right]^2$$

**7.9—Ratio for Changing $n$ When $\alpha$ Changes:**

$$\frac{n(\text{new})}{n(\text{old})} = \left[\frac{z_{\alpha/2}(\text{new})}{z_{\alpha/2}(\text{old})}\right]^2$$

# CHAPTER EIGHT

*You don't have to eat the whole ox to know that the meat is tough.*
*Samuel Johnson*

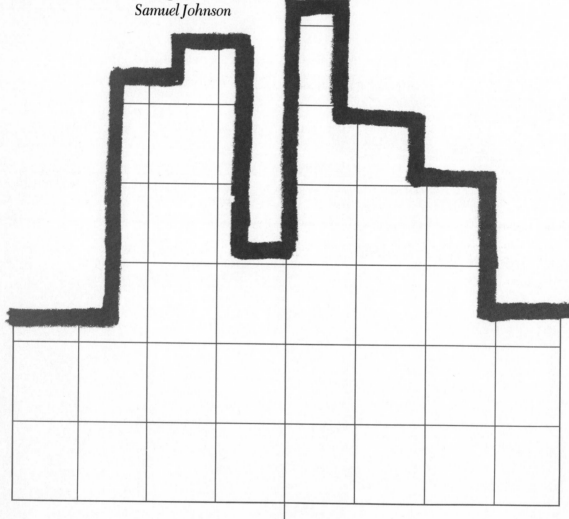

# HYPOTHESIS
# TESTING

# 8.1 INTRODUCTION

Business and economic decisions often depend on the correctness of assumptions about the value of a population parameter. Assumptions about a population parameter are called **hypotheses**. Judging the correctness of hypotheses is called **hypothesis testing**. As will be demonstrated in this chapter, the correctness of a statistical hypothesis is judged on the basis of sample information. The following examples illustrate the concept of hypothesis testing.

■ A production manager wants to test the hypothesis that the population proportion of defectives from a certain machine is the same as it was last year. Based on last year's records, the probability of observing 10 or more defects in a sample of 100 items is calculated to be only 0.001. Thus, if this year the machine *does* produce 10 or more defects in a sample of $n = 100$, the manager may reject the hypothesis that the population proportion of defects is the same as it was last year.

■ The manager of a fast-food franchise is concerned that the mean weight of the quarter-pound hamburgers it is serving is higher than 0.25 pound. A sample of $n = 200$ hamburgers resulted in a mean weight of 0.255 pound. The manager calculates the probability of a mean weight of 0.255 pound or larger (in a sample of $n = 200$) to be 0.27. Since 0.27 is not a particularly low probability, the manager decides not to reject the hypothesis that the population mean weight is 0.25 pound.

■ A marketing research analyst wants to determine if the mean price charged for a leading brand of hair shampoo is the same in New York City and Los Angeles. A random sample from 23 drug stores in New York City and 17 drug stores in Los Angeles results in mean prices of $1.79 and $1.63, respectively. The analyst calculates that a difference in sample means of $0.16 or more occurs with a probability of 0.02. Because 0.02 is a small probability, the analyst rejects the hypothesis that the mean prices are equal.

These examples illustrate business situations involving sampling and probability calculations designed to test hypotheses about population parameters. This chapter describes a five-step hypothesis testing procedure. By the end of this chapter you will be able to specify hypotheses for tests of population means or population proportions. You will also be able to use either the $z$ or the $t$ distribution to conduct these tests when appropriate conditions are met.

## The Tyrone Paper Company

You are the quality control manager for the Tyrone Paper Company. A new company directive states that you must cut costs without noticeably affecting the brightness of Tyrone's paper products. Paper brightness is measured by a machine, which results in a number ranging from 0 to 100. In the past, the more expensive bleach used by Tyrone resulted in a mean brightness of 78.35, with a standard deviation of 1.61. A new cheaper bleach is claimed to produce a brightness of at least 78.35. You question this claim and wish to test if the mean brightness of the new bleach is less than 78.35. For 30 sample batches of pulp, the new bleach yields a mean brightness of 77.61. In the population, is the mean brightness of the new bleach at least equal to that of the old bleach, or is it less?

# 8.2 The Process of Hypothesis Testing

Hypotheses in statistics always come in pairs, one called the **null hypothesis** and the other called the **alternative hypothesis**. The null and alternative hypotheses represent mutually exclusive and exhaustive theories about the value of a population parameter [such as a population mean ($\mu$) or a population proportion ($\pi$)]. From the presentation in Chapter 4, *mutually exclusive* in this context means that it is not possible for *both* the null hypothesis and the alternative hypothesis to be true. *Exhaustive* means that either the null or the alternative hypothesis is true.

The null hypothesis is traditionally designated by the symbol $H_0$, while the symbol for the alternative hypothesis is $H_A$. A colon always follows these symbols, and then a statement about a population parameter is made. The only statements we test in this chapter are statements about the value of population means and population proportions. Other population parameters (e.g., the median or variance) could be tested, but they will not be presented here.

In the case of the Tyrone Paper Company, the null hypothesis is

$$H_0: \mu_x \geq 78.35$$

This hypothesis says that one theory about the brightness of pulp is that the population mean of the new bleach is the same as the population mean for the old bleach (78.35), or some greater value. $H_0$ indicates that the population mean of $x$ is at least 78.35. The alternative hypothesis is

$$H_A: \mu_x < 78.35$$

This hypothesis says that the population mean is *not* 78.35, but rather some lower value. Under the alternative hypothesis, the mean using the new bleach may be any value smaller than 78.35, but it may not be 78.35 or larger. In this case $H_0$ and $H_A$ are mutually exclusive and exhaustive, since all values of $\mu$ are contained in either the null or alternative hypothesis. The alternative hypothesis $H_A: \mu_x < 78.35$ is said to be a **lower-sided alternative hypothesis** because values consistent with it are less than 78.35.

The decision to be made in hypothesis testing, on the basis of sample information, is whether to conclude that the null hypothesis or the alternative hypothesis is correct. We start by assuming that the null hypothesis is correct until sufficient sample information is obtained to refute this hypothesis. Thus, in the Tyrone Paper Company case, we assume that $H_0: \mu_x \geq 78.35$ is correct until we get sample information suggesting that $H_A: \mu_x < 78.35$. This procedure is similar to what takes place in a courtroom, where the defendant is presumed innocent until the weight of the evidence suggests guilt. In statistics, however, the weight of the evidence is always determined by the sample information and the probability of observing certain sample values.

---

**RULE**
**Hypothesis**
**Testing**

The standard procedure in hypothesis testing is to assume that the null hypothesis is correct until enough (sample) evidence is received to suggest that this assumption is unreasonable.

---

When the sample information suggests that the null hypothesis is inc rect, the null hypothesis is said to be *rejected*. In the Tyrone Paper Company case, if $H_0$: $\mu_x \geq 78.35$ is rejected, then $H_A$: $\mu_x < 78.35$ must be accepted. When the null hypothesis cannot be rejected, it is said to be *accepted*. Thus, if $H_0$: $\mu_x \geq 78.35$ is accepted, then $H_A$: $\mu_x < 78.35$ must be rejected. (Instead of saying that $H_0$ is accepted, because the truth of hypotheses is never known with certainty, some statisticians prefer to say that "$H_0$ cannot be rejected." For brevity, we treat the expression "accept $H_0$" as synonymous with "$H_0$ cannot be rejected.")

# 8.3 Hypothesis Testing Using a p Value

In the Tyrone Paper Company case, the sample evidence is $\bar{x} = 77.61$. This piece of information is used to decide whether to conclude that $H_0$: $\mu_x \geq 78.35$ is to be accepted or rejected in favor of accepting $H_A$. In this case you have to decide whether the sample result ($\bar{x} = 77.61$) is far enough away from the value specified under $H_0$ ($= 78.35$) to be reasonably certain that the null hypothesis is incorrect. The number 78.35 in the null hypothesis is called the **limiting value of $H_0$** because it represents the lower limit of the values $\mu_x \geq 78.35$.

The distance of the observed $\bar{x}$ value (77.61) from the limiting value of $H_0$ (78.35) can be expressed as a probability—namely, the probability that a sample of size $n = 30$ results in a value of $\bar{x} = 77.61$ or less when $\mu_x = 78.35$. This probability calculation is the same type of probability problem solved many times in Chapters 6 and 7. Now, however, this probability is called a *p* **value**. The *p* value for the Tyrone Paper Company is $P(\bar{x} \leq 77.61 | \mu_x = 78.35)$.

The *p* value always includes the probability of $\bar{x}$ values *more extreme* than the observed $\bar{x}$ value. If the observed $\bar{x}$ value is below the limiting value of $H_0$, then the more extreme $\bar{x}$ values are less than the observed $\bar{x}$ value, as in the Tyrone Paper Company case. [Remember from Chapter 6 that $P(\bar{x} \leq 77.61) = P(\bar{x} < 77.61)$ because probability at a single point is defined to be zero for a continuous probability density function (p.d.f.).] If the observed $\bar{x}$ value is above the limiting value of $H_0$, then the more extreme $\bar{x}$ values are greater than the observed $\bar{x}$ value.

To calculate a *p* value for the Tyrone Paper Company we must first determine the appropriate p.d.f. From the central limit theorem, we know that $\bar{x}$ is normally distributed. The $H_0$ limiting value of 78.35 is used to center the $\bar{x}$ distribution. The $p$ value is the area for $\bar{x}$ values below 77.61, as shown in Fig. 8.1(a).

To calculate $P(\bar{x} \leq 77.61)$, we must first standardize $\bar{x}$ as we did in Chapter 6, using Eq. (6.3). Now, however, the calculated value of $z$ is denoted as $z_c$.

$$z_c = \frac{\bar{x} - \mu_{\bar{x}}}{\sigma_{\bar{x}}} = \frac{\bar{x} - \mu_x}{\sigma_x/\sqrt{n}} = \frac{77.61 - 78.35}{1.61/\sqrt{30}} = -2.52$$

From Appendix Table B.4, $P(z \leq -2.52) = P(z \geq 2.52) = 1 - 0.9941 = 0.0059$ (Fig. 8.1b, c). Thus the probability of observing a sample mean of $\bar{x} = 77.61$ or less if the true population mean is 78.35 is 0.0059 (Fig. 8.1d). The value 0.0059 is called the $p$ value. This probability indicates that when $H_0$ is true, the sample mean will be no larger than 77.61 in 59 out of every 10,000 samples, on average, where each sample is $n = 30$.

The $p$ value is our indication of how far the sample result is from the limiting null hypothesis value. A small $p$-value indicates a highly unlikely sample result (i.e., one far away from the limiting $H_0$ value). If we observe a highly unlikely sample result we must question the assumption that $H_0$ is true. A large $p$ value indicates that the sample result is close to the $H_0$ value and thus does not cast doubt on the correctness of $H_0$. What size of $p$ values is considered small or large is a topic we will discuss shortly. In general, however, we know that a sample result far away from $H_0$ (a small $p$ value) is evidence against the null hypothesis ($H_0$). Similarly, a sample result that is close to $H_0$ (a large $p$ value) is evidence in favor of the null hypothesis. Thus we can specify the following decision rule:

---

**RULE**
**$H_0$ versus $H_A$**
$H_0$ is rejected for small $p$ values.
$H_0$ is not rejected for large $p$ values.

---

Again using the legal analogy, the defendant ($H_0$) is presumed innocent (true) until there is sufficient evidence (a small $p$ value) to declare this person ($H_0$) guilty (false). Sometimes in a court of law the defendant may appear to be guilty, but there is not enough evidence for a conviction. The same is true in hypothesis testing, where the sample evidence sometimes seems to be far away from $H_0$ but the $p$ value is not small enough to reject $H_0$. On the other hand, comparable to finding an innocent person guilty in court is the possibility of incorrectly rejecting $H_0$ in hypothesis testing.

**Figure 8.1**
Calculating the $p$ value in the Tyrone Paper Company case.

(a) Shaded area is the p-value to be determined.

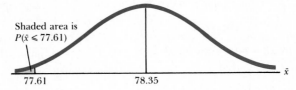

Shaded area is
$P(\bar{x} \leqslant 77.61)$

77.61    78.35    $\bar{x}$

(b) Transform the $\bar{x}$-value to a $z$-value, via Formula 6.3, and shade the desired area.

$$z_c = \frac{\bar{x} - \mu_{\bar{x}}}{\sigma_{\bar{x}}} = \frac{\bar{x} - \mu_x}{\sigma_x/\sqrt{n}} = \frac{77.61 - 78.35}{1.61/\sqrt{30}} = -2.52$$

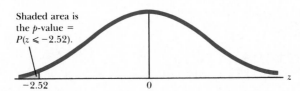

Shaded area is
the $p$-value =
$P(z \leqslant -2.52)$.

-2.52    0    $z$

(c) Recognize that $P(z \leqslant -2.52) = P(z \geqslant 2.52)$. Use Appendix Table B.4 to determine $P(z \geqslant 2.52) = 1 - 0.9941$.

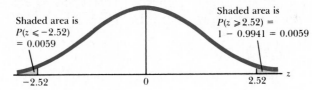

Shaded area is
$P(z \leqslant -2.52)$
$= 0.0059$

Shaded area is
$P(z \geqslant 2.52) =$
$1 - 0.9941 = 0.0059$

-2.52    0    2.52    $z$

(d) Solve for the $p$-value using results from (c).

$p$-value =
$P(\bar{x} \leqslant 77.61)$
$= 0.0059$

78.35    $\bar{x}$

To almost any jury, the $p$ value of 0.0059 in the Tyrone Paper case would be judged a small probability. An event that occurs with such a low probability (of 0.0059) is so unlikely that when it does occur, we have good reason to suspect that $H_0$ is not correct after all. The low $p$ value of 0.0059 means that you, as the Tyrone manager, should reject $H_0$: $\mu_x \geq 78.35$ and accept the alternative hypothesis, $H_A$: $\mu_x < 78.35$. This decision implies that your tests indicate that the new bleach is not sufficiently bright, and thus Tyrone should not switch from the old bleach. In reaching this conclusion, however, you must acknowledge that there is some chance (0.0059) that you are wrong.

---

**WORKED EXAMPLE 8.1**

The claim is made that the average level of schooling of applicants seeking jobs in a local trade union does not exceed the 11th grade, with a standard deviation of $\sigma = 1.0$. You decide to test this claim about the population mean using the following null and alternative hypotheses:

$H_0$: $\mu \leq 11.0$ (the average grade level does not exceed 11.0)
$H_A$: $\mu > 11.0$ (the average grade level does exceed 11.0)

A sample of 100 applicants is taken and the sample mean is found to equal 11.3. Do you have sufficient evidence to reject $H_0$?

ANSWER:

The $p$ value can be computed by first calculating the $z$ value that corresponds to $\bar{x} = 11.3$ and $\mu = 11.0$.

$$z_c = \frac{\bar{x} - \mu_{\bar{x}}}{\sigma_{\bar{x}}} = \frac{\bar{x} - \mu_x}{\sigma_x/\sqrt{n}} = \frac{11.3 - 11.0}{1.0/\sqrt{100}} = 3.0$$

From Appendix Table B.4 we find that $P(z \geq 3.0) = 0.0013$, so the $p$ value is $P(\bar{x} \geq 11.3 | \mu_x = 11.0) = 0.0013$. Since this $p$ value is very low, we know that a sample mean of 11.3 or larger is very unlikely. Thus the decision should be to reject $H_0$ and conclude that the average grade level of schooling in the population exceeds 11.0. We recognize that there is some probability (0.0013) that this conclusion is incorrect.

---

**8.1** What is the meaning of a $p$ value in a hypothesis test where the alternative hypothesis involves a greater-than sign, as in Worked Example 8.1?

**8.2** Why does an extremely low $p$ value imply that the null hypothesis should be rejected?

**8.3** Determine the $p$ value in the following cases:

a) $P(z \leq z_c)$, where $z_c = -1.48$

b) $P(\bar{x} \geq 120)$, where $\mu_0 = 120$, $\sigma_x = 100$, and $n = 64$

**8.4** Test the following null and alternative hypotheses:

$H_0: \mu_x \geq 18$

$H_A: \mu_x < 18$

The population standard deviation is 6.

a) For a random sample of 81 observations, $\bar{x} = 16$.

b) For a random sample of 81 observations, $\bar{x} = 20$.

c) For a random sample of 81 observations, $\bar{x} = 17.5$.

ACT **8.5** Many states require financial institutions to give the state any funds left in inactive accounts. In testimony before the state legislature, a bank executive stated that the average size of such accounts does not exceed $100, with a standard deviation of $25. As an auditor for the state you are told to check this claim. You set up the following hypotheses: $H_0: \mu_x \leq 100$ and $H_A: \mu_x > 100$. You draw a random sample of 36 accounts from state banks and find that the average balance of inactive accounts is $113.25. What conclusion can you draw, assuming that $\sigma_x = 25$?

# 8.4 General Procedures for Hypothesis Testing

Hypothesis testing can involve literally hundreds of different hypotheses and many different test statistics. Fortunately, however, the procedure for testing hypotheses almost always follows the same five basic steps. Although explicit attention was not given to these steps in the Tyrone Paper case, all five were followed. These five steps can now be summarized as follows:

<table>
<tr><td>RULES<br>Steps in<br>Hypothesis<br>Testing</td><td>
1. Establish the null and alternative hypotheses.<br><br>
2. Formulate a decision rule for rejecting or accepting the null hypothesis based on tolerable error levels.<br><br>
3. Select a test statistic, draw a sample, and calculate the value of the test statistic based on your sample data.<br><br>
4. Calculate the $p$ value associated with the value of the calculated test statistic.<br><br>
5. Reach a conclusion (accept or reject $H_0$) using the $p$ value calculated in step 4 and the decision rule formulated in step 2.
</td></tr>
</table>

The following sections will explain and demonstrate these five steps.

# 8.5 The Null and Alternative Hypotheses (Step 1)

The null and alternative hypotheses represent complementary hypotheses about a population parameter. This means that the values specified under $H_0$ and $H_A$ must be mutually exclusive and exhaustive.

In many testing situations it may not be easy to determine the appropriate null and alternative hypotheses, for there may be several different (correct) ways of formulating the same problem into $H_0$ and $H_A$. Although we will present some rules for establishing $H_0$ and $H_A$, the reader should remember that other formulations are possible.

Often an analyst is interested in testing a new theory against an established or current theory. In this situation the current theory is usually designated as the null hypothesis and the theory to be tested as the alternative hypothesis. For example, perhaps the established theory is that 50% or less of Indiana residents would vote for a state lottery, while the alternative is that more than 50% would vote for a lottery. Or if the established theory is that unemployment will not fall below 6% in the next year, the alternative to be tested could be that unemployment will fall below this level.

Recall that $H_0$ is not rejected unless sufficient sample evidence is collected to disprove this theory. This procedure causes a built-in bias toward the null hypothesis, which is exactly what one would want for an established theory. Because the null hypothesis is the current theory, the evidence against this theory must be strong before it is rejected. For example, suppose a current theory is that there is no cure for arthritis, and the alternative theory is that a new medicine will cure this disease. To comply with U.S. Food and Drug Administration (FDA) regulations in this case, the company must be very sure that the sample evidence clearly indicates that the null hypothesis is incorrect before it is rejected. Thus the null hypothesis states that there is no cure for arthritis, while the alternative hypothesis states that there is a cure. Conceptually, either of two hypotheses can be designated as the null hypothesis, and for some problems there may be no established theory. However, whenever possible we recommend the following rule:

| RULE Determining Hypotheses | In determining hypotheses, if a current or established theory exists, this theory should be designated as the null hypothesis. The new theory being tested should be designated as the alternative hypothesis. |
|---|---|

For the Tryone Paper Company, the new bleach is claimed to have a brightness level at least as high as the old one, 78.35. In the absence of any other information, you cannot refute this claim. Hence, the null hypothesis is

$$H_0: \mu_x \geq 78.35$$

If you question this claim, you must put forward a new theory. The alternative hypothesis represents this new theory. That is, the alternative hypothesis is that the new bleach gives less brightness than the old one, or

$$H_A: \mu_x < 78.35$$

This $H_A$ is called a **lower-sided alternative hypothesis** because it specifies values of $\mu_x$ that lie only below the number specified by $H_0$. In other words, $H_A$ is true only for values *less* than 78.35. $H_0$ and $H_A$ are mutually exclusive because no other values of $\mu_x$ are possible,

As another example, consider the problem of testing hypotheses about the proportion of Indiana residents who would vote for a lottery. Current opinion is that the population proportion ($\pi$) who would vote for a lottery is 50% or less. The alternative hypothesis is that $\pi$ is greater than 50%. Thus the hypotheses are

$$H_0: \pi \leq 0.50 \qquad \text{versus} \qquad H_A: \pi > 0.50$$

Here the population parameter being tested is $\pi$. The alternative hypothesis is an **upper-sided alternative** because only proportions greater than 0.50 are consistent with its acceptance.

The examples just presented used **one-sided hypothesis tests** because the alternative hypothesis allows for values of the parameter that are only on one side of the value stated in the null hypothesis. In contrast to one-sided hypotheses, a **two-sided** alternative allows for values on either side of the value stated in the null hypothesis. A two-sided alternative hypothesis, however, is possible only when the null hypothesis specifies a single value.

As an example of a two-sided testing situation, consider a *Wall Street Journal* (*WSJ*) article on how many tissues should be put in a box. A Kimberly-Clark marketing expert was quoted as saying 60, "because that's the average number of times people blow their noses during a cold." Here the expert is saying that the established theory is $\mu_x = 60$. If you question this theory, you might specify $\mu_x \neq 60$ as the alternative theory, since the expert stated only one value and gave no indication of whether the average might be more or less than 60. The null and alternative hypotheses are thus

$$H_0: \mu_x = 60 \qquad \text{versus} \qquad H_A: \mu_x \neq 60$$

In general, a one-sided hypothesis is appropriate whenever one of the two hypotheses is stated in words that indicate direction (e.g., "at least," "at most," "inferior to," "superior to," "greater than," or "less than"). One-sided hypothesis testing situations will always have either a $\geq$ or a $\leq$ sign in the null hypothesis and either a $<$ or $>$ sign in the alternative hypothesis. On the other hand, when no direction is suggested by $H_0$, then a two-sided alternative is required. For a two-sided test, the null hypothesis always involves an $=$ sign and the alternative hypothesis involves a $\neq$ sign. Table 8.1 indicates the type of null and alternative hypotheses we will be using in this chapter. In this table the symbol $\mu_0$ represents a specific value of $\mu$ (such as 78.35), while $\pi_0$ represents a specific value of $\pi$ (such as 0.50).

While it is always possible to determine if a population mean or population proportion is to be tested, sometimes it is not possible to determine which of two theories about $\mu$ or $\pi$ is the established view and which is the

**Table 8.1**

| Null and Alternative Hypotheses |
|---|
| **One-sided, lower-tail alternative hypothesis** |

| *Population Mean* | *Population Proportion* |
|---|---|
| $H_0: \mu \geq \mu_0$ | $H_0: \pi \geq \pi_0$ |
| $H_A: \mu < \mu_0$ | $H_A: \pi < \pi_0$ |

**One-sided, upper-tail alternative hypothesis**

| *Population Mean* | *Population Proportion* |
|---|---|
| $H_0: \mu \leq \mu_0$ | $H_0: \pi \leq \pi_0$ |
| $H_A: \mu > \mu_0$ | $H_A: \pi > \pi_0$ |

**Two-sided alternative hypothesis**

| *Population Mean* | *Population Proportion* |
|---|---|
| $H_0: \mu = \mu_0$ | $H_0: \pi = \pi_0$ |
| $H_A: \mu \neq \mu_0$ | $H_A: \pi \neq \pi_0$ |

Note: $\mu_0$ indicates the specific or limiting value of the population mean of interest and $\pi_0$ indicates the specific or limiting value of the population proportion of interest.

challenging view. In such cases, the cost of making an error in rejecting either theory should be considered.

> **RULE**
> **Null Hypothesis**
>
> The null hypothesis should always contain the theory that implies the greatest cost if it is erroneously rejected.

A statistical test is (again) similar to a court of law, where it is better to let the guilty go free (incorrectly accept $H_0$) rather than send an innocent person to prison (incorrectly reject $H_0$). Making an error in hypothesis testing is described in the next section.

# 8.6  The Probability of Type I and II Errors (Introduction to Step 2)

Because hypothesis testing decisions are based on sample information, an analyst may not make the correct decision. There are two types of errors in hypothesis testing: **type I errors** and **type II errors**.

To illustrate these errors in the Tyrone Paper case, a type I error is made whenever $H_A$: $\mu_x < 78.35$ is accepted but $\mu_x \geq 78.35$ is true. A type II error is made whenever $H_0$: $\mu_x \geq 78.35$ is accepted but $\mu_x < 78.35$ is true.

Unfortunately, since the true value of a population parameter is unknown without a census, we never know for sure whether a conclusion based on sample information is correct or incorrect. Thus in hypothesis testing the possibility always exists of making a type I error (when $H_0$ is rejected) or a type II error (when $H_0$ is accepted). The results of a decision to accept $H_0$ or to reject $H_A$ are summarized in Table 8.2.

In hypothesis testing, prior to taking a sample, the analyst must establish a decision rule for determining exactly when $H_0$ is to be rejected ($H_A$ accepted) and when $H_0$ is to be accepted ($H_A$ rejected). This decision rule will be based on an explicit probability of a type I error and at least implicit concern for the probability of a type II error. The probability of making a type I error is denoted by the Greek letter alpha ($\alpha$), while the probability of making a type II error is denoted by the Greek letter beta ($\beta$).

Ideally, the analyst would like to make both $\alpha$ and $\beta$ as small as possible and to take into account the *cost* of making both a type I and a type II error. While low levels of $\alpha$ can be specified, calculating $\beta$ is often an involved process, and the cost of making an error may not be easy to determine. To avoid the difficulties in calculating $\beta$, many analysts rely on the fact that for a fixed sample size there is an inverse relationship between $\alpha$ and $\beta$. This $\alpha$, $\beta$ trade-off, and the effect of sample size on $\beta$, are demonstrated in the

**Table 8.2** The Results of a Decision in Hypothesis Testing

| | | Population Situation | |
|---|---|---|---|
| | | $H_0$ *True* | $H_A$ *True* |
| **Decision Based on the Sample** | $H_0$ *Accepted* | Correct decision | Type II error |
| | $H_0$ *Rejected* | Type I error | Correct decision |

appendix to this chapter. To actually perform hypothesis tests, however, you only need to know that the α, β trade-off exists.

**DEFINITION**
**α, β Trade-off**

As the probability of a type I error (α) is made smaller, the probability of a type II error (β) rises.

Recall from the definition of a type I error that if $\alpha = 0.10$, then the decision maker is willing to make a type I error (reject $H_0$ incorrectly) no more than 10% of the time. If a type I error is very costly, the decision maker might specify a much lower value of α, such as 0.0001. From the α, β trade-off, however, we know that lowering α means that the probability of a type II error will increase. If a type II error is also very costly, then setting α as low as 0.0001 might not be wise. Usually α is not set as high as 0.10 or as low as 0.0001, but rather at some intermediate value, such as $\alpha = 0.05$ or 0.01.

Suppose that as the Tyrone Paper Company's manager you had specified that $\alpha = 0.05$. This means that you are willing to be wrong 5% of the time when you reject $H_0$: $\mu_x \geq 78.35$ in favor of $H_A$: $\mu_x < 78.35$. The probability when $\alpha = 0.05$ is shown in Fig. 8.2(a). The shaded area corresponding to $\alpha = 0.05$ represents the set of $\bar{x}$ values for which $H_0$ will be rejected. These values are in the *lower* tail because the alternative hypothesis is true only when the population mean is less than 78.35. As shown in Fig. 8.2, the value of $\bar{x}$ that puts 5% of the $\bar{x}$ values below it is $\bar{x} = 77.87$. This value is called the **critical value** of $\bar{x}$ and is designated by the letter $b$. The critical value

$b = 77.87$ is found using a slight variation of Eq. (6.3) from Chapter 6. In particular, substituting $b$ for $\bar{x}$ in Eq. (6.3) yields Eq. (8.1).

---

Critical value of $\bar{x}$ is $b$

**(8.1)**
$$z = \frac{b - \mu_0}{\sigma_{\bar{x}}} = \frac{b - \mu_0}{\sigma_x/\sqrt{n}}$$

---

From the discussion in Chapter 6, Eq. (8.1) implies that $b$ is $z$ standard deviations away from $\mu_0$, where $\sigma_{\bar{x}}$ is the standard deviation of the $\bar{x}$ distribution. Now $\mu_0$ is the limiting value (right-hand side) of $H_0$. The value of $\sigma_{\bar{x}}$ is calculated by dividing the population standard deviation ($\sigma_x = 1.61$ for the Tyrone Paper Company) by the square root of the sample size ($n = 30$), $\sigma_{\bar{x}} = 1.61/\sqrt{30} = 0.294$. The value of $z$ is determined using Appendix Table B.4. Since $\alpha = 0.05$, the appropriate $z$ value is the one cutting off 5% in the lower tail. Using Appendix Table B.4, as described in Chapter 6, we determine that

$$P(z \leq -1.645) = 0.05$$

$z = -1.645$ is called the **critical $z$ value**. This critical value is shown in Fig. 8.1(a).

Substituting $z = -1.645$, $\mu_0 = 78.35$, $\sigma = 1.61$, and $n = 30$ into Eq. (8.1) yields

$$-1.645 = \frac{b - 78.35}{1.61/\sqrt{30}} = \frac{b - 78.35}{0.294}$$

To solve for $b$, multiply both sides of this equation by 0.294 and then add 78.35 to both sides:

$$-0.48 = b - 78.35$$
$$b = 77.87$$

Thus the critical value of $\bar{x}$ is $b = 77.87$. This critical value is shown in Fig. 8.2(b). It states that 77.87 is 1.645 standard deviations below 78.35 in the $\bar{x}$ distribution shown in Fig. 8.2.

Setting $\alpha = 0.05$ in the Tyrone Paper Company case implies that you recognize that 5% of the time $\bar{x}$ will be 77.87 or smaller when $\mu_x = 78.35$.

**Figure 8.2**
Probability of a type I
error in the Tyrone
Paper Company case.

(a): The critical $z$ value cutting off 5% in the lower tail.

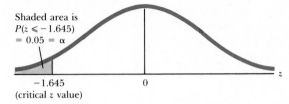

Shaded area is
$P(z \leqslant -1.645)$
$= 0.05 = \alpha$

$-1.645$
(critical $z$ value)

0

$z$

(b): Shaded area equals the probability of a Type I error, $\alpha = 0.05$.

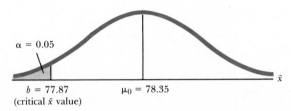

$\alpha = 0.05$

$b = 77.87$
(critical $\bar{x}$ value)

$\mu_0 = 78.35$

$\bar{x}$

Since values of 77.87 or lower are quite unlikely when $H_0$ is true, you are also stating that if one of these low values is observed, then you suspect that the true population mean is less than 78.35 and you will reject $H_0$. Because $\alpha = 0.05$, this decision will be wrong 5% of the time when $H_0$ is true.

# 8.7 A Decision Rule Based on $\alpha$ (A Continuation of Step 2)

The shaded area in Fig. 8.2(b) illustrates the area $\alpha = 0.05$ used for rejecting $H_0$ in the Tyrone Paper Company case. Either a critical $z$ value or a critical $\bar{x}$ value can be used to formulate a decision rule for rejecting $H_0$. In keeping with our earlier discussion of hypothesis testing, however, an equivalent decision rule based on a value of $\alpha$ and a comparison of this $\alpha$ with the $p$ value is preferred.

| | |
|---|---|
| **RULE** | Accept $H_0$ if the $p$ value is equal to or greater than $\alpha$. |
| **Decision** | Reject $H_0$ if the $p$ value is less than $\alpha$. |

**Figure 8.3**
One-sided lower-tail
decision rules.

(a): Illustrating accepting $H_0$ because $p$-value $\geqslant \alpha$

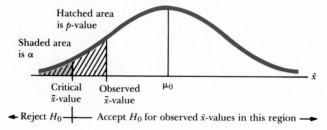

(b): Illustrating accepting $H_A$ because $p$-value $< \alpha$

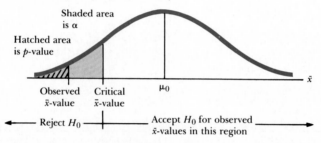

**Figure 8.4**
One-sided upper-tail
decision rules.

(a) Illustrating accepting $H_0$ because $p$-value $\geqslant \alpha$

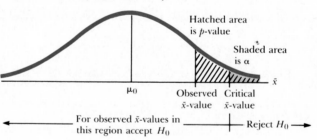

(b) Illustrating rejecting $H_0$ because $p$-value $< \alpha$

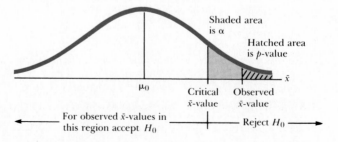

## One-Sided Hypothesis Tests

For one-sided tests, the decision rule just given is illustrated in Figs. 8.3 and 8.4. Notice in both graphs that $H_0$ is accepted if the $p$ value $\geq \alpha$ and $H_0$ is rejected if the $p$ value $< \alpha$. The same conclusion can be reached by comparing the calculated $\bar{x}$ (or calculated $z$) value with the critical $\bar{x}$ (or critical $z$) value.

Recall the Tyrone Paper Company case, where the $p$ value $= 0.0059$. Since this $p$ value is less than $\alpha = 0.05$, $H_A$: $\mu_x < 78.35$ is accepted (and $H_0$ $\mu_x \geq 78.35$ is rejected). In reaching this conclusion, we recognize that there is a 5% chance of making a type I error.

**Figure 8.5**
Two-sided decision rules.

(a) Illustrating accepting $H_0$, because the area below the observed $\bar{x}$ value is greater than $\alpha/2$.

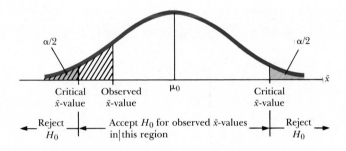

(b) Illustrating accepting $H_A$, because the area below the observed $\bar{x}$ value is less than $\alpha/2$.

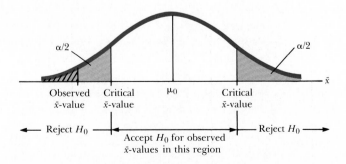

## Two-Sided Hypothesis Tests

When the alternative hypothesis is two-sided, the decision rule is the same as for a one-sided test: accept $H_0$ if the $p$ value is greater than or equal to $\alpha$; otherwise reject $H_0$. The process of finding critical $\bar{x}$ values and $p$ values is *not* the same for two-sided tests because the alternative hypothesis now permits values on either side of the single value specified in $H_0$. In this case, $\alpha$ is not put into one tail of the distribution, but rather is split equally between the two tails. That is, $\alpha/2$ is put into each tail, as shown in Fig. 8.5. As will be described in Section 8.9, the process for finding $p$ values also changes for two-sided tests. Figure 8.5 illustrates accepting or rejecting $H_0$ based on an observed value of $\bar{x}$.

## Exercises

**8.6** For each of the following situations, formulate an appropriate null and alternative hypothesis. Indicate whether $H_A$ is one- or two-sided.

a) The average number of applicants for assembly-line positions at the Radio Corporation of America (RCA) for the past 5 years has been 23.4. Recent studies suggest that the attractiveness of this type of job may be changing. What $H_0$ and $H_A$ values should be used to test for the average number of applicants now?

b) A national magazine predicts that starting salaries for computer programmers this year should increase no more than 7% over last year. The personnel director at an International Business Machines (IBM) facility in Greensburg, Indiana, believes that salaries will rise by more than this amount. The mean salary last year was $\mu_x = \$32{,}340$.

c) A machine stamping gaskets for automobiles produces a defective gasket approximately 8% of the time when it is working correctly. When the machine is working incorrectly, the defective rate is 15%.

d) A manager thinks that a new plastic will have an average breaking strength that is greater than that of the old plastic. The old breaking strength averaged 3000 pounds per square foot.

**8.7** Indicate an appropriate null and alternative hypothesis for each of the following situations. State whether a one- or a two-sided test is appropriate.

a) A market research study hopes to determine if average sales of potato chips will increase in a test market with the introduction of a new package. Sales with the old package averaged 153 packages per day.

b) A union study was designed to determine if earnings from piecework have changed since last year, when the average income was $378 per week.

c) An accountant wishes to assess whether or not there has been an increase in the percentage of overdue accounts receivable for a certain company. At the last audit, 5% of the accounts receivable were overdue.

d) An econometric analysis has been conducted to see if the rate of unemployment has changed from last month, when it was 8.1%.

**8.8** Describe a type I and a type II error for each part of Exercise 8.6.

**8.9** List some of the factors that determine whether a one- or a two-sided test is appropriate. Are there some circumstances in which either a one- or a two-sided test could be used? If so, which one should be used?

**8.10** What rules of thumb can be used to assist you in determining what statement should be presented in the null hypothesis?

ADM **8.11** Suppose the personnel director of your local First National Bank believes that the average work experience of the present tellers at that bank exceeds the national mean, which is $\mu_x = 4.1$ years.

a) If the personnel director's statement is the alternative hypothesis, what is the null hypothesis?

b) What is a type I and a type II error in this situation?

ADM **8.12** Assume that the personnel director in Exercise 8.11 has specified that the average work experience is less than the national average.

a) If this is the alternative hypothesis, what is $H_0$?

b) What is a type I and a type II error in this case?

c) What might be the consequences of a type I and a type II error in this situation? Which is possibly more serious?

MKT    **8.13** Radial, Inc., claims to have developed a new radial tire that will last for more than 70,000 miles on the average.

a) Formulate $H_0$ and $H_A$ and indicate the consequences of an incorrect decision.

b) If you worked as a statistician for Radial, how might you prefer to specify $H_0$ and $H_A$? Could the way the hypotheses are specified make a difference in the conclusion reached on the basis of sample information? Explain.

c) Let $H_0$: $\mu_x \geq 70,000$ and $H_A$: $\mu_x < 70,000$, and assume that a sample of size $n = 30$ yields $\bar{x} = 66,280$. Calculate a $p$ value using $P(z \leq z_c)$, where $z_c = (\bar{x} - \mu_0)/(\sigma/\sqrt{n})$ and $\sigma = 5000$.

d) Does the $p$ value in part (c) lead to acceptance or rejection of $H_0$, assuming $\alpha = 0.01$?

**8.14** Why are both $\alpha$ and $\beta$ important in hypothesis testing? Why is it especially important to limit the value of $\alpha$? Why have users in practical hypothesis testing problems traditionally focused only on $\alpha$, virtually ignoring $\beta$?

**8.15** What process does the decision maker follow in deciding to accept or reject $H_0$? What role does $\alpha$ play in this process? What role do the critical values play? Explain the relationship between $\alpha$ and the critical values.

ACT    **8.16** An accountant has been informed by a local bank that the average balance at the end of last month, for all customers with checking accounts, was \$232.10. As the auditor, you want to verify that the average balance is *no larger* than \$232.10.

a) Establish $H_0$ and $H_A$ (use a one-sided alternative).

b) Describe a type I and a type II error and the potential costs of each type of error. Which error would appear to be more serious?

c) Sketch a figure illustrating the critical $z$ values and shade the area leading to acceptance of $H_A$, assuming $\alpha = 0.05$.

d) Suppose a sample of size $n = 100$ customers yields $\bar{x} = \$248.95$. Assume that $\sigma_x = \$150$ and calculate a value of the test statistic $z_c = (\bar{x} - \mu_0)/(\sigma/\sqrt{n})$.

e) Calculate the $p$ value [use $P(z \leq z_c)$].

f) If $\alpha = 0.05$, would the $p$ value in part (e) lead to acceptance of $H_0$ or of $H_A$?

**8.17** Find the critical $z$ value for each part.

a) The null hypothesis is $H_0$: $\mu = \mu_0$, the alternative hypothesis is two-sided, and $\alpha = 0.05$.

b) For a one-sided, upper-tailed alternative hypothesis, $\alpha = 0.02$.

c) For a two-sided alternative hypothesis, $\alpha = 0.02$.

d) For a one-sided, lower-tailed alternative hypothesis, $\alpha = 0.01$.

**8.18** Find the critical $\bar{x}$ value(s) for both (a) and (b).

a) $H_0$: $\mu_x = 17.5$, $H_A$: $\mu_x \neq 17.5$, and $\sigma = 2.3$, $n = 100$, and $\alpha = 0.05$.

b) $H_0$: $\mu_x \leq 1078$, $H_A$: $\mu_x > 1078$, and $n = 100$, $\sigma = 12.7$, $\alpha = 0.04$.

# 8.8  Determine the Appropriate Test Statistic (Step 3)

A test statistic is a formula based on a sampling distribution. In this chapter we use only two familiar formulas as test statistics, the $z$ and the $t$ statistics (both introduced in Chapter 6).

> *z test statistic:*  Used for testing hypotheses about population means when the population standard deviation is known (also used for testing hypotheses about population proportions). The following formula represents one of the several $z$ test statistics presented in this chapter. (Note that this is Eq. (6.3), which was presented in Chapter 6 for standardizing $\bar{x}$ when $\sigma_x$ is known.)

---

$z$ statistic for testing $H_0$: $\mu_x = \mu_0$ or $H_0$: $\mu_x \leq \mu_0$ or $H_0$: $\mu_x \geq \mu_0$

**(8.2)**
$$z = \frac{\bar{x} - \mu_0}{\sigma_x/\sqrt{n}}$$

where $\mu_0$ is the number on the right-hand side of the null hypothesis and $\sigma_x$ is the population standard deviation.

---

Equation (8.2) is the correct test statistic for hypotheses about $\mu_x$ whenever

1. the population standard deviation $\sigma_x$ is known, and
2. the parent population ($x$) is normally distributed or $n = \geq 30$.

The test statistic in Eq. (8.2) gives the standardized $\bar{x}$ value about the hypothesized value $H_0$. The denominator of Eq. (8.2), $\sigma_x/\sqrt{n}$, is called the *standard error of the mean*. The standard error is the standard deviation of the distribution of all possible $\bar{x}$ values. The use of this formula has already been demonstrated in the Tyrone Paper Company case, where the calculated $z$ value was

$$z_c = \frac{\bar{x} - \mu_{\bar{x}}}{\sigma_{\bar{x}}} = \frac{\bar{x} - \mu_x}{\sigma_x/\sqrt{n}} = \frac{77.61 - 78.35}{1.61/\sqrt{30}} = -2.52$$

*t test statistic:* Used for testing hypotheses about the population mean when the population standard deviation is unknown. [Note that this is Eq. (6.4) from Chapter 6.]

---

$t$ statistic for testing $H_0$: $\mu_x = \mu_0$ or $H_0$: $\mu_x \leq \mu_0$ or $H_0$: $\mu_x \geq \mu_0$

(8.3)
$$t^* = \frac{\bar{x} - \mu_0}{s_x/\sqrt{n}}$$

where $\mu_0$ is the number on the right-hand side of the null hypothesis and $s_x$ is the sample standard deviation.

---

Equation (8.3) gives the standardized value of $\bar{x}$ values drawn from a normal parent population with a mean of $\mu_0$ and an unknown standard deviation. This formula is the correct statistic for testing hypotheses about $\mu_x$ whenever

1. the population standard deviation ($\sigma_x$) is unknown and
2. the parent population ($x$) is normal or $n \geq 30$.

**EXAMPLE** To illustrate the use of the $t$ test statistic, consider the example of the Kimberly-Clark marketing executive who claimed that the average number of times people blow their nose during a cold is 60. The null and alternative hypotheses were given as $H_0$: $\mu_x = 60$ versus $H_A$: $\mu_x \neq$

60. To test these hypotheses we draw a random sample of 30 people and pay them to keep a count of their Kleenex use when they catch a cold. For this sample of 30 people the average number of Kleenex used in nose blowing was 64.03 and the sample standard deviation was 13. Since we do not know the population standard deviation, the appropriate test statistic is $t$ and its calculated value $t_c$ is

$$t_c = \frac{\bar{x} - \mu_0}{s_x/\sqrt{n}} = \frac{64.03 - 60}{13/\sqrt{30}} = 1.698$$

As indicated earlier, there are test statistics other than the $z$ and the $t$, and there are other forms of the $z$ and the $t$. For now, let's make use of the previous test statistics in determining $p$ values.

# 8.9   Determining $p$ Values (Step 4)

As already shown, a $p$ value is a probability. If the test statistic is $z$, then the general way of denoting the probability associated with a $p$ value in a one-sided test is either $P(z \le z_c)$ or $P(z \ge z_c)$. Notice that these two probabilities differ only in that the first one contains the inequality $\le$, while the second one contains the inequality $\ge$. For one-sided tests, the inequality sign in the $p$ value is always the same as the inequality sign in the null hypothesis.

| | |
|---|---|
| **RULES**<br>**Determining**<br>**$p$ values** | $H_A$ one-sided upper: $p$ value $= P(z \ge z_c)$<br><br>$H_A$ one-sided lower: $p$ value $= P(z \le z_c)$ |

Determining $p$ values using the $t$ test follows the same rules as those just given. To demonstrate this process we will first consider a one-sided $t$ test and then the $p$ value in a two-sided test.

## Determining the $p$ Value for a One-Sided $t$ Test

A $p$ value for a one-sided $t$ test involves the same steps used in a $z$ test, except that the probabilities are obtained from Appendix Table B.5.

**EXAMPLE**   Assume that in a test of weekly grocery budgets the null and alternative hypotheses are as follows:

$H_0$: $\mu_x \leq \$90$ (average grocery budget is $90 or less)
$H_A$: $\mu_x > \$90$ (average grocery budget is more than $90).

Assume that the population is known to be normally distributed. A sample of 15 yields $\bar{x} = 105.37$ and $s_x = 20$. The calculated $t$ test statistic is

$$t_c = \frac{\bar{x} - \mu_0}{s_x/\sqrt{n}} = \frac{105.37 - 90}{20/\sqrt{15}} = 2.976$$

Since this is an upper-tail test the $p$ value is $P(t \geq 2.976)$. To determine this probability look in Appendix Table B.5 for the row with 14 d.f. (Recall from Chapter 6 that the degrees of freedom is d.f. $= n - 1$.) From Appendix Table B.5, the closest $t$ value to 2.976, with 14 d.f., is 2.977; that is, $P(t \leq 2.977|\text{d.f.} = 14) = 0.995$. Thus the approximate $p$ value is $P(\bar{x} \geq 105.37) = 1 - 0.995 = 0.005$. This area is represented in Fig. 8.6. (As discussed in Chapters 6 and 7, the exact probability associated with each calculated $t$ value cannot always be obtained from Appendix Table B.5. When this happens a computer program can be used to get exact probabilities for all possible $t$ values.)

**Figure 8.6**
The $p$ value for an upper-sided $t$ test statistic.

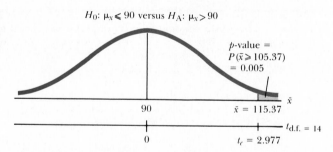

$H_0$: $\mu_x \leq 90$ versus $H_A$: $\mu_x > 90$

$p$-value = $P(\bar{x} \geq 105.37)$ = 0.005

$\bar{x}$

90    $\bar{x} = 115.37$

$t_{\text{d.f.}} = 14$

0    $t_c = 2.977$

## Determining a $p$ Value for a Two-Sided Test

The determination of $p$ values for a two-sided alternative hypothesis requires special attention because the sample value can fall on either side of the null hypothesized value.

*The $p$ value in two-sided hypothesis tests is determined by doubling the area for $\bar{x}$ values more extreme than the observed $\bar{x}$ value.*

**EXAMPLE**   Reconsider the Kleenex example: the null and alternative hypotheses were $H_0$: $\mu_x = 60$ versus $H_A$: $\mu_x \neq 60$. For a sample of size 30, the mean was 64.03 and the calculated $t$-test statistic was 1.698. The area beyond 1.698 can be obtained from Appendix Table B.5, where d.f. $= 29$. The closest $t$ value in Table B.5 is 1.699. Thus the approximate area beyond 1.698 is 0.05, that is, $P(t > 1.699) = 1 - 0.95 = 0.05$. This is the $p$ value for an upper-sided test. A two-tail test must account for $\bar{x}$ values on both sides of the null hypothesized mean. Thus the $p$ value for this two-sided test is twice as large as the one-sided $p$ value. The $p$ value for this two-sided test is thus 0.10, as shown in Fig. 8.7. Remember, in a two-sided test the $p$ value is twice the area corresponding to $\bar{x}$ values that are more extreme than the observed $\bar{x}$ value.

**Figure 8.7**
The $p$ value in the two-sided Kleenex test.

The shaded areas added together give a two-sided $p$-value of 0.10

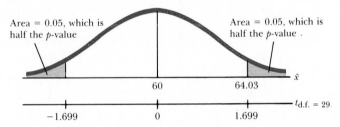

Area = 0.05, which is half the $p$-value

Area = 0.05, which is half the $p$-value .

$60$      $64.03$      $\bar{x}$

$-1.699$      $0$      $1.699$      $t_{\text{d.f.}} = 29$

## 8.10   Reach a Conclusion (Accept or Reject $H_0$)

As we indicated earlier, the decision to accept or reject $H_0$ can be made by comparing the $p$ value with the $\alpha$ value. Again, the rule is:

Accept $H_0$ if the $p$ value is greater than or equal to $\alpha$.

Reject $H_0$ if the $p$ value is less than $\alpha$.

If $H_0$ is rejected, the sample is said to be **significantly different** from the $H_0$ value. If $H_0$ is accepted, the sample is said to be *not significantly different* from the $H_0$ value. The examples introduced so far will now be reviewed in terms of this decision rule.

**EXAMPLE**   In the Tyrone Paper Company case, the null and alternative hypotheses were $H_0$: $\mu_x \geq 78.35$ versus $H_A$: $\mu_x < 78.35$. The observed

$\bar{x}$ value, 77.61, resulted in a calculated $z$ test statistic of $-2.52$ and a one-sided $p$ value of 0.0059. If $\alpha = 0.05$, the $p$ value is less than $\alpha$, and the decision is to reject $H_0$. That is, 77.61 is significantly below 78.35. (Note: any $\alpha$ greater than 0.0059 would lead to rejection of $H_0$ in this case.)

**EXAMPLE** For weekly grocery budgets, the null and alternative hypotheses were $H_0$: $\mu_x \leq \$90$ versus $H_A$: $\mu_x > \$90$. Setting $\alpha$ at 0.01 means rejecting $H_0$, since the $\bar{x}$ value of 105.37 and the resulting calculated $t$ value of 2.976 lead to a $p$ value (of about 0.005) that is less than $\alpha = 0.01$. We thus conclude the average weekly budget is significantly larger than $90. (Note: any $\alpha$ greater than or equal to 0.005 leads to rejection of $H_0$.)

**EXAMPLE** In the Kleenex example, the null and alternative hypotheses were $H_0$: $\mu_x = 60$ versus $H_A$: $\mu_x \neq 60$. For a sample mean of 64.03, the calculated $t$ test statistic was 1.698 and the two-sided $p$ value was 0.10. Since this $p$ value is not less than the established $\alpha$ of 0.05, $H_0$ must be accepted. Thus there is no significant difference between 60 and 64.03.

---

**WORKED EXAMPLE 8.2**

A small pharmaceutical company has announced a new headache remedy that it claims will give relief just as fast as the more expensive and more popular brand. The established brand is known to relieve a headache in an average of 28 minutes or less, with a standard deviation of 5.2 minutes. Skeptics suspect that the new brand may take longer to relieve a headache. A test of 100 users of the new brand indicated an average relief time of 28.6 minutes. The skeptics are willing to assume that the standard deviation of the new brand is the same as that of the established brand, $\sigma = 5.2$. The Food and Drug Administration (FDA) has decided that a test at the 0.05 type I error level is needed. What should the FDA conclude?

**ANSWER:**

STEP 1.   This is clearly a test about means, and the established theory is that $\mu_x \leq 28$ (minutes). The appropriate alternative hypothesis is dictated by the skeptics, namely, $\mu_x > 28$ minutes.

$H_0$: $\mu_x \leq 28.0$     versus     $H_A$: $\mu_x > 28.0$

STEP 2.   The $\alpha$ is determined by the FDA to be 0.05. Thus the decision rule is to reject $H_0$ if the $p$ value is less than 0.05.

STEP 3. Because the hypotheses are about a population mean and $\sigma$ is known, the $z$ distribution (Eq. 8.2) is appropriate. To find the calculated value of $z$, the sample mean $\bar{x} = 28.6$, $\mu_0 = 28.0$, $\sigma = 5.2$, and $n = 100$ are substituted in Eq. (8.2).

$$z_c = \frac{\bar{x} - \mu_0}{\sigma/\sqrt{n}} = \frac{28.6 - 28}{5.2/\sqrt{100}} = 1.15$$

STEP 4. This is a one-sided test, so the $p$ value is simply the area beyond 28.6. From Appendix Table B.4, the $p$ value $= P(z \geq 1.15) = (1 - 0.8747) = 0.1253$.

STEP 5. The $p$ value (0.1253) is considerably larger than the $\alpha$ value (0.05), so the decision must be to accept $H_0$. This comparison is illustrated in Fig. 8.8, where the critical values are shown to be $\bar{x} = 28.858$ and $z = 1.645$. (Note: comparisons can be made in terms of $p$ values, $\bar{x}$ values, or $z$ values.) Although the average relief time for the new brand is longer than that of the established brand, the difference is not significant. Thus we accept the theory that the two remedies have the same average relief time but acknowledge that there is some probability that this conclusion could be wrong.

**Figure 8.8**
Testing $H_0$: $\mu \leq 28$ versus $H_A$: $\mu > 28$.

In this graph the $p$-value $= 0.1253$ is greater than $\alpha = 0.05$. Thus, $H_0$ is accepted.

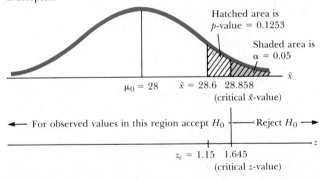

## Exercises

**8.19** What is a test statistic? What test statistics are used in this chapter? What is a calculated value of a test statistic?

**8.20** Indicate whether a $z$ or a $t$ test statistic should be used in each of the following situations involving sample means.

a) The population is normal, the sample size is small, and $\sigma$ is unknown.

b) The population is normal, the sample size is small, and $\sigma$ is known.

c) The population may not be normal, the sample size is large, and $\sigma$ is unknown.

d) The population is not normal, the sample size is small, and $\sigma$ is known.

e) The population is not normal, the sample size is large, $\sigma$ is unknown.

**8.21** Explain intuitively why a low $p$ value is evidence against the null hypothesis. For hypothesis testing in business and economics, how low does the $p$ value have to be (typically) before $H_0$ is rejected?

**8.22** Indicate the decision to be reached (accept or reject $H_0$) in the following cases:

a) The $p$ value is 0.0244 and $\alpha = 0.02$.

b) For a two-sided alternative, $P(z \geq z_c) = 0.0375$, and $\alpha = 0.05$.

c) For a one-sided upper test, $z_c = 1.85$ and $\alpha = 0.05$.

d) For a one-sided lower test, $z_c = -0.45$ and the level of significance is 0.10.

PUB **8.23** A study by the Institute for Highway Safety indicated that for 1978 the average number of miles driven by licensed drivers 20 years of age was 7235. Test the hypothesis that 20-year-olds drove more miles in 1986, using $\alpha = 0.05$. In a 1986 random sample of 100 people, all 20-year-old licensed drivers, the average number of miles driven was 7787. The standard deviation is known to be $\sigma = 3000$ miles. (Complete all five hypothesis testing steps.)

FIN **8.24** For 1983 the number of shares traded on the New York Stock Exchange averaged 58.7 million per day, with a standard deviation of 14.3. The improved economic conditions in 1985 led many people to anticipate more activity. A random sample of 50 days in the first half of 1985 indicated an average volume of 61.3 shares per day. Complete the five hypothesis testing steps.

ACT **8.25** The Internal Revenue Service (IRS) is attempting to determine the reasonableness of their assumption that the waiters or waitresses in a typical restaurant earn $5 per hour in tips. They take a random sample of 200 different hours (different locations and different times of day) and find the average tip to be $5.23. Is this sufficient evidence for the IRS to conclude that the average is no longer $5? Use $\alpha = 0.02$ and assume that $\sigma = \$1.46$. (Complete the five hypothesis testing steps.)

ADM    **8.26**   Eastman Kodak is concerned that the quality of the students they interview for permanent jobs may be decreasing. Last year, the average grade point average (GPA) over all students interviewed was 3.32. This year, the first 145 students interviewed had an average GPA of 3.25. If these 145 students are considered a random sample, is the company's concern justified? Assume that $\sigma = 0.19$ and let $\alpha = 0.04$. Does a lower average GPA necessarily mean that the quality of the students is lower? Explain.

MKT    **8.27**   A Mexican restaurant is attempting to determine whether their weekday lunch business has changed with their new menu. Previously, the average revenue per weekday lunch was $1740. A random sample of 25 weekdays after the menu change resulted in a mean revenue of $1985. Has the revenue changed significantly if $\sigma = \$221$ and $\alpha = 0.05$?

FIN    **8.28**   Midwest corn growers were overjoyed when Pepsico, Inc., announced that they would replace liquid sugar with corn sweetener. A spokesman for the Iowa Corn Promotion Bureau predicted that Pepsi's switch would increase corn prices by $0.02 or more per bushel in the first year. A sample of 100 growers 1 year later indicated an average increase in price of $0.19, with a standard deviation of $0.02. Complete the five hypothesis testing steps, using $\alpha = 0.05$.

MKT    **8.29**   In a classic study by Bohemia beer, the brewer of the Mexican beer hypothesized that they would increase sales by reducing the quantity in each bottle from 12 to 11 ounces and using the cost savings for a fancier container and a bigger advertising budget. Skeptics believed that sales would stay the same or even decrease. In a test market using the 12-ounce bottle, sales averaged 223 bottles per week. For the same test market using the 11-ounce bottle, sales in 100 outlets averaged 258 bottles, with a standard deviation of 51. Using $\alpha = 0.02$, complete the five hypothesis testing steps. Be sure to specify the critical $\bar{x}$ and $z$ values.

# 8.11 Hypothesis Tests Involving Parameters Other Than $\mu$

Hypothesis testing almost always follows the five steps described in Section 8.4. In fact, only steps 1 and 3 change from situation to situation. For step 1, many different types of hypotheses are possible, so one must be careful to specify correctly the parameters to be tested and the numerical values upon which the test will be based. For step 3 there are many different test statistics, and sometimes more than one can be used in a given situation. In steps 2, 4, and 5, however, the process of specifying the probability of a type I error, the determination of a $p$ value, and the reaching of a conclusion typically vary only slightly from one problem to another. Thus the remaining sections of this chapter focus on developing hypotheses and presenting test statistics, but do not elaborate greatly on steps 2, 4, and 5.

# 8.12 A One-Sample Test Involving a Population Proportion

Recall from the discussion in Section 8.5, and Chapters 6 and 7, that a population proportion is denoted by the letter $\pi$, where $\pi$ may represent the proportion of females in a workforce, the proportion of smokers flying commercial airlines, the proportion of defective units on an assembly line, or a shampoo's market share.

Suppose Procter and Gamble (P&G) wishes to test if Prell's market proportion this year will equal Prell's known market proportion last year. If P&G has population data from last year but only sample data for this year, a hypothesis test based on sample data is necessary. Suppose last year's population proportion was known to be $\pi = 0.17$ (17% of the market). The appropriate null and alternative hypotheses might be

$H_0$: $\pi = 0.17$ (the population percent is 17)
$H_A$: $\pi \neq 0.17$ (the population percent is not 17)

**EXAMPLE** Consider a consumer protection agency that is interested in testing a statement by General Electric that 80% of their 100-watt Soft-White light bulbs last longer than 750 hours. In this case the following one-sided test would be appropriate:

$H_0$: $\pi \leq 0.80$ (the population percent is 80 or less)

$H_A$: $\pi > 0.80$ (the population percent exceeds 80)

Notice that in this case the null hypothesis is the complement of the company statement. Because the null hypothesis has a built-in bias, this means that we have (purposely) constructed the most difficult test for the company. If $H_A$ is accepted, the public should be very confident that no favoritism was shown to any commercial interest the company may have in the results of the test.

We use a $z$ test statistic for testing population proportions. This test is appropriate when the sample size is not small, which we will arbitrarily assume means a sample of at least $n = 30$. Although smaller samples can be tested using the binomial distribution, we will not present this approach here. The one-sample $z$ test for proportions is:

---

$z$ test for a population proportion:

**(8.4)**

$$z = \frac{(x/n) - \pi_0}{\sqrt{\dfrac{\pi_0(1 - \pi_0)}{n}}}$$

where $\pi_0$ is the value on the right-hand side of the null hypothesis and there are $x$ successes in a sample of size $n > 30$.

---

A calculated value for this test statistic is determined by substituting in the sample proportion $x/n$, where $x$ is the number of successes in the sample, and substituting for $\pi_0$ the limiting null hypothesis $\pi$ value (that is, the right-hand side of $H_0$). As before, a $p$ value is determined using the calculated $z$ test statistic. Either $H_0$ or $H_A$ is accepted by comparing the $p$ value with the probability of a type I error ($\alpha$). A conclusion must be presented and then interpreted.

---

**WORKED EXAMPLE 8.3**

U.S. courts have ruled that for a company to have nondiscriminatory hiring practices, it must hire workers in proportions that are representative of the available workforce. In one area, 25% of the accountants available for new accounting jobs are women. Thus a company in this area that has not discriminated against female applicants should hire a proportion of women that is not significantly different from 0.25. One company in this area hired 80 new accountants over the past several years, 16 of whom were women. Does this indicate discriminatory hiring, using $\alpha = 0.05$?

**ANSWER:**

STEP 1. The appropriate null and alternative hypotheses are:

$$H_0: \pi \geq 0.25 \text{ (the company is not discriminating)}$$
$$H_A: \pi < 0.25 \text{ (the company is discriminating)}.$$

STEP 2. The level of significance is set at $\alpha = 0.05$.

STEP 3. The calculated $z$ test statistic is

$$z_c = \frac{\dfrac{x}{n} - \pi_0}{\sqrt{\dfrac{\pi_0(1 - \pi_0)}{n}}} = \frac{\dfrac{16}{80} - 0.25}{\sqrt{\dfrac{0.25(0.75)}{80}}} = \frac{-0.05}{0.0484} = -1.03$$

STEP 4. The $p$ value is

$$p \text{ value} = P(z \leq -1.03) = 1 - 0.8485 = 0.1515$$

STEP 5. Because the $p$ value (0.1515) exceeds $\alpha = 0.05$, the null hypothesis is accepted. We conclude that while the company has hired less than 25% women, the sample evidence is not strong enough to accept $H_A$ that the company is descriminating against women.

# 8.13 Two-Sample Tests Involving Tests of Means

In some statistical problems the analyst wants to compare two different populations. For example, a company may wish to compare sales in two different cities or the number of units sold by two different sales representatives. Perhaps two different brands of paint are being compared for durability or two factories for efficiency. Hypotheses in this situation typically involve comparisons between the two population means. The test statistic will still be a $z$ or a $t$ test, but will take a slightly different form than the test statistics presented thus far. Otherwise, the five steps for hypothesis testing are the same ones discussed previously.

The null hypothesis in a two-sample test is often that the two populations have the same mean, or equivalently, that there is no difference between the two means. If the mean of the first population is $\mu_1$ and that of the second population is $\mu_2$, then the null hypothesis is that the difference between the two means equals zero:

$$H_0: \mu_1 - \mu_2 = 0$$

The alternative hypothesis is that the difference does not equal zero:

$$H_A: \mu_1 - \mu_2 \neq 0$$

When a theory suggests that one population mean is less than the other, a one-sided, two-sample test is appropriate. The null and alternative hypotheses used to test the theory that $\mu_1$ is less than $\mu_2$ are

$$H_0: \mu_1 - \mu_2 \geq 0 \qquad \text{versus} \qquad H_A: \mu_1 - \mu_2 < 0$$

To test whether $\mu_1$ is greater than $\mu_2$, the null and alternative hypotheses are

$$H_0: \mu_1 - \mu_2 \leq 0 \qquad \text{versus} \qquad H_A: \mu_1 - \mu_2 > 0$$

In a two-sample test, the right-hand side can be *any* number. Usually, however, the limiting value is zero.

The test statistic for the difference between two population means is a $z$ test if the two population variances are known and a $t$ test if the variances are unknown. The following notation is used in both situations:

| Population 1 | | Population 2 |
|---|---|---|
| $\mu_1$ | population mean | $\mu_2$ |
| $\sigma_1^2$ | population variance | $\sigma_2^2$ |
| $n_1$ | sample size | $n_2$ |
| $\bar{x}_1$ | sample mean | $\bar{x}_2$ |
| $s_1^2$ | sample variance | $s_2^2$ |

## Two-Sample $z$ Test When the Population Variances Are Known

The two-sample $z$ test is appropriate when

1. the population variances are known.

**2.** both random samples are independent of each other and

    **a)** of at least size $n = 30$ or

    **b)** are drawn from a normal parent population.

---

Test statistic for the two-sample $z$ test

(8.5)
$$z = \frac{\bar{x}_1 - \bar{x}_2 - 0}{\sqrt{\dfrac{\sigma_1^2}{n_1} + \dfrac{\sigma_2^2}{n_2}}}$$

where 0 is the difference specified by the right-hand side of $H_0$.

---

**WORKED EXAMPLE 8.4**

A 1984 study by the Environmental Protection Agency (EPA) compared the highway fuel economy of domestic and imported passenger cars. In the 2500-pound weight class, a test of 25 domestic cars resulted in an average of 35.2 miles per gallon (mpg), and a test of 18 imported cars resulted in an average of 34.2 mpg. The population gas mileage is known to be normal in both cases, and the variances are known to be $\sigma_1^2 = 2.3$ (domestic) and $\sigma_2^2 = 1.8$ (imported). Test the hypothesis that the population means are equal at $\alpha = 0.05$.

**ANSWER:**

STEP 1. Since $H_0$ is a hypothesis of equality, the hypotheses are

$$H_0: \mu_1 - \mu_2 = 0 \qquad \text{versus} \qquad H_A: \mu_1 - \mu_2 \neq 0$$

STEP 2. The level of significance is given as $\alpha = 0.05$.

STEP 3. The sample means are $\bar{x} = 35.2$ and $\bar{x} = 34.2$. Although one sample is relatively small ($n_2 = 18$), the populations are known to be normal, with $\sigma_1^2 = 2.3$ and $\sigma_2^2 = 1.8$. Thus a $z$ test is appropriate. Substituting into Eq. (8.5) yields

$$z = \frac{\bar{x}_1 - \bar{x}_2 - 0}{\sqrt{\dfrac{\sigma_1^2}{n_1} + \dfrac{\sigma_2^2}{n_2}}} = \frac{35.2 - 34.2}{\sqrt{\dfrac{2.3}{25} + \dfrac{1.8}{18}}} = \frac{1.0}{0.44} = 2.27$$

STEP 4. The $p$ value for this two-tail test requires the doubling of $P(z \geq 2.27)$, as obtained from Appendix Table B.4; that is, $p$ value $= 2P(z \geq 2.27) = 2(1 - 0.9884) = 0.0232$.

STEP 5. The two-sided $p$ value (0.0232) is much less than the $\alpha$ value (0.05). Hence $H_0$ must be rejected. The EPA can thus conclude that the average mpg for domestic cars in the 2500-pound weight class is significantly different from that of imported cars. Figure 8.9 illustrates this result.

In this example (as in all two-tailed tests), the correct $p$ value is twice the area beyond the calculated value $z_c = 2.27$. For two-tailed tests, the critical $\bar{x}$ and $z$ values cut off $\alpha/2$ in each tail of the sampling distribution (see Fig. 8.9). As before, if the sample result falls beyond the critical value, then $H_0$ must be rejected.

**Figure 8.9**
Reaching a decision for the EPA study of gas mileage.

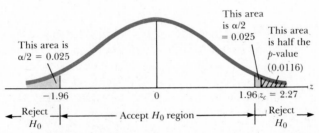

Note: The decision based on these values is to reject $H_0$, since $\alpha = 0.05$ is greater than the $p$-value $= 0.0232$.

## Two-Sample $t$ Test When the Variances Are Unknown

The two-sample $z$ test in the last section was appropriate because the population variances were known. Now let's assume that the population variances are *unknown*. The two-sample $t$ test makes the following assumptions:

1. The population variances are unknown. However, it must be reasonable to assume that they are equal.

2. Both random samples are independent of each other and

   a) of at least size $n = 15$ or

   b) are drawn from a normal parent population.

The test statistic in this situation is:

Test statistic for the two-sample $t$ test

(8.6)
$$t = \frac{\bar{x}_1 - \bar{x}_2 - 0}{\sqrt{\left(\dfrac{s_1^2(n_1 - 1) + s_2^2(n_2 - 1)}{n_1 + n_2 - 2}\right)\left(\dfrac{n_1 + n_2}{n_1 n_2}\right)}}$$

with $n_1 + n_2 - 2$ d.f. and where 0 is the value on the right-hand side of $H_0$.

**WORKED EXAMPLE 8.5**

In a December 22, 1983, *WSJ* advertisement, Leading Edge Products, Inc., claimed that its microcomputer was more dependable (in terms of the mean time between failures of disk drives) than the IBM-PC. The ad stated that the mean time between failures for their disk drives was 20,000 hours ($\bar{x}_1 = 20{,}000$), compared to only 8000 hours for the IBM ($\bar{x}_2 = 8000$). Test this claim using $\alpha = 0.01$ and the following information for a sample of five Leading Edge and five IBM machines.

| (1)<br>**Leading Edge** | (2)<br>**IBM** |
|---|---|
| $\bar{x}_1 = 20{,}000$ | $\bar{x}_2 = 8{,}000$ |
| $s_1 = 3{,}000$ | $s_2 = 2{,}000$ |
| $n_1 = 5$ | $n_2 = 5$ |

**ANSWER:**

STEP 1. In this example Leading Edge is claiming superiority with a new theory that $\mu_1 - \mu_2 > 0$. Thus the null and alternative hypotheses are

$$H_0: \mu_1 - \mu_2 \leq 0 \qquad \text{versus} \qquad H_A: \mu_1 - \mu_2 > 0$$

STEP 2. The probability of a Type I error is set at $\alpha = 0.01$.

STEP 3. Since the population standard deviations are not known, the sample standard deviations must be used in the $t$ test statistic. To use this statistic we must assume that the populations are normal and have equivalent variances. (It is worth noting that because of sampling error, the populations can have equal variances and yet, for any two samples drawn at random, the sample standard deviations $s_1$ and $s_2$ may differ, as they do here.) The calculated value of the $t$ test statistic is

$$t_c = \frac{\bar{x}_1 - \bar{x}_2 - 0}{\sqrt{\left(\dfrac{s_1^2(n_1 - 1) + s_2^2(n_2 - 1)}{n_1 + n_2 - 2}\right)\left(\dfrac{n_1 + n_2}{n_1 n_2}\right)}}$$

$$= \frac{(20{,}000 - 8000) - 0}{\sqrt{\left[\dfrac{(3000)^2(4) + (2000)^2(4)}{5 + 5 - 2}\right]\left[\dfrac{5 + 5}{(5)(5)}\right]}}$$

$$= \frac{12{,}000}{1612.45} = 7.44$$

STEP 4. From Appendix Table B.5 the $p$ value, the probability of being above 7.44, with $n_1 + n_2 - 2 = 8$ d.f., cannot be determined exactly. The closest we can get is $P(t \geq 5.041 | \text{d.f.} = 8) = 1 - 0.9995 = 0.0005$. Using a computer program, the exact $p$ value is 0.00004, as shown in the following output:

| | |
|---|---|
| **Student's $t$ Distribution** | Computer Output |
| | d.f.: 8 |
| | $t$: 7.44 |
| | $p = 0.99996$    $1 - p = 0.00004$ |

STEP 5. The $p$ value of 0.00004 is less than $\alpha = 0.01$, so $H_0$ must be rejected. On the basis of this sample, the conclusion is that the mean time between failures of the disk drives of the Leading Edge computer is significantly greater than that of the IBM-PC, as claimed in the ad.

As Fig. 8.10 indicates, the test could have been carried out by comparing the critical $t$ value (2.896) with the calculated $t$ value, $t_c = 7.44$. Since the calculated value falls beyond the critical value, $H_0$ is rejected.

Figure 8.10
Testing the difference
between Leading
Edge and IBM disk
durability.

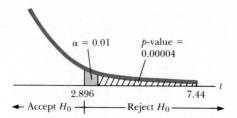

## 8.14 Summary

The hypothesis tests presented in this chapter represent just a small part of all those we could have presented. To mention just a few, there are two-sample tests for population proportions, multiple-sample tests for population proportions, tests for comparing means when the observations are matched, and both one- and two-sample tests about variances. There are also nonparametric tests that can handle small samples without the assumption of a normal parent population. Many of these tests are presented in a later chapter.

No matter what testing situation you are confronted with in the future, remember that in any testing situation there are always five steps:

1. Establish the null and alternative hypotheses.

2. Formulate a decision rule for rejecting or accepting the null hypothesis based on tolerable ($\alpha$ and $\beta$) error levels.

3. Select a test statistic, draw a sample, and calculate the value of the test statistic based on your sample data.

4. Calculate the $p$ value associated with the value of the calculated test statistic.

5. Reach a conclusion (accept or reject $H_0$) using the $p$ value calculated in step 4 and the decision rule formulated in step 2.

As we demonstrated in the later sections of this chapter, only steps 1 and 3 vary greatly from one type of problem to another. The process of specifying the probability of a type I error, determining a $p$ value, and reaching a conclusion typically vary only slightly from problem to problem.

PUB **8.30** In the 1984 presidential election, President Reagan asked voters to think about whether they were better off than they had been 4 years before. An October 1984 *Money* magazine article surveyed 2465 people, and 59 percent said they were better off in 1984. Is this sufficient evidence to reject the null hypothesis that 50% or less are better off? Use $\alpha = 0.01$ and present all five hypothesis testing steps.

ADM **8.31** According to a July 26, 1984, article in the *WSJ*, a survey of 1200 hourly workers found that "only 45% of hourly workers think their firm is a good place to work." Using a 0.10 probability of a type I error, is this sufficient evidence to conclude that less than 50% of all hourly workers think their firm is a good place to work?

ADM **8.32** A recent study by *Science Digest* suggests that "University scientists make more money than their industry counterparts." Use the following information to test this claim at $\alpha = 0.10$:

| University Scientists | Industry Scientists |
|---|---|
| $\bar{x}_1 = \$55,000$ | $\bar{x}_2 = \$52,000$ |
| $s_1 = \$5,000$ | $s_2 = \$7,000$ |
| $n_1 = 15$ | $n_2 = 14$ |

MKT **8.33** A new print size for a newspaper ad is expected to involve the same average reading time for both older and younger readers. Previously, older people took longer. The standard deviations are known to be $\sigma_1 = 0.02$ minute and $\sigma_2 = 0.01$ minute for older and younger readers, respectively. Changing the print size is not expected to change these standard deviations. For a sample of 30 older people the average time needed to read the new ad is 0.9 minute. For a sample of 35 younger readers it is 0.85 minute. Do the reading times differ significantly? Test this hypothesis using $\alpha = 0.05$.

LAW **8.34** A report by the American Bar Association claims that two-thirds of the lawyers in private practice work 45 hours a week or more. To test this claim for your home town you take a random sample of 50 lawyers in private practice. Thirty worked 45 hours or more. Use $\alpha = 0.05$. What conclusion can you draw?

MKT **8.35** A report by the *Power Newsletter* suggests that car buyers who are 25 years old or less purchase less than 10% of the new cars in the United States. Recent buying patterns suggest that this percentage may have increased. In a sample of 728 new-car buyers, 79 were 25 or less. Construct and test appropriate hypotheses, using $\alpha = 0.10$.

MKT **8.36** An ad in the *WSJ* provided the following data on the cost of renting a compact Hertz car at 26 selected locations. Test the null hypothesis that the mean cost is $45, using a two-sided alternative and $\alpha = 0.05$.

| City | Hertz |
|------|-------|
| Atlanta | $46 |
| Boston | 61 |
| Chicago (O'Hare) | 59 |
| Cleveland | 55 |
| Denver | 54 |
| Detroit | 52 |
| Honolulu | 34 |
| Houston (IAH) | 50 |
| Kansas City | 49 |
| Los Angeles | 46 |
| Miami | 41 |
| New Orleans | 54 |
| New York (JFK) | 68 |
| New York (LGA) | 68 |
| Newark | 65 |
| Orlando | 44 |
| Philadelphia | 57 |
| Phoenix | 45 |
| Pittsburgh | 56 |
| St. Louis | 50 |
| Salt Lake City | 50 |
| San Francisco | 47 |
| San Jose | 48 |
| Seattle | 47 |
| Wash., D.C. (Nat'l) | 62 |
| West Palm Beach | 45 |

**8.37** Compare the process of constructing a confidence interval (as presented in Chapter 7) and testing a two-sided hypothesis.

OPS   **8.38** A manufacturer wants to know whether or not the rate of production in a plant will be changed by the introduction of a new production process. Historically, a worker has produced 90 units per hour. A sample of 36 workers try the new process. The sample average is 86 units per hour with a standard deviation of 20. Construct a test using $\alpha = 0.05$.

**8.39** State several rules of thumb that could be used to assist in deciding whether an inference is to be made about a population proportion or population mean.

MKT   **8.40** A cigarette manufacturer is considering the introduction of one of three new low-tar cigarettes. The marketing department believes that if customers could choose among the three types, more than one-third would pick brand A. To find out, the company surveys 200 smokers and finds that 36% prefer brand A, 30% prefer brand B, and 34% prefer brand C. Is it reasonable to conclude that more than one-third of the smokers prefer brand A over brands B and C? Use $\alpha = 0.04$.

PUB   **8.41** To win a clear-cut victory in a local election, a union leader wants to get more than 55% of the vote. To test whether or not this type of victory can be anticipated, the labor leader surveys 64 of the voting members; 40 of these people intend to vote for this person. At the $\alpha = 0.01$ level of significance, should the leader be confident about a clear-cut victory?

MKT   **8.42** An advertisement in *Time* magazine for Hasselblad camera stated that the cameras are inspected, and "sixty percent are rejected for the slightest imperfections." To test this assertion, you observe the inspection of a random selection of 30 cameras and find that 15 are rejected. Construct a test, using $\alpha = 0.05$.

FIN   **8.43** A *Business Week* article indicated that Miller beer had 20% of the market in 1983. In a random sample of 1000 liquor stores, Miller had 23% of the market. Does this result indicate a significant increase in Miller's market share, using $\alpha = 0.02$?

ECN **8.44** A 1984 *Time* magazine study indicated that the average yearly housing cost for a family of four was $12,983. A random sample of 200 families in Seattle resulted in a mean of $14,039, with a standard deviation of $2129. Is the Seattle sample mean significantly higher than the population mean, using $\alpha = 0.04$?

**8.45** Using diagrams such as Figs. 8.11 and 8.12 (in Ch. 8 Appendix), show why it is not necessarily true that the probability of a type I error equals $1 -$ the probability of a type II error. Under what condition will the probability of a type I error equal the probability of a type II error?

MKT **8.46** An ad in the *WSJ* provided the following prices for renting a compact car from Avis or Hertz at 26 selected locations. Determine if the two sample means differ significantly, using $\alpha = 0.05$.

| City | Hertz | Avis |
|---|---|---|
| Atlanta | $46 | $46 |
| Boston | 61 | 57 |
| Chicago (O'Hare) | 59 | 58 |
| Cleveland | 55 | 54 |
| Denver | 54 | 54 |
| Detroit | 52 | 52 |
| Honolulu | 34 | 34 |
| Houston (IAH) | 50 | 49 |
| Kansas City | 49 | 49 |
| Los Angeles | 46 | 46 |
| Miami | 41 | 41 |
| New Orleans | 54 | 50 |
| New York (JFK) | 68 | 63 |
| New York (LGA) | 68 | 63 |
| Newark | 65 | 61 |
| Orlando | 44 | 44 |
| Philadelphia | 57 | 53 |
| Phoenix | 45 | 45 |
| Pittsburgh | 56 | 52 |
| St. Louis | 50 | 50 |
| Salt Lake City | 50 | 50 |
| San Francisco | 47 | 47 |
| San Jose | 48 | 48 |
| Seattle | 47 | 47 |
| Wash., D.C. (Nat'l) | 62 | 59 |
| West Palm Beach | 45 | 45 |

ADM **8.47** A *WSJ* article of (1/18/85), on computer product design systems quoted Henry Eichfield, an official at the Computervision Corporation, as saying, "Thirty percent down time isn't atypical for the world of data processing." To determine if average down time is 30%, you check with 25 firms and find average down time to be 32%, with a standard deviation of 5%. At the 0.05 type I error level, is Eichfield's claim refutable?

LAW **8.48** In Worked Example 8.3, under the null hypothesis we treated the company's 80 new accountants as a random sample from the available workforce. In what sense can these 80 employees be considered the outcome of a random sample?

# Glossary

$\alpha$: The probability of a type I error.

**alternative hypothesis:** A statement about a population parameter being tested. Traditionally designated by the symbol $H_A$, it is a statement that is anticipated to be true if the null hypothesis is false.

$\beta$: The probability of a type II error.

**calculated test statistic:** The standardized value of the observed sample value.

**critical $t$ value:** The $t$ value beyond which $H_0$ is rejected. The area beyond the critical value(s) is of size $\alpha$.

**critical $\bar{x}$ value:** The $\bar{x}$ value beyond which $H_0$ is rejected. The area beyond the critical value(s) is of size $\alpha$.

**critical $z$ value:** The $z$ value beyond which $H_0$ is rejected. The area beyond the critical value(s) is of size $\alpha$.

**hypothesis:** Statement about population parameters.

**hypothesis testing:** The process of judging the correctness of two mutually exclusive and exhaustive hypotheses.

**limiting value of $H_0$:** The number appearing on the right-hand side of the null hypothesis.

**lower-sided alternative hypothesis:** A one-sided alternative hypothesis that specifies values less than the limiting value stated in the null hypothesis.

**null hypothesis:** A statement about a population parameter (or difference in parameters) that is assumed to be true until sufficient contrary sample evidence is presented. Traditionally designated by the symbol $H_0$, it is a statement that typically reflects an existing theory or belief.

**one-sided hypothesis test:** A test in which the alternative hypothesis specifies values on one side of the limiting value specified by $H_0$.

***p* value:** The probability of observing a sample value, assuming the null hypothesis is true. In the case of a one-sided alternative hypothesis, the *p* value is the probability of obtaining sample statistic values more extreme than the observed (or calculated) value of the sample statistic. In the case of a two-sided alternative hypothesis, the *p* value is twice the probability of obtaining sample statistic values more extreme than the observed (or calculated) value of the sample statistic.

**significantly different:** A sample estimate sufficiently far away from the population parameter value in the null hypothesis that the null hypothesis is rejected.

**two-sided hypothesis test:** A test in which the alternative hypothesis specifies values both less than and greater than the value in the null hypothesis.

**type I error:** Rejecting the null hypothesis when it is true.

**type II error:** Accepting the null hypothesis when it is false.

**upper-sided alternative hypothesis:** A one-sided alternative hypothesis that specifies values greater than the limiting value stated in the null hypothesis.

## Formulas

**8.1—For a $z$ Test in which the Null Hypothesis Is $H_0$: $\mu = \mu_0$, the Critical Value of $\bar{x}$ Is Defined by $b$ in the Ratio**

$$z = \frac{b - \mu_0}{\sigma_x / \sqrt{n}}$$

**8.2—$z$ Statistic for Testing $H_0$: $\mu_x = \mu_0$ ($\sigma$ Known)**

$$z = \frac{\bar{x} - \mu_0}{\sigma_x / \sqrt{n}}$$

where $\mu_0$ is the number on the right-hand side of the null hypothesis and $\sigma_x$ is the population standard deviation.

**8.3—$t$ Statistic for Testing $H_0$: $\mu_x = \mu_0$ ($\sigma$ Unknown)**

$$t = \frac{\bar{x} - \mu_0}{s_x / \sqrt{n}}$$

*single mean compared to null value*

Chapter 8  Hypothesis Testing

where $\mu_0$ is the number on the right-hand side of the null hypothesis and $s_x$ is the sample standard deviation.

**8.4—$z$ Test for a Population Proportion Where $H_0$: $\pi = \pi_0$**

$$z = \frac{(x/n) - \pi_0}{\sqrt{\dfrac{\pi_0(1 - \pi_0)}{n}}}$$

where $\pi_0$ is the value on the right-hand side of the null hypothesis and the sample size is at least $n = 30$.

**8.5—Test Statistic for a Two-Sample $z$ Test, Where $H_0$: $\mu_1 - \mu_2 = 0$ ($\sigma_1$ and $\sigma_2$ Both Known)**

$$z = \frac{\bar{x}_1 - \bar{x}_2 - 0}{\sqrt{\dfrac{\sigma_1^2}{n_1} + \dfrac{\sigma_2^2}{n_2}}}$$

**8.6—Test Statistic for a Two-Sample $t$ Test, Where $H_0$: $\mu_1 - \mu_2 = 0$ ($\sigma_1$ and $\sigma_2$ Unknown)**

$$t = \frac{\bar{x}_1 - \bar{x}_2 - 0}{\sqrt{\left(\dfrac{s_1^2(n_1 - 1) + s_2^2(n_2 - 1)}{n_1 + n_2 - 2}\right)\left(\dfrac{n_1 + n_2}{n_1 n_2}\right)}}$$

with $n_1 + n_2 - 2$ d.f.

---

# APPENDIX — Type I and Type II Error Trade-off and the Effect of Sample Size

As indicated in Section 8.3, there is a trade-off between the probability of a type I and a type II error. For a given sample size, as the probability of a type I error ($\alpha$) is reduced, the probability of a type II error ($\beta$) rises. Similarly, if $\beta$ is reduced, $\alpha$ will increase. To illustrate this inverse relationship, consider a national consumer group's claim that retailers of a new sports car are not selling this car at the $10,000 list price "because demand for the car is far less than expected." To see if such discounting is occurring locally, a TV station consumer affairs reporter intends to survey area car dealers. The reporter decides to test at $\alpha = 0.05$. The null and alternative hypotheses to be tested are

$$H_0: \mu_x \geq \$10,000 \qquad \text{versus} \qquad H_A: \mu_x < \$10,000$$

where $\mu_x$ is the average purchase price of the sports car locally and $\$10,000$ is the suggested manufacturer's selling price.

Under the null hypothesis, the mean purchase price paid for this sports car should be centered at $\$10,000$, as shown in Fig. 8.11(a). If $H_0$ is true, 5% of the $\bar{x}$ values from samples of size $n$ will lie below the critical value, $b$. If $H_0$ is not true, then the true average selling price might be some lower number, such as $\$9400$ (see (Fig. 8.11b). If the true mean price is $\$9400$,

(a) Assuming $H_0: \mu_x = \$10,000$ is true, and $\alpha = 0.05$, the decision rule is that

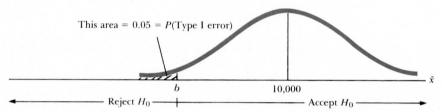

(b) If $H_A$ is true (e.g. $\mu_x = \$9,400$), then the shaded area is the probability of incorrectly accepting $H_0$ (a Type II error).

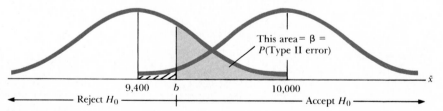

(c) Assuming $\mu_x = \$10,000$ and $\alpha$ is increased to $\alpha = 0.10$,

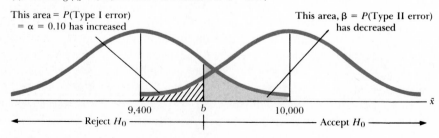

**Figure 8.11**
Illustrating the relationship between $\alpha$ and $\beta$, holding $n$ constant.

then the probability that $H_0$ is incorrectly accepted (type II error) is indicated by the shaded area in Fig. 8.11(b).

If the probability of making a type I error ($\alpha$) is increased, say from 0.05 to 0.10, the critical $\bar{x}$ value ($b$) will increase (move to the right, as in Fig. 8.11c). As $b$ is moved to the right (in Fig. 8.11), the set of $\bar{x}$ values leading to rejection of $H_0$ becomes larger (Fig. 8.11c). By comparing Figs. 8.11(b) and 8.11(c), this also implies that $\beta$ is smaller. In general, for any fixed sample size, raising (lowering) the probability of a type I error will lower (raise) the probability of a type II error.

The probability of a type II error can be reduced, for any given $\alpha$ level, by increasing the sample size. To see this relationship consider the previous example, where now we add the information that the initial sample size was $n = 100$. Figure 8.12(a), shows the initial probabilities of type I and type II errors when $\mu_x$ is assumed to equal \$10,000 ($H_0$) but actually equals \$9400 ($H_A$). If the sample size is increased to $n = 200$ the standard deviation of the $\bar{x}$ distribution is reduced. The effect of this reduction in $\sigma_{\bar{x}}$ is shown in Fig. 8.12(b). When $\alpha$ is held constant, increasing the sample size moves the critical value $b$ closer to the null hypothesized value of $\mu_x$. As $b$ moves closer to \$10,000, the probability of incorrectly accepting $H_0$ is reduced (the $\beta$ area is smaller in Fig. 8.12(b) than in 8.12(a)).

(a) If $H_A$ is true (e.g. $\mu_x = \$9,400$), then the shaded area is the probability of incorrectly accepting $H_0$ if $\mu_x = \$10,000$ and the hatched area is the probability of incorrectly rejecting $H_0$ if $\mu_x = \$10,000$, based on a sample size of $n = 100$.

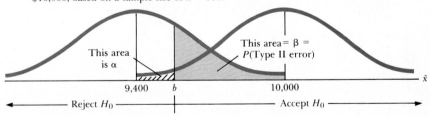

(b) Assuming $\mu_x = \$10,000$ and $n$ is increased to $n = 200$,

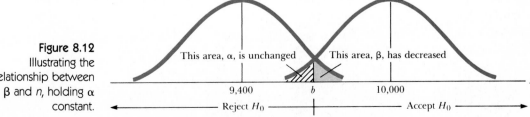

**Figure 8.12**
Illustrating the relationship between $\beta$ and $n$, holding $\alpha$ constant.

# CHAPTER NINE

*I have a great subject (statistics) to write upon, but feel keenly my literary incapacity to make it easily intelligible without sacrificing accuracy and thoroughness.*
*Sir Francis Galton*

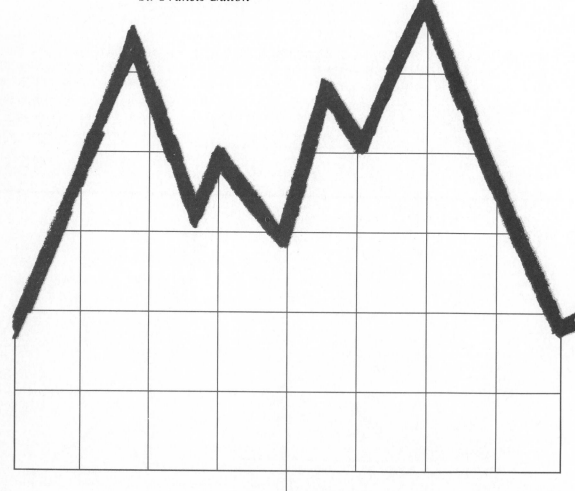

# SIMPLE LINEAR REGRESSION AND CORRELATION

This chapter provides an introduction to regression and correlation. Regression analysis is used to study the relationship that may exist between variables and to make predictions based on such relationships. Correlation analysis is used to study the strength of the relationship between variables. It is difficult to find a business, a governmental unit, or an academic area that does not make use of regression and correlation.

■ Economists use regression analysis to predict changes in personal income that may result from proposed changes in the tax structure.

■ A marketing analyst uses regression to forecast how sales may respond to various advertising campaigns.

■ Steel companies have used regression and correlation to predict the strength of steel relative to various combinations of the elements carbon, manganese, silicon, and sulfur.

■ Insurance companies use regression to forecast how long an individual is expected to live on the basis of age, weight, sex, and smoking history.

■ Legal researchers use regression to investigate claims of discrimination in the treatment of minorities (such as in making hiring decisions and determining salaries).

By the end of this chapter you will be able to interpret and make predictions using a regression equation involving two variables. You will also be able to calculate least-squares regression estimates and correlation coefficients. You will know the conditions required to use least-squares estimates in a regression analysis. Finally, you will be able to perform statistical tests to assess the strength of the relationship between two variables. (In the next chapter you will learn about the use of regression and correlation analysis when more than two variables are involved.)

## Gas Mileage Prediction

You are a systems analyst for General Motors (GM). Your current project is to analyze and estimate the gas mileage (city and highway combined) that GM can expect to achieve from its newest entry into the car market, the front-wheel-drive, four-cylinder Tiger. Based on past experience, you expect most of the difference in gas mileage (MPG) between cars to depend on the weight of the cars. Some cars will be heavier because of the model type (two door versus four door), and others will be heavier because of optional equipment purchased (such as air conditioning, radio, automatic transmission, etc.). Your task is to try to relate the weight of each car to its MPG using experimental data from numerous prototypes that have already been produced and tested.

# 9.2 Linear Regression

The techniques of regression analysis can be traced to a nineteenth-century English expert on heredity, Sir Francis Galton. Galton's studies related the height of sons to that of their fathers. He found that while a son's height could be estimated by his father's height (taller than average fathers tend to have taller than average sons), sons of tall fathers tended to be shorter than their fathers and sons of short fathers tended to be taller than their fathers. Thus son heights appeared to be pulled to the average height of all sons. Galton called this phenomenon *regressing to the mean*, hence the term *regression*.

The variable being predicted in regression analysis is called the **dependent variable**. In the Tiger car case MPG is the dependent variable, while in Galton's studies the son's height was the dependent variable. One or more **independent variables** are used to predict a dependent variable. For the Tiger car, weight is the independent variable; in Galton's research the father's height was the independent variable.

Other independent variables might be considered in the Tiger gas mileage case, such as whether the car has power steering and power brakes, a

In a regression study the dependent variable is the variable being predicted or explained. The independent variable is the variable used to predict or explain the dependent variable.

fifth forward gear or overdrive, automatic transmission, cruise control, and so forth. As a starting point, however, only one independent variable is used: weight. Our objective is to find a formula relating the weight of a Tiger to its MPG.

The population consists of all possible combinations of weight and the resulting MPG for all Tiger cars. Since it is impossible to test all Tiger cars (some haven't been made yet), a random sample of 10 cars is tested for weight and MPG. The results of this sample are shown in Table 9.1.

The first entry in Table 9.1 indicates that car 1 had a weight of 2530 pounds and achieved 40.8 miles per gallon. The second car weighed 2620 pounds and achieved 39.8 miles per gallon. From a review of Table 9.1, MPG does appear to be related to weight; in general, the more a car weighs, the lower its gas mileage. From a visual inspection, however, we cannot tell exactly how MPG and weight are related or the strength of this relationship.

The first step in studying the relationship between any two variables is to plot the sample data on a **scatter diagram**. Such diagrams traditionally place the variable to be explained (the dependent variable) on the vertical axis and the variable that may explain it (the independent variable) on the horizontal axis. The vertical axis is the $y$ axis (thus the letter $y$ stands for the dependent variable). The horizontal axis is the $x$ axis (thus the letter $x$ represents the independent variable). The scatter diagram for our Tiger cars is

Table 9.1

| Miles Per Gallon and Weight for 10 Tiger Cars | | | | | |
|---|---|---|---|---|---|
| Car | Weight (lb) | MPG | Car | Weight (lb) | MPG |
| 1 | 2530 | 40.8 | 6 | 2710 | 38.9 |
| 2 | 2620 | 39.8 | 7 | 2740 | 38.2 |
| 3 | 2630 | 40.3 | 8 | 2720 | 39.1 |
| 4 | 2690 | 38.4 | 9 | 2810 | 37.4 |
| 5 | 2670 | 39.7 | 10 | 2780 | 37.9 |

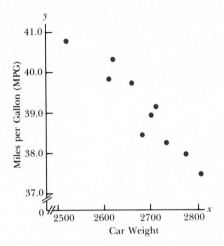

**Figure 9.1**
Scatter diagram of Tiger gas mileage and weight.

shown in Fig. 9.1, where MPG is the dependent variable and weight is the independent variable.

In Fig. 9.1 there is an *inverse* relationship between MPG and weight; the heavier the car, the lower the gas mileage. Notice in Fig. 9.1 that a straight line could be drawn through the scatter diagram so that the points in our sample appear to fall randomly around the line drawn. Thus we say that there is an inverse *linear* relationship between MPG and weight. (As will be discussed later, if the points did not appear to fall on or randomly around a straight line, then no linear relationship would exist.)

The straight line that best fits the data is the one that would be drawn through the scatter diagram so that the points appeared to fall randomly around the line. Although a straight-edge rule could be used to draw this line, there is a mathematical procedure for finding it. This procedure is called the *method of least squares*.

# 9.3 The Least-Squares Regression Equation

Using a straight-edge ruler or the mathematical procedures to be discussed in Section 9.4, the straight line that best fits the scatter diagram in Fig. 9.1 has the following equation form:

$$\hat{y} = 72.94 - 0.0126x$$

This equation is written in slope-intercept form. The symbol $\hat{y}$, (read *y hat*) represents the values of $y$ associated with the line. The number (72.94) is the *y intercept,* of the line, and the number $(-0.0126)$ is the *slope.* The y intercept is the point where the straight line intersects with the y (or vertical) axis. The slope indicates the change predicted in y for a one-unit change in x that is, how much $\hat{y}$ changes for each one-unit change in x. Figure 9.2 shows this equation.

The general form for an equation in slope-intercept form is

$$\hat{y} = a + bx$$

In this form, the letter $a$ denotes the point where the line crosses or intersects the y axis ($a = 72.94$ in Fig. 9.2). The letter $b$ denotes the slope of the line ($b = -0.0126$ in Fig. 9.2). The slope indicates how $\hat{y}$ changes for a one-unit change in x. (In Fig. 9.2, the slope indicates that $\hat{y}$ decreases by 1.26 MPG when x increases by 100 pounds.) The best-fitting regression line is thus written as follows:

---

(9.1)

Slope-intercept form

$$\hat{y} = a + bx$$

where

$\hat{y}$ is the predicted dependent variable
$x$ is the independent variable
$a$ is the y intercept
$b$ is the slope

---

The equation $\hat{y} = 72.94 - 0.0126x$ is called the **sample regression line**. It may be used to make predictions and to estimate the population relationship between x and y. As we will see, under certain conditions the sample intercept ($a = 72.94$) is the best estimate of the intercept of the population regression line. Similarly, the sample slope ($b = -0.0126$) is the best estimate of the population slope. Section 9.8 describes the assumptions about the population necessary for estimation and testing of hypotheses about the relationship between x and y in the population. For now, we will use the sample regression line only to predict values of the dependent variable.

**Figure 9.2**
The equation $\hat{y} = 72.94 - 0.0126x$.

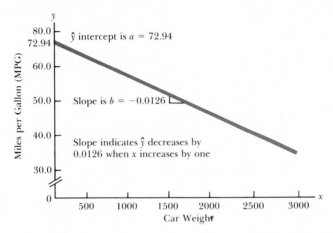

To predict MPG for various Tiger cars, the weight of the car of interest is substituted (for $x$) in the regression equation. This means that the car's weight is multiplied by the slope, and then this product is subtracted (because $b$ is negative) from the intercept. For every *additional* pound of weight, the predicted MPG of the Tiger will decrease by 0.0126 miles per gallon. For example, if we want to estimate the mileage for a car weighing 2700 pounds, we would substitute $x = 2700$ into Eq. (9.1) as follows:

$$\hat{y} = 72.94 - 0.0126(2700) = 38.92$$

The value $\hat{y} = 38.92$ indicates that our best guess for Tiger cars weighing 2700 pounds is that they will average 38.92 miles per gallon. Similarly, by this process, the prediction for Tiger cars weighing 2800 pounds is found to be 37.66 miles per gallon. The difference between the predicted mileage of a car weighing 2700 pounds and one weighing 2800 pounds is $-1.26$ miles per gallon. (Note that this difference could have been obtained by multiplying the slope by the weight change, that is, $-0.0126 \times 100 = -1.26$.) These two points [namely, ($x = 2700$, $\hat{y} = 38.92$) and ($x = 2800$, $\hat{y} = 37.66$) are shown in Fig. 9.3.]

We should point out that the regression equation previously given is not necessarily meaningful for all weights. For example, we cannot realistically substitute WEIGHT = 0 (a weightless car?) into the equation. Similarly, it might be risky to let WEIGHT = 4000 pounds, for the largest weight in the sample was 2810 pounds. In general, we should use values for the independent variable that are within the range of the sample (for Tiger cars, weights ranged from 2530 to 2810 pounds).

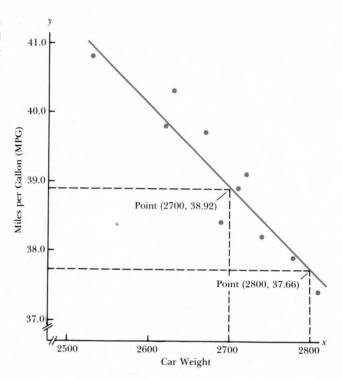

**Figure 9.3**
Scatter diagram and regression line for Tiger cars.

Miles per Gallon (MPG)

Point (2700, 38.92)

Point (2800, 37.66)

Car Weight

# 9.4 Calculating the Least-Squares Equation

Figure 9.4 presents each $(x, y)$ point for the Tiger cars in Table 9.1. In that figure we have labeled the vertical difference between each $y$ value and the line $(\hat{y})$ as an error. That is, for each $x$ value the error in predicting the associated $y$ is $e = (y - \hat{y})$. These differences are called errors because they measure the amount by which the regression line differs (errors) in predicting the actual $y$ values in our sample.

In Fig. 9.4, we added the subscript $i$ to indicate which $y$ and $\hat{y}$ values are used to calculate the $e$ value. Thus $e_i = y_i - \hat{y}_i$ indicates that the $i$th error is obtained by subtracting the $i$th $\hat{y}$ value from the $i$th $y$ value. For example, in Table 9.1 the MPG of the second car in our sample (i.e., $i = 2$) was $y_2 = 39.8$. Using the weight of this car ($x_2 = 2620$) and the regression equation, the predicted MPG for cars of this weight is $\hat{y}_2 = 39.93$ [$= 72.94 - 0.0126(2620)$]. Hence the error is $e_2 = y_2 - \hat{y}_2 = 39.8 - 39.93 = -0.13$.

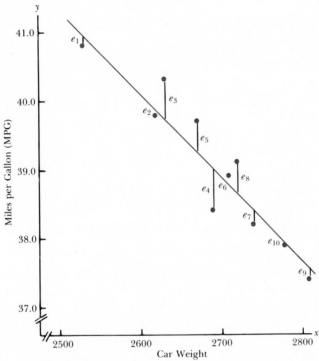

**Figure 9.4**
Errors in predicting
Tiger gas mileage.

Note: Errors are numbered in the same order as the cars in Table
9.1. Thus, for example, $e_2$ represents the error for the
second car.

The error for predicting the MPG of the eighth Tiger car in our sample is
$e_8 = y_8 - \hat{y}_8 = 39.1 - 38.67 = 0.43$. There are 10 such errors in Fig. 9.4.

The method of **least-squares regression** makes the errors as small as
possible in two ways. First, this method derives a line in which the errors
sum to zero [i.e., $\Sigma(y_i - \hat{y}_i) = 0$]. There are, however, many different lines
in which $\Sigma e_i = 0$. Thus the second objective of the least-squares approach is
to find the line that minimizes the sum of the *squared* errors—that is, it
makes $\Sigma(y_i - \hat{y}_i)^2$ as small as possible. This is why the approach is called the
method of least squares. Since the line shown in Fig. 9.4 is the least-squares
regression line, it can be shown that there is no other straight line that would
make the sum of squared errors smaller.

Computers are used to find the least-squares regression line in most
practical problems. However, to demonstrate the calculation process, we will
present the relevant formulas and show how to solve for the least-squares
estimates $a$ and $b$.

Least-squares estimators

(9.2)
$$b = \frac{\Sigma x_i y_i - n\bar{x}\bar{y}}{\Sigma x_i^2 - n\bar{x}^2}$$

$$a = \bar{y} - b\bar{x}$$

These equations are illustrated in Table 9.2, using the Tiger car data. Notice in Eq. (9.2) and Table 9.2 that the value of $b$ must be determined first, since it is used in the calculation of $a$.

The sample regression line $\hat{y}_i = 72.94 - 0.0126x_i$ can be used to verify the 10 errors shown in Fig. 9.4. Using a computer program, we generated Table 9.3 to show the $x$ and $y$ values, the predicted value of $\hat{y}$ for each $x$ value, the error for each sample point, and finally, the squared error for each point. (Because of rounding errors in hand calculations, the 10 errors that could be calculated from the regression equation in Table 9.2 will differ slightly from the computer-generated errors in Table 9.3.)

**Table 9.2**

| | | Calculating $a$ and $b$ for 10 Tiger Cars | | |
|---|---|---|---|---|
| $i$ | Weight ($x_i$) | MPG ($y_i$) | $x_i y_i$ | $x_i^2$ |
| 1 | 2,530 | 40.8 | 103,224 | 6,400,900 |
| 2 | 2,620 | 39.8 | 104,276 | 6,864,400 |
| 3 | 2,630 | 40.3 | 105,989 | 6,916,900 |
| 4 | 2,690 | 38.4 | 103,296 | 7,236,100 |
| 5 | 2,670 | 39.7 | 105,999 | 7,128,900 |
| 6 | 2,710 | 38.9 | 105,419 | 7,344,100 |
| 7 | 2,740 | 38.2 | 104,668 | 7,507,600 |
| 8 | 2,720 | 39.1 | 106,352 | 7,398,400 |
| 9 | 2,810 | 37.4 | 105,094 | 7,896,100 |
| 10 | 2,780 | 37.9 | 105,362 | 7,728,400 |
| Sum = | 26,900 | 390.5 | $\Sigma x_i y_i = 1,049,679$ | $72,421,800 = \Sigma x_i^2$ |

Mean: $\bar{x} = 2690$, $\bar{y} = 39.05$

$$b = \frac{\Sigma x_i y_i - n\bar{x}\bar{y}}{\Sigma x_i^2 - n\bar{x}^2} = \frac{1,049,679 - 10(2690)(39.05)}{72,421,800 - 10(2690)^2} = \frac{-766}{60,800} = -0.0126$$

$$a = \bar{y} - b\bar{x} = 39.05 - (-0.0126)(2690) = 72.94$$

Chapter 9   Simple Linear Regression and Correlation

Table 9.3

| | | | Predicted Values ($\hat{y}$), Errors ($y - \hat{y}$), and Squared Errors ($y - \hat{y}$)$^2$ | | |
|:---:|:---:|:---:|:---:|:---:|:---:|
| $i$ | Weight ($x_i$) | MPG ($y_i$) | $\hat{y}_i$ | $y_i - \hat{y}_i$ | $(y_i - \hat{y}_i)^2$ |
| 1 | 2530 | 40.8 | 41.066 | −0.266 | 0.071 |
| 2 | 2620 | 39.8 | 39.932 | −0.132 | 0.017 |
| 3 | 2630 | 40.3 | 39.806 | +0.494 | 0.244 |
| 4 | 2690 | 38.4 | 39.050 | −0.650 | 0.423 |
| 5 | 2670 | 39.7 | 39.302 | +0.398 | 0.158 |
| 6 | 2710 | 38.9 | 38.798 | +0.102 | 0.010 |
| 7 | 2740 | 38.2 | 38.420 | −0.220 | 0.048 |
| 8 | 2720 | 39.1 | 38.672 | +0.428 | 0.183 |
| 9 | 2810 | 37.4 | 37.538 | −0.138 | 0.019 |
| 10 | 2780 | 37.9 | 37.916 | −0.016 | 0.000 |
| | | | Sum = | 0.000 | 1.173 = Sum of squares error |

Notice in Table 9.3 that the sum of the errors (or **residuals**, as they are sometimes called) equals zero. The total amount by which some MPG's are overpredicted is exactly equal to the total amount by which others are underpredicted. This will always be the case if the least-squares regression line has been determined correctly. Also note that the **sum of the squares error** (denoted as SSE) equals 1.173. This is the sum that was minimized in finding the least-squares regression line. No other regression line will give a sum of squares error smaller than SSE = 1.173.

---

**DEFINITION**
**Least Squares:**
**Regression**
**Method**

The regression method of least squares finds the straight line that best fits the sample data by minimizing the sum of the squared errors (SSE), where

$$SSE = \Sigma(y_i - \hat{y}_i)^2$$

---

**WORKED EXAMPLE 9.1**

A real estate appraiser wishes to use a regression line to predict the selling price of a house with 2700 square feet. The following information on selling price and house size are the only data available.

| | Selling Price and Floor Space for 10 Homes (in Thousands of Dollars and Thousands of Square Feet) | | | | | | | | | |
|---|---|---|---|---|---|---|---|---|---|---|
| Price (y) | 94 | 136 | 120 | 135 | 110 | 125 | 140 | 100 | 105 | 85 |
| Size (x) | 2.1 | 4.0 | 3.0 | 3.2 | 2.5 | 2.9 | 4.1 | 2.5 | 2.8 | 1.9 |

**ANSWER:**

Since price is to be predicted, it is the dependent variable and size is the independent variable. The calculations necessary for determining the least-square values of $a$ and $b$ by Eq. (9.2) are as follows:

| Price ($y_i$) | Size ($x_i$) | $x_i y_i$ | $x_i^2$ |
|---|---|---|---|
| 94 | 2.1 | 197.4 | 4.41 |
| 136 | 4.0 | 544.0 | 16.00 |
| 120 | 3.0 | 360.0 | 9.00 |
| 135 | 3.2 | 432.0 | 10.24 |
| 110 | 2.5 | 275.0 | 6.25 |
| 125 | 2.9 | 362.5 | 8.41 |
| 140 | 4.1 | 574.0 | 16.81 |
| 100 | 2.5 | 250.0 | 6.25 |
| 105 | 2.8 | 294.0 | 7.84 |
| 85 | 1.9 | 161.5 | 3.61 |
| Sum = 1150 | 29.0 | 3450.4 | 88.82 |

Means: $\bar{y} = 115$, $\bar{x} = 2.9$

$$b = \frac{\Sigma x_i y_i - n\bar{x}\bar{y}}{\Sigma x_i^2 - n\bar{x}^2} = \frac{3450.4 - 10(2.9)(115)}{88.82 - 10(2.9)^2} = \frac{115.4}{4.72} = 24.45$$

$$a = \bar{y} - b\bar{x} = 115 - 24.45(2.9) = 44.10$$

The sample regression equation that best fits the data is thus

$$\hat{y}_i = 44.10 + 24.45x_i$$

This equation is represented by the straight line drawn through the scatter diagram in Fig. 9.5. For a house with 2700 square feet of floor space, the predicted selling price is calculated by setting $x_i = 2.7$.

$$\hat{y}_i = 44.10 + 24.45(2.7) = 110.115$$

Since $y$ is measured in thousands of dollars, the predicted selling price is $110,115.

**Figure 9.5**
Regression line and
scatter diagram of the
selling price and floor
space of a house.

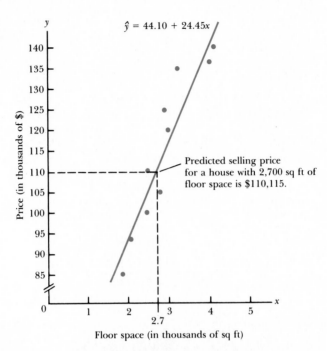

$\hat{y} = 44.10 + 24.45x$

Price (in thousands of $)

140
135
130
125
120
115
110
105
100
95
90
85

Predicted selling price
for a house with 2,700 sq ft of
floor space is $110,115.

0    1    2    3    4    5

2.7

Floor space (in thousands of sq ft)

---

## Exercises

**9.1** Use the following diagrams in parts (a) through (c).

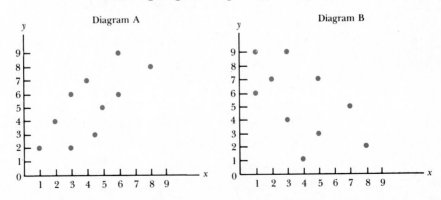

Diagram A

Diagram B

a) With a ruler, draw the regression lines that best fit the sample data in each diagram.

b) For each diagram, is the relationship between $x$ and $y$ positive or negative?

c) Use a ruler to determine the slope and $y$ intercept of the lines you drew in part (a). Write the equation for each line.

9.2 Suppose a sample of $n = 100$ observations results in the following least-squares regression line:

$$\hat{y}_i = -15 + 3.2x_i$$

a) Is there a negative or positive relationship between $x$ and $y$?

b) Sketch this line on graph paper.

c) What value do you predict for $y$ if $x_i = 50$?

9.3 Suppose a sample of $n = 100$ observations results in the following least-squares regression line:

$$\hat{y}_i = 15 - 3.2x_i$$

a) Is there a negative or positive relationship between $x$ and $y$?

b) Sketch this line on graph paper.

c) What value do you predict for $y_i$ if $x_i = 50$?

9.4 The method of least squares minimizes the error sum of squares around the fitted regression line and forces the sum of errors to equal zero. Does this imply that the number of sample points that fall above the fitted regression line will necessarily equal the number that fall below it? (Show by means of an example why this implication always holds or show an example for which it does not hold.)

REL 9.5 For the regression in Worked Example 9.1:

a) In terms of the selling price and house size, what does the slope indicate? What does the intercept indicate?

b) Calculate all 10 residuals. Do they sum to zero? Why or why not?

c) What is the predicted selling price of a house with 800 square feet?

d) What is the meaning of your predicted value in part (c)?

e) Why should you question the actual use of the prediction in part (c)?

ADM 9.6 A study of textile workers was designed to relate the number of years of work experience (rounded to the nearest year) and the number of pieces of finished product returned because of imperfect work. Consider the following sample of five workers, where $x$ = number of years worked and $y$ = number of imperfections.

**Years Worked ($x$) and Number of Imperfections ($y$)**

| $y$: | 12 | 8 | 6 | 2 | 2 |
|------|----|---|---|---|---|
| $x$: | 0 | 2 | 4 | 4 | 5 |

a) Find the least-squares regression line.

b) Calculate the five residuals (errors). Do they sum to zero? Find the sum of the squared errors and indicate the role that this sum played in the method of least squares.

c) Plot these data, indicating the five residuals on your graph.

ACT  **9.7**  A certified public accounting (CPA) firm interviewing a large number of accounting students about to receive their undergraduate degree is trying to estimate starting salaries. The firm traditionally adjusts offers to the student's grade point average (GPA). For this year, the firm has collected information on nine randomly selected students who graduated last year. The personnel director has indicated that starting salaries should be 10% higher this year for accounting majors.

| Salary: | $22,000 | 24,000 | 21,000 | 22,000 | 23,000 | 25,500 | 20,500 | 26,000 | 23,000 |
|---------|---------|--------|--------|--------|--------|--------|--------|--------|--------|
| GPA: | 3.5 | 3.6 | 2.9 | 3.0 | 3.3 | 3.7 | 3.0 | 3.9 | 3.4 |

a) Plot these data on a scatter diagram. Does a linear relationship seem reasonable?

b) Determine the least-squares regression line using last year's data (given in the preceding tabulation) and add this line to your scatter diagram in part (a).

c) Predict the starting salary for a person with a GPA of 3.2. Does it make a difference if you first raise the last year's salaries by 10% and then estimate your regression or use your regression in part (b) and then raise the predicted salary by 10%? Explain.

d) Find the nine residuals from your regression in part (a) and show that they sum to zero.

e) What is the value of the sum of the squared errors for the regression in part (b)?

MKT 9.8 A market researcher wants to predict the relationship between sales (in $10,000 units) and the number of people who see a billboard advertisement (in 10 thousands of people) for a particular product. The following values are calculated for a sample of 10 billboards:

$$\Sigma xy = 924.8 \qquad \Sigma x^2 = 9.28 \qquad \Sigma x = 9.4 \qquad \Sigma y = 959$$

a) Find the least-squares regression line.

b) Sketch the regression line.

c) Predict the sales if 10,000 people see a billboard.

FIN 9.9 Use the five tobacco companies listed in Appendix A.1 to find a regression line relating each company's 1984 sales ($x$) to their 12-month earnings per share ($y$).

a) Sketch the data and the resulting least-squares regression line.

b) What is the intercept for this regression?

c) What is the slope for this regression and what does it indicate?

# 9.5 Measures of Variability

Once a regression line has been calculated a natural question is, how well does the line fit the sample data? If the line fits the sample data well, then we may have some confidence that the independent variable helps to explain the $y$ values. Even for a well-fitting line, however, we must be careful not to infer that the changes in $x$ cause the changes in $y$. For example, an aptitude test may be helpful to an employer in estimating how well a prospective employee will perform in a particular job, but no one would argue that the tests themselves cause differences in performance. On the other hand, we could easily argue that weight differences among the Tiger cars do cause differences in MPG. The point is to be cautious in making cause-and-effect statements in describing relationships in regression analysis.

One important measure of how well a regression line fits the data is the percentage of the variability in the dependent variable that is "explained by" or "associated with" the independent variable. Variability in the dependent variable $y$ is measured by the sum of the squared deviations of $y$ around the sample mean ($\bar{y}$). This measure is called the *sum of squares total* (*SST*) and is defined as follows:

(9.3)    $$\text{SST} = \Sigma(y_i - \bar{y})^2$$

the variability to be explained.

For the Tiger data, this measure can be calculated from the sample data in Table 9.1, where $\bar{y} = 39.05$ (remember, 39.05 is the average MPG of the Tiger cars in our sample of 10). Subtracting this mean $y$ value from each of the 10 estimated values of $y$ in our sample, squaring each of these differences (or residuals), and then summing the 10 numbers results in SST = 10.8250 (see Table 9.4, column 3). [Although computer programs are typically used to calculate SST, recall from Chapter 3 that algebraically $\Sigma(y_i - \bar{y})^2 = \Sigma y_i^2 - n\bar{y}^2$. Either form of SST will give equivalent results, with the exception of rounding errors.]

To measure the fit of the regression line, the SST is broken down into the sum of two parts, one part representing the variation that is "unexplained," and the other representing the part that is "explained." The part that is unexplained is called the sum of squares error (SSE), while the part that is explained is called the *sum of squares regression (SSR)*.

**Table 9.4**

| Calculating the Sum of Squares Total (SST) | | |
|---|---|---|
| $y_i$ | $(y_i - \bar{y})$ | $(y_i - \bar{y})^2$ |
| 40.8 | 1.75 | 3.0625 |
| 39.8 | 0.75 | 0.5625 |
| 40.3 | 1.25 | 1.5625 |
| 38.4 | −0.65 | 0.4225 |
| 39.7 | 0.65 | 0.4225 |
| 38.9 | −0.15 | 0.0225 |
| 38.2 | −0.85 | 0.7225 |
| 39.1 | 0.05 | 0.0025 |
| 37.4 | −1.65 | 2.7225 |
| 37.9 | −1.15 | 1.3225 |
| Sum = 390.5 | Sum = 0 | SST = 10.8250 |

<table>
<tr>
<td>
DEFINITION<br>
Sum of<br>
Squares Total
</td>
<td>
Sum of squares total = sum of squares error + sum of squares regression

$$SST = SSE + SSR$$
</td>
</tr>
</table>

The method of least squares is designed to minimize the SSE. But least-squares estimation cannot force the SSE to be zero, since the regression line typically does not predict all $y$ values perfectly. The SSE for the Tiger Company was previously calculated to be 1.173 (see Table 9.3).

Since total variability in $y$ (SST) must equal unexplained variability (SSE) plus explained variability (SSR), we can solve for the variability in $y$ that our regression is explaining by simply substracting SSE from SST.

<table>
<tr>
<td>(9.4)</td>
<td>
Sum of squares regression (SSR):

$$SSR = SST - SSE,$$

the explained variability in $y$.
</td>
</tr>
</table>

For Tiger cars the amount of variability in $y$ that is explained by the fitted regression is

$$SSR = 10.825 - 1.173 = 9.652$$

Computer programs such as BMD, SPSS, SAS, IDA, and MICROSTAT typically provide SST, SSE, and SSR. In some computer outputs errors are referred to as *residuals*, in which case SSE represents the *sum of squares residual*.

## 9.6 Goodness-of-Fit Measures

As stated in Section 9.5, the proportion of the variability in the dependent variable that is "explained by" the independent variable is a measure of how well a regression line fits the data. For example, in the Tiger car case the total variability in $y$ is SST = 10.8250. The proportion of variability explained

Chapter 9   Simple Linear Regression and Correlation

by the regression line is SSR = 9.6520. Thus the proportion of total variability explained is

$$\frac{\text{SSR}}{\text{SST}} = \frac{9.6520}{10.8250} = 0.89$$

This result indicates that 89% of the variability in gas mileage ($y$) for Tiger cars is explained by weight ($x$). Since this number is close to 1.00, the sample regression line is said to fit the data relatively well. That is, weight does a good job of predicting gas mileage. The measure of goodness of fit, SSR/SST, is called the **coefficient of determination** and is designated by the symbol $r^2$.

---

(9.5)

The coefficient of determination $r^2$ is a number between 0 and 1 that indicates the proportion of variability in the dependent variable explained by the independent variable.

$$r^2 = \frac{\text{SSR}}{\text{SST}}$$

---

If the value of $r^2 = 1.00$, then 100% of the variability in $y$ is explained by the regression equation. When the value of $r^2 = 0$, none of the variability in $y$ is explained by $x$. A value of $r^2 = 0.60$ means that 60% of the variability in $y$ is explained by $x$.

Some books and research reports present the square root of the coefficient of determination as a measure of goodness of fit. This measure, called the **correlation coefficient**, is designated by the letter $r$. If the slope of the regression line is positive, then the sign of $r$ is also positive. If the slope of the regression line is negative, then the sign of $r$ is negative.

---

**DEFINITION**
**Correlation**
**Coefficient**

The correlation coefficient $r$ is the (negative or positive) square root of the coefficient of determination.

$$r = \pm \sqrt{r^2}$$

The sign of $r$ is always the same as the sign of the regression slope.

---

The correlation coefficient is often used in test statistics for hypotheses concerned with goodness of fit. It is also reported in statistical studies since the sign of $r$ has meaning (a minus sign indicates that the slope is negative, while a positive sign indicates a positive relationship). In general, however, $r^2$ is easier to interpret than $r$. Thus we recommend always changing $r$ values to $r^2$ values.

**WORKED EXAMPLE
9.2**

Suppose teachers' salaries $(y)$ and years in service $(x)$ in a school have a correlation coefficient of $r = 0.90$. What can you conclude from this value?

**ANSWER:**

An $r$ of $+0.90$ indicates that salary and years of service are positively related in the sample. In addition, if this value is squared $(r^2 = 0.81)$, the interpretation is that 81% of the variability in salaries is explained by the variable years in service.

**Figure 9.6**
Coefficient of
determination and
correlation coefficient.

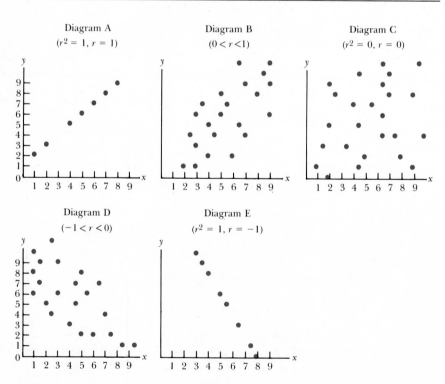

Chapter 9   Simple Linear Regression and Correlation

Figure 9.6 illustrates some values of $r$ and $r^2$. In diagrams A and E, $x$ and $y$ are said to be perfectly correlated because the $y$ values all fall on a straight line. Diagram A represents a perfect positive correlation ($r = 1.0$ and $r^2 = 1.0$), while diagram E represents perfect negative correlation ($r = -1.0$ and $r^2 = 1.0$). Diagrams B and D illustrate less than perfect correlation. Note that the sign of $r$ is always the same as the sign of the slope of the regression line. When $r$ (or $r^2$) equals zero, there is no correlation (see diagram C).

**WORKED EXAMPLE 9.3**

For the real estate data in Worked Example 9.1, calculate the coefficient of determination and the correlation coefficient and interpret these measures.

**ANSWER:**

To calculate $r^2$, it is first necessary to calculate the SST and the SSE.

| $y_i$ | $y_i - \bar{y}$ | $(y_i - \bar{y})^2$ | $\hat{y}_i$ | $y_i - \hat{y}_i$ | $(y_i - \hat{y}_i)^2$ |
|---|---|---|---|---|---|
| 94 | −21 | 441 | 95.44 | −1.44 | 2.0736 |
| 136 | 21 | 441 | 141.89 | −5.89 | 34.6921 |
| 120 | 5 | 25 | 117.45 | 2.55 | 6.5025 |
| 135 | 20 | 400 | 122.33 | 12.67 | 160.5289 |
| 110 | −5 | 25 | 105.22 | 4.78 | 22.8484 |
| 125 | 10 | 100 | 115.00 | 10.00 | 100.0000 |
| 140 | 25 | 625 | 144.34 | −4.34 | 18.8356 |
| 100 | −15 | 225 | 105.22 | −5.22 | 27.2484 |
| 105 | −10 | 100 | 112.56 | −7.56 | 57.1536 |
| 85 | −30 | 900 | 90.55 | −5.55 | 30.8025 |
| $\bar{y} = 115$ | | SST = 3282 | | | SSE = 460.6856 |

The SSR is

$$\text{SSR} = \text{SST} - \text{SSE} = 3282.00 - 460.69 = 2821.31$$

The coefficient of determination and correlation coefficient are thus

$$r^2 = \text{SSR/SST} = 2821.31/3282.00 = 0.86$$
$$r = \sqrt{0.86} = 0.93$$

Because there is a positive relationship between price and house size (i.e., the slope of the regression line in Worked Example 9.1 was positive), the sign of $r$ is positive. From the coefficient of determination, we know that 86% of the variability in selling price is explained by the floor space.

# 9.7 Mean Square Errors

In regression analysis it is often useful to have a measure of *average* variability. An average (or mean) variability is defined as a sum of squares divided by its degrees of freedom and is called a *mean square*. In regression analysis there are two mean squares of interest—**mean square error (MSE)** and **mean square regression (MSR)**.

---

**DEFINITIONS**
**MSE**
**MSR**

Mean square error

$$MSE = \frac{SSE}{n - 2}$$

Mean square regression

$$MSR = \frac{SSR}{1}$$

---

The first mean square (MSE) represents the average square error about the regression line. SSE is divided by $n - 2$ because after the slope and intercept are specified, only $n - 2$ sample points are free to vary. The 1 d.f. for the second mean square (MSR) is determined by the number of independent variables included in the regression—in simple regression, one.

The square root of the MSE is called the **standard error of the estimate** and is denoted by the symbol $s_e$. This measure represents the standard deviation of the errors about the regression line.

---

**DEFINITION**
**$s_e$**

Standard error of the estimate ($s_e$)

$$s_e = \sqrt{\frac{SSE}{n - 2}}$$

---

The value of $s_e$ provides an indication of the variability in sample points around the regression line. A small value for $s_e$ indicates little dispersion, while a larger value indicates greater dispersion. In the extreme case where all the sample points are on the regression line, $s_e = 0$.

**EXAMPLE** Suppose a sales prediction using regression analysis yields $\hat{y} = 120$ and $s_e = 3$. A measure of dispersion for this prediction can be determined by calculating the predicted value ($\hat{y}$) plus or minus two times the standard error of the estimate ($s_e$):

$120 \pm 2(3)$ or [114 to 126]

In general, most of the sample $y$ values will lie within two standard errors of $\hat{y}$. This process of finding two numbers (such as 114 and 126) is similar to that used to find confidence intervals for $\mu_x$ described in Chapter 7. Now, however, we are forming an interval estimate for the predicted value of the dependent variable (such as sales).

## Exercises

**9.10** Give an interpretation of 1) the sign of a correlation coefficient and 2) the coefficient of determination.

**9.11** What do we know about the SSE when $r = +1$, $r = -1$, and $r = 0$?

**9.12** Is there any relationship between the magnitude of $r^2$ or $r$ and the number or percentage of sample points falling on the fitted regression line? Is there any relationship between the magnitude of $r$ or $r^2$ and the proportion of sample points that fall above versus below the fitted regression line? (Explain the conditions, if any, under which information about $r$ gives information about where the sample values fall relative to the sample regression line.)

**9.13** What, if any, is the relationship between the distance between sample points and the fitted regression line and the size of the coefficient of determination?

**9.14** If $r = -0.90$, what does this indicate about the relationship between the dependent and independent variables?

**9.15** The data for the sample points shown in diagram A of Fig. 9.6 are as follows:

$x$: 1 2 3 4 5 6 7 8
$y$: 2 3 4 5 6 7 8 9

a) Use the least-squares formulas to estimate the regression lines that best fit these data.

b) Determine the values of SST, SSE, and SSR.

c) Calculate the coefficient of determination and coefficient of correlation. Interpret $r^2$.

d) Determine MSE, MSR, and the standard error of the estimate. If $x = 5$, what is the estimate of $y$? What numbers constitute a region that is $\hat{y}$ minus or plus two standard errors?

**9.16** Repeat Exercise 9.15 using the data in diagram B of Fig. 9.6. These data are as follows:

| $x$ | $y$ | $x$ | $y$ |
|-----|-----|-----|-----|
| 2   | 1   | 5   | 6   |
| 2   | 1   | 9   | 6   |
| 4   | 2   | 3.5 | 7   |
| 6   | 2   | 5.5 | 7   |
| 3   | 3   | 5   | 8   |
| 2.5 | 4   | 8   | 8   |
| 4.5 | 4   | 7   | 9   |
| 7   | 4   | 9   | 9   |
| 4   | 5   | 8.5 | 10  |
| 6.5 | 5   | 6.5 | 11  |
| 3   | 6   | 9   | 11  |

ADM **9.17** For the data on work experience and imperfections given in Exercise 9.6, what is the value and sign of $r$? What percent of the variability in imperfections is explained by experience?

ADM **9.18** For the data in Exercise 9.6, calculate an interval that reflects two standard errors around the predicted $y$ value for $x = 3$. Interpret this interval.

FIN **9.19** Use the data in Exercise 9.9 to find SST, SSE, SSR, $r^2$, MSE, and MSR. Interpret these values and indicate how each is related to the others.

# 9.8 Assumptions About the Population

For most regression analysis problems, the analyst would like to estimate a population relationship and test hypotheses about the population. The data from our 10 Tiger cars, for instance, can be used to make inferences and test theories about the population of all Tiger cars. For such tests and inferences to be meaningful, certain assumptions about the population must be made.

To discuss the regression assumptions, we present the **population linear model**. This model specifies the relationship between the values of independent and dependent variables in the population as follows.

---

(9.6)

Population linear model

$$y = \alpha + \beta x + \epsilon$$

---

In this model, $\alpha$ is the **population intercept** to be estimated, $\beta$ is the **population slope** to be estimated, and $\epsilon$ is the **population error term**. Both $\alpha$ and $\beta$ are *population parameters*. In contrast, the population error term $\epsilon$ is a random variable. To make inferences and test hypotheses about the population parameters $\alpha$ and $\beta$, four assumptions about the population model are required:

---

ASSUMPTION 1: The population relationship between $y$ and $x$ is the linear equation $y = \alpha + \beta x + \epsilon$ where the expected value of $\epsilon$ is zero.

Because $E(\epsilon) = 0$, this assumption implies that the average (or expected) value of $y$ is related to $x$ in the population by a straight line. Since we cannot examine the entire population, one way to check assumption 1 is to look for a straight line relationship between $x$ and $y$ in the sample. If the sample data do not appear linear then assumption 1 may be violated.

---

Figure 9.7
Violations of
assumption 1.

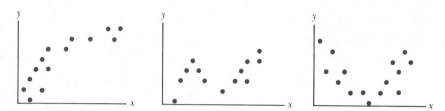

If we reexamine the scatter diagram for the Tiger cars in Fig. 9.2, non-linearity (the lack of a straight line $x,y$ relation) does not seem a problem; $x$ and $y$ appear linearly related. Similarly, for the three scatter diagrams in Exercise 9.1, assumption 1 appears to be reasonable. For the three scatter diagrams presented in Fig. 9.7, however, the $x,y$ relationship does appear to be nonlinear. Predicted values of $y$ from a straight line drawn through the data would not yield residuals that appear to fall randomly about the line. Hence assumption 1 may be violated.

---

**ASSUMPTION 2**   **The variance of $\epsilon$ is constant**

This assumption states that the distribution of the error has a variance that is the same for all values of $x$. It implies that we should not have small errors about the population regression equation for some values of $x$ and large errors for other values of $x$. Since the distribution of $\epsilon$ is unknown, the sample scatter diagram is often used to look for violations of this assumption. Figure 9.8 illustrates data that contain more variability (larger errors) for the high values of $x$ than for the low ones, suggesting a violation of assumption 2.

---

Figure 9.8
Nonconstant errors—a
violation of
assumption 2.

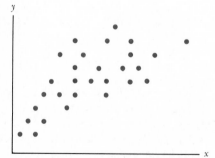

**ASSUMPTION 3**     Population errors cannot be related to *x* or to any other possible explanatory variable, including themselves.

This assumption says that the errors must be truly random. That is, $x$ and $\epsilon$ must be independent, and no one error can be predicted on the basis of any other error. The values of $\epsilon$ must be completely unpredictable.

If we knew that the first two Tiger cars off the production line both have positive errors, this would be a violation of assumption 3. Another violation would exist if large errors tended to occur with the heaviest cars. Similarly, if there are variables other than car weight that are believed to influence gas mileage, and if these other variables are correlated with weight, then assumption 3 may be violated. (If these other variables are not included in the regression equation, then their effect is part of the error term and the error term will thus be correlated with weight.) Unfortunately, from sample data the correctness of assumption 3 is not easily verified. In addition, errors may tend to be related to each other over time; for example, if overpredictions in one period are followed by overpredictions in the next period, this is a violation of assumption 3 (as demonstrated in Section 9.12).

**ASSUMPTION 4**     For any *x* value, the error $\epsilon$ must be normally distributed, with a mean of zero (as in assumption 1) and a constant variance (as in assumption 2).

From assumption 1 we know that the expected value of $y$ is $\alpha + \beta x$, since the mean of $\epsilon$ is zero. If $\epsilon$ is normally distributed with a constant variance, deviations in $y$ values around $\alpha + \beta x$ are also normally distributed with a constant variance.

Consider all Tiger cars weighing 2700 pounds. Suppose the population mean mileage for all Tiger cars of this weight is 37.9 MPG. Assumption 4 says that the distribution of population errors ($\epsilon = y - \alpha - \beta x$) for these Tiger cars must have a mean of zero and must be normally distributed. Thus the MPG distribution for all Tiger cars weighing 2700 pounds must be cen-

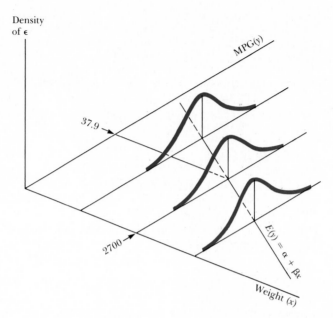

**Figure 9.9**
The normality of errors
for Tiger cars.

tered on 37.9 and must be normally distributed, as shown by the middle distribution in Fig. 9.9. The constant variance assumption implies that for all Tiger cars the distributions of the errors look the same, as demonstrated by comparing the three distributions in Fig. 9.9.

Although detecting violations of assumption 4 is usually not easy, care must be taken to avoid obvious problems. For example, consider the problem facing a university administrator attempting to predict college grades on the basis of Scholastic Aptitude Test (SAT) scores. For students with test scores totaling 1500, the predicted grades should be very high, such as 3.90 (on a 4.00-point scale). It is hard to imagine any group of students (including those with SAT scores of 1500) having grades normally distributed about 3.90. In this case the limit of 4.0 on grades causes the problem.

When the assumptions hold, then it can be shown that the average $b$ value equals $\beta$ (i.e., $E[b] = \beta$) and the average $a$ value equals $\alpha$ (i.e., $E[a] = \alpha$.) This means that if all possible samples (an infinite number) could be drawn and separate regression lines fit to each sample, then the average $b$ value for the many lines estimated would be the population parameter $\beta$ and the average value of $a$ would be the population parameter $\alpha$. Thus $a$ and $b$ are unbiased estimators of the population parameters $\alpha$ and $\beta$. Since hy-

Figure 9.10
The sampling
distribution of b.

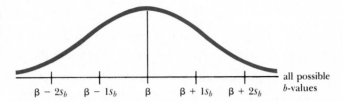

pothesis testing in regression analysis is generally concerned with tests of $\beta$, the sampling distribution of $b$ is of special interest.

The distribution of all possible $b$ values is called the *sampling distribution of b*. Since $b$ is an unbiased estimator of $\beta$, the mean of this sampling distribution is $\beta$. The sample standard deviation of $b$ is denoted as $s_b$, and is referred to as the **standard error of b**.

**(9.7)**

Standard error of $b$ $(s_b)$

$$s_b = \sqrt{\frac{\text{SSE}/(n - 2)}{\Sigma x_i^2 - n\bar{x}^2}}$$

The sampling distribution of $b$ and its standard error are illustrated in Fig. 9.10.

## 9.9 Testing the Relationship Between x and y

In most regression problems one is interested in determining whether $x$ is positively (or negatively) related to $y$ in the population. That is, when we consider all values of $y$ that might be associated with a given $x$ value, are we better off using the regression line $(\hat{y})$ to estimate and forecast $y$ values or might $\bar{y}$ do just as good a job?

Typically, the relationship between $x$ and $y$ is tested against a null hypothesis that states there is no relationship, i.e., $H_0$: $\beta = 0$. There are three alternative hypotheses that can be considered:

$H_A$: $\beta \neq 0$ ($x$ and $y$ are related in the population).

$H_A$: $\beta < 0$ ($x$ and $y$ are negatively related in the population).

$H_A$: $\beta > 0$ ($x$ and $y$ are positively related in the population).

If a theory does not suggest a direction for the $x,y$ population relationship, use $H_0$: $\beta = 0$ versus $H_A$: $\beta \neq 0$. If the alternative hypothesis does suggest a direction, then the inequality in the null hypothesis is either $\geq 0$ or $\leq 0$. In our Tiger car case, for example, we want to test if there is a negative population relationship between car weight ($x$) and gas mileage ($y$). Thus our null and alternative hypotheses are $H_0$: $\beta \geq 0$ versus $H_A$: $\beta < 0$.

In general, hypotheses about the population slope are tested by comparing the sample slope ($b$) with the population value specified in the null hypothesis, designated by $\beta_0$. (Typically, $\beta_0$ is zero.) This comparison is made by the five-step procedure described in Chapter 8. Now, however, the test statistic is the following $t$ ratio:

---

**(9.8)**

The $t$ statistic for $b$

$$t = \frac{b - \beta_0}{s_b}$$

where d.f. $= n - 2$, $\beta_0$ is the right-hand side of $H_0$, and $s_b$ is calculated as follows:

$$s_b = \sqrt{\frac{\text{SSE}/(n-2)}{\Sigma x_i^2 - n\bar{x}^2}}$$

---

The degrees of freedom is $n - 2$ because once $a$ and $b$ are fixed, there are only $n - 2$ observations in a sample of size $n$ that are free to vary.

In the Tiger car case, SSE $= 1.173$. From previous calculations we know that $\Sigma x_i^2 - n\bar{x}^2 = 60,800$ (see Table 9.2). Since there are 10 observations, d.f. $= 8$. Substituting these values and $b = -0.0126$ into Eq. (9.8) yields

$$t_c = \frac{b - \beta_0}{s_b} = \frac{-0.0126 - 0}{\sqrt{\dfrac{1.173/8}{60800}}} = -8.114$$

**Figure 9.11**
The $t$ ratio for $b$,
given $\beta = 0$.

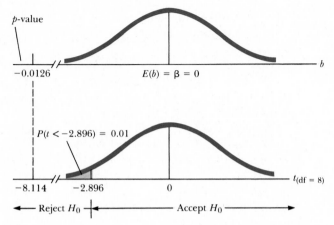

The relationship between the sample $b$ value of $-0.0126$ and this calculated $t$ value of $-8.114$ is shown in Fig. 9.11. As can be seen, because the absolute value of $t = -8.114$ is large, the probability of observing a $b$ value of $-0.0126$ or less is very small; that is, the $p$ value is approximately zero. This leads us to reject $H_0$. For instance, if the probability of a type I error is set at 0.01, from Appendix Table B.5 we see that the $H_0$ rejection region, with d.f. $= 8$, is $t < -2.896$. Since the calculated $t$ ratio of $-8.114$ is in the $H_0$ rejection region (see Fig. 9.11), $H_0$ is rejected and $H_A$ is accepted. We conclude that $\beta < 0$ and that there is a negative relationship between car weight and gas mileage in the population. Thus our regression line should be useful in estimating the expected value of $y$.

It cannot be overemphasized that the preceding use of the $t$ statistic and the conclusion reached depend on the four least-squares assumptions. If one or more of those assumptions is false, then the use of the $t$ statistic is questionable. In the next chapter we will address some of the steps that a researcher might take to handle suspected violations of the least-squares assumptions.

---

**WORKED EXAMPLE
9.3**

In contrast to the real estate appraiser in Worked Example 9.1, a real estate salesperson claims that there is no relationship between the size of a house and its price. Using the information in Worked Examples 9.1 and 9.3, test the hypotheses related to this claim at the 0.05 type I error level.

**Figure 9.12**
The *t* ratio for *b*,
given β = 0.

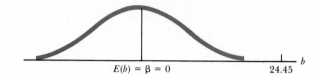

$E(b) = \beta = 0$                          $b$
                                         24.45

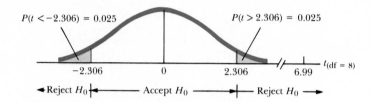

$P(t < -2.306) = 0.025$                  $P(t > 2.306) = 0.025$

    $-2.306$           $0$          $2.306$         $6.99$    $t_{(df = 8)}$

◄Reject $H_0$ |◄——— Accept $H_0$ ———►| — Reject $H_0$ ►

**ANSWER:**

The null and alternative hypotheses are

$H_0$: β = 0 (There is no relationship.)

$H_A$: β ≠ 0 (There is a relationship.)

From Worked Example 9.1 we know that $\Sigma x_i^2 - n\bar{x}^2 = 4.72$ and $b = 24.45$; from Worked Example 9.3 we know that SSE = 460.69. Thus the *t* ratio is

$$t_c = \frac{b - \beta_0}{s_b} = \frac{24.45}{\sqrt{\dfrac{460.69/8}{4.72}}} = 6.99$$

With 8 d.f., the $H_0$ rejection region is $t > 2.306$ or $t < -2.306$ (because the alternative hypothesis calls for two tails). This rejection region and the calculated *t* ratio are shown in Fig. 9.12. Since the calculated *t* ratio falls in the $H_0$ rejection region, $H_0$ is rejected and we conclude that house size and selling price are related.

## Exercises

**9.20** What does it mean to say that the least-squares estimator *b* is an unbiased estimator of the population parameter β?

**9.21** Explain how *x* and *y* could be positively related in a sample and negatively related in the population.

**9.22** For each of the following scatter diagrams, indicate whether it appears that all four assumptions for linear regression have been met.

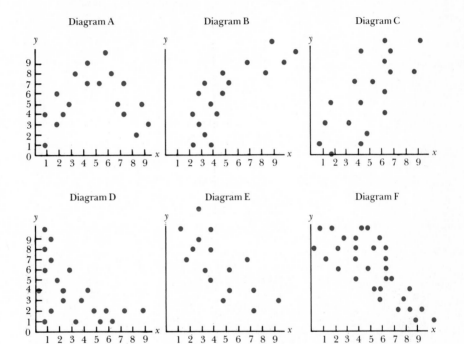

Diagram A    Diagram B    Diagram C

Diagram D    Diagram E    Diagram F

**9.23** Explain what happens to the magnitude of MSE, $s_b$, and $t = (b - \beta_0)/s_b$ as $n$ is increased.

ADM **9.24** Use the data in Exercise 9.6 to test the alternative hypothesis that an inverse relationship exists between work experience and imperfections, for a 5% probability of a type I error.

FIN **9.25** Use the data in Exercise 9.9 to test the alternative hypothesis that no relationship exists between sales and earnings per share in the tobacco industry, for a 1% probability of a type I error.

OPS **9.26** The engineer for a production process has determined that the time it takes a certain plastic to harden is directly related to the temperature of the mixture during a preliminary stage. Temperature $(x)$ and hardening time in minutes $(y)$ for the last five batches are as follows:

| $y$: | 48 | 36 | 32 | 30 | 34 |
|------|-----|-----|-----|-----|-----|
| $x$: | 450 | 480 | 500 | 510 | 500 |

a) Determine the least-squares regression line and use this line to estimate the hardening time for a batch with a temperature of 490°F.

b) Determine the percentage of hardening time explained by temperature by calculating SSE, SST, and SSR. Calculate $r^2$ and $r$.

c) Test $H_0: \beta = 0$ versus $H_A: \beta \neq 0$, using $\alpha = 0.05$.

9.27 Explain why each of the following is true or false.

a) If the four least-squares assumptions are true, then $b = \beta$.

b) The $\hat{y}$ value may be used as both a predictor of individual $y$ values and an estimator of the mean $y$ for a given $x$.

c) The method of least squares minimizes the sum of the absolute deviations of the errors in the population.

d) If SSE = 0, the resulting line is the least-squares regression line.

e) Simple linear regression (one $x$ variable) is of little use because practical problems almost always involve more than one independent variable.

FIN   9.28 An article in the *WSJ* related 11 business slumps. In each case the article presented the percentage drop in industrial output and the peak jobless rate.

| Period | Drop in Industrial Output (%) | Peak Jobless Rate (%) |
|---|---|---|
| 1929–1933 | 53.4 | 24.9 |
| 1937–1938 | 32.4 | 20.0 |
| 1945–1945 | 38.3 | 4.3 |
| 1948–1949 | 9.9 | 7.9 |
| 1953–1954 | 10.0 | 6.1 |
| 1957–1958 | 14.3 | 7.5 |
| 1960–1961 | 7.2 | 7.1 |
| 1969–1970 | 8.1 | 6.1 |
| 1973–1975 | 14.7 | 9.0 |
| 1980–1980 | 8.7 | 7.8 |
| 1981–1982 | 12.3 | 10.7 |

a) Find the least-squares regression line relating the percentage drop in industrial output $(x)$ to the jobless rate $(y)$.

b) Test the null hypothesis of no linear relationship against the alternative of a relationship for a 5% probability of a type I error.

c) Determine SST, SSE, and SSR, and then find and interpret the coefficient of determination and the correlation coefficient.

# 9.10 Regression and Correlation Using the Computer

Computer programs are typically used to do the computations required in least-squares estimation. In problems involving large sets of data, using the computer is the only practical way to do the tedious calculations involved in regression analysis.

Least-squares regression programs are readily available in any computer center. Typical programs in large mainframe installations include Statistical Program for the Social Sciences (SPSS), Biomedical Series (BMD), Statistical Analysis System (SAS), Minitab, and Interactive Data Analysis (IDA). In addition to some of these mainframe packages, a large number of additional packages are available for microcomputers. All of the available least-squares computer programs use some variation of the formulas given previously to do the required calculations. Some provide numerous options for the user and frequently are difficult to use. Others, such as Microstat, are menu driven and very easy to learn, but provide fewer options.

Most companies, government agencies, colleges, and universities have a staff to assist users with the mechanical operations. The analyst's job, however, is to determine what data are fed into the computer and to interpret the results obtained. As an example of what a canned computer program will do, consider the following case.

## Salary Determination

You are a new personnel director faced with two lingering problems. First, in 1979, one of the scientists working for the company complained about not receiving compensation comparable to that of others of similar age. (this scientist was born in 1940). Second, at the same time, a group of female scientists claimed they were being paid less than the males. In 1979, the research unit had 180 salaried scientists (37 females) engaged in applied research. Salaries have always been set by the unit manager, who says that they are determined by experience, productivity, and the contribution to the corporation. No information exists on productivity or contribution to the corporation, but salary and age (birth date) are available for all 180 scientists. Your job is to investigate these claims.

To investigate the two claims, you decide to use a computer to fit three regression lines:

1. Relating salary $(y)$ to birth date $(x)$ for all 180 employees. The population model is $y = \alpha + \beta x + \epsilon$.

2. Relating salary $(y_f)$ to the birth date $(x_f)$ of the 37 female scientists in the corporation. The model is $y_f = \alpha_f + \beta_f x_f + \epsilon_f$ (where the subscript $f$ indicates female).

3. Relating salary $(y_m)$ to the birth date $(x_m)$ of the 143 males in the corporation. The model is $y_m = \alpha_m + \beta_m x_m + \epsilon_m$ (where the subscript $m$ indicates male).

The first regression is run to investigate the claim of the scientist who complains of being paid less than other scientists of similar age. If salary is related to age (birth date), then a regression analysis can be used to predict the salary for this person based on age alone. This predicted salary can then be compared with his actual salary. The next two regressions are used to investigate the claim of sex discrimination. If there is no discrimination, then the regression equation for men should be similar to that for women. In all three regressions, the last two digits of the year in which a person was born are used for $x$. If age is related to salary, then we expect the population relationship to be $\beta < 0$ (i.e., someone born in 1952 should have a salary lower than someone born in 1942).

You decide to run these regressions on the corporation's mainframe computer using SPSS. These data are on magnetic tape, where the tape includes (among other data) each person's ID number, each scientist's sex (1 for males and 0 for females), salary (in 1979 dollars), and the last two digits of each person's year of birth. With the help of the computer personnel, you specify in the SPSS program how to locate on the tape each piece of information. As a test of the linearity assumption for regression analysis (assumption 1), you first request a printout of the salary-age scatter diagram for all 180 scientists. As anticipated, there is a negative relationship between salary and year of birth (see Fig. 9.13). Although there is considerable variability in salaries around a line drawn through these data, no obvious nonlinear relationship exists. The least-squares regression line generated by SPSS is given in Table 9.5.

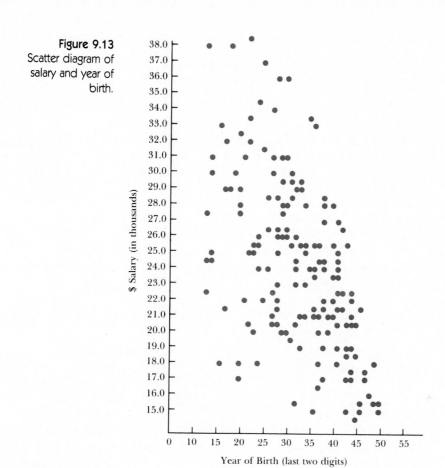

**Figure 9.13**
Scatter diagram of salary and year of birth.

**Table 9.5**

| Salary and Year of Birth Regression: SPSS Regression Computer Printout | | | | |
|---|---|---|---|---|
| DEPENDENT VARIABLE.. Y SALARY | | | | |
| MEAN RESPONSE 24201.8500 STD DEV 5422.1649 | | | | |
| VARIABLE(S) ENTERED.... : X BIRTH | | | | |
| MULTP R | .5202 | ANALYSIS OF VARIANCE | DF | SUM OF SQUARES |
| R SQUARE | .2706 | REGRESSION | 1. | 1424215379.9864 |
| ADJ R SQUARE | .2665 | RESIDUAL | 178. | 3838361758.9642 |
| STD DEVIAT | 4643.6871 | COEFF OF VARIABILITY | 19.2 PCT | |
| | | VARIABLES IN THE EQUATION | | |
| VARIABLE | B | STD ERROR B | F | |
| X | -302.2397 | 37.1900 | 66.0449 | |
| CONSTANT | 33969.23 | 1250.70 | 737.6656 | |

# 9.11 Reading and Interpreting a Computer Output

The least-squares regression output in Table 9.5 uses some abbreviations and several measures not yet introduced. All of these abbreviations and measures are described, at least briefly, in this section. For some, however, elaboration will be postponed until Chapter 10. We have modified the SPSS output to avoid scientific notation, although the notation is not difficult. For example, if the symbol E+2 occurs at the end of a number, this indicates that the decimal must be moved two places to the *right*. Similarly, E−3 indicates the decimal must be moved three places to the *left*. Thus, 2.128E+2 is really 212.8 and 5.392E−3 is actually 0.005392.

The top of the SPSS output gives the name of the dependent variable ($y$ or salary) and the mean and standard deviation of this variable ($\bar{y} = \$24{,}201.85$ and $s_y = \$5422.16$). The next line gives the independent variable(s) entered. In simple linear regression there is only one independent variable—in this case, $x$ or birth. The next group of titles and numbers in the left-hand column are interpreted as follows:

MULTP R .5202 This is the correlation coefficient. It should be printed as $r = -.5202$, but most programs do not include the proper sign (+ or −) and most print a capital $R$ rather than lowercase $r$. The value 0.5202 is interpreted using R SQUARE.

R SQUARE .2706 $R^2$ is the coefficient of determination and is used to interpret the strength of the relationship between $x$ and $y$. Thus 27.06% of the variability in salaries ($y$) is explained by our age measure ($x$).

ADJ R SQUARE .2665 Although not discussed in this text, this measure "adjusts" $R^2$ to account for the sample size and the number of independent variables included.

STD DEVIAT 4643.6871 The value 4643.6871 is the standard error of the estimate ($s_e$), where

$$s_e = \sqrt{\text{SSE}/(n-2)}$$

The set of numbers in the middle columns provides information about the variability in the data. This information is referred to as *analysis of variance*, which is abbreviated as ANOVA. ANOVA information is as follows:

$\text{SSR} = 1424215379.9864$     with d.f. = 1
$\text{SSE} = 3838361758.9642$     with d.f. = $n - 2 = 178$

The value of SST must be the sum SSE + SSR. Note that

$$R \ SQUARE = \frac{SSR}{SST} = \frac{1424215379.9864}{5262577138.9506} = 0.2706$$

Although not emphasized in this text, the coefficient of variability is

$$\frac{s_e}{\bar{y}} \times 100 = \frac{4643.6871}{24201.850} \times 100 = 19.2\%$$

This coefficient indicates that the standard error $(s_e)$ is 19.2% of the mean of $y$ $(\bar{y})$.

The section VARIABLES IN THE EQUATION presents the least-squares regression line, the standard error of $b$, and the associated $t$ values. The first value in the "B" column is the regression slope, $b = -302.2397$, and the second value is the constant, $a = 33969.23$. Thus the sample regression line is

$$\hat{y} = 33969.23 - 302.2397x$$

The standard error of $b$ is $s_b = 37.19$. To test the null hypothesis $H_0$: $\beta \geq 0$ versus $H_A$: $\beta < 0$ (a one-sided alternative stating that birth year and salary are negatively related), we form the $t$ ratio

$$t_c = \frac{-302.2397}{37.19} = -8.1269$$

Notice that the square of this $t$ value is shown on the right side of the SPSS output, under the heading "F" (The $F$ distribution is discussed in Chapter 10.) For now, however, it is only necessary to know that for single-parameter tests the calculated $t$ is simply the square root of the SPSS reported $F$.) This high $t$ value clearly suggests that for any reasonable probability of a type I error, $H_0$ should be rejected and we can conclude that salary and birth year are negatively related (i.e., salary and age are positively related).

## Settling Discrimination Claims with this Regression Line

You now want to use the regression equation to estimate the salary for a scientist born in 1940. Substituting $x = 40$ into the regression equation yields

$$\hat{y} = 33969.23 - 302.2397(40) = \$21,879.64$$

This means that scientists born in 1940 are predicted to earn an average of $21,879.64. The standard error $s_e = 4643.69$ is one indication of the variability about this predicted salary. The scientist claiming to be underpaid according to age was making $21,000 in 1979 when the complaint was issued. The difference of $879.64 between the predicted salary of $21,879.64 and this actual salary of $21,000 is not particularly large in light of the standard error of $4643.69. Thus, as the personnel manager, you should be justified in emphasizing to the scientist that while experience (as measured by age) is only one part of the salary determination (explaining about 27%), a salary of $21,000 is not that much lower than would be predicted for someone born

**Table 9.6**

| Separate Male and Female Salary–Age Regressions |
|---|

Male Regression Computer Printout

```
DEPENDENT VARIABLE.. Y    MALE SALARY
MEAN RESPONSE  24780.9400     STD.DEV  5190.8515
VARIABLE(S) ENTERED ON STEP NUMBER 1.   X  BIRTH


MULTP R          .5243   ANALYSIS OF VARIANCE   DF      SUM OF SQUARES
R SQUARE         .2749   REGRESSION             1.    1051681096.4615
ADJ R SQUARE     .2697   RESIDUAL             141.    2774500265.0912
STD DEVIAT    4435.9111  COEFF OF VARIABILITY  17.9 PCT

                    VARIABLES IN THE EQUATION
VARIABLE            B               STD ERROR B         F
X              -304.2689              41.6197        53.4463
CONSTANT       34668.62              1402.44        611.0784
```

Female Regression Computer Printout

```
DEPENDENT VARIABLE.. Y    FEMALE SALARY
MEAN RESPONSE 21963.7300     STD.DEV  5780.9577
VARIABLE(S) ENTERED ON STEP NUMBER 1.   X  BIRTH


MULTP R          .5903   ANALYSIS OF VARIANCE  DF    SUM OF SQUARES
R SQUARE         .3484   REGRESSION             1.    419180865.33414
ADJ R. SQUARE    .3298   RESIDUAL              35.    783920125.96327
STD DEVIAT    4732.6227  COEFF OF VARIABILITY  21.5 PCT

                    VARIABLES IN THE EQUATION
VARIABLE            B               STD ERROR B         F
X              -315.5924              72.9504        18.7143
CONSTANT       31943.28              2434.4851       172.1606
```

in 1940. (Statistical tests of the difference between a predicted and an actual $y$ value exist but will not be presented here.)

Table 9.6 provides the separate computer printouts (for males and females) for the analysis of the sex discrimination charge by the female scientists. A comparison of the mean salaries (for males and females) reported in Table 9.6 shows that females receive less salary, on the average, than males ($21,963.73 versus $24,780.94). This comparison, however, overlooks any possible difference in experience (age) between the men and women. The original data in this case (not presented here) show that the males are considerably older than the females and thus would be expected to have a higher average salary.

One way to take experience into account is to compare the two regression lines to see if men and women are rewarded equally for each additional year of experience. This involves a comparison of slopes. For the male scientists, the slope is a negative $304.2689, representing the men's predicted change in salary for a 1-year birth change. For the females, the predicted change in salary is a negative $315.5924 per year. It appears that men and women are being rewarded about the same for experience. Given the relatively high amount of unexplained variability in salaries (as reflected in the low coefficients of determination, 0.2749 and 0.3484, respectively), variables other than age may be needed to explain male and female salaries more fully. This is the subject of Chapter 10.

# 9.12 Analyzing Residuals Using a Computer

In Section 9.4 we discussed the calculation of residuals or errors in prediction, $y - \hat{y}$. Section 9.8 stated that an analysis of these residuals in a scatter diagram could shed light on the correctness of the least-squares assumptions. To see how this analysis is facilitated using a computer program, consider a macroeconomic example involving the prediction of consumption from income.

From *The Economic Report of the President* we obtained data on real disposable personal income, net income in the United States, and real consumption. Using yearly 1952–1981 data, measured in billions of constant 1972 dollars, and running a regression of real consumption ($y$) on real disposable personal income ($x$), the Microstat computer program yields the results in

| Table 9.7 | Regression of Personal Consumption on Personal Disposable Income (1952–1981, Measured in Billions of 1972 Dollars) |
|---|---|

```
INDEX        NAME           MEAN        STD.DEV.
  1          INCOME        676.9933     214.8417
DEP. VAR.:   CONSUMP       614.3233     193.3873

DEPENDENT VARIABLE: CONSUMPTION (y)
             REGRESSION
VAR.         COEFFICIENT  STD. ERROR   T(DF = 28)
INCOME (x)      .8996        .0061      146.930
CONSTANT       5.3303

STD. ERROR OF EST. = 7.0833
       r SQUARE = .9987
            r = .9994

         ANALYSIS OF VARIANCE TABLE

SOURCE        SUM OF SQUARES   D.F.   MEAN SQUARE
REGRESSION      1083156.3580    1     1083156.3580
RESIDUAL           1404.8350   28          50.1727
TOTAL           1084561.1930   29
```

Table 9.7. Although arranged differently, these results are interpreted the same way as in the SPSS printouts previously given.

From Table 9.7 we see that the sample regression equation is

$$\hat{y} = 5.3303 + 0.8996x$$

This equation fits well, as $R^2 = 0.9987$. Unlike the SPSS printout, in the Microstat printout the calculated $t$ statistic for the independent variable is reported in the column T(DF = 28) that is, $t_c = 146.930$, with 28 d.f.

To make predictions and calculate prediction errors in the 30 years represented by this data, we could substitute each value of income into the equation, predict consumption, and then calculate the 30 residuals. For instance, in 1981 real personal disposable income was $1043.1 billion and consumption was $947.6 billion. Thus the prediction error or residual is

$$y - \hat{y} = 947.6 - [5.3303 + 0.8996(1043.1)] = 947.6 - 943.7 = 3.9$$

All the remaining 29 residuals could likewise be calculated. It is faster, however, to use a computer to calculate these residuals. The computer-generated residuals appear in Table 9.8. Notice in Table 9.8 that the observed

**Table 9.8**

## Residuals of Personal Consumption–Personal Disposable Income Regression

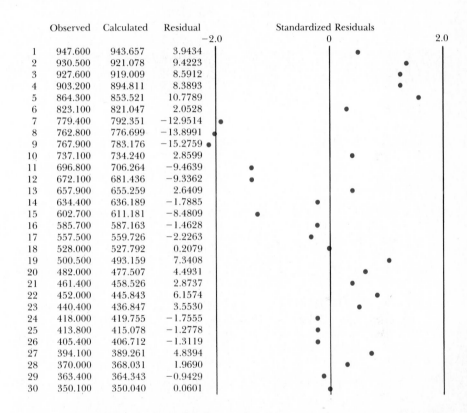

| | Observed | Calculated | Residual | Standardized Residuals |
|---|---|---|---|---|
| | | | −2.0 | 0      2.0 |
| 1 | 947.600 | 943.657 | 3.9434 | |
| 2 | 930.500 | 921.078 | 9.4223 | |
| 3 | 927.600 | 919.009 | 8.5912 | |
| 4 | 903.200 | 894.811 | 8.3893 | |
| 5 | 864.300 | 853.521 | 10.7789 | |
| 6 | 823.100 | 821.047 | 2.0528 | |
| 7 | 779.400 | 792.351 | −12.9514 | |
| 8 | 762.800 | 776.699 | −13.8991 | |
| 9 | 767.900 | 783.176 | −15.2759 | |
| 10 | 737.100 | 734.240 | 2.8599 | |
| 11 | 696.800 | 706.264 | −9.4639 | |
| 12 | 672.100 | 681.436 | −9.3362 | |
| 13 | 657.900 | 655.259 | 2.6409 | |
| 14 | 634.400 | 636.189 | −1.7885 | |
| 15 | 602.700 | 611.181 | −8.4809 | |
| 16 | 585.700 | 587.163 | −1.4628 | |
| 17 | 557.500 | 559.726 | −2.2263 | |
| 18 | 528.000 | 527.792 | 0.2079 | |
| 19 | 500.500 | 493.159 | 7.3408 | |
| 20 | 482.000 | 477.507 | 4.4931 | |
| 21 | 461.400 | 458.526 | 2.8737 | |
| 22 | 452.000 | 445.843 | 6.1574 | |
| 23 | 440.400 | 436.847 | 3.5530 | |
| 24 | 418.000 | 419.755 | −1.7555 | |
| 25 | 413.800 | 415.078 | −1.2778 | |
| 26 | 405.400 | 406.712 | −1.3119 | |
| 27 | 394.100 | 389.261 | 4.8394 | |
| 28 | 370.000 | 368.031 | 1.9690 | |
| 29 | 363.400 | 364.343 | −0.9429 | |
| 30 | 350.100 | 350.040 | 0.0601 | |

value of consumption in 1981 is the first value. It is followed by the predicted value of consumption (labeled "Calculated") and the residual. Row 2 gives the values for 1980, and so on. These residuals, divided by the standard error ($s_e$), are then graphed in the column labeled "Standardized Residuals."

From the printout of residuals in Table 9.8 we can see that several of the least-squares assumptions may be violated. For instance, to make inferences about the population parameters and forecast future values, we have to assume that the population error term $\epsilon$ is purely random and not dependent on other things. The residuals in Table 9.8, however, appear to follow a serpentine pattern where negative and positive residuals tend to follow each other and occur in groups. Such a pattern is not consistent with a random process. This residual pattern suggests that in the population $\epsilon$ may contain a component that does not behave randomly over time. Such *residual correlation* is a common problem in time series analysis. Time series analysis will be discussed in Chapter 10.

## Exercises

ECN **9.29** The output in the following table represents the Microstat output for a simple linear regression analysis:

```
INDEX          NAME       MEAN            STD.DEV.
  1            X          32.3100
DEP. VAR.:     Y         24201.8500       5422.1649

DEPENDENT VARIABLE: y

               REGRESSION
VAR.           COEFFICIENT   STD. ERROR   T(D.F. = 178)
x              -302.2397        37.1900        8.1268
CONSTANT      33969.2300      1250.7000       27.1600

STD.ERROR OF EST. = 4643.6871
       r SQUARE = .2706
            r = .5202
```

### ANALYSIS OF VARIANCE TABLE

| SOURCE | SUM OF SQUARES | D.F. | MEAN SQUARE |
|---|---|---|---|
| REGRESSION | 1424215379.9864 | 1 | 1424215379.9864 |
| RESIDUAL | 3838361758.9642 | 178 | 21563837.9722 |
| TOTAL | 5252587127.9506 | 179 | |

Use these data to:

a) Determine the correlation coefficient and the coefficient of determination.

**b)** Find the value of SSE, SSR, and SST.

**c)** Find the means of $x$ and $y$ and the sample size.

**d)** Determine the least-squares regression equation.

**e)** Find the $t$ ratio to test the null hypothesis $H_0$: $\beta = 0$.

**f)** Determine the standard error of the estimate.

**g)** Explain why these data look familiar.

ECN  **9.30** A common belief until 1972 was that there was a negative linear relationship between the rate of unemployment and the rate of inflation (the "Phillip's curve"). The following data are for unemployment and inflation in the United States, during the period 1952–1982.

| Year | Unemploy-ment Rate | Rate of Inflation | Year | Unemploy-ment Rate | Rate of Inflation | Year | Unemploy-ment Rate | Rate of Inflation |
|------|------|------|------|------|------|------|------|------|
| 1952 | 3.0 | 2.2 | 1963 | 5.7 | 1.2 | 1974 | 5.6 | 11.0 |
| 1953 | 2.9 | 0.8 | 1964 | 5.2 | 1.3 | 1975 | 8.5 | 9.1 |
| 1954 | 5.5 | 0.5 | 1965 | 4.5 | 1.7 | 1976 | 7.7 | 5.8 |
| 1955 | 4.4 | −0.4 | 1966 | 3.8 | 2.9 | 1977 | 7.1 | 6.5 |
| 1956 | 4.1 | 1.5 | 1967 | 3.8 | 2.9 | 1978 | 6.1 | 7.7 |
| 1957 | 4.3 | 3.6 | 1968 | 3.6 | 4.2 | 1979 | 5.8 | 11.3 |
| 1958 | 6.8 | 2.7 | 1969 | 3.5 | 5.4 | 1980 | 7.1 | 13.5 |
| 1959 | 5.5 | 0.8 | 1970 | 4.9 | 5.9 | 1981 | 7.6 | 10.4 |
| 1960 | 5.5 | 1.6 | 1971 | 5.9 | 4.3 | 1982 | 9.7 | 6.1 |
| 1961 | 6.7 | 1.0 | 1972 | 5.6 | 3.3 | 1983 | | |
| 1962 | 5.5 | 1.1 | 1973 | 4.9 | 6.2 | 1984 | | |

**a)** To determine a least-squares regression line for these data, is it clear whether the unemployment rate or the rate of inflation is the dependent variable?

**b)** Use a computer program to determine the least-squares regression line for the data prior to 1973. (Assume that unemployment is the dependent variable.) Does the same line hold for the data after 1972?

**c)** Check to see if a linear relationship is appropriate for these data by looking at a plot of the residuals. Do you detect any possible violations of the four assumptions?

REL **9.31** Analyze the data on house size and selling price in Worked Example 9.1 using a computer package. Why do your results from this computer estimation differ slightly from those in Worked Example 9.3?

ADM **9.32** A personnel manager claims that scores on the company's application test are positively related to a person's first-year raise following job placement. This claim is based on the following sample data:

| Score | Raise | Score | Raise | Score | Raise |
|-------|-------|-------|-------|-------|-------|
| 80 | $2000 | 69 | $1800 | 55 | $1390 |
| 90 | 2300 | 61 | 1380 | 60 | 1440 |
| 55 | 1400 | 59 | 1480 | 53 | 1400 |
| 74 | 1800 | 88 | 1500 | 91 | 2900 |
| 67 | 1770 | 73 | 1390 | 59 | 1360 |
| 43 | 1200 | 57 | 1700 | 66 | 1750 |
| 61 | 1950 | 51 | 1600 | 80 | 1800 |
| 90 | 1960 | 50 | 1570 | 79 | 1800 |
| 82 | 1600 | 94 | 1600 | 81 | 1850 |
| 62 | 1400 | 63 | 1300 | 63 | 1700 |
| 65 | 1510 | 58 | 1800 | 83 | 2800 |
| 49 | 1750 | 82 | 2790 | 52 | 1900 |
| 53 | 1600 | 71 | 1700 | 96 | 2500 |

a) Specify the population model to be estimated.

b) Use a computer program to estimate the relationship between raises and scores. How well does your sample regression fit the data?

c) At the 0.01 type I error level, are scores related to raises?

ECN **9.33** Human capital theory states that individuals invest in education because there is a positive return from schooling. That is, the more years of schooling, the higher one's income should be. As an initial test of this theory, the following small regression was run on the average income ($y$) received by individuals who completed 8, 10, 12, 14, 16, 18, and 20 years of schooling ($x$)

| INDEX | NAME | MEAN | STD. DEV. |
|-------|------|------|-----------|
| 1 | x—ed yrs | 14.00000 | 4.32049 |
| DEP. VAR.: | y—income | 24471.42857 | 7437.90165 |

```
DEPENDENT VARIABLE: y-income

                 REGRESSION
VAR.             COEFFICIENT    STD. ERROR    T(D.F. = 5)
x-ed yrs         1517.85714      363.26538        4.178
CONSTANT         3221.42857

STD. ERROR OF EST. = 3844.43940
         r SQUARED =  .7774
               r =  .8817


              ANALYSIS OF VARIANCE TABLE

   SOURCE          SUM OF SQUARES   D.F.      MEAN SQUARE
REGRESSION         258035714.30000    1     258035714.30000
RESIDUAL            73898571.40000    5      14779714.28000
TOTAL              331934285.70000    6
```

a) State the meaning of all of the numbers in this printout.

b) What is the expected salary of someone who completes 13 years of schooling?

c) At a 1% probability of a type I error, is there a positive relationship between years of schooling and income?

ECN   **9.34**  Following is a residual plot for the income–education regression given in Exercise 9.33. Why do these residuals cast doubt on the validity of the estimation and hypothesis test you performed in Exercise 9.33?

| | Observed | Calculated | Residual | | Standardized Residuals | |
|---|---|---|---|---|---|---|
| | | | | −2.0 | 0 | 2.0 |
| 1 | 10000.000 | 15364.286 | −5364.28571 | • | | |
| 2 | 200000.00 | 18400.000 | 1600.00000 | | • | |
| 3 | 25000.000 | 21435.714 | 3564.28572 | | | • |
| 4 | 25800.000 | 24471.429 | 1328.57143 | | • | |
| 5 | 30000.000 | 27507.143 | 2492.85714 | | • | |
| 6 | 31500.000 | 30542.857 | 957.14286 | | • | |
| 7 | 29000.000 | 33578.571 | −4578.57143 | • | | |

FIN   **9.35**  Assume that the banks and bank holding companies in Appendix Table A.1 represent a random sample. Run a regression relating profits ($y$) to sales ($x$). Interpret all parts of your computer output. Predict profits for a company with sales of $500 million.

**9.36** Indicate whether each statement is true or false and why.

a) In the regression model $y = \alpha + \beta x + \epsilon$, the population parameters to be estimated are $\alpha$, $\beta$, and $\epsilon$. The least-squares estimators are $a$, $b$, and $e$.

b) The least-squares method minimizes the squared errors around the population regression line.

c) If SSE $= 0$, then $r^2 = 1$ and the sample regression line perfectly predicts each $y$ value in the sample.

d) If SSE $=$ SSR, then 25% of the variability in $y$ is explained by $x$.

e) If $\Sigma(y_i - \hat{y}_i) = 0$, then the expected value of the population error term $\epsilon$ must be zero.

MKT **9.37** A marketing research analyst has determined a least-squares regression line relating advertising to sales $(y)$ to be

$$\hat{y} = 15 + 1000x$$

a) What is the meaning of the numbers 15 and 1000?

b) Is it possible to get a slope as large as $b = 1000$ and still accept $H_0: \beta = 0$? Explain.

ECN **9.38** A *WSJ* article reported that in the past, automobile producers had used a fixed sales forecast in setting car prices. According to the article, "First, the auto companies' pricing committees would decide how many cars they expected to sell. Then they added up costs and putting in a healthy margin for profit, they arrived at the average prices by simply dividing." From 1920 to 1981 this method of pricing worked well because car prices themselves had little or no impact on sales. In 1981, however, sales became extremely price sensitive. For example, a $300 rebate (equivalent to a $300 price cut) by Chrysler resulted in a 30% jump in sales.

a) Working from an initial net purchase price of $7000 and monthly sales of 40,000 cars, which of the following regression equations best represents the monthly demand for an automobile before 1981? After 1981? (*P* is the net price paid by an auto purchaser in thousands of current dollars and $Q$ is the quantity of autos demanded per month in thousands of units.)

1. $\hat{P} = 8 + 0.025Q$    3. $\hat{P} = 8 - 0.025Q$
2. $\hat{P} = 7$             4. $\hat{Q} = 40$

b) Graph each of the four regression equations in part (a) and show the change in the quantity demanded resulting from a drop in the price from $7000 to $6700. What is the percentage change in quantity demanded associated with each of the four regression equations?

c) How does your work in part (b) relate to your answer in part (a) and the statement about the use of fixed forecasts when demand is price sensitive?

d) If you were on the pricing committee of one of the auto producers, would you continue to use fixed forecasts or recommend another technique? (Explain and defend your recommendation to the other committee members.)

FIN    9.39   The owners of a new indoor tennis facility are attempting to determine the relationship between the average outside temperature ($x$) and the amount of gas ($y$ in thousands of cubic centimeters) used per day for heating. Five observations were taken during a period in January.

$y$:  10   27   5   13   9
$x$:  21   −4   35   25   31

a) Compute the least-squares regression line.
b) Determine SSE, SSR, and SST and then find $r^2$ and $r$.
c) Test $H_0$ using a one-sided alternative and type I error level of 0.05.
d) Find MSE and $s_e$. If the average temperature is $x = 15$, what is the predicted value of $y$? Form an interval to reflect two standard errors around this predicted $y$ value.

ECN    9.40   In *Forbes* on March 8, 1982, Daniel Seligman commented in his article on how tenuous projected federal deficits can be. He used official deficit projections (by the administration in office) between 1970 and 1982. These data (in billions of dollars) are:

| Fiscal year | Projected Deficit | Actual Deficit |
|:---:|:---:|:---:|
| 1970 | −3.4 | 2.8 |
| 1971 | −1.3 | 23.0 |
| 1972 | 11.6 | 23.4 |
| 1973 | 25.5 | 14.9 |
| 1974 | 12.7 | 4.7 |
| 1975 | 9.7 | 45.2 |
| 1976 | 51.9 | 66.4 |
| 1977 | 59.1 | 57.9 |
| 1978 | 47.0 | 48.8 |
| 1979 | 60.6 | 27.7 |
| 1980 | 29.9 | 59.6 |
| 1981 | 15.8 | 57.9 |
| 1982 | 27.5 | 98.6 |

a) Construct a scatter diagram for these 13 values, using actual deficit as the dependent variable. What do you think it means to have a negative deficit for 1970 and 1971?

b) Find the least-squares sample regression line.

c) The Reagan administration projected a deficit of 91.5 billion for 1983. What actual deficit would you predict on the basis of the regression line? Do you think your regression line provides a good fit to the sample data?

d) Construct an interval to reflect two standard errors around your predicted deficit value in part (c).

e) From these data can you conclude that projected deficits influence actual deficits?

ADM **9.41** In an attempt to predict knowledge at the end of a training program, an instructional design specialist tested all trainees prior to the course $(x)$ and again at the end $(y)$. The specialist recorded the following results:

$x$ (pretest score):   75 40 51 80 50 52 49 52 50 66 58 50 51
$y$ (posttest score):   98 75 65 96 71 80 62 51 44 93 67 59 61

a) Obtain the least-squares regression for these sample data.

b) If the claim is made that there is a one-to-one relationship between the pretest and the posttest, with the exception of random error, what population model is being specified? What value of $\beta$ is being suggested? (Hint: a one-to-one relationship can be interpreted to mean that if a person with a 50 on the pretest scores a 60 on the posttest, then a person with a 70 on the pretest should score an 80 on the posttest, on the average.)

c) Test the claim in part (b) at the 0.01 type I error level.

d) In drawing your conclusion in part (c), are there any violations of the four least-squares assumptions that should concern you?

MKT **9.42** An executive wants to determine the relationship between corporate sales and the amount spent on advertising over the past 15 years. The following yearly data are available:

| Year | Corporate Sales (in $1000) | Advertising Expense (in $1000) | Year | Corporate Sales (in $1000) | Advertising Expense (in $1000) |
|------|------|------|------|------|------|
| 1 | 900 | 50 | 9 | 989 | 69 |
| 2 | 1234 | 52 | 10 | 1000 | 69 |
| 3 | 978 | 53 | 11 | 1690 | 71 |
| 4 | 879 | 60 | 12 | 1400 | 75 |
| 5 | 900 | 58 | 13 | 1489 | 80 |
| 6 | 1076 | 61 | 14 | 1398 | 76 |
| 7 | 1105 | 67 | 15 | 1698 | 80 |
| 8 | 1230 | 70 | | | |

A computer program was used to obtain the following results:

```
                REGRESSION
VAR.            COEFFICIENT      STD. ERROR      T(D.F. = 13)
EXPENSE          20.4493          5.3725            3.806
CONSTANT       -153.2859
STD. ERROR OF EST. = 199.5031
        r SQUARE =    .5271
            r =    .7260

 SOURCE        SUM OF SQUARES   D.F.   MEAN SQUARE
REGRESSION       576635.7402     1      576635.7402
RESIDUAL         517419.1938    13       39801.4765
TOTAL           1094054.9340    14
```

a) Give the estimated sample regression line.

b) Predict sales if the advertising expense is $60,000. What is the average prediction error for this sample?

c) Predict sales if the advertising expense is $100,000. Why is (or isn't) this prediction questionable? Construct a $\hat{y} \pm 2s_e$ interval for this prediction. Interpret the interval.

d) What does the coefficient of determination tell you in this exercise?

MKT **9.43** The head of advertising for the company described in Exercise 9.42 claims that there is a positive relationship between sales and advertising expense.

a) Test this claim using the output in Exercise 9.42.

b) Use the following residuals plot to state why you would or would not question the test in part (a).

| | Observed | Calculated | Residual | Standardized Residuals |
|---|---|---|---|---|
| | | | −2.0 | 0 ... 2.0 |
| 1 | 900.00 | 869.181 | 30.8193 | |
| 2 | 1234.000 | 910.079 | 323.9206 | |
| 3 | 978.000 | 930.529 | 47.4713 | |
| 4 | 879.000 | 1073.674 | −194.6740 | |
| 5 | 900.000 | 1032.775 | −132.7754 | |
| 6 | 1076.000 | 1094.123 | −18.1234 | |
| 7 | 1105.000 | 1216.819 | −111.8194 | |
| 8 | 1230.000 | 1278.167 | −48.1674 | |
| 9 | 989.000 | 1257.718 | −268.7180 | |
| 10 | 1000.000 | 1257.718 | −257.7180 | |
| 11 | 1690.000 | 1298.617 | 391.3833 | |
| 12 | 1400.000 | 1380.414 | 19.5860 | |
| 13 | 1489.000 | 1482.661 | 6.3393 | |
| 14 | 1398.000 | 1400.863 | −2.8634 | |
| 15 | 1698.000 | 1482.661 | 215.3393 | |

**9.44** According to recent press releases, psychologists have found that more than 50% of the variability in IQ can be explained by "speed thinking," as measured by a visual test in which subjects identify the length of lines. For example, a 1982 *Newsweek* article stated that subjects who required only $\frac{1}{50}$th of a second to identify the length of lines also scored well on standard intelligence tests (predicted IQ of 135). Those who took $\frac{1}{10}$th of a second scored low (predicted IQ of 75).

a) Write the general form of the population and sample regression equation suggested by the preceding statement. (Define notation.)

b) Draw a graph showing the suggested regression line and label the points identified.

c) What are the slope and intercept of the line drawn in part (b)?

**coefficient of determination $r^2$:** A number between 0 and 1 that indicates the proportion of variability in the dependent variable explained by the independent variable.

**correlation coefficient $r$:** A relative measure of the variability in the dependent variable that is explained by the sample regression. It is the square root of the coefficient of determination and has a range $-1 \leq r \leq +1$. The minus or plus sign of $r$ is determined by the negative or positive relationship between $x$ and $y$.

**dependent variable:** The variable being predicted or explained.

**independent variable:** The variable used to predict or explain the dependent variable.

**least-squares regression:** A method for finding the line that best fits the sample data by minimizing the sum of the squared errors.

**mean square error (MSE):** A measure of the average variability unexplained by the independent variable.

**mean square regression (MSR):** A measure of the average variability explained by the independent variable.

**population error term:** The source of randomness in a population model, designated by $\epsilon$.

**population intercept $\alpha$:** The parameter that represents a point where the population regression line intersects the $y$ axis.

**population linear model:** The assumed theoretical relationship that exists between a dependent variable $y$, an independent variable $x$, and an error term $\epsilon$. The linear model is $y = \alpha + \beta x + \epsilon$, where $\alpha$ and $\beta$ are parameters.

**population slope $\beta$:** The parameter that indicates the change in the expected value of the dependent variable with each one-unit change in the independent variable.

**predicted dependent variable $\hat{y}$:** The values of the dependent variable that are calculated from the sample regression line $\hat{y} = a + bx$.

**regression parameters:** Fixed values that describe the population relationship between the dependent and independent variables.

**residual:** (also called **sample error**): The difference between the predicted and observed values of the dependent variable in a sample, designated by $e = y - \hat{y}$.

**sample error term:** (also called *residual*): The difference between the predicted and observed values of the dependent variable in a sample, designated by $e = y - \hat{y}$.

**sample regression intercept $a$:** The point where the sample regression line intersects the $y$ axis.

**sample regression line:** The least squares line that best fits the sample data.

**sample regression slope $b$:** The slope of the sample regression line. It indicates how the predicted value of the dependent variable will change with each one-unit change in the independent variable.

**scatter diagram:** A plot of sample $y$ and $x$ values, where traditionally the variable to be explained ($y$) is on the vertical axis and the variable that may explain it ($x$) is on the horizontal axis.

**standard error of $b$:** (also called *standard deviation of $b$*): A measure of the variability in the least-squares slope estimator $b$, designated by $s_b$.

**standard error of the estimate:** A measure of the variability of the errors about the regression line, designated by $s_e = \sqrt{\text{SSE}/(n - 2)}$.

**sum of squares error (SSE):** A measure of the unexplained variability in the dependent variable in the sample.

**sum of squares regression (SSR):** A measure of the amount of variability in the dependent variable that is explained by the independent variable.

**sum of squares total (SST):** A measure of the variability in the dependent variable to be explained by the regression analysis.

## Formulas

**9.1—Slope-Intercept Form of the Sample Regression Equation**

$$\hat{y} = a + bx$$

where

$\hat{y}$ is the predicted dependent variable

$x$ is the independent variable

$a$ is the $y$ intercept

$b$ is the slope

**9.2—Least-Squares Estimators**

$$\text{slope: } b = \frac{\Sigma x_i y_i - n\bar{x}\bar{y}}{\Sigma x_i^2 - n\bar{x}^2}$$

intercept: $a = \bar{y} - b\bar{x}$

**9.3—Sum of Squares Total (SST)**

$$\text{SST} = \Sigma(y_i - \bar{y})^2$$

**9.4—Sum of Squares Regression (SSR)**

$$\text{SSR} = \text{SST} - \text{SSE}$$

**9.5—Coefficient of Determination**

$$r^2 = \text{SSR/SST}$$

**9.6—Population Linear Model**

$$y = \alpha + \beta x + \epsilon$$

where

$y$ is the dependent variable

$x$ is the independent variable

$\alpha$ is the $y$ intercept to be estimated

$\beta$ is the slope to be estimated

$\epsilon$ is the population error term

**9.7—Standard Error of $b$**

$$s_b = \sqrt{\frac{\text{SSE}/(n - 2)}{\Sigma x_i^2 - n\bar{x}^2}}$$

**9.8—The $t$ Statistic for $b$**

$$t = \frac{b - \beta_0}{s_b} \text{ with d.f. } = n - 2$$

# CHAPTER TEN

*It ain't so much the things we don't know that get us into trouble. It's the things we know that ain't so.*
Artemus Ward

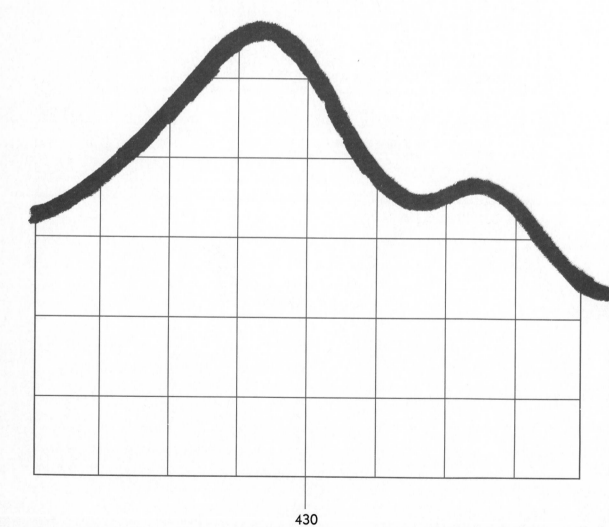

# MULTIPLE REGRESSION: CROSS-SECTION AND TIME-SERIES ANALYSIS

# 10.1 INTRODUCTION

In the last chapter we studied the process of using a single independent variable to predict the value of a dependent variable. In most real-world situations more than one independent variable is used to predict the dependent variable. For example:

■ The treasurer of a major daily newspaper is trying to improve the methods used for cash forecasting. Because much of the variability in cash flows occurs as a result of varying subscription levels from month to month, the treasurer uses the following independent variables in an attempt to forecast subscriptions: advertising expenditures, local population, the price of a subscription, and the local median income.

■ In a long-range forecast for the brewing industry, the consumption of beer (per adult) in a given state was predicted on the basis of the price of beer and the per capita income in the state.

■ The compensation received by corporate executives has been estimated using the independent variables such as corporate profits, corporate sales, and years of service.

■ The enrollment at institutions of higher learning has been predicted by using a variety of independent variables, including tuition costs, number of eligible students, and economic conditions (e.g., unemployment rate, median income, and the rate of inflation).

In this chapter you will learn how to set up and interpret the output of computer regression programs when more than one independent variable is used to predict or forecast the dependent variable. By the end of this chapter you will be able to build multiple regression models (specify a hypothetical relationship between a dependent variable and several independent variables), estimate these models and test hypotheses about the parameters of the specified model. In addition, you will be able to describe possible shortcomings in regression results when the analysis is based on either a cross section of data (collected at a point in time) or a time series of data.

Many of the concepts associated with multiple linear regression are direct extensions of the concepts of simple linear regression. To illustrate the similarity between simple and multiple regression, the first three sections of this chapter present a multiple regression case, with a brief accompanying description of the major concepts. These concepts are covered in more detail in subsequent sections.

## Forecasting for Hosply, Inc.

You are a marketing research analyst for Hosply, Inc., which sells high-quality hospital supplies throughout the United States. The firm is considering opening a retail outlet in Indianapolis to serve central Indiana. Your concern is with forecasting sales in the Indianapolis area using sales data from the 20 retail outlets Hosply has in comparable cities throughout the United States. You also have data on three other variables that may be related to sales—the dollar value of advertising (abbreviated ADVERT), the number of hospitals in the area served by the outlet (NUMBR), and the number of competing firms in the area (COMP). The 20 observations for these variables are displayed in Table 10.1. In the Indianapolis area, there are nine hospitals and four competing firms, and the amount to be spent on advertising has been initially set at $14,500. Since the advertising budget is the only value under your control, you are particularly interested in its relationship to predicted sales.

# 10.2 Inspecting the Data

As in simple linear regression, the first step in multiple regression is to make sure that your data are adequate for regression analysis. This requires an understanding of the units in which each variable is measured, a check that all variables have a sufficient number of observations, and a check that predictions with a sample linear regression are meaningful.

In Table 10.1, the first column identifies each of the 20 outlets. In the second column sales are reported in $1000 units. The first entry, 321, represents the $321,000 in sales of the first outlet last year. This outlet spent

| Table 10.1 | Data for 20 Outlets of Hosply, Inc. | | | |
|---|---|---|---|---|
| Outlet Number | SALES (in Thousands of Dollars) | ADVERT (in Hundreds of Dollars) | NUMBR (No. of Hospitals in the Area) | COMP (No. of Competitors in the Area) |
| 1 | 321 | 125 | 7 | 5 |
| 2 | 412 | 144 | 11 | 3 |
| 3 | 295 | 98 | 8 | 6 |
| 4 | 512 | 181 | 10 | 5 |
| 5 | 439 | 137 | 9 | 5 |
| 6 | 193 | 103 | 5 | 6 |
| 7 | 277 | 107 | 8 | 4 |
| 8 | 442 | 129 | 9 | 4 |
| 9 | 602 | 164 | 10 | 3 |
| 10 | 384 | 113 | 11 | 6 |
| 11 | 238 | 139 | 6 | 5 |
| 12 | 563 | 154 | 9 | 4 |
| 13 | 302 | 121 | 9 | 6 |
| 14 | 366 | 149 | 10 | 6 |
| 15 | 486 | 134 | 8 | 3 |
| 16 | 422 | 110 | 7 | 2 |
| 17 | 189 | 115 | 7 | 5 |
| 18 | 505 | 160 | 11 | 3 |
| 19 | 281 | 139 | 9 | 7 |
| 20 | 317 | 142 | 9 | 5 |

$12,500 in advertising last year. Because advertising is measured in hundreds of dollars, only 125 is recorded under the heading ADVERT in the third column. (Dropping zeros makes data entry and data manipulation easier.) The remaining columns indicate that there were seven hospitals in the first outlet's area and five competing firms. Finally, note that each variable has 20 cases, so there are no missing observations.

Although most real-world problems will have more than 20 observations, this number of cases is sufficient to illustrate a multiple regression in which sales will be predicted by the three independent variables (ADVERT, NUMBR, and COMP) and a constant. As long as the number of observations on each independent variable exceeds the number of independent variables plus one, a multiple regression can be run. For this case the condition is met, as $n = 20 > 3 + 1 = 4$.

Just looking at the data in Table 10.1 does not indicate how well sales can be predicted. As with simple regression, the method of least squares is used to formulate the predicting equation, and as before, care must be taken to check for linear relationships in the data.

The first step is to check the data for any atypical observations. For example, suppose one of our outlets had an advertising expenditure of $35,000. This is nearly twice the expense of any other outlet; hence we might decide not to include this particular outlet in our sample (i.e., to throw it out). While such "censoring" of data involves a subjective decision that may differ from person to person, a check of Table 10.1 does not indicate any such inconsistencies. Next we need to make sure that the Indianapolis situation is, in fact, comparable to that of the 20 outlets in our sample. If Indianapolis had only one hospital, for example, we probably would not want to make a sales forecast based on Table 10.1, where the smallest number of hospitals is five.

As with a simple linear regression, we might also consider a visual inspection of a scatter diagram. Unfortunately, when there is more than one independent variable, a *single* diagram is difficult to construct prior to actually estimating the best-fitting sample regression line. One approach is to construct a separate scatter diagram for the dependent variable and each independent variable. While this method is useful, a better one is to use a single scatter diagram relating the dependent variable to the residuals. The process of looking for patterns in the residuals was introduced at the end of Chapter 9 and is continued in Section 10.7.

# 10.3 Least-Squares Multiple Regression Estimation Using a Computer

In multiple regression the letter $m$ represents the number of independent variables. This means that simple linear regression is a special case of multiple regression where $m = 1$. For the Hosply case, $m = 3$, since three independent variables (ADVERT, NUMBR, and COMP) are used to predict sales.

Because the equations for calculating the least-squares estimators in multiple regression involve many computations, computer programs (such as BMD, Minitab, IDA, or SPSS) are used to find the sample regression equation that best fits the data. This process is almost identical to the least-squares method for simple linear regression except that more than one independent variable is used. For multiple regression the method of least squares minimizes the sum of the squared errors around a plane rather than around a

**Table 10.2**

| | | Computer Output for Hosply, Where the Dependent Variable Is Sales ($\hat{y}$) | | |
|---|---|---|---|---|
| VARIABLE | REGRESSION COEFFICIENT | STD. ERROR | T(D.F. = 16) | PROBABILITY OR SIGNIFICANCE |
| ADVERT | 2.0195 | 0.8483 | 2.381 | 0.03005 |
| NUMBR | 24.7174 | 11.0512 | 2.237 | 0.03990 |
| COMP | -41.0554 | 11.5762 | -3.547 | 0.00269 |
| CONSTANT: | 85.4053 | | | |

line. The computer output in Table 10.2 (which is similar to that of many computer regression packages) presents the least-squares regression equation (all of Table 10.2 will be explained shortly).

# 10.4 The Regression Equation

The sample equation for multiple regression has the following form:

**(10.1)**

Sample equation for multiple regression

$$\hat{y} = a + b_1 x_1 + b_2 x_2 + \cdots + b_m x_m$$

In Eq. (10.1), $x_1$, $x_2$, ..., $x_m$ are the $m$ independent variables, and $a$, $b_1$, $b_2$, ..., $b_m$ are the regression coefficients. Note that there are $m + 1$ regression coefficients [one intercept ($a$) and $m$ slopes (the $b$'s)]. As with simple regression, the sample regression coefficients provide estimates of the population regression parameters, where the population regression model takes the following form:

**(10.2)**

Population model for multiple regression

$$y = \alpha + \beta_1 x_1 + \beta_2 x_2 + \cdots + \beta_m x_m + \epsilon$$

In Eq. (10.2), $\alpha$, $\beta_1$, $\beta_2$, . . . and $\beta_m$ are the parameters to be estimated by $a$, $b_1$, $b_2$, . . . and $b_m$. The population error term is $\epsilon$.

The sample regression equation for the Hosply case is:

$$\hat{y} = a + b_1\text{ADVERT} + b_2\text{NUMBR} + b_3\text{COMP}$$

where $\hat{y}$ is predicted sales, and the associated population model is

$$y = \alpha + \beta_1\text{ADVERT} + \beta_2\text{NUMBR} + \beta_3\text{COMP} + \epsilon$$

To begin interpreting the output in Table 10.2, let's obtain the sample regression equation, using the information in the columns titled VARIABLE and REGRESSION COEFFICIENT. The first column lists the independent variables and then the word *constant*. The next column gives the value of each regression coefficient, as well as the value of the constant. Thus the sample regression equation is:

$$\hat{y} = 85.4053 + 2.0195\text{ADVERT} + 24.7174\text{NUMBR} - 41.0554\text{COMP}$$

To predict SALES for Indianapolis we substitute into the preceding equation the given values stated in the case, namely, ADVERT = 145, NUMBR = 9, and COMP = 4.

$$\hat{y} = 85.4053 + 2.0195(145) + 24.7174(9) - 41.0554(4) = 436.468$$

This means that our predicted sales are $436,468, since SALES (i.e., $\hat{y}$) are measured in thousands of dollars.

Each regression coefficient (2.0195, 24.7174, and $-41.0554$) should be interpreted as representing the predicted change in sales resulting from a one-unit change in the respective independent variable, *holding the other variables constant*. For instance, if advertising is increased by $100 (such as increasing ADVERT from 145 to 146), and nothing else changes, then we would predict sales to increase by $2019.50 (because $\hat{y}$ rises by 2.0195 but SALES are measured in thousands of dollars). Similarly, if the number of competitors increases by one (COMP goes from 4 to 5) and nothing else changes, then sales are predicted to *decrease* (because the sign of the coefficient is negative) by $41,055.40

# 10.5 Standard Errors of the Coefficients and *t* Statistics

Moving across the computer printout in Table 10.2 to the column headed STD. ERROR, the next set of values are the standard errors for each regression coefficient. These standard errors are comparable to the value of

$s_b$ determined for simple linear regression. Just as in simple regression, there is a probability distribution representing the possible values for each regression coefficient. The standard error is the standard deviation of this distribution. Thus, from Table 10.2,

Standard error for $\mathtt{ADVERT}$ coefficient $= s_{\mathtt{ADVERT}} = 0.8483$

Standard error for $\mathtt{NUMBR}$ coefficient $= s_{\mathtt{NUMBR}} = 11.0512$

Standard error for $\mathtt{COMP}$ coefficient $= s_{\mathtt{COMP}} = 11.5762$

These standard errors are used to test hypotheses about the population parameters using the same procedures presented in Chapter 9. Estimation of population parameters and hypothesis testing require certain assumptions about the population that are presented in Section 10.7.

Typically, the null hypothesis is that a population slope equals zero, although values other than zero can be tested. To illustrate, consider the slope parameter for $\mathtt{NUMBR}$ and the following hypotheses.

$H_0: \beta_2 = 0$ $\quad$ ($\mathtt{NUMBR}$ is not related to $\mathtt{SALES}$)

$H_A: \beta_2 \neq 0$ $\quad$ ($\mathtt{NUMBR}$ and $\mathtt{SALES}$ are related)

The right-hand value in a hypothesis is denoted by the symbol $\beta_0$. In the example above, where $H_0: \beta_2 = 0$ and $H_A: \beta_2 \neq 0$, the $\beta_0$ value is 0. This notation is used in a $t$ statistic similar to that presented in Chapter 9.

---

Test statistic for testing a regression coefficient

$$ t = \frac{b_i - \beta_0}{\text{standard error of } b_i} $$

(10.3)

where $\beta_0$ is the value of $\beta_i$ specified in $H_0$ and there are $n - m - 1$ degrees of freedom.

---

In Table 10.2, each value in the column titled $\mathtt{T(D.F. = 16)}$ was calculated using Eq. (10.3), with $\beta_0 = 0$ and $n - m - 1 = 20 - 3 - 1 = 16$ d.f. For instance, to test the preceding hypothesis of no linear relationship between $\mathtt{NUMBR}$ and $\mathtt{SALES}$, the calculated $t$ is

$$ t_{\mathtt{NUMBR}} = \frac{b_2 - 0}{\text{standard error for } \mathtt{NUMBR}} = \frac{24.7174}{11.0512} = 2.237 $$

The final column in Table 10.2 presents the computed $p$ value for each coefficient. The $p$ value shown is for a two-sided alternative hypothesis. Thus the probability of getting a $t$ value greater than 2.237 or less than $-2.237$, with 16 d.f., is 0.0399. As in Chapter 9, we test hypotheses by comparing the $p$ value with the probability of making a type I error. For instance, if the probability of making a type I error is initially set at $\alpha = 0.05$, then $H_0$: $\beta_2 = 0$ is rejected and $H_A$: $\beta_2 \neq 0$ is accepted because the $p$ value of 0.0399 is less than the 0.05 type I error level (see Fig. 10.1). As long as the probability of a type I error is greater than 0.0399, $H_0$ is rejected. Thus $b_2 = 24.7174$ is said to be *significantly different from zero at the 0.0399 level.*

In Fig. 10.1, a two-sided alternative was used because it may not be clear before the data collection whether the population slope relating SALES and NUMBR is positive or negative. In the case of SALES and ADVERT, we certainly would predict a positive relationship, for sales generally are not *hurt* by advertising. Hence this alternative hypothesis should be one-sided.

$H_0$: $\beta_1 \leq 0$     (no positive linear relationship)

$H_A$: $\beta_1 > 0$     (a positive relationship)

While some computer programs (such as SPSS, for example) will calculate the $p$ value for a one-sided test, computer programs like Microstat do not. Thus it is essential to check the manual in order to learn whether a one- or two-sided $p$ value is being calculated. In the case of programs giving two-

**Figure 10.1**
A test of $H_0$: $\beta_2 = 0$ versus $H_A$: $\beta_2 \neq 0$.

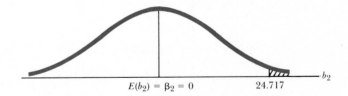

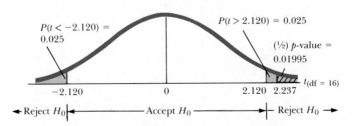

Figure 10.2
A test of $H_0$: $\beta_1 = 0$
versus $H_A$: $\beta_1 > 0$.

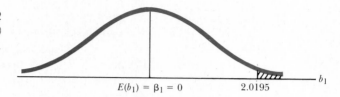

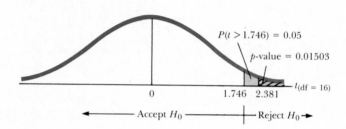

sided probability, such as in Table 10.2, the probability of 0.03005 associated with ADVERT in the last column must be divided by 2 to get a one-sided $p$ value of $(1/2)(0.03005) = 0.01503$. Again using the 0.05 probability of a type I error, the null hypothesis of no linear relationship is rejected and the alternative hypothesis of a positive relationship between ADVERT and SALES is accepted (see Fig. 10.2).

Similar to the test of ADVERT, a one-sided test of COMP results in the rejection of $H_0$: $\beta_3 \geq 0$ (accept $H_A$: $\beta_3 < 0$), since the $p$ value (0.00134) is small. Thus advertising is significant at the 0.01503 level and COMP is significant at the 0.00134 level.

In multiple regression analysis, if some variables are judged not to be significant (i.e., have a large $p$ value), common practice is to remove the insignificant variables from the regression equation and rerun the equation with only the significant variables. The new regression equation will yield coefficient estimates and levels of significance that differ from the estimates in the original regression because fewer independent variables are included. Econometricians refer to the search for regressions that include only significant variables as *data mining* because models built in this way may involve going back to the same sample several times to check various combinations of variables.

# 10.6 Coefficient of Determination, Multiple Correlation, and the Correlation Matrix

To continue our analysis of the Hosply data, we present an expanded version of Table 10.2, including additional computer output. The center section of the computer output in Table 10.3 describes the fit of the regression equation to the sample data. The R SQUARED value (which is also called the **multiple coefficient of determination**) is 0.7401. As in the case of simple regression, this means that 74.01% of the variability in the dependent variable (SALES) is explained by the independent variables. This $R^2$ value is calculated by dividing the regression sum of squares (SSR) by the total sum of squares (SST).

---

Multiple coefficient of determination

(10.4)

$$R^2 = \frac{SSR}{SST}$$

---

The values of SSR and SST are provided in the ANOVA table at the bottom of the computer output in Table 10.3.

SSR = 199829.6083     and     SST = 270020.2000

Thus the value of the coefficient of determination is

$$R^2 = \frac{199829.6083}{270020.2000} = 0.7401$$

The square root of the multiple coefficient of determination is called the *multiple correlation coefficient*, or just **multiple R**. For Hosply,

$$R = \sqrt{0.7401} = 0.8603$$

In Section 10.8, the significance of this multiple $R$ value (which is $p = 0.00006102$) will be determined using the $F$ value of 15.184.

From the computer printout in Table 10.3, SSE is shown as the residual

**Table 10.3**

| | | | | |
|---|---|---|---|---|
| Extended Computer Output for Hosply, Dependent Variable = SALES | | | | |
| VARIABLE | REGRESSION COEFFICIENT | STD. ERROR | T(D.F. 16) | PROBABILITY OR SIGNIFICANCE |
| ADVERT | 2.0195 | 0.8483 | 2.381 | 0.03005 |
| NUMBR | 24.7174 | 11.0512 | 2.237 | 0.03990 |
| COMP | -41.0554 | 11.5762 | -3.547 | 0.00269 |
| CONSTANT: | 85.4053 | | | |

R SQUARED = 0.7401
MULTIPLE R = 0.8603
STD. ERR. OF EST. = 66.2338

ANALYSIS OF VARIANCE TABLE

| SOURCE | SUM OF SQUARES | D.F. | MEAN SQUARE | F RATIO | SIGNIFICANCE |
|---|---|---|---|---|---|
| REGRESSION | 199829.6083 | 3 | 66609.8694 | 15.184 | 6.102E-05 |
| RESIDUAL | 70190.5917 | 16 | 4386.9120 | | |
| TOTAL | 270020.2000 | 19 | | | |

sum of squares = 70190.5917. As with simple linear regression, SSE divided by its degrees of freedom is called the *standard error of the estimate*.

**(10.5)**

Standard error of the estimate

$$s_e = \sqrt{\text{SSE}/(n - m - 1)}$$

For the data in Table 10.3,

$$s_e = \sqrt{70190.5917/(20 - 3 - 1)} = 66.2338$$

The standard error of the estimate indicates the average variability about the regression equation, measured in the same units as the dependent variable.

**WORKED EXAMPLE 10.1**

An economist states that corporate stock prices are related to adjusted earnings (the inverse of the more frequently used composite price/earnings ratio), and the interest rate (Moody's composite Aaa corporate bond rate). To estimate this relationship you use 15 years of data on the Standard and Poor's composite stock price index (stocks) as the dependent variable and use a composite earnings/price ratio (ern/pric) and Moody's interest rate measure (rate) as independent variables. The results are:

DEPENDENT VARIABLE: stocks

| VAR. | REGRESSION COEFFICIENT | STD. ERROR | T(D.F. = 12) | PROB. |
|------|------------------------|------------|--------------|-------|
| ern/pric | -1.7120 | 0.6908 | -2.478 | 0.0145 |
| rate | 5.2826 | 1.5191 | 3.477 | 0.0046 |
| CONSTANT | 70.1189 | | | |

R SQUARED = 0.5490
MULTIPLE R = 0.7409

ANALYSIS OF VARIANCE TABLE

| SOURCE | SUM OF SQUARES |
|--------|----------------|
| REGRESSION | 1327.7450 |
| RESIDUAL | 1090.8730 |
| TOTAL | 2418.6180 |

Use these regression results to predict the value of the Standard and Poor's index for an earnings/price ratio of 8.9 and a bond rate of 8.43. Also indicate the meaning of all the quantities contained in this computer printout.

ANSWER:

The prediction equation is

$$\hat{y} = 70.1189 + 5.2826(\text{rate}) - 1.7120(\text{ern/pric})$$

To predict the Standard and Poor's index, we substitute into this equation the bond rate of 8.43 and the earnings/price ratio of 8.9.

$$\hat{y} = 70.1189 + 5.2826(8.43) - 1.7120(8.9) = 99.414$$

The $\hat{y}$ intercept for this equation is 70.1189. The change in $\hat{y}$ resulting from a one-unit change in rate is 5.2826 (holding the ern/pric fixed). The $-1.712$ coefficient is the change in $\hat{y}$ resulting from a one-unit change in ern/pric (holding the rate fixed). The standard errors of these coefficients are 1.5191 and 0.6908, and their $t$ ratios are 3.477 and $-2.478$, respectively.

If the probability of a type I error is 0.05, the rate coefficient is significantly different from zero ($p$ value = 0.0046 for a two-sided alternative), as is the ern/pric coefficient ($p$ value = 0.0145 for a two-sided alternative). The multiple coefficient of determination of 0.549 indicates that 54.9% of the variability in $y$ (as indicated by SST = 2418.6180) is explained by the two independent variables (as indicated by SSR = 1327.7450). That is, $R^2$ = 0.549 = 1327.745/2418.618.

In some multiple regression problems it may be helpful (in trying to assess an independent variable's contribution to the regression sum of squares, for example) to look at the simple correlation between pairs of variables. The relationship between pairs of variables is given in the **correlation matrix**. This matrix shows the simple correlation coefficients for each variable with itself and the other variables. Table 10.4 shows such a correlation matrix for the Hosply data given in Table 10.1. In this matrix the values along the diagonal (the 1's) represent the correlation of each variable with itself (which must, of course, be perfect). The remaining values give the correlation coefficient ($r$) between pairs of variables.

The first column in Table 10.4 presents the correlation between SALES ($y$) and each of the independent variables. For example, the correlation between SALES and ADVERT is $r$ = 0.67435. This implies that 45.47% [= $(0.67435)^2$] of the variability in SALES is explained by ADVERT. Note that the percent of variability in $y$ explained by the three independent variables sums to more than 100%. This occurs because the so-called independent $x$ variables are typically not independent of one another. Hence two or more such variables may be explaining much of the same variability in $y$. For example, the correlation between ADVERT and NUMBR, $r$ = 0.56254, indicates that these variables are not truly independent; rather, 31.65% [= $(0.56254)^2$] of ADVERT is explained by NUMBR. (It is equally correct to say that 31.65% of NUMBR is explained by ADVERT).

Table 10.4

| | Correlation Matrix for Hosply Data | | | |
|---|---|---|---|---|
| | SALES | ADVERT | NUMBR | COMP |
| SALES | 1.00000 | | | |
| ADVERT | 0.67435 | 1.00000 | | |
| NUMBR | 0.61459 | 0.56254 | 1.00000 | |
| COMP | -0.59420 | -0.22914 | -0.12790 | 1.00000 |

When two or more $x$ variables are *highly* related to one another, a problem of **multicollinearity** is said to exist. Assessing the consequences of multicollinearity involves advanced concepts beyond the scope of this book. We close this discussion about correlation by mentioning that the least-squares method breaks down completely if two (or more) of the independent variables are *perfectly* related to one another. In this case, a common practice is to remove one of the two offending variables.

## Exercises

**10.1** Use the following equation to answer parts (a) through (d).

$$\hat{y} = -1.67 + 2.46x_1 - 5.48x_2$$

a) What is the meaning of the numbers $-1.67$, $2.46$, and $-5.48$?
b) Graph the relationship between $\hat{y}$ and $x_1$ for $x_2 = 10$.
c) Graph the relationship between $\hat{y}$ and $x_1$ for $x_2 = 20$.
d) What is the difference between the lines you graphed in parts (b) and (c)?

**10.2** How can you determine if a computer program is calculating $p$ values (or significance levels) on the basis of a one- or a two-sided alternative hypothesis?

**10.3** Use the following regression results to answer questions (a) through (f).

DEPENDENT VARIABLE: y

| VAR. | REGRESSION COEFFICIENT | STD. ERROR | T(D.F. = 16) | PROB. |
|------|------|------|------|------|
| X₁ | -1.6374 | 4.3743 | -.374 | 0.71307 |
| X₂ | 26.6923 | 19.5192 | 1.367 | 0.19037 |
| X₃ | -423.9598 | 293.3541 | -1.445 | 0.16770 |
| CONSTANT | 11562.7524 | | | |

STD. ERROR OF EST. = 1327.7748
R SQUARED = 0.2805
MULTIPLE R = 0.5296

## ANALYSIS OF VARIANCE TABLE

| SOURCE | SUM OF SQUARES | D.F. | MEAN SQUARE | F RATIO | PROB. |
|--------|----------------|------|-------------|---------|-------|
| REGRESSION | 10996949.7400 | 3 | 3665649.9130 | 2.079 | 0.1433 |
| TOTAL | 39204724.9700 | 19 | | | |

a) What is the $y$ intercept and what does it indicate?

b) Describe the effect of $x_2$ on $\hat{y}$.

c) How was the $t$ statistic for $b_2$ calculated? What does it indicate?

d) How was the coefficient of multiple determination calculated? What does it indicate?

e) Determine the SSE. What does SSE measure?

f) At what level is $x_1$ significant? What does this imply?

REL  **10.4**  Use a computer program and the following data on the selling price, floor space, and number of rooms to predict the selling price of a house with nine rooms and 2800 square feet of floor space.

Selling price (in thousands of dollars): 105 130 189 99 150 124 119 100
Floor space (in thousands of sq. ft.):  2.7 2.9 3.4 2.1 2.5 2.7 2.9 2.8
Number of rooms:               8  11  14  7  8  9  9  7

REL  **10.5**  Test the null hypothesis $H_0$: $\beta \le 0$ versus the alternative $H_A$: $\beta > 0$ for each independent variable in Exercise 10.4 at a 0.05 type I error level. Are both variables significant? What is the meaning of significance in this case?

REL  **10.6**  In Exercise 10.4 a multiple regression equation was used to predict the selling price of a house, while in Worked Example 9.1 a simple regression was used to predict the selling price. What is the advantage of multiple regression over simple regression?

ECN  **10.7**  An economist states that wages should be inversely related to the rate of unemployment and should be positively related to prices. At the 0.10 type I error level, test these claims using the following data in a multiple regression specification. Report a $p$ value (the significance) for each coefficient.

Average dollar wage: 266 255 235 220 207 189 175 163 154 145 136 127 120
Unemployment rate: 9.7 7.6 7.1 5.8 6.1 7.1 7.7 8.5 5.6 4.9 5.6 5.9 4.9
Price index:    289 272 246 217 195 181 170 161 147 133 125 121 116

ECN  **10.8**  In Exercise 10.7 wages were stated to be positively related to prices and negatively related to the unemployment rate. What is the difference between testing these relationships by running two simple regressions (wages on prices and then wages on the rate of unemployment) and using a multiple regression of wages on both prices and the unemployment rate?

FIN   **10.9**   The following output is the result of a regression analysis using 11 companies. The dependent variable is stock price (1983) and the independent variables are (1) return on common equity (return) and (2) 12 months' earnings per share. Write the least-squares regression equation, indicating the significance of each variable.

## REGRESSION ANALYSIS

DEPENDENT VARIABLE: price

| VAR. | REGRESSION COEFFICIENT | STD. ERROR | T(D.F. = 8) | PROB. |
|------|------------------------|------------|-------------|-------|
| return | 0.2151 | 0.5628 | 0.382 | 0.71227 |
| earnings | 2.2000 | 2.0185 | 1.090 | 0.30748 |
| CONSTANT | 1.2181 | | | |

STD. ERROR OF EST. = 5.0439
R SQUARED = 0.3459
MULTIPLE R = 0.5882

## ANALYSIS OF VARIANCE TABLE

| SOURCE | SUM OF SQUARES | D.F. | MEAN SQUARE | F RATIO | PROB. |
|--------|----------------|------|-------------|---------|-------|
| REGRESSION | 107.6398 | 2 | 53.8199 | 2.115 | .1830 |
| RESIDUAL | 203.5292 | 8 | 25.4412 | | |
| TOTAL | 311.1691 | 10 | | | |

**10.10**  The following regression output used these data.

| $y$: | 1 | 3 | 6 | 9 | 11 | 12 |
|------|---|---|---|---|----|----|
| $x$: | 2 | 3 | 4 | 8 | 9 | 11 |
| $z$: | 5 | 9 | 8 | 4 | 3 | 0.5 |

a) Write the sample regression equation in slope intercept form.

b) Are both $x$ and $z$ significant at typical type I error levels? Explain.

c) Determine the predicted $y$ value if $x = 6$ and $z = 7$.

d) Use the least-squares regression line to find the residual for each set of the sample data. Verify the value of SSE given in the ANOVA table. Do the residuals sum to zero?

e) Is the least-squares fit a good one? Explain why or why not, using an appropriate measure of overall fit.

f) What proportion of the variable $z$ is explained by the variable $x$? What proportion of $y$ is explained by $x$?

## REGRESSION ANALYSIS

| INDEX | NAME | MEAN | STD. DEV. |
|---|---|---|---|
| 1 | x | 6.1667 | 3.6560 |
| 2 | z | 4.9167 | 3.1689 |
| DEP. VAR.: | y | 7.0000 | 4.4272 |

DEPENDENT VARIABLE: y

| VAR. | REGRESSION COEFFICIENT | STD. ERROR | T(D.F. = 3) | PROB. |
|---|---|---|---|---|
| x | 1.4564 | 0.2013 | 7.236 | 0.00544 |
| z | 0.3787 | 0.2322 | 1.631 | 0.20146 |
| CONSTANT | -3.8428 | | | |

STD. ERROR OF EST. = 0.9034
R SQUARED = 0.9750
MULTIPLE R = 0.9874

## ANALYSIS OF VARIANCE TABLE

| SOURCE | SUM OF SQUARES | D.F. | MEAN SQUARE | F RATIO | PROB. |
|---|---|---|---|---|---|
| REGRESSION | 95.5516 | 2 | 47.7758 | 58.540 | 3.949E-03 |
| RESIDUAL | 2.4484 | 3 | 0.8161 | | |
| TOTAL | 98.0000 | 5 | | | |

## CORRELATION MATRIX

| | y | x | z |
|---|---|---|---|
| y | 1.00000 | | |
| x | 0.97615 | 1.00000 | |
| z | -0.73419 | -0.83582 | 1.00000 |

FIN **10.11** Use the Office Equipment, Computer companies data in Appendix A.1 to find a regression line in which the price/earnings ratio is predicted by sales and profits. How well does your regression line for the 42 companies fit the data?

ECN **10.12** The following correlation matrix is for the data in Exercise 10.7. What is the correlation between the two independent variables? Interpret this value. Which independent variable is more highly correlated with the dependent variable?

|  | WAGE | RATE | INDEX |
|---|---|---|---|
| WAGE | 1.00000 | | |
| RATE | 0.65459 | 1.00000 | |
| INDEX | 0.99242 | 0.68977 | 1.00000 |

REL **10.13** The following correlation matrix is for the data in Exercise 10.4. Explain each value in this matrix.

|  | PRICE | SPACE | ROOMS |
|---|---|---|---|
| PRICE | 1.00000 | | |
| SPACE | 0.65945 | 1.00000 | |
| ROOMS | 0.84861 | 0.82665 | 1.00000 |

# 10.7 Assumptions About the Population

Recall that we made four assumptions about the population for simple linear regression. These assumptions, modified for multiple regression, are as follows.

**ASSUMPTION 1** The population relationship between the x values and y is the linear equation $y = \alpha + \beta_1 x_1 + \beta_2 x_2 + \cdots + \beta_m x_m + \epsilon$ where the expected value of $\epsilon$ is zero.

This assumption implies that for the population, the dependent variable $y$ cannot have a nonlinear relationship with any of the independent variables $x_1, x_2, x_3, \ldots, x_m$ and the expected value of $y$, for given values of the x's, is $\alpha + \beta_1 x_1 + \beta_2 x_2 + \cdots + \beta_m x_m$. One way to check for linearity is to construct $m$ scatter diagrams, between $y$ and $x_1$, between $y$ and $x_2$, and so on. A better method is to plot $y$ versus the residuals (as described in Chapter 9), as shown in Fig. 10.3.

Figure 10.3
Looking for patterns
in residuals.

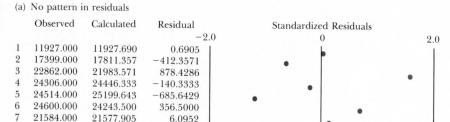

(a) No pattern in residuals

| | Observed | Calculated | Residual | Standardized Residuals |
|---|---|---|---|---|
| 1 | 11927.000 | 11927.690 | 0.6905 | |
| 2 | 17399.000 | 17811.357 | −412.3571 | |
| 3 | 22862.000 | 21983.571 | 878.4286 | |
| 4 | 24306.000 | 24446.333 | −140.3333 | |
| 5 | 24514.000 | 25199.643 | −685.6429 | |
| 6 | 24600.000 | 24243.500 | 356.5000 | |
| 7 | 21584.000 | 21577.905 | 6.0952 | |

(b) Residuals suggest that $y$ is not a linear function of the $x$'s.

| | Observed | Calculated | Residual | Standardized Residuals |
|---|---|---|---|---|
| 1 | 11927.000 | 16203.321 | −4276.3214 | |
| 2 | 17399.000 | 17811.357 | −412.3571 | |
| 3 | 22862.000 | 19419.393 | 3442.6071 | |
| 4 | 24306.000 | 21027.429 | 3278.5714 | |
| 5 | 24514.000 | 22635.464 | 1878.5357 | |
| 6 | 24600.000 | 24243.500 | 356.5000 | |
| 7 | 21584.000 | 25851.536 | −4267.5357 | |

If there is no pattern to the residuals, then the assumption of a linear relationship between $y$ and the $x$'s may be justified. Figure 10.3(a) illustrates residuals with no pattern, while Fig. 10.3(b) illustrates a pattern.

---

**ASSUMPTION 2**   **The variance of $\epsilon$ is constant.**

Assumption 2 says that the variance of the distribution of errors (around the population regression equation) is the same for all possible sets of $x$ values. In other words, there cannot be a tendency to get only small errors about the population regression equation for one set of $x$ values and large errors for another set of $x$ values. Since the distribution of $\epsilon$ is never actually observed, a plot of the sample regression residuals may be used to get an indication of nonconstant variance. For example, in Fig. 10.4, the variability in the residuals appears to increase with the predicted $y$ values.

---

Errors that violate assumption 2 are said to be **heteroscedastic**. If the errors do have a constant variance, they are **homoscedastic**. Heteroscedasticity can be a problem in cross-sectional analysis, where data are collected on subjects at a point in time, or in time-series analysis, where data are collected over time.

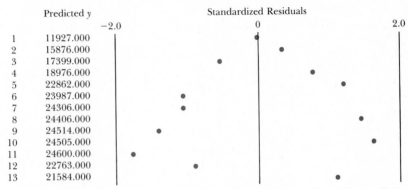

**Figure 10.4**
Heteroscedastic errors.

| | Predicted $y$ |
|---|---|
| 1 | 11927.000 |
| 2 | 15876.000 |
| 3 | 17399.000 |
| 4 | 18976.000 |
| 5 | 22862.000 |
| 6 | 23987.000 |
| 7 | 24306.000 |
| 8 | 24406.000 |
| 9 | 24514.000 |
| 10 | 24505.000 |
| 11 | 24600.000 |
| 12 | 22763.000 |
| 13 | 21584.000 |

Note: As the predicted $y$-values rise, the residuals from the sample regression tend to get larger.

---

**ASSUMPTION 3**  **The population errors cannot be related to any of the $x$ variables or to themselves.**

This assumption means that the $x$ variables and $\epsilon$ must be unrelated. As in simple regression, the error term $\epsilon$ is the unknown random element in regression analysis, which means that it must be unpredictable. A violation of this assumption may be caused by omitting variables that should have been included as independent variables. When data are collected over time, this assumption may also be violated because errors in one period may be associated with errors in the next period (called **serial correlation**).

---

**ASSUMPTION 4**  **For any set of $x$ values, the errors must be normally distributed with a mean of zero (as in Assumption 1) and a constant variance (as in Assumption 2).**

Normality of $\epsilon$ implies that the distribution of $y$ values around the expected value of $y$ ($\alpha + \beta_1 x_1 + \beta_2 x_2 + \cdots + \beta_m x_m$) is also normal.

When the first three multiple regression assumptions hold, it can be shown that the expected values of the least-squares point estimators ($b_1$, $b_2$,

..., $b_m$) are the respective parameters in the population model ($\beta_1$, $\beta_2$, ..., $\beta_m$). Although regression coefficients and standard errors can be calculated even when these assumptions are false, it is the correctness of all four assumptions that determines our ability to make inferences and perform hypothesis tests about the parameters of the population regression model.

The newspaper article mentioned in Worked Example 10.1 stated that daily stock prices tend to fall as interest rates rise because investors shift out of stocks and into bonds to get higher yields. Similarly, stock prices tend to fall as corporate earnings fall. Your regression results in Worked Example 10.1 suggested the opposite relationships. Is the newspaper article in error?

ANSWER:

Whenever regression results are counterintuitive, the checking of data and assumptions is critical. A check of the data in Worked Example 10.1 shows that these data were based on average yearly observations, while the newspaper article referred to daily changes. While interest rates may be negatively correlated with movements in the stock market on a daily basis, over a longer period of time they may be positively related.

Before putting much faith in any regression result a check should be made of the least-squares assumptions. One starting point is to look at the residuals, as shown in Fig. 10.5. There is a possible pattern to these residuals as negative and positive values tend to occur in groups and follow each other in a serpentine pattern over time.

**Figure 10.5**
Regression residuals from Worked Example 10.1.

| | Observed | Calculated | Residual | Standardized Residuals |
|---|---|---|---|---|
| | | | | −2.0 ... 0 ... 2.0 |
| 1 | 119.710 | 122.422 | −2.7116 | |
| 2 | 128.050 | 124.497 | 3.5526 | |
| 3 | 118.780 | 111.519 | 7.2611 | |
| 4 | 103.010 | 97.947 | 5.0634 | |
| 5 | 96.020 | 95.640 | 0.3796 | |
| 6 | 98.200 | 94.013 | 4.1873 | |
| 7 | 102.010 | 99.414 | 2.5958 | |
| 8 | 86.160 | 101.099 | −14.9392 | |
| 9 | 82.850 | 95.549 | −12.6985 | |
| 10 | 107.430 | 97.232 | 10.1982 | |
| 11 | 109.200 | 98.790 | 10.4097 | |
| 12 | 98.290 | 99.895 | −1.6052 | |
| 13 | 83.220 | 101.548 | −18.3284 | |
| 14 | 97.840 | 96.846 | 0.9935 | |
| 15 | 98.700 | 93.058 | 5.6418 | |

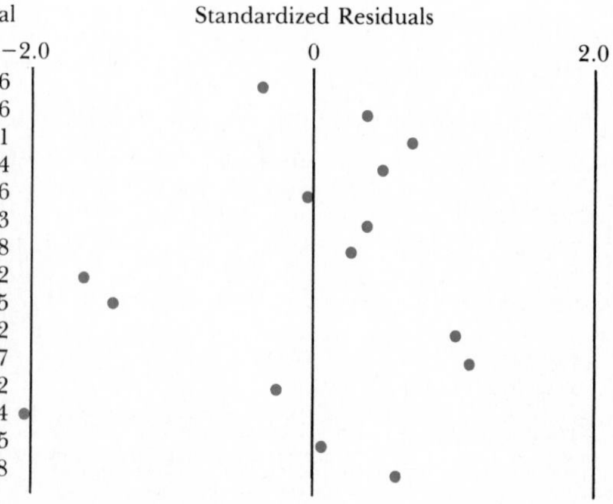

Variability in the residuals in Fig. 10.5 may be related to the magnitude of the predicted or calculated stock index. For instance, the two highest calculated $y$ values (1 and 2) have relatively small residuals, while the two lowest calculated $y$ values (6 and 15) have somewhat larger residuals. Hence, heteroscedasticity may be a problem. Because of these possible violations of the least-squares assumptions, we need to be very cautious when interpreting the test results. This implies that the newspaper article cannot be discredited with this regression.

# 10.8 A Test of the Overall Fit of the Regression Equation

The analysis of variance (ANOVA) table presented in a regression analysis provides useful information for testing hypotheses about the overall fit of the regression equation. In multiple regression, as in simple regression,

Sum of squares total = sum of squares error + sum of squares regression
SST       =       SSE     +       SSR

This relationship says that the total variability in any regression problem is composed of two parts: (1) SSR, which is that part explained by the regression line (i.e., by the independent variables), and (2) SSE, which is that part unexplained by the regression equation (i.e., the residuals or errors). In a regression output the ANOVA table gives the values of SST, SSR, and SSE (see Table 10.5).

If there is no relationship between $y$ and any of the $x$ values in the *sample*, then SSE would equal SST and all the $b$'s would be zero. If there is no relationship between $y$ and any of the $x$ values in the *population*, then all the $\beta$'s must equal zero. To test for no linear relationship in the population, the

**Table 10.5**

| ANOVA Table for the Hosply Data in Table 10.2 | | | | | |
|---|---|---|---|---|---|
| SOURCE | SUM OF SQUARES | D.F. | MEAN SQUARE | F RATIO | SIGNIFICANCE |
| REGRESSION | 199829.6083 | 3 | 66609.8694 | 15.184 | 6.102E-05 |
| RESIDUAL | 70190.5917 | 16 | 4386.9120 | | |
| TOTAL | 270020.2000 | 19 | | | |

null and alternative hypotheses are:

$$H_0: \beta_1 = \beta_2 = \cdots = \beta_m = 0 \qquad \text{(there is no population linear}$$
relationship between $y$ and the $x$'s.)

$$H_A: \text{at least one } \beta_i \neq 0 \qquad \text{(there is some linear regression)}.$$

These hypotheses are tested using a statistic that is based on the $F$ distribution. The appropriate test statistic is the $F$ ratio given in Eq. (10.6).

---

The $F$ ratio to test $H_0: \beta_1 = \beta_2 = \cdots = \beta_m = 0$

$$(10.6) \qquad F = \frac{SSR/m}{SSE/(n - m - 1)} = \frac{MSR}{MSE}$$

where the degrees of freedom are $m$ (numerator) and $n - m - 1$ (denominator).

---

Note that this test statistic has two separate degrees of freedom, one for the numerator ($m$) and one for the denominator ($n - m - 1$). For the Hosply data in Table 10.5, $m = 3$ and $n = 20$, so there are $m = 3$ d.f. in the numerator and $n - m - 1 = 16$ d.f. in the denominator. The $F$ ratio given in Table 10.5 is calculated using Eq. (10.5).

$$F = \frac{199829.6083/3}{70190.5917/16} = \frac{66609.8694}{4386.9120} = 15.184$$

Testing hypotheses with the $F$ statistic follows the same general pattern as the tests in Chapter 8. Large $F$ values lead to the rejection of the null hypothesis, and hence to the conclusion that the independent variables (taken as a group) are useful in estimating the dependent variable. As before, $p$ values are used to indicate the probability of the observed sample result.

Most computer programs provide the appropriate $p$ value under the heading SIGNIFICANCE or PROBABILITY in the ANOVA section of the printout. Thus the $p$ value shown in Table 10.5 for $F = 15.184$ is 0.00006. This indicates that only 6 out of 100,000 times, on average, will we get an $F$ value more extreme than 15.184 if $H_0$ is true.

As before, our procedure for testing hypotheses is to compare the probability of a type I error with the $p$ value. A $p$ value of 0.00006 is very small ($F$ is very large). Thus $H_0$ is rejected at any reasonable type I error level. That is, for any type I error level higher than 0.00006, the null hypothesis of no linear regression between sales and the three independent variables is rejected. So our regression is said to be significant for explaining sales at the 0.00006 level.

**10.14** Why are both $t$ tests and $F$ tests used in the same multiple regression problem?

**10.15** For each of the following three residual plots, indicate a possible violation of a least-squares assumption.

(a) Regression based on sales collected at a point in time.

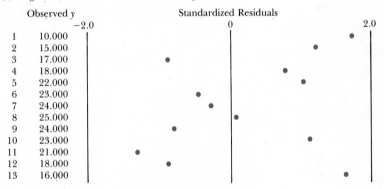

(b) Regression based on sales data collected over time.

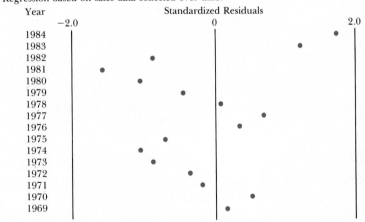

(c) From a regression of earnings on ten year intervals of age.

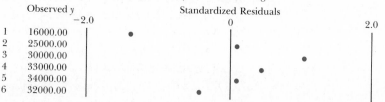

| | Observed y | | Standardized Residuals | | |
|---|---|---|---|---|---|
| | | −2.0 | 0 | | 2.0 |
| 1 | 16000.00 | | | | |
| 2 | 25000.00 | | | | |
| 3 | 30000.00 | | | | |
| 4 | 33000.00 | | | | |
| 5 | 34000.00 | | | | |
| 6 | 32000.00 | | | | |

ECN **10.16** The output of a certain coal mining operation depends on two independent variables, the amount of labor (number of workers) and the amount of physical equipment, measured in horsepower. The output is measured in tons/day. The regression based on these variables is as follows:

## REGRESSION ANALYSIS

| INDEX | NAME | MEAN | STD. DEV. |
|---|---|---|---|
| 1 | labor | 4.5000 | 2.3155 |
| 2 | horsepr | 3500.0000 | 1725.8979 |
| DEP. VAR.: | output | 68.2917 | 37.8108 |

DEPENDENT VARIABLE: output

| VAR. | REGRESSION COEFFICIENT | STD. ERROR | T(D.F. = 45) | PROB. |
|---|---|---|---|---|
| labor | 12.7857 | 0.9426 | 13.564 | 0.00000 |
| horsepr | 0.0107 | 0.0013 | 8.432 | 0.00000 |
| CONSTANT | −26.5690 | | | |

STD. ERROR OF EST. = 14.9641
R SQUARED = 0.8500
MULTIPLE R = 0.9220

## ANALYSIS OF VARIANCE TABLE

| SOURCE | SUM OF SQUARES | D.F. | MEAN SQUARE | F RATIO | PROB. |
|---|---|---|---|---|---|
| REGRESSION | 57117.3500 | 2 | 28558.6750 | 127.538 | 0.000E+00 |
| RESIDUAL | 10076.5666 | 45 | 223.9237 | | |
| TOTAL | 67193.9166 | 47 | | | |

a) Write the least-squares regression line. Use this line to predict output for labor $= 5$, horsepower $= 4000$.

b) Test the significance of both independent variables, and the overall relationship, using a 0.10 type I error level.

c) What proportion of the variability in output is explained by the independent variables? What is the average variability about the regression equation?

**10.17** A regression analysis has two independent variables $(x_1, x_2)$.

a) What does it mean if $x_1$ and $x_2$ are independent of one another? In that case, what is the correlation between them?

b) Is saying that $x_1$ and $x_2$ are independent variables the same as saying that they are independent of one another? Explain.

MKT **10.18** A business executive has established a least-squares line relating sales to advertising and another least-squares line relating sales to price. In order to determine a multiple regression line relating sales to both advertising and price, the executive forms a single equation by adding the two intercepts and using the two simple linear regression slopes. Comment on this approach.

# 10.9 Dummy Variables

Recall that Chapter 9 began with the problem of predicting the gas mileage (MPG) of a new car, the Tiger, based on its weight. As the systems analyst for this project, you were pleased to find a strong correlation between MPG and WEIGHT. Now you are concerned because you have learned that some of the drivers in your sample of 10 observations were more experienced than others. Perhaps driver experience affects gas mileage. Fortunately, this concern is relatively easy to handle using dummy variables.

**Dummy variables** are variables added to a regression analysis to divide the data into qualitative parts. In our example, one part is for cars driven by less experienced drivers and the other part is for cars driven by more experienced drivers. We could add other dummy variables to reflect the presence or absence of air conditioning. Another dummy variable could capture differences in cars equipped with radial versus bias ply tires.

**Table 10.6**

| | | | | Using Dummy Variables to Represent Driver Experience | | | | |
|---|---|---|---|---|---|---|---|---|
| GROUP | MPG | WEIGHT | DUMMY | | GROUP | MPG | WEIGHT | DUMMY |
| 1 | 35.0 | 2405 | 0 | | 13 | 42.1 | 2016 | 1 |
| 2 | 36.5 | 2379 | 0 | | 14 | 40.9 | 2098 | 1 |
| 3 | 36.9 | 2310 | 0 | | 15 | 41.2 | 2125 | 1 |
| 4 | 37.1 | 2290 | 0 | | 16 | 39.4 | 2173 | 1 |
| 5 | 38.1 | 2247 | 0 | | 17 | 40.5 | 2155 | 1 |
| 6 | 37.7 | 2184 | 0 | | 18 | 39.8 | 2203 | 1 |
| 7 | 38.2 | 2155 | 0 | | 19 | 39.2 | 2241 | 1 |
| 8 | 38.7 | 2131 | 0 | | 20 | 40.1 | 2220 | 1 |
| 9 | 39.2 | 2075 | 0 | | 21 | 38.3 | 2310 | 1 |
| 10 | 37.9 | 2226 | 0 | | 22 | 38.9 | 2292 | 1 |
| 11 | 36.1 | 2363 | 0 | | 23 | 37.1 | 2363 | 1 |
| 12 | 34.7 | 2477 | 0 | | 24 | 38.2 | 2344 | 1 |

**Table 10.7**

| | Car Mileage Related to Weight and Driver Experience | | |
|---|---|---|---|
| INDEX | NAME | MEAN | STD. DEV. |
| 1 | WEIGHT | 2240.9167 | 115.2566 |
| 2 | DUMMY | 0.5000 | 0.5108 |
| DEP. VAR.: | MPG | 38.4083 | 1.8692 |

DEPENDENT VARIABLE: MPG

| VAR. | REGRESSION COEFFICIENT | STD. ERROR | T(D.F. = 21) | PROB. |
|---|---|---|---|---|
| WEIGHT | -0.0119 | 7.65542E-04 | -15.542 | 0.00000 |
| DUMMY | 1.7706 | 0.1728 | 10.250 | 0.00000 |
| CONSTANT | 64.1850 | | | |

STD. ERROR OF EST. = 0.4087
R SQUARED = 0.9564
MULTIPLE R = 0.9779

ANALYSIS OF VARIANCE TABLE

| SOURCE | SUM OF SQUARES | D.F. | MEAN SQUARE | F RATIO | PROB. |
|---|---|---|---|---|---|
| REGRESSION | 76.8508 | 2 | 38.4254 | 230.057 | 0.0000 |
| RESIDUAL | 3.5075 | 21 | 0.1670 | | |
| TOTAL | 80.3583 | 23 | | | |

**Table 10.7 (cont.)**

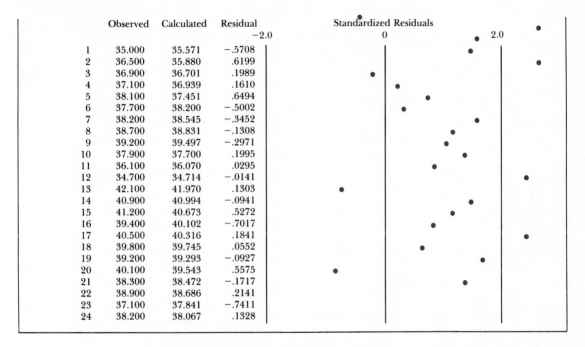

| | Observed | Calculated | Residual |
|---|---|---|---|
| 1 | 35.000 | 35.571 | −.5708 |
| 2 | 36.500 | 35.880 | .6199 |
| 3 | 36.900 | 36.701 | .1989 |
| 4 | 37.100 | 36.939 | .1610 |
| 5 | 38.100 | 37.451 | .6494 |
| 6 | 37.700 | 38.200 | −.5002 |
| 7 | 38.200 | 38.545 | −.3452 |
| 8 | 38.700 | 38.831 | −.1308 |
| 9 | 39.200 | 39.497 | −.2971 |
| 10 | 37.900 | 37.700 | .1995 |
| 11 | 36.100 | 36.070 | .0295 |
| 12 | 34.700 | 34.714 | −.0141 |
| 13 | 42.100 | 41.970 | .1303 |
| 14 | 40.900 | 40.994 | −.0941 |
| 15 | 41.200 | 40.673 | .5272 |
| 16 | 39.400 | 40.102 | −.7017 |
| 17 | 40.500 | 40.316 | .1841 |
| 18 | 39.800 | 39.745 | .0552 |
| 19 | 39.200 | 39.293 | −.0927 |
| 20 | 40.100 | 39.543 | .5575 |
| 21 | 38.300 | 38.472 | −.1717 |
| 22 | 38.900 | 38.686 | .2141 |
| 23 | 37.100 | 37.841 | −.7411 |
| 24 | 38.200 | 38.067 | .1328 |

Standardized Residuals: −2.0, 0, 2.0

By definition, dummy variables must have either a value of 0 or a value of 1. For Tiger cars, we could let the dummy variable = 0 for cars driven by less experienced drivers and 1 for drivers with more experience. (Which group is defined as 0 or a 1 is arbitrary.) A new sample with 24 observations is collected and reported in Table 10.6.

Notice in Table 10.6 that the first 12 cars had the less experienced drivers (since their dummy variable equals 0). The remaining 12 cars had more experienced drivers (their dummy equals 1). The resulting least-squares regression analysis, with two independent variables (weight and the dummy variable), and the dependent variable MPG is shown in Table 10.7.

From the middle part of this computer output, the least-squares regression equation is found to be:

PREDICTED MPG = 64.1850 − 0.0119(WEIGHT) + 1.7706(DUMMY)

The independent variables WEIGHT and DUMMY explain 95.64% of the variability in MPG (given by $R^2$). The $F$ ratio in the ANOVA table ($F =$

230.057) and the associated $p$ value of 0.0000 indicate that the null hypothesis of no linear regression can easily be rejected. In addition, the residuals appear to be randomly distributed with a constant variance. (Note: although some of the positively signed residuals appear to be grouped together, this grouping has no meaning because the order of the cars, and hence of the residuals, is arbitrary; cars can be placed in any order. Serial correlation is a problem typically with data collected over time. For data collected at a point in time, the major concern is that the residuals have a constant variance.)

The question of whether or not the dummy variable is related to gas mileage in the Tiger population is answered by looking at the $p$ value for the dummy variable coefficient. This $p$ value, shown next to the $t$ ratio of 10.25, is 0.0000. Such a low probability indicates that the null hypothesis $H_0$: $\beta_{DUMMY} = 0$ should be rejected for any reasonable type I error level. This means that we have a lot of confidence that the level of driving experience represented by the dummy variable is related to gas mileage in the population.

Remember that the value of the dummy variable equals either 0 or 1. Substituting 0 for the dummy variable into the regression equation yields the regression line for less experienced drivers.

If DUMMY = 0, then

$$\text{MPG EST.} = 64.1850 - 0.0119(\text{WEIGHT}) + 1.7706(0)$$
$$= 64.1850 - 0.0119(\text{WEIGHT})$$

Substituting 1 for the dummy variable yields the regression line for more experienced drivers.

If DUMMY = 1, then

$$\text{MPG EST.} = 64.1850 - 0.0119(\text{WEIGHT}) + 1.7706(1)$$
$$= 65.9556 - 0.0119(\text{WEIGHT})$$

These two regression lines have the same slope ($-0.0119$) but different intercepts (64.1850 versus 65.9556). The difference in intercepts reflects the difference in gas mileage predicted for less experienced versus more experienced drivers. These two equations are graphed in Fig. 10.6. (Note that the two lines are parallel.)

Suppose we want to determine the MPG for a Tiger car weighing 2100 pounds for both types of drivers. Figure 10.6 can be used for this purpose by finding the two MPG values corresponding to WEIGHT = 2100. A more accurate way is to substitute WEIGHT = 2100 in the two regression equations. The result is a prediction of 39.195 MPG for less experienced drivers and 40.966 MPG for more experienced drivers.

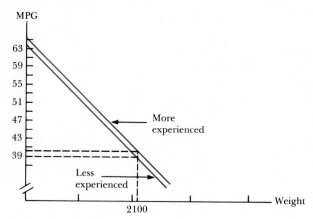

**Figure 10.6**
The effect of experience on gas mileage for cars of different weight.

---

**WORKED EXAMPLE 10.3**

Professional employees beginning to work for a large company are given a 3-day training program. As the educational director for this corporation, you have measured the skill level of each new employee before the training program (a pretest) as well as after it (a posttest). You want to use these data to assess the importance of the skills each person brings to the new job. A second objective is to determine if a new training program results in a different skill level than the traditional program.

If a trainee participated in the new program, dummy = 1. For the old program, dummy = 0. Following are the regression results for a sample of 16 trainees (8 from each type of program). Is there a relationship between the dependent variable posttest score and the independent variables pretest score and type of program? How strongly is the posttest score related to the pretest score? Is the new training program better than the old one?

```
DEPENDENT VARIABLE: post
               REGRESSION
VAR.           COEFFICIENT    STD. ERROR    T(D.F. = 13)    PROB.
pre            1.5151         0.1103        13.733          0.00000
dum            1.6250         0.8103         2.006          0.06618
CONSTANT      -2.9718

STD. ERROR OF EST. = 1.6205
        R SQUARED = 0.9368
      MULTIPLE R = 0.9679
```

### ANALYSIS OF VARIANCE TABLE

| SOURCE | SUM OF SQUARES | D.F. | MEAN SQUARE | F RATIO | PROB. |
|---|---|---|---|---|---|
| REGRESSION | 505.7990 | 2 | 252.8995 | 96.304 | 1.610E-08 |
| RESIDUAL | 34.1385 | 13 | 2.6260 | | |
| TOTAL | 539.9375 | 15 | | | |

**ANSWER:**

In this problem there are three sets of hypotheses:

1. To test for no linear regression.

   $H_0$: $\beta_{dum} = \beta_{pre} = 0$      versus      $H_A$: at least one $\beta_i \neq 0$

2. To test if pretest and posttest scores are not related.

   $H_0$: $\beta_{pre} = 0$      versus      $H_A$: $\beta_{pre} \neq 0$

3. The null hypothesis that the program (old versus new) is not related to skill level versus the alternative that the new program is better.

   $H_0$: $\beta_{dum} = 0$      versus   $H_A$: $\beta_{dum} > 0$

In the following tests of these three hypotheses, we assume that the least-squares assumptions are true.

The computer results indicate a significant overall relationship (since the $F$ ratio is large and the $p$ value is low, $p = 0.0000000161$), so the first null hypothesis is rejected. The second null hypothesis is also rejected ($t = 13.733$ and $p = 0.0000$), and we conclude that the pretest and posttest scores are related.

The $t$ ratio 2.006 and PROB $= 0.0668$ can be used for the third hypothesis (the new program versus the old one). This computer program, however, reports two-tailed probabilities. Since the third alternative hypothesis is one-sided, the significance level indicated in the PROB column must be divided in half. Thus the $p$ value is $p = \frac{1}{2}(0.06618) = 0.03309$. If the probability of a type I error is 0.05, then $H_0$ should be rejected, and we would conclude that the new program is better than the old one.

# 10.10 Time Series Analysis

In the Hosply and Tiger examples we used observations collected in different cities and on different cars. The order in which observations were collected or arranged was not important because they had no time dimension. When data are collected at regular time intervals, both the magnitude and the order of the observations take on meaning. For example, knowledge of the magnitude of the Consumer Price Index (CPI) is required to adjust wages to reflect inflation. The pattern of changes in the CPI over time is also important in forecasting future changes in prices.

Data that accumulate over regular time intervals are called a **time series**. For example, the cost data in the second column of Table 10.8 were collected and recorded at the end of each quarter from 1980 to 1985. Time series for costs, prices, inventories, and interest rates are important in business because they can be used to extract information regarding variations that might be time related.

A time series can be composed of four different components—trend, seasonal variations, cyclical variations, and purely random variations. **Trend** is the long-run movement of the time series, such as the steady rise in starting

**Table 10.8**

| | | Time Series of Cost Data | | | | | |
|---|---|---|---|---|---|---|---|
| Year and Quarter | | Cost (in Thousands of Dollars) | Trend Variable | Year and Quarter | | Cost (in Thousands of Dollars) | Trend Variable |
| 1980 | I | 37.50 | 1.00 | 1983 | I | 61.10 | 13.00 |
| | II | 34.30 | 2.00 | | II | 57.90 | 14.00 |
| | III | 38.70 | 3.00 | | III | 64.20 | 15.00 |
| | IV | 38.90 | 4.00 | | IV | 62.50 | 16.00 |
| 1981 | I | 42.80 | 5.00 | 1984 | I | 67.30 | 17.00 |
| | II | 41.50 | 6.00 | | II | 67.00 | 18.00 |
| | III | 46.90 | 7.00 | | III | 71.90 | 19.00 |
| | IV | 48.00 | 8.00 | | IV | 69.40 | 20.00 |
| 1982 | I | 51.20 | 9.00 | 1985 | I | 77.50 | 21.00 |
| | II | 49.90 | 10.00 | | II | 75.00 | 22.00 |
| | III | 56.10 | 11.00 | | III | 80.00 | 23.00 |
| | IV | 53.60 | 12.00 | | IV | 77.60 | 24.00 |

salaries for college graduates, the continual increase in the number of residents in Florida, or the decline in the price of computers over the past 20 years. **Seasonal variations** represent deviations from a trend that occur regularly within 1 year, such as the increase in swimwear sales in the summer and the increase in sales of new cars every fall.

**Cyclical variations** are the longer swings in a time series, lasting for more than 1 year. Periods of rising and falling interest rates or long-term swings in residential construction represent cyclical variations. Because such fluctuations may vary greatly in length and can be over 15 years long, removing the effect of such business cycles is often difficult, if not impossible. We will not attempt to isolate cyclical patterns in this chapter. Finally, **random variation** is the unpredictable or irregular movement in a time series. Fluctuations caused by unpredictable changes in the weather, by fads, or by unforeseen political activities are examples of random variation.

# 10.11  Trend

Trend refers to the increase or decrease in a time series over time. The steady rise in the CPI is an example of a trend. The cost data in Table 10.8 provide another example of a series with a trend. These cost data fluctuate from quarter to quarter, but over the 4 years the trend is up (see Fig. 10.7).

The trend line is a straight line that best fits the data. Such a trend line can be estimated, using the method of least squares, by letting time be the independent variable. The values of this variable consist of a series of consecutive numbers designed to represent time. In Table 10.8, for example, the numbers 1, 2, . . ., 24 are used to represent time. In this case, $x = 1$ represents the first quarter of 1980, $x = 2$ the second quarter of 1980, and so forth, with $x = 24$ representing the fourth quarter of 1985.

To calculate a trend line using regression, the **trend variable** is treated in the same manner as were the independent variables in Chapter 9. For the data in Table 10.8, the dependent variable is cost, which means that the regression line to be estimated is

Predicted cost = $a$ + $b$(trend)

Figure 10.7
Plot of cost data.

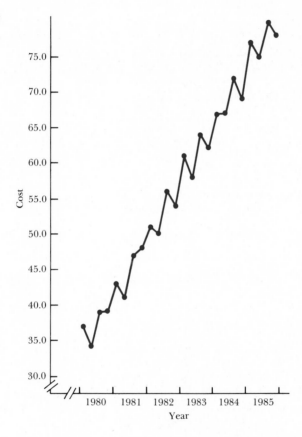

Microstat was used with the data in Table 10.8. The resulting least-squares regression line, Table 10.9, is

Predicted cost = 32.2232 + 1.9915(trend)

This equation indicates that cost is predicted to rise by $1991.50 in each quarter. While this equation appears to provide a good fit to the data in Table 10.8 (resulting in a high $R^2$ and significant test statistics), a review of the residuals suggests a problem. Notice in Table 10.9 and Fig. 10.7 that the residuals alternate in sign throughout the series. Any pattern to a set of residuals in a time series indicates a possible violation of the assumption that the errors are independent of one another. Such a pattern may be due to seasonal variation, to be discussed in the next section.

**Table 10.9**

<table>
<tr><td colspan="6" align="center">**Estimating the Trend Line in Fig. 10.7**</td></tr>
</table>

DEPENDENT VARIABLE: cost

| VAR. | REGRESSION COEFFICIENT | STD. ERROR | T(D.F. = 22) | PROB. |
|------|------------------------|------------|--------------|-------|
| trend | 1.9915 | 0.0620 | 32.108 | 0.00000 |
| CONSTANT | 32.2232 | | | |

STD. ERROR OF EST. = 2.1034
r SQUARED = 0.9791
r = 0.9895

ANALYSIS OF VARIANCE TABLE

| SOURCE | SUM OF SQUARES | D.F. | MEAN SQUARE | F RATIO | PROB. |
|--------|----------------|------|-------------|---------|-------|
| REGRESSION | 4560.8835 | 1 | 4560.8835 | 1030.922 | 5.000E-10 |
| RESIDUAL | 97.3298 | 22 | 4.4241 | | |
| TOTAL | 4658.2133 | 23 | | | |

| | Observed | Calculated | Residual | Standardized Residuals |
|----|----------|------------|----------|------------------------|
| 1 | 37.500 | 34.215 | 3.2853 | |
| 2 | 34.300 | 36.206 | −1.9061 | |
| 3 | 38.700 | 38.198 | 0.5024 | |
| 4 | 38.900 | 40.189 | −1.2891 | |
| 5 | 42.800 | 42.181 | 0.6194 | |
| 6 | 41.500 | 44.172 | −2.6721 | |
| 7 | 46.900 | 46.164 | 0.7365 | |
| 8 | 48.000 | 48.155 | −0.1550 | |
| 9 | 51.200 | 50.146 | 1.0535 | |
| 10 | 49.900 | 52.138 | −2.2380 | |
| 11 | 56.100 | 54.129 | 1.9706 | |
| 12 | 53.600 | 56.121 | −2.5209 | |
| 13 | 61.100 | 58.112 | 2.9876 | |
| 14 | 57.900 | 60.104 | −2.2039 | |
| 15 | 64.200 | 62.095 | 2.1046 | |
| 16 | 62.500 | 64.087 | −1.5868 | |
| 17 | 67.300 | 66.078 | 1.2217 | |
| 18 | 67.000 | 68.070 | −1.0698 | |
| 19 | 71.900 | 70.061 | 1.8387 | |
| 20 | 69.400 | 72.053 | −2.6528 | |
| 21 | 77.500 | 74.044 | 3.4558 | |
| 22 | 75.000 | 76.036 | −1.0357 | |
| 23 | 80.000 | 78.027 | 1.9728 | |
| 24 | 77.600 | 80.019 | −2.4187 | |

Standardized Residuals axis: −2.0    0    2.0

# 10.12 Seasonal Variation

*Seasonal variations* are the patterns of change that tend to repeat themselves from year to year. Sales of garden equipment, for example, increase regularly every spring and decrease every fall. There are many business variables that tend to repeat on a seasonal basis, such as Christmas spending, summer vacation travel, and spring housing starts. Economists often want to "deseasonalize" data—that is, to remove the seasonal variation in order to make comparisons over time. On the other hand, a business executive forecasting a variable over time (on the basis of a trend) will want to account for seasonality in order to predict as accurately as possible. Thus it is important to identify the seasonal component of a time series.

Dummy variables can be used to identify the seasonal component of a time series. For data reported on a quarterly basis, three dummy variables is the maximum number that can be used. (For some situations, as we will describe, fewer dummy variables may be sufficient.) The regression line to predict cost ($\hat{y}$) is

$$\hat{y} = a + b_1(\text{1-quart}) + b_2(\text{2-quart}) + b_3(\text{3-quart}) + b_4(\text{trend})$$

where the variables 1-quart, and 2-quart, and 3-quart represent the first, second, and third quarters, respectively. Each of these variables is a 0–1 dummy variable, and no dummy variable is used for the fourth quarter because its effect is reflected in the constant term $a$. The values assigned to each dummy variable in the three quarters are shown in Table 10.10 (the last three columns). Notice in this table that the appropriate quarter dummy equals 1 in the quarter it represents and 0 otherwise.

The regression analysis for the data in Table 10.10 is shown in Table 10.11. Notice that the residuals in Table 10.11 no longer have a distinct pattern. Thus the dummy variables have controlled for the seasonal variation. The least-squares regression equation shown in Table 10.11 is

$$\hat{y} = 30.1433 + 2.0136(\text{trend}) + 3.9407(\text{1-quart})$$
$$- 0.0395(\text{2-quart}) + 3.3136(\text{3-quart})$$

From Table 10.11 we see that the $p$ value for the coefficient of the dummy variable 2-quart is very high ($p = 0.94321$). This means that dummy variable 2-quart is contributing very little to the explanation of the dependent variable, and we can consider eliminating it from the time series analysis. Table 10.12

Table 10.10

| Year and Quarter | | Cost (in Thousands of Dollars) | Trend | 1-quart | 2-quart | 3-quart |
|---|---|---|---|---|---|---|
| | | **Table 10.8 with Three Dummy Variables Added** | | | | |
| 1980 | I | 37.50 | 1.00 | 1 | 0 | 0 |
| | II | 34.30 | 2.00 | 0 | 1 | 0 |
| | III | 38.70 | 3.00 | 0 | 0 | 1 |
| | IV | 38.90 | 4.00 | 0 | 0 | 0 |
| 1981 | I | 42.80 | 5.00 | 1 | 0 | 0 |
| | II | 41.50 | 6.00 | 0 | 1 | 0 |
| | III | 46.90 | 7.00 | 0 | 0 | 1 |
| | IV | 48.00 | 8.00 | 0 | 0 | 0 |
| 1982 | I | 51.20 | 9.00 | 1 | 0 | 0 |
| | II | 49.90 | 10.00 | 0 | 1 | 0 |
| | III | 56.10 | 11.00 | 0 | 0 | 1 |
| | IV | 53.60 | 12.00 | 0 | 0 | 0 |
| 1983 | I | 61.10 | 13.00 | 1 | 0 | 0 |
| | II | 57.90 | 14.00 | 0 | 1 | 0 |
| | III | 64.20 | 15.00 | 0 | 0 | 1 |
| | IV | 62.50 | 16.00 | 0 | 0 | 0 |
| 1984 | I | 67.30 | 17.00 | 1 | 0 | 0 |
| | II | 67.00 | 18.00 | 0 | 1 | 0 |
| | III | 71.90 | 19.00 | 0 | 0 | 1 |
| | IV | 69.40 | 20.00 | 0 | 0 | 0 |
| 1985 | I | 77.50 | 21.00 | 1 | 0 | 0 |
| | II | 75.00 | 22.00 | 0 | 1 | 0 |
| | III | 80.00 | 23.00 | 0 | 0 | 1 |
| | IV | 77.60 | 24.00 | 0 | 0 | 0 |

(page 470) shows the least-squares regression analysis after eliminating the second-quarter dummy from the analysis and rerunning the regression using the remaining variables.

The least squares regression equation in Table 10.12 is

$$\hat{y} = 30.1208 + 2.0138(\text{trend}) + 3.9609(\text{1-quart}) + 3.3333(\text{3-quart})$$

This equation is really three different regression equations; the first and the third quarters are two distinct lines, and the second and the fourth quarters are the same line. The equation for each quarter is derived by substituting the dummy-variable values, as follows.

**Table 10.11**

| Regression with Three Quarter Dummies to Control for Seasonality |
|---|

DEPENDENT VARIABLE: cost

| VAR. | REGRESSION COEFFICIENT | STD. ERROR | T(D.F. = 19) | PROB. |
|---|---|---|---|---|
| TREND | 2.0136 | 0.0282 | 71.436 | 0.00000 |
| 1-quart | 3.9407 | 0.5511 | 7.150 | 0.00000 |
| 2-quart | -0.0395 | 0.5475 | -0.072 | 0.94321 |
| 3-quart | 3.3136 | 0.5454 | 6.076 | 0.00001 |
| CONSTANT | 30.1433 | | | |

STD. ERROR OF EST. = 0.9433
R SQUARED = 0.9964
MULTIPLE R = 0.9982

ANALYSIS OF VARIANCE TABLE

| SOURCE | SUM OF SQUARES | D.F. | MEAN SQUARE | F RATIO | PROB. |
|---|---|---|---|---|---|
| REGRESSION | 4641.3063 | 4 | 1160.3266 | 1303.965 | 0.000E+00 |
| RESIDUAL | 16.9070 | 19 | 0.8898 | | |
| TOTAL | 4658.2133 | 23 | | | |

| | Observed | Calculated | Residual | Standardized Residuals |
|---|---|---|---|---|
| 1 | 37.500 | 36.098 | 1.4024 | |
| 2 | 34.300 | 34.131 | 0.1690 | |
| 3 | 38.700 | 39.498 | -0.7976 | |
| 4 | 38.900 | 38.198 | 0.7024 | |
| 5 | 42.800 | 44.152 | -1.3519 | |
| 6 | 41.500 | 42.185 | -0.6852 | |
| 7 | 46.900 | 47.552 | -0.6519 | |
| 8 | 48.000 | 46.252 | 1.7481 | |
| 9 | 51.200 | 52.206 | -1.0062 | |
| 10 | 49.900 | 50.240 | -0.3395 | |
| 11 | 56.100 | 55.606 | 0.4938 | |
| 12 | 53.600 | 54.306 | -0.7062 | |
| 13 | 61.100 | 60.260 | 0.8395 | |
| 14 | 57.900 | 58.294 | -0.3938 | |
| 15 | 64.200 | 63.660 | 0.5395 | |
| 16 | 62.500 | 62.360 | 0.1395 | |
| 17 | 67.300 | 68.315 | -1.0148 | |
| 18 | 67.000 | 66.348 | 0.6519 | |
| 19 | 71.900 | 71.715 | 0.1852 | |
| 20 | 69.400 | 70.415 | -1.0148 | |
| 21 | 77.500 | 76.369 | 1.1310 | |
| 22 | 75.000 | 74.402 | 0.5976 | |
| 23 | 80.000 | 79.769 | 0.2310 | |
| 24 | 77.600 | 78.469 | -0.8690 | |

Standardized Residuals scale: -2.0, 0, 2.0

**Table 10.12**

| Regression for Table 10.8 with Two Dummy Variables | | | | |
|---|---|---|---|---|
| DEPENDENT VARIABLE: cost | | | | |
| VAR. | REGRESSION COEFFICIENT | STD. ERROR | T(D.F. = 20) | PROB. |
| trend | 2.0138 | 0.0273 | 73.681 | 0.00000 |
| 1-quart | 3.9609 | 0.4630 | 8.555 | 0.00000 |
| 3-quart | 3.3333 | 0.4598 | 7.250 | 0.00000 |
| CONSTANT | 30.1208 | | | |
| STD. ERROR OF EST. = 0.9196 | | | | |
| R SQUARED = 0.9964 | | | | |
| MULTIPLE = 0.9982 | | | | |

For the first quarter, let 1-quart = 1, 3-quart = 0.

$$\hat{y} = 30.1208 + 2.0138(\text{trend}) + 3.9609(1) + 3.3333(0)$$
$$= 34.0817 + 2.0138(\text{trend})$$

For the third quarter, let 1-quart = 0, 3-quart = 1.

$$\hat{y} = 30.1208 + 2.0138(\text{trend}) + 3.9609(0) + 3.3333(1)$$
$$= 33.4514 + 2.0138(\text{trend})$$

**Figure 10.8**
Seasonal regression lines for Table 10.12.

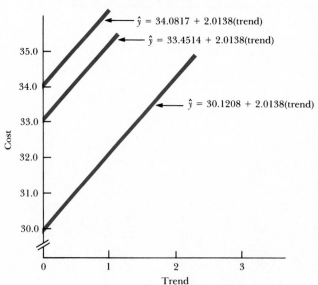

$\hat{y} = 34.0817 + 2.0138(\text{trend})$

$\hat{y} = 33.4514 + 2.0138(\text{trend})$

$\hat{y} = 30.1208 + 2.0138(\text{trend})$

Chapter 10  Multiple Regression: Cross-Section and Time-Series Analysis

For the second and fourth quarters, let 1-quart = 0, 3-quart = 0.

$$\hat{y} = 30.1208 + 2.0138(\text{trend}) + 3.9609(0) + 3.3333(0)$$
$$= 30.1208 + 2.0138(\text{trend})$$

These three lines are shown in Fig. 10.8.

Suppose we want to use this regression line to forecast costs in the third quarter of 1986. The trend value for this period is $x = 27$, and the dummy variable is 1-quart = 0, 3-quart = 1. Thus the predicted cost is \$87,826.70.

$$\hat{y} = 30.1208 + 2.0138(27) + 3.9609(0) + 3.3333(1) = 87.8267$$

---

**WORKED EXAMPLE 10.4**

The following plot represents the residuals resulting from a linear trend for *bimonthly* observations on retail trade at a large shopping mall in a resort city. Specify the sample regression line that should be used to identify all possible seasonal variations in this type of situation. Indicate what value you would assign to each dummy variable.

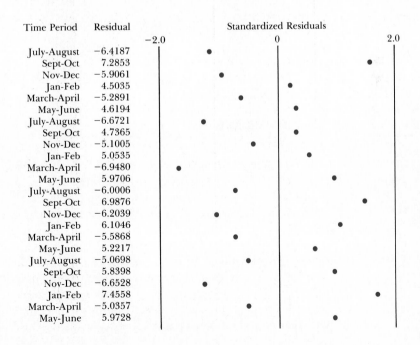

| Time Period | Residual |
| --- | --- |
| July-August | −6.4187 |
| Sept-Oct | 7.2853 |
| Nov-Dec | −5.9061 |
| Jan-Feb | 4.5035 |
| March-April | −5.2891 |
| May-June | 4.6194 |
| July-August | −6.6721 |
| Sept-Oct | 4.7365 |
| Nov-Dec | −5.1005 |
| Jan-Feb | 5.0535 |
| March-April | −6.9480 |
| May-June | 5.9706 |
| July-August | −6.0006 |
| Sept-Oct | 6.9876 |
| Nov-Dec | −6.2039 |
| Jan-Feb | 6.1046 |
| March-April | −5.5868 |
| May-June | 5.2217 |
| July-August | −5.0698 |
| Sept-Oct | 5.8398 |
| Nov-Dec | −6.6528 |
| Jan-Feb | 7.4558 |
| March-April | −5.0357 |
| May-June | 5.9728 |

**ANSWER:**

Five dummy variables are necessary to be assured of identifying all possible seasonal variation when the data consist of six data points per year (bimonthly data). Thus the regression equation is

$$\hat{y} = a + b_1(\text{Dum1}) + b_2(\text{Dum2}) + b_3(\text{Dum3}) + b_4(\text{Dum4}) + b_5(\text{Dum5}) + b_6(\text{trend})$$

where: $\hat{y}$ is retail trade, trend = 1, 2, 3, . . . for time, and the dummy variables are Dum1, Dum2, Dum3, Dum4, and Dum5. The values assigned to the dummy variables are as follows:

| | Values Assigned to: | | | | |
|---|---|---|---|---|---|
| **Time Period** | *Dum1* | *Dum2* | *Dum3* | *Dum4* | *Dum5* |
| July–Aug. | 1 | 0 | 0 | 0 | 0 |
| Sept.–Oct. | 0 | 1 | 0 | 0 | 0 |
| Nov.–Dec. | 0 | 0 | 1 | 0 | 0 |
| Jan.–Feb. | 0 | 0 | 0 | 1 | 0 |
| Mar.–Apr. | 0 | 0 | 0 | 0 | 1 |
| May–June | 0 | 0 | 0 | 0 | 0 |

## 10.13 Data Transformations

A *data transformation* is a change in one or more of the variables. Data transformations have already been used in this text in several places. As one example, in the salary discrimination case in Chapter 9 we did not use salaries such as $24,000; rather, we used 24.0. In other words, we transformed each salary by dividing it by 1000 to make data entry easier. As another example, suppose that $x_1$ was initially defined to represent the number of years of undergraduate college education a person has completed, while $x_2$ was the number of years of graduate education. If we now want to assess the combined effects of all postsecondary school education, a logical data transformation would be to create a new variable, $x_3$, representing the *total* number of years of higher education, where $x_3 = x_1 + x_2$.

Some transformations are used to provide a better fit of the regression equation to the data. Economic data, for example, are often transformed using a lagged variable, which enables a forecast for a current time period to depend on data occurring in a previous time period. In other situations, transformations are used to avoid violations of the least-squares regression assumptions. For example, some transformations attempt to "straighten" data that are nonlinear. Others may attempt to correct for heteroscedastic errors.

There are many different transformations that can be applied to a data set, only a few of which will be illustrated here. Most of these transformations are relatively simple with the aid of a computer. What is not so simple is trying to decide which transformation to use, especially if the objective is to avoid a possible violation of one or more least-squares assumptions.

## Lagging a Variable

In a time series, the value of the dependent variable in the current period often depends on the value of this variable in a prior period. For example, many businesses estimate sales for one period on the basis of the sales in the last period. Starting salaries for business school graduates this year are highly related to comparable starting salaries last year. A variable related to itself in a previous period is called a **lagged variable**.

Lagging the dependent variable and including it as a regressor provides a way of capturing the dynamic nature of a time series. Including lagged dependent variables on the right-hand side of a regression equation may capture the growth or decay in a dependent variable that appears to be approaching an equilibrium (or target value, as shown in Fig. 10.9a and b) or appears to be unbounded (or explosive, as shown in Fig. 10.9c and d). If the correct lag lengths can be found, lagged dependent variables can also be used to capture seasonal and cyclical variations.

As an illustration of a lagged dependent variable, consider the quarterly sales data in Table 10.13, column 2. There are 20 observations on sales; the first value, 103, occurs in the fourth quarter of 1980 and the last value, 128, occurs in the third quarter of 1985. Lagging this time series one quarter creates the new variable called "Sales$(t - 1)$," column 3. The first value of Sales$(t - 1)$ is 103, but this value is now associated with the first quarter of 1981, while the last value, which occurs in the third quarter of 1985, is 126. Here one observation (128) is lost in lagging.

By regressing sales on Sales$(t - 1)$, we can estimate the relationship between sales in consecutive periods and use information on sales in one period to forecast sales in the next one. Before running this regression, re-

**Figure 10.9**
Scatter diagrams for a
dynamic time series
process.

For the dynamic model $y_t = \alpha + \beta y_{t-1}$, where $y_{t-1}$ is a one period lag of $y_t$, there are four paths which $y_t$ can follow over time.

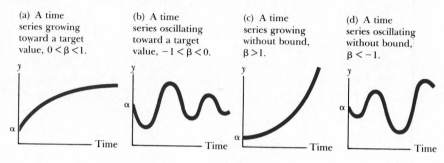

(a) A time
series growing
toward a target
value, $0 < \beta < 1$.

(b) A time
series oscillating
toward a target
value, $-1 < \beta < 0$.

(c) A time
series growing
without bound,
$\beta > 1$.

(d) A time
series oscillating
without bound,
$\beta < -1$.

**Table 10.13**

| Sales and One-Quarter Lag of Sales (in Thousands of Dollars) | | | | | |
|---|---|---|---|---|---|
| Year and Quarter | Sales | Sales $(t-1)$ | **Seasonal Dummies** | | |
| | | | 3-quart | 2-quart | 1-quart |
| 1980 IV | 103.0 | not known | | | |
| 1981 I | 106.0 | 103.0 | 0.0 | 0.0 | 1.0 |
| II | 108.0 | 106.0 | 0.0 | 1.0 | 0.0 |
| III | 112.0 | 108.0 | 1.0 | 0.0 | 0.0 |
| IV | 112.5 | 112.0 | 0.0 | 0.0 | 0.0 |
| 1982 I | 114.0 | 112.5 | 0.0 | 0.0 | 1.0 |
| II | 116.0 | 114.0 | 0.0 | 1.0 | 0.0 |
| III | 119.0 | 116.0 | 1.0 | 0.0 | 0.0 |
| IV | 118.0 | 119.0 | 0.0 | 0.0 | 0.0 |
| 1983 I | 119.5 | 118.0 | 0.0 | 0.0 | 1.0 |
| II | 121.0 | 119.5 | 0.0 | 1.0 | 0.0 |
| III | 123.5 | 121.0 | 1.0 | 0.0 | 0.0 |
| IV | 122.0 | 123.5 | 0.0 | 0.0 | 0.0 |
| 1984 I | 123.0 | 122.0 | 0.0 | 0.0 | 1.0 |
| II | 124.0 | 123.0 | 0.0 | 1.0 | 0.0 |
| III | 126.4 | 124.0 | 1.0 | 0.0 | 0.0 |
| IV | 125.0 | 126.4 | 0.0 | 0.0 | 0.0 |
| 1985 I | 125.5 | 125.0 | 0.0 | 0.0 | 1.0 |
| II | 126.0 | 125.5 | 0.0 | 1.0 | 0.0 |
| III | 128.0 | 126.0 | 1.0 | 0.0 | 0.0 |

member that our sample now contains only 19 quarters for which data are available on both Sales and Sales$(t - 1)$ as only the first quarter of 1981 through the third quarter of 1985 contain data on both Sales and Sales$(t - 1)$. (Lagging a variable one period results in the loss of one observation. Lagging a variable two periods results in the loss of two observations, and so on.) In addition, since we have quarterly data, our initial regression should include three seasonal dummy variables to control for any seasonal effects that may not be part of the dynamic time process. Thus the sample regression equation is

$$\text{Predicted sales} = a + b_1(\text{1-quart}) + b_2(\text{2-quart})$$
$$+ b_3(\text{3-quart}) + b_4[\text{sales}(t - 1)]$$

where 1-quart, 2-quart, and 3-quart are the three 0–1 dummy variables represented in Table 10.13. [The first observation on each variable is Sales $=$ 106.0, Sales$(t - 1) = 103.0$, 3-quart $= 0$, 2-quart $= 0$, and 1-quart $= 1.0$, with a total of only 19 observations on each variable.] The least-squares regression estimates for these data are given in Table 10.14.

As the R SQUARED value in Table 10.14 indicates, this regression equation fits well, $R^2 = 0.9984$. (Although not shown, the residuals also appear to be random.) There are strong seasonal factors in the data, since all three dummy variable coefficients are highly significant, and sales in one quarter are highly related to sales in the next, since the lag coefficient, 0.8988, is

**Table 10.14**

| Regression of Sales on a One-Quarter Lag of Sales and Seasonal Dummies | | | | |
|---|---|---|---|---|
| DEPENDENT VARIABLE: Sales | | | | |
| VAR. | REGRESSION COEFFICIENT | STD. ERROR | T(D.F. = 14) | PROB. |
| Sales(t − 1) | 0.8988 | 0.0100 | 89.970 | 0.00000 |
| 3-quart | 3.5060 | 0.1981 | 17.694 | 0.00000 |
| 2-quart | 1.9843 | 0.1995 | 9.947 | 0.00000 |
| 1-quart | 1.9325 | 0.2020 | 9.566 | 0.00000 |
| CONSTANT | 11.3180 | | | |

STD. ERROR OF EST. $= 0.2948$
R SQUARED $= 0.9984$
MULTIPLE R $= 0.9992$

highly significant. Using this equation, we forecast sales in the fourth quarter of 1985 to be $126,364.40.

$$\text{Predicted sales} = 11.3180 + 1.9325(0) + 1.9843(0)$$
$$+ 3.5060(0) + 0.8988(128) = 126.3644$$

In making forecasts or predictions about the future it is important to remember that such predictions are outside the sample time period. The further into the future we attempt to predict, the less confidence we can have in the forecast. As stated in Chapter 9, predictions with a sample regression equation have meaning only within the range of sample values and the conditions under which the sample was drawn. Regressions that are estimated under one set of economic conditions may have little meaning if those conditions change.

## Straightening Nonlinear Data

Economic variables often change at a constant *proportion*, rather than by a constant amount. A variable that starts at $100 and then changes to $110, $120, $130, . . ., is increasing by a constant amount ($10). A variable that starts at $100 and then changes to $110, $121, $133.10, . . . is increasing by a constant proportion (namely, 10% each period). Proportional changes occur frequently in financial data.

The investment in Fig. 10.10 is growing by a proportional amount. Notice in this figure that the best approximation to the data is not a straight line, but rather a curved line. If a straight line is fit to the data, the result is a line that tends to underestimate future values (see the right side of Fig. 10.10). Thus we would like to "straighten" these data so that least squares can be used. One way to straighten a nonlinear data set that is changing at a proportional rate is to transform the data by using logarithms. (Even if you don't remember much about logarithms, you will see in a moment that the computer and some hand calculators can do all the computations anyway.) We will use natural logarithms here (logs to the base $e$, denoted as $Ln$), but logs to the base 10 work equally well.

In order to use a log transformation on the data in Fig. 10.10, take the natural log of each value of the dependent variable (Net Value). We call this new dependent variable $Ln(NV)$. As before, Time is the independent variable, with Time $= 0, 1, 2, 3, . . .$ The second column of log data in Table 10.15 was generated from the original data in the first column, letting the computer program find each value of $Ln(NV)$. (For an algebraic demonstration of why this log transformation is necessary, see Exercise 10.24.)

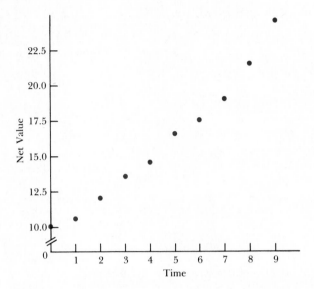

**Figure 10.10**
Growth in net value over time.

Figure 10.11 is the scatter diagram of Time versus $Ln(NV)$. Notice how much more linear the relationship is in Fig. 10.11 compared to Fig. 10.10.

The data in Table 10.15 are used in Table 10.16 to present the least-squares output. The regression line using $Ln(NV)$ as the dependent variable is

Predicted $Ln(NV) = 2.3024 + 0.0954$(Time).

**Table 10.15**

| Growth of an Investment Over Time | | |
|---|---|---|
| NV (Net value in Thousands of Dollars) | Ln(NV) (Logarithm of Net Value) | Time |
| 10.00 | 2.30 | 0.00 |
| 10.90 | 2.39 | 1.00 |
| 12.20 | 2.50 | 2.00 |
| 13.40 | 2.60 | 3.00 |
| 14.50 | 2.67 | 4.00 |
| 16.30 | 2.79 | 5.00 |
| 17.60 | 2.87 | 6.00 |
| 19.50 | 2.97 | 7.00 |
| 21.30 | 3.06 | 8.00 |
| 23.70 | 3.17 | 9.00 |

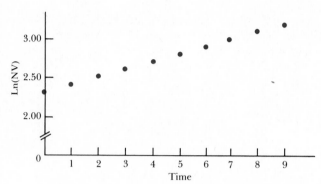

**Figure 10.11**
The data in Table 10.15 using a logarithm transformation.

Now suppose we want to predict the value of this investment at Time = 10. Substituting Time = 10 into the regression equation,

Predicted $Ln(NV) = 2.3024 + 0.0954(10) = 3.2564$

But 3.2564 is the logarithm of the predicted net value. To convert logarithms back to the original units of measurement we take *antilogs*, which is the reverse process of taking logs. Using a table of logs or an appropriate hand calculator,

Antilog $(3.2564) = 25.956$

Because our original data were in thousands of dollars, the predicted value of the net value at Time = 10 is $25,956.

The preceding example reminds us that after transforming the dependent variable and running a regression, the prediction value must be transformed back into the original units of measurement. Also, after any nonlinear trans-

**Table 10.16**

| Estimating the Growth of Investments | | | | |
|---|---|---|---|---|
| DEPENDENT VARIABLE: Ln(NV) | | | | |
| VAR. | REGRESSION COEFFICIENT | STD. ERROR | T(D.F. = 8) | PROB. |
| Time | 0.0954 | 9.08105E-04 | 105.017 | 0.00000 |
| CONSTANT | 2.3024 | | | |
| STD. ERROR OF EST. = 0.0082 | | | | |
| r SQUARED = 0.9993 | | | | |
| r = 0.9996 | | | | |

formation, the resulting least-squares residuals should be checked for possible violations of the regression assumptions. For future reference, the following diagrams represent two transformations that may help straighten data in certain types of regression problems.

If your data look like this . . .          try this transformation.

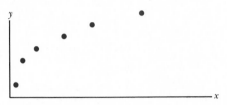

$$\hat{y} = a + bLn(x)$$

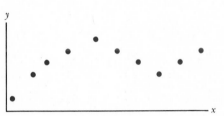

$$\hat{y} = a + b_1x + b_2x^2 + b_3x^3$$

---

**WORKED EXAMPLE 10.5**

A union executive claims that members at two different plants receive different salaries for doing the same work. After controlling for seniority, does the following sample information on years of seniority and salary support this claim? (Test at the 0.05 type I error level.)

| Worker | Salary (in Thousands of Dollars) | Plant | Years of Seniority | Worker | Salary (in Thousands of Dollars) | Plant | Years of Seniority |
|--------|--------|--------|--------|--------|--------|--------|--------|
| 1 | 15.50 | 1.00 | 5.00 | 9 | 39.20 | 0.00 | 20.00 |
| 2 | 34.50 | 0.00 | 15.00 | 10 | 30.00 | 1.00 | 15.00 |
| 3 | 24.00 | 1.00 | 10.00 | 11 | 16.90 | 0.00 | 5.00 |
| 4 | 33.30 | 1.00 | 20.00 | 12 | 17.00 | 1.00 | 20.00 |
| 5 | 28.10 | 0.00 | 10.00 | 13 | 31.00 | 1.00 | 20.00 |
| 6 | 29.50 | 1.00 | 15.00 | 14 | 33.00 | 0.00 | 20.00 |
| 7 | 18.00 | 0.00 | 5.00 | 15 | 25.00 | 1.00 | 10.00 |
| 8 | 42.10 | 0.00 | 25.00 | 16 | 43.00 | 0.00 | 25.00 |

**ANSWER:**

Using salary as the dependent variable, years of seniority as one independent variable, and plant number as a dummy variable number, there appears to be no difference in the salary schedules at the two plants (for the coefficient of the plant dummy, $p = 0.05231$ exceeds the 0.05 type I error level).

DEPENDENT VARIABLE: salary

| VAR. | REGRESSION COEFFICIENT | STD. ERROR | T(D.F. = 13) | PROB. |
|------|------------------------|------------|--------------|-------|
| Plant Dummy | -2.6031 | 1.2189 | -2.136 | 0.05231 |
| Years | 1.1470 | 0.0884 | 12.979 | 0.00000 |
| CONSTANT | 13.9279 | | | |

A careful review of the original data (a scatter diagram) indicates that salaries and years of seniority are not linearly related. Rather, it appears as if salaries increase at a decreasing rate. In this case, we use a logarithm transformation on the independent variable (yrs) to straighten the relationship. Thus the correct regression equation is

Predicted salary $= a + b_1 Ln(\text{yrs}) + b_2(\text{Plant Dummy})$.

After a logarithm transformation on Years, a least-squares analysis gives the following results:

DEPENDENT VARIABLE: salary

| VAR. | REGRESSION COEFFICIENT | STD. ERROR | T(D.F. = 13) | PROB. |
|------|------------------------|------------|--------------|-------|
| Plant Dummy | -3.7712 | 0.9842 | -3.832 | 0.00208 |
| Ln(yrs) | 13.5453 | 0.8443 | 16.042 | 0.00000 |
| CONSTANT | -3.1285 | | | |

The $p$ value for the coefficient of the dummy variable in this output is very low ($p = 0.00208$), which means that we should conclude that there is a significant difference in salaries.

**10.19** In using a dummy variable, does it matter which characteristic is assigned a 0? Explain.

**10.20** Define each of the four principal components of a time series and give an example of each.

MKT **10.21** Which of the four components of a time series best describes the effect of Christmas and Easter sales at department stores?

FIN **10.22** Which of the four components of a time series best describes the general decline of the steel industry in the United States?

**10.23** Use the following regression to answer parts (a) and (b):

$$\hat{y} = 2 + 3x_1 - 4x_2$$

where

$x_1$ is a trend variable ($x_1 = 1, 2, 3, \ldots$)
$x_2 = 1$ if $x_1$ is even and 0 if $x_2$ is odd.

a) In the third period ($x_1 = 3$), what is $\hat{y}$?
b) Draw a two-dimensional diagram to show the effect of $x_2$.

FIN **10.24** The expected growth ($g$) in the net value of the investment represented in Table 10.15 can be represented by the equation $NV = 10(1 + g)^t$, where $t$ is the time period. For example, if $t = 0$, $NV = 10$. Taking logarithms of both sides of this equation gives $Ln(NV) = Ln(10) + Ln(1 + g)t$. The least-squares regression equation is

Predicted $Ln(NV) = 2.3024 + 0.0954t$

What is the expected rate of return from this investment (i.e., what is $g$)?

ECN **10.25** Two sets of regression results were obtained using a least-squares approach on the following data, where $y$ = earnings (in dollars), $x$ = years of school completed, and $Ln(yrs)$ = logarithm of $x$.

| Earnings: | 12,500 | 20,000 | 25,000 | 25,800 | 30,000 | 31,500 | 34,000 |
|---|---|---|---|---|---|---|---|
| Years (yrs): | 8 | 10 | 12 | 14 | 16 | 18 | 20 |
| Ln(yrs): | 2.079 | 2.303 | 2.485 | 2.639 | 2.773 | 2.890 | 2.996 |

```
DEPENDENT VARIABLE: y-Earnings

                REGRESSION
VAR.            COEFFICIENT    STD. ERROR     T(D.F. = 5)      PROB.
x-yrs           1651.7857       200.4316        8.241         0.00043
CONSTANT        2417.8571

STD. ERROR OF EST. = 2121.1688
        R SQUARED =    0.9314
              R =    0.9651

DEPENDENT VARIABLE: y-Earnings

                REGRESSION
VAR.            COEFFICIENT    STD. ERROR     T(D.F. = 5)      PROB.
Ln(yrs)         22267.0947     1614.3471       13.793        0.00004
CONSTANT       -32239.2463

STD. ERROR OF EST. = 1296.2485
        R SQUARED =    0.9744
              R =    0.9871
```

a) Draw two scatter diagrams, one for each regression. In the first, place the actual number of years of schooling on the horizontal axis. In the second, place the logarithm of years on the horizontal axis.

b) To predict earnings for someone who has completed 22 years of school, which regression is more appropriate and why?

c) Predict earnings for someone with 22 years of schooling.

10.26 Run a least-squares regression on the following sales data, using a 12-month lag, plus a trend variable. What value do you predict for Jan. 1986?

| Year | Jan. | Feb. | Mar. | Apr. | May | June | July | Aug. | Sept. | Oct. | Nov. | Dec. |
|------|------|------|------|------|-----|------|------|------|-------|------|------|------|
| 1983 | 67 | 71 | 72 | 73 | 71 | 70 | 67 | 64 | 66 | 74 | 82 | 99 |
| 1984 | 80 | 86 | 89 | 89 | 84 | 83 | 79 | 76 | 77 | 87 | 98 | 114 |
| 1985 | 92 | 98 | 101 | 103 | 96 | 96 | 89 | 87 | 90 | 99 | 112 | 131 |

10.27 Consider the following sales data for soft drinks in central Indiana (in thousands of cases)

| Year | $x_1$ | $x_2$ | $x_3$ | Year | $x_1$ | $x_2$ | $x_3$ |
|---|---|---|---|---|---|---|---|
| 1983 | Jan. 2300 | Feb. 2500 | Mar. 2600 | | July 6300 | Aug. 5900 | Sept. 4500 |
| | Apr. 3100 | May 3800 | June 4700 | | Oct. 3700 | Nov. 3300 | Dec. 2800 |
| | July 5900 | Aug. 5800 | Sept. 4300 | 1985 | Jan. 2700 | Feb. 2600 | Mar. 2800 |
| | Oct. 3500 | Nov. 3200 | Dec. 2800 | | Apr. 3500 | May 4400 | June 5000 |
| 1984 | Jan. 2500 | Feb. 2700 | Mar. 2900 | | July 6500 | Aug. 6100 | Sept. 4800 |
| | Apr. 3200 | May 4200 | June 4900 | | Oct. 3900 | Nov. 3600 | Dec. 3000 |

a) Create a computer file for these data using the three variables shown: $x_1$, $x_2$ and $x_3$. Transform these data by dividing each sales value by 100. Then transform these monthly data into quarterly data by creating a new variable $y$, where $y = x_1 + x_2 + x_3$. Run a least-squares regression on the transformed $y$, using a trend variable (let Jan. 1983 = 1) plus a four-quarter lagged variable. Are the independent variables significantly different from zero, using $\alpha = 0.10$? What sales value do you predict for the fourth quarter of 1986?

b) Repeat the preceding analysis, using three dummy variables rather than a four-quarter lag. Would you recommend using the dummy variable approach or the four-quarter lag approach to predict for the fourth quarter of 1986? Explain.

c) Sketch the four regression lines in part (b).

# Chapter Exercises

10.28 In the following regression, $x_2$ is a dummy variable that is equal to 1 or 0 and $x_1$ is a continuous variable.

$$\hat{y} = a + b_1x_1 + b_2x_2$$

**a)** If $x_2 = 1$, what is the intercept of this line?

**b)** If $x_2 = 0$, what is the intercept of this line?

**c)** Sketch the regression lines in parts (a) and (b) on one graph.

MKT **10.29** Why might a researcher want to consider including a trend variable in a regression analysis of the selling price of hand calculators?

**10.30** In the regression $\hat{y} = 10 + 0.75x_1 - 1.05x_2$, what is the meaning of the coefficient for $x_2$?

**10.31** When data are collected at a point in time, why isn't serial correlation in the residuals a problem?

**10.32** For each of the following indicate whether the statement is true or false, and if false, explain why.

**a)** In the population regression model

$$y = \alpha + \beta_1 x_1 + \beta_2 x_2 + \epsilon$$

$\beta_2$ is the change in the expected value of $y$ if and only if $x_2$ is held fixed at its mean.

**b)** In the model described in part (a), the parameters to be estimated are $\alpha$, $\beta_1$, and $\beta_2$.

**c)** The higher the value of the $F$ ratio, the more significance there is to the overall regression.

**d)** Multicollinearity occurs in multiple regression when the dependent variable is highly related to one or more of the independent variables.

**e)** The method of least squares for multiple linear regression, when $m = 2$, minimizes the sum of squared errors about a plane, while in simple regression the sum of squared errors is minimized around a line.

**f)** In assigning a 1 or a 0 to a dummy variable to represent a qualitative variable, it is necessary to assign the 1 to the attribute that causes $\hat{y}$ to rise.

ACT **10.33** You wish to use the data set in Section 9.6 (on salaries and grade point averages of accounting majors) to check for possible differences in the starting salaries of males and females. The first four starting salaries ($22,000, $24,000, $21,000, and $22,000) were those of females, the rest were those of males. Is gender related to starting salaries?

ADM **10.34** Some people hypothesize that prices are related to profits and productivity. To test this theory, a regression was run with a price index as the dependent variable and profits per unit of output and output per hour as the independent variables. For 15 consecutive years of observations, the results were:

| INDEX | NAME | MEAN | STD. DEV. |
|-------|------|------|-----------|
| 1 | profit | 0.127867 | 0.027245 |
| 2 | productivity | 7.697667 | 0.488782 |
| DEP. VAR.: | price | 160.193333 | 53.458495 |

DEPENDENT VARIABLE: price

| VAR. | REGRESSION COEFFICIENT | STD. ERROR | T(D.F. = 12) | PROB. |
|------|------------------------|------------|--------------|-------|
| profit | 465.096072 | 353.187000 | 1.317 | 0.21248 |
| productivity | 77.876707 | 19.686557 | 3.956 | 0.00191 |
| CONSTANT | −498.745883 | | | |

STD. ERROR OF EST. = 26.096579
R SQUARED = 0.7957
MULTIPLE R = 0.8920

ANALYSIS OF VARIANCE TABLE

| SOURCE | SUM OF SQUARES | D.F. | MEAN SQUARE | F RATIO | PROB. |
|--------|----------------|------|-------------|---------|-------|
| REGRESSION | 31836.972070 | 2 | 15918.486040 | 23.374 | 7.263E−05 |
| RESIDUAL | 8172.377270 | 12 | 681.031439 | | |
| TOTAL | 40009.349340 | 14 | | | |

a) How well does this regression fit the sample data?

b) Is the overall theory supported by these results? Why?

c) As individual regressors, are both productivity and profit related to price? Explain.

d) What information would you like to have in order to check the least-squares regression assumptions?

**e)** What is the predicted price level if output per man-hour $= 1$ and profits $= 0$?

**f)** Why isn't the prediction in part (e) meaningful?

ADM **10.35** The following residuals were obtained from the regression described in Exercise 10.34. What can you conclude about the least-squares assumptions from them?

| | Observed | Calculated | Residual |
|---|---|---|---|
| 1 | 272.400 | 225.228 | 47.171719 |
| 2 | 246.800 | 203.938 | 42.862325 |
| 3 | 217.400 | 211.624 | 5.776337 |
| 4 | 195.400 | 219.303 | −23.903159 |
| 5 | 181.500 | 211.293 | −29.792679 |
| 6 | 170.500 | 191.397 | −20.897361 |
| 7 | 161.200 | 164.340 | −3.139550 |
| 8 | 147.700 | 131.471 | 16.228715 |
| 9 | 133.100 | 162.274 | −29.173670 |
| 10 | 125.300 | 147.866 | −22.566479 |
| 11 | 121.300 | 127.480 | −6.180096 |
| 12 | 116.300 | 96.275 | 20.024658 |
| 13 | 109.800 | 105.646 | 4.153517 |
| 14 | 104.200 | 111.221 | −7.021144 |
| 15 | 100.000 | 93.543 | 6.456869 |

Standardized Residuals (−2.0, 0, 2.0)

ECN **10.36** Some analysts believe that the trend in money growth changed after 1973. Use a trend and a dummy variable on the following information on the money stock to assess the correctness of this assertion.

Year:
1982  81  80  79  78  77  76  75  74  73  72  71  70  69  68  67  66  65

Money stock
(in billions):
478  441  414  389  363  336  310  291  277  265  251  230  216  206  199  185  174  170

ADM **10.37** In a study of bank teller efficiency, the following data were collected on the dollar value of the transactions, the type of teller used (human or automated), and the amount of time required to complete the transaction.

| Observation Period | Average Amount Transacted During Observation Period | Average Time to Complete Transaction (Min.) | Teller Type: 1 If Human 0 If Automatic |
|---|---|---|---|
| 1 | $2314 | 2.0 | 1 |
| 2 | 1178 | 1.0 | 0 |
| 3 | 897 | 0.9 | 0 |
| 4 | 987 | 1.1 | 1 |
| 5 | 2037 | 2.5 | 1 |
| 6 | 1987 | 2.3 | 0 |
| 7 | 1005 | 2.1 | 1 |
| 8 | 1764 | 2.2 | 0 |
| 9 | 987 | 1.2 | 1 |
| 10 | 1741 | 2.0 | 1 |
| 11 | 1200 | 0.9 | 0 |
| 12 | 876 | 0.9 | 1 |
| 13 | 1435 | 1.7 | 1 |
| 14 | 1143 | 1.1 | 0 |
| 15 | 1998 | 2.0 | 1 |
| 16 | 2345 | 1.9 | 0 |
| 17 | 1067 | 1.1 | 0 |
| 18 | 958 | 0.9 | 1 |
| 19 | 2978 | 1.5 | 0 |
| 20 | 1591 | 1.0 | 0 |

a) Use a regression analysis to predict the time necessary to complete a transaction using as independent variables the value of the transaction and the type of teller involved.

b) What is the predicted amount of time it takes an automatic teller versus a human teller to complete a $1500 transaction?

c) How well does the regression equation fit the sample data?

d) Were the automatic tellers more efficient than the human ones?

10.38 Use the following regression information to write the least-squares equation. Calculate the predicted $y$ value for an $x$ value of 40. (Note: X-SQUARED is $x^2$.)

```
                     REGRESSION
VAR.                 COEFFICIENT    STD. ERROR    T(D.F. = 2)    PROB.
x                    1175.0043      165.3061          7.108      0.01922
x-SQUARED            -10.5243         1.6580         -6.348      0.02393
CONSTANT             -7808.9240

STD. ERROR OF EST. = 620.3516
        R SQUARED =   0.9774
       MULTIPLE R =   0.9886
```

$$\text{ANALYSIS OF VARIANCE TABLE}$$

| SOURCE | SUM OF SQUARES | D.F. | MEAN SQUARE | F RATIO | PROB. |
|---|---|---|---|---|---|
| REGRESSION | 33222092.5700 | 2 | 16611046.2900 | 43.164 | .0226 |
| RESIDUAL | 769672.2300 | 2 | 384836.1150 | | |
| TOTAL | 33991764.8000 | 4 | | | |

**10.39** Answer the following questions using the information in Exercise 10.38.

a) How well does the sample regression fit the data?

b) Test $\beta_1 = \beta_2 = 0$ against the alternative hypothesis that either $\beta_1$ or $\beta_2$ or both do not equal 0.

c) Test $H_0$: $\beta_2 = -10$ against the alternative hypothesis, $H_A$: $\beta_2 < -10$.

d) Why do you think $x^2$ was included as an independent variable?

MKT **10.40** A marketing study was designed to investigate the relationship between the number of bus rides (in millions) and five independent variables: (1) fare, (2) city population (in thousands), (3) per capita income, (4) advertising and promotion expenditures, and (5) automobile operating costs. This investigation involved 12 comparable cities.

| Rides | Fare | Pop. | Income | Advert. | Auto. |
|---|---|---|---|---|---|
| 116.980 | 0.50 | 1655 | 12860 | 9790 | 2200 |
| 114.880 | 0.50 | 1550 | 12980 | 9830 | 2200 |
| 113.550 | 0.50 | 1479 | 13120 | 9890 | 2360 |
| 115.060 | 0.50 | 1614 | 13330 | 9811 | 2360 |
| 122.900 | 0.50 | 1645 | 13530 | 11656 | 2500 |
| 126.890 | 0.60 | 1792 | 14020 | 11950 | 2576 |
| 121.050 | 0.60 | 1600 | 14344 | 13200 | 2576 |

| Rides | Fare | Pop. | Income | Advert. | Auto. |
|-------|------|------|--------|---------|-------|
| 115.200 | 0.80 | 1555 | 14454 | 14600 | 2576 |
| 103.100 | 0.80 | 1480 | 14768 | 13200 | 3010 |
| 94.334 | 0.80 | 1440 | 15316 | 15300 | 3010 |
| 91.006 | 0.80 | 1390 | 16071 | 22419 | 3010 |
| 85.460 | 0.80 | 1370 | 16200 | 16700 | 3240 |

A regression analysis on these data produced the following output:

DEPENDENT VARIABLE: rides

| VAR. | REGRESSION COEFFICIENT | STD. ERROR | T(D.F. = 6) | PROB. |
|------|------------------------|------------|-------------|-------|
| fare | 8.9324 | 26.7014 | 0.335 | 0.74936 |
| pop | 0.0720 | 0.0185 | 3.885 | 0.00813 |
| income | −0.0042 | 0.0101 | −0.415 | 0.69253 |
| advert | 2.80094E−04 | 0.0015 | 0.187 | 0.85761 |
| auto | −0.0066 | 0.0227 | −0.292 | 0.78017 |
| CONSTANT | 66.4820 | | | |

STD. ERROR OF EST. = 5.5162
R SQUARED = 0.9072
MULTIPLE R = 0.9525

ANALYSIS OF VARIANCE TABLE

| SOURCE | SUM OF SQUARES | D.F. | MEAN SQUARE | F RATIO | PROB. |
|--------|----------------|------|-------------|---------|-------|
| REGRESSION | 1784.9954 | 5 | 356.9991 | 11.732 | 4.706E−03 |
| RESIDUAL | 182.5733 | 6 | 30.4289 | | |
| TOTAL | 1967.5687 | 11 | | | |

a) Run a regression analysis on these data to verify the output given.

b) What variables are significant in explaining bus ridership? Is the overall relationship significant? Explain.

c) Rerun these data, using only the population variable. How much does $R^2$ decrease? Is the fit better using all five independent variables or just population? Explain.

MKT   10.41   A study was conducted to determine what factors influence the sale of roses. The dependent variable was sales (in dozens), while the independent variables were (1) average price of roses, (2) average price of carnations, (3) average unemployment rate, (4) number of births, (5) number of deaths, (6) number of marriages, and (7) average weekly family disposable income. Sixteen observations yielded the following:

DEPENDENT VARIABLE: SALES

| VAR. | REGRESSION COEFFICIENT | STD. ERROR | T(D.F. = 8) | PROB. |
|------|------------------------|------------|-------------|-------|
| PRICE | -1531.2562 | 1307.2371 | -1.171 | 0.27515 |
| CARN PRI | 2528.5416 | 985.5808 | 2.566 | 0.03336 |
| UNEMP | -65.5141 | 219.4712 | -0.299 | 0.77292 |
| BIRTHS | 0.7119 | 0.5156 | 1.381 | 0.20471 |
| DEATHS | -0.0132 | 0.8750 | -0.015 | 0.98834 |
| MARRIAGE | 0.4295 | 0.2622 | 1.638 | 0.13998 |
| DIS INC | -20.7374 | 41.8060 | -0.496 | 0.63321 |
| CONSTANT | -7536.7087 | | | |

STD. ERROR OF EST. = 950.6382
R SQUARED =   0.8994
MULTIPLE R =   0.9484

| SOURCE | SUM OF SQUARES | D.F. | MEAN SQUARE | F RATIO | PROB. |
|--------|----------------|------|-------------|---------|-------|
| REGRESSION | 64650867.9100 | 7 | 9235838.2730 | 10.220 | 1.948E-03 |
| RESIDUAL | 7229703.5200 | 8 | 903712.9400 | | |
| TOTAL | 71880571.4300 | 15 | | | |

Write down the least-squares regression equation. What variables are most important in explaining the sale of roses? Are the signs of all the regression coefficients what you would have expected? How much of the variability in sales is explained by these independent variables? Use this regression equation to predict sales when the price of roses = 3.00, the price of carnations = 3.50, unemployment = 7.3%, the number of births = 17,500, deaths = 9120, marriages = 10,200, and disposable income = 178.00.

MKT   10.42   The following data represent quarterly sales (in thousands of dollars) for a large department store in Boston between the years 1970 and 1985. Also shown is the dollar amount spent quarterly on advertising (in hundreds of dollars).

| | Quarter | | | | | | | |
|---|---|---|---|---|---|---|---|---|
| | I | | II | | III | | IV | |
| Year | Sales | Adv. | Sales | Adv. | Sales | Adv. | Sales | Adv. |
| 1970 | 4,910 | 96 | 5,070 | 100 | 5,790 | 210 | 7,720 | 474 |
| 1971 | 5,100 | 98 | 5,280 | 118 | 5,800 | 240 | 7,800 | 488 |
| 1972 | 5,120 | 115 | 5,340 | 145 | 6,000 | 250 | 7,980 | 512 |
| 1973 | 5,240 | 123 | 5,390 | 156 | 6,670 | 280 | 8,520 | 550 |
| 1974 | 5,580 | 141 | 6,110 | 183 | 7,090 | 310 | 9,190 | 570 |
| 1975 | 6,070 | 179 | 6,650 | 191 | 7,720 | 330 | 10,400 | 630 |
| 1976 | 6,790 | 198 | 6,980 | 208 | 8,230 | 360 | 10,880 | 650 |
| 1977 | 6,910 | 220 | 7,640 | 221 | 8,700 | 400 | 11,370 | 710 |
| 1978 | 7,520 | 238 | 8,020 | 243 | 9,720 | 420 | 13,700 | 780 |
| 1979 | 7,850 | 250 | 8,380 | 259 | 10,100 | 450 | 13,950 | 840 |
| 1980 | 8,010 | 278 | 8,510 | 281 | 9,690 | 450 | 14,130 | 890 |
| 1981 | 9,840 | 280 | 10,380 | 288 | 11,400 | 480 | 15,100 | 940 |
| 1982 | 10,250 | 300 | 11,080 | 299 | 12,390 | 489 | 16,120 | 970 |
| 1983 | 10,750 | 305 | 11,500 | 311 | 12,840 | 480 | 16,960 | 1,000 |
| 1984 | 11,550 | 315 | 12,650 | 321 | 13,630 | 490 | 17,010 | 1,000 |
| 1985 | 11,280 | 330 | 12,730 | 339 | 14,480 | 524 | 19,020 | 1,010 |

a) Run a least-squares regression analysis on these data, with sales as the dependent variable and using two independent variables, advertising and trend (first quarter of 1970 = 1). Have the program plot the residuals. Describe any pattern you see in them. What might be causing such patterns?

b) Transform the data by taking the natural logarithm of the dependent variable. Rerun the regression analysis, plot the residuals, and again answer the questions in part (a). Has the log transformation helped?

c) To control for seasonality, add three dummy variables to the regression in part (b) and plot the residuals. Is there significant seasonality (i.e., has this transformation helped)?

d) Add a four-quarter lagged variable to the log of sales in part (c). Does this lagged variable improve the fit of the model?

e) Predict a sales value for the second quarter of 1986, assuming an advertising expenditure of $35,000.

FIN  **10.43** The treasurer of a major daily newspaper has been attempting to forecast the number of subscribers each month on the basis of the advertising budget, local population figures, and the subscription rate charged for the paper (per month). Thirty months of data are available. Use these data to forecast sales for the next 6 months. The subscription rate will increase to $5.25 3 months from now (in month 33). The advertising budget for the next 6 months is 25, 20, 20, 15, 8, and 15 (in thousands of dollars). Use a trend variable in your analysis, and be sure to try (at least) a one-period lag using the subscription rate.

| Subscribers (in Thousands) | Adv. Budget (in Thousands of Dollars) | Population (in Thousands) | Sub. Rate/Month (in Dollars) |
|---|---|---|---|
| 370 | 15 | 3478 | 5.00 |
| 377 | 21 | 3480 | 5.00 |
| 381 | 21 | 3493 | 5.00 |
| 380 | 25 | 3520 | 5.00 |
| 383 | 26 | 3525 | 5.00 |
| 379 | 21 | 3530 | 5.00 |
| 385 | 21 | 3530 | 5.00 |
| 386 | 16 | 3540 | 5.00 |
| 389 | 17 | 3560 | 5.25 |
| 359 | 10 | 3581 | 5.25 |
| 366 | 9 | 3600 | 5.25 |
| 361 | 15 | 3620 | 5.25 |
| 366 | 21 | 3640 | 5.10 |
| 388 | 21 | 3680 | 5.10 |
| 394 | 26 | 3710 | 5.10 |
| 399 | 26 | 3764 | 5.10 |
| 402 | 21 | 3768 | 5.10 |
| 404 | 21 | 3810 | 5.10 |
| 403 | 16 | 3815 | 5.10 |
| 408 | 16 | 3838 | 5.15 |
| 405 | 8 | 3877 | 5.15 |
| 410 | 8 | 3890 | 5.15 |
| 410 | 6 | 3930 | 5.15 |
| 417 | 14 | 3950 | 5.15 |
| 420 | 19 | 3991 | 5.15 |
| 426 | 20 | 4018 | 5.15 |
| 422 | 27 | 4028 | 5.20 |
| 420 | 27 | 4066 | 5.20 |
| 426 | 30 | 4120 | 5.20 |
| 427 | 31 | 4126 | 5.20 |

MKT **10.44** Fit a linear trend variable to the 20 observations on sales in Table 10.13, including the three quarter dummy variables to control for seasonality. Compare your results with those in Table 10.14, where the lag of sales was used to control for trend. Explain why the results in Table 10.14 constitute a better fit.

FIN **10.45** Using the 24 observations on cost in Table 10.10, create a one-quarter lag variable of cost. Fit this lag variable to cost, including the three quarter dummy variables to control for seasonality. Compare your results with those in Table 10.11, where a linear trend variable was used to control for trend in cost. Explain why the linear trend variable may be more appropriate than the lag variable in controlling for trend in this time series.

FIN **10.46** Using the 21 quarterly observations on net income and assets of Workingmens Federal Savings and Loan Association in Appendix A.3 (from the first quarter of 1980 through the first quarter of 1985), estimate a regression equation to predict quarterly net income based on assets and seasonal effects. After taking account of any significant seasonal effects, are assets significantly related to net income at the 0.05 level?

FIN **10.47** You are to fit a trend line to the yearly assets of the Workingmens Federal Savings and Loan Association in Appendix A.3. Use the 10 yearly asset totals reported for 1970 through 1979 plus the five fourth-quarter asset totals as the yearly totals for 1980 through 1984. For these 15 observations, what is the best-fitting trend line?

## Glossary

**correlation matrix:** An array of simple correlation coefficients that shows the relationship of each variable to itself and to the other variables included in a regression.

**cross-sectional data:** A set of values collected on subjects at a point in time.

**cyclical variations:** Patterns of change in a time series that tend to recur over long intervals.

**dummy variables:** Variables whose value is 0 or 1, added to a regression analysis to divide the data into parts, where each part represents possible qualitative differences in the data.

**heteroscedastic errors:** A violation of Assumption 2, where the error terms do not possess a constant variance.

**homoscedastic errors:** Constant variance of the error terms.

**lagged variable:** A variable that is created by setting the original time-specific values back one or more periods.

**mean square error:** The sum of squared residual or regression errors divided by the appropriate degrees of freedom.

**multicollinearity:** The high correlation of two or more independent variables in a regression.

**multiple coefficient of determination ($R^2$):** The proportion of total variability explained by the regression equation (SSR/SST).

**multiple R:** The multiple correlation coefficient.

**multiple regression:** A regression with more than one independent variable ($m > 1$).

**random variation:** The unpredictable or irregular movement in a time series.

**seasonal variations:** Pattern of change in a time series that tend to recur during the same time period every year.

**serial correlation:** The correlation of residuals over time.

**significance level:** The $p$ value. It gives the lowest probability of a type I error for which a null hypothesis could be rejected.

**time series:** A series of values that occur or are observed over regular intervals of time.

**trend:** The long-run change in a variable over time.

**trend variable:** An independent variable included in a regression to reflect the effect of the change in the dependent variable over time.

## Formulas

### 10.1—Sample Regression Equation

$$\hat{y} = a + b_1x_1 + b_2x_2 + \cdots + b_mx_m$$

where $a$ and the $b$'s are least-squares estimators.

### 10.2—Population Regression Model

$$y = \alpha + \beta_1 x_1 + \beta_2 x_2 + \cdots + \beta_m x_m + \epsilon$$

where $\alpha$ and the $\beta$'s are parameters to be estimated.

### 10.3—$t$ Statistic for Individual Coefficients

$$t = \frac{b_i - \beta_0}{\text{standard error of } b_i}$$

where $\beta_0$ is a the value of $\beta_i$ given by the null hypothesis, $b_i$ is the estimator of $\beta_i$, and the degrees of freedom are $n - m - 1$.

### 10.4—Multiple Coefficient of Determination

$$R^2 = \frac{\text{SSR}}{\text{SST}}$$

### 10.5—Standard Error of the Estimate

$$S_e = \sqrt{\text{SSE}/(n - m - 1)}$$

### 10.6—$F$ Statistic to Test $H_0$: $\beta_1 = \beta_2 = \cdots = \beta_m = 0$

$$F = \frac{(\text{variability in } y \text{ explained by regression})/m}{(\text{unexplained variability in } y)/(n - m - 1)}$$

$$= \frac{\text{mean square regression}}{\text{mean square error}}$$

where the degrees of freedom are $m$ and $n - m - 1$.

# CHAPTER ELEVEN

*Education is . . . hanging around until you've caught on.*
*Robert Frost*

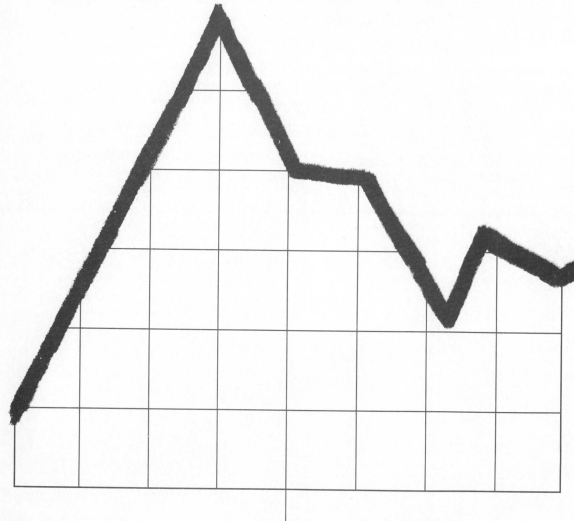

# ANALYSIS OF VARIANCE

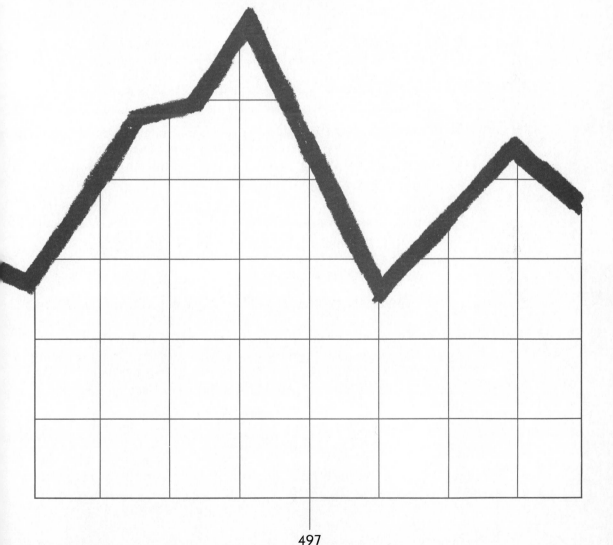

# 11.1 INTRODUCTION

**Analysis of variance (ANOVA)** is used to test hypotheses about two or more population means. Previously we studied one form of ANOVA in testing hypotheses about the overall fit of a regression equation. Examples of the types of problems we will now consider with ANOVA include the following:

- *Tennis* magazine published a study on the weight of new tennis balls. Samples of Dunlop, Wilson, Penn, MacGregor, Slazenger, and Tretorn balls were weighed. Tennis officials could use ANOVA to determine if the mean weight is significantly different across these brands.

- A financial analyst compares price-earning ratios across four industries. A random sample of companies is taken from each industry, and ANOVA is used to determine if the mean ratio differs significantly across industries.

- The personnel manager for a large company wants to compare the salaries of middle managers by gender in four cities. A random sample of male and female salaries is taken from these cities, and ANOVA is used to determine if the mean salaries differ significantly across cities and gender.

In general, ANOVA tests hypotheses by comparing the variability in a data set attributed to chance with the variability caused by systematic differences among the populations under study. The test statistic used for ANOVA is the same $F$ ratio used in Chapter 10 for regression. Sir Ronald Fisher, a British statistician, laid much of the foundation for ANOVA in his research in the early 1900s on agriculture in England. In fact, the $F$ test was named for Fisher.

Although there are numerous ANOVA models, only two fundamental ones will be described in this chapter: the one-factor model and the two-factor model. By the end of this chapter, you will be able to distinguish between these two models, to specify the appropriate test statistics, and to interpret a computer output in order to test hypotheses. The following example will be used to illustrate ANOVA.

## Assessing Taxes

You are an accountant working for the Indiana State Tax Board. The charge has been made that residential property taxes have been reassessed differently in the three townships in King County. Two of these townships used a local person for their reassessments, while the third used an outside assessor. One of the tasks of the Tax Board is to make sure that taxes in the county are equitable. To study the charge of unfair reassessment, the Tax Board took a random sample of residential houses in each township and recorded the ratio of new to old house values, as shown in Table 11.1. Your job is to determine if these mean ratios are significantly different across townships, which would indicate unequitable reassessments.

**Table 11.1**

| | Ratio of New to Old Tax Assessment | | |
|---|---|---|---|
| Sample Observation | Township | | |
| | 1 | 2 | 3 |
| 1 | 1.05 | 1.15 | 1.09 |
| 2 | 1.10 | 1.16 | 0.98 |
| 3 | 1.09 | 1.12 | 1.03 |
| 4 | 1.21 | 1.07 | 1.10 |
| 5 | 1.07 | 1.18 | 1.03 |
| 6 | 1.14 | 1.22 | 1.00 |
| 7 | 1.11 | 1.15 | 0.97 |
| 8 | 1.17 | 1.09 | 1.16 |
| 9 | 1.13 | 1.24 | 1.13 |
| 10 | 1.19 | 1.19 | 1.01 |
| 11 | 1.22 | 1.13 | 1.11 |
| 12 | 1.13 | 1.17 | 1.15 |
| 13 | 1.22 | 1.25 | 1.08 |
| 14 | 1.01 | 1.16 | 1.13 |

# 11.2 Overview of the One-Factor Model

In ANOVA, the three townships represented in Table 11.1 are called *treatments* rather than *populations*. We think of each tax assessor as "treating" a particular township in a certain manner. The effect a treatment (an assessor) has on a population (a township) is called the **treatment effect**.

For the Tax Board case the hypotheses to be tested concern the mean ratio (new assessment/old assessment) in each township.

$H_0$: The mean ratio for the first population (township 1) = the mean ratio for the second population (township 2) = the mean ratio for the third population (township 3).

$H_A$: At least two of the population mean ratios are not equal.

The null hypothesis is that the column means are all equal, or (equivalently) that treatment effects do not differ. The alternative hypothesis is that the treatment effects do differ (or that the column means are significantly different) and the Tax Board should conclude that taxes were assessed differently.

To test hypotheses in ANOVA, a comparison is made between two measures of variability. As in Chapter 10, the measure of variability used is the *mean square*, which equals the average of the squared variability. The two mean squares needed for the one-factor ANOVA model are the mean square columns and the mean square error.

1. **Mean square columns (MSC)** measure the amount of variability *between* the columns in an ANOVA problem. The more the column means differ, the larger the value of MSC. Because we can explain why column means might differ (because they have been treated differently), MSC is called a measure of the explained variability in an ANOVA problem. In some textbooks and computer programs, mean square columns is called *mean square between (MSB)*. We use MSC because this notation is consistent with the notation in the two-factor model introduced in Section 11.5.

2. **Mean square error (MSE)** measures the amount of variability *within* the columns in an ANOVA problem. This variability is the error in using the values in a column to measure the treatment effect. The more variability there is within each column, the larger the value of MSE. Thus MSE is said to measure the unexplained variability in an ANOVA problem. Mean square error is called *mean square within (MSW)* in some textbooks. We

use MSE because this notation is consistent with the notation in the two-factor model.

The test statistic for ANOVA is the $F$ ratio of MSC to MSE.

---

Test statistic for ANOVA

(11.1)
$$F = \frac{MSC}{MSE}$$

---

Large values of this $F$ ratio lead to rejection of $H_0$, while small values lead to its acceptance. Notice how similar this $F$ ratio is to the $F$ for regression analysis. For regression analysis the numerator of the $F$ ratio is the explained variability (MSR), while for ANOVA the numerator is the variability explained (by different treatments—MSC). In both regression and ANOVA the unexplained variability is MSE. The $F$ ratio in both cases has the explained measure in the numerator and the unexplained measure in the denominator.

---

**WORKED EXAMPLE 11.1**

Without doing any calculations, estimate whether data set A or data set B (in Table 11.2) has the larger $F$ ratio.

**Table 11.2**

| Two Data Sets for ANOVA | | | | | | | |
|---|---|---|---|---|---|---|---|
| Data Set A | | | | Data Set B | | | |
| Observa-tion | Treat-ment 1 | Treat-ment 2 | Treat-ment 3 | Observa-tion | Treat-ment 1 | Treat-ment 2 | Treat-ment 3 |
| 1 | 1.10 | 2.10 | 3.10 | 1 | 1.10 | 2.20 | 3.00 |
| 2 | 1.00 | 2.00 | 3.00 | 2 | 2.00 | 1.10 | 2.10 |
| 3 | 1.10 | 2.10 | 3.10 | 3 | 3.10 | 3.00 | 1.10 |
| 4 | 1.00 | 2.00 | 3.00 | 4 | 1.00 | 2.10 | 1.00 |
| 5 | 1.10 | 2.10 | 3.10 | 5 | 2.10 | 1.10 | 2.00 |
| Means = | 1.06 | 2.06 | 3.06 | Means = | 1.86 | 1.90 | 1.84 |

**ANSWER:**

Compared to data set B, data set A shows little variability within each column. For example, for treatment 1 in A, the range of variability is only from 1.00 to 1.10, while for B the range is from 1.00 to 3.10, and similarly for treatments 2 and 3. Yet, in data set A there is more variability between the treatment means (1.06, 2.06, and 3.06) than there is between the treatment means in data set B (1.86, 1.90, and 1.84). Thus we should anticipate a larger $F$ ratio for data set A than for data set B.

# 11.3 The Formal One-Factor Model

The one-factor ANOVA model describes the relationship between the dependent variable, the various treatments (or populations), and the random error. To describe the populations, consider the matrix in Table 11.3. Notice in this table that the numbering or counting of population values (such as the number of residential properties in our case) occurs down the left margin. This count is denoted by the letter $i$, where $i$ runs from 1 to $N$ and $N$ is the population size. The treatments levels (populations) are denoted by the letter $j$, where $j$ runs from 1 to $J$ and $J$ is the number of treatments.

**Table 11.3**

| ANOVA Notation for a Population of $N$ Observations and $J$ Treatments | | | | | | | | |
|---|---|---|---|---|---|---|---|---|
| | | **Treatment** | | | | | | |
| | | 1 | 2 | 3 | $\cdots$ | $j$ | | $J$ |
| | 1 | | | | $\cdots$ | | $\cdots$ | |
| | 2 | | | | $\cdots$ | | $\cdots$ | |
| **Count of** | 3 | | $y_{3,2}$ | | $\cdots$ | | $\cdots$ | |
| **Population** | $\vdots$ | | | | $\cdots$ | | $\cdots$ | |
| **Values** | $i$ | | | | | $y_{i,j}$ | | |
| | $\vdots$ | | | | | | | |
| | $N$ | | | | | | | |
| **Means** | | $\mu_1$ | $\mu_2$ | $\mu_3$ | | $\mu_j$ | | $\mu_J$  $\mu$ = Grand mean |

The following population notation is used for ANOVA (and Table 11.3).

$y_{i,j}$ = value of the dependent variable in the $i$th row and the $j$th column. This is the variable under investigation.

**EXAMPLE** In our Tax Board problem, $y_{i,j}$ represents the ratio new assessment/previous assessment. Thus $y_{3,2}$ is the ratio for the third piece of residential property (on the tax rolls) in the second township; $J = 3$ in this problem because there are three columns.

$\mu_j$ = mean of the $j$th column. This is the average value for the $j$th treatment.

**EXAMPLE** $\mu_3$ is the mean of the third treatment.

$\mu$ = grand mean. This is the mean of all the column means.

$\tau_j$ = *treatment effect* for the $j$th column, defined as the difference $\mu_j - \mu$. This is the difference between a column mean and the grand mean. The value of $\tau$ indicates how much effect a particular treatment has on the grand mean.

$$\tau_j = \mu_j - \mu$$

**EXAMPLE** Suppose the mean of treatment (column) 5 is $\mu_5 = 1.06$ and the grand mean is $\mu = 1.02$. The treatment effect for the fifth population is $\tau_3 = 1.06 - 1.02 = 0.04$.

$\epsilon_{i,j}$ = random error associated with $y_{i,j}$, defined as the difference between $y_{i,j}$ and $\mu_j$. This is the amount by which a particular value of the dependent variable differs from the mean of all values in that column.

$$\epsilon_{i,j} = y_{i,j} - \mu_j$$

**EXAMPLE** Suppose $\mu_3 = 7.15$ and $y_{2,3} = 7.06$. The error $\epsilon_{2,3} = y_{2,3} - \mu_3 = 7.15 - 7.06 = 0.09$.

The population model for ANOVA states that any value $y_{i,j}$ is the sum of the grand mean ($\mu$) plus the treatment effect ($\tau_j$) plus the random error ($\epsilon_{i,j}$). In symbols,

---

**(11.2)**

The one-factor ANOVA model

$$y_{i,j} = \mu + \tau_j + \epsilon_{i,j}$$

---

Using the notation in Table 11.3, the null and alternative hypotheses in the one-factor ANOVA model are

$$H_0: \mu_1 = \mu_2 = \cdots = \mu_J$$

$H_A$: at least two of the population means are not equal.

From Eq. (11.2), it can be shown that if the expected value of $\epsilon_{i,j}$ is zero and these errors are independent, then the null and alternative hypotheses can also be written as

$$H_0: \tau_1 = \tau_2 = \cdots = \tau_J = 0$$

$H_A$: at least one of the treatment effects does not equal zero.

In order to test the null hypothesis that the treatment effects are all equal to zero, two assumptions are necessary:

1. The random error terms $\epsilon_{ij}$ are normally distributed, with a mean of zero and a variance that is constant for all populations.
2. The random error terms $\epsilon_{ij}$ are independent.

# 11.4 Testing Hypotheses

The test in one-factor ANOVA is based on the $F$ distribution, Appendix Table B.6, where there are $(J - 1)$ and $(n - J)$ degrees of freedom and $n$ is the total number of observations on all $J$ treatments. That is,

---

$F$ test for one-factor ANOVA

(11.3)     $$F = \frac{\text{MSC}}{\text{MSE}}$$

with $(J-1)$ d.f. for the numerator and $(n-J)$ d.f. for the denominator

---

If the calculated value of the $F$ ratio in Eq. (11.3) exceeds the critical value of $F$ obtained from Appendix Table B.6, with $(J - 1)$ and $(n - J)$ degrees of freedom, then the null hypothesis is rejected. If the $F$ ratio is less than the critical value, then the null hypothesis is not rejected. (In the following discussion, we first present a hand calculation method for determining the $F$ ratio in Worked Example 11.1. Next, for the larger data set in the Tax Board case, we demonstrate the use of a computer for the $F$ test in ANOVA.)

## Hand Calculation of the $F$ Ratio

A mean square is a sum of squared deviations divided by the degrees of freedom. Because we need two mean squares, two sums of squares are needed—sum of squares columns (SSC) and sum of squares error (SSE). To calculate these sums of squares, the following notation is used:

$\bar{y}$ = average of all values in the sample. It is the grand mean of the data set. This is our estimator for $\mu$.

$\bar{y}_j$ = average of the $j$th column in the sample. This is our estimator for the $j$th treatment effect ($\mu_j$).

$f_j$ = frequency of observations in the $j$th column in the sample.

$n$ = total number of observations in the sample. $n = \Sigma f_j$.

---

Mean square columns

(11.4)    $$MSC = \frac{SSC}{J - 1} = \frac{\Sigma f_j(\bar{y}_j - \bar{y})^2}{J - 1}$$

(Note: $J - 1$ is the degrees of freedom for SSC.)

---

Mean square error

(11.5)    $$MSE = \frac{SSE}{n - J} = \frac{\Sigma\Sigma(y_{ij} - \bar{y}_j)^2}{n - J}$$

(Note: $n - J$ is the degrees of freedom for SSE.)

---

For data set A in Worked Example 11.1, MSC, MSE, and the $F$ ratio are now calculated in the following manner:

| Treatment 1 | Treatment 2 | Treatment 3 |
|:---:|:---:|:---:|
| 1.10 | 2.10 | 3.10 |
| 1.00 | 2.00 | 3.00 |
| 1.10 | 2.10 | 3.10 |
| 1.00 | 2.00 | 3.00 |
| 1.10 | 2.10 | 3.10 |
| $\bar{y}_1 = 1.06$ | $\bar{y}_2 = 2.06$ | $\bar{y}_3 = 3.06$ |

$\bar{y}$ = grand mean = $(1.06 + 2.06 + 3.06)/3 = 2.06$
$J = 3, f_1 = f_2 = f_3 = 5, n = 15$

$$\text{MSC} = \frac{\text{SSC}}{J - 1} = \frac{\Sigma f_j(\bar{y}_j - \bar{y})^2}{J - 1}$$

$$= \frac{5(1.06 - 2.06)^2 + 5(2.06 - 2.06)^2 + 5(3.06 - 2.06)^2}{3 - 1}$$

$$= \frac{10}{2} = 5$$

$$\text{MSE} = \frac{\text{SSE}}{n - J} = \frac{\Sigma\Sigma(y_{i,j} - \bar{y}_j)^2}{n - J}$$

$$= \frac{(1.10 - 1.06)^2 + \cdots + (3.10 - 3.06)^2}{15 - 3}$$

$$= \frac{0.036}{12} = 0.003$$

The calculated $F$ ratio is $F = \dfrac{5}{0.003} = 1666.67$.

To conduct the $F$ test we must specify the probability of a type I error, say $\alpha = 0.05$. From Appendix Table B.6, we now find the critical value of $F$ to be 3.89, with $(J - 1) = 2$ and $(n - J) = 12$ d.f. Since the calculated $F = 1666.67$ exceeds the critical value of 3.89, we reject $H_0$ and conclude that the three treatment effects are not all equal to zero.

---

**WORKED EXAMPLE 11.2**

A corporate recruiter arranges to hire MBA students from five universities. Over the past several years this recruiter has placed 30 students from each university. Because the commission for placing students is tied to starting salaries, the recruiter wishes to know if there is a difference in starting salaries for these five schools. The following information is available on starting salaries, in thousands of dollars.

| | University | | | | |
|---|---|---|---|---|---|
| | *1* | *2* | *3* | *4* | *5* |
| Mean | 31.5 | 30.9 | 33.1 | 32.4 | 33.8 |
| Standard deviation | 2.4 | 2.0 | 2.5 | 2.5 | 2.6 |
| Sample size | 30 | 30 | 30 | 30 | 30 |

Conduct an ANOVA on these data to determine if there is a difference in mean starting salaries for the five schools, at $\alpha = 0.05$.

**ANSWER:**

From these data the grand mean is calculated as follows:

Grand mean $= (31.5 + 30.9 + 33.1 + 32.4 + 33.8)/5 = 32.34$

Using Eq. (11.4), MSC (Universities) is calculated as follows:

$$MSC = [(30)(31.5 - 32.34)^2 + (30)(30.9 - 32.34)^2$$
$$+ (30)(33.1 - 32.34)^2 + (30)(32.4 - 32.34)^2$$
$$+ (30)(33.8 - 32.34)^2]/(5 - 1) = 41.19$$

Rather than use Eq. (11.5) to calculate MSE, a special variation of the equations from Chapter 3 can be used. This equation is

$$MSE = \Sigma(f_j - 1)s_j^2/(n - J)$$

Thus

$$MSE = [(29)(2.4)^2 + (29)(2.0)^2 + (29)(2.5)^2 + (29)(2.5)^2$$
$$+ (29)(2.6)^2]/(150 - 5) = 5.80$$

The calculated $F$ ratio is $F = MSC/MSE = 41.19/5.80 = 7.10$. With 4 and 145 d.f., the critical $F$ value at the 0.05 type I error level is 5.66 (approximately, from Table B.6). Since the calculated $F$ exceeds the critical $F$, we reject the null hypothesis of no differences in column means and conclude that there is a difference in the mean starting salaries among the five universities.

## Computer-Generated ANOVA

Using a computer program such as Microstat, ANOVA tables can be obtained that contain all the information for the preceding $F$ test. Table 11.4, for instance, gives the computer output for data set A in Worked Example 11.1. Notice in this table that the computer output uses the word *between* where we used the word *column* and the word *within* where we use the word *error*. Thus the sum of squares within is 0.036, which is what we calculated as SSE. The MSE is reported in scientific notation to be $3.0000E-03$, which is what we calculated as MSE $= 0.003$. Notice also that the computer program gives the $p$ value for the calculated $F$. If this $p$ value is less than the $\alpha$ level, then $H_0$ is rejected. Since the $p$ value in this example is approximately zero $(0.000E+00)$, we again conclude that there is a significant treatment effect.

**Table 11.4**

| A Computer-Generated ANOVA Table for Data Set A in Worked Example 11.1 | | | | | |
|---|---|---|---|---|---|
| SOURCE | SUM OF SQUARES | D.F. | MEAN.SQUARE | F RATIO | PROB. |
| BETWEEN | 10.000 | 2 | 5.000 | 1666.667 | 0.000E+00 |
| WITHIN | 0.036 | 12 | 3.0000E-03 | | |
| TOTAL | 10.036 | 14 | | | |

Returning to our Tax Board case, we can now use the computer printout in Table 11.5 to test for equity across the three townships. After the 42 observations in Table 11.1 are entered into an ANOVA computer program, Table 11.5 is the output.

Table 11.5 shows the calculated $F$ ratio to be 8.553 (MSC/MSE $= 0.032/0.0037115$). The $p$ value is 0.0008318, which is quite small. Thus, for any reasonable $\alpha$ level, the Tax Board should conclude that taxes were not reassessed equitably. Remember that this test requires the assumption that the $\epsilon$'s are normally distributed, with a mean of zero, and that these errors are independent of one another.

**Table 11.5**

| Tax Assessment ANOVA Table for the Data in Table 11.1 | | | | | |
|---|---|---|---|---|---|
| SOURCE | SUM OF SQUARES | D.F. | MEAN SQUARE | F RATIO | PROB. |
| BETWEEN | 0.063 | 2 | 0.032 | 8.553 | 8.318E-04 |
| WITHIN | 0.145 | 39 | 3.7115E-03 | | |
| TOTAL | 0.208 | 41 | | | |

**WORKED EXAMPLE 11.3**

Use the data in Worked Example 11.1, data set B, to show that $F$ is small, as was predicted. Use these data to find an estimate of $\tau_2$, the second treatment effect, and an estimate of the random error in the third row, second column, $\epsilon_{3,2}$. Show how the sample estimates of the ANOVA model (Eq. 11.2) work for the value $y_{3,2}$.

**ANSWER:**

|  | Treatment 1 | Treatment 2 | Treatment 3 |
|---|---|---|---|
|  | 1.10 | 2.20 | 3.00 |
|  | 2.00 | 1.10 | 2.10 |
|  | 3.10 | 3.00 | 1.10 |
|  | 1.00 | 2.10 | 1.00 |
|  | 2.10 | 1.10 | 2.00 |
|  | $\bar{y}_1 = 1.86$ | $\bar{y}_2 = 1.90$ | $\bar{y}_3 = 1.84$ |

GRAND MEAN $= \bar{y} = 1.867$    $n = 15$

| SOURCE | SUM OF SQUARES | D.F. | MEAN SQUARE | F RATIO | PROB. |
|---|---|---|---|---|---|
| BETWEEN | 9.3333E-03 | 2 | 4.6667E-03 | 6.7928E-03 | 0.9932 |
| WITHIN | 8.244 | 12 | 0.687 | | |
| TOTAL | 8.253 | 14 | | | |

The value of $F$ is indeed small, and the $p$ value is very large. An estimate of the second treatment effect is $\bar{y}_2 - \bar{y} = 1.90 - 1.867 = 0.033$. An estimate of the error $\epsilon_{3,2}$ is $y_{3,2} - \bar{y}_2 = 3.00 - 1.90 = 1.10$. Using the estimates for Eq. (11.2),

$$y_{3,2} = \text{est. of } \mu + \text{est. of } \tau_2 + \text{est. of } \epsilon_{3,2}$$
$$3.00 = 1.867 + 0.033 + 1.10$$

## Exercises

**11.1** In an ANOVA, can the calculated $F$ statistic ever be negative? Explain. How would you interpret an $F$ ratio that is (a) 0, (b) less than 1?

ADM   **11.2** An agribusinessman wishes to know the effects of three different fertilizers on tomato yield. The following yearly yields were obtained per plant tested:

| Fertilizer 1 | | Fertilizer 2 | | Fertilizer 3 | |
|:---:|:---:|:---:|:---:|:---:|:---:|
| 44 | 34 | 37 | 32 | 35 | 42 |
| 38 | 49 | 35 | 38 | 33 | 37 |
| 40 | 36 | 40 | 39 | 36 | 38 |

a) What is the mean yield for each fertilizer?

b) What is the variance of the yield for each fertilizer?

c) Calculate the $F$ statistic for a test of fertilizers.

d) At the 0.05 type I error level, is there a difference in the yield of these three fertilizers?

e) Estimate the three treatment effects.

FIN 11.3 A *Wall Street Journal* article on the legendary summer rally of stocks contained data that also showed stock prices crashing in the summer months. Following are the rally and crash percentage changes in the Dow Jones Industrial Averages reported in this article. To determine if the so-called summer rally was offset by the summer crash, a one-factor ANOVA can be employed. Conduct this test by specifying the null and alternative hypotheses, showing your computations of the test statistic and the specification of the critical test statistic value. (Note: to test for percentage differences in the crash and rally series, the signs in one of the series must be reversed.)

| Year: | 1983 | 1982 | 1981 | 1980 | 1979 | 1978 | 1977 | 1976 | 1975 | 1974 |
|---|---|---|---|---|---|---|---|---|---|---|
| Rally percent change, low for May–June to high in July–Sept. | +6.3 | +18.5 | +0.4 | +21.0 | +8.9 | +11.8 | +2.8 | +5.9 | +8.2 | +1.4 |
| Crash percent change, high for May–June to low in July–Sept. | −6.1 | −10.6 | −18.6 | −1.7 | −3.7 | −7.0 | −11.5 | −4.7 | −9.9 | −29.8 |
| Year | 1973 | 1972 | 1971 | 1970 | 1969 | 1968 | 1967 | 1966 | 1965 | 1964 |
| Rally percent change | +9.7 | +5.2 | +5.5 | +22.5 | +1.9 | +5.2 | +11.2 | +3.5 | +11.6 | +9.4 |
| Crash percent change | −10.9 | −6.3 | −10.7 | −8.8 | −17.2 | −5.5 | −5.5 | −17.7 | −8.3 | −1.0 |

**FIN** **11.4** In Exercise 11.3 why did the signs in one of the series have to be reversed to conduct the ANOVA tests?

**FIN** **11.5** For a 10-year period, the yearly portfolio returns for three different investment firms are listed. Do these data show a statistically significant difference in the firms' performance? Assume that the population errors meet the conditions necessary for ANOVA.

|  | Firm 1 | Firm 2 | Firm 3 |
|---|---|---|---|
| Mean return | 12.0 | 10.0 | 11.5 |
| Standard deviation | 2.0 | 2.4 | 3.0 |

**FIN** **11.6** Why might the ANOVA assumptions be questioned in Exercise 11.5? Explain carefully.

**MKT** **11.7** A national mail order firm wants to know if more sales result from placing ads in newspapers or on the radio. For 24 days the firm keeps track of the daily source of orders, with the following results. Assume that the ANOVA assumptions hold.

|  | Newspaper | Radio |
|---|---|---|
| Mean daily orders | 96 | 30 |
| Standard deviation | 11 | 10 |

a) What is the grand mean of these sample data?

b) Calculate the $F$ statistic for a test of newspaper–radio differences in orders.

c) Test for newspaper–radio differences at $\alpha = 0.05$.

**MFG** **11.8** A tire manufacturer is testing a new rubber compound. Tires produced with this new compound are given to race car drivers for high-speed testing at the Indianapolis 500 race track. The following tire wear is recorded for the old and new compound tires after an identical number of laps on each set of tires. Use ANOVA to test for a difference in tire wear between the old and new compounds at $\alpha = 0.05$.

Old: 0.05  0.09  0.08  0.07  0.10  0.08  0.06  0.07
New: 0.06  0.07  0.08  0.06  0.08  0.06  0.07  0.06

OPS **11.9** A clothing manufacturer tested the durability of four kinds of fabric. The following data show the weight loss after laundry tests on four samples of each fabric.

| Fabric | | | |
|---|---|---|---|
| A | B | C | D |
| 22.5 | 24.3 | 23.0 | 22.9 |
| 29.0 | 21.9 | 27.5 | 24.1 |
| 26.7 | 22.6 | 26.3 | 25.7 |
| 25.1 | 23.6 | 24.5 | 26.8 |

a) What is the mean weight loss for each fabric?

b) What is the grand mean for this sample?

c) What is the variance for each fabric weight loss?

d) What is the calculated $F$ statistic for ANOVA?

e) Test for a difference in weight loss at $\alpha = 0.05$.

f) Estimate each of the four treatment effects.

OPS **11.10** What is the value of $y_{4,2}$ in Exercise 11.9? What is your estimate of $\mu$, $\tau_2$, and $\epsilon_{4,2}$? Show that these estimates correspond to the relationship specified by Eq. (11.2).

**11.11** Consider the following ANOVA computer output:

| GROUP | MEAN | n |
|---|---|---|
| 1 | 1.113 | 4 |
| 2 | 1.123 | 4 |
| 3 | 1.168 | 4 |
| GRAND MEAN | 1.134 | 12 |

| SOURCE | SUM OF SQUARES | D.F. | MEAN SQUARE | F RATIO | PROB. |
|---|---|---|---|---|---|
| BETWEEN | 6.8667E-03 | 2 | 3.4333E-03 | 1.206 | 0.3436 |
| WITHIN | 0.026 | 9 | 2.8472E-03 | | |
| TOTAL | 0.032 | 11 | | | |

a) Use the information on group means to show that the grand mean is correctly calculated by this program.

b) What is the value of MSC and MSE in this problem?

c) Is there a significant difference in the three groups? (Explain your answer in terms of the $p$ value.)

**11.12** Consider the following ANOVA computer output:

| GROUP | MEAN | n |
|:-----:|:----:|:-:|
| 1 | 61.070 | 20 |
| 2 | 53.035 | 20 |
| GRAND MEAN | 57.053 | 40 |

| SOURCE | SUM OF SQUARES | D.F. | MEAN SQUARE | F RATIO | PROB. |
|--------|----------------|------|-------------|---------|-------|
| BETWEEN | 645.612 | 1 | 645.612 | 4.530 | 0.0398 |
| WITHIN | 5415.708 | 38 | 142.519 | | |
| TOTAL | 6061.320 | 39 | | | |

a) Use the information on group means to show that the grand mean is correctly calculated by this program.

b) What is the value of MSC and MSE in this problem?

c) Is there a significant difference in the two groups? (Explain your answer in terms of the $p$ value.)

# 11.5 Overview of the Two-Factor Model

Two-factor ANOVA extends the model presented in Section 11.3 by adding a second possible variable (or treatment) that might influence the dependent variable. The two possible influences on a two-factor model are usually called *factor A* and *factor B*. For example, the company testing for differences in the weight of tennis balls may use two-factor ANOVA to compare brands (factor A) as well as the type of ball (factor B could be "regular duty," "extra duty," or "pressureless").

In the case of the Tax Board at the beginning of this chapter, the board might wish to classify residential property as either rural or urban and use ANOVA to test for significant differences on both factor A (the township) and factor B (rural versus urban). Suppose the Tax Board finds that the first seven houses in each township sample were urban and the remaining seven were rural. The sample data would then look like Table 11.6.

Table 11.6

| | | Township 1 | Township 2 | Township 3 | Means |
|---|---|---|---|---|---|
| | | **Tax Assessment in Urban and Rural Townships** | | | |
| | | 1.05 | 1.15 | 1.09 | |
| | | 1.10 | 1.16 | 0.98 | |
| | | 1.09 | 1.12 | 1.03 | |
| | 1 (Urban) | 1.21 | 1.07 | 1.10 | 1.096 |
| | | 1.07 | 1.18 | 1.03 | |
| | | 1.14 | 1.22 | 1.00 | |
| Location (Factor B) | | 1.11 | 1.15 | 0.97 | |
| | | 1.17 | 1.09 | 1.16 | |
| | | 1.13 | 1.24 | 1.13 | |
| | | 1.19 | 1.19 | 1.01 | |
| | 2 (Rural) | 1.22 | 1.13 | 1.11 | 1.144 |
| | | 1.13 | 1.17 | 1.15 | |
| | | 1.22 | 1.25 | 1.08 | |
| | | 1.01 | 1.16 | 1.13 | |
| | Means | 1.131 | 1.159 | 1.069 | 1.120 = Grand mean |

The Tax Board must now test for three different effects. First, are there differences in the way taxes were assessed across townships (i.e., column differences)? Second, are there differences in the way taxes were assessed across the urban–rural classification (i.e., row differences)? These two tests are called tests of **main effects**. The third test is called a test of the **interaction effect**. An interaction effect is any *systematic* influence on the dependent variable that is not explained by the row and column effects (the main effects).

Any influence on the dependent variable that is not either a main effect or an interaction effect is called **random error**. In summary, the variability in a two-factor ANOVA model is assumed to be composed of four parts:

1. Row effect ⎱
2. Column effect ⎰ main effects
3. Interaction effect
4. Random error

## Main Effects

The test of column differences is similar to the test in the one-factor model, but now account is taken of the interaction between rows and columns. Thus this test is called a test of the main effect. It involves the following hypotheses:

$H_0$: The column means are all equal.

$H_A$: At least two of the column means are not equal.

To test these hypotheses, we again calculate the test statistic $F$ = MSC/MSE, where MSC is exactly the same as in a one-way ANOVA but MSE may now be smaller because any relationship between rows and columns is being explained as an interaction effect.

The test of row differences is similar to the test of column differences, except that now the data are classified by the labels assigned to the rows (in the Tax case, urban versus rural). This main effect test involves the following hypotheses:

$H_0$: The row means are all equal.

$H_A$: At least two of the row means are not equal.

These hypotheses are the same as the first set, except that they apply to rows rather than columns. In the Tax Board case there are only two row classifications—urban and rural. We are trying to determine if the two urban and rural sample means (1.096 and 1.144) differ significantly. The $F$ ratio in this case is $F$ = MSR/MSE, where MSR = mean square rows. For this test, all the urban properties are grouped together, as are the rural properties. In Section 11.7, we will calculate this $F$ ratio and complete the test of rows.

## Interaction Effect

An interaction effect is any systematic influence on the dependent variable that is not explained by the two main effects. For example, suppose the assessor in township 1 has a bias toward rural properties and consistently assesses them lower. This influence may not show up in the main effect for factor B (perhaps the assessor in township 2 has a preference for urban properties). These two preferences might cancel each other out in terms of the main effects, but they could appear as a significant interaction effect. Because an interactive effect is a *systematic* influence on the dependent variable, the presence of any interaction will tend to lower the random error (and hence the MSE). The hypotheses are:

$H_0$: There is no interaction effect in any of the cells.

$H_A$: There is an interaction effect in one or more cells.

An interaction effect is tested with the $F$ ratio $F$ = MSI/MSE, where MSI = mean square interaction.

We might further describe an interaction effect by thinking of Sir Ronald Fisher's agricultural experiments (in England) involving fertilizers. In this experiment two different fertilizers are applied to the same piece of land. The two fertilizers may act independently of one another, so their net effect is the sum of their separate main effects. Alternatively, the two fertilizers may interact; perhaps they cancel one another out, or perhaps the two in combination are even better than the sum of both taken individually. As an agribusiness executive, you would want to know of any interactive effect before buying fertilizer.

# 11.6 The Formal Two-Factor Model

For the two-factor model we use three subscripts. As in the one-factor model, the letter $j$ represents column treatments, where $j$ runs from 1 to $J$. The letter $k$ represents the row treatments, where $k$ runs from 1 to $K$. The letter $i$ represents the number of the observations in a cell, where $i$ runs from $i$ to $n$. For simplicity, we will assume that all cells have the same number of observations. Notice in the Tax Board case (Table 11.6) that there are three column treatments (three townships), so $J = 3$. Since there are two row treatments (urban and rural), $K = 2$. Within each of the six cells created by the three column and two row classifications are seven sample observations, so $n = 7$.

To calculate an $F$ ratio for a two-way ANOVA it is necessary to introduce new notation to describe the observations. This notation for the population model is shown in Table 11.7. Notice in this table that the observations on $y$ are denoted by subscripts; the first subscript denotes the observation number, the second subscript denotes the column, and the third subscript denotes the row.

Table 11.7 uses the following notation:

$$y_{i,j,k} = \text{ith population value in the jth column and the kth row.}$$
$$\mu_j = \text{population mean of the jth column}$$
$$\mu_k = \text{population mean of the kth row}$$
$$\mu_{j,k} = \text{mean of the cell in the jth column, kth row}$$
$$\mu = \text{grand mean of the population}$$
$$\tau_j = \text{treatment effect of the jth column, where } \tau_j = \mu_j - \mu$$
$$(\tau\lambda)_{j,k} = \text{interaction effect in the jth column, kth row, where } (\tau\lambda)_{j,k}$$
$$= \mu_{j,k} - \mu_j - \mu_k + \mu$$

**Table 11.7**

| | | | | The Two-Factor ANOVA Model | | | | | |
|---|---|---|---|---|---|---|---|---|---|

| | | | | | Levels of Factor A | | | | |
|---|---|---|---|---|---|---|---|---|---|
| | | 1 | 2 | 3 | $\cdots$ | $j$ | | $J$ | |
| | 1 | | | | $\cdots$ | | $\cdots$ | | $\mu_1$ |
| | 2 | | | | $\cdots$ | | $\cdots$ | | $\mu_2$ |
| Levels of | 3 | $y_{1,2,3}$ $y_{2,2,3}$ $y_{3,2,3}$ | | | $\cdots$ | | $\cdots$ | | $\mu_3$ |
| Factor | $\vdots$ | | | | $\cdots$ | | $\cdots$ | | |
| B | $k$ | | | | | $y_{i,j,k}$ | | | $\mu_k$ |
| | $\vdots$ | | | | $\cdots$ | | $\cdots$ | | |
| | $K$ | | | | $\cdots$ | | $\cdots$ | | $\mu_K$ |
| Means | | $\mu_1$ | $\mu_2$ | $\mu_3$ | | $\mu_j$ | | $\mu_J$ | $\mu$ = Grand mean |

$\epsilon_{i,j,k}$ = the random error of the $i$th value in the $j$th column, $k$th row, where $\epsilon_{i,j,k} = y_{i,j,k} - \mu_{j,k}$

(This is the error of values in a cell about the mean of that cell.)

To understand the population notation in Table 11.7, an example using the corresponding sample notation is presented. Table 11.8 identifies the sample observations in Table 11.6 using the notation suggested in Table 11.7. In Table 11.8, we see that $y_{3,2,1}$ (= 1.12) represents the third observation in the second column treatment and the first row treatment. The grand mean in the population, $\mu$ in Table 11.7, is estimated by the sample grand mean $\bar{y}$ = 1.120 in Table 11.8. The population mean of the third township, $\mu_3$ in Table 11.7, is estimated by the sample mean $\bar{y}_3$ = 1.069 in Table 11.8, and the population mean of the urban townships is estimated by the sample mean $\bar{y}_1$ = 1.096 on the right-hand side of Table 11.8.

In the two-factor model the value of $y_{i,j,k}$ is the sum of five components: (1) the grand mean [$\mu$], (2) the column treatment effect [$\tau_j$], (3) the row treatment effect [$\lambda_k$], (4) the interactive effect [$(\tau\lambda)_{j,k}$], and (5) the error term [$\epsilon_{i,j,k}$]. Thus

The two-factor model

(11.6)
$$y_{i,j,k} = \mu + \tau_j + \lambda_k + (\tau\lambda)_{jk} + \epsilon_{i,j,k}$$

Table 11.8

| | Township 1 | Township 2 | Township 3 | Means $(\bar{y}_k)$ |
|---|---|---|---|---|
| | **Sample Data on Tax Assessment in Urban and Rural Townships** | | | |
| 1 (Urban) | $y_{1,1,1} = 1.05$<br>$y_{2,1,1} = 1.10$<br>$y_{3,1,1} = 1.09$<br>$y_{4,1,1} = 1.21$<br>$y_{5,1,1} = 1.07$<br>$y_{6,1,1} = 1.14$<br>$y_{7,1,1} = 1.11$ | $y_{1,2,1} = 1.15$<br>$y_{2,2,1} = 1.16$<br>$y_{3,2,1} = 1.12$<br>$y_{4,2,1} = 1.07$<br>$y_{5,2,1} = 1.18$<br>$y_{6,2,1} = 1.22$<br>$y_{7,2,1} = 1.15$ | $y_{1,3,1} = 1.09$<br>$y_{2,3,1} = 0.98$<br>$y_{3,3,1} = 1.03$<br>$y_{4,3,1} = 1.10$<br>$y_{5,3,1} = 1.03$<br>$y_{6,3,1} = 1.00$<br>$y_{7,3,1} = 0.97$ | $\bar{y}_1 = 1.096$ |
| 2 (Rural) | $y_{1,1,2} = 1.17$<br>$y_{2,1,2} = 1.13$<br>$y_{3,1,2} = 1.19$<br>$y_{4,1,2} = 1.22$<br>$y_{5,1,2} = 1.13$<br>$y_{6,1,2} = 1.22$<br>$y_{7,1,2} = 1.01$ | $y_{1,2,2} = 1.09$<br>$y_{2,2,2} = 1.24$<br>$y_{3,2,2} = 1.19$<br>$y_{4,2,2} = 1.13$<br>$y_{5,2,2} = 1.17$<br>$y_{6,2,2} = 1.25$<br>$y_{7,2,2} = 1.16$ | $y_{1,3,2} = 1.16$<br>$y_{2,3,2} = 1.13$<br>$y_{3,3,2} = 1.01$<br>$y_{4,3,2} = 1.11$<br>$y_{5,3,2} = 1.15$<br>$y_{6,3,2} = 1.08$<br>$y_{7,3,2} = 1.13$ | $\bar{y}_2 = 1.144$ |
| Means $(\bar{y}_j)$ | $\bar{y}_1 = 1.131$ | $\bar{y}_2 = 1.159$ | $\bar{y}_3 = 1.069$ | $\bar{y} = 1.120$<br>Grand mean |

**WORKED EXAMPLE 11.4**

Use the population data in Table 11.9 to determine the treatment effect for column 2, the treatment effect for row 3, and the interaction effect for column 2 and row 3. Show how the two-factor model in Eq. (11.6) describes the value $y_{4,2,3}$.

**ANSWER:**

We know the following about the population model. The treatment effect for column 2 is $\tau_2 = 1.11 - 1.09 = 0.02$. The treatment effect for row 3 is $\lambda_3 = 1.06 - 1.09 = -0.03$. Using the formula on page 516, the interaction effect for cell (2, 3) is

$$(\tau\lambda)_{2,3} = 1.07 - 1.06 - 1.11 + 1.09 = -0.01$$

The error $\epsilon_{2,3} = 1.15 - 1.07 = 0.08$.

Putting all this together in the model (Eq. 11.6) gives

$$
\begin{aligned}
y_{i,j,k} &= \mu + \tau_j + \lambda_k + (\tau\lambda)_{jk} + \epsilon_{i,j,k} \\
1.15 &= 1.09 + 0.02 + (-0.03) + (-0.01) + 0.08
\end{aligned}
$$

**Table 11.9**

| | | | Population Data | | | | | | |
|---|---|---|---|---|---|---|---|---|---|
| | | | **Levels of Factor A** | | | | | | |
| | | 1 | 2 | 3 | $\cdots$ | $j$ | | $J$ | |
| | 1 | | | $\cdots$ | | $\cdots$ | | | $\mu_1$ |
| | 2 | | | $\cdots$ | | $\cdots$ | | | $\mu_2$ |
| **Levels of Factor B** | 3 | | fourth value in this cell is 1.15 and the cell mean is $\mu_{2,3} = 1.07$ | | $\cdots$ | | $\cdots$ | | $\mu_3 = 1.06$ |
| | $\vdots$ | | | | $\cdots$ | | $\cdots$ | | |
| | $k$ | | | | | | | | $\mu_k$ |
| | $\vdots$ | | | | $\cdots$ | | $\cdots$ | | |
| | $K$ | | | | $\cdots$ | | $\cdots$ | | $\mu_K$ |
| Means | | $\mu_1$ | $\mu_2 = 1.11$ | $\mu_3$ | | $\mu_j$ $\cdot$ | | $\mu_J$ | 1.09 = Grand mean |

---

# 11.7 Testing Hypotheses Using the Two-Factor Model

The three null hypotheses in the two-factor model are tested with three different $F$ ratios. For these $F$ ratios we need three mean squares and four sums of squares. Because a computer is usually used to calculate these sums of squares and mean squares, we present the formulas at the end of this chapter as reference material and will not discuss their use in hand calculations. This section emphasizes the computer-generated $F$ ratio for each of our three sets of hypotheses and their interpretation. As discussed in Section 11.5, the three hypotheses to be tested in a two-factor ANOVA model are:

1. Testing the treatment effect for factor A (columns):

$$H_0: \tau_1 = \tau_2 = \cdots = \tau_J = 0 \quad \text{(the column treatment affects all = 0)}$$

$$H_A: \text{At least one } \tau_j \neq 0$$

$$F \text{ test}: F = \frac{\text{MSC}}{\text{MSE}} \quad \text{with } J - 1, JK(n - 1) \text{ d.f.}$$

2. Testing the treatment effect for factor B (rows):

$H_0: \lambda_1 = \lambda_2 = \cdots = \lambda_K = 0$     (the row treatment affects all $= 0$)
$H_A$: at least one $\lambda_k \neq 0$.

$$F \text{ test}: F = \frac{\text{MSR}}{\text{MSE}} \quad \text{with } K - 1, JK(n - 1) \text{ d.f.}$$

3. Testing the interaction effect:

$H_0: (\tau\lambda)_{j,k} = 0$     for all combinations of $j$ and $k$
$H_A$: at least one $(\tau\lambda)_{j,k} \neq 0$

$$F \text{ test}: F = \frac{\text{MSI}}{\text{MSE}} \quad \text{with } (J - 1)(K - 1), JK(n - 1) \text{ d.f.}$$

The assumptions necessary for the two-factor model are similar to those presented earlier for the one-factor model.

1. The random error terms $\epsilon_{ijk}$ for each $jk$ cell are normally distributed, with a mean of zero and a variance that is constant for all treatment combinations.

2. The random error terms are independent.

In addition, if the hypothesis that interaction exists is accepted, then one needs to be cautious in interpreting the main effects (see Worked Example 11.6).

Using a computer program the two-factor ANOVA table for the Tax Board assessment data in Table 11.8 can be generated and used to test the preceding three hypotheses, where $\alpha = 0.05$. The ANOVA table is given in Table 11.10.

**Table 11.10**

| Two-Factor ANOVA Table for Tax Data (Table 11.8) | | | | | |
|---|---|---|---|---|---|
| SOURCE | SUM OF SQUARES | D.F. | MEAN SQUARE | F RATIO | PROB. |
| COLS | 0.063 | 2 | 0.032 | 10.131 | 3.232E-04 |
| ROWS | 0.026 | 1 | 0.026 | 8.378 | 6.415E-03 |
| INTERACTION | 5.7000E-03 | 2 | 2.8500E-03 | 9.096E-01 | 0.4117 |
| ERROR | 0.113 | 36 | 3.1333E-03 | | |
| TOTAL | 0.208 | 41 | | | |

The formulas used to calculate MSC, MSR, MSI and MSE are given on pages 534 and 535.

The first row in Table 11.10 presents the results for testing the column treatment effects. The $F$ value is 10.131 and its associated $p$ value is $p = 0.0003232$. Since this $p$ value is less than $\alpha = 0.05$, the null hypothesis of no column main effect is rejected. The null hypothesis of no row main effect is also rejected, since the row $F$ is 8.378, with $p$ value $= 0.006415$. Finally, the null hypothesis of no interaction is not rejected, since its $p$ value (0.4117) is larger than $\alpha$.

These results suggest that taxes are not assessed equitably across townships (as we knew before) and are not assessed equitably between rural and urban locations. However, there is no significant interaction between townships and the classification of urban versus rural.

---

**WORKED EXAMPLE 11.5**

Find the estimated treatment effect for the rows in Table 11.8. Find the estimated interaction effect for the second column and the first row. Find an estimate of the error associated with the last observation in the first column and the second row.

**ANSWER:**

The sample means are:

| COL | MEAN | n | ROW | MEAN | n |
|-----|------|---|-----|------|---|
| 1 | 1.131 | 14 | 1 | 1.096 | 21 |
| 2 | 1.159 | 14 | 2 | 1.144 | 21 |
| 3 | 1.069 | 14 | | | |

CELL MEANS

| ROW | COL | MEAN | n | ROW | COL | MEAN | n |
|-----|-----|------|---|-----|-----|------|---|
| 1 | 1 | 1.110 | 7 | 2 | 2 | 1.169 | 7 |
| 2 | 1 | 1.153 | 7 | 1 | 3 | 1.029 | 7 |
| 1 | 2 | 1.150 | 7 | 2 | 3 | 1.110 | 7 |

GRAND MEAN = 1.120   42

Estimate of $\lambda_1 = 1.096 - 1.120 = -0.024$

Estimate of $\lambda_2 = 1.144 - 1.120 = \phantom{-}0.024$

Estimate of $(\tau\lambda)_{2,1} = 1.150 - 1.159 - 1.096 + 1.120 = 0.015$

Estimate of $\epsilon_{7,1,2} = 1.01 - 1.153 = -0.143$

Consider the values in Table 11.11 as a random sample of the weight of both regular-duty and extra-duty tennis balls (some of these data were reported in an article in *Tennis* magazine). Use these data and the computer output given at the bottom of Table 11.11 to answer the following questions:

**Table 11.11**

| Tennis Ball Data | | | | |
|---|---|---|---|---|
| | | Wilson | Penn | Dunlop | MacGregor |

| | | Wilson | Penn | Dunlop | MacGregor |
|---|---|---|---|---|---|
| Regular Duty | 1 | 1.97 | 2.02 | 2.04 | 2.01 |
| | 2 | 1.99 | 1.98 | 1.99 | 2.05 |
| | 3 | 2.01 | 2.01 | 2.02 | 2.04 |
| | 4 | 1.96 | 2.00 | 1.97 | 2.09 |
| | 5 | 1.97 | 2.04 | 2.03 | 2.03 |
| Extra Duty | 6 | 1.96 | 2.04 | 2.00 | 2.09 |
| | 7 | 1.91 | 2.07 | 2.05 | 2.08 |
| | 8 | 1.92 | 2.05 | 2.03 | 2.09 |
| | 9 | 1.96 | 2.03 | 2.08 | 2.06 |
| | 10 | 1.95 | 2.06 | 2.04 | 2.08 |

MEANS

| COL | MEAN | n | ROW | MEAN | n |
|---|---|---|---|---|---|
| 1 | 1.960 | 10 | 1 | 2.011 | 20 |
| 2 | 2.030 | 10 | 2 | 2.028 | 20 |
| 3 | 2.025 | 10 | | | |
| 4 | 2.062 | 10 | | | |

CELL MEANS

| ROW | COL | MEAN | n | ROW | COL | MEAN | n |
|---|---|---|---|---|---|---|---|
| 1 | 1 | 1.980 | 5 | 1 | 3 | 2.010 | 5 |
| 2 | 1 | 1.940 | 5 | 2 | 3 | 2.040 | 5 |
| 1 | 2 | 2.010 | 5 | 1 | 4 | 2.044 | 5 |
| 2 | 2 | 2.050 | 5 | 2 | 4 | 2.080 | 5 |

GRAND MEAN        2.019        40

| SOURCE | SUM OF SQUARES | D.F. | MEAN SQUARE | F RATIO | PROB. |
|---|---|---|---|---|---|
| COLS | 0.055 | 3 | 0.018 | 33.028 | 0.000E+00 |
| ROWS | 2.7225E-03 | 1 | 2.7225E-03 | 4.916 | 0.0338 |
| INTERACTION | 0.011 | 3 | 3.5892E-03 | 6.482 | 1.492E-03 |
| ERROR | 0.018 | 32 | 5.5375E-04 | | |
| TOTAL | 0.086 | 39 | | | |

1. Is either main effect significant? Is the interaction effect significant? Interpret these results. Use $\alpha = 0.05$.

2. What assumptions about the population are necessary?

3. Estimate the main effects, both column and row.

4. Determine an estimate of the interaction effect $(\tau\lambda)_{4,2}$.

5. Find an estimate of the random error $\epsilon_{3,4,2}$.

6. Show that the value of $y_{3,4,2}$ equals the sample grand mean + the estimated column effect + the estimated row effect + the estimated interaction effect + the estimated random error.

## ANSWER:

1. The main effect for columns is significant ($p$ value $= 0.0000$), as is the main effect for rows ($p$ value $= 0.0338$). The interaction effect is also significant ($p$ value $= 0.001492$). Thus there is a significant difference in the weight across brands, with Wilson weighing the least and MacGregor the most. The weights by type (regular versus extra-duty) are also significantly different, with the extra-duty balls weighing more. The significant interaction indicates that we must be careful in interpreting the main effects as they do not account for all the differences. For example, although extra-duty balls generally weigh more, this is not the case for Wilson balls, where the regular-duty balls weigh more on the average.

2. The necessary assumptions are that the eight cells have independent random error terms that are each normally distributed, with a mean of zero and a constant variance.

3. The estimated main effects are:

   Estimate of column 1 effect: $1.96 - 2.019 = -0.059$
   Estimate of column 2 effect: $2.03 - 2.019 = 0.011$
   Estimate of column 3 effect: $2.025 - 2.019 = 0.006$
   Estimate of column 4 effect: $2.062 - 2.019 = 0.043$
   Estimate of row 1 effect: $2.011 - 2.019 = -0.008$
   Estimate of row 2 effect: $2.028 - 2.019 = 0.009$

4. Estimate of the interaction $(\tau\lambda)_{4,2}$:

   $2.08 - 2.062 - 2.028 + 2.019 = 0.009$

5. Estimate of the random error $\epsilon_{3,4,2}$: $2.09 - 2.08 = 0.01$

6. $y_{3,4,2} =$ grand mean + col. eff. + row eff. + inter. eff. + error
   $2.09 = 2.019 + 0.043 + 0.009 + 0.009 + 0.01$

**11.13** In Table 11.5, the column $F$ ratio for the three townships was calculated to be 8.553. In Table 11.10, the column $F$ ratio for the three townships was calculated to be 10.131. Why do these two $F$ ratio values differ if they both represent a test statistic for the difference between columns?

ADM **11.14** For each of the three fertilizers described in Exercise 11.2, it is learned that the first three plants for each fertilizer (first column of numbers for each fertilizer) came from the north end of a field, while the last three plants came from the south end. Draw up a two-factor ANOVA table and use a computer program to calculate the three $F$ statistics for the fertilizer treatment effect, the north–south field effect and the interaction effect. Test these effects at $\alpha = 0.05$.

OPS **11.15** You have just learned that the four fabrics in Exercise 11.9 were washed in different machines. The first two observations on each fabric came from one washing machine, while the last two observations came from another machine. State $H_0$ and $H_A$. Does this information affect your answer in Exercise 11.9? Explain.

MFG **11.16** The first four observations on the old and new tires in Exercise 11.8 came from one race car driver, while the last four observations came from another driver. State $H_0$ and $H_A$. After controlling for interaction effects, is there a difference in tire wear? Is there a difference in drivers?

MKT **11.17** In a marketing experiment, four male and four female subjects were asked to give their perception of the selling price of three different products (marked A, B, and C). Following are the results for the eight subjects.

|  | Product | | |
|---|---|---|---|
|  | *A* | *B* | *C* |
| *Males* | 5.35 | 4.78 | 9.87 |
|  | 6.89 | 5.38 | 6.78 |
|  | 5.78 | 4.90 | 7.79 |
|  | 6.50 | 4.58 | 5.00 |
| *Females* | 6.50 | 5.79 | 5.80 |
|  | 6.10 | 4.80 | 7.00 |
|  | 4.68 | 6.00 | 5.00 |
|  | 5.90 | 5.00 | 6.00 |

**a)** State the null and alternative hypotheses for this problem and the required assumptions.

**b)** At the 0.05 type I level, is there any difference in the average dollar value placed on the three brands? Does gender appear to affect this dollar value? Is there any interaction between gender and the three product values?

MKT **11.18** For Exercise 11.17, estimate $\mu$, the five column/row means, and the five main treatment effects. Find $e_{3,1,2}$. Verify that $y_{3,1,2}$ can be determined using estimates of the values in Eq. (11.6).

**11.19** The following computer printout is for a two-factor ANOVA:

| COL | MEAN | n |
|---|---|---|
| 1 | 377.300 | 20 |
| 2 | 133.200 | 20 |
| 3 | 12528.950 | 20 |

| ROW | MEAN | n |
|---|---|---|
| 1 | 4243.600 | 30 |
| 2 | 4449.367 | 30 |

CELL MEANS

| ROW | COL | MEAN | n |
|---|---|---|---|
| 1 | 1 | 387.700 | 10 |
| 2 | 1 | 366.900 | 10 |
| 1 | 2 | 130.100 | 10 |
| 2 | 2 | 136.300 | 10 |
| 1 | 3 | 12213.000 | 10 |
| 2 | 3 | 12844.900 | 10 |

GRAND MEAN 4346.483 60

| SOURCE | SUM OF SQUARES | D.F. | MEAN SQUARE | F RATIO | PROB. |
|---|---|---|---|---|---|
| COLS | 2009178675.000 | 2 | 1004589338.000 | 1447.181 | 0.000E+00 |
| ROWS | 635098.816 | 1 | 635098.816 | 0.915 | 0.3431 |
| INTERACTION | 1363740.184 | 2 | 681870.092 | 0.982 | 0.3810 |
| ERROR | 37485163.000 | 54 | 694169.685 | | |
| TOTAL | 2048662677.000 | 59 | | | |

a) How many cells are represented in this ANOVA table, and what is each cell's mean?

b) What values are used to calculate the column $F$ ratio of 1447.181? What are the degrees of freedom for the column $F$ statistic? What is the value and meaning of the column $p$ value?

c) Are there any column, row, or interaction effects? Estimate each main effect.

**11.20** The following computer printout is for a two-factor ANOVA:

| SOURCE | SUM OF SQUARES | D.F. | MEAN SQUARE | F RATIO | PROB. |
|---|---|---|---|---|---|
| COLS | 31336.966 | 2 | 15668.483 | 1072.203 | 0.000E+00 |
| ROWS | 1503.001 | 1 | 1503.001 | 102.851 | 1.000E-09 |
| INTERACTION | 1023.133 | 2 | 511.566 | 35.008 | 2.000E-10 |
| ERROR | 789.121 | 54 | 14.613 | | |
| TOTAL | 34652.222 | 59 | | | |

a) How many observations are represented in this ANOVA table?

b) What values are used to calculate the row $F$ ratio of 102.851? What are the degrees of freedom for the row $F$ statistic? What is the value and meaning of the row $p$ value?

c) Are there any significant column, row, or interaction effects?

**11.21** In the following ANOVA table, how many observations are represented? Are there any significant column, row, or interaction effects indicated at the 0.05 type I error level?

| SOURCE | SUM OF SQUARES | D.F. | MEAN SQUARE | F RATIO | PROB. |
|---|---|---|---|---|---|
| COLS | 42996.218 | 2 | 21498.109 | 1016.352 | 0.000E+00 |
| ROWS | 2640.222 | 1 | 2640.222 | 124.820 | 1.000E-09 |
| INTERACTION | 1776.444 | 2 | 888.222 | 41.992 | 0.000E+00 |
| ERROR | 1396.047 | 66 | 21.152 | | |
| TOTAL | 48808.931 | 71 | | | |

**11.22** For Exercise 11.21, how many column treatments are there? How many row treatments?. How many replications in each cell?

# 11.8 Other ANOVA Models

The models presented thus far are just two of the many ANOVA models. Many universities devote entire courses to the study of ANOVA. We will not present additional models here, but will mention some of the more popular ones.

1. *Models with more than two factors.* It is possible to consider the influence of three or more factors in an ANOVA model. However, as the number of factors increases, so does the complexity of analysis of interactions. For example, with three factors ($A$, $B$, $C$), there are four different interaction terms: $A \times B$, $A \times C$, $B \times C$, and $A \times B \times C$.

2. *Contrasts.* In some ANOVA models the difference between two specific treatments (a *contrast*) is of special interest. Techniques are available for determining if the specific treatments of interest differ significantly. The procedure in this case is to form a confidence interval for the difference in treatment effects. If this confidence interval does not include zero, then the pair of treatments is significantly different from zero.

3. *Experimental design.* In most statistical analysis, the researcher wishes to design a data collection procedure that maximizes the information obtained for a given sample size. This process is called *experimental design.* For ANOVA the statistician uses experimental design in an attempt to control or modify certain influences on the dependent variable. For example, suppose a researcher is studying the influence (on gas mileage) of car speed (factor A) and number of cylinders (factor B). It would be unwise to try to determine gas mileage for all possible car speeds. Instead, a controlled experiment could be used where only certain specified speeds are studied.

   As another example, suppose an ANOVA model has three factors, with five levels of each factor. In this case the number of cells in the ANOVA model is $(5)(5)(5) = 125$. With four replications in each cell, this analysis would require $4(125) = 500$ random observations, a number that may be impractical for many research problems. A careful experimental design, however, may be able to reduce the sample size dramatically. In one approach for three factors, called a *Latin square* design, only one level of factor C is used with each combination of factors A and B. Two other designs used to reduce the sample size are called *incomplete block* and *fractional factorial.*

4. *Randomized blocks models.* An extension of the one-factor ANOVA model permits the researcher to control for influences on the dependent variable without adding additional factors to the model. For example, in the Tax Board problem, it may be that the differences between the class of the residential property (classified as A, B, C, D, or E according to value) in a township could be considered an influence on the reassessment. The ANOVA procedure in this case might select three classes of houses to sample. The class is the *block*. Within each block, a random sample of houses is taken, hence the name *randomized blocks*.

## Chapter Exercises

**11.23** How and under what conditions is a one-factor ANOVA $F$ test comparable to the $t$ or $z$ test of the difference between two population means described in Chapter 8?

**11.24** Why is a one-factor ANOVA similar to simple regression analysis? Explain.

**11.25** Explain the similarities between two-factor ANOVA and multiple regression analysis. Could multiple regression be used to solve an ANOVA problem? Explain.

**11.26** A researcher concludes that there is no difference in the column treatments in a one-factor model. Upon reanalysis of the same data using two-factor ANOVA, the researcher concludes that there is a difference in the column treatments. Did the researcher make a mistake? Which if either conclusion is true? (Explain how these contradictory conclusions can or cannot be justified.)

MKT **11.27** Following are the results of a pilot study of a new product. As a marketing executive, you want to know if there is a difference in mean ages of the people who bought, did not buy, or may buy the product. If there is a difference in ages, then your advertising campaign will be tailored to age groups. If there is no difference, then the campaign will be general.

| Buy* | Not Buy* | May Buy* |
|------|----------|----------|
| 21 | 33 | 30 |
| 35 | 65 | 46 |
| 50 | 29 | 25 |
| 44 | 22 | 19 |
| 23 | 46 | 23 |

*Age in years.

a) State the null and alternative hypotheses.

b) Calculate the test statistics.

c) State the level of significance at which $H_0$ could be rejected.

d) Should a general or age-specific advertising campaign be planned?

MKT   **11.28**   For Exercise 11.27, estimate the column effects. Estimate the random error for row 4, column 3. Show that $y_{4,3}$ equals the sum of the grand mean plus the estimated column effect plus the random error.

OPS   **11.29**   A car magazine tests the acceleration (0 to 60 MPH) of three expensive sports cars and gets the following results in seconds:

| Car 1 | Car 2 | Car 3 |
|-------|-------|-------|
| 6.01 | 7.10 | 5.90 |
| 7.00 | 6.05 | 6.89 |
| 6.70 | 6.90 | 6.30 |
| 6.03 | 6.50 | 6.50 |
| 5.90 | 6.30 | 6.25 |
| 6.80 | 5.92 | 5.89 |

Can the magazine conclude that there is a difference in the mean acceleration time for these three cars?

OPS   **11.30**   If you learned that the first three time trials for each car in Exercise 11.29 were made by one driver, while the last three were made by another, would you want to reconsider your conclusion? Explain.

ACT   **11.31**   For three different stores in 25 randomly selected weeks, the dollar value of goods damaged and destroyed is recorded. Below are the average dollar values and standard deviations.

|  | Store 1 | Store 2 | Store 3 |
|---|---|---|---|
| *Average* | 725 | 876 | 800 |
| *Standard deviation* | 100 | 125 | 120 |

a) What is the grand mean dollar value of goods damaged and destroyed? What are the values of MSC and MSE?

b) Is there a difference in the average dollar value of goods damaged and destroyed among these three stores. (Test at the 0.05 type I error level).

c) Why would an accountant be interested in performing this test?

MKT 11.32 In a marketing study aimed at assessing the knowledge consumers gain from watching a commercial, 16 subjects were tested prior to and after watching the commercial. The following ANOVA results were obtained:

| SOURCE | SUM OF SQUARES | D.F. | MEAN SQUARE | F RATIO | PROB. |
|---|---|---|---|---|---|
| BETWEEN | 457.531 | 1 | 457.531 | 18.164 | 1.851E-04 |
| WITHIN | 755.688 | 30 | 25.190 | | |
| TOTAL | 1213.219 | 31 | | | |

a) State the null and alternative hypotheses for a test of the effect of the commercial on knowledge.

b) At the 0.05 type I error level, would you reject or accept the null hypothesis?

c) Is your result in part (b) sensitive to the $\alpha$ level? Why or why not?

11.33 Use the following computer printout in parts (a) through (d).

| SOURCE | SUM OF SQUARES | D.F. | MEAN SQUARE | F RATIO | PROB. |
|---|---|---|---|---|---|
| COLS | 457.531 | 1 | 457.531 | 24.821 | 2.912E-05 |
| ROWS | 225.781 | 1 | 225.781 | 12.249 | 1.577E-03 |
| INTERACTION | 13.781 | 1 | 13.781 | 0.748 | 0.3946 |
| ERROR | 516.125 | 28 | 18.433 | | |
| TOTAL | 1213.219 | 31 | | | |

a) How many row and column effects are represented?

b) How many observations are represented?

c) What are the critical $F$ values to test the row, column, and interaction effects at $\alpha = 0.05$?

d) Are there any row, column, or interaction effects?

11.34 Use the following computer printout to answer the questions (a) through (c).

| SOURCE | SUM OF SQUARES | D.F. | MEAN SQUARE | F RATIO | PROB. |
|--------|------|------|-------------|---------|-------|
| COLS | 6767400.449 | 2 | 3383700.225 | 513.957 | 0.000E+00 |
| ROWS | 1296456.041 | 1 | 1296456.041 | 196.921 | 4.000E-10 |
| INTERACTION | 575879.757 | 2 | 287939.879 | 43.736 | 0.000E+00 |
| ERROR | 553024.900 | 84 | 6583.630 | | |
| TOTAL | 9192761.147 | 89 | | | |

a) How many row and column effects are represented?

b) How many observations are represented?

c) For $\alpha = 0.01$, are there any row, column, or interaction effects?

ECN 11.35 Select a sample of 20 price-earnings ratios from Appendix Table A.1 by *randomly* picking five companies from each of these four categories: Banks and Bank Holding Companies, Service Industries, Electrical, Office Equipment. Do the means of these price-earnings ratios differ significantly? Use $\alpha = 0.05$.

11.36 An ANOVA model has four factors, A, B, C, and D. Specify the hypotheses that could be tested in such a model.

11.37 A researcher has an ANOVA problem with five columns (treatments). Would you recommend testing for differences between the columns by looking at pairs of columns? Explain why. How many pairs are there?

11.38 Explain intuitively why it is that when the confidence interval for a contrast overlaps zero, the two treatments being compared are not significantly different.

11.39 Construct three $2 \times 2$ contingency tables that have the following characteristics. Verify your tables with a computer output.

a) A significant column effect, a significant row effect, and a significant interaction effect.

b) A significant row and column effect, but no significant interaction effect.

c) A significant interaction effect, but no significant main effects.

**11.40** Think of the following square as a farm that has been divided into nine plots of land. The farm is testing three types of fertilizer (A1, A2, A3), three types of pest control (B1, B2, B3), and three types of wheat (C1, C2, C3). Explain what advantages (efficiencies) and disadvantages you see in the following *Latin-square* design. What pattern is there in this design?

|  |  | **Factor B** | | |
|---|---|---|---|---|
|  |  | *B1* | *B2* | *B3* |
|  | *A1* | C1 | C3 | C2 |
| **Factor A** | *A2* | C2 | C1 | C3 |
|  | *A3* | C3 | C2 | C1 |

**11.41** Construct an example illustrating a randomized block design. What efficiencies does your design provide?

## Glossary

**analysis of variance (ANOVA):** A statistical technique used to test the equality of two or more means. It is used to make inferences about whether multiple samples come from populations having the same means.

**grand mean:** The overall mean of the data set. It is the mean of all the column or row means.

**interaction effect:** Any systematic influence on the dependent variable that is not explained by the two main effects.

**main effects:** The treatment effect of either the columns or rows.

**mean square columns (MSC):** A measure of the amount of variability *between* the columns in an ANOVA problem. The more the column means differ, the larger the value of MSC. (MSC is also called the *explained* or *between variability*.)

**mean square error (MSE):** A measure of the amount of variability within the columns in an ANOVA problem. This variability is the error in using the values in a column to measure the treatment effect. The more variability there is within each column, the larger the value of MSE. (MSE is also called the *unexplained* or *within variability*.)

**treatment effect:** The difference between a column (or row) mean and the grand mean. This difference indicates how much influence a particular treatment has on the grand mean.

## FORMULAS

**11.1—Test Statistic for ANOVA**

$$F = \frac{\text{MSC}}{\text{MSE}}$$

**11.2—Notation and Formulas for the One-Factor Model**

The one-factor ANOVA model is

$$y_{i,j} = \mu + \tau_j + \epsilon_{i,j},$$

where

$y_{i,j}$ = the value of the *i*th observation in the *j*th column
$\mu$ = grand mean (mean of all values in the population)
$\tau_j$ = treatment effect of the *j*th column = $\mu_j - \mu$
$\epsilon_{i,j}$ = error of the *i*th value in the *j*th column = $y_{i,j} - \mu_j$

The relevant sample notation and formulas are:

$y_{i,j}$ = value of the *i*th observation in the *j*th column
$\bar{y}$ = grand mean of all values in the sample
$\bar{y}_j$ = mean of the *j*th column in the sample
$f_j$ = frequency of observations in the *j*th sample column
$n$ = total number of observations in the sample ($n = \Sigma f_j$)

**11.3—*F* Ratio d.f. for One-Factor Model**

$$F = \text{MSC}/\text{MSE} \qquad \text{with } J - 1, n - J \text{ d.f.}$$

### 11.4—Mean Square Column (MSC) for One-Factor Model

$$\text{MSC} = \frac{\text{SSC}}{J-1} = \frac{\Sigma f_j(\bar{y}_j - \bar{y})^2}{J-1}$$

### 11.5—Mean Square Error (MSE) for One-Factor Model

$$\text{MSE} = \frac{\text{SSE}}{n-J} = \frac{\Sigma\Sigma(y_{i,j} - \bar{y}_j)^2}{n-J}$$

### 11.6—Notation and Formulas for the Two-Factor Model
The two-factor ANOVA model is

$$y_{i,j,k} = \mu + \tau_j + \lambda_k + (\tau\lambda)_{j,k} + \epsilon_{i,j,k}$$

where

$\mu$ = grand mean of all values in the population

$\mu_j$ = mean of the $j$th column

$\mu_k$ = mean of the $k$th column

$\mu_{j,k}$ = mean of observations for the cell in the $j$th column, $k$th row

$\tau_j$ = treatment effect of the $j$th column = $\mu_j - \mu$

$\lambda_k$ = treatment effect of the $k$th row = $\mu_k - \mu$

$(\tau\lambda)_{j,k}$ = interaction effect of the $j$th column and the $k$th row

= $\mu_{j,k} - \mu_j - \mu_k + \mu$

$\epsilon_{i,j,k}$ = error of the $i$th observation in the $j$th column and the
$k$th row = $y_{i,j,k} - \mu_{j,k}$

The relevant notation and formulas for two-factor ANOVA are:

$y_{i,j,k}$ = value of the $i$th observation in the $j$th column in the
$k$th row

$\bar{y}_j$ = sample mean of the $j$th column

$\bar{y}_k$ = sample mean of the $k$th row

$\bar{y}$ = the grand mean of the sample

$n$ = the number of observations in each cell

### Mean Square Columns (MSC) for Two-Factor Model

$$\text{MSC} = \frac{\text{SSC}}{J-1} = \frac{\Sigma Kn(\bar{y}_j - \bar{y})^2}{J-1}$$

**Mean Square Rows (MSR) for Two-Factor Model**

$$\text{MSR} = \frac{\text{SSR}}{K-1} = \frac{\Sigma Jn(\bar{y}_k - \bar{y})^2}{K-1}$$

**Mean Square Interaction (MSI) for Two-Factor Model**

$$\text{MSI} = \frac{\text{SSI}}{(J-1)(K-1)} = \frac{\Sigma\Sigma n(\bar{y}_{j,k} - \bar{y}_j - \bar{y}_k + \bar{y})^2}{(J-1)(K-1)}$$

**Mean Square Error (MSE) for Two-Factor Model**

$$\text{MSE} = \frac{\text{SSE}}{JK(n-1)} = \frac{\Sigma\Sigma\Sigma(y_{i,j,k} - \bar{y}_{jk})^2}{JK(n-1)}$$

**F Ratios for Two-Factor Model**

$$F = \text{MSR}/\text{MSE}, \ F = \text{MSC}/\text{MSE}, \text{ and } F = \text{MSI}/\text{MSE}$$

# CHAPTER TWELVE

*The man who insists on seeing with perfect clearness before he decides, never decides.*
*Henri Frederic Amiel*

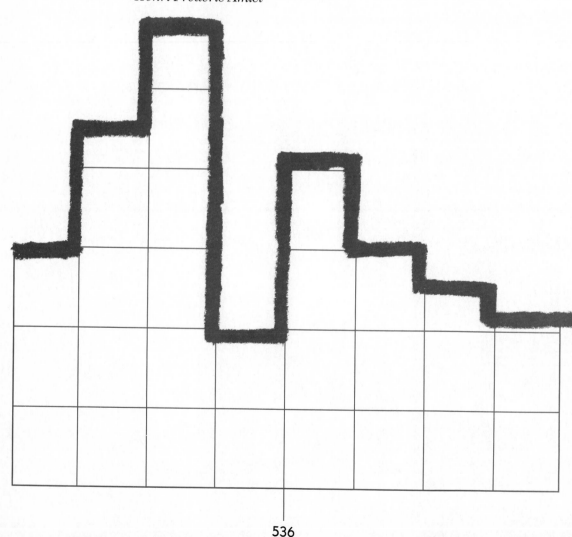

536

# STATISTICAL
# DECISION THEORY

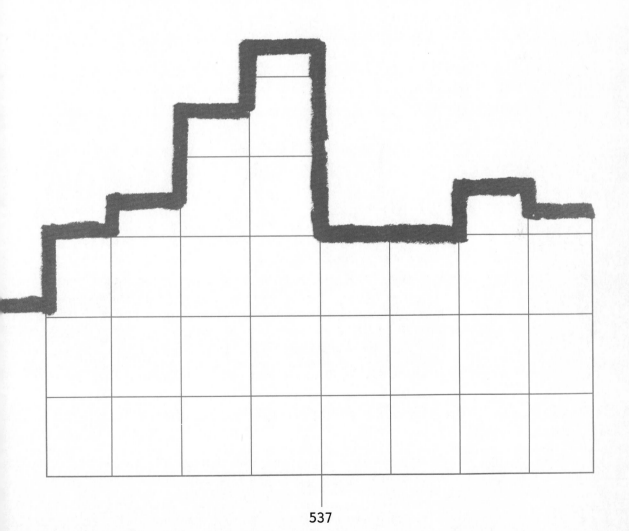

# 12.1 INTRODUCTION

A new branch of statistics, called *statistical decision theory* developed rapidly in the 1950s based on research by Howard Raiffa, John Pratt, and Leonard Savage (among others), and now occupies an important place in statistical literature. The term *Bayesian statistics* is often used to denote this branch, in honor of research presented over 200 years ago by an English philosopher, the Reverend Thomas Bayes (1702–1761). The focus of statistical decision theory is on the process of making a decision. This is in contrast to classical statistics, where the focus is on estimation, constructing confidence intervals, and hypothesis testing. Consider the following examples of statistical decision theory problems.

- A corporation president is deciding whether or not to build an addition to an existing plant. If sales continue to increase at the present rate, the new wing will be necessary. If sales level off, the new addition will be unnecessary.

- The Ford Motor Company is considering three options regarding car prices for next year: (1) raising prices by an average of 4.9%, (2) raising prices by an average of 2.3%, or (3) not raising prices at all. The decision will be based at least partly on what General Motors and Chrysler are expected to do.

- A manager, concerned because the number of defective items on a production line is slightly larger than usual, must decide whether or not to stop the line for repairs. If the process is not working correctly, then the line should be stopped and repaired. However, stopping a line that doesn't need repair is very costly.

Statistical decision theory is concerned with determining which of a set of possible decisions is optimal for a particular decision maker. In many circumstances one of the set of possible decisions is to delay the decision until additional information (sample data) can be gathered. Sample information is usually not free, so the decision maker must decide how much additional data (if any) should be gathered.

By the end of this chapter you should be able to recognize a statistical decision theory problem and determine the optimal action both before and after obtaining sample information. You should also be able to use decision trees to aid the analysis process. Finally, you should be able to indicate how the optimal sample size could be determined for a given problem, and should be aware of how various attitudes toward risk can be incorporated into the decision-making process.

## Semiconductor Memories, Inc.

Semiconductor Memories, Inc., manufactures memory chips containing 256,000 bits of memory. Each chip is a single integrated circuit used primarily for storing computer programs or data. The failure of a single bit in a chip constitutes an unacceptable failure of the product. The company carefully tests all chips, scrapping some 50% of them (those that fail at any time in the test process). In the past, about one-half of the chips in each production run (of 500 chips) have been defective.

A recent suggestion is that defective chips can be used for TV displays, where small failures may not distort a picture composed of thousands of small multicolor dots (called *pixels*). If the failure rate of pixels is only a small proportion of the 200,000 bits needed for a typical TV picture, then this difference would not be evident to the viewer. Defective chips are classified as either acceptable or not acceptable for a TV picture. Past records indicate that among defective chips the proportion acceptable for a TV picture is always either 90% or 60%. There is no way to tell for sure if there are 90% or 60% acceptable chips without testing each chip. Three-fourths of the time there have been 90% acceptable, and one-fourth there have been 60% acceptable.

As an advisor to Semiconductor, you have investigated various options for the use of defective chips. The scrap value of the defective chips from a single run (about 250 defectives) is $1250. Semiconductor can completely test each chip, in which case the average value of a run (net of the testing costs) depends on whether the run has 90% acceptable or 60% acceptable chips. For 90% runs, the average value of the (defective) chips is $3000. For 60% runs, Semiconductor incurs a loss of $250. A third alternative for Semiconductor is to sell the entire set of defective chips to an independent dealer. This dealer will test each chip and then pay Semiconductor $2500 if the run is 90% acceptable or $750 if the run is 60% acceptable. You prepare Table 12.1 to assist in your analysis.

Table 12.1

| | State of Defective Chips | |
|---|---|---|
| | **90% Acceptable** | **60% Acceptable** |
| Test | $3000 | −$250 |
| Sell | $2500 | $750 |
| Scrap | $1250 | $1250 |
| Probability | 0.75 | 0.25 |

# 12.2 The Elements of a Decision

Four elements are needed to analyze a decision-making problem: actions, states of nature, payoffs, and probabilities.

*Actions*: The choices available to the decision maker are called **actions**, (or sometimes *alternatives*). Although the approach in this book assumes that the decision maker can specify a finite number of mutually exclusive and exhaustive actions, problems with an infinite number of outcomes can also be analyzed.

**EXAMPLE**   In Table 12.1 the actions listed down the left side are Test, Sell, or Scrap.

*States of nature*: The uncertain elements in a problem are referred to as **states of nature**. As with actions, we assume that the states of nature are finite, mutually exclusive, and exhaustive—but again, it is possible to analyze a problem with an infinite number.

**EXAMPLE**   The states of nature listed across the top of Table 12.1 are "90% acceptable" and "60% acceptable."

*Payoffs*: A **payoff** is needed for each combination of an action and a state of nature. Payoffs are usually in dollars, but nonmonetary units (such as *utils* as described later) can also be used.

**EXAMPLE** Six payoffs are shown in Table 12.1, which is often referred to as a *payoff table*.

*Probabilities*: A probability must be associated with each state of nature. These probabilities, called **prior probabilities**, may be determined by historical data, expert opinion, or any other factors (including personal judgment) the decision maker wishes to use. Since the states of nature are mutually exclusive and exhaustive, the prior probabilities must sum to 1.0.

**EXAMPLE** The prior probabilities in Table 12.1 are 0.75 (for the state of nature "90% acceptable") and 0.25 (for "60% acceptable"). These probabilities sum to 1.0.

# 12.3 Expected Monetary Value

After constructing a payoff table (such as Table 12.1), the decision maker wants to determine the optimal action. The first step in this determination is to calculate an **expected monetary value (EMV)** for each action. An EMV is merely the average payoff an action would yield over many trials. This average is determined by multiplying each payoff by its probability and then summing these values.

Expected monetary value (average payoff)

(12.1)     $EMV = \Sigma(\text{payoff})(\text{probability})$

where this sum is over all payoffs associated with a given action.

**EXAMPLE** Calculate the EMV for each action in Table 12.1.

$$EMV(\text{Test}) = (\$3000)(0.75) + (-\$250)(0.25) = \$2187.50$$
$$EMV(\text{Sell}) = (\$2500)(0.75) + (\$750)(0.25) = \$2062.50$$
$$EMV(\text{Scrap}) = (\$1250)(0.75) + (\$1250)(0.25) = \$1250.00$$

The optimal action is the one with the largest EMV. Since EMV(Test) = \$2187.50 is the largest in the preceding example, the Test action is best. Semiconductor should thus test each chip and expect to earn an average of \$2187.50 for the defective chips in a run.

## Drawing Decision Trees

Decision trees are often used in decision analysis to illustrate graphically the process of determining the optimal action. Notice in the decision tree in Fig. 12.1 that the first set of branches represents the actions, while the second set of branches represents the states of nature. Each square (□) in the tree is a point where a decision has to be made. The value inside each square is the dollar value of the best decision for the decision maker. Each circle (○) is a point where nature makes the decision, and the value inside each circle is the EMV of the branches to the right of that point. The probability of each state of nature is listed below the tree branch. The payoffs in a decision tree are determined by working from right to left (called **backward induction**). Once all the payoffs are entered on the right-hand side, then the EMV's are calculated by multiplying payoffs by probabilities and adding.

The first EMV in Fig. 12.1, \$2187.50, is determined by adding \$3000(0.75) and −\$250(0.25); the \$2187.50 is placed in the circle near the top of the tree. The other EMV, \$2062.50, is placed in the circle near the bottom of the tree. The next step is to choose between the three values, \$2187.50 (Test), \$2062.50 (Sell), and \$1250 (Scrap). The best of these three actions is Test, so \$2187.50 is placed in the decision square at the beginning of the tree. Notice in Fig.

**Figure 12.1**
Decision tree for
Semiconductor, Inc.

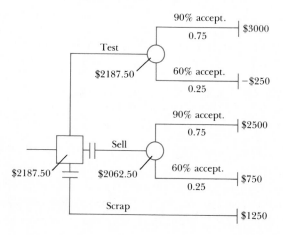

12.1 that we have used an arrow ($\rightarrow$) to mark the optimal decision and the symbol $-\|-$ to indicate branches that should not be taken (i.e., they have been "pruned").

## 12.4 Using Sample Information to Revise Probabilities

Among the four elements of a decision problem (actions, states of nature, payoffs, and probabilities), probabilities are generally the most difficult to determine. Unfortunately, if the probabilities are in error, then an incorrect optimal action may be selected. Thus it is important that probabilities be assessed as accurately as possible.

In decision problems there is usually an opportunity to gather (sample) information about the states of nature and to use this information to assess the probability of each state. Most companies gather sample information regularly—for example, using test markets to evaluate a new product, using a marketing research firm to survey potential customers, or conducting a panel study to evaluate a new advertising campaign. As a student you also gather information before making a major decision. You may have investigated a number of colleges before making your choice and perhaps looked at various majors within the college. Before taking a course you may try to find out how hard it is or who is teaching a particular section. This process can be thought of as gathering the information necessary for assessing probabilities.

Sample information is usually not free. Generally, it takes time and money to collect the data necessary to help evaluate the probabilities in a decision-making context. If the improvement in the decision process is not worth the time and money spent, then the sample information should not be purchased. Thus a primary focus of statistical decision theory is on determining if sample information should be purchased, and if so, how much.

**EXAMPLE** Semiconductor is considering a complete test of a random sample of chips from each group of defectives. They plan to use this sample information to help decide whether to test, sell, or scrap the entire set of defective chips. The sample information costs $10 per chip. Is this type of information worth purchasing? If so, how many chips should they sample?

As we indicated earlier, probabilities determined before (new) sample information is considered are called prior probabilities. Probabilities determined after considering this sample information are called **posterior probabilities**. Thus a posterior probability is the probability of a state of nature given the sample information, or

---

**DEFINITION**
**Posterior**
**Probability**

$P$(state of nature|sample information)

---

**EXAMPLE** Suppose Semiconductor takes a sample of two chips and, after testing, finds that one is acceptable and the other is unacceptable. The two posterior probabilities are:

1. The probability of the state "90% acceptable" given the sample result of one out of two acceptable, or

   $P$(90% accept.|1 of 2 accept.)

2. The probability of the state "60% acceptable," given the sample result of one out of two acceptable, or

   $P$(60% accept.|1 of 2 accept.)

Bayes' rule, described in the next section, is the formula used to revise prior probabilities into posterior probabilities. For now, we will use Fig. 12.2 to summarize the revision process. Notice the question mark between the first two blocks. This indicates that the decision maker is *considering* collecting sample information. That is, the process in Fig. 12.2 does not include actual collection of sample data. Instead, the decision maker determines the value of sample information by determining the optimal course of action for each possible sample result. Since posterior probabilities in this approach are

**Figure 12.2**
Using sample
information to revise
probabilities.

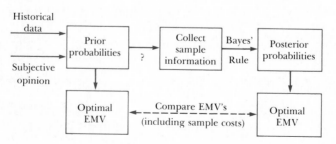

Chapter 12 Statistical Decision Theory

calculated *before* the sample is taken (on the basis of assumed sample results), this method is often called *preposterior analysis*. The EMV resulting from this set of optimal actions is then compared with the EMV based on the prior probabilities to determine if the sample is worth purchasing.

**EXAMPLE**   If Semiconductor is considering taking a sample of two chips, there are three possible sample results: (1) both chips are unacceptable, (2) one chip is acceptable and one is unacceptable, and (3) both chips are acceptable. Semiconductor must decide what their optimal action will be for each of the sample outcomes. These outcomes are shown as sample branches in the tree diagram in Fig. 12.3. The cost of a sample of two is

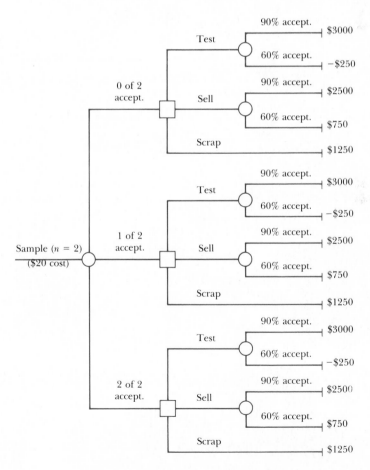

**Figure 12.3**
The sample branches for Semiconductor, $n = 2$.

$20. Notice that each of the sample branches is an exact duplicate of the branches in Fig. 12.1. Thus Fig. 12.3 can be thought of as delaying the decision between testing, selling, and scrapping until sample information has been evaluated. If the sample information is free, then the sample information should always be gathered.

A probability is necessary for each branch in Fig. 12.3 where nature is making the decision (that is, following each ○ symbol). The next section illustrates how to calculate these probabilities.

# 12.5 Calculating Posterior and Marginal Probabilities

A type of probability we haven't presented yet, called a **likelihood**, indicates how likely it is for a particular sample to occur for some state of nature. A likelihood is defined as follows:

---

**DEFINITION**
**Likelihood**    $P$(sample information|state of nature).

---

Compare this definition of a likelihood with the definition of a posterior probability given earlier, and notice that the terms in parentheses are the same, but in reverse order. For a posterior probability, the sample information is given. For a likelihood, on the other hand, the state of nature is given.

**EXAMPLE**    Assume (again) that Semiconductor is considering taking a random sample of two chips. There are four likelihoods to be found in this situation:

$P$(0 of 2 accept.|90% accept.)    and    $P$(0 of 2 accept.|60% accept.)
$P$(1 of 2 accept.|90% accept.)    and    $P$(1 of 2 accept.|60% accept.)
$P$(2 of 2 accept.|90% accept.)    and    $P$(2 of 2 accept.|60% accept.)

## Determining Likelihoods

For all the problems in this textbook, likelihoods can be determined using Appendix Table B.2 (the binomial table). For this table we need to know $n$, $\pi$, and $x$. The sample size is $n$, $\pi$ is the probability of one success on one draw, and $x$ is the number of successes of interest.

**EXAMPLE** Consider the Semiconductor likelihood,

$$P(1 \text{ of } 2 \text{ accept.}|90\% \text{ accept.})$$

In this case, $n = 2$. If a run is 90% acceptable, then the probability of one success on one draw is $\pi = 0.90$. The number of successes of interest is $x = 1$ (out of two chips). Using Table B.2, we find that

$$P(1 \text{ of } 2 \text{ accept.}|90\% \text{ accept.}) = 0.1800$$

This says that if a run is 90% acceptable, then the probability of exactly one success in a sample of two is 0.1800.

The likelihood $P(1 \text{ of } 2 \text{ accept.}|60\% \text{ accept.})$ is determined the same way. From Table B.2, $n = 2$, $\pi = 0.60$, and $x = 1$:

$$P(1 \text{ of } 2 \text{ accept.}|60\% \text{ accept.}) = 0.4800$$

Thomas Bayes developed the following formula (generally called **Bayes' rule**) for determining a posterior probability:

---

Bayes' Rule

(12.2)  $\quad P(\text{state of nature}|\text{ sample info.}) = \dfrac{(\text{prior})(\text{likelihood})}{\Sigma(\text{priors})(\text{likelihoods})}$

where the sum in the denominator is over all states of nature.

---

**EXAMPLE** Calculate the posterior probability $P(90\% \text{ accept.}|1 \text{ of } 2 \text{ accept.})$ for Semiconductor. Recall that the prior for 90% is $P(90\% \text{ accept.}) = 0.75$, and the likelihoods are 0.1800 (for 90%) and 0.4800 (for 60%).

$$P(90\% \text{ accept.}|1 \text{ of } 2 \text{ accept.}) = \frac{(0.75)(0.1800)}{(0.75)(0.1800) + (0.25)(0.4800)}$$

$$= \frac{0.1350}{0.2550} = 0.5294$$

The posterior probability 0.5294 indicates that the state of nature "90% acceptable" has only slightly more than a 50-50 chance of being the correct state of nature given one acceptable in a sample of two. This posterior probability is considerably lower than the prior probability (of 0.75) because the sample information (one of two) agrees more closely with the 60% state of nature.

The posterior probability that the state of nature is "60% acceptable" is the complement of 0.5294:

$$P(60\% \text{ accept.}|1 \text{ of } 2 \text{ accept.}) = 1 - 0.5294 = 0.4706$$

The denominator of Bayes' rule is important in decision problems, because it is the (marginal) probability of the sample information itself. Thus, from the denominator calculated previously, we know that

$$P(1 \text{ of } 2 \text{ accept.}) = 0.2550$$

## The Tabular Approach to Bayes' Rule

In most problems in this chapter a tabular approach will facilitate the calculation of posterior probabilities. Each possible sample outcome is treated separately in this approach. Table 12.2 uses the tabular method to calculate the probabilities associated with the three outcomes for a sample of two chips.

The first step in the tabular approach is to specify the sample result under consideration. In Table 12.2 the samples considered are "0 of 2 acceptable," "1 of 2 acceptable" (a repeat of what we did previously), and "2 of 2 acceptable." Then the states of nature are listed on the left, and next to each state is its prior probability and its likelihood (from Appendix Table B.2). Column 4 is the product of the (prior) × (likelihood), and the sum of this column is the probability of the sample information. Finally, each (prior) × (likelihood) is divided by the sum of all such products of (priors) × (likelihoods), which gives the posteriors.

Notice in Table 12.2 that the three marginal probabilities sum to 1.00, as they must in all decision problems.

**Table 12.2**

| | | | | |
|---|---|---|---|---|
| | | **Tabular Approach to Bayes's Rule** | | |

Sample result is 0 of 2 acceptable

| State of Nature | Prior | Likelihood | (Prior) × (Likelihood) | Posterior |
|---|---|---|---|---|
| 90% accept. | 0.75 | 0.0100 | 0.0075 | 0.0075/0.0475 = 0.1579 |
| 60% accept. | 0.25 | 0.1600 | 0.0400 | 0.0400/0.0475 = 0.8421 |
| | | | P(0 of 2 accept.) = 0.0475 | 1.0000 |

[Note: these likelihoods are from Appendix Table B.2, $n = 2$, $x = 0$, and $\pi = 0.90$ (the 90% row) and $\pi = 0.60$ (the 60% row).]

Sample result is 1 of 2 acceptable

| State of Nature | Prior | Likelihood | (Prior) × (Likelihood) | Posterior |
|---|---|---|---|---|
| 90% accept. | 0.75 | 0.1800 | 0.1350 | 0.1350/0.2550 = 0.5294 |
| 60% accept. | 0.25 | 0.4800 | 0.1200 | 0.1200/0.2550 = 0.4706 |
| | | | P(1 of 2 accept.) = 0.2550 | 1.0000 |

[Note: these likelihoods are from Appendix Table B.2, $n = 2$, $x = 1$, and $\pi = 0.90$ (the 90% row) and $\pi = 0.60$ (the 60% row).]

Sample result is 2 of 2 acceptable

| State of Nature | Prior | Likelihood | (Prior) × (Likelihood) | Posterior |
|---|---|---|---|---|
| 90% accept. | 0.75 | 0.8100 | 0.6075 | 0.6075/0.6975 = 0.8710 |
| 60% accept. | 0.25 | 0.3600 | 0.0900 | 0.0900/0.6975 = 0.1290 |
| | | | P(2 of 2 accept.) = 0.6975 | 1.0000 |

[Note: these likelihoods are from Appendix Table B.2, $n = 2$, $x = 2$, and $\pi = 0.90$ (the 90% row) and $\pi = 0.60$ (the 60% row).]

$$P(0 \text{ of } 2 \text{ accept.}) + P(1 \text{ of } 2 \text{ accept.}) + P(2 \text{ of } 2 \text{ accept.}) = 1.00$$
$$0.0475 \quad + \quad 0.2550 \quad + \quad 0.6975 \quad = 1.00$$

These probabilities indicate that over many samples of size $n = 2$, we expect about 5% to have no acceptable chips, about 25% to have one acceptable chip, and about 70% to have two acceptable chips.

# 12.6  Determining the Value of Sample Information

Once the posterior and marginal probabilities have been calculated, the optimal action for each sample branch in a decision tree can be determined. Figure 12.4 is a reproduction of Fig. 12.3, with both posterior and marginal probabilities added.

Figure 12.4 was evaluated by the backward induction process, that is, from right to left. For example, the EMV in the upper right, $263.18, is the sum of $0.1579(\$3000) + 0.8421(-\$250)$ and represents the average payoff of

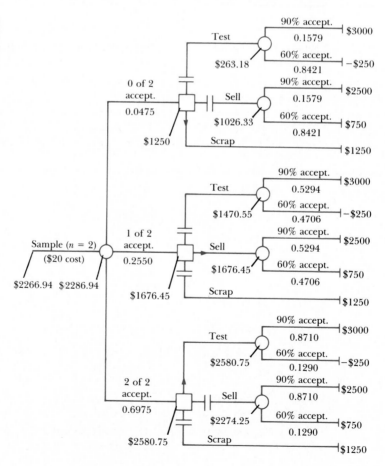

**Figure 12.4**
The completed decision tree for Semiconductor.

the Test branch if the sample is 0 of 2 acceptable. The average of the comparable Sell branch is $1026.33. The scrap branch has an EMV of $1250. Scraping is clearly the best choice (highest EMV). Hence, the value $1250 is placed in the decision box to the left.

Following the same process for the other two sample branches results in EMV's of $1676.45 and $2580.75 (placed in the other two boxes). Finally, we calculate an EMV that includes all three sample branches (but does not include the cost of the sample):

$$0.0475(\$1250.00) + 0.2550(\$1676.45) + 0.6975(\$2580.75) = \$2286.94$$

The total EMV for the sample branch is the preceding value minus the cost of the sample ($20). This value is placed at the beginning of the tree.

$$\text{EMV}(n = 2) = \$2286.94 - \$20.00 = \$2266.94$$

The EMV($n = 2$) of $2266.94 is compared with the prior optimal decision (with no sample information), which was (from Fig. 12.1) $2187.50. Since sampling leads to a higher EMV, the decision maker is better off taking the sample of $n = 2$.

Two measures are used to determine how much better (or worse) off the decision maker is with sample information—the **expected value of sample information (EVSI)** and the **expected net gain from sampling (ENGS)**.

---

**DEFINITION**
**EVSI**
**ENGS**

*Expected value of sample information (EVSI).* This measure is the difference between the optimal EMV using sample information and the optimal EMV without sample information, *not including any sample costs*. That is,

$$\text{EVSI} = \text{EMV(optimal after sample)}$$
$$- \text{EMV(optimal before sample)}$$

*Expected net gain from sampling (ENGS).* This measure is identical to EVSI, except that now sample costs *are* included. Thus

$$\text{ENGS} = \text{EVSI} - \text{cost of the sample}$$

---

ENGS indicates the value of the sample information to the decision maker, including sample costs. This is the more important measure of the two if sample costs are known. In some cases, however, the decision maker may not know the cost of the sample. Perhaps costs are still being negotiated or are in the process of being calculated. In such cases, EVSI is important because it indicates the value of the information itself. EVSI can never be negative, as the prospect of free information is, at worst, of no value to us (we can ignore information we know to be misleading). *EVSI tells the decision maker the maximum amount to pay for the sample information.*

**EXAMPLE**   For Semiconductor, EVSI can be determined by comparing the optimal EMV's given in Figs. 12.1 and 12.3. Remember, sample costs are not considered.

$$\text{EVSI}(n = 2) = \text{EMV(after sample)} - \text{EMV(before sample)}$$
$$= \$2286.94 - \$2187.50$$
$$= \$99.44$$

The maximum Semiconductor should pay for a sample of $n = 2$ is \$99.44.

$$\text{ENGS}(n = 2) = \text{EVSI} - \text{cost of sample}$$
$$= \$99.44 - \$20.00 = \$79.44$$

The net worth of the sample branch is \$79.44.

# 12.7   The Value of $n = 3$ for Semiconductor—An Example

As a further illustration of evaluating sample information, this section extends the Semiconductor analysis to consider a sample of size $n = 3$. This sample will cost \$30 (a sample of $n = 2$ costs \$20). There are four possible sample outcomes to this problem: (1) 3 accept., 0 unaccept., (2) 2 accept., 1 unaccept., (3) 1 accept., 2 unaccept., and (4) 0 accept., 3 unaccept. Each of these possible outcomes is treated separately in Table 12.3. In this table notice that the four marginal probabilities sum to 1.0000:

$$P(3 \text{ of } 3) + P(2 \text{ of } 3) + P(1 \text{ of } 3) + P(0 \text{ of } 3) = 1.0000$$
$$0.60075 + 0.29025 + 0.09225 + 0.01675 = 1.0000$$

Figure 12.5 presents the decision tree for the $n = 3$ sample branches. Using this figure we can determine EVSI and ENGS for $n = 3$.

**Table 12.3**

| Probabilities for $n = 3$ |
|---|

### Sample result is 0 of 3 acceptable

| State of Nature | Prior | Likelihood | (Prior) × (Likelihood) | Posterior |
|---|---|---|---|---|
| 90% accept. | 0.75 | 0.0010 | 0.00075 | 0.00075/0.01675 = 0.0448 |
| 60% accept. | 0.25 | 0.0640 | 0.01600 | 0.01600/0.01675 = 0.9552 |
| | | | P(0 of 3 accept.) = 0.01675 | 1.0000 |

[Note: these likelihoods are from Appendix Table B.2, $n = 3$, $x = 0$, and $\pi = 0.90$ (the 90% row) and $\pi = 0.60$ (the 60% row).]

### Sample result is 1 of 3 acceptable

| State of Nature | Prior | Likelihood | (Prior) × (Likelihood) | Posterior |
|---|---|---|---|---|
| 90% accept. | 0.75 | 0.0270 | 0.02025 | 0.02025/0.09225 = 0.2195 |
| 60% accept. | 0.25 | 0.2880 | 0.07200 | 0.07200/0.09225 = 0.7805 |
| | | | P(1 of 3 accept.) = 0.09225 | 1.0000 |

[Note: these likelihoods are from Appendix Table B.2, $n = 3$, $x = 1$, and $\pi = 0.90$ (the 90% row) and $\pi = 0.60$ (the 60% row).]

### Sample result is 2 of 3 acceptable

| State of Nature | Prior | Likelihood | (Prior) × (Likelihood) | Posterior |
|---|---|---|---|---|
| 90% accept. | 0.75 | 0.2430 | 0.18225 | 0.18225/0.29025 = 0.6279 |
| 60% accept. | 0.25 | 0.4320 | 0.10800 | 0.10800/0.29025 = 0.3721 |
| | | | P(2 of 3 accept.) = 0.29025 | 1.0000 |

[Note: these likelihoods are from Appendix Table B.2, $n = 3$, $x = 2$, and $\pi = 0.90$ (the 90% row) and $\pi = 0.60$ (the 60% row).]

### Sample result is 3 of 3 acceptable

| State of Nature | Prior | Likelihood | (Prior) × (Likelihood) | Posterior |
|---|---|---|---|---|
| 90% accept. | 0.75 | 0.7290 | 0.54675 | 0.54675/0.60075 = 0.9101 |
| 60% accept. | 0.25 | 0.2160 | 0.05400 | 0.05400/0.60075 = 0.0899 |
| | | | P(3 of 3 accept.) = 0.60075 | 1.0000 |

[Note: these likelihoods are from Appendix Table B.2, $n = 3$, $x = 3$, and $\pi = 0.90$ (the 90% row) and $\pi = 0.60$ (the 60% row).]

**Figure 12.5**
Semiconductor
decision tree for
$n = 3$.

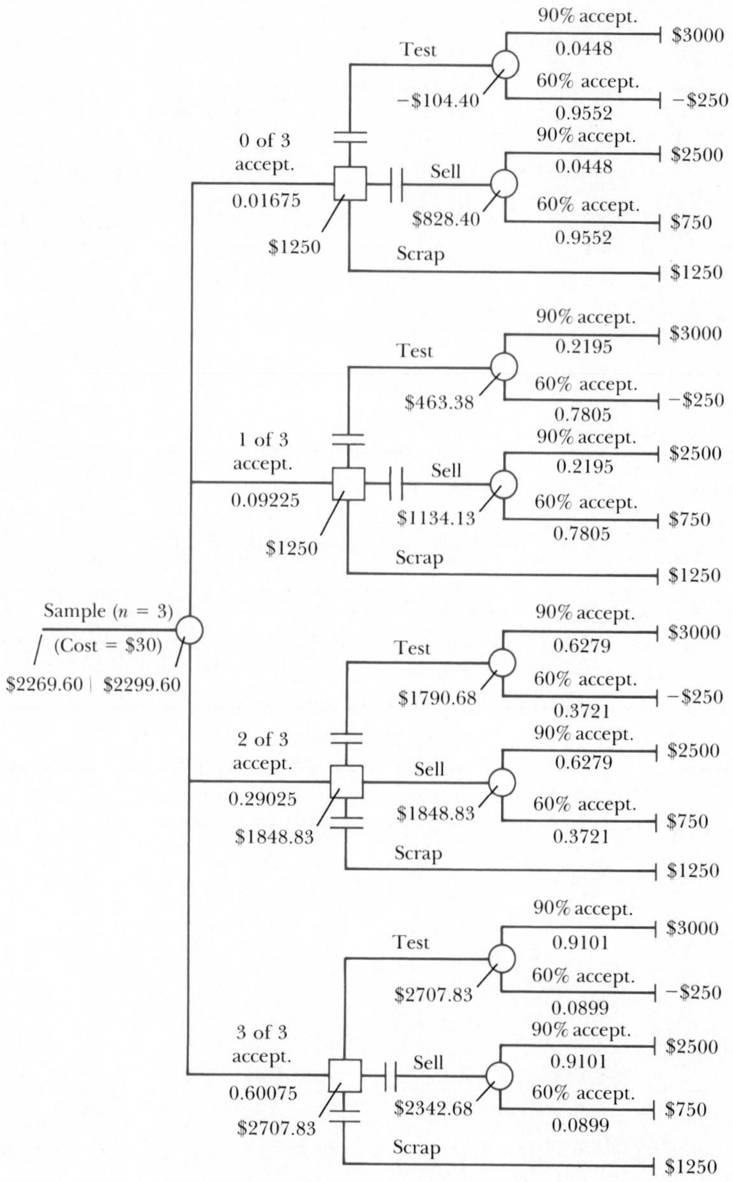

Chapter 12   Statistical Decision Theory

$$\begin{aligned}
\text{EVSI}(n \ = \ 3) \ &= \ \text{EMV(optimal after sample)} \\
&\quad - \ \text{EMV(optimal before sample)} \\
&= \ \$2299.60 \ - \ \$2187.50 \ = \ \$112.10 \\
\text{ENGS}(n \ = \ 3) \ &= \ \text{EVSI} \ - \ \text{cost of sample} \\
&= \ \$112.10 \ - \ \$30.00 \ = \ \$82.10
\end{aligned}$$

These results indicate that Semiconductor is better off with a sample of three ($82.10) than a sample of two ($79.44), and the maximum they should pay for $n \ = \ 3$ is $112.10.

## 12.8 Determining the Optimal Sample Size

In statistical decision theory problems the optimal sample size can be determined by finding the $n$ that gives the largest value of ENGS. In most problems, as $n$ increases, ENGS will at first increase and then will begin to decrease. This is because posterior probabilities change quite rapidly when $n$ is small and more slowly when $n$ is larger. At the point where the additional information gained with another observation is not worth the additional sample cost, then ENGS will begin to decline. For some problems the optimal sample size may be very small ($n \ = \ 1$), while for others it may be very large (in the hundreds). Since ENGS is typically calculated on a computer, any charges for computer time should be part of the sample cost.

Figure 12.6 shows a typical relationship between $n$ and ENGS. This figure gives ENGS for Semiconductor for $n \ = \ 1$ through 5. The costs are $10 for $n \ = \ 1$, $20 for $n \ = \ 2$, $30 for $n \ = \ 3$, $60 for $n \ = \ 4$, and $120 for $n \ = \ 5$. The reader is encouraged to verify at least the $n \ = \ 1$ value (the $n \ = \ 4$

**Figure 12.6**
Determining the optimal sample size for Semiconductor.

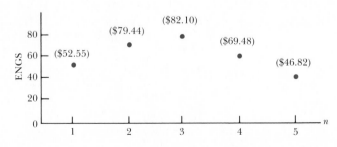

and 5 values take considerably more time). The optimal sample size is shown in Fig. 12.6 to be $n = 3$.

## Exercises

**12.1** Name the elements needed for analyzing a decision problem. Which of these elements is typically the most difficult to assess?

**12.2** Would you have any trouble describing the states of nature corresponding to tomorrow's weather? Is it possible for various people to define these states differently? What does this imply for specifying the elements of a decision problem?

**12.3** Return to Table 12.1 and suppose that the probabilities across the bottom of this table are unknown. How might you determine the best action to take? Name several possible approaches.

**12.4** What does it mean to maximize EMV? Can you think of any weaknesses in this approach to decision making?

MFG **12.5** Draw the decision tree for the Semiconductor problem for $n = 4$, assuming cost $(n = 4) = \$60$. Show the calculations of ENGS.

MFG **12.6** Draw the decision tree for the Semiconductor problem for $n = 1$. Verify that ENGS $= 52.55$, assuming cost $(n = 1) = \$10$.

**12.7** Refer to the definitions of subjective and objective probabilities in Chapter 4. Why would a prior probability be considered a subjective probability?

OPS **12.8** A classic study in decision making was made in 1966 by a California wine-making company, Mirassou Wines. Mirassou was considering purchasing a machine to pick grapes, something that had not been tried before. The machine, costing almost $50,000, could pick an acre of grapes in approximately 120 minutes. This mechanical harvester would cut labor costs substantially and would result in the harvesting of only ripe grapes (hand laborers tended to pick all grapes, ripe or not). Unfortunately, the grape vines had to be replanted with more space between them in order for the machine to have enough room. The number of vines per acre was then cut approximately in half.

Mirassou was concerned with the ability of the machine to harvest the grapes successfully, since earlier machines had cut the grapes, making them unsuitable. Another concern was public acceptance of the product. The fear was that people might not buy it when they learned of the mechanical harvester, thinking that the taste was different.

Mirassou had approximately 600 acres in vines. They were also considering purchasing the machine and experimenting on 20 acres of undeveloped land. Any new land planted would take 2 years before the first harvest.

Draw the decision tree for Mirassou, putting in as much detail as possible from the preceding information.

12.9 A national manufacturer of refrigerators is trying to decide whether to purchase either $\frac{1}{2}$, 1, or $1\frac{1}{2}$ minutes of advertising during next year's Super Bowl. The slots cost $200,000 for each 30 seconds. The company is unsure of how many potential buyers watch the Super Bowl, but it is estimating 20, 30, or 40%. Its prior probabilities for these states of nature are 0.50, 0.40, and 0.10, respectively. It has determined the following payoff matrix, which does not include the purchase cost.

| Payoff Table | | | |
|---|---|---|---|
| | **20%** | **30%** | **40%** |
| $\frac{1}{2}$ min. | $-$100,000 | $600,000 | $1,000,000 |
| 1 min. | $300,000 | $550,000 | $1,300,000 |
| $1\frac{1}{2}$ min. | $450,000 | $700,000 | $2,000,000 |
| Probability | 0.50 | 0.40 | 0.10 |

The company has the option to purchase, for a cost of $10,000, a study by a marketing research firm. The firm will provide sample information regarding the number of potential refrigerator buyers who watched last year's Super Bowl. The sample result will be either "low" or "high." The likelihoods (based on past experience) are:

$P(\text{low}|20\%) = 0.70 \quad P(\text{high}|20\%) = 0.30$
$P(\text{low}|30\%) = 0.50 \quad P(\text{high}|30\%) = 0.50$
$P(\text{low}|40\%) = 0.10 \quad P(\text{high}|40\%) = 0.90$

a) Draw the decision tree for the prior problem and indicate the optimal action.

b) Draw the decision tree for a sample of $n = 1$, and then determine EVSI and ENGS.

**c)** Assume that another survey could be conducted, independent of the first, with the same likelihoods and a cost of $20,000. Draw the decision tree for $n = 2$, and determine EVSI and ENGS. Is a sample of $n = 2$ better than a sample of $n = 1$?

**12.10** A small firm that makes high-speed electrical switches for telephone companies has just received an order for 2000 switches. Each perfectly operating switch should yield the firm a profit of $1, but the cost of handling and repairing a defective switch is $4. The machine used to make switches is not working perfectly now, and the firm is considering making either minor or major repairs to it. This machine is known to produce defects at a rate of 12%, when minor repairs are needed, and at a rate of 24%, when major repairs are needed. If minor repairs are made when major repairs are required, the defect rate falls to 6%. If minor repairs are all that is required, then the defect rate falls to zero. Major repairs will reduce the defect rate to zero regardless of whether minor or major repairs are needed. Major repairs, however, cost $400, while minor repairs cost only $200. Defects are produced randomly, so there is no way that the firm can tell if the machine needs major or minor repair. Furthermore, no repairs can be made once the machine is started and production of switches begins. Prior to starting production, however, the firm can sample switches from a short test run at a cost of $5 per switch. The prior probabilities of repair needs are $P(\text{major}) = 0.40$ and $P(\text{minor}) = 0.60$.

**a)** Draw the decision tree and find the optimal action for the firm if it is trying to decide between not sampling at all and sampling one switch. Calculate ENGS and EVSI.

**b)** Draw the decision tree and find the optimal action when the firm is willing to consider sampling either one or two switches. Calculate ENGS and EVSI.

# 12.9  Incorporating Risk into the Decision Analysis

Thus far we have determined the optimal action by maximizing expected monetary value. The EMV approach means that only the average payoff is considered. The variability in payoffs, is ignored. As the following payoff table illustrates, considering only EMV may not be the best approach.

| Payoff Table | | | |
|---|---|---|---|
| | **State of Nature** | | |
| | *I* | *II* | *EMV* |
| Outcome $A_1$ | $900,000 | − $800,000 | $50,000 |
| $A_2$ | − $1.00 | $1.00 | 0 |
| Probability | 0.50 | 0.50 | |

Assume that only one payoff is to be made. Although action $A_1$ has the higher EMV, many people would pick $A_2$ in order to avoid the possibility of losing $800,000. Obviously, any decision maker would like to gain $900,000, but for most of us (including the authors), the possible loss of $800,000 is too much of a risk to take. If this situation were repeated over and over, and the decision maker could afford one or more losses of $800,000, then action $A_1$ is the better choice. *If a decision is repeated over and over, the optimal action should be determined by maximizing EMV; otherwise, risk needs to be taken into account.*

# 12.10 Utility Analysis

The utility approach to decision making was developed by John Von Neumann and Oskar Morgenstern and presented in their classic book *The Theory of Games and Economic Behavior* (1944). Their approach is to develop for each decision maker a *utility function* that relates dollar values to utility. **Utility** is the measure that indicates the amount of pleasure derived from a dollar amount. A utility function might look like Fig. 12.7.

Suppose we let $U(\$x)$ represent the utility of $x$ dollars. From Fig. 12.7, the utility of $50 is 150, or $U(\$50) = 150$. Similarly, $U(\$1000) = 330$, $U(\$2000) = 420$, and $U(\$3000) = 475$. The utility values (such as 150, 330, 420, and

**Figure 12.7**
A utility function.

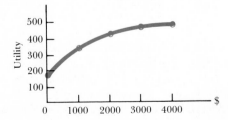

475) have no inherent meaning, and some other scale could have been used. However, utilities values can be ranked, so that $475 > 420 > 330 > 150$. This means that $3000 is preferred to $2000, which is preferred to $1000, which is preferred to $50 (as we would expect). Such comparisons are more meaningful when comparing actions in decision analysis.

The Von Neumann–Morgenstern method derives a function (such as Fig. 12.7) by asking the decision maker a series of questions. Each question determines a point on the function (the *'s), and these points are then connected by a smooth curve. The questions asked relate to a hypothetical gamble, such as the following:

Flip a fair coin once:
  If heads, you win $4000
  If tails, you win $0.

The decision maker is asked to indicate how much the gamble is worth; that is, how much he or she would be willing to pay to participate in the gamble.

Note that the EMV of our gamble is

$$0.50(\$4000) + 0.50(\$0) = \$2000$$

The gamble between $4000 and $0 is illustrated in Fig. 12.8. The straight line connecting the two points represents the expected utility of the gamble for various probabilities of winning. If $p = 0.50$, the expected utility of the gamble is halfway between $U(\$4000)$ and $U(\$0)$. In general, the expected utility for a gamble between $A, received with probability $p_1$, and $B, received with probability $1 - p$, is

$$pU(\$A) + (1 - p) U(\$B)$$

For gambles such as the one shown in Fig. 12.8, a decision maker can be classified as either risk neutral, a risk taker, or a risk avoider, according to the amount the person indicates the gamble is worth.

**Figure 12.8**
A gamble between $4000 and $0, with $p = 0.50$.

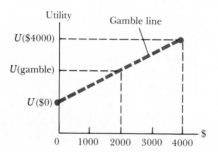

Chapter 12   Statistical Decision Theory

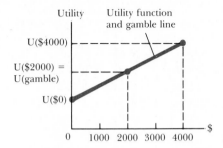

**Figure 12.9**
The utility function for a risk-neutral person.

1. A decision maker who considers the gamble to be worth exactly the same as the EMV of the gamble is called **risk neutral**. A risk-neutral person neither avoids nor seeks risk. The gamble given previously would be worth $2000 to this type of person. For a risk-neutral person, the utility function is the same as the gamble line, as shown in Fig. 12.9.

2. A decision maker who considers the gamble to be worth *more* than the EMV of the gamble is called a **risk taker**. This person would answer that the gamble is worth more than $2000 in our example. Because a risk taker values a gamble more than its equivalent EMV, the gamble line of such a person lies above (more pleasure) the utility function, as shown in Fig. 12.10.

3. A decision maker who considers the gamble to be worth less than its EMV is called a **risk avoider**. In our example a risk avoider would indicate that the gamble is worth less than $2000. The gamble line of a risk avoider lies below the utility function, as shown in Fig. 12.11 (page 562).

## A Typical Utility Function

Research on utility functions suggests that most people probably are not consistently risk neutral, risk takers, or risk avoiders. Rather, it suggests that

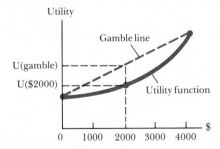

**Figure 12.10**
The utility function of a risk taker.

Figure 12.11
The utility function of
a risk avoider.

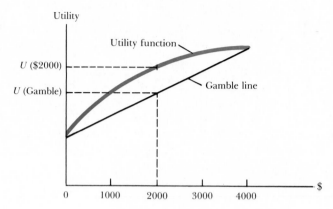

a typical person may be willing to gamble for small dollar amounts (such as buying a lottery ticket or playing cards for money), but this same person will avoid gambles involving large dollar amounts (for example, by buying insurance on a home or an automobile). Such a person might have the utility function shown in Fig. 12.12.

Notice in Fig. 12.12 that the utility function around the origin (near $0 amounts), indicates a risk taker. At the high and low ends of the function the curve is that of a risk avoider. For the most part, this person will be a conservative decision maker, unwilling to take risks. It is important to recognize that a utility function is for a single person at a single point in time. Utility functions do change over time, and group utility functions are difficult (if not impossible) to define.

Figure 12.12
A typical utility
function.

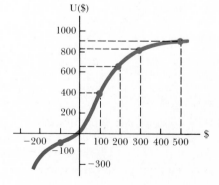

# 12.11 Incorporating Utility into a Decision

Once a utility function has been derived, the utility values reflected in this analysis can be used in place of the dollar values used previously. That is, the payoffs on the right-hand margin of a decision tree are replaced with utilities. Then, instead of calculating EMV, the decision maker calculates expected utility (EU). The process of backward inductions is followed exactly as before, except that now the process is one of *maximizing expected utility*. Consider the following example.

## DuPont Plastic for Automobiles

An article in the *Wall Street Journal* announced a breakthrough by DuPont in the development of plastic materials suitable for use in automobile bodies. Despite the success of Pontiac's Fiero, currently plastic is not widely used in automobile bodies, and DuPont is unsure of the extent to which plastic will replace metal. Assume that you are advising DuPont on their long-range planning to handle the demand for the plastic. The decision is whether to build a new plant or to modify existing facilities. The potential profit to the company over the next 5 years is substantial, totalling hundreds of millions of dollars. The company has classified possible industry acceptance of the new material as either low, medium, or high, with prior probabilities of 0.20, 0.50, and 0.30. The company has prepared the following payoff table.

| Payoff Table (in Millions of Dollars) | | | |
|---|---|---|---|
| | **Demand for Material** | | |
| | *Low* | *Medium* | *High* |
| Modify old plant | 100 | 200 | 300 |
| Build new plant | − 100 | 200 | 500 |
| Probability | 0.20 | 0.50 | 0.30 |

DuPont also has the option of organizing a panel of automobile experts who will report on their opinion of industry acceptance of the new plastic. The panel's report will be either favorable or unfavorable. Based on a variety of previous panel reports, DuPont estimates the following likelihoods:

$$P(\text{fav.}|\text{low}) = 0.20 \qquad P(\text{fav.}|\text{med}) = 0.50 \qquad P(\text{fav.}|\text{hi}) = 0.90$$
$$P(\text{unfav.}|,\text{low}) = 0.80 \qquad P(\text{unfav.}|\text{med}) = 0.50 \qquad P(\text{unfav.}|\text{hi}) = 0.10$$

Assume the utility function for the decision maker in this problem is that of the typical person shown in Fig. 12.12, where the dollar scale is millions of dollars. The cost of the panel study has not been estimated yet. What do you recommend?

Figure 12.13 presents the decision tree for the DuPont problem. Both dollar values (EMV, in millions of dollars) and utility (EU) were maximized in the analysis of this problem to show the contrast between the two. First, notice that building the new plant (EMV = \$230 million) is better than modifying existing facilities (EMV = \$210 million). However, sampling is even better (EMV = \$256.02 million). The value of the sample information to DuPont is

$$\text{EVSI} = \$256.02 - \$230.00 = \$26.02 \text{ million}$$

ENGS cannot be calculated because the cost of the sample is unknown.

All of the utility values in Fig. 12.13 are shown in color. The utilities in the right margin are taken directly from Fig. 12.12, which gives the following values:

$$U(-100) = -100, \quad U(100) = 400, \quad U(200) = 650, \quad U(300) = 830,$$
$$\text{and } U(500) = 900$$

The expected utility on the upper right, $EU = 654$, was calculated as follows:

$$0.20(400) + 0.50(650) + 0.30(830) = 654$$

The first interesting aspect of the expected utility analysis in Fig. 12.13 is that now the modify plant branch ($EU = 654$) is better than the branch for building a new plant ($EU = 575$). This reversal of the EMV decision is due to the conservative nature of our typical decision maker (from Fig. 12.12). The decision to modify is better for this person because there is less variability in payoffs than in the decision to build a new plant.

A second interesting aspect of Fig. 12.13 is that the $EU$ of the sample branch is exactly the same as for the modify branch ($EU = 654$ in both cases). The reason they are the same is that, after the sample has been collected, the expected utility analysis always leads to the same decision—to modify the existing facilities. Anytime the sample information *always* leads to the same decision, there is obviously no need to take the sample, and the value of the sample information must equal zero. In this case there is no utility to be gained by taking the sample, because our conservative decision maker will modify the existing plant no matter what the sample says.

**Figure 12.13**
The decision tree for
the DuPont plastic
problem.

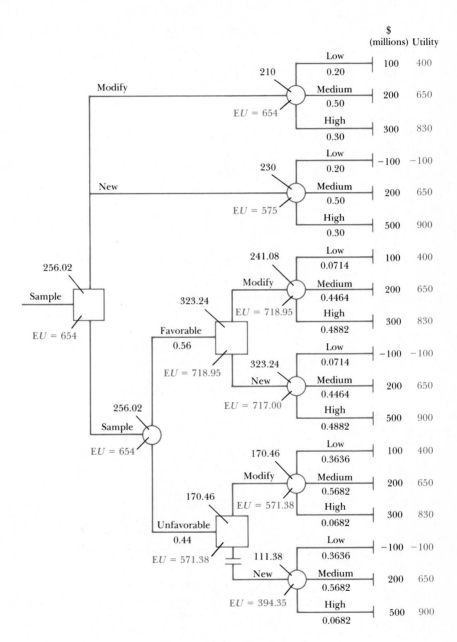

The purpose of this utility example is to show that maximizing expected utility may not lead to the same decision as maximizing EMV. When the decision situation is repeated over and over again (as in our chip example at the beginning of this chapter), then maximizing EMV is correct. When the decision situation occurs only once (as with DuPont), then utility should be maximized.

# 12.12  Overview of the Statistical Decision Theory Approach

The Bayesian approach to statistics has gained considerable popularity over the past 30 years. One of the difficulties with this approach is that a number of subjective judgments are required, and the classical statistician questions the ability of the decision maker to make such judgments. The Bayesian would counterargue that classical statistics also requires subjective judgments (such as the size of $\alpha$ in hypothesis testing), and such judgments should be made explicitly rather than implicitly.

Another concern with statistical decision theory is that the process of constructing a utility function and drawing the decision tree is often time-consuming and tedious. Perhaps for these reasons, the number of companies actively using statistical decision theory remains relatively small. Some companies, such as DuPont, General Electric, Pillsbury, and the Ford Motor Company, have tried this approach, and most often have been pleased with the result.

## Exercises

12.11  Under what circumstances should a decision maker maximize EMV, and when should $EU$ be used? Explain.

12.12  Sketch your own utility function for dollar values running from $-\$1000$ to $+\$1000$. Specify the types of questions you asked yourself to determine this function. Are you a risk taker, a risk avoider, risk neutral, or some mixture? Explain.

12.13  Verify that the posterior probabilities shown in Fig. 12.13 are correct.

12.14  In Fig. 12.13, could we have substituted utilities for dollar value at some point other than the right-hand margin? Explain why or why not.

12.15  Classify each of the following answers as that of a risk taker, a risk avoider, or a risk-neutral person.

a) $1000 guaranteed is preferred to a gamble between $2000 and $0 using $p = 0.50$.

b) A gamble between $1000 and $200 at $p = 0.50$ is preferred to $600 guaranteed.

c) A decision maker is indifferent between receiving $-$100 guaranteed and a gamble between $500 and $-$500 with $p = 0.50$.

d) A decision maker prefers $900 guaranteed to a gamble where $3000 is received with $p = 0.20$ and $400 is received with $p = 0.80$.

**12.16** Use Fig. 12.12 to answer the following questions:

a) What is the expected utility of a bet between $100 and $-$100, using $p = 0.50$? Would the decision maker accept $0 in place of this bet? Explain.

b) What is the expected utility of a gamble between $100 and $300, using $p = 0.50$? Would the decision maker accept $200 guaranteed in place of this gamble?

c) What is the expected utility of a gamble between $-$100 and $500 using $p = 0.50$? Is the decision maker a risk taker or a risk avoider in this range? Would this person accept $200 guaranteed in place of this gamble? Explain.

d) What dollar value gives the decision maker exactly the same utility as a gamble between $500 and $100 using $p = 0.50$?

## Chapter Exercises

OPS **12.17** Repeat the DuPont utility analysis in Fig. 12.13, assuming that it is possible to conduct two separate panel studies (i.e., $n = 2$). Assume that the panel results are independent but that the same type of outcome occurs (favorable/unfavorable), and the same likelihoods apply.

LAW **12.18** Two engineers quit their respective jobs with two different companies and started their own company to produce an integrated high-resolution computer monitor and graphics video board. They are now being sued separately for patent infringement and theft by a TV company for which one of the engineers worked previously, and by a computer company for which the other engineer worked previously. The engineers have not tooled up for mass production of their two products and are considering the wisdom of doing so, given the possible outcomes of the lawsuits. Following is the payoff table (in thousands of dollars).

| Possible Lawsuit Outcomes | Tool Up For: | | | |
|---|---|---|---|---|
| | Both Boards and Monitors | Boards Only | Monitors Only | Neither |
| Engineers win both suits | 1500 | 1425 | 1200 | 1200 |
| Engineers win TV company suit only | 1375 | 1450 | 1150 | 1150 |
| Engineers win computer company suit only | 725 | 850 | 900 | 900 |
| Engineers lose both suits | 425 | 800 | 850 | 875 |

Of the four different courses of action (tool up for both, one of the two, or neither) which actions should the engineers consider as viable alternatives? Explain.

**12.19** For the payoff table in Exercise 12.18, why can't you specify the best action?

**12.20** A decision maker who is extremely cautious will wish to maximize the minimum payoff from any course of action. In accordance with this criterion, what action in Exercise 12.18 should the engineers take?

FIN **12.21** In planning to run for public office, Mrs. Becker has to decide how many letters to mail out in soliciting contributions to support her campaign. Letters and follow-up telephone calls will be done by a clerical and word-processing firm, which requires orders in multiples of 50. The contributions to be received are uncertain, but from previous campaigns Mrs. Becker knows that an average contribution of $50 or more per letter is a large return, $25 to $50 is a moderate, and less than $20 is small. The payoff table (net dollars) is as follows:

| | Solicitation Letter Order Size | | | | |
|---|---|---|---|---|---|
| Contribution level | 50 | 100 | 150 | 200 | 250 |
| Large | 225 | 350 | 475 | 550 | 475 |
| Moderate | 225 | 350 | 300 | 225 | 175 |
| Small | 225 | 175 | 125 | 100 | 0 |

a) Which solicitation letter order sizes are viable alternatives? Explain.

b) If Mrs. Becker wishes to maximize her minimum payoff, which action should she take?

c) From these payoffs, does it appear that Mrs. Becker should consider letter order sizes larger than 250? Explain.

FIN **12.22** In Exercise 12.21, suppose Mrs. Becker assigns probabilities to each contribution outcome as follows:

$P(\text{large}) = 0.25$, $P(\text{moderate}) = 0.55$, and $P(\text{small}) = 0.20$.

a) What is the expected payoff of each action (letter order)?

b) If Mrs. Becker is risk neutral, how many letters should she order?

OPS **12.23** A small software company has just come out with a new program that can be used with the U.S. Bureau of Labor Statistics work life table to calculate expected earnings in wrongful death and personal injury litigation. This company can order 1000, 5000, or 10,000 disks with copy-protected versions of its program at a cost of $1000 for the initial order (fixed cost) and $5 per copy (variable cost). It can produce the disks internally at a fixed start-up cost of $5000 and a variable cost of $4.50 per copy. The company estimates that the probability of selling exactly 1000 copies is 0.55. The probability of selling exactly 5000 copies is 0.40, and the probability of selling exactly 10,000 copies is 0.05. The finished disk will sell for $80. Unsold disks are assumed to have no worth. If this software company wishes to maximize the expected net return, what action should it take? Draw the decision tree.

**12.24** In Exercise 12.23, if you learned that the owner of the software company was a risk taker, how might this affect the optimal decision?

PUB **12.25** A new method of identifying drunk drivers has been shown in experiments to correctly identify a drunk driver 90% of the time. One percent of the time, however, the test will identify someone as being drunk who is not. If 0.05% of the drivers on the road are drunk, what is the probability that a person who is identified as a drunk driver by this test is in fact not drunk? Why would the courts be interested in this probability?

OPS **12.26** A company can ship its product by train or truck. There is a possibility of damage with either type of transit, but because of differences in insurance coverage and shipping charges, the costs of these two methods of shipping are different. The dollar cost of shipping and damage is as follows:

|  | No Damage | Damage |
|---|---|---|
| Ship by train | $4000 | $5000 |
| Ship by truck | $4200 | $4000 |

If the probability of damage is 0.04, what are the expected costs of each method of shipping?

OPS **12.27** Suppose in Exercise 12.26 you hear that because of worker unrest, your goods may be damaged. The possibilities of this unrest, conditioned on no damage or damaged goods is given by the likelihoods $P(\text{unrest true}|\text{no damage}) = 0.55$ and $P(\text{unrest true}|\text{damage}) = 0.75$. If you find there is unrest, how would this new information cause you to revise the probability of damage (0.04) given in Exercise 12.26? Using this revised probability, what is the best way to ship your goods in Exercise 12.26, assuming you are risk neutral?

PUB **12.28** A relatively new rock star is planning a stop in Indianapolis. The local committee can schedule the concert at the Market Square Arena (seating 17,000) or the Hoosier Dome (seating 35,000). The committee assesses potential attendance to be normally distributed, with a mean of 15,000 and a standard deviation of 3000. What is the committee's prior probability that the demand for tickets will exceed the capacity of the Market Square Arena?

FIN **12.29** An article in the *WSJ* reported that a number of grocery chains, including Safeway and A & P, have begun using plastic bags. As manager of XTRA Foods, Inc., you are attempting to decide whether to order plastic or paper bags for the next 6 months. The *WSJ* article reported that Giant Foods of Washington, D.C., pays $0.026 per plastic bag versus $0.044 per paper bag. Plastic bags take less storage space, cause fewer problems when wet, and can carry more weight. However, some customers do not like plastic bags because they do not stand up in the trunk of a car. Your order is for 500,000 bags. The following payoff matrix includes your estimate of the cost of the bags as well as the gain or loss in the value of customer goodwill.

|  | Most Customers | | |
|---|---|---|---|
|  | *Prefer Plastic* | *Are Neutral* | *Prefer Paper* |
| Plastic | $10,000 | $13,000 | $30,000 |
| Paper | $25,000 | $22,000 | $20,000 |
| Probability | 0.20 | 0.30 | 0.50 |

a) What decision is optimal based on the prior probability?

b) You can purchase a survey of customers thoughts on plastic for $2000. The outcome of this survey will be either favorable, unfavorable, or neutral. You estimate the following likelihoods:

$P(\text{unfav.}|\text{most prefer plastic}) = 0.10$    $P(\text{neutral}|\text{most prefer plastic}) = 0.40$
$P(\text{unfav.}|\text{most are neutral}) = 0.30$    $P(\text{neutral}|\text{most are neutral}) = 0.50$
$P(\text{unfav.}|\text{most prefer paper}) = 0.50$    $P(\text{neutral}|\text{most prefer paper}) = 0.30$

Draw the decision tree and determine the optimal decision. Calculate ENGS and EVSI.

**12.30** Suppose that a person's utility for $50 is 100 ($U(\$50) = 100$), and the utility of $10 is 50. This person is also indifferent between a bet when $50 occurs with a probability of 0.5, $10 occurs with a probability 0.5, and $20 occurs with certainty. What is $U(\$20)$?

**12.31** Is the person described in Exercise 12.30 risk neutral, a risk taker, or a risk avoider? Explain.

**12.32** Is it possible for a person to be a risk taker for some gambles and a risk avoider for others? If yes, give an example of such gambles. If no, explain why not.

**12.33** A decision maker's utility function for money is $U(\text{money}) = 0.3(\text{money}) - 0.002(\text{money})^2$, where the money values are between $0 and $100 and money is measured in thousands of dollars.

a) Plot this utility function for $0–$100.

b) Is this decision maker a risk taker or a risk avoider?

**12.34** For the decision maker described in Exercise 12.33, which of the following gambles would be preferred?

a) A lottery in which a win of $0 or $80,000 is equally likely.

b) $20,000 for certain.

**12.35** A lumber mill produces sawdust as a by-product. A decision is to be made on whether to sell this dust through the mill's regular distribution network ($D_1$) or to use an independent distributor ($D_2$). A second-stage decision will be necessary if the mill selects $D_1$ but is unsuccessful. As sawdust builds up in the yard, the mill will either have to unload the packaged dust in individual packages at substantial discounts ($E_1$) or dispose of large lots at periodic auctions ($E_2$). The decision tree for this problem is as follows (payoffs are expected future returns in thousands of dollars).

**a)** What are the expected payoffs from alternative actions?

**b)** What is the optimal strategy?

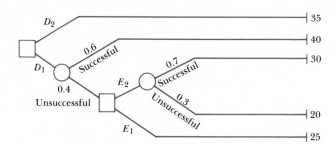

## Glossary

**actions:** The choices (or alternatives) available to the decision maker.

**backward induction:** Working from the payoffs in a decision tree to the action to be taken—working from right to left on a decision tree.

**Bayes' rule:** The formula used to revise prior probabilities to posterior probabilities.

**expected monetary value (EMV):** The mean dollar value of the payoffs.

**expected net gain from sampling (ENGS):** EVSI net of sample costs.

**expected value of sample information (EVSI):** The difference between the optimal expected monetary value (EMV) using sample information and the optimal EMV without sample information, excluding sample costs.

**likelihood:** A probability that indicates how likely it is for a particular sample to occur for some state of nature. A likelihood is defined as a conditional probability, that is, $P$(sample information|state of nature).

**optimal action:** The action with the highest expected monetary value.

**payoff:** The benefit (or cost) associated with each combination of an action and a state of nature. Payoffs are usually in dollars, but nonmonetary units can also be used.

**posterior probabilities:** Probabilities determined after considering new sample information. A posterior probability is the probability of a state of nature given the sample information.

**prior probabilities:** Probabilities associated with each state of nature. Prior probabilities may be determined by historical data, expert opinion, or any other factors (including personal judgment) the decision maker wishes to use.

**risk avoider:** A decision maker who considers the gamble to be worth less than its EMV.

**risk neutral:** A gamble considered to be worth exactly the same as its EMV. A risk-neutral decision maker neither avoids nor seeks risk and is indifferent to the size of the variance associated with the payoffs in a gamble.

**risk taker:** A decision maker who considers the gamble to be worth more than its EMV.

**states of nature:** The uncertain elements in a problem.

**statistical decision theory:** Statistical analysis that focuses on the process of making a decision as opposed to estimation and hypothesis testing.

**utility:** A measure of the amount of pleasure or satisfaction derived from a dollar amount.

## Formulas

**12.1—Expected Monetary Value (Average Payoff)**

$$EMV = \Sigma(\text{payoff})(\text{probability})$$

where this sum is over all payoffs associated with a given action.

**12.2—Bayes' Rule**

$$P(\text{state of nature}|\text{sample info.}) = \frac{(\text{prior})(\text{likelihood})}{\Sigma(\text{priors})(\text{likelihoods})}$$

where the sum in the denominator is over all states of nature.

# CHAPTER THIRTEEN

*If a problem has really big numbers in it, the answer is always "one million."*
Peppermint Patty, in Peanuts

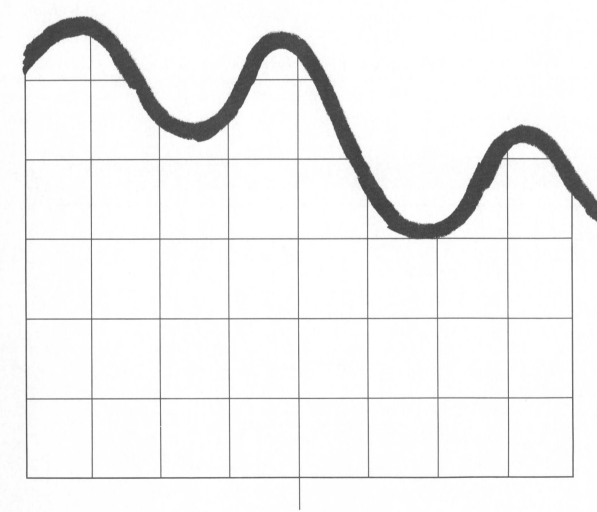

# NONPARAMETRIC STATISTICS

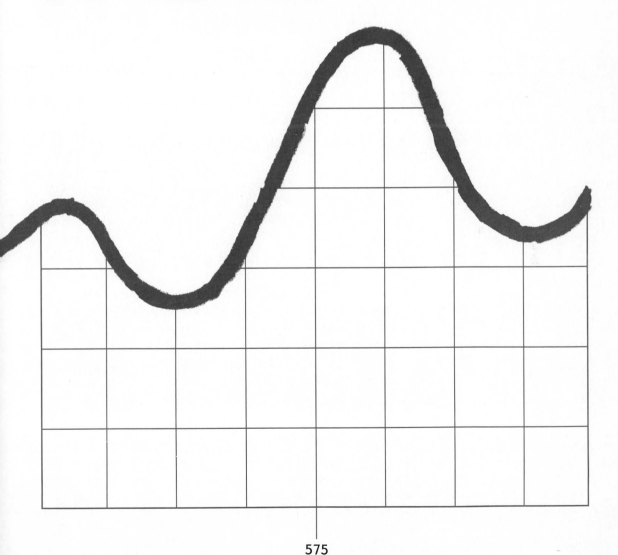

# 13.1 INTRODUCTION

The confidence intervals and tests of hypotheses given in the preceding seven chapters often required certain assumptions about the population from which samples are drawn. For example, $t$ tests and $F$ tests require the assumption that the population is normally distributed. This assumption of normality is especially critical when the sample size is small. Because $t$, $F$, and $z$ tests depend on assumptions about the parameters of the population, they are called **parametric tests**. The opposite of a parametric test is a **nonparametric test**, where no assumptions are made about the population. Consider the following examples.

- A company manufacturing toothpaste has developed a new brand that is supposed to reduce plaque more effectively than the leading brand. A study is made of 12 people using the new brand and 12 using the leading brand. Records suggest that the distribution of plaque reduction is skewed. Thus a nonparametric statistic is used to determine if the new brand is more effective than the leading brand.

- *Consumer Reports* has 10 tennis players (of varying skill) rate the two most popular types of oversize tennis rackets. Because *Consumer Reports* is only interested in the order of the rankings, it uses nonparametric statistics to determine the correlation in the rankings of the two rackets and to determine if one racket is judged to be significantly better than the other.

- A recruiter for a major corporation thinks that the grades of college students are not independent of their major. To test this claim across many majors, this recruiter may use a nonparametric statistic on a random sample of students.

In this chapter you will learn more about the difference between parametric and nonparametric methods. A number of the nonparametric methods presented are substitutes for parametric tests presented earlier in this book. In addition, we present several methods designed to determine the goodness of fit between two variables. By the end of this chapter you should be able to recognize when a non-parametric approach is required. You should be able to specify an appropriate nonparametric test and to complete the computational analysis.

## Testing Tennis Balls

You work for Wilson Sporting Goods, in quality control for tennis balls. In a recent article in the magazine *Tennis*, Wilson was the only U.S. manufacturer to have a sample of balls not fall within the weight limits specified by the International Tennis Federation: more than 2 ounces and less than $2\frac{1}{16}$ ounces. The sample of Wilson Championship balls weighed an average of 1.96 ounces, while the Wilson Championship Heavy Extra Duty balls weighed an average of 1.94 ounces. Assuming three plants make Wilson tennis balls, your concern now is whether defective balls are associated with the producing plants. To study the association between balls and plants, a random sample of 300 balls is taken, and each ball is classified as either acceptable or defective (not falling within the weight limits). The results are reported in Table 13.1. Are defective balls and the three plants independent or dependent?

**Table 13.1**

| Number of Acceptable and Defective Tennis Balls Produced by Plants | | | |
|---|---|---|---|
| | *Plant* | | |
| | *A* | *B* | *C* | *Total* |
| Acceptable | 80 | 75 | 115 | 270 |
| Defective | 5 | 15 | 10 | 30 |
| Total | 85 | 90 | 125 | 300 |

# 13.2 Parametric versus Nonparametric Tests

Although nonparametric statistics avoid the assumptions inherent in parametric tests, many nonparametric tests are less powerful than comparable parametric tests. **Power** is the ability of a statistical test to accept the alternative hypothesis correctly. This means that one may have to take more observations with the nonparametric test to achieve comparable power. For example, one nonparametric test about a population mean (based on the sample median) requires 150 observations to have the same power achieved by 100 observations using the (parametric) $z$ test presented in Chapter 8. Yet, nonparametric tests are more often used only for small samples (such as $n < 30$). There are two reasons: (1) the parametric assumptions about the parent population are far less critical when $n$ is large (remember the central limit theorem) and (2) nonparametric tests are often tedious to calculate when $n$ is large. In addition, nonparametric tests often use the rankings of a set of numbers. Thus the exact magnitude of each value in the set is not required.

This chapter will cover only a few of the numerous nonparametric tests. Two nonparametric measures of goodness of fit will be presented, the chi-square test and Spearman's rank correlation coefficient. We will also consider two nonparametric alternatives to the $t$ tests of Chapter 8, the sign test and the Mann–Whitney U test. In general, the same steps presented in Chapter 8 for testing hypotheses hold for nonparametric tests.

# 13.3 Chi-Square Test for Independence

The chi-square test is a goodness of fit test designed to test whether or not two variables are independent. Suppose we call the two variables "attribute A" and "attribute B." Each item in the population is classified according to the two attributes. For example, in testing tennis balls, attribute A might be the plant that manufactured a particular ball, either plant $A_1$, $A_2$, or $A_3$. Similarly, attribute B might be whether a particular ball is acceptable or unacceptable. The hypotheses for this test are:

$H_0$: attributes A and B are independent.

$H_A$: attributes A and B are not independent
  (i.e., they are dependent).

Before presenting the test statistics for these hypotheses, we need to present some notation. The test for these hypotheses determines the goodness of fit between a set of observed frequencies and a set of expected fre-

| Table 13.2 | Observed Frequencies in Table 13.1 | | | | |
|---|---|---|---|---|---|
| | | **Plant (Attribute A)** | | | |
| | | $A_1$ | $A_2$ | $A_3$ | *Total* |
| **State of Ball** | Acceptable | $O_{11} = 80$ | $O_{12} = 75$ | $O_{13} = 115$ | 270 |
| **(Attribute B)** | Defective | $O_{21} = 5$ | $O_{22} = 15$ | $O_{23} = 10$ | 30 |
| | Total | 85 | 90 | 125 | 300 |

quencies. The observed frequencies are typically presented in what is called a **contingency table**. Such a table was presented at the beginning of this chapter, for tennis balls, and earlier in chapter 4. Attribute A is shown across the top of the table and attribute B down the left side. The symbol $O_{ij}$ represents the observed frequency in the $i$th row and the $j$th column. Table 13.2 repeats the tennis ball frequencies observed in Table 13.1 using this notation.

This contingency table shows that in our sample of 300 tennis balls, 85 came from plant $A_1$. Of these 85, 5 were defective, that is, $O_{21} = 5$. Similarly, 125 balls from plant $A_3$ were tested, and 115 of these were acceptable, that is, $O_{13} = 115$. Out of the sample total of 300 balls, 270 were acceptable and 30 were defective.

The next step in our goodness of fit procedure is to determine the expected frequency for each cell in the contingency table. The expected frequency for each cell $(E_{ij})$ is calculated from the observed marginal totals, under the assumption, that attributes A and B are independent (i.e., that $H_0$ is true). From Chapter 4 we know that when two events are independent, the product of their marginal probabilities equals the probability of their intersection. Thus, if $H_0$ is true, the expected number of acceptable balls from plant A equals the probability that a ball is accepted (approximately equal to 270/300, from Table 3.2) times the probability that it comes from plant A (approximated from Table 3.2 by 85/300) times the total number of balls sampled (from Table 3.2, $n = 300$):

$$E_{11} = \frac{270}{300} \times \frac{85}{300} \times 300 = \frac{(270)(85)}{300} = 76.5$$

Equation (13.1) indicates how to determine the expected frequency for any cell. $E_{ij}$ represents the expected frequency for the $i$th row and the $j$th column.

Determining Expected Frequencies

(13.1)

$$E_{ij} = \frac{(\text{marginal total for } i\text{th row})(\text{marginal total for } j\text{th column})}{\text{total number of observations}}$$

To illustrate how Eq. (13.1) works, let's calculate all the expected frequencies for Table 13.2.

$$E_{11} = \frac{(\text{marg. total for row 1})(\text{marg. total for col 1})}{\text{total number of observations}}$$

$$= \frac{(270)(85)}{300} = 76.5$$

$$E_{12} = \frac{(\text{marg. total for row 1})(\text{marg. total for col 2})}{\text{total number of observations}}$$

$$= \frac{(270)(90)}{300} = 81.0$$

$$E_{13} = \frac{(270)(125)}{300} = 112.5 \qquad E_{21} = \frac{(30)(85)}{300} = 8.5$$

$$E_{22} = \frac{(30)(90)}{300} = 9.0 \qquad E_{23} = \frac{(30)(125)}{300} = 12.5$$

This entire set of expected frequencies is presented in Table 13.3.

The chi-square goodness-of-fit test compares the observed and expected frequencies. Remember, the expected frequencies are derived under the assumption that the two attributes are independent. If the fit is good (i.e., if the frequencies in the two tables are fairly close), then the null hypothesis of independence should be accepted. If the fit is not good, then the alternative

**Table 13.3**

| | | **Expected Frequencies** | | | |
|---|---|---|---|---|---|
| | | **Plant (Attribute A)** | | | |
| | | $A_1$ | $A_2$ | $A_3$ | *Total* |
| **State of Ball** | Acceptable | 76.5 | 81.0 | 112.5 | 270 |
| **(Attribute B)** | Defective | 8.5 | 9.0 | 12.5 | 30 |
| | Total | 85 | 90 | 125 | 300 |

hypothesis (of dependence) should be accepted. To determine whether or not the fit is good, we calculate the following chi-square (the Greek letter χ, squared) test statistic. (As before, the subscript $c$ denotes a calculated value of the test statistic.)

---

Chi-square Test Statistic

(13.2)
$$\chi_c^2 = \sum_{i=1}^{r} \sum_{j=1}^{c} \frac{(O_{ij} - E_{ij})^2}{E_{ij}}$$

where $O_{ij}$ is the observed frequency in cell $i,j$, $E_{ij}$ is the expected frequency in cell $i,j$, and there are $(r - 1)(c - 1)$ d.f.

---

Using the tennis ball information in Tables 13.2 and 13.3, the chi-square test statistic is calculated using Eq. (13.2) as follows:

$$\chi^2 = \sum_{i=1}^{2} \sum_{j=1}^{3} \frac{(O_{ij} - E_{ij})^2}{E_{ij}}$$

$$= \frac{(80 - 76.5)^2}{76.5} + \frac{(75 - 81.0)^2}{81.0} + \frac{(115 - 112.5)^2}{112.5}$$

$$+ \frac{(5 - 8.5)^2}{8.5} + \frac{(15 - 9.0)^2}{9.0} + \frac{(10 - 12.5)^2}{12.5} = 6.60$$

Thus $\chi_c^2 = 6.60$, with 2 d.f. $[= (r - 1)(c - 1) = (2 - 1)(3 - 1)]$.

The $p$ value in a chi-square test is the probability $P(\chi^2 \geq \chi_c^2)$, which in the tennis ball case is the probability of receiving a number equal to or larger than $\chi_c^2 = 6.60$, with 2 d.f. As noted in Chapter 8, if the $p$ value is less than the $\alpha$ value, then $H_0$ is rejected. If the $p$ value exceeds $\alpha$, then $H_0$ is accepted.

The $p$ values are readily determined using a computer program. We would see that the probability of obtaining a chi-square value of 6.60 or larger [i.e., $P(\chi^2 \geq 6.60)$ with 2 d.f.] is 0.0369. This tells us that for any probability of a type I error greater than 0.0369 (e.g., $\alpha = 0.05$) the null hypothesis of independence is rejected, and the conclusion is that the state of a tennis ball *does* depend on the manufacturing plant.

A method equivalent to finding $p$ values is to determine the appropriate chi-square critical value for $(r - 1)(c - 1)$ degrees of freedom. Appendix Table B.7 presents critical values for the chi-square distribution. If the

Figure 13.1
Family of chi-square
distributions.

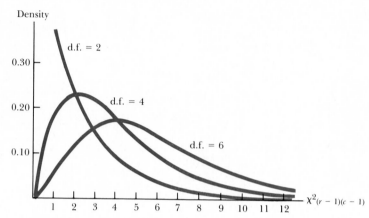

calculated $\chi^2_c$ value exceeds the critical value shown in this table for $(r - 1)(c - 1)$ degrees of freedom, then $H_0$ should be rejected. If $\chi^2_c$ does not exceed the critical value, then $H_0$ should be accepted.

## The Chi-Square Distribution and Finding Critical Values

The chi-square distribution is a continuous distribution that depends on the degrees of freedom (d.f.). As indicated above, d.f. = $(r - 1)(c - 1)$. Like the $t$ distribution, the chi-square distribution is a family of distributions, one for each degree of freedom. A few of these distributions are shown in Fig. 13.1.

Notice in Fig. 13.1 that the chi-square distribution becomes more and more symmetrical as the degrees of freedom become larger. For d.f. > 30 the chi-square distribution is very close to being normally distributed (if $n$ = infinity, the chi-square distribution is identical to the normal distribution.) Appendix Table B.7 provides the critical values for various degrees of freedom and $\alpha$ levels. Figure 13.2 shows the chi-square distribution for d.f. = 2, using the critical values shown in Appendix Table B.7.

The values in Fig. 13.2 are critical for d.f. = 2. They can be used in any test of independence where the contingency table is 2 × 3 or 3 × 2. For example, if the null hypothesis is true (i.e., the attributes are independent), then the calculated value of $\chi^2_2$ will be larger than 4.61 10% of the time. (Note: The subscript on $\chi^2$ denotes the d.f.) In other words, if there is no association between two attributes and d.f. = 2, the value calculated by using Eq. (13.2) will be less than 4.61 90% of the time and greater than 4.61 10%

Figure 13.2
The chi-square
distribution for 2 d.f.

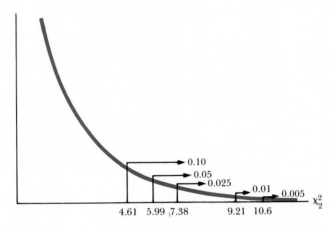

of the time. Similarly, a calculated value of $\chi_2^2$ will exceed 5.99 5% of the time when $H_0$ is true. Only the right-hand tail of the chi-square distribution is used in the chi-square test for independence.

In our tennis ball case there were 2 d.f. and $\chi_c^2 = 6.60$. If the probability of a type I error is $\alpha = 0.05$, the critical value (from Fig. 13.2 and Appendix Table B.7) is 5.99. As shown in Fig. 13.3, since the calculated chi-square value (6.60) exceeds this critical value (5.99), or alternatively, since the $p$ value (0.0369) is less than $\alpha$, we reject $H_0$ and conclude that the state of a tennis ball (acceptable or defective) does depend on the manufacturing plant.

Figure 13.3
Chi-square test of
tennis balls.

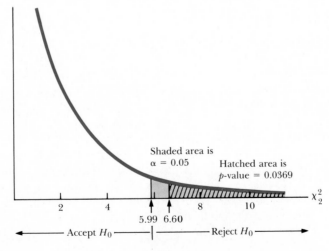

The plant manager for a large midwestern company is concerned with the number of clerical workers who are absent from their jobs. The manager believes that there is a relationship between the day of the week and the classification level of the employee. Clerical employees are classified as CL01, CL02, and CL03. A random sample of 300 days absent was taken over the past year, including an employee only once. Use the data in Table 13.4 to test the null hypothesis of independence, with $\alpha = 0.025$.

**ANSWER:**

The hypotheses in this situation are:

$H_0$: For days absent, the level of the worker and the day of the week are independent.

$H_A$: For days absent, the level of the worker and the day of the week are dependent.

The expected frequencies, calculated using Eq. (13.1), are given in Table 13.5.

$$\chi_c^2 = \frac{(28 - 26.4)^2}{26.4} + \frac{(24 - 24.0)^2}{24.0} + \frac{(20 - 21.6)^2}{21.6}$$

$$+ \frac{(20 - 16.9)^2}{16.9} + \frac{(18 - 15.3)^2}{15.3} + \frac{(18 - 13.8)^2}{13.8}$$

$$+ \frac{(13 - 20.5)^2}{20.5} + \frac{(15 - 18.7)^2}{18.7} + \frac{(18 - 16.8)^2}{16.8}$$

$$+ \frac{(17 - 17.6)^2}{17.6} + \frac{(16 - 16.0)^2}{16.0} + \frac{(15 - 14.4)^2}{14.4}$$

$$+ \frac{(32 - 28.6)^2}{28.6} + \frac{(27 - 26.0)^2}{26.0} + \frac{(19 - 23.4)^2}{23.4} = 7.416$$

From Appendix Table B.7, the critical value for d.f. $= (r - 1)(c - 1) = (5 - 1)(3 - 1) = 8$ and $\alpha = 0.025$ is 14.4. Since $14.4 > 7.416$, the null hypothesis of independence should not be rejected, and the conclusion is that clerical level and days of the week absent are not related. [Alternatively, using a computer, the $p$ value for this problem is $P(\chi_8^2 \geq 7.416) = 0.2841$. This $p$ value is larger than the $\alpha = 0.025$ specified in the problem. Hence, $H_0$ is not rejected.]

| Table 13.4 | Days Absent Among Clerical Workers | | | | |
|---|---|---|---|---|---|
| | | Level of the Worker (Attribute A) | | | |
| | | CL01 | CL02 | CL03 | Totals |
| | Monday | 28 | 24 | 20 | 72 |
| | Tuesday | 20 | 18 | 18 | 56 |
| Day | Wednesday | 13 | 15 | 18 | 46 |
| (Attribute B) | Thursday | 17 | 16 | 15 | 48 |
| | Friday | 32 | 27 | 19 | 78 |
| | Totals | 110 | 100 | 90 | 300 |

| Table 13.5 | Expected Frequencies for Days Absent | | | | |
|---|---|---|---|---|---|
| | | Level of the Worker (Attribute A) | | | |
| | | CL01 | CL02 | CL03 | Totals |
| | Monday | 26.4 | 24.0 | 21.6 | 72 |
| | Tuesday | 16.9 | 15.3 | 13.8 | 46 |
| Day | Wednesday | 20.5 | 18.7 | 16.8 | 56 |
| (Attribute B) | Thursday | 17.6 | 16.0 | 14.4 | 48 |
| | Friday | 28.6 | 26.0 | 23.4 | 78 |
| | Totals | 110 | 100 | 90 | 300 |

## Exercises

**13.1** If two events A and B are independent and the probability of A is 0.20 while that of B is 0.15, then for a sample of 200, what is the expected frequency of A and B?

**13.2** Specify the $H_0$ rejection region for the chi-square test of independence for the following contingency table sizes and type I error levels.

a) The contingency table is $r = 4$ by $c = 5$ and $\alpha = 0.01$.

b) The contingency table has three rows and six columns, and the probability of a type I error is 0.05.

c) The contingency table is 2 by 2 and $\alpha = 0.10$.

OPS  13.3  A plant manager wants to know if there is a difference in the number of machine breakdowns during the plant's three shifts. The following sample information is collected on four machines. At the 0.05 level of significance, are breakdowns on the four machines independent of the shifts?

| Time of | Machine Number | | | |
|---|---|---|---|---|
| Shift | *1* | *2* | *3* | *4* |
| 7:30–3:30 | 9 | 15 | 9 | 11 |
| 3:30–11:30 | 10 | 13 | 8 | 10 |
| 11:30–7:30 | 11 | 14 | 11 | 14 |

ADM  13.4  It is often stated that gender and occupation are related. Is this statement supported by the following information from the 1980 U.S. Census? (Use a chi-square test.)

| **Male and Female Occupations** (in Millions) | | |
|---|---|---|
| Occupation | Male | Female |
| Management and professional | 13.5 | 9.2 |
| Technical, sales, administrative support | 11.0 | 19.9 |
| Service occupations | 5.6 | 8.0 |
| Farming, forestry, fishing | 2.6 | 0.5 |
| Precision production, craft, repairing | 12.5 | 1.6 |
| Operators, fabricators, laborers | 14.5 | 5.5 |

PUB  13.5  A *USA Today* article on the composition of delegates to the Democratic and Republican national conventions (August 20, 1984) showed the following survey results on the yearly income of 2142 responding Democrats and 1448 responding Republicans.

| | $10,000 or less | $10,001– $20,000 | $20,001– $40,000 | $40,001– $50,000 | More than $50,000 |
|---|---|---|---|---|---|
| Republican | 2% | 9% | 29% | 14% | 46% |
| Democrat | 5% | 13% | 40% | 12% | 30% |

a) Construct a contingency table (frequency of each income–party cell) for these data.

**b)** Is income level related to party affiliation?

**c)** To perform the test in part (a), what did you have to assume about the survey method?

FIN **13.6** *The Business Failure Record*, compiled by Dun and Bradstreet in 1979, shows the following number of business failures (in hundreds) by industry type and selected years. Is the type of business independent of the year in which failures occurred?

| Industry | Number of Failures in | | | |
|---|---|---|---|---|
| | *1940* | *1950* | *1960* | *1970* |
| Mining and manufacturing | 25 | 21 | 26 | 20 |
| Wholesale trade | 13 | 10 | 15 | 10 |
| Retail trade | 85 | 44 | 74 | 47 |
| Construction | 8 | 9 | 26 | 17 |
| Commercial service | 6 | 7 | 14 | 14 |

# 13.4 Rank Correlation Measures

**Rank correlation** is a nonparametric method of correlation designed to measure the strength of association between two sets of ranked data. There are two methods of calculating rank correlation—Kendall's tau (named after the statistician Maurice Kendall) and Spearman's rho (named after the statistican C. Spearman). Although both of these methods were developed in the early 1900s, today **Spearman's rho** is the more widely used. It is the nonparametric equivalent of the simple coefficient of correlation presented in Chapter 9 and is the only nonparametric measure of correlation we will describe here.

## Electronic Work Stations

You are a systems analyst for General Motors. You are assigned to the evaluation of two different brands of work stations. The brand selected will be installed at the desks of over 1000 professional employees in the Detroit area. The choice between the two will depend, in part, on how "user friendly" each system is, as well as on the response time of each. For testing purposes, the two companies involved (labeled A and B) provide seven stations each. In the first phase of testing, seven professional employees are randomly assigned to use both brands. In a second phase of testing, seven other employees are randomly assigned to usage. All 14 employees rate the work stations on a scale from 0 to 100 for user friendliness and response time (Table 13.6). Your task is to compare the rankings of the two groups of users and to compare the brands in terms of these rankings.

**Table 13.6**

| Computer Work Station Comparison | | | | | | | | |
|---|---|---|---|---|---|---|---|---|
| | **Brand A** | | **Brand B** | | | **Brand A** | | **Brand B** | |
| User | *Friend-liness* | *Resp. Time* | *Friend-liness* | *Resp. Time* | User | *Friend-liness* | *Resp. Time* | *Friend-liness* | *Resp. Time* |
| 1 | 81 | 75 | 80 | 78 | 8 | 91 | 74 | 95 | 77 |
| 2 | 60 | 60 | 90 | 84 | 9 | 77 | 61 | 48 | 86 |
| 3 | 90 | 40 | 48 | 69 | 10 | 90 | 50 | 75 | 68 |
| 4 | 95 | 55 | 61 | 79 | 11 | 79 | 52 | 59 | 80 |
| 5 | 77 | 82 | 66 | 90 | 12 | 88 | 81 | 71 | 92 |
| 6 | 85 | 70 | 75 | 82 | 13 | 81 | 72 | 61 | 82 |
| 7 | 55 | 50 | 71 | 65 | 14 | 85 | 51 | 66 | 63 |

Spearman's rho is used as the measure of correlation when numerical values reflect only order; they do not reflect relative magnitudes. For example, in the work station case, an increase in numerical value from 50 to 60 need not imply a 20% increase in user friendliness across all judges. This change may simply imply a nonquantifiable feeling of increased friendliness. Spearman's rho is customarily denoted by $r_s$ and is defined as follows:

Spearman's Rho

(13.3)
$$r_s = 1 - \left( \frac{6\Sigma d_i^2}{n^3 - n} \right)$$

If two sets of rankings are identical, then $r_s = +1$. If two sets of ranks are perfectly related in an inverse manner, then $r_s = -1$. If two sets of ranks are uncorrelated, then $r_s = 0$. Thus $-1 \leq r_s \leq +1$. The $d_i^2$ in Eq. (13.3) is the square of the difference in the ranks of the two data sets. That is, $d_1^2$ is the square of the difference between the ranks of the first pair of observations in the sample, $d_2^2$ is the square of the difference in ranks of the second pair of observations, and so forth. The number of observations in each sample is $n$. If two observations are the same, the average rank is given to each.

We will first find the rank correlation coefficient between the two brand ratings on the "friendly" scale by users 1 through 7. Table 13.7 gives the rank of each observation for the two brands. Notice that rank 1 is the lowest score, rank 2 is the second lowest score, and rank 7 is the highest score. Column 6 ($d_i$) in Table 13.7 shows the difference in ranks between the two brands, and column 7 ($d_i^2$) gives the square of these differences.

In the first row in Table 13.7, user 1 gave brand A a score of 81. There are three user-friendly scores lower than 81. Hence, the user-friendly rank for employee 1 is 4. Similarly, the user-friendly rank for brand B from employee 1 is 6, since five of these scores are lower than employee 1's score of 80. Thus $d_1 = 4 - 6 = -2$, and $d_1^2 = (-2)^2 = 4$.

Spearman's rho is calculated using the sum of $d_i^2 = 88$ in Table 13.7 as follows:

$$ r_s = 1 - \left( \frac{6 \Sigma d_i^2}{n^3 - n} \right) = 1 - \left( \frac{6(88)}{7^3 - 7} \right) = 1 - 1.57 = -0.57 $$

This result indicates an inverse relationship between the ranking of friendliness on the two brands.

**Table 13.7**

| Calculating $r_s$ for Friendliness of Brand A and Brand B | | | | | | |
|---|---|---|---|---|---|---|
| | **Brand A** | | **Brand B** | | | |
| *User* | *Friendly* | *Rank* | *Friendly* | *Rank* | $d_i$ | $d_i^2$ |
| 1 | 81 | 4 | 80 | 6 | −2 | 4 |
| 2 | 60 | 2 | 90 | 7 | −5 | 25 |
| 3 | 90 | 6 | 48 | 1 | +5 | 25 |
| 4 | 95 | 7 | 61 | 2 | +5 | 25 |
| 5 | 77 | 3 | 66 | 3 | 0 | 0 |
| 6 | 85 | 5 | 75 | 5 | 0 | 0 |
| 7 | 55 | 1 | 71 | 4 | −3 | 9 |
| | | | | | Sum = | 88 |

## Testing Rank Correlation Hypotheses

The null and alternative hypotheses for rank correlation are:

$H_0$: The ranks of the two population data sets are not correlated

$H_A$: The ranks of the two population data sets are correlated.

For small sample sizes ($n < 10$), tables are available for determining if $r_s$ is significantly different from zero. For example, if $n = 7$ (such as the computer work station case), $r_s$ must be larger than 0.714 or less than $-0.714$ to be significant when $\alpha = 0.10$. Since our calculated value of $-0.57$ falls between these values, we accept $H_0$ and conclude that the rankings are not significantly correlated. People who rank brand A high do not necessarily rank brand B high.

If $n > 10$, the following test statistic can be used to determine if $r_s$ is significantly different from zero:

---

$t$ Test Statistic for Spearman's Rho ($n \geq 10$):

(13.4) $$t_c = r_s \sqrt{\frac{n - 2}{1 - r_s^2}}$$

where d.f. $= n - 2$.

---

**WORKED EXAMPLE 13.2**

In a ranked correlation problem with $n = 50$ observations, the sum of the squared differences between the ranked observations is $d_i^2 = 12{,}200$. Calculate $r_s$ and determine if the rank correlation is significantly different from zero. Use $\alpha = 0.05$.

**ANSWER:**

Using Eq. (13.3),

$$r_s = 1 - \frac{6(12{,}200)}{50^3 - 50} = 1 - 0.586 = 0.414$$

Using Eq. (13.4),

$$t_c = 0.414 \sqrt{\frac{50 - 2}{1 - (0.414)^2}} = 3.151$$

Chapter 13  Nonparametric Statistics

The critical value from the $t$ table for $n - 2 = 48$ d.f. is approximately 2.021 (using d.f. $= 40$ as the closest value and the column headed 0.025 because this is a two-sided test). Since our calculated value of 3.151 clearly exceeds the critical value, we reject the null hypothesis of no rank correlation.

**WORKED EXAMPLE 13.3**

Find Spearman's rho for the brand B scores given by the first seven users for friendliness and response time in the computer work station case. Test for significance, assuming that the critical value for $r_s$ when $n = 7$ is $\pm 0.893$ (we found this in a table of $r_s$ critical values for $\alpha = 0.02$ and a two-sided test).

**ANSWER:**

| User | Friend-liness | Rank | Response Time | Rank | $d_i$ | $d_i^2$ |
|------|------|------|------|------|------|------|
| 1 | 80 | 6 | 78 | 3 | 3 | 9 |
| 2 | 90 | 7 | 84 | 6 | 1 | 1 |
| 3 | 48 | 1 | 69 | 2 | $-1$ | 1 |
| 4 | 61 | 2 | 79 | 4 | $-2$ | 4 |
| 5 | 66 | 3 | 90 | 7 | $-4$ | 16 |
| 6 | 75 | 5 | 82 | 5 | 0 | 0 |
| 7 | 71 | 4 | 65 | 1 | 3 | 9 |
|  |  |  |  |  | Sum = | 40 |

$$r_s = 1 - \frac{6(40)}{7^3 - 7} = 1 - \frac{240}{336} = 1 - 0.71 = 0.29$$

This rank correlation does not exceed the critical value of 0.893. Hence, $H_0$ of no rank correlation between friendliness and response time for brand B must be accepted.

## Exercises

**13.7** For the scores on friendliness given to brands A and B by users 8 through 14 (Table 13.6), what is Spearman's rho? What does this value indicate?

**13.8** Under what conditions is Spearman's rho a more appropriate measure of the relationship between two variables than the simple coefficient of correlation described in Chapter 9?

ADM **13.9** For the data on occupation and gender in Exercise 13.4, calculate the Spearman rank correlation coefficient. Why would the $t$ statistic for Spearman's rho be questionable for a test of the relationship between occupation and gender?

ECN **13.10** A *Journal of Economic Literature* article reported on the most frequently cited journals in economics. The adjusted ranking of the top 18 journals follows:

1 *American Economic Review*
2 *Journal of Political Economy*
3 *Econometrica*
4 *Journal of Monetary Economics*
5 *Journal of Economic Theory*
6 *Review of Economic Studies*
7 *International Economic Review*
8 *Bell Journal of Economics*
9 *Journal of Finance*
10 *Journal of Econometrics*
11 *Scandinavian Journal of Economics*
12 *Brookings Papers*
13 *Journal of Public Economics*
14 *Journal of Financial Economics*
15 *Review of Economics and Statistics*
16 *Journal of the American Statistical Association*
17 *Quarterly Journal of Economics*
18 *Journal of Human Resources*

An informal survey of economists aimed at assessing the overall quality of journals suggests the following ranking:

1 *Journal of Political Economy*
2 *Econometrica*
3 *American Economic Review*
4 *Journal of Monetary Economics*
5 *Journal of Finance*
6 *Review of Economic Studies*
7 *Journal of Financial Economics*
8 *Review of Economics and Statistics*
9 *Quarterly Journal of Economics*
10 *Journal of Economic Theory*
11 *Bell Journal of Economics*
12 *Journal of Econometrics*
13 *Journal of the American Statistical Association*
14 *Brookings Papers*
15 *International Economic Review*
16 *Scandinavian Journal of Economics*
17 *Journal of Human Resources*
18 *Journal of Public Economics*

a) Calculate Spearman's rank correlation coefficient for the journal citation ranking and the quality ranking.

b) At the 0.05 type I error level, is there a relationship between the citation and the quality ranking?

ECN 13.11 In Exercise 13.10, why should you use Spearman's rank correlation coefficient to measure the relationship between the journal citation ranking and the journal quality ranking, rather than the simple coefficient of correlation defined in Chapter 9?

ADM 13.12 For the following, use the data on pre- and posttest results in Exercise 9.41.

a) Calculate Spearman's rho for the pre- and posttests.

b) Using the rho value calculated in part (a), test whether there is a relationship between the pre- and posttest results.

c) Why might the use of Spearman's rho and the testing procedure used in part (b) be preferred to the testing procedure followed in Exercise 9.41?

ADM 13.13 For the following, use the data on test scores and raises in Exercise 9.32. Use only the first 13 observations.

a) Calculate Spearman's rho for scores and raises.

b) Using the rho value calculated in part (a), test whether there is a relationship between scores and raises. Use $\alpha = 0.05$.

c) Why might the use of Spearman's rho and the testing procedure used in part (b) be preferred to the testing procedure followed in Exercise 9.32?

# 13.5 Runs Tests

A *runs test* is a nonparametric method for determining if a set of observations occur at random. A *run* is a set of consecutive observations that have the same characteristic. To illustrate, a financial analyst interested in determining whether or not movements in the stock market are random might observe consecutive days on the New York Stock Exchange and classify the Dow Jones Industrial Index as either increasing (I) or decreasing (D). Fifteen consecutive trading days might look like this:

$$\underbrace{\text{I I I I}}_{\text{run 1}} \quad \underbrace{\text{D D D D}}_{\text{run 2}} \quad \underbrace{\text{I I I I}}_{\text{run 3}} \underbrace{\text{D D}}_{\text{run 4}}$$

There are four runs ($r = 4$) to these data, where a run is a series of consecutive I's or D's.

In a runs test we compare samples that might come from two populations. The null hypothesis in a runs test is that the two samples are drawn randomly from the same population. The alternative hypothesis is that the samples are drawn from different populations. Again consider the data in our work station case, where the two populations are now brand A and brand B, for users 8 through 14. We are interested in the ratings on the "friendliness" scale for users 8 through 14, and want to know if the scores for brand A differ significantly from those for brand B. To do this test, we arrange the scores from the two brands from lowest to highest and count the number of brand runs, as shown in Table 13.8.

If the alternative hypothesis is true, then the A and B scores are drawn from different populations; that is, the brands are different in terms of friendliness. In that case, we would expect some pattern to the mixture of sample A and B scores. For example, suppose in the population that B scores are generally less than A scores. Then we would expect a pattern such as that seen in Table 13.8, where most of the sample B scores are bunched at the lower end. When the B scores are bunched (at either end), then the number of runs will be small. If the null hypothesis is correct (that the A and B scores were drawn from the same population, i.e., no difference in brands), then the sample A and B scores should be randomly intermixed (resulting in a relatively large number of runs).

To test hypotheses in a runs test we need to know the critical number of runs. If the number of runs in the sample is greater than this critical value, then the null hypothesis is accepted. If the number of runs in the sample is less than or equal to the critical value, then $H_0$ is rejected. The critical value depends on the number of sample values drawn from each population. In our work station example, the sample sizes are $n_1 = 7$ and $n_2 = 7$.

**Table 13.8**

| Brand A and Brand B Runs |
|---|

| Brand: | B | B | B | B | B | B | A | A | A | A | A | A | A | B |
|---|---|---|---|---|---|---|---|---|---|---|---|---|---|---|
| Score: | 48 | 59 | 61 | 66 | 71 | 75 | 77 | 79 | 81 | 85 | 88 | 90 | 91 | 95 |

$$\underbrace{\phantom{48 \ 59 \ 61 \ 66 \ 71 \ 75}}_{\text{run 1}} \quad \underbrace{\phantom{77 \ 79 \ 81 \ 85 \ 88 \ 90 \ 91}}_{\text{run 2}} \quad \underbrace{\phantom{95}}_{\text{run 3}}$$

Chapter 13 Nonparametric Statistics

Appendix Table B.8 provides the critical values for a runs test using $\alpha = 0.05$. The two sample sizes are in the margins of this table (note: it makes no difference which sample is called 1 and which is called 2). Critical values are shown in the center. Thus, for $n_1 = 7$ and $n_2 = 7$, Table B.8 shows the critical value for $\alpha = 0.05$ to be three runs. With three or fewer runs, $H_0$ should be rejected. Since our work station example had exactly three runs (see Table 13.8), we reject the null hypothesis that the A and B scores are drawn from the same population, and conclude that the two brands differ significantly.

---

**WORKED EXAMPLE 13.4**

The residuals in Table 13.9 are taken from Fig. 10.5. Are these residuals random?

**Table 13.9**

| Residuals | | |
|---|---|---|
| Observation | Residual | Run |
| 1 | −2.7116 } | 1 |
| 2 | 3.5526 ⎫ | |
| 3 | 7.2611 ⎪ | |
| 4 | 5.0634 ⎪ | 2 |
| 5 | 0.3796 ⎬ | |
| 6 | 4.1873 ⎪ | |
| 7 | 2.5958 ⎭ | |
| 8 | −14.9392 ⎫ | 3 |
| 9 | −12.6985 ⎭ | |
| 10 | 10.1982 ⎫ | 4 |
| 11 | 10.4097 ⎭ | |
| 12 | −1.6052 ⎫ | 5 |
| 13 | −18.3284 ⎭ | |
| 14 | 0.9935 ⎫ | 6 |
| 15 | 5.6418 ⎭ | |

**ANSWER:**

A runs test can be used to test for a pattern in a time series. After counting the runs in Table 13.9, it is seen that there are $n_1 = 5$ minus signs and $n_2 = 10$ plus signs. The critical number of runs for $n_1 = 5$ and $n_2 = 10$ is $r = 3$. To be significant, the calculated number of runs must be fewer than three (see Appendix Table B.8). Since the calculated number is six, we do not reject $H_0$ that the data are random. In other words, this sample does not provide enough evidence to conclude that there is a pattern to the residuals using the runs test.

## Exercises

**13.14** Perform a runs test on the response time scores given brand A and B by user employees 8 through 14 (Table 13.6).

ADM **13.15** The following sequence indicates whether daily production of defective automobiles coming off an assembly line was above (indicated by an A) or below (B) the long-term median number of defective autos.

A B B B A A B A B A A B B B A A B B A A A B B B A B A B B A

a) Does this series suggest a departure from randomness? (Test at the 0.05 type I error level.)

b) Why would the production manager care if this series did or did not suggest randomness?

PUB **13.16** The following sequence indicates whether or not an accident occurred at a given intersection during the 3:00 to 6:00 P.M. rush period. (A indicates accident and N no accident.)

A N N A N A A N N N A N N A A A N N A A

a) Is there an indication of departure from randomness at the 0.05 type I error level?

b) Why would a transportation official be concerned about the nonrandom occurrence of accidents?

ECN **13.17** Perform a runs test on the consumption–income regression residuals given in Table 9.8. At the 0.05 type I error level, would you conclude that these residuals suggest a nonrandom error term?

ECN **13.18** Perform a runs test on the cost–trend regression residuals given in Table 10.11. At the 0.05 type I error level, would you conclude that these residuals suggest a nonrandom error term?

ECN **13.19** Econometricians criticize the use of the runs test for nonrandomness in time series because this test assesses only the changing of signs and not the pattern in residuals themselves between sign changes. Is there any merit in their warning?

# 13.6 The Mann–Whitney $U$ and the Two-Sample $t$ Test on Rank

The Mann–Whitney test is similar to the runs test in that it tests the null hypothesis that two populations are identical. This test, however, is more powerful than the runs test because it takes account of the rank of an observation, not just the grouping of observations.

The **Mann–Whitney test** starts with the assumption that two samples are drawn independently of each other (i.e., they are not matched pairs). As in the runs test, the sample observations are arranged from lowest to highest in a single ordering. But now, the rank of the observations is identified as shown in Table 13.10, where we have ranked the brand A friendliness scores given by users 1 through 7 and the brand B friendliness scores given by users 8 through 14. (Notice that the high score of 95 was given to both brands A and B. Thus each brand receives the average of the 13th and 14th rank.)

**Table 13.10**

| Table 13.8 Repeated with Ranks | | | | | | | | | | | | | |
|---|---|---|---|---|---|---|---|---|---|---|---|---|---|
| Brand: | B | A | B | A | B | B | B | B | A | A | A | A | A | B |
| Score: | 48 | 55 | 59 | 60 | 61 | 66 | 71 | 75 | 77 | 81 | 85 | 90 | 95 | 95 |
| Rank: | 1 | 2 | 3 | 4 | 5 | 6 | 7 | 8 | 9 | 10 | 11 | 12 | 13.5 | 13.5 |

For the Mann–Whitney test, the following null and alternative hypotheses are used:

$H_0$: The two populations are identical

$H_A$: The two populations are not identical

The Mann–Whitney test determines the similarity between the two rankings by first calculating a value of $T_A$ and $T_B$.

Calculating the Mann–Whitney test

(13.5)
$$T_A = n_A n_B + \frac{n_A(n_A + 1)}{2} - r_A$$
$$T_B = n_A n_B - T_A$$
$$U = \min[T_A, T_B]$$

The symbol $r_A$ denotes the sum of the ranks of the A values, and $n_A$, $n_B$ are the sample sizes taken from the A and B populations, respectively. The statistic for the Mann–Whitney test is $U$, where $U$ is defined as

$$U = \min[T_A, T_B]$$

Critical values of $U$ are provided in books of statistical tables (not presented in this text). In general, if $U$ is small (less than the critical value), then the null hypothesis that the two populations are identical should be rejected. If $U$ is large (larger than the critical value), then $H_0$ should be accepted. Some statistical tables give the $p$ value for certain values of $U$.

The data in Table 13.10 can be used to demonstrate the calculation of the Mann–Whitney $U$. Recall that for this problem $n_A = n_B = 7$. The sum of the ranks, $r_A$, is as follows:

$$r_A = 2 + 4 + 9 + 10 + 11 + 12 + 13.5 = 61.5$$

$$T_A = n_A n_B + \frac{n_A(n_A + 1)}{2} - r_A$$

$$= (7)(7) + (7)(8)/2 - 61.5 = 15.5$$

Thus

$$T_B = n_A n_B - T_A = (7)(7) - 15.5 = 33.5$$

and

$$U = \min[15.5, 33.5] = 15.5$$

An extensive table of Mann–Whitney $U$ values (not given in this book) for $n_A = n_B = 7$ shows the $p$ value to be approximately 0.145. Thus we accept the null hypothesis (that the two populations are identical) and conclude that brand A and brand B are not different in terms of user friendliness.

In the absence of tables for the Mann–Whitney $U$, the researcher may use the two-sample $t$ test presented in Chapter 8. The two-sample $t$ test requires the two populations to have the same variance. Now, however, the observations are defined by their rank. As an illustration of this test, consider the response time scores given for brand A by users 1 through 7 and for brand B by users 8 through 14 (see Table 13.11).

Note in Table 13.11 that the response time score of 82 occurs twice. Thus its rank of 11.5 is the average of the 11th and 12th positions, both of which equal 82. Using Eq. (8.6) and the null hypothesis of identical populations,

| | | Table 13.11 | | Response Time Rank of Brand A by Users 1 through 7 and of Brand B by Users 8 through 14 (from Table 13.6) | | | |

**Table 13.11** — Response Time Rank of Brand A by Users 1 through 7 and of Brand B by Users 8 through 14 (from Table 13.6)

| | Brand A | | | Brand B | |
| --- | --- | --- | --- | --- | --- |
| User | Response Time | Rank | User | Response Time | Rank |
| 1 | 75 | 8 | 8 | 77 | 9 |
| 2 | 60 | 4 | 9 | 86 | 13 |
| 3 | 40 | 1 | 10 | 68 | 6 |
| 4 | 55 | 3 | 11 | 80 | 10 |
| 5 | 82 | 11.5 | 12 | 92 | 14 |
| 6 | 70 | 7 | 13 | 82 | 11.5 |
| 7 | 50 | 2 | 14 | 63 | 5 |

Average brand rank: $\overline{R}_A = 5.21$ $\overline{R}_B = 9.79$

Variance of brank rank: $s_A^2 = 14.15$ $s_B^2 = 11.49$

the calculated $t$ statistic for ranks is

$$t = \frac{\overline{R}_A - \overline{R}_B}{\sqrt{\left(\frac{s_A^2(n_A - 1) + s_B^2(n_B - 1)}{n_A + n_B - 2}\right)\left(\frac{n_A + n_B}{n_A n_B}\right)}}$$

$$= \frac{5.21 - 9.79}{\sqrt{\left(\frac{(14.15)(6) + (11.49)(6)}{7 + 7 - 2}\right)\left(\frac{7 + 7}{7 \times 7}\right)}}$$

$$= -2.393$$

With $n_A + n_B - 2 = 12$ d.f. and $\alpha = 0.05$, for a two-tail test the critical $t$ value is $-2.179$. Thus the null hypothesis of no population difference is rejected, and we conclude that there is a significant difference in the response time of the two brands.

## Exercises

ADM  **13.20**  A company wishes to compare the accuracy in typing on two different types of computer keyboards. Thirteen experienced typists type the same 500 words. Keyboard A is used six times and keyboard B seven times with the following results:

Board A: 12 9 14 15 9 13     Board B: 16 8 17 10 16 20 19

Compute the Mann–Whitney $U$ and state the assumptions for a $U$ test. What does a large calculated $U$ value indicate?

ADM    **13.21** For the following questions, use the typing data in Exercise 13.20.

    **a)** Using both the Mann–Whitney $U$ and the $t$ statistic rank test, is there a population difference between errors on the two keyboards? (Test at the 0.10 type I error level.)

    **b)** Why couldn't you test for a mean difference in errors using the $t$ or $z$ statistic from Chapter 8?

ADM    **13.22** The owner of two 24-hour convenience stores is concerned that the register shortages are higher at the north-side store than at the south-side store. For 12 randomly selected days the following dollar shortages were reported:

| North-Side Store | | | | South-Side Store | | | |
|---|---|---|---|---|---|---|---|
| 7.10 | 4.55 | 14.30 | 37.70 | 9.85 | 7.00 | 2.10 | 11.12 |
| 8.95 | 9.60 | 10.30 | 8.45 | 2.71 | 3.80 | 4.78 | 30.00 |
| 7.54 | 5.00 | 15.00 | 21.90 | 29.00 | 9.00 | 3.00 | 15.00 |

Use the $t$ statistic rank test to check for any difference in the dollar shortage at the two stores at $\alpha = 0.01$.

MKT    **13.23** For the following, use the data on car rental prices in Exercise 8.46.

    **a)** Using both the Mann–Whitney $U$ and the $t$ statistic rank test, is there a population difference between Avis and Hertz car rental prices at the 0.05 type I error level?

    **b)** Why might your nonparametric test in part (a) be preferred to the test used in Exercise 8.46?

PUB    **13.24** As a statistical analyst for the Federal Trade Commission, you want to determine if brand A's car batteries last as long as brand B's, as claimed in an advertisement. You randomly select 12 batteries of each brand and obtain the following results (measured in months):

| Brand A | | | | Brand B | | | |
|---|---|---|---|---|---|---|---|
| 36.50 | 37.25 | 38.75 | 38.12 | 37.50 | 37.75 | 37.75 | 39.50 |
| 39.00 | 41.50 | 40.00 | 41.00 | 38.50 | 40.50 | 39.25 | 38.50 |
| 37.75 | 38.25 | 39.00 | 38.75 | 38.50 | 39.25 | 42.00 | 39.50 |

a) You could test the null hypothesis of a difference in mean time to
   · failure using a $t$ statistic, or you could use a nonparametric rank test
   such as the Mann–Whitney $U$ or $t$ statistic rank test. What are the
   different assumptions required for each test?

b) Test for a difference in the two populations of batteries using both the
   Mann–Whitney $U$ and the $t$ statistic rank test. What is your conclusion
   at $\alpha = 0.05$?

# 13.7 Sign Tests Using the Binomial Distribution

As indicated in Chapter 8, we can test hypotheses about population proportions. For example, we might test the null hypothesis that the proportion of
airline passengers requesting the nonsmoking section for a flight is 0.80. The
null and alternative hypotheses could be:

$$H_0: \pi = 0.80 \qquad \text{versus} \qquad H_A: \pi \neq 0.80$$

These hypotheses could be tested using the $z$ test given in Chapter 8. A
nonparametric alternative is the **sign test**. We will present two versions of
the sign test—a one-sample test and a two-sample test.

## One-Sample Sign Test

In some samples it is possible to look at the sample values and to place each
observation into one of two groups. For example, a certified public accountant
(CPA) review board might want to look at the most recent CPA exam scores
and identify each score as belonging to either the pass or the fail group.
Similarly, candidates selected for job interviews at a corporation might be
classified as either minority or nonminority. In the preceding airline illustration, passengers can be classified as requesting either smoking or nonsmoking
sections.

To conduct a one-sample sign test, we observe the sign of each observation in the sample. Each sign is either a plus or a minus. Observations in one category are given a plus sign, and observations in the other category are given a minus sign. It is convenient to let $x$ = the number of plus signs. The binomial distribution (Appendix Table B.2) is then used to determine the probability (a $p$ value) of the recorded number of pluses and minuses, assuming the null hypothesis is correct. If the $p$ value exceeds $\alpha$, $H_0$ is accepted. If the $p$ value is less than $\alpha$, then $H_0$ is rejected.

Consider again the airline reviewing requests for the nonsmoking section. Past records indicate that 80% of passengers request this section, although there is some indication that more people may currently be requesting it. The following null and one-sided alternative hypotheses might be appropriate:

$$H_0: \pi \leq 0.80 \qquad \text{versus} \qquad H_A: \pi > 0.80$$

Suppose a random sample of size $n = 100$ is taken of recent airline passengers, and 88 of these people request the nonsmoking section. Thus, if a plus sign $(x)$ is a request for the nonsmoking section, $x = 88$. Now go to Appendix Table B.2 for $n = 100$ (the sample size) under $\pi = 0.80$ (the null hypothesis) and determine the probability of 88 or more successes. Remember, with discrete distributions, the $p$ value is always the sum of a set of probabilities. From Appendix Table B.2,

$$
\begin{aligned}
P(x \geq 88) &= P(x = 88) + P(x = 89) + P(x = 90) + \cdots \\
&= 0.0128 + 0.0069 + 0.0034 + 0.0015 + 0.0006 \\
&\quad + 0.0002 + 0.0001 \\
&= 0.0255
\end{aligned}
$$

Thus the $p$ value is 0.0255. If the probability of a type I error is set at $\alpha = 0.05$, then this $p$ value is less than $\alpha$, which means that the null hypothesis $H_0: \pi \leq 0.80$ should be rejected. We can conclude that the proportion of nonsmoking requests has increased.

---

**WORKED EXAMPLE 13.5**

A company is using newspaper and television ads to encourage minority candidates to apply for a certain administrative position. For comparable positions in the past, only about 10 percent of the applicants have been from minority groups. The new position has 50 applicants, 12 of whom can be classified as members of minority groups. Does this evidence suggest that the advertising campaign was successful, using $\alpha = 0.04$?

**ANSWER:**

The hypotheses are

$$H_0: \pi \le 0.10 \qquad \text{versus} \qquad H_A: \pi > 0.10$$

The two groups are "minority" (a plus sign) and "nonminority" (a minus sign). There were 12 minority group applicants, which means that $x = 12$ (12 plus signs). Using Appendix Table B.2 for $n = 50$ (the sample size), $\pi = 0.10$, we calculate the probability of 12 or more successes.

$$P(x \ge 12) = P(x = 12) + P(x = 13) + \cdots$$
$$= 0.0022 + 0.0007 + 0.0002 + 0.0001 = 0.0032$$

Since the $p$ value of 0.0032 is less than $\alpha = 0.05$, $H_0: \pi \le 0.10$ is rejected and we conclude that the advertising campaign was successful.

## Two-Sample Sign Test

The two-sample sign test is used to compare a sample of scores from one population with a sample of scores from another population. The data must be from **matched pair samples**. That is, each element in one sample must share one common characteristic or more with an element in the other sample. For each matched pair, the score from sample A is compared with the score from sample B. If $A > B$, then a plus $(+)$ sign is associated with this pair. If $B < A$, then a minus $(-)$ sign is associated with this pair. The null hypothesis is that the probability of a plus sign, $P(+)$, equals the probability of a minus sign, $P(-)$, and thus $P(+) = P(-) = \frac{1}{2}$. Another way of stating this null hypothesis is to say that the median difference is zero.

For a given sample, the number of plus and minus signs is recorded. (If a matched pair shows no difference, then this pair is dropped from the analysis.) If $H_0$ is correct, then we would expect the number of plus and minus signs in the matched pairs to be approximately equal. As with the one-sample test, the binomial distribution is used to determine if $H_0$ is accepted or rejected.

As an example of the two-sample sign test, consider the user-friendly and response-time scores given by users 1 through 7 to brand A work stations in Table 13.6. Here the common characteristic processed by both scores is the user who gave each score. Suppose that the user-friendly score is hypothe-sized to be larger than the response-time scores. Given this supposition, the null and alternative hypotheses are:

$H_0$: there is no difference in scores.

$H_A$: friendliness exceeds responsiveness.

This is a one-sided, two-sample test, since the alternative hypothesis is that the user-friendly score is larger than the response-time score. The appropriate data for this test are reported in Table 13.12.

Table 13.12

| | **Data for the Sign Test Using Information on Brand A in Table 13.6** | | |
|---|---|---|---|
| **User** | **User Friendly** | **Response Time** | **Sign** |
| 1 | 81 | 75 | + |
| 2 | 60 | 60 | Neither |
| 3 | 90 | 40 | + |
| 4 | 95 | 55 | + |
| 5 | 77 | 82 | − |
| 6 | 85 | 70 | + |
| 7 | 55 | 50 | + |

Since employee 2 gave the same score to brand A on both measures, we ignore this person's scores. Now there are only six ($n = 6$) matched pairs we can use. For the six pairs, there are five plus signs and one minus sign. Thus the probability to be determined is $P(x \geq 5 | n = 6, \pi = \frac{1}{2})$. From Appendix Table B.2, for $n = 6$ the probability of getting five or more successes is

$$P(x \geq 5) = 0.0937 + 0.0156 = 0.1093$$

This $p$ value of 0.1093 is relatively large (e.g., greater than $\alpha = 0.05$), so we do not reject the null hypothesis of no differences.

**WORKED EXAMPLE 13.6**

Suppose that in a matched-pairs problem involving 50 paired observations there are 19 plus signs and 31 minus signs. Using $\alpha = 0.10$ and a two-sided test, determine if $H_0$, should be accepted or rejected.

**ANSWER:**

We need to determine the probability of 19 or fewer successes in $n = 50$ trials when $\pi = 0.50$. From Appendix Table B.2 this probability is

$$P(x \le 19 | n = 50, \pi = 0.50) = 0.0270 + 0.0160 + 0.0087 + 0.0044$$
$$+ 0.0020 + 0.0006 + 0.0003 + 0.0001$$
$$= 0.0591$$

This probability must be doubled because the alternative hypothesis was specified (in the problem) to be two-sided. Thus the $p$ value is 0.1182. Since the $p$ value exceeds $\alpha = 0.10$, the null hypothesis cannot be rejected. Thus this sample does not provide enough evidence to reject the hypothesis that the population difference is zero.

## Exercises

PUB  **13.25**  An army proficiency test is supposed to be designed so that 50% of the recruits can complete it in 30 minutes. Fifty recruits are given the test; 21 finish before 30 minutes are up and 29 require more than 30 minutes.

a) At the 0.05 level of significance, test whether the population median time needed to finish is 30 minutes.

b) What assumptions about the population did you have to make in part (a)?

MKT  **13.26**  An advertising executive claims that the majority of people (50%) can read and understand a certain ad in 2 seconds. To test this claim, a sample of 18 people are tested, with the following times (in seconds) recorded for reading the ad.

2.9  1.3  4.0  2.1  1.1  3.3  0.8  1.9  2.4
3.5  1.6  3.9  2.8  3.6  0.7  3.9  3.2  2.5

Is the median time required to read the ad 2 seconds? (Test at the 0.01 type I error level.)

MKT  **13.27**  Using the data in Exercise 8.36, test the claim that the median rental price of Hertz compact cars is $45. (Test at the 0.05 level of significance.) Compare these results with those obtained in Exercise 8.36. Are the two tests designed to test the same hypotheses? Are the assumptions required for both tests the same? Explain why or why not.

MKT  **13.28**  An oil company claims that there is a 10% median increase in horsepower resulting from the use of its new oil additive. A consumer group tests the oil additive on 100 cars and finds that in 31 of them the new additive results in an increase in horsepower of more than 10%. In 69 cars there is an increase of less than 10%. Using the sign test, is the oil company's claim reasonable? (Test at the 0.05 type I error level.)

**13.29**  To use the two-sample sign test, why must the observations in the two samples be matched pairs?

**13.30**  Use a two-sample sign test to determine whether brand B's user-friendly score is significantly different from its response-time score based on the sample data in Table 13.6 (at $\alpha = 0.10$).

MKT  **13.31**  A paint company asks six customers to rate its paint (A) and a competitor's paint (B) to determine which one is preferred. For the following results, is paint A significantly preferred to paint B at $\alpha = 0.05$?

| Customer: | 1 | 2 | 3 | 4 | 5 | 6 |
|-----------|---|---|---|---|---|---|
| Preference: | A over B | A over B | B over A | A over B | B over A | A over B |

ADM  **13.32**  In a management training program, 10 trainees were pre- and posttested to assess the impact of the program on management skill acquisition. The following results were recorded:

| Trainee | Skill Acquisition | Trainee | Skill Acquisition |
|---------|-------------------|---------|-------------------|
| 1 | Positive | 6 | No change |
| 2 | Negative | 7 | Positive |
| 3 | Positive | 8 | Positive |
| 4 | Positive | 9 | Negative |
| 5 | Positive | 10 | No change |

At the 0.05 type I error level, does this program appear to produce positive skill acquisition?

ADM **13.33** A *Wall Street Journal* article on how executives rate the performance of accountants, lawyers, and other specialists provided the following ratings of 782 chief executives.

| Performance of | Very Good (%) | Fairly Good (%) | Poor (%) | No Opinion (%) |
|---|---|---|---|---|
| Accountants | 45 | 47 | 6 | 2 |
| Lawyers | 39 | 43 | 14 | 4 |
| PR specialists | 15 | 45 | 27 | 13 |
| Business journalists | 13 | 46 | 29 | 12 |
| Executive recruiters | 11 | 42 | 27 | 20 |

a) Construct a contingency table (frequency of each rating–occupation cell) for these data.

b) Are executive ratings related to the occupations being rated?

ADM **13.34** An industrial trainer makes the following tally of final scores received by persons in her training program and the supervisor's judgment about their performance on the job. Test the hypothesis that the score received is independent of on-the-job performance at the 0.05 level of significance.

| Test Score (%) | On-the-Job Rating | |
|---|---|---|
| | *Acceptable* | *Unacceptable* |
| 70–100 | 60 | 15 |
| 40– 70 | 95 | 20 |
| 0– 40 | 25 | 45 |

PUB **13.35** A *USA Today* article on the composition of delegates to the Democratic and Republican national conventions showed the following survey results on the ethnic background of 2142 responding Democrats and 1448 responding Republicans:

|             | Black | White | Hispanic | Other |
|-------------|-------|-------|----------|-------|
| Republican  | 3%    | 92%   | 3%       | 2%    |
| Democrat    | 15%   | 78%   | 4%       | 3%    |

a) Construct a contingency table (frequency of each income–party cell) for these data. Round to the nearest person.

b) Is race related to party affiliation?

c) Why might one question the results of your test in part (b)?

**FIN** **13.36** For the data on business failure rates in Exercise 13.6, calculate Spearman's rho for failures in 1960 and 1970. Why wouldn't it be meaningful to calculate a simple coefficient of correlation as defined in Chapter 9?

**13.37** For the data on deficits in Exercise 9.40, calculate Spearman's rho and a simple coefficient of correlation. Why do these two measures of correlation differ?

**MKT** **13.38** In Exercise 9.42 the simple coefficient of correlation for sales and advertising expense was $r = 0.726$. Using the data on sales and advertising expense given in that exercise, calculate Spearman's rho. Why do these two measures of correlation differ?

**ACT** **13.39** An accountant concerned with the number of errors being made in filling out invoices wants to determine if a new procedure will result in a change in the number of errors made. To test for change, the accountant draws a sample of 11 people and observes the following error record:

|           | Person |    |    |    |    |    |    |    |    |    |    |
|-----------|--------|----|----|----|----|----|----|----|----|----|----|
| Procedure | *1*    | *2* | *3* | *4* | *5* | *6* | *7* | *8* | *9* | *10* | *11* |
| New       | 12     | 11 | 13 | 9  | 10 | 12 | 10 | 13 | 8  | 14 | 7  |
| Old       | 11     | 15 | 9  | 10 | 13 | 12 | 8  | 12 | 10 | 13 | 9  |

Use both the Mann–Whitney $U$ and the $t$ statistic rank test to test for a change in errors at the 0.05 level of significance. What did you have to assume about the sample of new and old procedures? Why might this be questioned?

**ADM** **13.40** An industrial psychologist claims that the time required to perform a certain task is highly skewed but is not related to a person's gender.

To test this claim, an affirmative action officer asks 10 men and 8 women to perform the task. The times recorded (in minutes) are:

Men: 2.5 1.3 4.0 2.1 1.1 3.3 0.8 1.9 2.4 3.5
Women: 1.6 3.9 2.8 3.6 0.7 3.9 3.2 2.9

a) Is a parametric or nonparametric test more appropriate to test for no gender difference in time? Explain.

b) At the 0.05 type I error level, are the data consistent with the psychologist's claim of no difference?

MKT **13.41** A real estate salesperson claims that the median selling price of houses in a given area of the city is about $100,000. To check this claim, you randomly select 10 houses that recently sold in this area and record the following prices (in thousands of dollars):

110  105  90  103  93  107  97  117  101  89

Using the sign test, is the salesperson's claim reasonable? (Test at the 0.05 level of significance.)

ECN **13.42** The distribution of income is known to be right skewed. Thus the median is typically used as the best measure of central tendency. What test statistic can be used to test hypotheses about median income levels?

**13.43** Using a computer random number generator or a random number table, generate 20 random numbers. Let even numbers be denoted by E and odd numbers by O. How many runs of E's and O's should there be in your sample, on the average? How many are there? Why would the number of E's and O's differ in a sample? Using the runs test, is there any evidence from the numbers generated that your method of generating them might not have been random? Explain.

MKT **13.44** Perform a runs test on the department store regression requested in Exercise 10.41 using only the first 9 years (1970–1978). At the 0.05 type I error level, do your residuals indicate a nonrandom error term?

**13.45** Why can a runs test be used to test for nonrandomness only in regression residuals that are time specific (i.e., in time series and not cross-sectional analysis)?

FIN **13.46** Calculate the yearly change in net income for the first 10 years (1970–1979) of net income data for Workingmans Federal Savings and

Loan in Appendix Table A.3. Use a runs test to check if the change in net income appears to be random.

FIN    13.47    Using the first four companies (AAR, AGS, Action, and Air Express) in the Service Industry category of Appendix Table A.1 as a sample, test for no change in the overall service industry earnings per share for the 5-year period 1980–84, $\alpha = 0.05$. For this period, what was the industry's composite growth rate? Is this rate consistent with your test results? If not, indicate why your test may not be valid.

## Glossary

**contingency table:** A table showing the observed frequencies on multiple attributes.

**matched pair samples:** Each element in one sample shares one or more common characteristics with an element in the other sample.

**Mann-Whitney U test:** A nonparametric method for testing the null hypothesis that two populations are identical.

**nonparametric tests:** Tests that do not require assumptions about the parent population distribution.

**parametric tests:** Tests that depend on assumptions about the parameter's population distribution.

**power (of the test):** The ability of a statistical test to accept the alternative hypothesis correctly.

**rank correlation:** A nonparametric measure of correlation that is based on the rank of the observations in two sets of data.

**runs test:** A nonparametric method for determining if a set of observations occur at random, where a run is a set of consecutive observations that have the same characteristic.

**sign test:** A nonparametric method for determining if plus and minus observations occur with a probability $\frac{1}{2}$.

**Spearman's rho:** A nonparametric measure of the correlation between two sets of ranked data.

**13.1—Determining Expected Frequencies**

$$E_{ij} = \frac{(\text{marginal total for } i\text{th row})(\text{marginal total for } j\text{th column})}{\text{total number of observations}}$$

**13.2—Calculating Chi-Square**

$$\chi_c^2 = \sum_{i=1}^{r} \sum_{j=1}^{c} \frac{(O_{ij} - E_{ij})^2}{E_{ij}}$$

where $O_{ij}$ is the observed frequency in cell $i,j$, $E_{ij}$ is the expected frequency in cell $i,j$, and where d.f. $= (r - 1)(c - 1)$.

**13.3—Spearman's Rho**

$$r_s = 1 - \left( \frac{6\Sigma d_i^2}{n^3 - n} \right)$$

where $d_i^2$ is the square of the difference in ranks.

**13.4—$t$ Test Statistic for Spearman's Rho ($n > 10$)**

$$t_c = r_s \sqrt{\frac{n - 2}{1 - r_s^2}}$$

where d.f. $= n - 2$

**13.5—Calculating $T_A$ and $T_B$ in the Mann–Whitney $U$ Test**

$$T_A = n_A n_B + \frac{n_A(n_A + 1)}{2} - r_A$$

$$T_B = n_A n_B - T_A$$

$$U = \min[T_A, T_B]$$

**13.6—Two-Sample $t$ Statistic for Testing Average Rank (Modified Eq. 8.6)**

$$t = \frac{\overline{R}_A - \overline{R}_B}{\sqrt{\left( \dfrac{s_A^2(n_A - 1) + s_B^2(n_B - 1)}{n_A + n_B - 2} \right)\left( \dfrac{n_A + n_B}{n_A n_B} \right)}}$$

where d.f. $= n_A + n_B - 2$

# APPENDIX A:
# DATA SETS

Table A.1

# CORPORATE SCOREBOARD
## THE FULL YEAR'S RESULTS QUARTER BY QUARTER

**GLOSSARY**  **Sales:** Includes all sales and other operating revenues. For banks, includes all operating revenues. Most quarterly data as originally reported; some data as restated. Annual data as restated.

**Profits:** Net income before extraordinary items. Most quarterly data as originally reported; some data as restated. Annual data as restated.

| | SALES | | | | | | | PROFITS | | | | | | |
| | Reported | | | | Change from 4Q 1983 % | Restated | Change from 1983 % | Reported | | | | Change from 4Q 1983 % | Restated | Change from 1983 % |
| | 1st quarter 1984 $ mil. | 2nd quarter 1984 $ mil. | 3rd quarter 1984 $ mil. | 4th quarter 1984 $ mil. | | 12 months 1984 $ mil. | | 1st quarter 1984 $ mil. | 2nd quarter 1984 $ mil. | 3rd quarter 1984 $ mil. | 4th quarter 1984 $ mil. | | 12 months 1984 $ mil. | |
|---|---|---|---|---|---|---|---|---|---|---|---|---|---|---|
| **BANKS AND BANK HOLDING COMPANIES** | | | | | | | | | | | | | | |
| Allied Bancshares* | 235.1 | 269.4 | 292.4 | 286.7 | 22 | 1083.6 | 32 | 27.9 | 29.6 | 30.3 | 31.0 | 21 | 118.8 | 15 |
| Banc One | 228.1 | 253.7 | 276.1 | 291.5 | 37 | 1049.5 | 41 | 25.0 | 26.6 | 28.6 | 27.8 | 18 | 108.0 | 30 |
| Bank of Boston | 673.4 | 798.8 | 864.7 | 1065.2 | 55 | 3402.2 | 31 | 24.9 | 30.9 | 33.7 | 74.6 | 115 | 164.1 | 21 |
| Bank of New England | 183.4 | 198.0 | 214.8 | 214.6 | 25 | 810.2 | 30 | 9.4 | 10.8 | 11.6 | 14.5 | 64 | 46.3 | 26 |
| Bank of New York | 359.5 | 401.6 | 408.2 | 407.7 | 17 | 1577.0 | 18 | 25.9 | 26.3 | 26.9 | 28.4 | 21 | 107.5 | 19 |
| BankAmerica | 3383.0 | 3538.0 | 3683.0 | 3794.0 | 12 | 14398.0 | 8 | 101.0 | 110.0 | 91.0 | 44.0 | −16 | 346.0 | −11 |
| Bankers Trust New York | 1054.4 | 1178.2 | 1283.0 | 1318.5 | 29 | 4834.2 | 25 | 74.1 | 72.0 | 79.8 | 81.0 | 19 | 306.8 | 19 |
| Barnett Banks of Florida* | 292.2 | 329.7 | 368.0 | 367.6 | 37 | 1357.5 | 37 | 24.0 | 25.3 | 26.7 | 27.4 | 24 | 103.4 | 26 |
| Chase Manhattan | 2237.6 | 2329.4 | 2706.4 | 2607.9 | 17 | 9881.3 | 16 | 102.5 | 90.2 | 93.0 | 120.1 | 9 | 405.8 | −6 |
| Chemical New York | 1286.3 | 1480.2 | 1592.7 | 1523.6 | 17 | 5857.0 | 19 | 81.3 | 76.8 | 77.2 | 105.5 | 20 | 340.8 | 12 |
| Citicorp | 4727.0 | 4989.0 | 5266.0 | 5512.0 | 21 | 20494.0 | 20 | 223.0 | 206.0 | 200.0 | 261.0 | 30 | 890.0 | 3 |
| Citizens & Southern Georgia | 186.6 | 203.6 | 217.8 | 220.0 | 19 | 832.1 | 20 | 14.6 | 18.0 | 19.2 | 20.1 | 18 | 72.4 | 21 |
| Comerica | 228.5 | 246.6 | 266.0 | 282.0 | 26 | 1023.1 | 31 | 12.4 | 14.9 | 14.5 | 15.2 | 34 | 56.9 | 17 |
| Continental Illinois | 1219.8 | 993.2 | 995.8 | 882.1 | −21 | 4090.9 | −7 | 29.4 | −1158.2 | 4.4 | 36.7 | 44 | −1087.7 | NM |
| CoreStates Financial | 244.2 | 266.2 | 283.5 | 288.0 | 14 | 1081.9 | 20 | 23.7 | 26.9 | 27.2 | 26.7 | 16 | 104.5 | 22 |
| Crocker National | 661.1 | 660.6 | 685.4 | 751.7 | 16 | 2758.7 | 8 | −120.8 | 6.1 | 6.4 | −216.1 | NM | −324.4 | NM |
| First Bank System | 540.3 | 574.1 | 612.3 | 623.6 | 17 | 2350.3 | 22 | 31.6 | 32.5 | 27.3 | 39.7 | 11 | 131.1 | 1 |
| First Chicago | 994.2 | 1104.6 | 1240.5 | 1186.4 | 22 | 4525.7 | 23 | 49.8 | 53.0 | −71.8 | 55.5 | 16 | 86.4 | −53 |
| First City Bancorp. of Texas | 431.2 | 470.4 | 503.6 | 495.2 | 16 | 1900.3 | 17 | 23.4 | 25.6 | 15.9 | 16.2 | NM | 81.0 | 63 |
| First Interstate Bancorp | 1149.9 | 1207.3 | 1301.6 | 1306.0 | 11 | 4964.8 | 14 | 63.7 | 67.5 | 70.4 | 74.8 | 13 | 276.3 | 12 |
| First National State* | 252.5 | 266.4 | 277.8 | 267.9 | 8 | 1064.6 | 23 | 18.5 | 20.9 | 20.6 | 21.4 | 15 | 81.5 | 27 |
| InterFirst | 575.6 | 598.3 | 680.6 | 586.7 | 2 | 2441.2 | 14 | 9.6 | 13.4 | 81.3 | 13.6 | 77 | 117.9 | NM |
| Irving Bank | 495.5 | 534.2 | 565.3 | 547.5 | 13 | 2142.5 | 17 | 26.7 | 26.3 | 24.0 | 21.1 | −8 | 98.1 | 6 |
| MCorp | 313.1 | 343.6 | 368.2 | 602.8 | 94 | 1627.7 | 46 | 23.7 | 24.3 | 25.6 | 34.1 | 58 | 107.7 | 7 |
| Manufacturers Hanover | 1741.4 | 2011.6 | 2279.1 | 2282.7 | 31 | 8314.8 | 26 | 84.0 | 73.7 | 88.6 | 106.2 | 23 | 352.5 | 5 |
| Marine Midland Banks | 619.0 | 664.1 | 667.8 | 651.6 | 11 | 2602.5 | 21 | 22.6 | 26.4 | 27.8 | 13.6 | −50 | 90.4 | −11 |
| Maryland National | 154.3 | 178.2 | 200.1 | 206.0 | 37 | 738.6 | 35 | 10.8 | 12.5 | 12.5 | 13.2 | 29 | 49.0 | 27 |
| Mellon Bank | 671.4 | 762.7 | 804.5 | 823.3 | 15 | 3061.9 | 22 | 33.0 | 39.4 | 42.6 | 43.4 | −19 | 158.5 | −14 |
| Michigan National | 204.2 | 209.9 | 216.5 | 214.9 | 6 | 845.5 | 9 | 4.2 | 5.2 | 5.8 | 6.2 | NM | 21.4 | NM |
| Midlantic Banks | 162.5 | 174.7 | 187.8 | 189.7 | 23 | 714.6 | 39 | 14.2 | 15.6 | 17.3 | 18.0 | 23 | 65.0 | 33 |
| Morgan (J. P.) | 1541.7 | 1551.7 | 1709.1 | 1759.5 | 20 | 6562.0 | 14 | 146.0 | 103.7 | 120.4 | 167.5 | 33 | 537.6 | 17 |
| NBD Bancorp | 315.4 | 327.0 | 358.6 | 376.8 | 23 | 1377.8 | 20 | 20.6 | 22.3 | 24.2 | 27.4 | 31 | 94.5 | 16 |
| National City* | 171.0 | 177.4 | 188.1 | 289.2 | 69 | 825.7 | 27 | 13.5 | 14.3 | 16.7 | 21.4 | 50 | 65.9 | 37 |
| NCNB | 360.7 | 417.1 | 436.6 | 428.7 | 26 | 1643.0 | 31 | 28.3 | 29.1 | 30.8 | 31.1 | 30 | 119.2 | 29 |
| Norstar Bancorp | 137.1 | 180.8 | 203.9 | 208.8 | 56 | 730.6 | 55 | 15.9 | 19.2 | 21.5 | 20.7 | 31 | 77.3 | 33 |
| Northern Trust | 174.7 | 185.9 | 201.7 | 192.0 | 10 | 754.4 | 10 | 5.6 | 5.7 | 5.6 | 5.5 | 60 | 22.4 | 22 |
| Norwest | 630.5 | 675.7 | 667.5 | 708.9 | 18 | 2682.5 | 16 | 33.8 | 32.4 | −24.0 | 27.3 | 13 | 69.5 | −45 |
| PNC Financial | 335.9 | 374.9 | 381.3 | 407.3 | 29 | 1499.4 | 23 | 30.4 | 34.1 | 36.5 | 42.1 | 38 | 143.2 | 22 |
| Rainier Bancorporation | 185.1 | 203.5 | 217.1 | 209.7 | 14 | 811.6 | 17 | 13.3 | 15.2 | 17.4 | 15.5 | 14 | 61.4 | 30 |
| Republic New York | 247.3 | 261.0 | 310.4 | 312.3 | 21 | 1131.0 | 14 | 22.8 | 24.3 | 24.2 | 25.2 | 14 | 96.5 | 14 |
| RepublicBank | 485.0 | 532.2 | 606.9 | 580.7 | 25 | 2204.9 | 27 | 29.7 | 32.3 | 38.4 | 37.0 | 144 | 137.3 | 6 |
| Security Pacific | 1156.2 | 1231.1 | 1474.7 | 1387.3 | 20 | 5249.3 | 21 | 67.9 | 68.6 | 74.7 | 79.8 | 13 | 291.0 | 10 |
| Southeast Banking | 237.7 | 252.9 | 271.5 | 275.8 | 20 | 1038.0 | 20 | 16.3 | 16.2 | 17.2 | 14.4 | 6 | 64.1 | 18 |
| Sovran Financial | 213.0 | 222.9 | 234.1 | 241.4 | 15 | 911.5 | 12 | 18.2 | 19.7 | 21.1 | 21.2 | 53 | 80.2 | 22 |
| Sun Banks | 247.4 | 257.8 | 266.4 | 268.0 | 71 | 1039.5 | 75 | 19.2 | 17.7 | 16.2 | 11.8 | 8 | 64.9 | 40 |

**Margins:** Net income before extraordinary items as a percent of sales.

**Earnings per share:** For most recent 12-month period. Includes all common-stock equivalents.

**Price-earnings ratio:** Based on Feb. 28 common stock price and corporate earnings before extraordinary items for most recent 12-month period.

**Yield:** Indicated annual dividend as a percent of Feb. 28 stock price.

**Book value per share:** Sum of the company's common stock at nominal balance-sheet value, capital surplus, and retained earnings as shown in company accounts, divided by number of shares outstanding.

**Return on common equity:** Net income available for common stockholders (most recent 12 months) divided by latest available common equity, which includes common stock, capital surplus, and retained earnings.

**Five-year growth:** Annual percentage growth in common equity and earnings per share for latest five-year period. Per share growth includes all common-stock equivalents.

| MARGINS | | | | | | | PERFORMANCE | | | | | | | | |
|---|---|---|---|---|---|---|---|---|---|---|---|---|---|---|---|
| 1st quarter 1984 % | 2nd quarter 1984 % | 3rd quarter 1984 % | 4th quarter 1984 $ mil. | Change from 4Q 1983 % | 12 months 1984 % | Change from 1983 % | Share price 2-28 | 12 months earnings $ per share | Price-earnings ratio 2-28 | Yield % | Book value $ per share | Return on common equity 1984 % | 5-year growth rate in earnings per share | 5-year growth rate in common equity | |
| 11.9 | 11.0 | 10.4 | 10.8 | −1 | 11.0 | −13 | 25.25 | 2.89 | 9 | 3.33 | 14 | 20.8 | 21 | 34 | Allied Banc. |
| 11.0 | 10.5 | 10.3 | 9.5 | −13 | 10.3 | −8 | 29.38 | 2.88 | 10 | 3.40 | 17 | 16.6 | 13 | 25 | Banc One |
| 3.7 | 3.9 | 3.9 | 7.0 | 39 | 4.8 | −8 | 43.00 | 8.35 | 5 | 5.58 | 59 | 14.1 | 12 | 11 | Bank of Boston |
| 5.1 | 5.5 | 5.4 | 6.7 | 31 | 5.7 | −3 | 67.00 | 9.35 | 7 | 4.24 | 61 | 14.9 | 8 | 26 | Bank New Eng. |
| 7.2 | 6.5 | 6.6 | 7.0 | 4 | 6.8 | 1 | 39.63 | 6.40 | 6 | 5.15 | 42 | 14.9 | 13 | 12 | Bank New York |
| 3.0 | 3.1 | 2.5 | 1.2 | −25 | 2.4 | −18 | 19.25 | 1.77 | 11 | 7.90 | 29 | 6.1 | −17 | 8 | BankAmerica |
| 7.0 | 6.1 | 6.2 | 6.1 | −8 | 6.3 | −5 | 62.75 | 9.52 | 7 | 4.30 | 61 | 15.0 | 11 | 19 | Bankers Trust |
| 8.2 | 7.7 | 7.3 | 7.5 | −9 | 7.6 | −8 | 48.75 | 5.48 | 9 | 2.79 | 33 | 16.3 | 17 | 22 | Barnett Banks |
| 4.6 | 3.9 | 3.4 | 4.6 | −7 | 4.1 | −19 | 52.25 | 9.01 | 6 | 7.27 | 92 | 9.5 | 0 | 11 | Chase |
| 6.3 | 5.2 | 4.8 | 6.9 | 2 | 5.8 | −7 | 39.38 | 6.48 | 6 | 5.99 | 47 | 13.5 | 10 | 14 | Chemical |
| 4.7 | 4.1 | 3.8 | 4.7 | 7 | 4.3 | −14 | 41.88 | 6.45 | 7 | 4.92 | 46 | 14.3 | 11 | 10 | Citicorp |
| 7.8 | 8.8 | 8.8 | 9.1 | −1 | 8.7 | 1 | 19.75 | 2.26 | 9 | 3.85 | 14 | 16.4 | 21 | 14 | C&S |
| 5.4 | 6.0 | 5.4 | 5.4 | 7 | 5.6 | −11 | 39.00 | 4.81 | 8 | 5.38 | 42 | 11.6 | 3 | 7 | Comerica |
| 2.4 | NM | 0.4 | 4.2 | 83 | NM | NM | 8.25 | −26.99 | NM | 0.00 | 14 | −170.7 | NA | 7 | Conill |
| 9.7 | 10.1 | 9.6 | 9.3 | 2 | 9.7 | 2 | 47.88 | 6.30 | 8 | 4.34 | 37 | 16.9 | 16 | 11 | CoreStates |
| NM | 0.9 | 0.9 | NM | NM | NM | NM | 25.50 | −15.93 | NM | 1.57 | 42 | −37.8 | NA | 22 | Crocker |
| 5.9 | 5.7 | 4.5 | 6.4 | −5 | 5.6 | −17 | 33.25 | 4.15 | 8 | 4.81 | 37 | 12.0 | 5 | 10 | First Bank |
| 5.0 | 4.8 | NM | 4.7 | −5 | 1.9 | −62 | 23.38 | 1.19 | 20 | 5.65 | 34 | 3.4 | −4 | 6 | First Chicago |
| 5.4 | 5.4 | 3.2 | 3.3 | NM | 4.3 | 39 | 16.63 | 1.97 | 8 | 7.82 | 29 | 6.8 | −13 | 21 | First City |
| 5.5 | 5.6 | 5.4 | 5.7 | 1 | 5.6 | −2 | 47.13 | 6.16 | 8 | 4.97 | 51 | 12.3 | 2 | 13 | First Interstate |
| 7.3 | 7.9 | 7.4 | 8.0 | 7 | 7.7 | 3 | 48.38 | 6.67 | 7 | 5.95 | 49 | 13.6 | 11 | 14 | First Natl. State |
| 1.7 | 2.2 | 11.9 | 2.3 | 73 | 4.8 | NM | 12.00 | 1.76 | 7 | 5.00 | 17 | 10.2 | −5 | 18 | InterFirst |
| 5.4 | 4.9 | 4.2 | 3.9 | −19 | 4.6 | −9 | 32.13 | 5.11 | 6 | 6.10 | 46 | 11.2 | 3 | 10 | Irving Bank |
| 7.6 | 7.1 | 7.0 | 5.7 | −19 | 6.6 | −27 | 23.25 | 3.56 | 7 | 6.02 | 26 | 9.7 | 8 | 28 | MCorp |
| 4.8 | 3.7 | 3.9 | 4.7 | −6 | 4.2 | −17 | 38.00 | 7.12 | 5 | 8.42 | 65 | 10.8 | 3 | 10 | Man. Hanover |
| 3.7 | 4.0 | 4.2 | 2.1 | −55 | 3.5 | −26 | 33.13 | 4.17 | 8 | 4.83 | 53 | 7.9 | 7 | 17 | Marine Midland |
| 7.0 | 7.0 | 6.3 | 6.4 | −6 | 6.6 | −6 | 47.75 | 6.01 | 8 | 3.35 | 47 | 12.8 | 9 | 12 | Maryland Natl. |
| 4.9 | 5.2 | 5.3 | 5.3 | −29 | 5.2 | −29 | 49.50 | 5.64 | 9 | 5.41 | 56 | 9.9 | 5 | 12 | Mellon Bank |
| 2.1 | 2.5 | 2.7 | 2.9 | NM | 2.5 | NM | 24.50 | 1.81 | 14 | 0.00 | 30 | 6.0 | −24 | 4 | Michigan Natl. |
| 8.7 | 8.9 | 9.2 | 9.5 | 0 | 9.1 | −4 | 30.75 | 4.09 | 8 | 3.64 | 24 | 16.8 | 10 | 19 | Midlantic |
| 9.5 | 6.7 | 7.0 | 9.5 | 11 | 8.2 | 3 | 45.38 | 6.07 | 7 | 4.85 | 42 | 14.9 | 11 | 12 | Morgan |
| 6.5 | 6.8 | 6.7 | 7.3 | 7 | 6.9 | −3 | 56.13 | 7.90 | 7 | 4.28 | 72 | 11.0 | 5 | 7 | NBD Bancorp |
| 7.9 | 8.1 | 8.9 | 7.4 | −11 | 8.0 | 8 | 39.75 | 5.45 | 7 | 4.78 | 48 | 9.7 | 5 | 6 | National City |
| 7.8 | 7.0 | 7.0 | 7.3 | 3 | 7.3 | −1 | 35.75 | 4.07 | 9 | 3.69 | 26 | 14.8 | 12 | 20 | NCNB |
| 11.6 | 10.6 | 10.5 | 9.9 | −16 | 10.6 | −14 | 38.75 | 4.75 | 8 | 5.68 | 39 | 11.6 | 9 | 19 | Norstar |
| 3.2 | 3.1 | 2.8 | 2.9 | 45 | 3.0 | 11 | 64.25 | 4.06 | 16 | 4.23 | 72 | 5.6 | −9 | 6 | Northern Trust |
| 5.4 | 4.8 | NM | 3.9 | −5 | 2.6 | −52 | 26.00 | 1.90 | 14 | 6.92 | 36 | 5.2 | −12 | 9 | Norwest |
| 9.1 | 9.1 | 9.6 | 10.3 | 8 | 9.5 | −1 | 50.75 | 6.51 | 8 | 4.57 | 42 | 15.2 | 12 | 18 | PNC Financial |
| 7.2 | 7.5 | 8.0 | 7.4 | 0 | 7.6 | 11 | 24.00 | 3.14 | 8 | 4.17 | 23 | 13.8 | 7 | 11 | Ranier |
| 9.2 | 9.3 | 7.8 | 8.1 | −5 | 8.5 | 0 | 42.88 | 5.49 | 8 | 3.73 | 50 | 11.2 | 11 | 27 | Republic NY |
| 6.1 | 6.1 | 6.3 | 6.4 | 95 | 6.2 | −17 | 32.75 | 4.66 | 7 | 5.01 | 37 | 12.5 | 6 | 17 | RepublicBank |
| 5.9 | 5.6 | 5.1 | 5.8 | −6 | 5.5 | −9 | 28.63 | 3.96 | 7 | 4.26 | 27 | 14.8 | 10 | 14 | Security |
| 6.8 | 6.4 | 6.4 | 5.2 | −11 | 6.2 | −2 | 27.75 | 3.30 | 8 | 4.32 | 27 | 12.8 | 2 | 17 | Southeast Bkg. |
| 8.5 | 8.8 | 9.0 | 8.8 | 34 | 8.8 | 10 | 42.50 | 4.73 | 9 | 3.95 | 29 | 15.9 | 13 | 23 | Sovran |
| 7.8 | 6.9 | 6.1 | 4.4 | −37 | 6.2 | −20 | 31.25 | 2.95 | 11 | 3.84 | 25 | 11.7 | 8 | 32 | Sun Banks |

# Corporate Scoreboard (cont.)

| | SALES Reported 1st quarter 1984 $ mil. | 2nd quarter 1984 $ mil. | 3rd quarter 1984 $ mil. | 4th quarter 1984 $ mil. | Change from 4Q 1983 % | SALES Restated 12 months 1984 $ mil. | Change from 1983 % | PROFITS Reported 1st quarter 1984 $ mil. | 2nd quarter 1984 $ mil. | 3rd quarter 1984 $ mil. | 4th quarter 1984 $ mil. | Change from 4Q 1983 % | PROFITS Restated 12 months 1984 $ mil. | Change from 1983 % |
|---|---|---|---|---|---|---|---|---|---|---|---|---|---|---|
| **BANKS AND HOLDING COMPANIES (cont.)** | | | | | | | | | | | | | | |
| Texas Commerce Bancshrs. | 470.1 | 510.5 | 545.6 | 541.2 | 22 | 2067.4 | 24 | 45.8 | 46.4 | 46.4 | 44.7 | 3 | 183.3 | 3 |
| U.S. Bancorp | 170.2 | 189.8 | 199.0 | 209.9 | 23 | 768.9 | 18 | 12.7 | 14.6 | 16.0 | 16.7 | 31 | 60.1 | 15 |
| Valley National | 222.0 | 237.7 | 249.5 | 258.9 | 22 | 968.1 | 19 | 13.2 | 15.1 | 15.8 | 16.4 | 51 | 60.4 | 32 |
| Wachovia | 217.7 | 224.5 | 232.9 | 239.2 | 17 | 914.4 | 17 | 24.3 | 23.7 | 25.9 | 26.4 | 30 | 100.3 | 19 |
| Wells Fargo | 788.0 | 842.3 | 876.5 | 884.9 | 13 | 3391.6 | 13 | 40.0 | 40.9 | 43.8 | 44.5 | 10 | 169.3 | 9 |
| **INDUSTRY COMPOSITE** | 33812.2 | 36092.9 | 38940.8 | 39577.7 | 20 | 148396.3 | 19 | 1711.5 | 644.0 | 1747.0 | 1871.6 | 16 | 5974.7 | −10 |
| **ELECTRICAL, ELECTRONICS** | | | | | | | | | | | | | | |
| AMP | 458.7 | 477.2 | 453.6 | 423.3 | 1 | 1812.8 | 20 | 53.7 | 58.3 | 49.5 | 39.9 | −14 | 201.3 | 23 |
| AVX | 55.3 | 61.1 | 59.3 | 55.2 | 20 | 230.9 | 44 | 3.9 | 4.5 | 3.5 | 3.7 | 4 | 15.5 | 79 |
| Advanced Micro Devices (9) | 192.2 | 234.3 | 257.1 | 238.6 | 54 | 922.2 | 89 | 30.6 | 38.2 | 42.1 | 29.3 | 45 | 140.2 | 198 |
| American District Telegraph | 119.9 | 127.6 | 126.2 | 136.8 | 10 | 510.6 | 6 | 1.3 | 2.7 | 3.7 | 4.3 | −24 | 12.0 | −55 |
| Ametek | 123.9 | 130.3 | 128.6 | 121.0 | 4 | 503.9 | 12 | 9.9 | 10.4 | 14.3 | 8.1 | 13 | 42.7 | 33 |
| Analog Devices (2) | 69.5 | 77.6 | 81.8 | 84.6 | 39 | 313.4 | 46 | 7.7 | 9.3 | 10.2 | 10.3 | 57 | 37.4 | 103 |
| Andrew (3) | 48.8 | 55.6 | 68.9 | 56.1 | 27 | 229.5 | 28 | 4.1 | 5.4 | 7.5 | 4.2 | 11 | 21.2 | 16 |
| ATCOR (3) | 79.6 | 84.7 | 76.0 | 69.1 | 14 | 309.4 | 14 | 2.4 | 2.8 | 3.0 | 0.5 | 24 | 8.7 | 18 |
| Augat | 63.5 | 68.3 | 62.8 | 62.4 | −3 | 257.1 | 12 | 7.6 | 7.4 | 4.8 | 4.4 | −44 | 24.1 | −6 |
| Avantek | 32.0 | 35.3 | 33.9 | 57.9 | 39 | 159.2 | 33 | 3.6 | 4.0 | 3.8 | 5.8 | 36 | 17.2 | 44 |
| Bairnco | 116.4 | 128.9 | 123.1 | 129.7 | 22 | 498.1 | 35 | 4.9 | 7.2 | 6.0 | 7.3 | 38 | 25.3 | 46 |
| Burndy | 59.5 | 60.9 | 54.6 | 57.4 | 8 | 232.4 | 10 | 3.2 | 3.3 | 2.9 | 3.4 | 11 | 12.8 | 6 |
| CTS | 94.1 | 90.2 | 85.4 | 78.5 | 26 | 327.2 | 37 | 3.7 | 4.4 | 7.3 | 4.9 | 17 | 25.0 | 112 |
| Champion Spark Plug | 213.1 | 212.3 | 180.7 | 210.4 | 0 | 816.5 | 7 | 9.6 | 9.6 | 0.2 | 8.0 | −34 | 27.3 | 1 |
| Cubic (3) | 70.2 | 65.4 | 74.6 | 71.4 | 10 | 281.6 | 2 | 4.1 | 2.6 | 3.4 | 3.6 | −8 | 13.7 | −23 |
| Digital Switch* | 69.3 | 87.2 | 97.2 | 98.5 | 61 | 352.2 | 78 | 12.3 | 10.1 | 16.5 | 18.4 | 69 | 57.3 | 70 |
| E-Systems | 193.0 | 211.7 | 195.6 | 219.1 | 5 | 819.4 | −1 | 15.8 | 14.9 | 14.5 | 15.9 | 13 | 61.1 | 11 |
| EG&G* | 246.5 | 267.8 | 270.2 | 287.1 | 24 | 1071.7 | 19 | 13.9 | 13.4 | 12.9 | 13.4 | 6 | 53.5 | 15 |
| Emerson Electric (3) | 1048.7 | 1121.3 | 1073.7 | 1077.0 | 15 | 4320.6 | 20 | 91.2 | 91.7 | 85.7 | 92.4 | 15 | 360.9 | 16 |
| Emerson Radio (9) | 46.6 | 61.5 | 98.2 | 107.8 | 101 | 314.1 | 96 | 1.4 | 2.0 | 4.1 | 4.8 | 130 | 12.4 | 4 |
| Federal Signal | 66.3 | 65.7 | 62.7 | 64.0 | 9 | 258.7 | 14 | 2.5 | 2.8 | 2.0 | 2.1 | NM | 9.4 | 32 |
| General Electric | 6583.0 | 6664.0 | 6723.0 | 7980.0 | 7 | 27950.0 | 4 | 485.0 | 579.0 | 564.0 | 652.0 | 13 | 2280.0 | 13 |
| General Instrument (10) | 250.0 | 238.7 | 268.6 | 260.4 | 14 | 1017.7 | 14 | 7.4 | 9.3 | 11.5 | 4.5 | −15 | 32.7 | −37 |
| Gould | 363.0 | 392.5 | 389.7 | 251.9 | −26 | 1397.1 | 5 | 20.9 | 22.7 | 22.5 | 23.2 | −8 | 89.3 | 13 |
| Harris (6) | 502.5 | 588.5 | 511.7 | 585.0 | 24 | 2187.7 | 18 | 19.8 | 23.9 | 25.3 | 21.7 | 18 | 90.6 | 30 |
| Hazeltine | 37.7 | 38.3 | 38.7 | 59.1 | 25 | 173.8 | 22 | 2.2 | 2.6 | 2.9 | 3.2 | NM | 10.7 | 310 |
| Hubbell (Harvey) | 113.6 | 120.7 | 117.4 | 115.5 | 3 | 467.1 | 11 | 9.1 | 11.2 | 10.2 | 11.5 | 12 | 42.0 | 13 |
| Intel | 371.6b | 410.1b | 431.6b | 416.1b | 25 | 1629.3 | 45 | 50.3 | 54.7 | 70.0 | 23.2 | −51 | 198.2 | 71 |
| KDI | 52.5 | 64.5 | 60.6 | 57.3 | 19 | 234.9 | 17 | 1.4 | 3.5 | 1.9 | 1.6 | 36 | 8.4 | 23 |
| Kollmorgen | 78.1 | 85.8 | 80.9 | 81.4 | 13 | 326.2 | 25 | 3.5 | 4.0 | 2.6 | 0.7 | −82 | 10.8 | 21 |
| Litton Industries (5) | 1141.6b | 1214.2b | 1146.4b | 1166.9b | 6 | 4669.1 | 16 | 67.3 | 75.9 | 73.9 | 67.8 | 12 | 284.8 | 12 |
| Loral (9) | 133.4 | 119.4 | 114.2 | 125.1 | 14 | 492.0 | 30 | 10.7 | 9.3 | 9.4 | 10.7 | 20 | 40.0 | 31 |
| M/A-COM (3) | 187.0 | 198.1 | 214.8 | 197.4 | 17 | 797.4 | 22 | 7.6 | 10.7 | 12.8 | 8.8 | 24 | 39.9 | 27 |
| McGraw-Edison | 549.2 | 580.0 | 560.5 | 445.7 | 9 | 1720.9 | 17 | 12.9 | 15.1 | 14.6 | 22.9 | 53 | 68.3 | 65 |
| Medtronic (8) | 103.1 | 110.6 | 100.2 | 99.0 | −6 | 413.0 | −1 | 13.9 | 17.9 | 11.9 | 12.6 | −10 | 56.4 | 0 |
| Molex (6) | 66.6 | 69.8 | 63.8 | 61.1 | 2 | 261.4 | 23 | 11.2 | 9.9 | 8.3 | 7.8 | −19 | 37.1 | 24 |
| Motorola | 1256.0b | 1416.0b | 1377.0b | 1485.0b | 17 | 5534.0 | 28 | 78.0 | 98.0 | 124.0 | 87.0 | −8 | 387.0 | 59 |
| National Semiconductor (7) | 382.8 | 470.8 | 529.0 | 435.4 | 18 | 1818.0 | 31 | 15.4 | 16.7 | 32.0 | 7.4 | −44 | 71.5 | 436 |
| National Service Inds. (4) | 249.5 | 276.2 | 292.0 | 290.7 | 14 | 1108.4 | 15 | 13.0 | 16.4 | 18.5 | 15.0 | 11 | 63.0 | 11 |
| North American Philips | 975.7 | 1033.8 | 1068.1 | 1248.4 | 11 | 4325.9 | 14 | 23.0 | 33.4 | 32.7 | 41.5 | 12 | 130.5 | 36 |
| Paradyne | 60.6 | 70.5 | 76.2 | 82.6 | 49 | 290.0 | 39 | 2.9 | 2.4 | 3.1 | 2.6 | NM | 11.0 | 203 |
| RCA* | 2363.7 | 2482.9 | 2472.2 | 2792.8 | 12 | 10111.6 | 13 | −42.4 | 108.0 | 78.0 | 102.8 | 85 | 246.4 | 66 |
| RTE | 84.6 | 92.8 | 89.7 | 83.3 | 15 | 350.4 | 30 | 2.7 | 3.6 | 3.3 | 3.5 | −43 | 13.0 | 10 |
| Raytheon* | 1494.7 | 1522.2 | 1411.3 | 1567.0 | 7 | 5995.3 | 6 | 79.6 | 85.0 | 85.9 | 89.6 | 8 | 340.1 | 10 |
| Sanders Associates (5) | 176.1 | 192.0 | 229.0 | 186.6 | 25 | 783.8 | 30 | 12.1 | 13.7 | 15.0 | 7.3 | −11 | 48.1 | 22 |
| Scientific-Atlanta (6) | 95.8 | 111.1 | 106.9 | 109.4 | 15 | 423.2 | 14 | 2.3 | 3.6 | 3.3 | 4.1 | 19 | 13.2 | 9 |
| Singer | 630.2 | 603.2 | 605.2 | 680.2 | 3 | 2518.8 | 2 | 11.8 | 11.9 | 8.6 | 18.0 | 140 | 50.3 | 211 |
| Square D | 326.3 | 338.3 | 378.9 | 322.0 | 7 | 1365.5 | 19 | 24.3 | 25.9 | 37.7 | 18.2 | 1 | 106.2 | 69 |
| TIE/communications | 123.4 | 145.1 | 132.5 | 100.0 | 13 | 501.1 | 55 | 11.3 | 0.5 | 3.8 | 0.3 | −95 | 15.9 | −55 |
| Texas Instruments | 1339.0 | 1464.1 | 1422.7 | 1515.8 | 17 | 5741.6 | 25 | 79.8 | 85.9 | 85.8 | 64.5 | −17 | 316.0 | NM |

| MARGINS | | | | | | | PERFORMANCE | | | | | | | | |
|---|---|---|---|---|---|---|---|---|---|---|---|---|---|---|---|
| | | | | Change from 4Q | 12 months | Change from | | 12 months earnings | Price-earnings | | Book value | Return on common | 5-year growth rate | | |
| 1st quarter 1984 % | 2nd quarter 1984 % | 3rd quarter 1984 % | 4th quarter 1984 $ mil. | 1983 % | 1984 % | 1983 % | Share price 2-28 | $ per share | ratio 2-28 | Yield % | $ per share | equity 1984 % | in earnings per share | in common equity | |
| 9.7 | 9.1 | 8.5 | 8.3 | −16 | 8.9 | −17 | 43.50 | 5.64 | 8 | 3.59 | 36 | 15.7 | 15 | 19 | Tex. Comm. |
| 7.5 | 7.7 | 8.0 | 8.0 | 7 | 7.8 | −2 | 27.25 | 3.05 | 9 | 3.67 | 27 | 11.5 | 1 | 12 | U.S. Bancorp |
| 5.9 | 6.4 | 6.3 | 6.3 | 23 | 6.2 | 11 | 33.50 | 3.60 | 9 | 3.58 | 28 | 12.7 | 0 | 15 | Valley National |
| 11.2 | 10.6 | 11.1 | 11.0 | 12 | 11.0 | 1 | 31.38 | 3.11 | 10 | 2.93 | 18 | 17.7 | 18 | 12 | Wachovia |
| 5.1 | 4.9 | 5.0 | 5.0 | −2 | 5.0 | −3 | 53.13 | 6.85 | 8 | 4.07 | 56 | 12.9 | 5 | 10 | Wells Fargo |
| 5.1 | 1.8 | 4.5 | 4.7 | −3 | 4.0 | −24 | 33.39 | 3.42 | 8 | 4.62 | 37 | 9.2 | −1 | 13 | |
| 11.7 | 12.2 | 10.9 | 9.4 | −15 | 11.1 | 3 | 33.25 | 1.87 | 18 | 2.17 | 8 | 22.4 | 9 | 15 | AMP |
| 7.0 | 7.3 | 5.9 | 6.7 | −14 | 6.7 | 25 | 24.00 | 1.65 | 15 | 1.33 | 12 | 14.1 | −1 | 23 | AVX |
| 15.9 | 16.3 | 16.4 | 12.3 | −6 | 15.2 | 58 | 33.25 | 2.41 | 14 | 0.00 | 7 | 38.4 | 20 | 34 | Adv. Micro |
| 1.1 | 2.1 | 2.9 | 3.1 | −31 | 2.3 | −57 | 25.38 | 0.92 | 28 | 3.63 | 16 | 5.7 | −3 | 7 | Am. District |
| 8.0 | 8.0 | 11.1 | 6.7 | 9 | 8.5 | 18 | 28.50 | 1.96 | 15 | 2.81 | 9 | 21.6 | 13 | 12 | Ametek |
| 11.1 | 11.9 | 12.4 | 12.1 | 13 | 11.9 | 38 | 27.75 | 1.38 | 20 | 0.00 | 8 | 19.1 | 29 | 42 | Analog |
| 8.4 | 9.7 | 10.9 | 7.4 | −13 | 9.2 | −9 | 36.25 | 2.12 | 17 | 0.00 | 12 | 17.5 | 27 | 27 | Andrew |
| 3.0 | 3.3 | 3.9 | 0.7 | 9 | 2.8 | 3 | 18.50 | 1.69 | 11 | 2.16 | 13 | 12.9 | NA | NA | ATCOR |
| 11.9 | 10.8 | 7.6 | 7.1 | −42 | 9.4 | −16 | 27.13 | 1.37 | 20 | 1.18 | 11 | 12.7 | 2 | 28 | Augat |
| 11.3 | 11.3 | 11.2 | 10.0 | −2 | 10.8 | 8 | 23.50 | 0.90 | 26 | 0.00 | NA | 15.8 | 22 | 56 | Avantek |
| 4.2 | 5.6 | 4.9 | 5.6 | 13 | 5.1 | 8 | 32.88 | 2.54 | 13 | 1.52 | 15 | 17.5 | 17 | 17 | Bairnco |
| 5.4 | 5.3 | 5.3 | 6.0 | 2 | 5.5 | −4 | 17.00 | 1.07 | 16 | 4.94 | 11 | 9.7 | −13 | 9 | Burndy |
| 4.0 | 4.8 | 8.5 | 6.2 | −7 | 7.6 | 54 | 39.88 | 4.35 | 9 | 2.51 | 23 | 19.0 | 4 | 7 | CTS |
| 4.5 | 4.5 | 0.1 | 3.8 | −34 | 3.4 | −5 | 8.75 | 0.71 | 12 | 4.57 | 9 | 7.6 | −13 | −1 | Champ. Spark |
| 5.8 | 3.9 | 4.6 | 5.1 | −16 | 4.9 | −25 | 22.25 | 1.73 | 13 | 1.75 | 13 | 13.5 | 17 | 18 | Cubic |
| 17.7 | 11.6 | 16.9 | 18.7 | 5 | 16.3 | −5 | 25.38 | 1.40 | 18 | 0.00 | 6 | 25.7 | NA | NA | Digital Switch |
| 8.2 | 7.1 | 7.4 | 7.3 | 8 | 7.5 | 12 | 29.13 | 2.02 | 14 | 1.72 | 9 | 22.2 | 30 | 21 | E-Systems |
| 5.6 | 5.0 | 4.8 | 4.7 | −14 | 5.0 | −3 | 38.50 | 1.88 | 20 | 1.25 | 5 | 41.4 | 18 | 28 | EG&G |
| 8.7 | 8.2 | 8.0 | 8.6 | −1 | 8.4 | −3 | 75.75 | 5.27 | 14 | 3.43 | 27 | 19.3 | 8 | 12 | Emerson Elec. |
| 3.1 | 3.3 | 4.2 | 4.5 | 15 | 4.0 | −47 | 14.50 | 0.79 | 18 | 0.00 | 3 | 26.8 | 12 | 20 | Emerson Rad. |
| 3.8 | 4.2 | 3.3 | 3.2 | NM | 3.6 | 15 | 19.13 | 1.13 | 17 | 4.18 | 10 | 11.1 | −5 | 20 | Federal Signal |
| 7.4 | 8.7 | 8.4 | 8.2 | 5 | 8.2 | 8 | 63.63 | 5.03 | 13 | 3.46 | 27 | 18.9 | 10 | 11 | GE |
| 3.0 | 3.9 | 4.3 | 1.7 | −26 | 3.2 | −45 | 19.38 | 1.04 | 19 | 2.58 | 20 | 5.0 | 2 | 25 | Gen. Inst. |
| 5.8 | 5.8 | 5.8 | 9.2 | 25 | 6.4 | 7 | 24.50 | 1.98 | 12 | 2.78 | 21 | 9.8 | −11 | 5 | Gould |
| 3.9 | 4.1 | 4.9 | 3.7 | −5 | 4.1 | 11 | 30.50 | 2.27 | 13 | 2.89 | 21 | 10.8 | −8 | 17 | Harris |
| 5.7 | 6.7 | 7.4 | 5.3 | NM | 6.2 | 236 | 25.63 | 1.72 | 15 | 1.40 | 8 | 21.0 | 9 | 3 | Hazeltine |
| 8.0 | 9.3 | 8.7 | 10.0 | 8 | 9.0 | 2 | 40.25 | 3.37 | 12 | 3.38 | 20 | 16.7 | 9 | 12 | Hubbell |
| 13.5 | 13.3 | 16.2 | 5.6 | −61 | 12.2 | 18 | 28.00 | 1.70 | 16 | 0.00 | 12 | 14.9 | 9 | 35 | Intel |
| 2.6 | 5.5 | 3.2 | 2.7 | 15 | 3.6 | 6 | 8.25 | 0.92 | 9 | 2.42 | 5 | 19.9 | 12 | 28 | KDI |
| 4.4 | 4.7 | 3.2 | 0.9 | −84 | 3.3 | −3 | 19.63 | 1.08 | 18 | 1.63 | 11 | 10.2 | −5 | 23 | Kollmorgen |
| 5.9 | 6.3 | 6.4 | 5.8 | 6 | 6.1 | −3 | 70.38 | 6.65 | 11 | 2.84 | 49 | 13.7 | 4 | 17 | Litton |
| 8.0 | 7.8 | 8.2 | 8.6 | 5 | 8.1 | 1 | 31.13 | 1.71 | 18 | 1.54 | NA | 16.8 | 12 | 33 | Loral |
| 4.1 | 5.4 | 6.0 | 4.5 | 6 | 5.0 | 4 | 20.38 | 0.94 | 22 | 1.08 | 10 | 9.4 | 9 | 49 | M/A-COM |
| 2.3 | 2.6 | 2.6 | 5.1 | 40 | 4.0 | 41 | 44.00 | 4.12 | 11 | 4.55 | 35 | 11.8 | −4 | 4 | McGraw-Ed. |
| 13.5 | 16.2 | 11.9 | 12.8 | −4 | 13.7 | 1 | 30.50 | 3.53 | 9 | 2.49 | 21 | 17.4 | 16 | 20 | Medtronic |
| 16.8 | 14.2 | 13.0 | 12.7 | −21 | 14.2 | 1 | 34.25 | 1.85 | 19 | 0.09 | 8 | 23.6 | 20 | 26 | Molex |
| 6.2 | 6.9 | 9.0 | 5.9 | −22 | 7.0 | 24 | 34.63 | 3.27 | 11 | 1.85 | 19 | 17.6 | 10 | 17 | Motorola |
| 4.0 | 3.5 | 6.1 | 1.7 | −52 | 3.9 | 308 | 11.75 | 0.81 | 15 | 0.00 | 8 | 10.6 | 0 | 25 | Natl. Semi. |
| 5.2 | 5.9 | 6.3 | 5.2 | −2 | 5.7 | −3 | 29.00 | 2.56 | 11 | 3.45 | 16 | 16.4 | 9 | 12 | Natl. Service |
| 2.4 | 3.2 | 3.1 | 3.3 | 0 | 3.0 | 20 | 43.25 | 4.53 | 10 | 2.31 | 33 | 13.7 | 7 | 12 | NA Philips |
| 4.8 | 3.4 | 4.1 | 3.2 | NM | 3.8 | 118 | 15.75 | 0.49 | 32 | 0.00 | 9 | 5.3 | −2 | 71 | Paradyne |
| NM | 4.4 | 3.2 | 3.7 | 64 | 2.4 | 48 | 39.25 | 2.15 | 18 | 2.65 | 25 | 8.8 | −12 | 4 | RCA |
| 3.2 | 3.8 | 3.6 | 4.2 | −51 | 3.7 | −16 | 17.13 | 1.75 | 10 | 3.27 | 12 | 15.0 | 24 | 12 | R T E |
| 5.3 | 5.6 | 6.1 | 5.7 | 1 | 5.7 | 3 | 46.75 | 4.02 | 12 | 3.42 | 23 | 17.5 | 4 | 22 | Raytheon |
| 6.9 | 7.1 | 6.6 | 3.9 | −29 | 6.1 | −6 | 43.00 | 2.51 | 17 | 1.30 | 17 | 15.0 | 16 | 34 | Sanders |
| 2.4 | 3.2 | 3.1 | 3.7 | 3 | 3.1 | −5 | 13.63 | 0.57 | 24 | 0.88 | 8 | 7.5 | −27 | 30 | Scien.-Atlanta |
| 1.9 | 2.0 | 1.4 | 2.6 | 133 | 2.0 | 205 | 36.00 | 2.57 | 14 | 0.28 | 24 | 10.9 | −5 | −1 | Singer |
| 7.5 | 7.7 | 9.9 | 5.7 | −5 | 7.8 | 41 | 41.88 | 3.71 | 11 | 4.39 | 19 | 19.3 | −2 | 13 | Square D |
| 9.1 | 0.4 | 2.9 | 0.3 | −96 | 3.2 | −71 | 8.38 | 0.47 | 18 | 0.00 | 8 | 6.1 | 46 | 121 | TIE |
| 6.0 | 5.9 | 6.0 | 4.3 | −29 | 5.5 | NM | 111.38 | 13.05 | 9 | 1.80 | 63 | 20.5 | 9 | 8 | Texas Insts. |

# Table A.1

Corporate Scoreboard (cont.)

|  | SALES | | | | | | | PROFITS | | | | | | |
|  | Reported | | | | Change from 4Q 1983 % | Restated 12 months 1984 $ mil. | Change from 1983 % | Reported | | | | Change from 4Q 1983 % | Restated 12 months 1984 $ mil. | Change from 1983 % |
|  | 1st quarter 1984 $ mil. | 2nd quarter 1984 $ mil. | 3rd quarter 1984 $ mil. | 4th quarter 1984 $ mil. | | | | 1st quarter 1984 $ mil. | 2nd quarter 1984 $ mil. | 3rd quarter 1984 $ mil. | 4th quarter 1984 $ mil. | | | |
|---|---|---|---|---|---|---|---|---|---|---|---|---|---|---|
| **ELECTRICAL, ELECTRONICS (cont.)** | | | | | | | | | | | | | | |
| Thermo Electron | 52.8 | 56.7 | 60.8 | 64.5 | 33 | 234.9 | 29 | 1.2 | 1.5 | 1.6 | 1.8 | 134 | 6.1 | NM |
| Thomas & Betts | 83.5 | 84.9 | 78.9 | 75.1 | 4 | 322.4 | 16 | 9.9 | 10.7 | 10.4 | 8.0 | 15 | 39.0 | 44 |
| Thomas Industries | 62.9 | 72.2 | 79.5 | 77.1 | 31 | 291.7 | 31 | 4.1 | 3.6 | 4.3 | 3.9 | 12 | 15.9 | 72 |
| Tracor | 125.4 | 128.4 | 128.7 | 130.4 | 17 | 512.9 | 21 | 7.6 | 7.9 | 9.0 | 8.8 | 23 | 33.2 | 35 |
| United Industrial | 72.1 | 76.6 | 74.8 | 70.0 | 10 | 246.2 | 10 | 4.0 | 4.7 | 4.5 | 4.4 | 4 | 15.8 | 13 |
| Varian Associates (3) | 227.3 | 235.0 | 269.7 | 229.2 | 17 | 961.2 | 22 | 14.2 | 15.7 | 18.4 | 12.5 | 7 | 60.7 | 29 |
| Watkins-Johnson | 49.9 | 52.2 | 53.0 | 55.5 | 11 | 210.5 | 13 | 3.9 | 8.5 | 4.3 | 5.2 | 19 | 21.9 | 24 |
| Westinghouse Electric | 2269.9 | 2559.6 | 2546.3 | 2888.7 | 11 | 10264.5 | 8 | 116.6 | 128.1 | 130.6 | 160.6 | 17 | 535.9 | 19 |
| Zenith Electronics | 372.7 | 424.0 | 435.7 | 484.0 | 33 | 1716.4 | 26 | 14.0 | 16.4 | 21.9 | 11.3 | −17 | 63.6 | 37 |
| **INDUSTRY COMPOSITE** | 26875.0 | 28528.8 | 28404.4 | 30581.6 | 11 | 113906.5 | 14 | 1499.6 | 1856.4 | 1875.9 | 1835.2 | 10 | 7072.8 | 34 |
| **OFFICE EQUIPMENT, COMPUTERS** | | | | | | | | | | | | | | |
| AM International (5) | 144.3 | 153.7 | 161.8 | 147.5 | 6 | 607.4 | 8 | 1.4 | 2.9 | 3.4 | 1.2 | −24 | 8.9 | −6 |
| Amdahl | 174.6 | 196.8 | 180.6 | 227.4 | 1 | 779.4 | 0 | 4.1 | 4.9 | 11.2 | 16.1 | 3 | 36.4 | −16 |
| American Business Prods. | 69.1 | 69.2 | 70.0 | 72.0 | 14 | 280.4 | 19 | 2.5 | 2.4 | 2.2 | 2.8 | 4 | 9.8 | 9 |
| Apollo Computer | 36.7 | 46.0 | 57.4 | 75.9 | 173 | 215.9 | 168 | 4.1 | 5.1 | 6.3 | 8.4 | 127 | 23.9 | 114 |
| Apple Computer (3) | 300.1 | 422.1 | 477.4 | 698.3 | 121 | 1897.9 | 75 | 9.1 | 18.3 | 30.8 | 46.1 | 692 | 104.3 | 77 |
| Automatic Data Process. (6) | 234.9 | 233.2 | 236.6 | 253.6· | 16 | 958.3 | 17 | 22.1 | 21.8 | 15.4 | 20.1 | 15 | 79.5 | 16 |
| Barry Wright | 47.9 | 49.9 | 47.5 | 56.4 | 20 | 201.8 | 24 | 4.1 | 3.7 | 3.4 | 3.9 | −13 | 15.0 | 10 |
| Bell & Howell | 165.7 | 176.4 | 182.6 | 188.9 | 3 | 713.5 | 5 | 5.0 | 7.7 | 12.6 | 7.7 | 11 | 33.0 | 34 |
| Burroughs | 1099.4b | 1233.7b | 1153.3b | 1389.2b | 6 | 4875.6 | 11 | 43.0 | 57.3 | 50.2 | 94.4 | 16 | 244.9 | 24 |
| COMPAQ Computer | 62.9 | 65.9 | 87.5 | 112.7 | 116 | 329.0 | 196 | 3.3 | 0.9 | 1.9 | 6.8 | 114 | 12.9 | 395 |
| Compugraphic | 90.0 | 94.8 | 101.4 | 105.1 | 25 | 391.2 | 23 | 5.1 | 6.0 | 6.6 | 6.7 | 51 | 24.4 | 44 |
| Computervision | 121.8 | 133.6 | 137.1 | 163.9 | 47 | 556.3 | 39 | 10.8 | 10.9 | 11.2 | 14.9 | 43 | 47.7 | 35 |
| Control Data | 1188.3 | 1256.3 | 1244.1 | 1338.2 | 7 | 5026.9 | 10 | 31.7 | 23.4 | −54.5 | 31.0 | −36 | 31.6 | −80 |
| Convergent Technologies* | 55.7 | 85.0 | 105.7 | 115.5 | 156 | 361.8 | 122 | 3.3 | 4.1 | 2.7 | −9.4 | NM | 0.7 | −96 |
| Cray Research | 44.2 | 42.1 | 71.6 | 70.9 | −14 | 228.8 | 35 | 5.7 | 4.1 | 19.6 | 16.0 | −17 | 45.4 | 74 |
| Data General (3) | 248.4 | 277.1 | 415.7 | 333.7 | 39 | 1274.9 | 44 | 12.6 | 16.1 | 42.1 | 23.0 | 128 | 93.8 | 211 |
| Datapoint (5) | 140.8 | 155.0 | 164.6 | 140.1 | 0 | 600.5 | 10 | 8.5 | 8.0 | 4.5 | 1.5 | −73 | 22.4 | 72 |
| Dataproducts (9) | 126.4 | 121.5 | 114.1 | 122.4 | 22 | 484.5 | 38 | 10.6 | 8.8 | 5.4 | 11.0 | 50 | 35.8 | 82 |
| Digital Equipment (6) | 1430.8 | 1655.5 | 1515.3 | 1628.1 | 14 | 6229.6 | 29 | 101.9 | 130.6 | 144.2 | 110.3 | 37 | 487.0 | 86 |
| Duplex Products (2) | 55.6 | 63.1 | 61.1 | 62.0 | 15 | 241.8 | 17 | 2.1 | 2.4 | 2.4 | 3.0 | 17 | 9.9 | 14 |
| Dynatech (9)* | 38.4 | 43.3 | 51.2 | 55.8 | 41 | 188.6 | 33 | 2.3 | 3.2 | 4.2 | 4.4 | 43 | 14.1 | 26 |
| Hewlett-Packard (2) | 1278.0 | 1519.0 | 1559.0 | 1688.0 | 27 | 6044.0 | 28 | 217.0 | 147.0 | 134.0 | 167.0 | 14 | 665.0 | 54 |
| Honeywell | 1392.3 | 1486.7 | 1496.4 | 1749.5 | 8 | 6073.6 | 7 | 39.6 | 74.3 | 93.3 | 110.4 | 7 | 334.8 | 34 |
| Intergraph | 78.7 | 98.8 | 105.5 | 120.8 | 43 | 403.8 | 60 | 10.3 | 16.5 | 17.4 | 18.8 | 77 | 62.9 | 115 |
| Intl. Business Machines | 9585.0 | 11199.0 | 10657.0 | 14496.0 | 14 | 45937.0 | 14 | 1202.0 | 1623.0 | 1585.0 | 2172.0 | 17 | 6582.0 | 20 |
| Mohawk Data Sciences (8) | 106.6 | 97.4 | 103.8 | 95.2 | −5 | 403.0 | 5 | 0.5 | −59.7 | 0.2 | −46.0 | NM | −105.0 | NM |
| NCR | 861.4 | 998.8 | 956.7 | 1257.4 | 10 | 4074.3 | 9 | 45.5 | 76.2 | 96.9 | 124.0 | 8 | 342.6 | 19 |
| Nashua | 152.8 | 146.1 | 144.8 | 148.3 | 5 | 591.9 | 5 | 5.9 | 6.2 | 3.9 | 3.9 | 46 | 19.9 | 149 |
| Pitney-Bowes | 421.3 | 425.5 | 410.4 | 474.9 | 7 | 1732.1 | 8 | 29.8 | 31.8 | 31.6 | 45.1 | 14 | 138.2 | 17 |
| Prime Computer | 145.6 | 161.4 | 165.0 | 170.8 | 20 | 642.8 | 24 | 10.2 | 12.8 | 21.9 | 14.8 | 48 | 59.7 | 84 |
| Reynolds & Reynolds (3) | 72.8 | 74.2 | 75.6 | 74.6 | 11 | 297.2 | 13 | 4.2 | 4.5 | 4.8 | 4.1 | 12 | 17.6 | 27 |
| SCI Systems (6) | 117.4 | 127.7 | 122.4 | 133.4 | 16 | 500.9 | 67 | 3.2 | 4.2 | 2.5 | 3.0 | 15 | 12.9 | 53 |
| Savin | 86.5 | 98.3 | 103.2 | 104.3 | 1 | 392.3 | −2 | −30.2 | −8.4 | −5.7 | −5.0 | NM | −49.3 | NM |
| Sperry (9) | 1478.8 | 1187.1 | 1247.1 | 1457.0 | 23 | 5370.0 | 13 | 81.4 | 20.1 | 99.5 | 61.2 | −10 | 262.2 | 50 |
| Standard Register | 101.4b | 102.8b | 100.0b | 109.3b | 11 | 413.5 | 13 | 5.6 | 5.8 | 5.3 | 7.8 | 22 | 24.5 | 21 |
| Tandem Computers (3) | 111.2 | 141.9 | 153.1 | 159.7 | 26 | 565.9 | 26 | 2.0 | 9.3 | 21.6 | 14.0 | 40 | 46.9 | 39 |
| Tandon (3) | 105.7 | 106.3 | 95.8 | 90.7 | −3 | 398.4 | 16 | 10.4 | 10.4 | −0.7 | −15.4 | NM | 4.8 | −83 |
| Tandy (6) | 656.1 | 599.2 | 595.8 | 893.3 | −1 | 2744.4 | 3 | 62.6 | 58.4 | 37.4 | 76.5 | −24 | 234.9 | −20 |
| Telex (9) | 94.5b | 97.1b | 167.0b | 165.3b | 98 | 523.9 | 71 | 10.1 | 10.8 | 12.4 | 14.4 | 53 | 47.6 | 41 |
| Wallace Computer Servs. (5) | 60.9 | 64.5 | 62.6 | 66.2 | 20 | 254.2 | 18 | 4.5 | 5.4 | 4.7 | 4.9 | 21 | 19.5 | 19 |
| Wang Laboratories (6) | 543.5 | 713.9 | 553.8 | 610.0 | 18 | 2421.2 | 35 | 49.8 | 73.8 | 51.2 | 56.3 | 18 | 231.0 | 29 |
| Xerox* | 2136.8 | 2257.9 | 2207.6 | 2508.0 | 14 | 8791.6 | 6 | 126.1 | 95.5 | 81.3 | 60.9 | −26 | 375.6 | −24 |
| **INDUSTRY COMPOSITE** | 25463.2 | 28277.6 | 27719.3 | 33930.0 | 15 | 115019.7 | 16 | 2183.7 | 2560.3 | 2624.1 | 3312.6 | 12 | 10709.7 | 20 |

| | MARGINS | | | | | | | PERFORMANCE | | | | | | |
|---|---|---|---|---|---|---|---|---|---|---|---|---|---|---|
| 1st quarter 1984 % | 2nd quarter 1984 % | 3rd quarter 1984 % | 4th quarter 1984 $ mil. | Change from 4Q 1983 % | 12 months 1984 % | Change from 1983 % | Share price 2-28 | 12 months earnings $ per share | Price-earnings ratio 2-28 | Yield % | Book value $ per share | Return on common equity 1984 % | 5-year growth rate in earnings per share | 5-year growth rate in common equity | |
| 2.3 | 2.6 | 2.6 | 2.9 | 77 | 2.6 | NM | 23.00 | 1.01 | 23 | 0.00 | 14 | 7.4 | −38 | 18 | Thermo |
| 11.8 | 12.6 | 13.2 | 10.7 | 10 | 12.1 | 25 | 39.75 | 2.51 | 16 | 3.12 | 13 | 18.7 | 1 | 10 | T&B |
| 6.5 | 4.9 | 5.4 | 5.1 | −15 | 5.4 | 31 | 18.38 | 1.87 | 10 | 3.36 | 11 | 16.3 | 2 | 8 | Thomas Inds. |
| 6.1 | 6.1 | 7.0 | 6.8 | 5 | 6.5 | 12 | 34.00 | 2.15 | 16 | 1.00 | 11 | 19.0 | 16 | 33 | Tracor |
| 5.5 | 6.2 | 6.0 | 6.4 | −5 | 6.4 | 3 | 21.63 | 1.30 | 17 | 2.19 | 8 | 18.6 | 17 | 18 | United Indl. |
| 6.2 | 6.7 | 6.8 | 5.5 | −8 | 6.3 | 6 | 37.75 | 2.76 | 14 | 0.69 | 20 | 14.2 | 25 | 21 | Varian |
| 7.8 | 16.3 | 8.1 | 9.4 | 7 | 10.4 | 9 | 27.00 | 2.26 | 12 | 1.19 | 11 | 19.8 | 28 | 12 | Watkins |
| 5.1 | 5.0 | 5.1 | 5.6 | 6 | 5.2 | 11 | 30.63 | 3.04 | 10 | 3.27 | 21 | 14.8 | 7 | 8 | Westinghouse |
| 3.8 | 3.9 | 5.0 | 2.3 | −38 | 3.7 | 9 | 22.63 | 2.88 | 8 | 0.00 | 19 | 14.8 | 24 | 5 | Zenith |
| 5.6 | 6.5 | 6.6 | 6.0 | −1 | 6.2 | 18 | 39.13 | 3.00 | 15 | 2.05 | 19 | 16.3 | 5 | 13 | |
| 1.0 | 1.9 | 2.1 | 0.8 | −28 | 1.5 | −13 | 4.63 | 0.79 | 6 | 0.00 | 2 | 11.0 | −5 | NA | AM Intl. |
| 2.4 | 2.5 | 6.2 | 7.1 | 2 | 4.7 | −16 | 16.50 | 0.80 | 21 | 1.21 | 10 | 9.3 | 9 | 20 | Amdahl |
| 3.6 | 3.5 | 3.1 | 3.8 | −9 | 3.5 | −8 | 25.25 | 1.73 | 15 | 2.53 | 12 | 13.9 | 6 | 13 | Am. Business |
| 11.1 | 11.2 | 11.1 | 11.0 | −17 | 11.1 | −20 | 28.13 | 0.75 | 38 | 0.00 | 3 | 25.8 | NA | NA | Apollo |
| 3.0 | 4.3 | 6.5 | 6.6 | 259 | 5.5 | 1 | 24.75 | 1.70 | 15 | 0.00 | 8 | 22.5 | 43 | 92 | Apple |
| 9.4 | 9.4 | 6.5 | 7.9 | −1 | 8.3 | −2 | 45.00 | 2.26 | 20 | 1.38 | 14 | 16.4 | 14 | 23 | Auto. Data |
| 8.5 | 7.5 | 7.1 | 6.9 | −27 | 7.4 | −12 | 25.50 | 1.68 | 15 | 2.35 | 10 | 16.1 | 8 | 29 | Barry Wright |
| 3.0 | 4.4 | 6.9 | 4.1 | 8 | 4.6 | 28 | 29.75 | 3.04 | 10 | 1.88 | 27 | 15.0 | −4 | 3 | Bell & Howell |
| 3.9 | 4.6 | 4.4 | 6.8 | 9 | 5.0 | 12 | 63.50 | 5.40 | 12 | 4.09 | 49 | 10.9 | 1 | 2 | Burroughs |
| 5.2 | 1.4 | 2.1 | 6.1 | −1 | 3.9 | 67 | 9.75 | 0.47 | 21 | 0.00 | 4 | 12.6 | NA | NA | COMPAQ |
| 5.7 | 6.3 | 6.5 | 6.4 | 20 | 6.2 | 17 | 33.00 | 2.93 | 11 | 1.82 | 21 | 14.6 | −5 | 16 | Compugraphic |
| 8.8 | 8.1 | 8.2 | 9.1 | −3 | 8.6 | −3 | 36.88 | 1.66 | 22 | 0.00 | 9 | 19.3 | 21 | 55 | Compvision |
| 2.7 | 1.9 | NM | 2.3 | −41 | 0.6 | −82 | 35.25 | 0.81 | 44 | 1.87 | 46 | 1.8 | −19 | 13 | Control Data |
| 5.9 | 4.8 | 2.6 | NM | NM | 0.2 | −98 | 10.13 | 0.02 | NM | 0.00 | 6 | 0.3 | −22 | NA | Convergent |
| 12.9 | 9.7 | 27.4 | 22.6 | −4 | 19.8 | 29 | 73.75 | 3.06 | 24 | 0.00 | 14 | 22.2 | 34 | 57 | Cray Research |
| 5.1 | 5.8 | 10.1 | 6.9 | 64 | 7.4 | 117 | 56.38 | 3.56 | 16 | 0.00 | 24 | 15.8 | −7 | 17 | Data General |
| 6.1 | 5.1 | 2.7 | 1.0 | −73 | 3.7 | 57 | 19.63 | 1.09 | 18 | 0.00 | 17 | 6.5 | −21 | 22 | Datapoint |
| 8.4 | 7.2 | 4.8 | 8.9 | 23 | 7.4 | 33 | 17.38 | 1.71 | 10 | 0.92 | 11 | 15.4 | 4 | 20 | Dataproducts |
| 7.1 | 7.9 | 9.5 | 6.8 | 20 | 7.8 | 44 | 112.00 | 8.29 | 14 | 0.00 | 71 | 11.8 | 4 | 29 | Digital Eq. |
| 3.8 | 3.9 | 3.9 | 4.8 | 2 | 4.1 | −3 | 29.50 | 2.61 | 11 | 2.85 | 20 | 13.2 | −4 | 11 | Duplex |
| 6.0 | 7.4 | 8.2 | 8.0 | 2 | 7.5 | −5 | 27.38 | 1.45 | 19 | 0.00 | 6 | 24.4 | 19 | 41 | Dynatech |
| 17.0 | 9.7 | 8.6 | 9.9 | −10 | 11.0 | 20 | 37.00 | 2.59 | 14 | 0.59 | 14 | 18.8 | 22 | 23 | H-P |
| 2.8 | 5.0 | 6.2 | 6.3 | −1 | 5.5 | 25 | 64.13 | 7.14 | 9 | 2.96 | 51 | 13.8 | 2 | 10 | Honeywell |
| 13.1 | 16.7 | 16.5 | 15.6 | 24 | 15.6 | 34 | 67.50 | 2.44 | 28 | 0.00 | 8 | 29.7 | 77 | 113 | Intergraph |
| 12.5 | 14.5 | 14.9 | 15.0 | 4 | 14.3 | 5 | 134.00 | 10.77 | 12 | 3.28 | 43 | 24.8 | 16 | 12 | IBM |
| 0.5 | NM | 0.2 | NM | NM | NM | NM | 11.50 | −7.20 | NM | 0.00 | 4 | −185.8 | NA | 15 | Mohawk |
| 5.3 | 7.6 | 10.1 | 9.9 | −2 | 8.4 | 9 | 30.00 | 3.30 | 9 | 2.67 | 20 | 17.1 | 7 | 9 | NCR |
| 3.8 | 4.2 | 2.7 | 2.6 | 39 | 3.4 | 138 | 28.25 | 4.22 | 7 | 0.00 | 26 | 16.5 | −11 | −5 | Nashua |
| 7.1 | 7.5 | 7.7 | 9.5 | 7 | 8.0 | 9 | 39.63 | 3.51 | 11 | 3.03 | 17 | 21.7 | 12 | 19 | Pitney-Bowes |
| 7.0 | 8.0 | 13.3 | 8.7 | 24 | 9.3 | 48 | 18.50 | 1.25 | 15 | 0.00 | 6 | 19.5 | 17 | 63 | Prime |
| 5.8 | 6.0 | 6.3 | 5.5 | 0 | 5.9 | 13 | 41.50 | 3.71 | 11 | 2.99 | 22 | 17.3 | 3 | 6 | Reynolds |
| 2.8 | 3.3 | 2.0 | 2.2 | −1 | 2.6 | −9 | 14.00 | 0.98 | 14 | 0.00 | 6 | 14.8 | 42 | 37 | SCI |
| NM | NM | NM | NM | NM | NM | NM | 7.00 | −3.25 | NM | 0.00 | 4 | −67.3 | NA | 2 | Savin |
| 5.5 | 1.7 | 8.0 | 4.2 | −27 | 4.9 | 32 | 51.75 | 4.79 | 11 | 3.71 | 52 | 9.0 | −16 | 10 | Sperry |
| 5.5 | 5.6 | 5.3 | 7.2 | 10 | 5.9 | 7 | 55.00 | 3.72 | 15 | 2.11 | 22 | 17.3 | 12 | 12 | Std. Register |
| 1.8 | 6.5 | 14.1 | 8.8 | 10 | 8.3 | 11 | 24.50 | 1.15 | 21 | 0.00 | 9 | 12.5 | 36 | 63 | Tandem |
| 9.9 | 9.8 | NM | NM | NM | 1.2 | −85 | 6.63 | 0.11 | 60 | 0.00 | 5 | 2.0 | 79 | 208 | Tandon |
| 9.5 | 9.8 | 6.3 | 8.6 | −24 | 8.6 | −22 | 31.75 | 2.46 | 13 | 0.00 | 11 | 24.1 | 29 | 42 | Tandy |
| 10.7 | 11.1 | 7.4 | 8.7 | −23 | 9.1 | −17 | 45.63 | 3.26 | 14 | 0.00 | 13 | 26.0 | 69 | 31 | Telex |
| 7.4 | 8.3 | 7.5 | 7.4 | 0 | 7.7 | 1 | 35.63 | 1.98 | 18 | 1.26 | 12 | 16.3 | 14 | 19 | Wallace |
| 9.2 | 10.3 | 9.2 | 9.2 | 0 | 9.5 | −4 | 26.38 | 1.64 | 16 | 0.61 | 9 | 17.9 | 37 | 61 | Wang |
| 5.9 | 4.2 | 3.7 | 2.4 | −35 | 4.3 | −28 | 45.38 | 3.42 | 13 | 6.61 | 44 | 7.7 | −14 | 8 | Xerox |
| 8.6 | 9.1 | 9.5 | 9.8 | −3 | 9.3 | 3 | 62.58 | 4.73 | 16 | 1.55 | 26 | 18.1 | 7 | 14 | |

# Corporate Scoreboard (cont.)

| | SALES | | | | | | | PROFITS | | | | | | |
|---|---|---|---|---|---|---|---|---|---|---|---|---|---|---|
| | Reported | | | | Change from 4Q 1983 % | Restated | | Reported | | | | Change from 4Q 1983 % | Restated | |
| | 1st quarter 1984 $ mil. | 2nd quarter 1984 $ mil. | 3rd quarter 1984 $ mil. | 4th quarter 1984 $ mil. | | 12 months 1984 $ mil. | Change from 1983 % | 1st quarter 1984 $ mil. | 2nd quarter 1984 $ mil. | 3rd quarter 1984 $ mil. | 4th quarter 1984 $ mil. | | 12 months 1984 $ mil. | Change from 1983 % |
| **SERVICE INDUSTRIES** | | | | | | | | | | | | | | |
| AAR (7) | 44.7 | 51.4 | 52.7 | 55.2 | 34 | 204.0 | 30 | 1.3 | 1.5 | 2.3 | 2.2 | 177 | 7.3 | 125 |
| AGS Computers | 53.0b | 52.9b | 56.1b | 62.0b | 33 | 221.6 | 52 | 1.6 | 1.3 | 1.8 | 1.8 | −20 | 6.8 | 17 |
| Action Industries (6) | 43.2 | 41.7 | 51.4 | 61.1 | 43 | 197.4 | 48 | 2.7 | 1.4 | 2.7 | 3.2 | 30 | 9.9 | 35 |
| Air Express International | 68.4 | 72.8 | 73.6 | 78.2 | 13 | 293.0 | 15 | 0.4 | 0.6 | 0.3 | −1.3 | NM | 0.0 | NM |
| Airborne Freight | 97.6 | 102.2 | 106.7 | 111.3 | 21 | 417.9 | 25 | 2.6 | 2.3 | 2.8 | 3.1 | 14 | 10.8 | 21 |
| Alexander & Baldwin | 106.9b | 115.8b | 135.0b | 128.3b | 9 | 486.0 | 7 | 12.5 | 17.5 | 20.2 | 16.3 | 12 | 66.6 | 25 |
| Allegheny Beverage (9)* | 150.7 | 168.1 | 167.3 | 130.7 | 35 | 519.2 | 32 | 1.7 | 3.0 | 2.5 | −0.1 | NM | 4.4 | −46 |
| Amer. Bldg. Maintenance (2) | 88.1 | 91.8 | 96.2 | 98.0 | 12 | 374.1 | 14 | 1.7 | 2.1 | 2.2 | 1.5 | −32 | 7.5 | −4 |
| American Medical Intl. (4) | 614.5 | 619.9 | 596.9 | 519.2 | 6 | 2450.8 | 6 | 14.7 | 44.6 | 41.5 | 42.6 | 18 | 143.4 | 0 |
| American Water Works | 94.3 | 102.1 | 110.9 | 100.2 | 7 | 407.6 | 10 | 9.0 | 12.6 | 14.7 | 10.8 | 33 | 47.0 | 23 |
| Amfac | 582.6b | 601.7b | 609.5b | 598.6b | 1 | 2392.4 | 6 | 6.2 | 3.9 | 5.4 | −30.6 | NM | −15.1 | NM |
| Angelica (11) | 55.4 | 59.8 | 63.0 | 63.0 | 11 | 241.3 | 11 | 3.5 | 3.8 | 4.1 | 4.5 | 10 | 15.8 | 6 |
| Anixter Bros. (5) | 135.6 | 157.8 | 164.7 | 165.7 | 19 | 623.8 | 18 | 2.9 | 4.6 | 5.1 | 4.4 | 12 | 17.1 | 55 |
| Apogee Enterprises (10) | 49.3 | 48.2 | 58.3 | 58.7 | 26 | 214.4 | 24 | 0.2 | 0.7 | 2.2 | 1.9 | 23 | 4.9 | −25 |
| Arrow Electronics | 190.4 | 196.2 | 190.4 | 163.0 | −2 | 740.0 | 31 | 3.8 | 4.3 | 2.9 | 1.7 | −27 | 12.8 | 151 |
| Avnet (6) | 427.7 | 456.6 | 432.4 | 395.1 | 0 | 1711.8 | 25 | 22.9 | 24.0 | 19.9 | 12.0 | −44 | 78.8 | 19 |
| BDM International | 41.6 | 45.7 | 48.8 | 55.2 | 32 | 191.4 | 27 | 1.7 | 1.9 | 2.1 | 2.4 | 20 | 8.1 | 27 |
| Barnes Group | 128.7 | 129.9 | 126.7 | 112.8 | 3 | 498.1 | 13 | 5.8 | 5.5 | 5.2 | 1.6 | −64 | 18.1 | 79 |
| BBDO International | 71.9 | 78.9 | 72.3 | 82.2 | 5 | 305.3 | 16 | 5.2 | 6.1 | 3.9 | 7.5 | 9 | 22.6 | 25 |
| Bearings (6) | 121.7 | 125.4 | 120.7 | 122.3 | 15 | 490.1 | 25 | 3.0 | 3.6 | 3.0 | 2.7 | 15 | 12.4 | 62 |
| Bell Industries (6) | 79.9 | 86.3 | 79.6 | 72.5 | 1 | 318.3 | 17 | 2.8 | 3.8 | 2.8 | 0.9 | −58 | 10.3 | 17 |
| Bergen Brunswig (4) | 418.8 | 441.6 | 445.8 | 492.5 | 24 | 1798.8 | 23 | 6.1 | 6.4 | 5.7 | 6.2 | 17 | 24.3 | 10 |
| Beverly Enterprises | 323.6 | 340.4 | 370.4 | 385.7 | 28 | 1420.1 | 30 | 9.4 | 11.6 | 12.3 | 13.8 | 24 | 47.0 | 33 |
| Bindley Western Industries | 131.4 | 133.5 | 141.2 | 160.6 | 21 | 566.7 | 18 | 1.0 | 1.3 | 1.0 | 1.3 | 73 | 4.7 | 64 |
| Blair (John) | 134.6 | 224.5 | 229.6 | 253.6 | 97 | 842.4 | 103 | 1.1 | 4.3 | 2.8 | 2.2 | −60 | 10.5 | −43 |
| Block (H&R) (8) | 52.4b | 274.8b | 41.8b | 56.6b | 20 | 425.7 | 25 | −5.9 | 59.5 | −4.5 | −1.2 | NM | 47.9 | 16 |
| Blount (10)† | 209.6b | 204.4b | 212.8b | 205.2b | −10 | 831.9 | 5 | 6.8 | 6.0 | 6.6 | 7.3 | 35 | 26.8 | 31 |
| BRAE (9) | 126.6b | 125.6b | 124.8b | 121.1b | −1 | 498.0 | 12 | 1.1 | 0.6 | 3.2 | −0.2 | NM | 4.7 | 16 |
| Browning-Ferris Inds. (3) | 231.1 | 259.2 | 277.4 | 265.6 | 14 | 1033.3 | 18 | 16.9 | 25.1 | 24.9 | 25.3 | 13 | 92.2 | 11 |
| Butler International | 92.2 | 100.0 | 80.6 | 83.8 | 23 | 313.7 | 22 | 0.6 | 1.5 | 1.8 | 1.7 | 28 | 6.3 | 30 |
| CDI (8) | 75.4 | 82.0 | 88.1 | 94.1 | 23 | 339.6 | 29 | 1.4 | 2.4 | 1.8 | 1.8 | −13 | 7.3 | 43 |
| CPI (11) | 44.3 | 37.8 | 41.1 | 62.3 | 28 | 185.5 | 29 | 4.1 | 1.6 | 1.8 | 3.9 | 0 | 11.3 | 18 |
| CRS Sirrine (6) | 73.1 | 75.3 | 65.9 | 71.3 | −12 | 285.6 | 8 | 0.2 | 0.8 | 2.1 | 1.1 | −12 | 4.2 | −29 |
| Cardinal Distribution (9) | 58.6 | 60.3 | 68.7 | 97.5 | 57 | 285.0 | 19 | 0.7 | 0.7 | 0.7 | 1.2 | 55 | 3.3 | 34 |
| Castle (A.M.) | 83.4 | 87.3 | 78.2 | 79.5 | 18 | 328.4 | 30 | 2.1 | 1.9 | 1.3 | 1.9 | 72 | 7.1 | 162 |
| Centex (9)* | 325.1 | 299.8 | 312.9 | 296.9 | 10 | 1234.7 | 13 | 12.4 | 10.1 | 11.2 | 8.5 | −18 | 42.1 | −1 |
| Charter Medical (3) | 108.2 | 108.7 | 110.2 | 123.0 | 26 | 450.1 | 20 | 9.8 | 9.5 | 8.5 | 9.4 | 27 | 37.1 | 30 |
| ChemLawn (2) | 17.7b | 55.3b | 106.3b | 110.5b | 21 | 289.7 | 27 | −17.0 | −8.7 | 16.2 | 25.1 | 27 | 15.6 | 24 |
| Comdisco (3) | 140.8 | 129.6 | 136.8 | 153.1 | 18 | 560.4 | 8 | 4.1 | 7.0 | 9.0 | 16.4 | 69 | 36.4 | −26 |
| Computer Sciences (9) | 185.0 | 173.9 | 172.0 | 178.7 | 6 | 709.6 | −1 | 7.1 | 4.6 | 3.4 | 12.4 | 194 | 27.6 | 74 |
| Deluxe Check Printers | 163.2 | 167.0 | 174.8 | 177.8 | 13 | 682.8 | 10 | 19.6 | 20.3 | 23.7 | 24.2 | 16 | 87.8 | 15 |
| Di Giorgio | 287.5 | 319.2 | 295.3 | 260.4 | 15 | 1036.5 | 25 | 0.6 | 1.3 | −1.0 | 0.9 | −70 | 6.6 | −28 |
| Dibrell Brothers (6) | 70.0 | 56.3 | 59.2 | 182.0 | 20 | 367.5 | 6 | 1.9 | 2.5 | 9.6 | 5.1 | 29 | 19.1 | 93 |
| Donnelley (R. R.) & Sons | 378.7 | 417.9 | 471.1 | 546.8 | 22 | 1814.5 | 17 | 23.3 | 30.3 | 39.2 | 41.1 | 19 | 133.9 | 17 |
| Dravo | 185.7 | 215.1 | 213.6 | 230.7 | 10 | 844.9 | 4 | −5.4 | −1.0 | −0.7 | −7.3 | NM | −11.2 | NM |
| Ducommun | 118.6 | 124.0 | 105.8 | 102.7 | 11 | 451.1 | 48 | 3.6 | 3.6 | 2.5 | 1.4 | −54 | 11.1 | 38 |
| Durr-Fillauer Medical | 81.4 | 83.2 | 86.1 | 91.0 | 25 | 341.7 | 30 | 1.0 | 1.4 | 1.6 | 1.8 | 10 | 5.8 | 14 |
| Dynalectron | 138.6 | 153.6 | 165.6 | 177.8 | 16 | 638.2 | 19 | 0.4 | 1.2 | 3.0 | 7.1 | 50 | 12.0 | 17 |
| Edgcomb Steel of New Eng. | 26.0 | 27.2 | 152.0 | 139.0 | 535 | 344.1 | 315 | 0.7 | 0.8 | 1.2 | 1.6 | 206 | 4.3 | 221 |
| Edwards (A. G.) (10) | 73.8 | 74.3 | 78.0 | 68.9 | −1 | 295.0 | −11 | 2.2 | 6.2 | 6.7 | 5.2 | −16 | 20.3 | −47 |

| | | | MARGINS | | | | | | | PERFORMANCE | | | | | | |
|---|---|---|---|---|---|---|---|---|---|---|---|---|---|---|---|---|
| | | | | Change from | 12 | Change from | | 12 months | Price- | | Book value | Return on common | 5-year growth rate | | |
| 1st quarter 1984 % | 2nd quarter 1984 % | 3rd quarter 1984 % | 4th quarter 1984 $ mil. | 4Q 1983 % | months 1984 % | 1983 % | Share price 2-28 | earnings $ per share | earnings ratio 2-28 | Yield % | $ per share | equity 1984 % | in earnings per share | in common equity | |
| 2.9 | 3.0 | 4.3 | 3.9 | 107 | 3.6 | 73 | 21.00 | 1.29 | 16 | 2.29 | 14 | 8.7 | -16 | 28 | AAR |
| 2.9 | 2.5 | 3.2 | 2.9 | -40 | 3.1 | -23 | 15.00 | 1.29 | 12 | 0.00 | 8 | 16.6 | 35 | NA | AGS |
| 6.2 | 3.3 | 5.2 | 5.2 | -9 | 5.0 | -8 | 17.00 | 1.54 | 11 | 0.00 | 6 | 24.1 | 126 | 17 | Action Inds. |
| 0.6 | 0.8 | 0.4 | NM | NM | 0.0 | NM | 7.00 | 0.00 | NM | 0.00 | 2 | 0.1 | -2 | 31 | Air Express |
| 2.7 | 2.3 | 2.6 | 2.8 | -6 | 2.6 | -3 | 24.00 | 1.85 | 13 | 2.50 | 13 | 14.6 | -2 | 15 | Airborne |
| 11.7 | 15.1 | 15.0 | 12.7 | 3 | 13.7 | 17 | 37.75 | 3.60 | 10 | 3.71 | 23 | 15.4 | 8 | 10 | A&B |
| 1.1 | 1.8 | 1.5 | NM | NM | 0.8 | -59 | 19.63 | 0.69 | 28 | 2.04 | 11 | 6.6 | 26 | 24 | Allegheny |
| 1.9 | 2.3 | 2.3 | 1.6 | -39 | 2.0 | -15 | 25.00 | 2.12 | 12 | 3.44 | 18 | 11.7 | 8 | 11 | Am. Building |
| 2.4 | 7.2 | 6.9 | 8.2 | 11 | 5.9 | -5 | 23.63 | 1.72 | 14 | 2.54 | 10 | 18.6 | 17 | 40 | Am. Medical |
| 9.5 | 12.3 | 13.3 | 10.7 | 25 | 11.5 | 12 | 45.00 | 6.15 | 7 | 4.44 | 42 | 14.7 | 20 | 9 | Am. Water |
| 1.1 | 0.7 | 0.9 | NM | NM | NM | NM | 26.25 | -0.99 | NM | 0.00 | 26 | -3.6 | NA | 6 | Amfac |
| 6.3 | 6.3 | 6.5 | 7.2 | -1 | 6.6 | -5 | 20.75 | 1.71 | 12 | 2.70 | 11 | 15.4 | 23 | 12 | Angelica |
| 2.1 | 2.9 | 3.1 | 2.6 | -5 | 2.7 | 31 | 18.25 | 0.93 | 20 | 1.53 | 11 | 8.8 | 1 | 34 | Anixter Bros. |
| 0.3 | 1.5 | 3.7 | 3.2 | -3 | 2.3 | -40 | 10.25 | 0.50 | 21 | 1.17 | 5 | 10.3 | 15 | 30 | Apogee |
| 2.0 | 2.2 | 1.5 | 1.1 | -25 | 1.7 | 92 | 16.13 | 2.00 | 8 | 1.24 | 12 | 16.3 | 4 | 15 | Arrow |
| 5.4 | 5.3 | 4.6 | 3.0 | -43 | 4.6 | -5 | 33.75 | 2.21 | 15 | 1.48 | 18 | 12.5 | 2 | 14 | Avnet |
| 4.2 | 4.2 | 4.2 | 4.3 | -10 | 4.2 | 0 | 37.38 | 1.63 | 23 | 0.35 | 7 | 22.3 | 22 | 34 | BDM |
| 4.5 | 4.2 | 4.1 | 1.5 | -65 | 3.6 | 59 | 22.50 | 2.51 | 9 | 3.56 | 18 | 13.8 | -10 | 2 | Barnes |
| 7.2 | 7.7 | 5.4 | 9.1 | 4 | 7.4 | 8 | 50.50 | 3.57 | 14 | 3.96 | 15 | 23.6 | 8 | 19 | BBDO |
| 2.5 | 2.9 | 2.5 | 2.2 | 0 | 2.5 | 30 | 35.50 | 3.10 | 11 | 2.82 | 33 | 9.5 | -11 | 7 | Bearings |
| 3.5 | 4.4 | 3.5 | 1.3 | -59 | 3.2 | 0 | 24.63 | 1.92 | 13 | 1.30 | 19 | 10.3 | 1 | 20 | Bell |
| 1.5 | 1.5 | 1.3 | 1.2 | -6 | 1.4 | -10 | 25.88 | 1.93 | 13 | 1.24 | 12 | 16.8 | 23 | 29 | Bergen |
| 2.9 | 3.4 | 3.3 | 3.6 | -4 | 3.3 | 2 | 34.00 | 1.80 | 19 | 0.94 | 16 | 11.1 | 25 | 87 | Beverly |
| 0.8 | 0.9 | 0.7 | 0.8 | 43 | 0.8 | 39 | 26.00 | 1.45 | 18 | 0.00 | 10 | 13.8 | NA | NA | Bindley |
| 0.8 | 1.9 | 1.2 | 0.9 | -80 | 1.2 | -72 | 22.63 | 1.31 | 17 | 2.48 | 16 | 8.2 | 10 | 17 | Blair |
| NM | 21.7 | NM | NM | NM | 11.2 | -7 | 48.50 | 3.87 | 13 | 4.95 | 17 | 22.3 | 7 | 15 | Block |
| 3.2 | 3.0 | 3.1 | 3.6 | 49 | 3.2 | 25 | 18.13 | 2.24 | 8 | 2.48 | 11 | 21.0 | 13 | 15 | Blount |
| 0.9 | 0.5 | 2.6 | NM | NM | 0.9 | 3 | 15.50 | 0.89 | 17 | 0.00 | 13 | 6.7 | -21 | 11 | BRAE |
| 7.3 | 9.7 | 9.0 | 9.5 | 0 | 8.9 | -6 | 41.50 | 2.68 | 15 | 2.60 | 14 | 19.7 | 21 | 23 | Browning |
| 0.7 | 1.5 | 2.2 | 2.0 | 5 | 2.0 | 7 | 19.50 | 0.96 | 20 | 2.67 | NA | 9.8 | -15 | 17 | Butler Intl. |
| 1.8 | 2.9 | 2.1 | 1.9 | -30 | 2.2 | 11 | 18.63 | 1.96 | 10 | 0.00 | 8 | 35.9 | 9 | 18 | CDI |
| 9.2 | 4.2 | 4.3 | 6.2 | -22 | 6.1 | -8 | 19.38 | 1.47 | 13 | 0.00 | 5 | 30.1 | NA | NA | CPI |
| 0.3 | 1.1 | 3.2 | 1.5 | -1 | 1.5 | -34 | 16.25 | 1.00 | 16 | 2.09 | 20 | 5.1 | -3 | 26 | CRS Sirrine |
| 1.1 | 1.1 | 1.1 | 1.3 | -2 | 1.2 | 13 | 18.00 | 1.06 | 17 | 0.22 | 9 | 9.7 | NA | NA | Cardinal |
| 2.5 | 2.2 | 1.7 | 2.3 | 46 | 2.2 | 102 | 19.00 | 2.28 | 8 | 4.21 | 17 | 13.8 | -11 | 5 | Castle |
| 3.8 | 3.4 | 3.6 | 2.8 | -25 | 3.4 | -12 | 24.00 | 2.12 | 11 | 1.04 | 16 | 13.2 | 3 | 23 | Centex |
| 9.1 | 8.7 | 7.7 | 7.6 | 1 | 8.3 | 8 | 37.00 | 1.86 | 20 | 0.65 | 7 | 27.1 | 45 | 46 | Charter Med. |
| NM | NM | 15.3 | 22.7 | 4 | 5.4 | -2 | 29.50 | 1.55 | 19 | 1.29 | 7 | 22.4 | 22 | 36 | ChemLawn |
| 2.9 | 5.4 | 6.5 | 10.7 | 43 | 6.5 | -31 | 16.00 | 1.33 | 12 | 1.25 | 7 | 19.3 | 30 | 46 | Comdisco |
| 3.8 | 2.7 | 2.0 | 6.9 | 177 | 3.9 | 76 | 15.75 | 2.00 | 8 | 0.00 | 11 | 16.6 | 0 | 24 | Comp. Sci. |
| 12.0 | 12.2 | 13.5 | 13.6 | 2 | 12.9 | 4 | 65.00 | 4.01 | 16 | 1.42 | 13 | 30.2 | 19 | 17 | Deluxe Check |
| 0.2 | 0.4 | NM | 0.3 | -74 | 0.6 | -42 | 14.63 | 0.95 | 15 | 4.38 | 18 | 5.3 | -11 | 4 | Di Giorgio |
| 2.8 | 4.4 | 16.2 | 2.8 | 7 | 5.2 | 82 | 30.00 | 6.52 | 5 | 3.33 | 25 | 27.4 | 23 | 12 | Dibrell |
| 6.1 | 7.2 | 8.3 | 7.5 | -3 | 7.4 | 0 | 53.38 | 3.50 | 15 | 2.17 | 20 | 17.4 | 16 | 12 | Donnelley |
| NM | NM | NM | NM | NM | NM | NM | 13.00 | -0.84 | NM | 3.85 | 16 | -5.3 | NA | 4 | Dravo |
| 3.0 | 2.9 | 2.4 | 1.4 | -59 | 2.5 | -7 | 32.75 | 3.38 | 10 | 2.44 | 29 | 11.8 | 0 | 20 | Ducommun |
| 1.2 | 1.7 | 1.8 | 2.0 | -12 | 1.7 | -12 | 15.00 | 0.92 | 16 | 1.07 | 7 | 12.6 | 15 | 22 | Durr-Fillauer |
| 0.3 | 0.8 | 1.8 | 4.0 | 29 | 1.9 | -1 | 14.88 | 1.23 | 12 | 1.68 | 10 | 12.7 | 17 | 28 | Dynalectron |
| 2.5 | 2.9 | 0.8 | 1.1 | -52 | 1.2 | -23 | 32.00 | 2.72 | 12 | 0.00 | 12 | 23.2 | 20 | 5 | Edgcomb |
| 3.0 | 8.3 | 8.6 | 7.6 | -15 | 6.9 | -40 | 31.88 | 1.49 | 21 | 2.51 | 14 | 10.9 | 16 | 34 | Edwards |

# Table A.1 Corporate Scoreboard (cont.)

| | SALES | | | | | | | PROFITS | | | | | | |
| | Reported | | | | Change from 4Q 1983 % | Restated | | Reported | | | | Change from 4Q 1983 % | Restated | |
| | 1st quarter 1984 $ mil. | 2nd quarter 1984 $ mil. | 3rd quarter 1984 $ mil. | 4th quarter 1984 $ mil. | | 12 months 1984 $ mil. | Change from 1983 % | 1st quarter 1984 $ mil. | 2nd quarter 1984 $ mil. | 3rd quarter 1984 $ mil. | 4th quarter 1984 $ mil. | | 12 months 1984 $ mil. | Change from 1983 % |
|---|---|---|---|---|---|---|---|---|---|---|---|---|---|---|
| **SERVICE INDUSTRIES (cont.)** | | | | | | | | | | | | | | |
| Emery Air Freight | 192.4b | 200.2b | 204.2b | 210.0b | 9 | 818.0 | 18 | 6.9 | 7.5 | 9.5 | 7.9 | 10 | 31.8 | 27 |
| Entre Computer Centers (4) | 42.2 | 48.3 | 54.7 | 63.9 | 117 | 209.1 | 230 | 1.6 | 2.0 | 2.3 | 2.5 | 127 | 8.3 | 372 |
| Equifax | 120.6b | 127.6b | 125.9b | 135.0b | 13 | 509.1 | 7 | 4.3 | 5.0 | 4.5 | 4.8 | 25 | 18.6 | 5 |
| Farm House Foods (9) | 347.2 | 447.0 | 407.6 | 179.0 | -51 | 1380.8 | -9 | -0.6 | 1.3 | 0.5 | 6.3 | NM | 7.4 | NM |
| Federal Express (7) | 375.1 | 413.2 | 439.1 | 485.2 | 42 | 1712.6 | 43 | 28.1 | 28.7 | 8.3 | 10.2 | -67 | 75.3 | -29 |
| Fischbach (3) | 225.0 | 237.1 | 220.5 | 282.7 | -2 | 965.3 | -25 | 2.4 | 0.7 | -1.5 | 0.4 | -90 | 1.9 | -92 |
| Fleming | 1575.2 | 1184.9 | 1227.3 | 1524.4 | 18 | 5511.8 | 13 | 13.9 | 10.7 | 9.6 | 15.4 | 22 | 49.6 | 19 |
| Fluor (2) | 1140.9 | 1153.6 | 1072.6 | 1034.0 | -18 | 4401.1 | -17 | 16.4 | 4.5 | 1.9 | -21.8 | NM | 1.0 | -99 |
| Foote Cone & Belding | 58.1 | 70.2 | 68.2 | 71.1 | 16 | 267.6 | 19 | 2.0 | 4.5 | 4.7 | 5.6 | NM | 16.8 | 137 |
| Foster Wheeler | 321.5 | 349.5 | 325.1 | 330.7 | -14 | 1326.9 | -14 | 8.4 | 8.4 | 7.8 | 10.8 | 16 | 35.4 | -20 |
| FoxMeyer (9) | 130.9b | 159.4 | 167.1 | 194.0 | 59 | 651.4 | 51 | 1.6 | 1.4 | 1.9 | 3.1 | 86 | 8.0 | 64 |
| Gelco (5) | 220.6 | 234.7 | 252.7 | 254.2 | 15 | 962.1 | 5 | 4.2 | 2.9 | 4.8 | 5.5 | 354 | 17.4 | NM |
| Genuine Parts | 562.3 | 587.6 | 602.3 | 551.5 | 8 | 2303.6 | 11 | 26.5 | 29.7 | 31.5 | 32.0 | 11 | 119.7 | 15 |
| Gilbert Associates | 63.3b | 63.7b | 59.2b | 59.6b | -1 | 245.9 | 2 | 1.0 | 0.8 | 2.4 | 1.9 | -1 | 6.2 | -8 |
| Grainger (W. W.) | 243.6 | 282.4 | 270.2 | 263.1 | 13 | 1059.4 | 20 | 14.1 | 18.2 | 18.2 | 18.5 | 20 | 68.9 | 33 |
| Grey Advertising | 40.4 | 55.5 | 49.8 | 58.4 | 23 | 204.1 | 26 | 1.0 | 4.2 | 2.0 | 3.0 | 14 | 10.2 | 27 |
| Greyhound | 493.4b | 570.4b | 574.9b | 545.1b | 23 | 2219.2 | 2 | 12.1 | 34.1 | 42.2 | 36.6 | NM | 125.0 | 78 |
| Handleman (8) | 87.4 | 86.7 | 82.4 | 97.7 | 42 | 354.2 | 45 | 4.6 | 5.2 | 4.1 | 5.5 | 59 | 19.3 | 76 |
| Harland (John H.) | 52.2 | 53.1 | 53.9 | 58.2 | 19 | 217.4 | 15 | 6.0 | 6.0 | 6.2 | 6.9 | 23 | 25.2 | 21 |
| HealthAmerica* | 36.1b | 40.3b | 51.0b | 56.6b | 82 | 183.9 | 76 | 3.1 | 3.2 | 3.3 | 3.0 | 62 | 12.6 | 165 |
| Hospital Corp. of America | 1093.9b | 1038.4b | 1001.7b | 1043.9b | 8 | 4178.0 | 7 | 86.5 | 73.9 | 69.1 | 67.2 | 20 | 296.8 | 22 |
| Hughes Supply (11) | 66.0 | 70.2 | 73.7 | 71.5 | 10 | 281.4 | 29 | 1.7 | 1.8 | 1.6 | 1.5 | -3 | 6.6 | 29 |
| Humana (4) | 482.4 | 507.1 | 503.3 | 515.1 | 10 | 2007.9 | 10 | 47.2 | 52.0 | 45.4 | 54.6 | 12 | 199.2 | 16 |
| I.M.S. International | 53.1 | 55.7 | 55.8 | 59.5 | 5 | 224.0 | 9 | 4.3 | 4.4 | 5.4 | 9.0 | 23 | 23.1 | 25 |
| IU International | 564.1 | 633.1 | 676.6 | 675.8b | 24 | 2550.1 | 23 | 7.7 | 11.8 | 5.6 | 2.1 | -86 | 7.9 | -82 |
| Informatics General* | 47.2 | 50.1 | 53.8 | 57.0 | 20 | 191.2 | 26 | 0.8 | 0.3 | 1.1 | 3.8 | 1 | 6.3 | 10 |
| Intermark (9)† | 50.3b | 49.6b | 49.9b | 111.1 | 159 | 404.2 | 197 | 1.6 | 1.3 | -0.6 | -2.3 | NM | 0.0 | NM |
| Interpublic Group | 146.4b | 169.5b | 145.0b | 183.5b | 3 | 644.4 | 7 | 4.8 | 14.7 | 3.2 | 10.0 | 4 | 32.8 | 29 |
| JWT Group | 118.8 | 126.0 | 123.8 | 139.6 | 9 | 508.2 | 13 | 3.8 | 6.2 | 4.8 | 5.8 | -12 | 20.5 | 17 |
| Jacobs Engineering (3) | 41.4 | 39.4 | 53.8 | 56.9 | 32 | 191.6 | 10 | -1.8 | -1.5 | -5.9 | 0.3 | NM | -8.8 | NM |
| Jorgensen (Earle M.) | 73.1 | 74.7 | 72.4 | 70.4 | 17 | 290.6 | 27 | 2.3 | 3.1 | 1.5 | 2.4 | -35 | 9.3 | 30 |
| Josephson International (6) | 71.8b | 69.1b | 69.7b | 84.5b | 54 | 295.1 | 59 | 0.7 | -3.2 | 0.4 | -0.4 | NM | -2.6 | NM |
| Kaman | 126.9b | 139.0b | 137.1b | 135.5b | 5 | 538.5 | 13 | 3.8 | 4.3 | 4.5 | 4.4 | 18 | 17.2 | 34 |
| Kay | 210.9b | 223.9b | 173.3b | 219.6b | -12 | 827.7 | 20 | -2.8 | -0.5 | -1.6 | 7.3 | 0 | 2.4 | 32 |
| Kelly Services | 165.9 | 180.7 | 199.3 | 195.2 | 30 | 741.2 | 41 | 5.2 | 6.2 | 8.4 | 6.9 | 26 | 26.7 | 53 |
| Ketchum (8) | 63.2 | 61.3 | 66.7 | 69.8 | 11 | 261.0 | 14 | 0.2 | 0.0 | 0.1 | 0.2 | -56 | 0.5 | -52 |
| LD Brinkman (5) | 67.3b | 72.0b | 77.2b | 69.5b | 7 | 286.0 | 20 | 2.2 | 2.5 | 3.2 | 3.2 | 29 | 11.0 | 32 |
| Little (Arthur D.) | 52.0b | 54.1b | 51.4b | 55.9b | 6 | 213.4 | 11 | 1.4 | 1.4 | 1.0 | -0.2 | NM | 3.6 | -41 |
| Mgmt. Science America | 32.3 | 31.0 | 31.2 | 56.4 | 19 | 141.8 | 21 | 0.5 | -1.7 | -1.8 | 11.2 | 26 | 13.7 | 25 |
| Manor Care (7) | 86.1 | 99.3 | 113.2 | 112.7 | 25 | 411.3 | 21 | 4.9 | 6.2 | 7.7 | 7.8 | 33 | 26.6 | 25 |
| Marshall Industries (7) | 63.4 | 77.1 | 77.1 | 69.4 | 25 | 287.0 | 62 | 2.8 | 3.8 | 2.9 | 1.6 | -27 | 11.2 | 114 |
| Mass Merchandisers | 77.7b | 78.6b | 82.5b | 87.4b | 16 | 326.3 | 17 | 1.2 | 1.4 | 1.4 | 1.5 | 22 | 5.5 | 46 |
| Maxicare Health Plans | 65.3b | 75.2b | 85.1b | 91.0b | 62 | 316.7 | 61 | 2.0 | 2.5 | 3.1 | 3.1 | 81 | 10.7 | 98 |
| McKesson (9) | 1099.1b | 1154.5b | 1171.0b | 1326.3b | 16 | 4750.9 | 15 | 13.5 | 14.7 | 16.7 | 17.8 | 0 | 62.8 | -3 |
| McLean Industries | 202.2 | 251.1 | 259.9 | 245.8 | 25 | 959.0 | 22 | 11.4 | 21.8 | 17.8 | 10.6 | NM | 61.6 | 132 |
| Morrison-Knudsen | 478.9b | 486.5b | 516.9b | 539.8b | -10 | 2022.1 | -7 | 7.4 | 9.5 | 9.9 | 16.8 | 8 | 43.6 | 5 |
| Nash Finch | 261.9b | 284.5b | 387.5b | 304.1b | 12 | 1238.0 | 8 | 1.3 | 3.0 | 3.7 | 3.6 | -5 | 11.7 | 6 |
| Natl. Medical Enterprises (7) | 632.8b | 570.0b | 683.8b | 708.3b | 16 | 2748.9 | 16 | 30.4 | 34.0 | 33.4 | 36.3 | 23 | 134.1 | 21 |
| Noland | 69.4 | 88.4 | 89.9 | 88.1 | 13 | 335.8 | 16 | 1.0 | 1.9 | 1.7 | 1.6 | 23 | 6.1 | 33 |
| Ogilvy & Mather Intl. | 95.2b | 110.3b | 102.5b | 131.2b | 20 | 439.2 | 23 | 3.1 | 6.4 | 4.6 | 11.7 | 30 | 25.8 | 45 |

| | | MARGINS | | | | | | | PERFORMANCE | | | | | | |
|---|---|---|---|---|---|---|---|---|---|---|---|---|---|---|---|
| | | | | Change from | | Change | | 12 months | Price- | | Book | Return on | 5-year growth rate | | |
| 1st quarter 1984 % | 2nd quarter 1984 % | 3rd quarter 1984 % | 4th quarter 1984 $ mil. | 4Q 1983 % | 12 months 1984 % | from 1983 % | Share price 2-28 | earnings $ per share | earnings ratio 2-28 | Yield % | value $ per share | common equity 1984 % | in earnings per share | in common equity | |
| 3.6 | 3.7 | 4.7 | 3.8 | 1 | 3.9 | 8 | 18.25 | 1.70 | 11 | 2.74 | 9 | 19.9 | 1 | 12 | Emery Air |
| 3.8 | 4.2 | 4.1 | 3.8 | 4 | 4.0 | 43 | 15.25 | 0.88 | 17 | 0.00 | 3 | 36.1 | NA | NA | Entre |
| 3.6 | 3.9 | 3.6 | 3.6 | 11 | 3.7 | −2 | 36.75 | 2.62 | 14 | 4.63 | 12 | 21.4 | 11 | 7 | Equifax |
| NM | 0.3 | 0.1 | 3.5 | NM | 0.5 | NM | 4.63 | 0.84 | 6 | 0.00 | 4 | 23.7 | −30 | 18 | Farm House |
| 7.5 | 6.9 | 1.9 | 2.1 | −76 | 4.4 | −51 | 37.00 | 1.60 | 23 | 0.00 | 16 | 10.0 | 31 | 52 | Fed. Express |
| 1.1 | 0.3 | NM | 0.1 | −90 | 0.2 | −89 | 36.50 | 1.04 | 35 | 2.74 | 45 | 2.2 | −7 | 12 | Fischbach |
| 0.9 | 0.9 | 0.8 | 1.0 | 4 | 0.9 | 6 | 36.13 | 2.70 | 13 | 2.44 | 17 | 14.6 | 15 | 24 | Fleming |
| 1.4 | 0.4 | 0.2 | NM | NM | 0.0 | −99 | 18.75 | 0.01 | NM | 2.13 | 21 | 0.1 | −56 | 34 | Fluor |
| 3.4 | 6.4 | 7.0 | 7.9 | NM | 6.3 | 100 | 54.75 | 4.71 | 12 | 4.02 | 25 | 19.0 | 4 | 15 | Foote Cone |
| 2.6 | 2.4 | 2.4 | 3.3 | 36 | 2.7 | −7 | 14.88 | 1.03 | 14 | 2.96 | 11 | 9.3 | −7 | 16 | Foster |
| 1.2 | 0.9 | 1.2 | 1.6 | 16 | 1.2 | 9 | 29.00 | 1.51 | 19 | 0.00 | 16 | 7.6 | NA | NA | FoxMeyer |
| 1.9 | 1.2 | 1.9 | 2.2 | 295 | 1.8 | NM | 18.38 | 1.24 | 15 | 3.05 | 15 | 8.3 | −18 | 14 | Gelco |
| 4.7 | 5.1 | 5.2 | 5.8 | 2 | 5.2 | 4 | 34.50 | 2.20 | 16 | 2.96 | 13 | 17.5 | 7 | 19 | Genuine Parts |
| 1.6 | 1.2 | 4.1 | 3.2 | 1 | 2.5 | −10 | 28.00 | 2.22 | 13 | 6.07 | 34 | 6.3 | 6 | 8 | Gilbert |
| 5.8 | 6.4 | 6.7 | 7.0 | 5 | 6.5 | 11 | 66.50 | 4.76 | 14 | 1.86 | 31 | 15.3 | 5 | 14 | Grainger |
| 2.5 | 7.5 | 4.0 | 5.2 | −7 | 5.0 | 1 | 145.00 | 16.02 | 9 | 2.34 | 82 | 20.9 | 9 | 16 | Grey |
| 2.5 | 6.0 | 7.3 | 6.7 | NM | 5.6 | 75 | 28.50 | 2.56 | 11 | 4.21 | 24 | 11.0 | −7 | 9 | Greyhound |
| 5.2 | 6.0 | 5.0 | 5.6 | 12 | 5.4 | 22 | 52.25 | 2.83 | 18 | 1.76 | 12 | 22.6 | 7 | 8 | Handleman |
| 11.5 | 11.4 | 11.5 | 11.9 | 3 | 11.6 | 5 | 58.75 | 2.96 | 20 | 1.91 | 12 | 23.7 | 22 | 20 | Harland |
| 8.6 | 8.0 | 6.4 | 5.3 | −11 | 6.8 | 50 | 19.00 | 0.58 | 33 | 0.00 | 2 | 27.7 | NA | NA | HealthAmerica |
| 7.9 | 7.1 | 6.9 | 6.4 | 11 | 7.1 | 14 | 45.88 | 3.35 | 14 | 1.09 | 21 | 16.4 | 28 | 45 | Hosp. Corp. |
| 2.6 | 2.5 | 2.1 | 2.1 | −12 | 2.3 | 0 | 20.50 | 2.11 | 10 | 1.56 | 20 | 10.3 | 0 | 10 | Hughes Supply |
| 9.8 | 10.3 | 9.0 | 10.6 | 2 | 9.9 | 5 | 29.13 | 2.02 | 14 | 2.33 | 8 | 25.8 | 37 | 36 | Humana |
| 8.0 | 7.9 | 9.6 | 15.2 | 17 | 10.3 | 15 | 40.38 | 2.36 | 17 | 0.74 | 8 | 31.2 | 14 | 6 | I.M.S. |
| 1.4 | 1.9 | 0.8 | 0.3 | −88 | 0.3 | −85 | 17.88 | 0.27 | 66 | 6.71 | 14 | 2.0 | −29 | −8 | IU Intl. |
| 1.7 | 0.7 | 2.0 | 6.6 | −15 | 3.3 | 12 | 17.13 | 1.12 | 15 | 0.00 | 17 | 6.8 | 6 | 53 | Informatics |
| 3.2 | 2.6 | NM | NM | NM | NM | NM | 13.25 | −0.01 | NM | 0.91 | 12 | −0.1 | −2 | 31 | Intermark |
| 3.3 | 8.7 | 2.2 | 5.5 | 1 | 5.1 | 21 | 35.63 | 3.03 | 12 | 3.03 | 16 | 19.3 | 5 | 14 | Interpublic |
| 3.2 | 4.9 | 3.8 | 4.1 | −19 | 4.0 | 3 | 28.25 | 2.24 | 13 | 3.96 | 13 | 18.1 | −8 | 5 | JWT Group |
| NM | NM | NM | 0.6 | NM | NM | NM | 6.88 | −1.95 | NM | 0.00 | 5 | −36.0 | NA | −2 | Jacobs |
| 3.1 | 4.1 | 2.1 | 3.4 | −45 | 3.2 | 2 | 24.63 | 1.46 | 17 | 4.06 | 26 | 5.7 | −19 | 9 | Jorgensen |
| 1.0 | NM | 0.6 | NM | NM | NM | NM | 10.00 | −0.52 | NM | 0.00 | 8 | −6.4 | −20 | 16 | Josephson |
| 3.0 | 3.1 | 3.3 | 3.3 | 12 | 3.2 | 18 | 26.88 | 2.41 | 11 | 2.08 | 14 | 17.1 | 16 | 12 | Kaman |
| NM | NM | NM | 3.3 | 14 | 0.3 | 10 | 13.25 | 0.66 | 20 | 1.51 | 7 | 8.6 | −39 | 5 | Kay |
| 3.1 | 3.4 | 4.2 | 3.5 | −3 | 3.6 | 8 | 34.00 | 2.06 | 17 | 1.88 | 8 | 25.7 | 9 | 15 | Kelly |
| 0.3 | 0.1 | 0.1 | 0.2 | −60 | 0.2 | −58 | 15.38 | 0.44 | 35 | 0.00 | 7 | 6.2 | 32 | −9 | Ketchum |
| 3.2 | 3.5 | 4.1 | 4.5 | 20 | 3.9 | 11 | 9.88 | 1.64 | 6 | 0.00 | 11 | 15.5 | 25 | 52 | LD Brinkman |
| 2.7 | 2.6 | 2.0 | NM | NM | 1.7 | −46 | 23.00 | 1.43 | 16 | 3.04 | 24 | 5.8 | −7 | 10 | Little |
| 1.5 | NM | NM | 19.8 | 6 | 9.7 | 3 | 12.50 | 0.77 | 16 | 0.00 | 7 | 11.3 | 26 | 115 | Mgmt. Science |
| 5.7 | 6.3 | 6.8 | 6.9 | 6 | 6.5 | 4 | 24.00 | 1.00 | 24 | 0.67 | 5 | 21.3 | 43 | 60 | Manor Care |
| 4.4 | 4.9 | 3.8 | 2.4 | −42 | 3.9 | 33 | 22.88 | 3.05 | 8 | 0.00 | 14 | 22.3 | 36 | 22 | Marshall |
| 1.6 | 1.7 | 1.7 | 1.8 | 5 | 1.7 | 24 | 11.63 | 0.81 | 14 | 1.38 | 6 | 12.6 | −1 | 19 | Mass Merch. |
| 3.1 | 3.3 | 3.6 | 3.4 | 12 | 3.4 | 23 | 27.50 | 0.65 | 42 | 0.00 | 3 | 23.4 | NA | NA | Maxicare |
| 1.2 | 1.3 | 1.4 | 1.3 | −14 | 1.3 | −16 | 38.25 | 3.43 | 11 | 6.27 | 31 | 11.4 | −2 | 10 | McKesson |
| 5.6 | 8.7 | 6.9 | 4.3 | NM | 6.4 | 90 | 14.38 | 1.53 | 9 | 0.00 | 8 | 18.1 | NA | NA | McLean |
| 1.5 | 2.0 | 1.9 | 3.1 | 21 | 2.2 | 13 | 39.63 | 4.13 | 10 | 3.74 | 34 | 12.6 | 6 | 20 | M-K |
| 0.5 | 1.1 | 1.0 | 1.2 | −15 | 0.9 | −3 | 23.00 | 2.30 | 10 | 4.26 | 19 | 12.0 | 6 | 8 | Nash Finch |
| 4.8 | 6.0 | 4.9 | 5.1 | 5 | 4.9 | 5 | 28.13 | 1.91 | 15 | 1.85 | 12 | 16.2 | 29 | 46 | Natl. Medical |
| 1.4 | 2.1 | 1.9 | 1.8 | 9 | 1.8 | 15 | 23.25 | 2.49 | 9 | 2.41 | 30 | 8.3 | 9 | 4 | Noland |
| 3.3 | 5.8 | 4.5 | 8.9 | 8 | 5.9 | 18 | 41.75 | 2.76 | 15 | 2.59 | 13 | 22.5 | 9 | 12 | Ogilvy |

# Table A.1

## Corporate Scoreboard (cont.)

| | SALES | | | | | | | PROFITS | | | | | | |
|---|---|---|---|---|---|---|---|---|---|---|---|---|---|---|
| | Reported | | | | Change from 4Q 1983 | Restated | | Reported | | | | Change from 4Q 1983 | Restated | |
| | 1st quarter 1984 $ mil. | 2nd quarter 1984 $ mil. | 3rd quarter 1984 $ mil. | 4th quarter 1984 $ mil. | % | 12 months 1984 $ mil. | Change from 1983 % | 1st quarter 1984 $ mil. | 2nd quarter 1984 $ mil. | 3rd quarter 1984 $ mil. | 4th quarter 1984 $ mil. | % | 12 months 1984 $ mil. | Change from 1983 % |
| **SERVICE INDUSTRIES (cont.)** | | | | | | | | | | | | | | |
| Olsten | 46.5 | 52.3 | 59.2 | 60.7 | 44 | 218.8 | 52 | 1.2 | 1.4 | 1.6 | 1.7 | 43 | 6.0 | 62 |
| Overseas Shipholding | 76.9b | 73.9b | 67.3b | 71.6b | −7 | 289.7 | −5 | 12.1 | 11.8 | 11.1 | 5.4 | −48 | 40.5 | −14 |
| Owens & Minor | 70.3 | 74.3 | 78.4 | 83.7 | 29 | 306.7 | 20 | 0.8 | 0.9 | 0.9 | 1.0 | 29 | 3.6 | 21 |
| PHH Group (8) | 126.2 | 142.2 | 155.2 | 148.9 | 21 | 572.7 | 1 | 9.4 | 9.6 | 9.4 | 9.9 | 13 | 38.3 | 8 |
| Perini | 202.2 | 201.2 | 214.4 | 218.3 | 3 | 836.2 | −2 | 2.6 | 2.1 | 0.7 | −3.4 | NM | 2.0 | −79 |
| Pioneer Std. Electronics (9) | 62.0 | 59.2 | 59.5 | 57.4 | −9 | 238.1 | 10 | 1.7 | 1.0 | 0.9 | 0.6 | −56 | 4.1 | 43 |
| Planning Research (6) | 79.5b | 84.9b | 78.2b | 81.8b | 7 | 324.3 | 1 | 2.3 | 2.7 | 0.7 | 1.6 | −44 | 7.2 | −36 |
| Premier Industrial (7) | 91.7 | 107.0 | 105.6 | 108.3 | 19 | 412.6 | 21 | 9.0 | 11.6 | 9.6 | 10.0 | 8 | 40.2 | 17 |
| Price (4) | 225.6b | 282.6b | 308.3b | 542.5 | 65 | 1359.0 | 70 | 6.0 | 6.0 | 8.3 | 13.7 | 65 | 34.0 | 80 |
| Purolator Courier | 201.8 | 201.4 | 193.8 | 193.3 | 4 | 790.3 | 11 | 6.5 | 4.9 | 2.7 | 1.4 | NM | 15.5 | −23 |
| Republic Health | 75.0 | 88.7 | 91.7 | 126.5 | 34 | 481.5 | 48 | 3.9 | 4.0 | 4.2 | 3.8 | 107 | 20.1 | 398 |
| Rollins (6) | 60.6 | 76.0 | 67.3 | 63.8 | 6 | 267.8 | 9 | 3.0 | 7.2 | 3.4 | 2.5 | 9 | 16.1 | NM |
| Ryder System | 572.4 | 634.5 | 629.7 | 649.3 | 17 | 2485.9 | 22 | 19.4 | 34.6 | 33.3 | 30.3 | 9 | 117.6 | 19 |
| Rykoff-Sexton (8) | 157.7 | 210.0 | 213.5 | 215.5 | 115 | 796.9 | 116 | 1.3 | 2.0 | 2.6 | 3.1 | 67 | 8.9 | 66 |
| Saunders Systems | 63.6 | 66.0 | 66.7 | 68.7 | 10 | 265.0 | 10 | 0.9 | 1.6 | 1.7 | 1.5 | −5 | 5.7 | 35 |
| Seligman & Latz (2) | 109.4 | 74.2 | 77.9 | 80.6 | 1 | 342.1 | 6 | 4.2 | −2.1 | −0.5 | −3.8 | NM | −2.2 | NM |
| ServiceMaster Industries | 202.7 | 207.3 | 215.6 | 224.2 | 17 | 849.7 | 21 | 6.1 | 7.8 | 7.4 | 9.2 | 20 | 30.5 | 19 |
| Shared Medical Systems | 59.8b | 62.8b | 65.7b | 68.4b | 20 | 256.8 | 22 | 7.5 | 8.2 | 8.7 | 9.3 | 25 | 33.8 | 24 |
| Southeastern Pub. Serv. (10) | 114.8 | 124.7 | 123.4 | 129.9 | −5 | 492.9 | 81 | −2.4 | 5.8 | 1.4 | −0.5 | NM | 4.2 | −64 |
| Spectro Industries (9) | 127.6 | 100.4 | 101.6 | 109.6 | 16 | 439.3 | 17 | 2.8 | 1.8 | 2.7 | 2.1 | 24 | 9.4 | 49 |
| Std. Comm. Tobacco (9) | 124.7 | 74.2 | 99.0 | 154.9 | 17 | 452.8 | 4 | 3.0 | 1.7 | 3.2 | 2.3 | 3 | 10.2 | 21 |
| Stone & Webster | 86.0b | 90.3b | 81.7b | 85.0b | 2 | 343.0 | 0 | 9.5 | 11.7 | 8.3 | 6.5 | 14 | 36.0 | 22 |
| Subaru of America (2) | 299.7 | 264.7 | 331.1 | 279.4 | 20 | 1174.9 | 11 | 14.4 | 14.9 | 16.7 | 14.0 | 26 | 60.0 | 21 |
| Summit Health (6) | 72.8b | 74.6b | 80.0b | 83.5b | 33 | 310.9 | 28 | 4.0 | 3.7 | 4.3 | 4.4 | 40 | 16.4 | 49 |
| Super Food Services (4) | 294.0b | 299.2b | 401.4b | 321.7b | 9 | 1316.3 | 6 | 1.5 | 1.5 | 2.6 | 1.9 | 15 | 7.5 | 28 |
| Super Rite Foods (10) | 83.9 | 79.2 | 78.1 | 79.7 | 11 | 321.0 | 21 | 1.2 | 1.1 | 1.1 | 1.4 | 28 | 4.8 | 37 |
| Super Valu Stores (10) | 1459.1 | 1895.0 | 1482.1 | 1576.5 | 14 | 6412.6 | 14 | 20.8 | 24.2 | 17.4 | 20.4 | 24 | 82.7 | 15 |
| SYSCO (6) | 588.0b | 622.5b | 636.3b | 658.6b | 15 | 2505.4 | 18 | 10.8 | 12.4 | 12.3 | 12.8 | 10 | 48.3 | 15 |
| TBC | 83.6 | 101.8 | 112.1 | 96.4 | 18 | 393.9 | 15 | 0.9 | 1.5 | 2.0 | 1.5 | 45 | 6.0 | 53 |
| Tiger International | 318.1 | 338.7 | 356.5 | 326.6 | 6 | 1209.9 | 14 | −7.0 | 0.7 | 14.7 | 28.4 | 509 | 44.2 | NM |
| U.S. Health Care Systems | 39.8b | 47.7b | 54.9b | 63.2b | 111 | 205.7 | 115 | 1.4 | 2.3 | 3.1 | 4.0 | 239 | 10.8 | 238 |
| United Stationers (4) | 113.3 | 115.0 | 105.5 | 145.0 | 39 | 478.7 | 43 | 3.6 | 3.6 | 3.7 | 3.8 | 30 | 14.7 | 49 |
| Univar (10) | 221.1 | 235.4 | 245.6 | 240.7 | 7 | 942.8 | 11 | 2.7 | 1.1 | 9.0 | 2.8 | 72 | 15.7 | 143 |
| Universal Health Services (6) | 84.9 | 88.8 | 86.1 | 112.5 | 48 | 372.3 | 35 | 4.0 | 3.6 | 3.6 | 3.8 | 84 | 14.9 | 52 |
| Universal Leaf Tobacco (6) | 209.0b | 256.0b | 139.0b | 515.5b | 18 | 1119.6 | 18 | 8.8 | 7.1 | 11.3 | 17.7 | 3 | 44.9 | 11 |
| Volt Inf. Sciences (2) | 86.8b | 99.0b | 107.8b | 120.2b | 32 | 413.8 | 24 | 2.5 | 3.2 | 3.7 | 3.5 | −37 | 13.0 | −22 |
| Waste Management | 277.0 | 308.8 | 341.0 | 387.9 | 41 | 1314.8 | 26 | 31.3 | 33.0 | 39.1 | 39.2 | 35 | 142.5 | 18 |
| Wetterau (9) | 671.3 | 717.6 | 782.5 | 808.1 | 16 | 2979.5 | 14 | 5.2 | 5.7 | 6.1 | 8.3 | 15 | 25.3 | 20 |
| Williams* | 1092.9 | 813.7 | 617.2 | 864.9 | −4 | 3388.7 | 97 | 82.8 | 44.8 | 1.4 | 15.5 | −53 | 144.5 | 194 |
| Wyle Laboratories (11) | 84.7 | 93.1 | 94.6 | 91.2 | 14 | 363.5 | 39 | 2.6 | 3.2 | 3.6 | 2.0 | −21 | 11.3 | 174 |
| **INDUSTRY COMPOSITE** | 29606.3 | 31081.9 | 31018.7 | 32845.5 | 14 | 124673.1 | 16 | 924.8 | 1126.7 | 1033.8 | 1058.7 | 14 | 4148.9 | 23 |
| **TOBACCO** | | | | | | | | | | | | | | |
| American Brands | 1836.5a | 1677.8a | 1837.3a | 1643.7a | −8 | 6995.2 | −1 | 106.7 | 95.0 | 106.1 | 106.2 | 2 | 414.1 | 6 |
| Culbro | 255.5c | 290.2c | 273.3c | 274.8c | 9 | 1093.8 | 49 | 2.0 | 6.6 | 2.6 | 2.6 | 34 | 13.7 | 67 |
| Philip Morris | 3249.3a | 3608.6a | 3666.4a | 3289.4a | 6 | 13813.7 | 6 | 205.1 | 257.3 | 321.6 | 104.5 | −51 | 888.5 | −2 |
| Reynolds (R.J.) Industries | 3170.0a | 3705.0a | 3224.0a | 3532.0a | 7 | 12974.0 | 5 | 165.0 | 241.0 | 229.0 | 259.0 | 30 | 843.0 | 20 |
| U.S. Tobacco | 101.0a | 112.6a | 115.4a | 114.8a | 12 | 443.8 | 16 | 18.6 | 21.1 | 22.1 | 22.0 | 16 | 83.7 | 19 |
| **INDUSTRY COMPOSITE** | 8612.3 | 9394.1 | 9116.4 | 8854.6 | 4 | 35320.5 | 5 | 497.4 | 621.0 | 681.4 | 494.3 | −8 | 2243.0 | 8 |

Most quarterly data as originally reported; annual data as restated. *Some quarterly sales and profits data as restated. (1) Fourth quarter ending Nov. 30. (2) Fourth quarter ending Oct. 31. (3) First quarter and most recent 12 months ending Dec. 31. (4) First quarter and most recent 12 months ending Nov. 30. (5) First quarter and most recent 12 months ending Oct. 31. (6) Second quarter and most recent 12 months ending Dec. 31. (7) Second quarter and most recent 12 months ending Nov. 30. (8) Second quarter and most recent 12 months ending Oct. 31. (9) Third quarter and most recent 12 months ending Dec.

| | | MARGINS | | | | | | | PERFORMANCE | | | | | | | |
|---|---|---|---|---|---|---|---|---|---|---|---|---|---|---|---|
| | | | | Change | | Change | | 12 | | | | Return | 5-year growth rate | | |
| 1st | 2nd | 3rd | 4th | from | 12 | from | | months | Price- | | Book | on | | | |
| quarter | quarter | quarter | quarter | 4Q | months | 1983 | Share | earnings | earnings | | value | common | in | in | |
| 1984 | 1984 | 1984 | 1984 | 1983 | 1984 | % | price | $ per | ratio | Yield | $ per | equity | earnings | common | |
| % | % | % | $ mil. | % | % | | 2-28 | share | 2-28 | % | share | 1984 % | per share | equity | |
| 2.6 | 2.7 | 2.8 | 2.8 | −1 | 2.7 | 6 | 25.50 | 1.67 | 15 | 0.94 | 10 | 17.3 | 12 | 23 | Olsten |
| 15.8 | 16.0 | 16.5 | 7.5 | −44 | 14.0 | −10 | 17.88 | 1.57 | 11 | 2.80 | 24 | 6.6 | −12 | 15 | Overseas |
| 1.1 | 1.3 | 1.1 | 1.2 | 0 | 1.2 | 1 | 15.00 | 1.43 | 10 | 2.40 | 12 | 11.6 | 14 | 14 | Owens & Minor |
| 7.5 | 6.7 | 6.1 | 6.6 | −7 | 6.7 | 6 | 30.00 | 2.41 | 12 | 2.93 | 14 | 17.0 | 18 | 29 | PHH Group |
| 1.3 | 1.1 | 0.3 | NM | NM | 0.2 | −78 | 27.13 | 0.60 | 45 | 2.95 | 32 | 1.8 | −12 | 7 | Perini |
| 2.7 | 1.6 | 1.5 | 1.0 | −52 | 1.7 | 30 | 8.75 | 0.77 | 11 | 1.37 | 6 | 13.4 | −7 | 12 | Pioneer |
| 2.9 | 3.1 | 0.8 | 2.0 | −47 | 2.2 | −37 | 13.88 | 1.07 | 13 | 1.44 | 10 | 11.5 | 17 | 11 | Plan. Research |
| 9.8 | 10.9 | 9.1 | 9.3 | −10 | 9.7 | −3 | 25.00 | 1.35 | 19 | 1.44 | 7 | 20.7 | 9 | 15 | Premier |
| 2.7 | 2.1 | 2.7 | 2.5 | 0 | 2.5 | 6 | 57.00 | 1.52 | 38 | 0.00 | 5 | 33.5 | 70 | 115 | Price |
| 3.2 | 2.4 | 1.4 | 0.7 | NM | 2.0 | −31 | 27.50 | 2.05 | 13 | 4.65 | 28 | 7.2 | 0 | 13 | Purolator |
| 5.2 | 4.6 | 4.6 | 3.0 | 54 | 4.2 | 236 | 14.63 | 1.04 | 14 | 0.00 | 13 | 12.7 | NA | NA | Rep. Health |
| 4.9 | 9.5 | 5.0 | 3.9 | 2 | 6.0 | NM | 11.50 | 0.65 | 18 | 4.00 | 1 | 46.3 | −21 | −20 | Rollins |
| 3.4 | 5.5 | 5.3 | 4.7 | −7 | 4.7 | −3 | 55.75 | 4.95 | 11 | 1.94 | 31 | 16.0 | 9 | 21 | Ryder System |
| 0.8 | 0.9 | 1.2 | 1.4 | −22 | 1.1 | −23 | 21.88 | 1.65 | 13 | 2.29 | 12 | 10.9 | 11 | 11 | Rykoff-Sexton |
| 1.5 | 2.4 | 2.6 | 2.2 | −14 | 2.2 | 23 | 6.25 | 0.85 | 7 | 3.20 | 7 | 11.9 | −6 | 7 | Saunders |
| 3.8 | NM | NM | NM | NM | NM | NM | 15.75 | −1.01 | NM | 0.00 | 17 | −5.9 | NA | 0 | Seligman |
| 3.0 | 3.8 | 3.4 | 4.1 | 3 | 3.6 | −2 | 36.38 | 1.40 | 26 | 3.08 | 3 | 47.4 | 22 | 15 | ServiceMaster |
| 12.6 | 13.0 | 13.2 | 13.6 | 4 | 13.1 | 2 | 33.13 | 1.37 | 24 | 1.45 | 5 | 28.5 | 25 | 25 | Shared Med. |
| NM | 4.6 | 1.1 | NM | NM | 0.9 | −80 | 8.00 | 0.39 | 21 | 0.00 | 9 | 4.4 | 2 | 20 | Southeast PS |
| 2.2 | 1.8 | 2.6 | 1.9 | 7 | 2.1 | 27 | 16.63 | 1.15 | 15 | 0.42 | 5 | 23.6 | 28 | 18 | Spectro |
| 2.4 | 2.2 | 3.3 | 1.5 | −12 | 2.3 | 16 | 20.00 | 3.55 | 6 | 2.50 | 25 | 13.9 | 9 | 17 | Std. Tobacco |
| 11.0 | 13.0 | 10.2 | 7.6 | 13 | 10.5 | 22 | 44.63 | 5.02 | 9 | 3.59 | 37 | 13.7 | 8 | 8 | S&W |
| 4.8 | 5.6 | 5.0 | 5.0 | 5 | 5.1 | 9 | 135.50 | 9.84 | 14 | 1.24 | 33 | 30.1 | 41 | 51 | Subaru |
| 5.5 | 5.0 | 5.4 | 5.3 | 6 | 5.3 | 17 | 10.63 | 0.53 | 20 | 6.59 | 2 | 23.7 | NA | NA | Summit Health |
| 0.5 | 0.5 | 0.7 | 0.6 | 6 | 0.6 | 20 | 27.38 | 2.17 | 13 | 1.61 | 16 | 13.9 | 21 | 17 | Super Food |
| 1.4 | 1.3 | 1.4 | 1.8 | 15 | 1.5 | 14 | 18.75 | 0.96 | 20 | 0.85 | 5 | 18.6 | NA | NA | Super Rite |
| 1.4 | 1.3 | 1.2 | 1.3 | 8 | 1.3 | 1 | 33.00 | 2.23 | 15 | 2.06 | 12 | 18.2 | 15 | 20 | Super Valu |
| 1.8 | 2.0 | 1.9 | 2.0 | −4 | 1.9 | −2 | 35.13 | 2.27 | 15 | 1.14 | 14 | 15.9 | 19 | 23 | SYSCO |
| 1.1 | 1.5 | 1.8 | 1.5 | 22 | 1.5 | 33 | 13.25 | 1.12 | 12 | 0.00 | 7 | 15.1 | NA | NA | TBC |
| NM | 0.2 | 4.1 | 8.7 | 477 | 3.7 | NM | 8.75 | 1.32 | 7 | 0.00 | 5 | 46.2 | NA | −19 | Tiger |
| 3.5 | 4.9 | 5.7 | 6.3 | 61 | 5.3 | 57 | 29.25 | 0.51 | 57 | 0.00 | 2 | 21.4 | NA | NA | U.S. Health |
| 3.2 | 3.2 | 3.5 | 2.6 | −6 | 3.1 | 4 | 24.25 | 1.07 | 23 | 0.82 | 5 | 20.8 | 28 | 48 | United |
| 1.2 | 0.5 | 3.7 | 1.2 | 61 | 1.7 | 119 | 18.25 | 2.83 | 6 | 3.73 | 17 | 16.9 | −8 | 6 | Univar |
| 4.7 | 4.0 | 4.2 | 3.3 | 24 | 4.0 | 12 | 14.50 | 1.05 | 14 | 0.00 | 8 | 13.4 | 29 | 131 | Univ. Health |
| 4.2 | 2.8 | 8.1 | 3.4 | −32 | 4.0 | −6 | 21.50 | 2.59 | 8 | 4.28 | 14 | 18.6 | 10 | 10 | Univ. Leaf |
| 2.9 | 3.3 | 3.4 | 2.9 | −52 | 3.1 | −37 | 21.50 | 1.70 | 13 | 0.00 | 16 | 11.3 | 6 | 34 | Volt |
| 11.3 | 10.7 | 11.5 | 10.1 | −4 | 10.8 | −6 | 51.00 | 2.93 | 17 | 1.57 | 18 | 16.7 | 22 | 40 | Waste Mgmt. |
| 0.8 | 0.8 | 0.8 | 1.0 | −1 | 0.9 | 5 | 26.50 | 2.39 | 11 | 3.32 | 15 | 15.5 | −3 | 14 | Wetterau |
| 7.6 | 5.5 | 0.2 | 1.8 | −51 | 4.3 | 49 | 27.88 | 4.21 | 7 | 5.02 | 37 | 11.3 | −5 | 11 | Williams |
| 3.1 | 3.4 | 3.8 | 2.2 | −31 | 3.1 | 97 | 14.00 | 1.49 | 9 | 2.29 | 11 | 13.9 | −4 | 11 | Wyle Labs. |
| 3.1 | 3.6 | 3.3 | 3.2 | 1 | 3.3 | 7 | 29.01 | 1.93 | 15 | 2.10 | 14 | 13.9 | 3 | 18 | |
| 5.8 | 5.7 | 5.8 | 6.5 | 11 | 5.9 | 8 | 68.13 | 7.20 | 9 | 5.72 | 38 | 19.0 | 2 | 9 | Am. Brands |
| 0.8 | 2.3 | 0.9 | 0.9 | 22 | 1.3 | 12 | 24.75 | 3.22 | 8 | 2.42 | 33 | 9.9 | 36 | 12 | Culbro |
| 6.3 | 7.1 | 8.8 | 3.2 | −54 | 6.4 | −8 | 90.63 | 7.24 | 13 | 3.75 | 34 | 21.0 | 13 | 14 | Philip Morris |
| 5.2 | 6.5 | 7.1 | 7.3 | 21 | 6.5 | 14 | 82.88 | 7.00 | 12 | 4.10 | 42 | 16.4 | 5 | 15 | Reynolds |
| 18.4 | 18.7 | 19.1 | 19.2 | 4 | 18.9 | 2 | 38.13 | 2.86 | 13 | 4.51 | 10 | 29.7 | 19 | 16 | U.S. Tobacco |
| 5.8 | 6.6 | 7.5 | 5.6 | −11 | 6.4 | 3 | 78.66 | 6.70 | 11 | 4.28 | 36 | 18.8 | 9 | 14 | |

31. (10) Third quarter and most recent 12 months ending Nov. 30. (11) Third quarter and most recent 12 months ending Oct. 31. (a) Includes excise taxes. (b) Includes other income. (c) Includes excise taxes and other income. †Revenues from some major subsidiaries not included in sales. Earnings per share are for latest 12 months, not necessarily for end of most recent fiscal year. They include all common stock equivalents but exclude extraordinary items. NA = not available. NM = not meaningful. SF = semiannual figure. Data: Standard & Poor's Compustat Services Inc.

**Table A.2**                        **Time Series Data**

Series on Prices, Productivity, Unemployment, and Business Transitions

| Year or Month | Consumer Price Index | Industrial Production Index | Unemployment Rates | | | Business Failures (number) | New Business Incorporations |
|---|---|---|---|---|---|---|---|
| | | | Total | Male | Female | | |
| 1948 | 72.1 | 41.1 | 3.8 | 3.6 | 4.1 | 5,250 | 96,346 |
| 1949 | 71.4 | 38.8 | 5.9 | 5.9 | 6.0 | 9,246 | 85,640 |
| 1950 | 72.1 | 44.9 | 5.3 | 5.1 | 5.7 | 9,162 | 93,092 |
| 1951 | 77.8 | 48.7 | 3.3 | 2.8 | 4.4 | 8,058 | 83,778 |
| 1952 | 79.5 | 50.6 | 3.0 | 2.8 | 3.6 | 7,611 | 92,945 |
| 1953 | 80.1 | 54.8 | 2.9 | 2.8 | 3.3 | 8,862 | 102,705 |
| 1954 | 80.5 | 51.9 | 5.5 | 5.3 | 6.0 | 11,086 | 117,411 |
| 1955 | 80.2 | 58.5 | 4.4 | 4.2 | 4.9 | 10,969 | 139,915 |
| 1956 | 81.4 | 61.1 | 4.1 | 3.8 | 4.8 | 12,686 | 141,163 |
| 1957 | 84.3 | 61.9 | 4.3 | 4.1 | 4.7 | 13,739 | 137,112 |
| 1958 | 86.6 | 57.9 | 6.8 | 6.8 | 6.8 | 14,964 | 150,781 |
| 1959 | 87.3 | 64.8 | 5.5 | 5.2 | 5.9 | 14,053 | 193,067 |
| 1960 | 88.7 | 66.2 | 5.5 | 5.4 | 5.9 | 15,445 | 182,713 |
| 1961 | 89.6 | 66.7 | 6.7 | 6.4 | 7.2 | 17,076 | 181,535 |
| 1962 | 90.6 | 72.2 | 5.5 | 5.2 | 6.2 | 15,782 | 182,057 |
| 1963 | 91.7 | 76.5 | 5.7 | 5.2 | 6.5 | 14,374 | 186,404 |
| 1964 | 92.9 | 81.7 | 5.2 | 4.6 | 6.2 | 13,501 | 197,724 |
| 1965 | 94.5 | 89.8 | 4.5 | 4.0 | 5.5 | 13,514 | 203,697 |
| 1966 | 97.2 | 97.8 | 3.8 | 3.2 | 4.8 | 13,061 | 200,010 |
| 1967 | 100.0 | 100.0 | 3.8 | 3.1 | 5.2 | 12,364 | 206,569 |
| 1968 | 104.2 | 106.3 | 3.6 | 2.9 | 4.8 | 9,636 | 233,635 |
| 1969 | 109.8 | 111.1 | 3.5 | 2.8 | 4.7 | 9,154 | 274,267 |
| 1970 | 116.3 | 107.8 | 4.9 | 4.4 | 5.9 | 10,748 | 264,209 |
| 1971 | 121.3 | 109.6 | 5.9 | 5.3 | 6.9 | 10,326 | 287,577 |
| 1972 | 125.3 | 119.7 | 5.6 | 5.0 | 6.6 | 9,566 | 316,601 |
| 1973 | 133.1 | 129.8 | 4.9 | 4.2 | 6.0 | 9,345 | 329,358 |
| 1974 | 147.7 | 129.3 | 5.6 | 4.9 | 6.7 | 9,915 | 319,149 |
| 1975 | 161.2 | 117.8 | 8.5 | 7.9 | 9.3 | 11,432 | 326,345 |
| 1976 | 170.5 | 130.5 | 7.7 | 7.1 | 8.6 | 9,628 | 375,766 |
| 1977 | 181.5 | 138.2 | 7.1 | 6.3 | 8.2 | 7,919 | 436,170 |
| 1978 | 195.4 | 146.1 | 6.1 | 5.3 | 7.2 | 6,619 | 478,019 |
| 1979 | 217.4 | 152.5 | 5.8 | 5.1 | 6.8 | 7,564 | 524,565 |

*Source:* Department of Commerce, Bureau of Economic Analysis

**Table A.2**                    **Time Series Data (Cont.)**

Series on Prices, Productivity, Unemployment, and Business Transitions

| Year or Month | Consumer Price Index | Industrial Production Index | Unemployment Rates | | | Business Failures (number) | New Business Incor- porations |
|---|---|---|---|---|---|---|---|
| | | | Total | Male | Female | | |
| 1980 | 246.8 | 147.0 | 7.1 | 6.9 | 7.4 | 11,742 | 533,520 |
| 1981 | 272.4 | 151.0 | 7.6 | 7.4 | 7.9 | 16,794 | 581,242 |
| 1982 | 289.1 | 138.6 | 9.7 | 9.9 | 9.4 | 24,908 | 566,942 |
| 1983 | 298.4 | 147.6 | 9.6 | 9.9 | 9.2 | 31,334 | 600,400 |
| 1984 | 311.1 | 163.5 | 7.5 | 7.4 | 7.6 | — | |
| 1983: | | | | | | | |
| Jan | 293.1 | 137.4 | 10.4 | 10.6 | 10.1 | 2,455 | 49,999 |
| Feb | 293.2 | 138.1 | 10.4 | 10.8 | 9.9 | 2,397 | 48,296 |
| Mar | 293.4 | 140.0 | 10.3 | 10.7 | 9.8 | 2,881 | 48,032 |
| Apr | 295.5 | 142.6 | 10.2 | 10.7 | 9.6 | 2,471 | 48,903 |
| May | 297.1 | 144.4 | 10.2 | 10.6 | 9.5 | 2,292 | 50,211 |
| June | 298.1 | 146.4 | 10.1 | 10.2 | 9.9 | 2,611 | 50,992 |
| July | 299.3 | 149.7 | 9.4 | 9.8 | 8.9 | 2,313 | 48,601 |
| Aug | 300.3 | 151.8 | 9.4 | 9.8 | 9.0 | 3,218 | 52,828 |
| Sept | 301.8 | 153.8 | 9.2 | 9.5 | 8.8 | 2,384 | 50,445 |
| Oct | 302.6 | 155.0 | 8.8 | 9.1 | 8.5 | 2,511 | 50,441 |
| Nov | 303.1 | 155.3 | 8.4 | 8.6 | 8.2 | 3,287 | 51,642 |
| Dec | 303.5 | 156.2 | 8.2 | 8.3 | 8.1 | 2,484 | 51,557 |
| 1984: | | | | | | | |
| Jan | 305.2 | 158.5 | 8.0 | 8.1 | 8.0 | | 53,044 |
| Feb | 306.6 | 160.0 | 7.8 | 7.8 | 7.9 | | 53,591 |
| Mar | 307.3 | 160.8 | 7.8 | 7.7 | 7.9 | | 53,424 |
| Apr | 308.8 | 162.1 | 7.8 | 7.7 | 7.8 | | 53,933 |
| May | 309.7 | 162.8 | 7.5 | 7.4 | 7.7 | | 51,166 |
| June | 310.7 | 164.4 | 7.2 | 7.2 | 7.3 | | 54,729 |
| July | 311.7 | 165.9 | 7.5 | 7.4 | 7.5 | | 52,992 |
| Aug | 313.0 | 166.0 | 7.5 | 7.2 | 7.8 | | 51,723 |
| Sept | 314.5 | 165.0 | 7.4 | 7.2 | 7.5 | | 51,892 |
| Oct | 315.3 | 164.5 | 7.3 | 7.1 | 7.7 | | |
| Nov | 315.3 | 165.2 | 7.1 | 7.0 | 7.3 | | |
| Dec | 315.5 | 166.2 | 7.2 | 7.1 | 7.2 | | |

**Table A.2**             Time Series Data (cont.)

Bond Yields and Interest Rates, 1929–84 (Percent per annum)

| Year and Month | U.S. Treasury Securities — Bills (New Issues)[1] 3-Month | U.S. Treasury Securities — Bills (New Issues)[1] 6-Month | Constant Maturities[a] 3 Years | Constant Maturities[a] 10 Years | Corporate Bonds (Moody's) Aaa[3] | Corporate Bonds (Moody's) Baa | High-Grade Municipal Bonds (Standard & Poor's) | New-Home Mortgage Yields (FHLBB)[4] | Commercial Paper, 6 Months[5] | Prime Rate Charged by Banks[6] High-Low | Discount Rate, Federal Reserve Bank of New York[8] High-Low | Federal Funds Rate[7] |
|---|---|---|---|---|---|---|---|---|---|---|---|---|
| **1980:** | | | | | | | | | | | | |
| Jan | 12.036 | 11.851 | 10.88 | 10.80 | 11.09 | 12.42 | 7.21 | 11.87 | 12.66 | 15.25-15.25 | 12.00-12.00 | 13.82 |
| Feb | 12.814 | 12.721 | 12.84 | 12.41 | 12.38 | 13.57 | 8.04 | 11.93 | 13.60 | 16.75-15.25 | 13.00-12.00 | 14.13 |
| Mar | 15.526 | 15.100 | 14.05 | 12.75 | 12.96 | 14.45 | 9.09 | 12.62 | 16.50 | 19.50-16.75 | 13.00-13.00 | 17.19 |
| Apr | 14.003 | 13.618 | 12.02 | 11.47 | 12.04 | 14.19 | 8.40 | 13.03 | 14.93 | 20.00-19.50 | 13.00-13.00 | 17.61 |
| May | 9.150 | 9.149 | 9.44 | 10.18 | 10.99 | 13.17 | 7.37 | 13.68 | 9.29 | 19.00-14.00 | 13.00-12.00 | 10.98 |
| June | 6.995 | 7.218 | 8.91 | 9.78 | 10.58 | 12.71 | 7.60 | 12.66 | 8.03 | 14.00-12.00 | 12.00-11.00 | 9.47 |
| July | 8.126 | 8.101 | 9.27 | 10.25 | 11.07 | 12.65 | 8.08 | 12.48 | 8.29 | 12.00-11.00 | 11.00-10.00 | 9.03 |
| Aug | 9.259 | 9.443 | 10.63 | 11.10 | 11.64 | 13.15 | 8.62 | 12.25 | 9.61 | 11.50-11.00 | 10.00-10.00 | 9.61 |
| Sept | 10.321 | 10.546 | 11.57 | 11.51 | 12.02 | 13.70 | 8.95 | 12.35 | 11.04 | 13.00-11.50 | 11.00-10.00 | 10.87 |
| Oct | 11.580 | 11.566 | 12.01 | 11.75 | 12.31 | 14.23 | 9.11 | 12.61 | 12.32 | 14.50-13.50 | 11.00-11.00 | 12.81 |
| Nov | 13.888 | 13.612 | 13.31 | 12.68 | 12.97 | 14.64 | 9.55 | 13.04 | 14.73 | 17.75-14.50 | 12.00-11.00 | 15.85 |
| Dec | 15.661 | 14.770 | 13.65 | 12.84 | 13.21 | 15.14 | 10.09 | 13.28 | 16.49 | 21.50-17.75 | 13.00-12.00 | 18.90 |
| **1981:** | | | | | | | | | | | | |
| Jan | 14.724 | 13.883 | 13.01 | 12.57 | 12.81 | 15.03 | 9.65 | 13.27 | 15.10 | 21.50-20.00 | 13.00-13.00 | 19.08 |
| Feb | 14.905 | 14.134 | 13.65 | 13.19 | 13.35 | 15.37 | 10.03 | 13.54 | 14.87 | 20.00-19.00 | 13.00-13.00 | 15.93 |
| Mar | 13.478 | 12.983 | 13.51 | 13.12 | 13.33 | 15.34 | 10.12 | 14.02 | 13.59 | 19.00-17.50 | 13.00-13.00 | 14.70 |
| Apr | 13.635 | 13.434 | 14.09 | 13.68 | 13.88 | 15.56 | 10.55 | 14.15 | 14.17 | 18.00-17.00 | 13.00-13.00 | 15.72 |
| May | 16.295 | 15.334 | 15.08 | 14.10 | 14.32 | 15.95 | 10.73 | 14.10 | 16.66 | 20.50-18.00 | 14.00-13.00 | 18.52 |
| June | 14.557 | 13.947 | 14.29 | 13.47 | 13.75 | 15.80 | 10.56 | 14.67 | 15.22 | 20.50-20.00 | 14.00-14.00 | 19.10 |
| July | 14.699 | 14.402 | 15.15 | 14.28 | 14.38 | 16.17 | 11.03 | 14.72 | 16.09 | 20.50-20.00 | 14.00-14.00 | 19.04 |
| Aug | 15.612 | 15.548 | 16.00 | 14.94 | 14.89 | 16.34 | 12.13 | 15.27 | 16.62 | 20.50-20.50 | 14.00-14.00 | 17.82 |
| Sept | 14.951 | 15.057 | 16.22 | 15.32 | 15.49 | 16.92 | 12.86 | 15.29 | 15.93 | 20.50-19.50 | 14.00-14.00 | 15.87 |
| Oct | 13.873 | 14.013 | 15.50 | 15.15 | 15.40 | 17.11 | 12.67 | 15.65 | 14.72 | 19.50-18.00 | 14.00-14.00 | 15.08 |
| Nov | 11.269 | 11.530 | 13.11 | 13.39 | 14.22 | 16.39 | 11.71 | 16.38 | 11.96 | 18.00-16.00 | 14.00-13.00 | 13.31 |
| Dec | 10.926 | 11.471 | 13.66 | 13.72 | 14.23 | 16.55 | 12.77 | 15.87 | 12.14 | 15.75-15.75 | 13.00-12.00 | 12.37 |
| **1982:** | | | | | | | | | | | | |
| Jan | 12.412 | 12.930 | 14.64 | 14.59 | 15.18 | 17.10 | 13.16 | 15.25 | 13.35 | 15.75-15.75 | 12.00-12.00 | 13.22 |
| Feb | 13.780 | 13.709 | 14.73 | 14.43 | 15.27 | 17.18 | 12.81 | 15.12 | 14.27 | 17.00-15.75 | 12.00-12.00 | 14.78 |
| Mar | 12.493 | 12.621 | 13.86 | 13.86 | 14.58 | 16.82 | 12.72 | 15.67 | 13.47 | 16.50-16.50 | 12.00-12.00 | 14.68 |
| Apr | 12.821 | 12.861 | 14.18 | 13.87 | 14.46 | 16.78 | 12.45 | 15.84 | 13.64 | 16.50-16.50 | 12.00-12.00 | 14.94 |
| May | 12.148 | 12.220 | 13.77 | 13.62 | 14.26 | 16.64 | 11.99 | 15.89 | 13.02 | 16.50-16.50 | 12.00-12.00 | 14.45 |
| June | 12.108 | 12.310 | 14.48 | 14.30 | 14.81 | 16.92 | 12.42 | 15.40 | 13.79 | 16.50-16.50 | 12.00-12.00 | 14.15 |
| July | 11.914 | 12.236 | 14.00 | 13.95 | 14.61 | 16.80 | 12.11 | 15.70 | 13.00 | 16.50-15.50 | 12.00-11.50 | 12.59 |
| Aug | 9.006 | 10.105 | 12.62 | 13.06 | 13.71 | 16.32 | 11.12 | 15.68 | 10.80 | 15.50-13.50 | 11.50-10.00 | 10.12 |
| Sept | 8.196 | 9.539 | 12.03 | 12.34 | 12.94 | 15.63 | 10.61 | 14.98 | 10.86 | 13.50-13.50 | 10.00-10.00 | 10.31 |
| Oct | 7.750 | 8.299 | 10.62 | 10.91 | 12.12 | 14.73 | 9.59 | 14.41 | 9.21 | 13.50-12.00 | 10.00-9.50 | 9.71 |
| Nov | 8.042 | 8.319 | 9.98 | 10.55 | 11.68 | 14.30 | 9.97 | 13.81 | 8.72 | 12.00-11.50 | 9.50-9.00 | 9.20 |
| Dec | 8.013 | 8.225 | 9.88 | 10.54 | 11.83 | 14.14 | 9.91 | 13.69 | 8.50 | 11.50-11.50 | 9.00-8.50 | 8.95 |

# Table A.2

## Time Series Data (cont.)
### Bond Yields and Interest Rates, 1929–84 (Percent per annum)

| Year and Month | U.S. Treasury Securities — Bills (New Issues)[1] 3-Month | 6-Month | Constant Maturities[a] 3 Years | 10 Years | Corporate Bonds (Moody's) Aaa[3] | Baa | High-Grade Municipal Bonds (Standard & Poor's) | New-Home Mortgage Yields (FHLBB)[4] | Commercial Paper, 6 Months[5] | Prime Rate Charged by Banks[6] High-Low | Discount Rate, Federal Reserve Bank of New York[8] High-Low | Federal Funds Rate[7] |
|---|---|---|---|---|---|---|---|---|---|---|---|---|
| **1983:** | | | | | | | | | | | | |
| Jan | 7.810 | 7.898 | 9.64 | 10.46 | 11.79 | 13.94 | 9.45 | 13.49 | 8.15 | 11.50-11.00 | 8.50-8.50 | 8.68 |
| Feb | 8.130 | 8.233 | 9.91 | 10.72 | 12.01 | 13.95 | 9.48 | 13.16 | 8.39 | 11.00-10.50 | 8.50-8.50 | 8.51 |
| Mar | 8.304 | 8.325 | 9.84 | 10.51 | 11.73 | 13.61 | 9.16 | 13.41 | 8.48 | 10.50-10.50 | 8.50-8.50 | 8.77 |
| Apr | 8.252 | 8.343 | 9.76 | 10.40 | 11.51 | 13.29 | 8.96 | 12.42 | 8.48 | 10.50-10.50 | 8.50-8.50 | 8.80 |
| May | 8.19 | 8.20 | 9.66 | 10.38 | 11.46 | 13.09 | 9.03 | 12.67 | 8.31 | 10.50-10.50 | 8.50-8.50 | 8.63 |
| June | 8.82 | 8.89 | 10.32 | 10.85 | 11.74 | 13.37 | 9.51 | 12.36 | 9.03 | 10.50-10.50 | 8.50-8.50 | 8.98 |
| July | 9.12 | 9.29 | 10.90 | 11.38 | 12.15 | 13.39 | 9.46 | 12.50 | 9.36 | 10.50-10.50 | 8.50-8.50 | 9.37 |
| Aug | 9.39 | 9.53 | 11.30 | 11.85 | 12.51 | 13.64 | 9.72 | 12.38 | 9.68 | 11.00-10.50 | 8.50-8.50 | 9.56 |
| Sept | 9.05 | 9.19 | 11.07 | 11.65 | 12.37 | 13.55 | 9.57 | 12.54 | 9.28 | 11.00-11.00 | 8.50-8.50 | 9.45 |
| Oct | 8.71 | 8.90 | 10.87 | 11.54 | 12.25 | 13.46 | 9.64 | 12.25 | 8.98 | 11.00-11.00 | 8.50-8.50 | 9.48 |
| Nov | 8.71 | 8.89 | 10.96 | 11.69 | 12.41 | 13.61 | 9.79 | 12.34 | 9.09 | 11.00-11.00 | 8.50-8.50 | 9.34 |
| Dec | 8.96 | 9.14 | 11.13 | 11.83 | 12.57 | 13.75 | 9.90 | 12.42 | 9.50 | 11.00-11.00 | 8.50-8.50 | 9.47 |
| **1984:** | | | | | | | | | | | | |
| Jan | 8.93 | 9.06 | 10.93 | 11.67 | 12.20 | 13.65 | 9.61 | 12.29 | 9.18 | 11.00-11.00 | 8.50-8.50 | 9.56 |
| Feb | 9.03 | 9.13 | 11.05 | 11.84 | 12.08 | 13.59 | 9.63 | 12.23 | 9.31 | 11.00-11.00 | 8.50-8.50 | 9.59 |
| Mar | 9.44 | 9.58 | 11.59 | 12.32 | 12.57 | 13.99 | 9.92 | 12.02 | 9.86 | 11.50-11.00 | 8.50-8.50 | 9.91 |
| Apr | 9.69 | 9.83 | 11.98 | 12.63 | 12.81 | 14.31 | 9.98 | 12.04 | 10.22 | 12.00-11.50 | 9.00-8.50 | 10.29 |
| May | 9.90 | 10.31 | 12.75 | 13.41 | 13.28 | 14.74 | 10.55 | 12.18 | 10.87 | 12.50-12.00 | 9.00-9.00 | 10.32 |
| June | 9.94 | 10.55 | 13.18 | 13.56 | 13.55 | 15.05 | 10.71 | 12.10 | 11.23 | 13.00-12.50 | 9.00-9.00 | 11.06 |
| July | 10.13 | 10.58 | 13.08 | 13.36 | 13.44 | 15.15 | 10.50 | 12.50 | 11.34 | 13.00-13.00 | 9.00-9.00 | 11.23 |
| Aug | 10.49 | 10.65 | 12.50 | 12.72 | 12.87 | 14.63 | 10.03 | 12.43 | 11.16 | 13.00-13.00 | 9.00-9.00 | 11.64 |
| Sept | 10.41 | 10.51 | 12.34 | 12.52 | 12.66 | 14.35 | 10.17 | 12.53 | 10.94 | 13.00-12.75 | 9.00-9.00 | 11.30 |
| Oct | 9.97 | 10.05 | 11.85 | 12.16 | 12.63 | 13.94 | 10.34 | 12.77 | 10.16 | 12.75-12.00 | 9.00-9.00 | 9.99 |
| Nov | 8.79 | 8.99 | 10.90 | 11.57 | 12.29 | 13.48 | 10.27 | 12.75 | 9.06 | 12.00-11.25 | 9.00-8.50 | 9.43 |
| Dec | 8.16 | 8.36 | 10.56 | 11.50 | 12.13 | 13.40 | 10.04 | 12.55 | 8.55 | 11.25-10.75 | 8.50-8.00 | 8.38 |

[1]Rate on new issues within period; bank-discount basis.

[2]Yields on the more actively traded issues adjusted to constant maturities by the Treasury Department.

[3]Series excludes public utility issues for January 17, 1984 through October 11, 1984 due to lack of appropriate issues.

[4]Effective rate (in the primary market) on conventional mortgages, reflecting fees and charges as well as contract rate and assuming, on the average, repayment at end of 10 years. Rates beginning January 1973 not strictly comparable with prior rates.

[5]Bank discount basis; prior to November 1979, data are for 4-6 months paper.

[6]For monthly data, high and low for the period. Prime rate for 1929–33 and 1947–48 are ranges of the rate in effect during the period.

[7]Since July 19, 1975, the daily effective rate is an average of the rates on a given day weighted by the volume of transactions at these rates. Prior to that date, the daily effective rate was the rate considered most representative of the day's transactions, usually the one at which most transactions occurred.

[8]From October 30, 1942, to April 24, 1946, a preferential rate of 0.50 percent was in effect for advances secured by Government securities maturing in 1 year or less.

Sources: Department of the Treasury, Board of Governors of the Federal Reserve System, Federal Home Loan Bank Board (FHLBB), Moody's Investors Service, and Standard & Poor's Corporation.

**Table A.2**          **Time Series Data** (cont.)

Corporate Profits with Inventory Valuation and Capital Consumption Adjustments,
1929–84
(Billions of Dollars; Quarterly Data at Seasonally Adjusted Annual Rates)

| Year or Quarter | Corporate Profits With Inventory Valuation and Capital Consumption Adjustments | Corporate Profits Tax Liability | Corporate Profits After Tax with Inventory Valuation and Capital Consumption Adjustments | | Undistributed Profits with Inventory Valuation and Capital Consumption Adjustments |
|---|---|---|---|---|---|
| | | | *Total* | *Dividends* | |
| 1929 | 9.0 | 1.4 | 7.7 | 5.8 | 1.9 |
| 1933 | −1.7 | .5 | −2.3 | 2.0 | −4.3 |
| 1939 | 5.3 | 1.4 | 3.9 | 3.8 | .1 |
| 1940 | 8.6 | 2.8 | 5.8 | 4.0 | 1.8 |
| 1941 | 14.1 | 7.6 | 6.5 | 4.4 | 2.1 |
| 1942 | 19.3 | 11.4 | 7.9 | 4.3 | 3.6 |
| 1943 | 23.5 | 14.1 | 9.5 | 4.4 | 5.0 |
| 1944 | 23.6 | 12.9 | 10.7 | 4.6 | 6.1 |
| 1945 | 19.0 | 10.7 | 8.4 | 4.6 | 3.8 |
| 1946 | 16.6 | 9.1 | 7.5 | 5.6 | 1.9 |
| 1947 | 22.3 | 11.3 | 11.0 | 6.3 | 4.7 |
| 1948 | 29.4 | 12.4 | 17.0 | 7.0 | 10.0 |
| 1949 | 27.1 | 10.2 | 16.9 | 7.2 | 9.7 |
| 1950 | 33.9 | 17.9 | 16.0 | 8.8 | 7.2 |
| 1951 | 38.7 | 22.6 | 16.1 | 8.5 | 7.6 |
| 1952 | 36.1 | 19.4 | 16.7 | 8.5 | 8.2 |
| 1953 | 36.3 | 20.3 | 16.0 | 8.8 | 7.2 |
| 1954 | 35.2 | 17.6 | 17.5 | 9.1 | 8.4 |
| 1955 | 45.5 | 22.0 | 23.4 | 10.3 | 13.1 |
| 1956 | 43.7 | 22.0 | 21.8 | 11.1 | 10.7 |
| 1957 | 43.3 | 21.4 | 21.8 | 11.5 | 10.3 |
| 1958 | 38.5 | 19.0 | 19.5 | 11.3 | 8.2 |
| 1959 | 49.6 | 23.6 | 26.0 | 12.2 | 13.8 |
| 1960 | 47.6 | 22.7 | 24.9 | 12.9 | 12.1 |
| 1961 | 48.6 | 22.8 | 25.8 | 13.3 | 12.5 |
| 1962 | 56.6 | 24.0 | 32.6 | 14.4 | 18.2 |
| 1963 | 62.1 | 26.2 | 35.9 | 15.5 | 20.4 |
| 1964 | 69.2 | 28.0 | 41.2 | 17.3 | 23.9 |
| 1965 | 80.0 | 30.9 | 49.1 | 19.1 | 30.0 |
| 1966 | 85.1 | 33.7 | 51.4 | 19.4 | 32.0 |
| 1967 | 82.4 | 32.5 | 49.9 | 20.2 | 29.7 |

## Table A.2      Time Series Data (cont.)
### Corporate Profits with Inventory Valuation and Capital Consumption Adjustments, 1929–84
(Billions of Dollars; Quarterly Data at Seasonally Adjusted Annual Rates)

| Year or Quarter | Corporate Profits With Inventory Valuation and Capital Consumption Adjustments | Corporate Profits Tax Liability | Corporate Profits After Tax with Inventory Valuation and Capital Consumption Adjustments | | Undistributed Profits with Inventory Valuation and Capital Consumption Adjustments |
|---|---|---|---|---|---|
| | | | *Total* | *Dividends* | |
| 1968 | 89.1 | 39.2 | 50.0 | 22.0 | 27.9 |
| 1969 | 85.1 | 39.5 | 45.6 | 22.5 | 23.1 |
| 1970 | 71.4 | 34.2 | 37.2 | 22.5 | 14.8 |
| 1971 | 83.2 | 37.5 | 45.7 | 22.9 | 22.8 |
| 1972 | 96.6 | 41.6 | 55.0 | 24.4 | 30.5 |
| 1973 | 108.3 | 49.0 | 59.3 | 27.0 | 32.3 |
| 1974 | 94.9 | 51.6 | 43.3 | 29.9 | 13.4 |
| 1975 | 110.5 | 50.6 | 59.9 | 30.8 | 29.1 |
| 1976 | 138.1 | 63.8 | 74.3 | 37.4 | 36.9 |
| 1977 | 167.3 | 72.7 | 94.6 | 40.8 | 53.7 |
| 1978 | 192.4 | 83.2 | 109.1 | 47.0 | 62.2 |
| 1979 | 194.8 | 87.6 | 107.2 | 52.7 | 54.5 |
| 1980 | 175.4 | 84.8 | 90.6 | 58.6 | 32.1 |
| 1981 | 189.9 | 81.1 | 108.8 | 66.5 | 42.3 |
| 1982 | 159.1 | 60.7 | 98.4 | 69.2 | 29.2 |
| 1983 | 225.2 | 75.8 | 149.4 | 72.9 | 76.5 |
| 1984 | 284.5 | 88.4 | 196.1 | 80.5 | 115.6 |
| 1982: | | | | | |
| I | 159.9 | 62.9 | 97.0 | 69.2 | 27.9 |
| II | 161.7 | 62.9 | 98.8 | 68.6 | 30.1 |
| III | 163.3 | 61.9 | 101.4 | 69.0 | 32.4 |
| IV | 151.6 | 55.0 | 96.6 | 70.2 | 26.4 |
| 1983: | | | | | |
| I | 179.1 | 59.1 | 120.0 | 71.1 | 48.8 |
| II | 216.7 | 74.8 | 141.9 | 71.7 | 70.2 |
| III | 245.0 | 84.7 | 160.2 | 73.3 | 86.9 |
| IV | 260.0 | 84.5 | 175.5 | 75.4 | 100.0 |
| 1984: | | | | | |
| I | 277.4 | 92.7 | 184.7 | 77.7 | 107.0 |
| II | 291.1 | 95.8 | 195.2 | 79.9 | 115.3 |
| III | 282.8 | 83.1 | 199.8 | 81.3 | 118.4 |

*Source:* Department of Commerce, Bureau of Economic Analysis.

**Table A.3**  Workingmens Federal Savings and Loan Association

| Net Income | | Assets | |
|---|---|---|---|
| 1970 | $   213,387 | 1970 | $  36,725,438 |
| 1971 | 205,523 | 1971 | 43,997,767 |
| 1972 | 431,033 | 1972 | 50,105,622 |
| 1973 | 438,762 | 1973 | 53,192,091 |
| 1974 | 387,671 | 1974 | 57,640,108 |
| 1975 | 272,043 | 1975 | 64,431,175 |
| 1976 | 442,432 | 1976 | 72,607,003 |
| 1977 | 577,245 | 1977 | 80,933,345 |
| 1978 | 780,987 | 1978 | 86,212,394 |
| 1979 | 1,015,262 | 1979 | 95,677,667 |
| 1st Qtr 1980 | 185,091 | 1st Qtr 1980 | 96,370,141 |
| 2nd Qtr 1980 | 39,509 | 2nd Qtr 1980 | 97,314,479 |
| 3rd Qtr 1980 | 42,231 | 3rd Qtr 1980 | 98,606,840 |
| 4th Qtr 1980 | 211,223 | 4th Qtr 1980 | 101,278,873 |
| 1st Qtr 1981 | 26,502 | 1st Qtr 1981 | 101,881,635 |
| 2nd Qtr 1981 | (97,554) | 2nd Qtr 1981 | 100,453,490 |
| 3rd Qtr 1981 | (70,368) | 3rd Qtr 1981 | 100,716,451 |
| 4th Qtr 1981 | (291,729) | 4th Qtr 1981 | 101,859,903 |
| 1st Qtr 1982 | (303,227) | 1st Qtr 1982 | 102,435,739 |
| 2nd Qtr 1982 | (279,667) | 2nd Qtr 1982 | 102,782,892 |
| 3rd Qtr 1982 | (295,941) | 3rd Qtr 1982 | 104,102,876 |
| 4th Qtr 1982 | (143,444) | 4th Qtr 1982 | 104,107,255 |
| 1st Qtr 1983 | (12,523) | 1st Qtr 1983 | 106,737,065 |
| 2nd Qtr 1983 | (38,019) | 2nd Qtr 1983 | 107,388,501 |
| 3rd Qtr 1983 | (80,498) | 3rd Qtr 1983 | 108,503,473 |
| 4th Qtr 1983 | 92,949 | 4th Qtr 1983 | 109,640,005 |
| 1st Qtr 1984 | (99,558) | 1st Qtr 1984 | 110,823,614 |
| 2nd Qtr 1984 | 96,653 | 2nd Qtr 1984 | 109,245,835 |
| 3rd Qtr 1984 | 39,191 | 3rd Qtr 1984 | 111,287,497 |
| 4th Qtr 1984 | 117,848 | 4th Qtr 1984 | 111,026,576 |
| 1st Qtr 1985 | 66,951 | 1st Qtr 1985 | 112,466,225 |

# APPENDIX B: RANDOM NUMBERS AND PROBABILITY FUNCTIONS

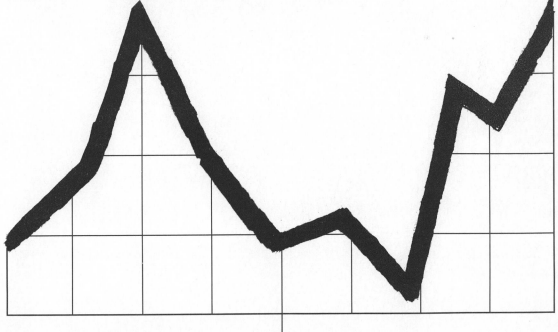

## Table B.1       Random Numbers

| | | | | | | |
|---|---|---|---|---|---|---|
| 46389 | 87437 | 23092 | 23988 | 11809 | 00826 | 97197 |
| 06218 | 69271 | 17918 | 06807 | 17834 | 10407 | 62125 |
| 21388 | 38052 | 48426 | 10275 | 93059 | 08944 | 06728 |
| 46159 | 62812 | 95214 | 99486 | 21683 | 13142 | 64595 |
| 72488 | 75788 | 58559 | 81198 | 51247 | 37079 | 86965 |
| | | | | | | |
| 55824 | 11156 | 84965 | 21592 | 80200 | 90622 | 03054 |
| 37080 | 83197 | 48692 | 84138 | 63048 | 33428 | 91568 |
| 82840 | 57952 | 82966 | 12036 | 41745 | 88006 | 11059 |
| 19838 | 11605 | 61116 | 82697 | 68569 | 00792 | 26999 |
| 20442 | 00620 | 90008 | 60867 | 19906 | 91433 | 68589 |
| | | | | | | |
| 79626 | 78430 | 52310 | 04791 | 22603 | 92953 | 22232 |
| 94405 | 24656 | 73998 | 16152 | 03246 | 29258 | 36207 |
| 28172 | 65833 | 49207 | 10259 | 53702 | 31945 | 85138 |
| 24593 | 55250 | 56568 | 29096 | 92112 | 01087 | 08006 |
| 01563 | 54844 | 82599 | 63547 | 97886 | 45001 | 78997 |
| | | | | | | |
| 03954 | 73168 | 06872 | 10690 | 77396 | 67933 | 79067 |
| 77964 | 26241 | 95040 | 37687 | 21382 | 14311 | 64713 |
| 61111 | 27603 | 17529 | 32020 | 67557 | 53208 | 87638 |
| 97861 | 27715 | 13045 | 20781 | 06147 | 63141 | 01961 |
| 23108 | 60807 | 50527 | 90977 | 22346 | 51612 | 36488 |
| | | | | | | |
| 57970 | 52760 | 90230 | 77747 | 32004 | 37867 | 89920 |
| 90262 | 05217 | 78527 | 82927 | 18339 | 59288 | 03588 |
| 75041 | 08560 | 56611 | 56132 | 59313 | 20722 | 24840 |
| 56872 | 25211 | 07823 | 27621 | 02037 | 00605 | 85640 |
| 93257 | 31809 | 75145 | 65364 | 21217 | 55078 | 64434 |
| | | | | | | |
| 13862 | 62672 | 83940 | 50451 | 53283 | 82739 | 77006 |
| 46547 | 67787 | 25828 | 71838 | 03498 | 56263 | 34533 |
| 26629 | 13913 | 37428 | 39222 | 20239 | 07280 | 38117 |
| 87171 | 54619 | 03367 | 89988 | 43139 | 72682 | 88761 |
| 89437 | 61905 | 57203 | 57077 | 97460 | 10392 | 64742 |
| | | | | | | |
| 61428 | 35260 | 21904 | 01420 | 15774 | 79443 | 40092 |
| 53336 | 77461 | 89279 | 70282 | 77159 | 70998 | 80642 |
| 25970 | 27319 | 63017 | 43080 | 24929 | 42378 | 22396 |
| 17897 | 77894 | 88788 | 61126 | 43599 | 81980 | 23070 |
| 17048 | 36505 | 48622 | 27170 | 60640 | 36701 | 10985 |

The binomial mass function is defined by

$$P(x) = \frac{n!}{x!\,(n-x)!}\,\pi^x(1-\pi)^{n-x}$$

This is the probability of $x$ successes in $n$ independent trials, where the probability of success on each trial is $\pi$. The values of $x$ in the left margin of each of the following sections are to be used in conjunction with the values of $\pi$ at the top of that section. The values of $x$ in the right margin of each section are to be used in conjunction with the values of $\pi$ at the bottom of that section.

**EXAMPLE**   To evaluate $P(x)$ for $n = 4$, $x = 1$, and $\pi = 0.20$, locate the section of the table for $n = 4$, the column for $\pi = 0.20$, and the row for $x = 1$ and read $P(x) = 0.4096$

This table gives the binomial distribution for $n = 1$ through $n = 10$, $n = 20$, and $n = 50$.

## Table B.2 — Binomial Distribution

### $n = 1$

| x | π | 01 | 02 | 03 | 04 | 05 | 06 | 07 | 08 | 09 | 10 | | |
|---|---|----|----|----|----|----|----|----|----|----|----|---|---|
| 0 |   | 9900 | 9800 | 9700 | 9600 | 9500 | 9400 | 9300 | 9200 | 9100 | 9000 | | 1 |
| 1 |   | 0100 | 0200 | 0300 | 0400 | 0500 | 0600 | 0700 | 0800 | 0900 | 1000 | | 0 |
|   |   | 99 | 98 | 97 | 96 | 95 | 94 | 93 | 92 | 91 | 90 | π | x |

| x | π | 11 | 12 | 13 | 14 | 15 | 16 | 17 | 18 | 19 | 20 | | |
|---|---|----|----|----|----|----|----|----|----|----|----|---|---|
| 0 |   | 8900 | 8800 | 8700 | 8600 | 8500 | 8400 | 8300 | 8200 | 8100 | 8000 | | 1 |
| 1 |   | 1100 | 1200 | 1300 | 1400 | 1500 | 1600 | 1700 | 1800 | 1900 | 2000 | | 0 |
|   |   | 89 | 88 | 87 | 86 | 85 | 84 | 83 | 82 | 81 | 80 | π | x |

| x | π | 21 | 22 | 23 | 24 | 25 | 26 | 27 | 28 | 29 | 30 | | |
|---|---|----|----|----|----|----|----|----|----|----|----|---|---|
| 0 |   | 7900 | 7800 | 7700 | 7600 | 7500 | 7400 | 7300 | 7200 | 7100 | 7000 | | 1 |
| 1 |   | 2100 | 2200 | 2300 | 2400 | 2500 | 2600 | 2700 | 2800 | 2900 | 3000 | | 0 |
|   |   | 79 | 78 | 77 | 76 | 75 | 74 | 73 | 72 | 71 | 70 | π | x |

| x | π | 31 | 32 | 33 | 34 | 35 | 36 | 37 | 38 | 39 | 40 | | |
|---|---|----|----|----|----|----|----|----|----|----|----|---|---|
| 0 |   | 6900 | 6800 | 6700 | 6600 | 6500 | 6400 | 6300 | 6200 | 6100 | 6000 | | 1 |
| 1 |   | 3100 | 3200 | 3300 | 3400 | 3500 | 3600 | 3700 | 3800 | 3900 | 4000 | | 0 |
|   |   | 69 | 68 | 67 | 66 | 65 | 64 | 63 | 62 | 61 | 60 | π | x |

| x | π | 41 | 42 | 43 | 44 | 45 | 46 | 47 | 48 | 49 | 50 | | |
|---|---|----|----|----|----|----|----|----|----|----|----|---|---|
| 0 |   | 5900 | 5800 | 5700 | 5600 | 5500 | 5400 | 5300 | 5200 | 5100 | 5000 | | 1 |
| 1 |   | 4100 | 4200 | 4300 | 4400 | 4500 | 4600 | 4700 | 4800 | 4900 | 5000 | | 0 |
|   |   | 59 | 58 | 57 | 56 | 55 | 54 | 53 | 52 | 51 | 50 | π | x |

Binomial Distribution (cont.)

### $n = 2$

| x | π | 01 | 02 | 03 | 04 | 05 | 06 | 07 | 08 | 09 | 10 | | |
|---|---|----|----|----|----|----|----|----|----|----|----|---|---|
| 0 | | 9801 | 9604 | 9409 | 9216 | 9025 | 8836 | 8649 | 8464 | 8281 | 8100 | | 2 |
| 1 | | 0198 | 0392 | 0582 | 0768 | 0950 | 1128 | 1302 | 1472 | 1638 | 1800 | | 1 |
| 2 | | 0001 | 0004 | 0009 | 0016 | 0025 | 0036 | 0049 | 0064 | 0081 | 0100 | | 0 |
| | | 99 | 98 | 97 | 96 | 95 | 94 | 93 | 92 | 91 | 90 | π | x |

| x | π | 11 | 12 | 13 | 14 | 15 | 16 | 17 | 18 | 19 | 20 | | |
|---|---|----|----|----|----|----|----|----|----|----|----|---|---|
| 0 | | 7921 | 7744 | 7569 | 7396 | 7225 | 7056 | 6889 | 6724 | 6561 | 6400 | | 2 |
| 1 | | 1958 | 2112 | 2262 | 2408 | 2550 | 2688 | 2822 | 2952 | 3078 | 3200 | | 1 |
| 2 | | 0121 | 0144 | 0169 | 0196 | 0225 | 0256 | 0289 | 0324 | 0361 | 0400 | | 0 |
| | | 89 | 88 | 87 | 86 | 85 | 84 | 83 | 82 | 81 | 80 | π | x |

| x | π | 21 | 22 | 23 | 24 | 25 | 26 | 27 | 28 | 29 | 30 | | |
|---|---|----|----|----|----|----|----|----|----|----|----|---|---|
| 0 | | 6241 | 6084 | 5929 | 5776 | 5625 | 5476 | 5329 | 5184 | 5041 | 4900 | | 2 |
| 1 | | 3318 | 3432 | 3542 | 3648 | 3750 | 3848 | 3942 | 4032 | 4118 | 4200 | | 1 |
| 2 | | 0441 | 0484 | 0529 | 0576 | 0625 | 0676 | 0729 | 0784 | 0841 | 0900 | | 0 |
| | | 79 | 78 | 77 | 76 | 75 | 74 | 73 | 72 | 71 | 70 | π | x |

| x | π | 31 | 32 | 33 | 34 | 35 | 36 | 37 | 38 | 39 | 40 | | |
|---|---|----|----|----|----|----|----|----|----|----|----|---|---|
| 0 | | 4761 | 4624 | 4489 | 4356 | 4225 | 4096 | 3969 | 3844 | 3721 | 3600 | | 2 |
| 1 | | 4278 | 4352 | 4422 | 4488 | 4550 | 4608 | 4662 | 4712 | 4758 | 4800 | | 1 |
| 2 | | 0961 | 1024 | 1089 | 1156 | 1225 | 1296 | 1369 | 1444 | 1521 | 1600 | | 0 |
| | | 69 | 68 | 67 | 66 | 65 | 64 | 63 | 62 | 61 | 60 | π | x |

| x | π | 41 | 42 | 43 | 44 | 45 | 46 | 47 | 48 | 49 | 50 | | |
|---|---|----|----|----|----|----|----|----|----|----|----|---|---|
| 0 | | 3481 | 3364 | 3249 | 3136 | 3025 | 2916 | 2809 | 2704 | 2601 | 2500 | | 2 |
| 1 | | 4838 | 4872 | 4902 | 4928 | 4950 | 4968 | 4982 | 4992 | 4998 | 5000 | | 1 |
| 2 | | 1681 | 1764 | 1849 | 1936 | 2025 | 2116 | 2209 | 2304 | 2401 | 2500 | | 0 |
| | | 59 | 58 | 57 | 56 | 55 | 54 | 53 | 52 | 51 | 50 | π | x |

### $n = 3$

| x | π | 01 | 02 | 03 | 04 | 05 | 06 | 07 | 08 | 09 | 10 | | |
|---|---|----|----|----|----|----|----|----|----|----|----|---|---|
| 0 | | 9703 | 9412 | 9127 | 8847 | 8574 | 8306 | 8044 | 7787 | 7536 | 7290 | | 3 |
| 1 | | 0294 | 0576 | 0847 | 1106 | 1354 | 1590 | 1816 | 2031 | 2236 | 2430 | | 2 |
| 2 | | 0003 | 0012 | 0026 | 0046 | 0071 | 0102 | 0137 | 0177 | 0221 | 0270 | | 1 |
| 3 | | 0000 | 0000 | 0000 | 0001 | 0001 | 0002 | 0003 | 0005 | 0007 | 0010 | | 0 |
| | | 99 | 98 | 97 | 96 | 95 | 94 | 93 | 92 | 91 | 90 | π | x |

**Binomial Distribution (cont.)**

### n = 3

| x | π | 11 | 12 | 13 | 14 | 15 | 16 | 17 | 18 | 19 | 20 | | |
|---|---|------|------|------|------|------|------|------|------|------|------|---|---|
| 0 | | 7050 | 6815 | 6585 | 6361 | 6141 | 5927 | 5718 | 5514 | 5314 | 5120 | | 3 |
| 1 | | 2614 | 2788 | 2952 | 3106 | 3251 | 3387 | 3513 | 3631 | 3740 | 3840 | | 2 |
| 2 | | 0323 | 0380 | 0441 | 0506 | 0574 | 0645 | 0720 | 0797 | 0877 | 0960 | | 1 |
| 3 | | 0013 | 0017 | 0022 | 0027 | 0034 | 0041 | 0049 | 0058 | 0069 | 0080 | | 0 |
| | | 89 | 88 | 87 | 86 | 85 | 84 | 83 | 82 | 81 | 80 | π | x |

| x | π | 21 | 22 | 23 | 24 | 25 | 26 | 27 | 28 | 29 | 30 | | |
|---|---|------|------|------|------|------|------|------|------|------|------|---|---|
| 0 | | 4930 | 4746 | 4565 | 4390 | 4219 | 4052 | 3890 | 3732 | 3579 | 3430 | | 3 |
| 1 | | 3932 | 4014 | 4091 | 4159 | 4219 | 4271 | 4316 | 4355 | 4386 | 4410 | | 2 |
| 2 | | 1045 | 1133 | 1222 | 1313 | 1406 | 1501 | 1597 | 1693 | 1791 | 1890 | | 1 |
| 3 | | 0093 | 0106 | 0122 | 0138 | 0156 | 0176 | 0197 | 0220 | 0244 | 0270 | | 0 |
| | | 79 | 78 | 77 | 76 | 75 | 74 | 73 | 72 | 71 | 70 | π | x |

| x | π | 31 | 32 | 33 | 34 | 35 | 36 | 37 | 38 | 39 | 40 | | |
|---|---|------|------|------|------|------|------|------|------|------|------|---|---|
| 0 | | 3285 | 3144 | 3008 | 2875 | 2746 | 2621 | 2500 | 2383 | 2270 | 2160 | | 3 |
| 1 | | 4428 | 4439 | 4444 | 4443 | 4436 | 4424 | 4406 | 4382 | 4354 | 4320 | | 2 |
| 2 | | 1989 | 2089 | 2189 | 2289 | 2389 | 2488 | 2587 | 2686 | 2783 | 2880 | | 1 |
| 3 | | 0298 | 0328 | 0359 | 0393 | 0429 | 0467 | 0507 | 0549 | 0593 | 0640 | | 0 |
| | | 69 | 68 | 67 | 66 | 65 | 64 | 63 | 62 | 61 | 60 | π | x |

| x | π | 41 | 42 | 43 | 44 | 45 | 46 | 47 | 48 | 49 | 50 | | |
|---|---|------|------|------|------|------|------|------|------|------|------|---|---|
| 0 | | 2054 | 1951 | 1852 | 1756 | 1664 | 1575 | 1489 | 1406 | 1327 | 1250 | | 3 |
| 1 | | 4282 | 4239 | 4191 | 4140 | 4084 | 4024 | 3961 | 3894 | 3823 | 3750 | | 2 |
| 2 | | 2975 | 3069 | 3162 | 3252 | 3341 | 3428 | 3512 | 3594 | 3674 | 3750 | | 1 |
| 3 | | 0689 | 0741 | 0795 | 0852 | 0911 | 0973 | 1038 | 1106 | 1176 | 1250 | | 0 |
| | | 59 | 58 | 57 | 56 | 55 | 54 | 53 | 52 | 51 | 50 | π | x |

### n = 4

| x | π | 01 | 02 | 03 | 04 | 05 | 06 | 07 | 08 | 09 | 10 | | |
|---|---|------|------|------|------|------|------|------|------|------|------|---|---|
| 0 | | 9606 | 9224 | 8853 | 8493 | 8145 | 7807 | 7481 | 7164 | 6857 | 6561 | | 4 |
| 1 | | 0388 | 0753 | 1095 | 1416 | 1715 | 1993 | 2252 | 2492 | 2713 | 2916 | | 3 |
| 2 | | 0006 | 0023 | 0051 | 0088 | 0135 | 0191 | 0254 | 0325 | 0402 | 0486 | | 2 |
| 3 | | 0000 | 0000 | 0001 | 0002 | 0005 | 0008 | 0013 | 0019 | 0027 | 0036 | | 1 |
| 4 | | 0000 | 0000 | 0000 | 0000 | 0000 | 0000 | 0000 | 0000 | 0001 | 0001 | | 0 |
| | | 99 | 98 | 97 | 96 | 95 | 94 | 93 | 92 | 91 | 90 | π | x |

**Binomial Distribution (cont.)**

### n = 4

| x \ π | 11 | 12 | 13 | 14 | 15 | 16 | 17 | 18 | 19 | 20 | |
|---|---|---|---|---|---|---|---|---|---|---|---|
| 0 | 6274 | 5997 | 5729 | 5470 | 5220 | 4979 | 4746 | 4521 | 4305 | 4096 | 4 |
| 1 | 3102 | 3271 | 3424 | 3562 | 3685 | 3793 | 3888 | 3970 | 4039 | 4096 | 3 |
| 2 | 0575 | 0669 | 0767 | 0870 | 0975 | 1084 | 1195 | 1307 | 1421 | 1536 | 2 |
| 3 | 0047 | 0061 | 0076 | 0094 | 0115 | 0138 | 0163 | 0191 | 0222 | 0256 | 1 |
| 4 | 0001 | 0002 | 0003 | 0004 | 0005 | 0007 | 0008 | 0010 | 0013 | 0016 | 0 |
| | 89 | 88 | 87 | 86 | 85 | 84 | 83 | 82 | 81 | 80 | π x |

| x \ π | 21 | 22 | 23 | 24 | 25 | 26 | 27 | 28 | 29 | 30 | |
|---|---|---|---|---|---|---|---|---|---|---|---|
| 0 | 3895 | 3702 | 3515 | 3336 | 3164 | 2999 | 2840 | 2687 | 2541 | 2401 | 4 |
| 1 | 4142 | 4176 | 4200 | 4214 | 4219 | 4214 | 4201 | 4180 | 4152 | 4116 | 3 |
| 2 | 1651 | 1767 | 1882 | 1996 | 2109 | 2221 | 2331 | 2439 | 2544 | 2646 | 2 |
| 3 | 0293 | 0332 | 0375 | 0420 | 0469 | 0520 | 0575 | 0632 | 0693 | 0756 | 1 |
| 4 | 0019 | 0023 | 0028 | 0033 | 0039 | 0046 | 0053 | 0061 | 0071 | 0081 | 0 |
| | 79 | 78 | 77 | 76 | 75 | 74 | 73 | 72 | 71 | 70 | π x |

| x \ π | 31 | 32 | 33 | 34 | 35 | 36 | 37 | 38 | 39 | 40 | |
|---|---|---|---|---|---|---|---|---|---|---|---|
| 0 | 2267 | 2138 | 2015 | 1897 | 1785 | 1678 | 1575 | 1478 | 1385 | 1296 | 4 |
| 1 | 4074 | 4025 | 3970 | 3910 | 3845 | 3775 | 3701 | 3623 | 3541 | 3456 | 3 |
| 2 | 2745 | 2841 | 2933 | 3021 | 3105 | 3185 | 3260 | 3330 | 3396 | 3456 | 2 |
| 3 | 0822 | 0891 | 0963 | 1038 | 1115 | 1194 | 1276 | 1361 | 1447 | 1536 | 1 |
| 4 | 0092 | 0105 | 0119 | 0134 | 0150 | 0168 | 0187 | 0209 | 0231 | 0256 | 0 |
| | 69 | 68 | 67 | 66 | 65 | 64 | 63 | 62 | 61 | 60 | π x |

| x \ π | 41 | 42 | 43 | 44 | 45 | 46 | 47 | 48 | 49 | 50 | |
|---|---|---|---|---|---|---|---|---|---|---|---|
| 0 | 1212 | 1132 | 1056 | 0983 | 0915 | 0850 | 0789 | 0731 | 0677 | 0625 | 4 |
| 1 | 3368 | 3278 | 3185 | 3091 | 2995 | 2897 | 2799 | 2700 | 2600 | 2500 | 3 |
| 2 | 3511 | 3560 | 3604 | 3643 | 3675 | 3702 | 3723 | 3738 | 3747 | 3750 | 2 |
| 3 | 1627 | 1719 | 1813 | 1908 | 2005 | 2102 | 2201 | 2300 | 2400 | 2500 | 1 |
| 4 | 0283 | 0311 | 0342 | 0375 | 0410 | 0448 | 0488 | 0531 | 0576 | 0625 | 0 |
| | 59 | 58 | 57 | 56 | 55 | 54 | 53 | 52 | 51 | 50 | π x |

### n = 5

| x \ π | 01 | 02 | 03 | 04 | 05 | 06 | 07 | 08 | 09 | 10 | |
|---|---|---|---|---|---|---|---|---|---|---|---|
| 0 | 9510 | 9039 | 8587 | 8154 | 7738 | 7339 | 6957 | 6591 | 6240 | 5905 | 5 |
| 1 | 0480 | 0922 | 1328 | 1699 | 2036 | 2342 | 2618 | 2866 | 3086 | 3280 | 4 |
| 2 | 0010 | 0038 | 0082 | 0142 | 0214 | 0299 | 0394 | 0498 | 0610 | 0729 | 3 |
| 3 | 0000 | 0001 | 0003 | 0006 | 0011 | 0019 | 0030 | 0043 | 0060 | 0081 | 2 |
| 4 | 0000 | 0000 | 0000 | 0000 | 0000 | 0001 | 0001 | 0002 | 0003 | 0004 | 1 |
| | 99 | 98 | 97 | 96 | 95 | 94 | 93 | 92 | 91 | 90 | π x |

**Table B.2**                    **Binomial Distribution (cont.)**

| | | | | | | $n = 5$ | | | | | | | |
|---|---|---|---|---|---|---|---|---|---|---|---|---|---|

| x | π | 11 | 12 | 13 | 14 | 15 | 16 | 17 | 18 | 19 | 20 | | |
|---|---|----|----|----|----|----|----|----|----|----|----|---|---|
| 0 | | 5584 | 5277 | 4984 | 4704 | 4437 | 4182 | 3939 | 3707 | 3487 | 3277 | | 5 |
| 1 | | 3451 | 3598 | 3724 | 3829 | 3915 | 3983 | 4034 | 4069 | 4089 | 4096 | | 4 |
| 2 | | 0853 | 0981 | 1113 | 1247 | 1382 | 1517 | 1652 | 1786 | 1919 | 2048 | | 3 |
| 3 | | 0105 | 0134 | 0166 | 0203 | 0244 | 0289 | 0338 | 0392 | 0450 | 0512 | | 2 |
| 4 | | 0007 | 0009 | 0012 | 0017 | 0022 | 0028 | 0035 | 0043 | 0053 | 0064 | | 1 |
| 5 | | 0000 | 0000 | 0000 | 0001 | 0001 | 0001 | 0001 | 0002 | 0002 | 0003 | | 0 |
| | | 89 | 88 | 87 | 86 | 85 | 84 | 83 | 82 | 81 | 80 | π | x |

| x | π | 21 | 22 | 23 | 24 | 25 | 26 | 27 | 28 | 29 | 30 | | |
|---|---|----|----|----|----|----|----|----|----|----|----|---|---|
| 0 | | 3077 | 2887 | 2707 | 2536 | 2373 | 2219 | 2073 | 1935 | 1804 | 1681 | | 5 |
| 1 | | 4090 | 4072 | 4043 | 4003 | 3955 | 3898 | 3834 | 3762 | 3685 | 3601 | | 4 |
| 2 | | 2174 | 2297 | 2415 | 2529 | 2637 | 2739 | 2836 | 2926 | 3010 | 3087 | | 3 |
| 3 | | 0578 | 0648 | 0721 | 0798 | 0879 | 0962 | 1049 | 1138 | 1229 | 1323 | | 2 |
| 4 | | 0077 | 0091 | 0108 | 0126 | 0146 | 0169 | 0194 | 0221 | 0251 | 0283 | | 1 |
| 5 | | 0004 | 0005 | 0006 | 0008 | 0010 | 0012 | 0014 | 0017 | 0021 | 0024 | | 0 |
| | | 79 | 78 | 77 | 76 | 75 | 74 | 73 | 72 | 71 | 70 | π | x |

| x | π | 31 | 32 | 33 | 34 | 35 | 36 | 37 | 38 | 39 | 40 | | |
|---|---|----|----|----|----|----|----|----|----|----|----|---|---|
| 0 | | 1564 | 1454 | 1350 | 1252 | 1160 | 1074 | 0992 | 0916 | 0845 | 0778 | | 5 |
| 1 | | 3513 | 3421 | 3325 | 3226 | 3124 | 3020 | 2914 | 2808 | 2700 | 2592 | | 4 |
| 2 | | 3157 | 3220 | 3275 | 3323 | 3364 | 3397 | 3423 | 3441 | 3452 | 3456 | | 3 |
| 3 | | 1418 | 1515 | 1613 | 1712 | 1811 | 1911 | 2010 | 2109 | 2207 | 2304 | | 2 |
| 4 | | 0319 | 0357 | 0397 | 0441 | 0488 | 0537 | 0590 | 0646 | 0706 | 0768 | | 1 |
| 5 | | 0029 | 0034 | 0039 | 0045 | 0053 | 0060 | 0069 | 0079 | 0090 | 0102 | | 0 |
| | | 69 | 68 | 67 | 66 | 65 | 64 | 63 | 62 | 61 | 60 | π | x |

| x | π | 41 | 42 | 43 | 44 | 45 | 46 | 47 | 48 | 49 | 50 | | |
|---|---|----|----|----|----|----|----|----|----|----|----|---|---|
| 0 | | 0715 | 0656 | 0602 | 0551 | 0503 | 0459 | 0418 | 0380 | 0345 | 0313 | | 5 |
| 1 | | 2484 | 2376 | 2270 | 2164 | 2059 | 1956 | 1854 | 1755 | 1657 | 1562 | | 4 |
| 2 | | 3452 | 3442 | 3424 | 3400 | 3369 | 3332 | 3289 | 3240 | 3185 | 3125 | | 3 |
| 3 | | 2399 | 2492 | 2583 | 2671 | 2757 | 2838 | 2916 | 2990 | 3060 | 3125 | | 2 |
| 4 | | 0834 | 0902 | 0974 | 1049 | 1128 | 1209 | 1293 | 1380 | 1470 | 1562 | | 1 |
| 5 | | 0116 | 0131 | 0147 | 0165 | 0185 | 0206 | 0229 | 0255 | 0282 | 0312 | | 0 |
| | | 59 | 58 | 57 | 56 | 55 | 54 | 53 | 52 | 51 | 50 | π | x |

| n = 6 | | | | | | | | | | |
|---|---|---|---|---|---|---|---|---|---|---|
| x  π | 01 | 02 | 03 | 04 | 05 | 06 | 07 | 08 | 09 | 10 | |
| 0 | 9415 | 8858 | 8330 | 7828 | 7351 | 6899 | 6470 | 6064 | 5679 | 5314 | 6 |
| 1 | 0571 | 1085 | 1546 | 1957 | 2321 | 2642 | 2922 | 3164 | 3370 | 3543 | 5 |
| 2 | 0014 | 0055 | 0120 | 0204 | 0305 | 0422 | 0550 | 0688 | 0833 | 0984 | 4 |
| 3 | 0000 | 0002 | 0005 | 0011 | 0021 | 0036 | 0055 | 0080 | 0110 | 0146 | 3 |
| 4 | 0000 | 0000 | 0000 | 0000 | 0001 | 0002 | 0003 | 0005 | 0008 | 0012 | 2 |
| 5 | 0000 | 0000 | 0000 | 0000 | 0000 | 0000 | 0000 | 0000 | 0000 | 0001 | 1 |
|  | 99 | 98 | 97 | 96 | 95 | 94 | 93 | 92 | 91 | 90 | π  x |
| x  π | 11 | 12 | 13 | 14 | 15 | 16 | 17 | 18 | 19 | 20 | |
| 0 | 4970 | 4644 | 4336 | 4046 | 3771 | 3513 | 3269 | 3040 | 2824 | 2621 | 6 |
| 1 | 3685 | 3800 | 3888 | 3952 | 3993 | 4015 | 4018 | 4004 | 3975 | 3932 | 5 |
| 2 | 1139 | 1295 | 1452 | 1608 | 1762 | 1912 | 2057 | 2197 | 2331 | 2458 | 4 |
| 3 | 0188 | 0236 | 0289 | 0349 | 0415 | 0486 | 0562 | 0643 | 0729 | 0819 | 3 |
| 4 | 0017 | 0024 | 0032 | 0043 | 0055 | 0069 | 0086 | 0106 | 0128 | 0154 | 2 |
| 5 | 0001 | 0001 | 0002 | 0003 | 0004 | 0005 | 0007 | 0009 | 0012 | 0015 | 1 |
| 6 | 0000 | 0000 | 0000 | 0000 | 0000 | 0000 | 0000 | 0000 | 0000 | 0001 | 0 |
|  | 89 | 88 | 87 | 86 | 85 | 84 | 83 | 82 | 81 | 80 | π  x |
| x  π | 21 | 22 | 23 | 24 | 25 | 26 | 27 | 28 | 29 | 30 | |
| 0 | 2431 | 2252 | 2084 | 1927 | 1780 | 1642 | 1513 | 1393 | 1281 | 1176 | 6 |
| 1 | 3877 | 3811 | 3735 | 3651 | 3560 | 3462 | 3358 | 3251 | 3139 | 3025 | 5 |
| 2 | 2577 | 2687 | 2789 | 2882 | 2966 | 3041 | 3105 | 3160 | 3206 | 3241 | 4 |
| 3 | 0913 | 1011 | 1111 | 1214 | 1318 | 1424 | 1531 | 1639 | 1746 | 1852 | 3 |
| 4 | 0182 | 0214 | 0249 | 0287 | 0330 | 0375 | 0425 | 0478 | 0535 | 0595 | 2 |
| 5 | 0019 | 0024 | 0030 | 0036 | 0044 | 0053 | 0063 | 0074 | 0087 | 0102 | 1 |
| 6 | 0001 | 0001 | 0001 | 0002 | 0002 | 0003 | 0004 | 0005 | 0006 | 0007 | 0 |
|  | 79 | 78 | 77 | 76 | 75 | 74 | 73 | 72 | 71 | 70 | π  x |
| x  π | 31 | 32 | 33 | 34 | 35 | 36 | 37 | 38 | 39 | 40 | |
| 0 | 1079 | 0989 | 0905 | 0827 | 0754 | 0687 | 0625 | 0568 | 0515 | 0467 | 6 |
| 1 | 2909 | 2792 | 2673 | 2555 | 2437 | 2319 | 2203 | 2089 | 1976 | 1866 | 5 |
| 2 | 3267 | 3284 | 3292 | 3290 | 3280 | 3261 | 3235 | 3201 | 3159 | 3110 | 4 |
| 3 | 1957 | 2061 | 2162 | 2260 | 2355 | 2446 | 2533 | 2616 | 2693 | 2765 | 3 |
| 4 | 0660 | 0727 | 0799 | 0873 | 0951 | 1032 | 1116 | 1202 | 1291 | 1382 | 2 |
| 5 | 0119 | 0137 | 0157 | 0180 | 0205 | 0232 | 0262 | 0295 | 0330 | 0369 | 1 |
| 6 | 0009 | 0011 | 0013 | 0015 | 0018 | 0022 | 0026 | 0030 | 0035 | 0041 | 0 |
|  | 69 | 68 | 67 | 66 | 65 | 64 | 63 | 62 | 61 | 60 | π  x |

## Table B.2        Binomial Distribution (cont.)

### n = 6

| x | π | 41 | 42 | 43 | 44 | 45 | 46 | 47 | 48 | 49 | 50 | |
|---|---|------|------|------|------|------|------|------|------|------|------|---|
| 0 |   | 0422 | 0381 | 0343 | 0308 | 0277 | 0248 | 0222 | 0198 | 0176 | 0156 | 6 |
| 1 |   | 1759 | 1654 | 1552 | 1454 | 1359 | 1267 | 1179 | 1095 | 1014 | 0937 | 5 |
| 2 |   | 3055 | 2994 | 2928 | 2856 | 2780 | 2699 | 2615 | 2527 | 2436 | 2344 | 4 |
| 3 |   | 2831 | 2891 | 2945 | 2992 | 3032 | 3065 | 3091 | 3110 | 3121 | 3125 | 3 |
| 4 |   | 1475 | 1570 | 1666 | 1763 | 1861 | 1958 | 2056 | 2153 | 2249 | 2344 | 2 |
| 5 |   | 0410 | 0455 | 0503 | 0554 | 0609 | 0667 | 0729 | 0795 | 0864 | 0937 | 1 |
| 6 |   | 0048 | 0055 | 0063 | 0073 | 0083 | 0095 | 0108 | 0122 | 0138 | 0156 | 0 |
|   |   | 59 | 58 | 57 | 56 | 55 | 54 | 53 | 52 | 51 | 50 | π | x |

### n = 7

| x | π | 01 | 02 | 03 | 04 | 05 | 06 | 07 | 08 | 09 | 10 | |
|---|---|------|------|------|------|------|------|------|------|------|------|---|
| 0 |   | 9321 | 8681 | 8080 | 7514 | 6983 | 6485 | 6017 | 5578 | 5168 | 4783 | 7 |
| 1 |   | 0659 | 1240 | 1749 | 2192 | 2573 | 2897 | 3170 | 3396 | 3578 | 3720 | 6 |
| 2 |   | 0020 | 0076 | 0162 | 0274 | 0406 | 0555 | 0716 | 0886 | 1061 | 1240 | 5 |
| 3 |   | 0000 | 0003 | 0008 | 0019 | 0036 | 0059 | 0090 | 0128 | 0175 | 0230 | 4 |
| 4 |   | 0000 | 0000 | 0000 | 0001 | 0002 | 0004 | 0007 | 0011 | 0017 | 0026 | 3 |
| 5 |   | 0000 | 0000 | 0000 | 0000 | 0000 | 0000 | 0000 | 0001 | 0001 | 0002 | 2 |
|   |   | 99 | 98 | 97 | 96 | 95 | 94 | 93 | 92 | 91 | 90 | π | x |

| x | π | 11 | 12 | 13 | 14 | 15 | 16 | 17 | 18 | 19 | 20 | |
|---|---|------|------|------|------|------|------|------|------|------|------|---|
| 0 |   | 4423 | 4087 | 3773 | 3479 | 3206 | 2951 | 2714 | 2493 | 2288 | 2097 | 7 |
| 1 |   | 3827 | 3901 | 3946 | 3965 | 3960 | 3935 | 3891 | 3830 | 3756 | 3670 | 6 |
| 2 |   | 1419 | 1596 | 1769 | 1936 | 2097 | 2248 | 2391 | 2523 | 2643 | 2753 | 5 |
| 3 |   | 0292 | 0363 | 0441 | 0525 | 0617 | 0714 | 0816 | 0923 | 1033 | 1147 | 4 |
| 4 |   | 0036 | 0049 | 0066 | 0086 | 0109 | 0136 | 0167 | 0203 | 0242 | 0287 | 3 |
| 5 |   | 0003 | 0004 | 0006 | 0008 | 0012 | 0016 | 0021 | 0027 | 0034 | 0043 | 2 |
| 6 |   | 0000 | 0000 | 0000 | 0000 | 0001 | 0001 | 0001 | 0002 | 0003 | 0004 | 1 |
|   |   | 89 | 88 | 87 | 86 | 85 | 84 | 83 | 82 | 81 | 80 | π | x |

**Table B.2**                                    **Binomial Distribution (cont.)**

| $n = 7$ |

| x | π | 21 | 22 | 23 | 24 | 25 | 26 | 27 | 28 | 29 | 30 | | |
|---|---|----|----|----|----|----|----|----|----|----|----|---|---|
| 0 |   | 1920 | 1757 | 1605 | 1465 | 1335 | 1215 | 1105 | 1003 | 0910 | 0824 | | 7 |
| 1 |   | 3573 | 3468 | 3356 | 3237 | 3115 | 2989 | 2860 | 2731 | 2600 | 2471 | | 6 |
| 2 |   | 2850 | 2935 | 3007 | 3067 | 3115 | 3150 | 3174 | 3186 | 3186 | 3177 | | 5 |
| 3 |   | 1263 | 1379 | 1497 | 1614 | 1730 | 1845 | 1956 | 2065 | 2169 | 2269 | | 4 |
| 4 |   | 0336 | 0389 | 0447 | 0510 | 0577 | 0648 | 0724 | 0803 | 0886 | 0972 | | 3 |
| 5 |   | 0054 | 0066 | 0080 | 0097 | 0115 | 0137 | 0161 | 0187 | 0217 | 0250 | | 2 |
| 6 |   | 0005 | 0006 | 0008 | 0010 | 0013 | 0016 | 0020 | 0024 | 0030 | 0036 | | 1 |
| 7 |   | 0000 | 0000 | 0000 | 0000 | 0001 | 0001 | 0001 | 0001 | 0002 | 0002 | | 0 |
|   |   | 79 | 78 | 77 | 76 | 75 | 74 | 73 | 72 | 71 | 70 | π | x |

| x | π | 31 | 32 | 33 | 34 | 35 | 36 | 37 | 38 | 39 | 40 | | |
|---|---|----|----|----|----|----|----|----|----|----|----|---|---|
| 0 |   | 0745 | 0672 | 0606 | 0546 | 0490 | 0440 | 0394 | 0352 | 0314 | 0280 | | 7 |
| 1 |   | 2342 | 2215 | 2090 | 1967 | 1848 | 1732 | 1619 | 1511 | 1407 | 1306 | | 6 |
| 2 |   | 3156 | 3127 | 3088 | 3040 | 2985 | 2922 | 2853 | 2778 | 2698 | 2613 | | 5 |
| 3 |   | 2363 | 2452 | 2535 | 2610 | 2679 | 2740 | 2793 | 2838 | 2875 | 2903 | | 4 |
| 4 |   | 1062 | 1154 | 1248 | 1345 | 1442 | 1541 | 1640 | 1739 | 1838 | 1935 | | 3 |
| 5 |   | 0286 | 0326 | 0369 | 0416 | 0466 | 0520 | 0578 | 0640 | 0705 | 0774 | | 2 |
| 6 |   | 0043 | 0051 | 0061 | 0071 | 0084 | 0098 | 0113 | 0131 | 0150 | 0172 | | 1 |
| 7 |   | 0003 | 0003 | 0004 | 0005 | 0006 | 0008 | 0009 | 0011 | 0014 | 0016 | | 0 |
|   |   | 69 | 68 | 67 | 66 | 65 | 64 | 63 | 62 | 61 | 60 | π | x |

| x | π | 41 | 42 | 43 | 44 | 45 | 46 | 47 | 48 | 49 | 50 | | |
|---|---|----|----|----|----|----|----|----|----|----|----|---|---|
| 0 |   | 0249 | 0221 | 0195 | 0173 | 0152 | 0134 | 0117 | 0103 | 0090 | 0078 | | 7 |
| 1 |   | 1211 | 1119 | 1032 | 0950 | 0872 | 0798 | 0729 | 0664 | 0604 | 0547 | | 6 |
| 2 |   | 2524 | 2431 | 2336 | 2239 | 2140 | 2040 | 1940 | 1840 | 1740 | 1641 | | 5 |
| 3 |   | 2923 | 2934 | 2937 | 2932 | 2918 | 2897 | 2867 | 2830 | 2786 | 2734 | | 4 |
| 4 |   | 2031 | 2125 | 2216 | 2304 | 2388 | 2468 | 2543 | 2612 | 2676 | 2734 | | 3 |
| 5 |   | 0847 | 0923 | 1003 | 1086 | 1172 | 1261 | 1353 | 1447 | 1543 | 1641 | | 2 |
| 6 |   | 0196 | 0223 | 0252 | 0284 | 0320 | 0358 | 0400 | 0445 | 0494 | 0547 | | 1 |
| 7 |   | 0019 | 0023 | 0027 | 0032 | 0037 | 0044 | 0051 | 0059 | 0068 | 0078 | | 0 |
|   |   | 59 | 58 | 57 | 56 | 55 | 54 | 53 | 52 | 51 | 50 | π | x |

| n = 8 | | | | | | | | | | |
|---|---|---|---|---|---|---|---|---|---|---|

| x  π | 01 | 02 | 03 | 04 | 05 | 06 | 07 | 08 | 09 | 10 | |
|---|---|---|---|---|---|---|---|---|---|---|---|
| 0 | 9227 | 8508 | 7837 | 7214 | 6634 | 6096 | 5596 | 5132 | 4703 | 4305 | 8 |
| 1 | 0746 | 1389 | 1939 | 2405 | 2793 | 3113 | 3370 | 3570 | 3721 | 3826 | 7 |
| 2 | 0026 | 0099 | 0210 | 0351 | 0515 | 0695 | 0888 | 1087 | 1288 | 1488 | 6 |
| 3 | 0001 | 0004 | 0013 | 0029 | 0054 | 0089 | 0134 | 0189 | 0255 | 0331 | 5 |
| 4 | 0000 | 0000 | 0001 | 0002 | 0004 | 0007 | 0013 | 0021 | 0031 | 0046 | 4 |
| 5 | 0000 | 0000 | 0000 | 0000 | 0000 | 0000 | 0001 | 0001 | 0002 | 0004 | 3 |
|  | 99 | 98 | 97 | 96 | 95 | 94 | 93 | 92 | 91 | 90 | π  x |

| x  π | 11 | 12 | 13 | 14 | 15 | 16 | 17 | 18 | 19 | 20 | |
|---|---|---|---|---|---|---|---|---|---|---|---|
| 0 | 3937 | 3596 | 3282 | 2992 | 2725 | 2479 | 2252 | 2044 | 1853 | 1678 | 8 |
| 1 | 3892 | 3923 | 3923 | 3897 | 3847 | 3777 | 3691 | 3590 | 3477 | 3355 | 7 |
| 2 | 1684 | 1872 | 2052 | 2220 | 2376 | 2518 | 2646 | 2758 | 2855 | 2936 | 6 |
| 3 | 0416 | 0511 | 0613 | 0723 | 0839 | 0959 | 1084 | 1211 | 1339 | 1468 | 5 |
| 4 | 0064 | 0087 | 0115 | 0147 | 0185 | 0228 | 0277 | 0332 | 0393 | 0459 | 4 |
| 5 | 0006 | 0009 | 0014 | 0019 | 0026 | 0035 | 0045 | 0058 | 0074 | 0092 | 3 |
| 6 | 0000 | 0001 | 0001 | 0002 | 0002 | 0003 | 0005 | 0006 | 0009 | 0011 | 2 |
| 7 | 0000 | 0000 | 0000 | 0000 | 0000 | 0000 | 0000 | 0000 | 0001 | 0001 | 1 |
|  | 89 | 88 | 87 | 86 | 85 | 84 | 83 | 82 | 81 | 80 | π  x |

| x  π | 21 | 22 | 23 | 24 | 25 | 26 | 27 | 28 | 29 | 30 | |
|---|---|---|---|---|---|---|---|---|---|---|---|
| 0 | 1517 | 1370 | 1236 | 1113 | 1001 | 0899 | 0806 | 0722 | 0646 | 0576 | 8 |
| 1 | 3226 | 3092 | 2953 | 2812 | 2670 | 2527 | 2386 | 2247 | 2110 | 1977 | 7 |
| 2 | 3002 | 3052 | 3087 | 3108 | 3115 | 3108 | 3089 | 3058 | 3017 | 2965 | 6 |
| 3 | 1596 | 1722 | 1844 | 1963 | 2076 | 2184 | 2285 | 2379 | 2464 | 2541 | 5 |
| 4 | 0530 | 0607 | 0689 | 0775 | 0865 | 0959 | 1056 | 1156 | 1258 | 1361 | 4 |
| 5 | 0113 | 0137 | 0165 | 0196 | 0231 | 0270 | 0313 | 0360 | 0411 | 0467 | 3 |
| 6 | 0015 | 0019 | 0025 | 0031 | 0038 | 0047 | 0058 | 0070 | 0084 | 0100 | 2 |
| 7 | 0001 | 0002 | 0002 | 0003 | 0004 | 0005 | 0006 | 0008 | 0010 | 0012 | 1 |
| 8 | 0000 | 0000 | 0000 | 0000 | 0000 | 0000 | 0000 | 0000 | 0001 | 0001 | 0 |
|  | 79 | 78 | 77 | 76 | 75 | 74 | 73 | 72 | 71 | 70 | π  x |

**Binomial Distribution (cont.)**

### n = 8

| x  π | 31 | 32 | 33 | 34 | 35 | 36 | 37 | 38 | 39 | 40 | |
|---|---|---|---|---|---|---|---|---|---|---|---|
| 0 | 0514 | 0457 | 0406 | 0360 | 0319 | 0281 | 0248 | 0218 | 0192 | 0168 | 8 |
| 1 | 1847 | 1721 | 1600 | 1484 | 1373 | 1267 | 1166 | 1071 | 0981 | 0896 | 7 |
| 2 | 2904 | 2835 | 2758 | 2675 | 2587 | 2494 | 2397 | 2297 | 2194 | 2090 | 6 |
| 3 | 2609 | 2668 | 2717 | 2756 | 2786 | 2805 | 2815 | 2815 | 2806 | 2787 | 5 |
| 4 | 1465 | 1569 | 1673 | 1775 | 1875 | 1973 | 2067 | 2157 | 2242 | 2322 | 4 |
| 5 | 0527 | 0591 | 0659 | 0732 | 0808 | 0888 | 0971 | 1058 | 1147 | 1239 | 3 |
| 6 | 0118 | 0139 | 0162 | 0188 | 0217 | 0250 | 0285 | 0324 | 0367 | 0413 | 2 |
| 7 | 0015 | 0019 | 0023 | 0028 | 0033 | 0040 | 0048 | 0057 | 0067 | 0079 | 1 |
| 8 | 0001 | 0001 | 0001 | 0002 | 0002 | 0003 | 0004 | 0004 | 0005 | 0007 | 0 |
|  | 69 | 68 | 67 | 66 | 65 | 64 | 63 | 62 | 61 | 60  π | x |

| x  π | 41 | 42 | 43 | 44 | 45 | 46 | 47 | 48 | 49 | 50 | |
|---|---|---|---|---|---|---|---|---|---|---|---|
| 0 | 0147 | 0128 | 0111 | 0097 | 0084 | 0072 | 0062 | 0053 | 0046 | 0039 | 8 |
| 1 | 0816 | 0742 | 0672 | 0608 | 0548 | 0493 | 0442 | 0395 | 0352 | 0312 | 7 |
| 2 | 1985 | 1880 | 1776 | 1672 | 1569 | 1469 | 1371 | 1275 | 1183 | 1094 | 6 |
| 3 | 2759 | 2723 | 2679 | 2627 | 2568 | 2503 | 2431 | 2355 | 2273 | 2187 | 5 |
| 4 | 2397 | 2465 | 2526 | 2580 | 2627 | 2665 | 2695 | 2717 | 2730 | 2734 | 4 |
| 5 | 1332 | 1428 | 1525 | 1622 | 1719 | 1816 | 1912 | 2006 | 2098 | 2187 | 3 |
| 6 | 0463 | 0517 | 0575 | 0637 | 0703 | 0774 | 0848 | 0926 | 1008 | 1094 | 2 |
| 7 | 0092 | 0107 | 0124 | 0143 | 0164 | 0188 | 0215 | 0244 | 0277 | 0312 | 1 |
| 8 | 0008 | 0010 | 0012 | 0014 | 0017 | 0020 | 0024 | 0028 | 0033 | 0039 | 0 |
|  | 59 | 58 | 57 | 56 | 55 | 54 | 53 | 52 | 51 | 50  π | x |

### n = 9

| x  π | 01 | 02 | 03 | 04 | 05 | 06 | 07 | 08 | 09 | 10 | |
|---|---|---|---|---|---|---|---|---|---|---|---|
| 0 | 9135 | 8337 | 7602 | 6925 | 6302 | 5730 | 5204 | 4722 | 4279 | 3874 | 9 |
| 1 | 0830 | 1531 | 2116 | 2597 | 2985 | 3292 | 3525 | 3695 | 3809 | 3874 | 8 |
| 2 | 0034 | 0125 | 0262 | 0433 | 0629 | 0840 | 1061 | 1285 | 1507 | 1722 | 7 |
| 3 | 0001 | 0006 | 0019 | 0042 | 0077 | 0125 | 0186 | 0261 | 0348 | 0446 | 6 |
| 4 | 0000 | 0000 | 0001 | 0003 | 0006 | 0012 | 0021 | 0034 | 0052 | 0074 | 5 |
| 5 | 0000 | 0000 | 0000 | 0000 | 0000 | 0001 | 0002 | 0003 | 0005 | 0008 | 4 |
| 6 | 0000 | 0000 | 0000 | 0000 | 0000 | 0000 | 0000 | 0000 | 0000 | 0001 | 3 |
|  | 99 | 98 | 97 | 96 | 95 | 94 | 93 | 92 | 91 | 90  π | x |

## Binomial Distribution (cont.)

### n = 9

| x | π | 11 | 12 | 13 | 14 | 15 | 16 | 17 | 18 | 19 | 20 | |
|---|---|------|------|------|------|------|------|------|------|------|------|---|
| 0 | | 3504 | 3165 | 2855 | 2573 | 2316 | 2082 | 1869 | 1676 | 1501 | 1342 | 9 |
| 1 | | 3897 | 3884 | 3840 | 3770 | 3679 | 3569 | 3446 | 3312 | 2169 | 3020 | 8 |
| 2 | | 1927 | 2119 | 2295 | 2455 | 2597 | 2720 | 2823 | 2908 | 2973 | 3020 | 7 |
| 3 | | 0556 | 0674 | 0800 | 0933 | 1069 | 1209 | 1349 | 1489 | 1627 | 1762 | 6 |
| 4 | | 0103 | 0138 | 0179 | 0228 | 0283 | 0345 | 0415 | 0490 | 0573 | 0661 | 5 |
| 5 | | 0013 | 0019 | 0027 | 0037 | 0050 | 0066 | 0085 | 0108 | 0134 | 0165 | 4 |
| 6 | | 0001 | 0002 | 0003 | 0004 | 0006 | 0008 | 0012 | 0016 | 0021 | 0028 | 3 |
| 7 | | 0000 | 0000 | 0000 | 0000 | 0000 | 0001 | 0001 | 0001 | 0002 | 0003 | 2 |
| | | 89 | 88 | 87 | 86 | 85 | 84 | 83 | 82 | 81 | 80 | π x |

| x | π | 21 | 22 | 23 | 24 | 25 | 26 | 27 | 28 | 29 | 30 | |
|---|---|------|------|------|------|------|------|------|------|------|------|---|
| 0 | | 1199 | 1069 | 0952 | 0846 | 0751 | 0665 | 0589 | 0520 | 0458 | 0404 | 9 |
| 1 | | 2867 | 2713 | 2558 | 2404 | 2253 | 2104 | 1960 | 1820 | 1685 | 1556 | 8 |
| 2 | | 3049 | 3061 | 3056 | 3037 | 3003 | 2957 | 2899 | 2831 | 2754 | 2668 | 7 |
| 3 | | 1891 | 2014 | 2130 | 2238 | 2336 | 2424 | 2502 | 2569 | 2624 | 2668 | 6 |
| 4 | | 0754 | 0852 | 0954 | 1060 | 1168 | 1278 | 1388 | 1499 | 1608 | 1715 | 5 |
| 5 | | 0200 | 0240 | 0285 | 0335 | 0389 | 0449 | 0513 | 0583 | 0657 | 0735 | 4 |
| 6 | | 0036 | 0045 | 0057 | 0070 | 0087 | 0105 | 0127 | 0151 | 0179 | 0210 | 3 |
| 7 | | 0004 | 0005 | 0007 | 0010 | 0012 | 0016 | 0020 | 0025 | 0031 | 0039 | 2 |
| 8 | | 0000 | 0000 | 0001 | 0001 | 0001 | 0001 | 0002 | 0002 | 0003 | 0004 | 1 |
| | | 79 | 78 | 77 | 76 | 75 | 74 | 73 | 72 | 71 | 70 | π x |

| x | π | 31 | 32 | 33 | 34 | 35 | 36 | 37 | 38 | 39 | 40 | |
|---|---|------|------|------|------|------|------|------|------|------|------|---|
| 0 | | 0355 | 0311 | 0272 | 0238 | 0207 | 0180 | 0156 | 0135 | 0117 | 0101 | 9 |
| 1 | | 1433 | 1317 | 1206 | 1102 | 1004 | 0912 | 0826 | 0747 | 0673 | 0605 | 8 |
| 2 | | 2576 | 2478 | 2376 | 2270 | 2162 | 2052 | 1941 | 1831 | 1721 | 1612 | 7 |
| 3 | | 2701 | 2721 | 2731 | 2729 | 2716 | 2693 | 2660 | 2618 | 2567 | 2508 | 6 |
| 4 | | 1820 | 1921 | 2017 | 2109 | 2194 | 2272 | 2344 | 2407 | 2462 | 2508 | 5 |
| 5 | | 0818 | 0904 | 0994 | 1086 | 1181 | 1278 | 1376 | 1475 | 1574 | 1672 | 4 |
| 6 | | 0245 | 0284 | 0326 | 0373 | 0424 | 0479 | 0539 | 0603 | 0671 | 0743 | 3 |
| 7 | | 0047 | 0057 | 0069 | 0082 | 0098 | 0116 | 0136 | 0158 | 0184 | 0212 | 2 |
| 8 | | 0005 | 0007 | 0008 | 0011 | 0013 | 0016 | 0020 | 0024 | 0029 | 0035 | 1 |
| 9 | | 0000 | 0000 | 0000 | 0001 | 0001 | 0001 | 0001 | 0002 | 0002 | 0003 | 0 |
| | | 69 | 68 | 67 | 66 | 65 | 64 | 63 | 62 | 61 | 60 | π x |

**Binomial Distribution (cont.)**

| | | | | | | | | | | | |
|---|---|---|---|---|---|---|---|---|---|---|---|
| | | | | | $n = 9$ | | | | | | |
| x  π | 41 | 42 | 43 | 44 | 45 | 46 | 47 | 48 | 49 | 50 | |
| 0 | 0087 | 0074 | 0064 | 0054 | 0046 | 0039 | 0033 | 0028 | 0023 | 0020 | 9 |
| 1 | 0542 | 0484 | 0431 | 0383 | 0339 | 0299 | 0263 | 0231 | 0202 | 0176 | 8 |
| 2 | 1506 | 1402 | 1301 | 1204 | 1110 | 1020 | 0934 | 0853 | 0776 | 0703 | 7 |
| 3 | 2442 | 2369 | 2291 | 2207 | 2119 | 2027 | 1933 | 1837 | 1739 | 1641 | 6 |
| 4 | 2545 | 2573 | 2592 | 2601 | 2600 | 2590 | 2571 | 2543 | 2506 | 2461 | 5 |
| 5 | 1769 | 1863 | 1955 | 2044 | 2128 | 2207 | 2280 | 2347 | 2408 | 2461 | 4 |
| 6 | 0819 | 0900 | 0983 | 1070 | 1160 | 1253 | 1348 | 1445 | 1542 | 1641 | 3 |
| 7 | 0244 | 0279 | 0318 | 0360 | 0407 | 0458 | 0512 | 0571 | 0635 | 0703 | 2 |
| 8 | 0042 | 0051 | 0060 | 0071 | 0083 | 0097 | 0014 | 0132 | 0153 | 0176 | 1 |
| 9 | 0003 | 0004 | 0005 | 0006 | 0008 | 0009 | 0011 | 0014 | 0016 | 0020 | 0 |
| | 59 | 58 | 57 | 56 | 55 | 54 | 53 | 52 | 51 | 50   π | x |

| | | | | | | | | | | | |
|---|---|---|---|---|---|---|---|---|---|---|---|
| | | | | | $n = 10$ | | | | | | |
| x  π | 01 | 02 | 03 | 04 | 05 | 06 | 07 | 08 | 09 | 10 | |
| 0 | 9044 | 8171 | 7374 | 6648 | 5987 | 5386 | 4840 | 4344 | 3894 | 3487 | 10 |
| 1 | 0914 | 1667 | 2281 | 2770 | 3151 | 3438 | 3643 | 3777 | 3851 | 3874 | 9 |
| 2 | 0042 | 0153 | 0317 | 0519 | 0746 | 0988 | 1234 | 1478 | 1714 | 1937 | 8 |
| 3 | 0001 | 0008 | 0026 | 0058 | 0105 | 0168 | 0248 | 0343 | 0452 | 0574 | 7 |
| 4 | 0000 | 0000 | 0001 | 0004 | 0010 | 0019 | 0033 | 0052 | 0078 | 0112 | 6 |
| 5 | 0000 | 0000 | 0000 | 0000 | 0001 | 0001 | 0003 | 0005 | 0009 | 0015 | 5 |
| 6 | 0000 | 0000 | 0000 | 0000 | 0000 | 0000 | 0000 | 0000 | 0001 | 0001 | 4 |
| | 99 | 98 | 97 | 96 | 95 | 94 | 93 | 92 | 91 | 90   π | x |
| x  π | 11 | 12 | 13 | 14 | 15 | 16 | 17 | 18 | 19 | 20 | |
| 0 | 3118 | 2785 | 2484 | 2213 | 1969 | 1749 | 1552 | 1374 | 1216 | 1074 | 10 |
| 1 | 3854 | 3798 | 3712 | 3603 | 3474 | 3331 | 3178 | 3017 | 2852 | 2684 | 9 |
| 2 | 2143 | 2330 | 2496 | 2639 | 2759 | 2856 | 2929 | 2980 | 3010 | 3020 | 8 |
| 3 | 0706 | 0847 | 0995 | 1146 | 1298 | 1450 | 1600 | 1745 | 1883 | 2013 | 7 |
| 4 | 0153 | 0202 | 0260 | 0326 | 0401 | 0483 | 0573 | 0670 | 0773 | 0881 | 6 |
| 5 | 0023 | 0033 | 0047 | 0064 | 0085 | 0111 | 0141 | 0177 | 0218 | 0264 | 5 |
| 6 | 0002 | 0004 | 0006 | 0009 | 0012 | 0018 | 0024 | 0032 | 0043 | 0055 | 4 |
| 7 | 0000 | 0000 | 0000 | 0001 | 0001 | 0002 | 0003 | 0004 | 0006 | 0008 | 3 |
| 8 | 0000 | 0000 | 0000 | 0000 | 0000 | 0000 | 0000 | 0000 | 0001 | 0001 | 2 |
| | 89 | 88 | 87 | 86 | 85 | 84 | 83 | 82 | 81 | 80   π | x |

# Table B.2

## Binomial Distribution (cont.)

### n = 10

| x | π | 21 | 22 | 23 | 24 | 25 | 26 | 27 | 28 | 29 | 30 | |
|---|---|----|----|----|----|----|----|----|----|----|----|---|
| 0 | | 0947 | 0834 | 0733 | 0643 | 0563 | 0492 | 0430 | 0374 | 0326 | 0282 | 10 |
| 1 | | 2517 | 2351 | 2188 | 2030 | 1877 | 1730 | 1590 | 1456 | 1330 | 1211 | 9 |
| 2 | | 3011 | 2984 | 2942 | 2885 | 2816 | 2735 | 2646 | 2548 | 2444 | 2335 | 8 |
| 3 | | 2134 | 2244 | 2343 | 2429 | 2503 | 2563 | 2609 | 2642 | 2662 | 2668 | 7 |
| 4 | | 0993 | 1108 | 1225 | 1343 | 1460 | 1576 | 1689 | 1798 | 1903 | 2001 | 6 |
| 5 | | 0317 | 0375 | 0439 | 0509 | 0584 | 0664 | 0750 | 0839 | 0933 | 1029 | 5 |
| 6 | | 0070 | 0088 | 0109 | 0134 | 0162 | 0195 | 0231 | 0272 | 0317 | 0368 | 4 |
| 7 | | 0011 | 0014 | 0019 | 0024 | 0031 | 0039 | 0049 | 0060 | 0074 | 0090 | 3 |
| 8 | | 0001 | 0002 | 0002 | 0003 | 0004 | 0005 | 0007 | 0009 | 0011 | 0014 | 2 |
| 9 | | 0000 | 0000 | 0000 | 0000 | 0000 | 0000 | 0001 | 0001 | 0001 | 0001 | 1 |
| | | 79 | 78 | 77 | 76 | 75 | 74 | 73 | 72 | 71 | 70 | π x |

| x | π | 31 | 32 | 33 | 34 | 35 | 36 | 37 | 38 | 39 | 40 | |
|---|---|----|----|----|----|----|----|----|----|----|----|---|
| 0 | | 0245 | 0211 | 0182 | 0157 | 0135 | 0115 | 0098 | 0084 | 0071 | 0060 | 10 |
| 1 | | 1099 | 0995 | 0898 | 0808 | 0725 | 0649 | 0578 | 0514 | 0456 | 0430 | 9 |
| 2 | | 2222 | 2107 | 1990 | 1873 | 1757 | 1642 | 1529 | 1419 | 1312 | 1209 | 8 |
| 3 | | 2662 | 2644 | 2614 | 2573 | 2522 | 2462 | 2394 | 2319 | 2237 | 2150 | 7 |
| 4 | | 2093 | 2177 | 2253 | 2320 | 2377 | 2424 | 2461 | 2487 | 2503 | 2508 | 6 |
| 5 | | 1128 | 1229 | 1332 | 1434 | 1536 | 1636 | 1734 | 1829 | 1920 | 2007 | 5 |
| 6 | | 0422 | 0482 | 0547 | 0616 | 0689 | 0767 | 0849 | 0934 | 1023 | 1115 | 4 |
| 7 | | 0108 | 0130 | 0154 | 0181 | 0212 | 0247 | 0285 | 0327 | 0374 | 0425 | 3 |
| 8 | | 0018 | 0023 | 0028 | 0035 | 0043 | 0052 | 0063 | 0075 | 0090 | 0106 | 2 |
| 9 | | 0002 | 0002 | 0003 | 0004 | 0005 | 0006 | 0008 | 0010 | 0013 | 0016 | 1 |
| 10 | | 0000 | 0000 | 0000 | 0000 | 0000 | 0000 | 0000 | 0001 | 0001 | 0001 | 0 |
| | | 69 | 68 | 67 | 66 | 65 | 64 | 63 | 62 | 61 | 60 | π x |

| x | π | 41 | 42 | 43 | 44 | 45 | 46 | 47 | 48 | 49 | 50 | |
|---|---|----|----|----|----|----|----|----|----|----|----|---|
| 0 | | 0051 | 0043 | 0036 | 0030 | 0025 | 0021 | 0017 | 0014 | 0012 | 0010 | 10 |
| 1 | | 0355 | 0312 | 0273 | 0238 | 0207 | 0180 | 0155 | 0133 | 0114 | 0098 | 9 |
| 2 | | 1111 | 1017 | 0927 | 0843 | 0763 | 0688 | 0619 | 0554 | 0494 | 0439 | 8 |
| 3 | | 2058 | 1963 | 1865 | 1765 | 1665 | 1654 | 1464 | 1364 | 1267 | 1172 | 7 |
| 4 | | 2503 | 2488 | 2462 | 2427 | 2384 | 2331 | 2271 | 2204 | 2130 | 2051 | 6 |
| 5 | | 2087 | 2162 | 2229 | 2289 | 2340 | 2383 | 2417 | 2441 | 2456 | 2461 | 5 |
| 6 | | 1209 | 1304 | 1401 | 1499 | 1596 | 1692 | 1786 | 1878 | 1966 | 2051 | 4 |
| 7 | | 0480 | 0540 | 0604 | 0673 | 0746 | 0824 | 0905 | 0991 | 1080 | 1172 | 3 |
| 8 | | 0125 | 0147 | 0171 | 0198 | 0229 | 0263 | 0301 | 0343 | 0389 | 0439 | 2 |
| 9 | | 0019 | 0024 | 0029 | 0035 | 0042 | 0050 | 0059 | 0070 | 0083 | 0098 | 1 |
| 10 | | 0001 | 0002 | 0002 | 0003 | 0003 | 0004 | 0005 | 0006 | 0008 | 0010 | 0 |
| | | 59 | 58 | 57 | 56 | 55 | 54 | 53 | 52 | 51 | 50 | π x |

# Binomial Distribution (cont.)

## n = 20

| x | π | 01 | 02 | 03 | 04 | 05 | 06 | 07 | 08 | 09 | 10 | |
|---|---|------|------|------|------|------|------|------|------|------|------|----|
| 0 | | 8179 | 6676 | 5438 | 4420 | 3585 | 2901 | 2342 | 1887 | 1516 | 1216 | 20 |
| 1 | | 1652 | 2725 | 3364 | 3683 | 3774 | 3703 | 3526 | 3282 | 3000 | 2702 | 19 |
| 2 | | 0159 | 0528 | 0988 | 1458 | 1887 | 2246 | 2521 | 2711 | 2828 | 2852 | 18 |
| 3 | | 0010 | 0065 | 0183 | 0364 | 0596 | 0860 | 1139 | 1414 | 1672 | 1901 | 17 |
| 4 | | 0000 | 0006 | 0024 | 0065 | 0133 | 0233 | 0364 | 0523 | 0703 | 0898 | 16 |
| 5 | | 0000 | 0000 | 0002 | 0009 | 0022 | 0048 | 0088 | 0145 | 0222 | 0319 | 15 |
| 6 | | 0000 | 0000 | 0000 | 0001 | 0003 | 0008 | 0017 | 0032 | 0055 | 0089 | 14 |
| 7 | | 0000 | 0000 | 0000 | 0000 | 0000 | 0001 | 0002 | 0005 | 0011 | 0020 | 13 |
| 8 | | 0000 | 0000 | 0000 | 0000 | 0000 | 0000 | 0000 | 0001 | 0002 | 0004 | 12 |
| 9 | | 0000 | 0000 | 0000 | 0000 | 0000 | 0000 | 0000 | 0000 | 0000 | 0001 | 11 |
| | | 99 | 98 | 97 | 96 | 95 | 94 | 93 | 92 | 91 | 90 | π x |

| x | π | 11 | 12 | 13 | 14 | 15 | 16 | 17 | 18 | 19 | 20 | |
|---|---|------|------|------|------|------|------|------|------|------|------|----|
| 0 | | 0972 | 0776 | 0617 | 0490 | 0388 | 0306 | 0241 | 0189 | 0148 | 0115 | 20 |
| 1 | | 2403 | 2115 | 1844 | 1595 | 1368 | 1165 | 0986 | 0829 | 0693 | 0576 | 19 |
| 2 | | 2822 | 2740 | 2618 | 2466 | 2293 | 2109 | 1919 | 1730 | 1545 | 1369 | 18 |
| 3 | | 2093 | 2242 | 2347 | 2409 | 2428 | 2410 | 2358 | 2278 | 2175 | 2054 | 17 |
| 4 | | 1099 | 1299 | 1491 | 1666 | 1821 | 1951 | 2053 | 2125 | 2168 | 2182 | 16 |
| 5 | | 0435 | 0567 | 0713 | 0868 | 1028 | 1189 | 1345 | 1493 | 1627 | 1746 | 15 |
| 6 | | 0134 | 0193 | 0266 | 0353 | 0454 | 0566 | 0689 | 0819 | 0954 | 1091 | 14 |
| 7 | | 0033 | 0053 | 0080 | 0115 | 0160 | 0216 | 0282 | 0360 | 0448 | 0545 | 13 |
| 8 | | 0007 | 0012 | 0019 | 0030 | 0046 | 0067 | 0094 | 0128 | 0171 | 0222 | 12 |
| 9 | | 0001 | 0002 | 0004 | 0007 | 0011 | 0017 | 0026 | 0038 | 0053 | 0074 | 11 |
| 10 | | 0000 | 0000 | 0001 | 0001 | 0002 | 0004 | 0006 | 0009 | 0014 | 0020 | 10 |
| 11 | | 0000 | 0000 | 0000 | 0000 | 0000 | 0001 | 0001 | 0002 | 0003 | 0005 | 9 |
| 12 | | 0000 | 0000 | 0000 | 0000 | 0000 | 0000 | 0000 | 0000 | 0001 | 0001 | 8 |
| | | 89 | 88 | 87 | 86 | 85 | 84 | 83 | 82 | 81 | 80 | π x |

**Table B.2**                          **Binomial Distribution (cont.)**

| | | | | | $n = 20$ | | | | | | |
|---|---|---|---|---|---|---|---|---|---|---|---|

| x  π | 21 | 22 | 23 | 24 | 25 | 26 | 27 | 28 | 29 | 30 | |
|---|---|---|---|---|---|---|---|---|---|---|---|
| 0 | 0090 | 0069 | 0054 | 0041 | 0032 | 0024 | 0016 | 0014 | 0011 | 0008 | 20 |
| 1 | 0477 | 0392 | 0321 | 0261 | 0211 | 0170 | 0137 | 0109 | 0087 | 0068 | 19 |
| 2 | 1204 | 1050 | 0910 | 0783 | 0669 | 0569 | 0480 | 0403 | 0336 | 0278 | 18 |
| 3 | 1920 | 1777 | 1631 | 1484 | 1339 | 1199 | 1065 | 0940 | 0823 | 0716 | 17 |
| 4 | 2169 | 2131 | 2070 | 1991 | 1897 | 1790 | 1675 | 1553 | 1429 | 1304 | 16 |
| 5 | 1845 | 1923 | 1979 | 2012 | 2023 | 2013 | 1982 | 1933 | 1868 | 1789 | 15 |
| 6 | 1226 | 1356 | 1478 | 1589 | 1686 | 1768 | 1833 | 1879 | 1907 | 1916 | 14 |
| 7 | 0652 | 0765 | 0883 | 1003 | 1124 | 1242 | 1356 | 1462 | 1558 | 1643 | 13 |
| 8 | 0282 | 0351 | 0429 | 0515 | 0609 | 0709 | 0815 | 0924 | 1034 | 1144 | 12 |
| 9 | 0100 | 0132 | 0171 | 0217 | 0271 | 0332 | 0402 | 0479 | 0563 | 0654 | 11 |
| 10 | 0029 | 0041 | 0056 | 0075 | 0099 | 0128 | 0163 | 0205 | 0253 | 0308 | 10 |
| 11 | 0007 | 0010 | 0015 | 0022 | 0030 | 0041 | 0055 | 0072 | 0094 | 0120 | 9 |
| 12 | 0001 | 0002 | 0003 | 0005 | 0008 | 0011 | 0015 | 0021 | 0029 | 0039 | 8 |
| 13 | 0000 | 0000 | 0001 | 0001 | 0002 | 0002 | 0003 | 0005 | 0007 | 0010 | 7 |
| 14 | 0000 | 0000 | 0000 | 0000 | 0000 | 0000 | 0001 | 0001 | 0001 | 0002 | 6 |
| | 79 | 78 | 77 | 76 | 75 | 74 | 73 | 72 | 71 | 70 | π  x |

| x  π | 31 | 32 | 33 | 34 | 35 | 36 | 37 | 38 | 39 | 40 | |
|---|---|---|---|---|---|---|---|---|---|---|---|
| 0 | 0006 | 0004 | 0003 | 0002 | 0002 | 0001 | 0001 | 0001 | 0001 | 0000 | 20 |
| 1 | 0054 | 0042 | 0033 | 0025 | 0020 | 0015 | 0011 | 0009 | 0007 | 0005 | 19 |
| 2 | 0229 | 0188 | 0153 | 0124 | 0100 | 0080 | 0064 | 0050 | 0040 | 0031 | 18 |
| 3 | 0619 | 0531 | 0453 | 0383 | 0323 | 0270 | 0224 | 0185 | 0152 | 0123 | 17 |
| 4 | 1181 | 1062 | 0947 | 0839 | 0738 | 0645 | 0559 | 0482 | 0412 | 0350 | 16 |
| 5 | 1698 | 1599 | 1493 | 1384 | 1272 | 1161 | 1051 | 0945 | 0843 | 0746 | 15 |
| 6 | 1907 | 1881 | 1839 | 1782 | 1712 | 1632 | 1543 | 1447 | 1347 | 1244 | 14 |
| 7 | 1714 | 1770 | 1811 | 1836 | 1844 | 1836 | 1812 | 1774 | 1722 | 1659 | 13 |
| 8 | 1251 | 1354 | 1450 | 1537 | 1614 | 1678 | 1730 | 1767 | 1790 | 1797 | 12 |
| 9 | 0750 | 0849 | 0952 | 1056 | 1158 | 1259 | 1354 | 1444 | 1526 | 1597 | 11 |
| 10 | 0370 | 0440 | 0516 | 0598 | 0686 | 0779 | 0875 | 0974 | 1073 | 1171 | 10 |
| 11 | 0151 | 1188 | 0231 | 0280 | 0336 | 0398 | 0467 | 0542 | 0624 | 0710 | 9 |
| 12 | 0051 | 0066 | 0085 | 0108 | 0136 | 0168 | 0206 | 0249 | 0299 | 0355 | 8 |
| 13 | 0014 | 0019 | 0026 | 0034 | 0045 | 0058 | 0074 | 0094 | 0118 | 0146 | 7 |
| 14 | 0003 | 0005 | 0006 | 0009 | 0012 | 0016 | 0022 | 0029 | 0038 | 0049 | 6 |
| 15 | 0001 | 0001 | 0001 | 0002 | 0003 | 0004 | 0005 | 0007 | 0010 | 0013 | 5 |
| 16 | 0000 | 0000 | 0000 | 0000 | 0000 | 0001 | 0001 | 0001 | 0002 | 0003 | 4 |
| | 69 | 68 | 67 | 66 | 65 | 64 | 63 | 62 | 61 | 60 | π  x |

# Binomial Distribution (cont.)

## n = 20

| x \ π | 41 | 42 | 43 | 44 | 45 | 46 | 47 | 48 | 49 | 50 | |
|---|---|---|---|---|---|---|---|---|---|---|---|
| 1 | 0004 | 0003 | 0002 | 0001 | 0001 | 0001 | 0001 | 0000 | 0000 | 0000 | 19 |
| 2 | 0024 | 0018 | 0014 | 0011 | 0008 | 0006 | 0005 | 0003 | 0002 | 0002 | 18 |
| 3 | 0100 | 0080 | 0064 | 0051 | 0040 | 0031 | 0024 | 0019 | 0014 | 0011 | 17 |
| 4 | 0295 | 0247 | 0206 | 0170 | 0139 | 0113 | 0092 | 0074 | 0059 | 0046 | 16 |
| 5 | 0656 | 0573 | 0496 | 0427 | 0365 | 0309 | 0260 | 0217 | 0180 | 0148 | 15 |
| 6 | 1140 | 1037 | 0936 | 0839 | 0746 | 0658 | 0577 | 0501 | 0432 | 0370 | 14 |
| 7 | 1585 | 1502 | 1413 | 1318 | 1221 | 1122 | 1023 | 0925 | 0830 | 0739 | 13 |
| 8 | 1790 | 1768 | 1732 | 1683 | 1623 | 1553 | 1474 | 1388 | 1296 | 1201 | 12 |
| 9 | 1658 | 1707 | 1742 | 1763 | 1771 | 1763 | 1742 | 1708 | 1661 | 1602 | 11 |
| 10 | 1268 | 1359 | 1446 | 1524 | 1593 | 1652 | 1700 | 1734 | 1755 | 1762 | 10 |
| 11 | 0801 | 0895 | 0991 | 1089 | 1185 | 1280 | 1370 | 1455 | 1533 | 1602 | 9 |
| 12 | 0417 | 0486 | 0561 | 0642 | 0727 | 0818 | 0911 | 1007 | 1105 | 1201 | 8 |
| 13 | 0178 | 0217 | 0260 | 0310 | 0366 | 0429 | 0497 | 0572 | 0653 | 0739 | 7 |
| 14 | 0062 | 0078 | 0098 | 0122 | 0150 | 0183 | 0221 | 0264 | 0314 | 0370 | 6 |
| 15 | 0017 | 0023 | 0030 | 0038 | 0049 | 0062 | 0078 | 0098 | 0121 | 0148 | 5 |
| 16 | 0004 | 0005 | 0007 | 0009 | 0013 | 0017 | 0022 | 0028 | 0036 | 0046 | 4 |
| 17 | 0001 | 0001 | 0001 | 0002 | 0002 | 0003 | 0005 | 0006 | 0008 | 0011 | 3 |
| 18 | 0000 | 0000 | 0000 | 0000 | 0000 | 0000 | 0001 | 0001 | 0001 | 0002 | 2 |
| | 59 | 58 | 57 | 56 | 55 | 54 | 53 | 52 | 51 | 50 | π \ x |

## n = 50

| x \ π | 01 | 02 | 03 | 04 | 05 | 06 | 07 | 08 | 09 | 10 | |
|---|---|---|---|---|---|---|---|---|---|---|---|
| 0 | 6050 | 3642 | 2181 | 1299 | 0769 | 0453 | 0266 | 0155 | 0090 | 0052 | 50 |
| 1 | 3056 | 3716 | 3372 | 2706 | 2025 | 1447 | 0999 | 0672 | 0443 | 0286 | 49 |
| 2 | 0756 | 1858 | 2555 | 2762 | 2611 | 2262 | 1843 | 1433 | 1073 | 0779 | 48 |
| 3 | 0122 | 0607 | 1264 | 1842 | 2199 | 2311 | 2219 | 1993 | 1698 | 1386 | 47 |
| 4 | 0015 | 0145 | 0459 | 0902 | 1360 | 1733 | 1963 | 2037 | 1973 | 1809 | 46 |
| 5 | 0001 | 0027 | 0131 | 0346 | 0658 | 1018 | 1359 | 1629 | 1795 | 1849 | 45 |
| 6 | 0000 | 0004 | 0030 | 0108 | 0260 | 0487 | 0767 | 1063 | 1332 | 1541 | 44 |
| 7 | 0000 | 0001 | 0006 | 0028 | 0086 | 0195 | 0363 | 0581 | 0828 | 1076 | 43 |
| 8 | 0000 | 0000 | 0001 | 0006 | 0024 | 0067 | 0147 | 0271 | 0440 | 0643 | 42 |
| 9 | 0000 | 0000 | 0000 | 0001 | 0006 | 0020 | 0052 | 0110 | 0203 | 0333 | 41 |
| 10 | 0000 | 0000 | 0000 | 0000 | 0001 | 0005 | 0016 | 0039 | 0082 | 0152 | 40 |
| 11 | 0000 | 0000 | 0000 | 0000 | 0000 | 0001 | 0004 | 0012 | 0030 | 0061 | 39 |
| 12 | 0000 | 0000 | 0000 | 0000 | 0000 | 0000 | 0001 | 0004 | 0010 | 0022 | 38 |
| 13 | 0000 | 0000 | 0000 | 0000 | 0000 | 0000 | 0000 | 0001 | 0003 | 0007 | 37 |
| 14 | 0000 | 0000 | 0000 | 0000 | 0000 | 0000 | 0000 | 0000 | 0001 | 0002 | 36 |
| 15 | 0000 | 0000 | 0000 | 0000 | 0000 | 0000 | 0000 | 0000 | 0000 | 0001 | 35 |
| | 99 | 98 | 97 | 96 | 95 | 94 | 93 | 92 | 91 | 90 | π \ x |

# Table B.2

## Binomial Distribution (cont.)

### n = 50

| x \ π | 11 | 12 | 13 | 14 | 15 | 16 | 17 | 18 | 19 | 20 | |
|---|---|---|---|---|---|---|---|---|---|---|---|
| 0 | 0029 | 0017 | 0009 | 0005 | 0003 | 0002 | 0001 | 0000 | 0000 | 0000 | 50 |
| 1 | 0182 | 0114 | 0071 | 0043 | 0026 | 0016 | 0009 | 0005 | 0003 | 0002 | 49 |
| 2 | 0552 | 0382 | 0259 | 0172 | 0113 | 0073 | 0046 | 0029 | 0018 | 0011 | 48 |
| 3 | 1091 | 0833 | 0619 | 0449 | 0319 | 0222 | 0151 | 0102 | 0067 | 0044 | 47 |
| 4 | 1584 | 1334 | 1086 | 0858 | 0661 | 0496 | 0364 | 0262 | 0185 | 0128 | 46 |
| 5 | 1801 | 1674 | 1493 | 1286 | 1072 | 0869 | 0687 | 0530 | 0400 | 0295 | 45 |
| 6 | 1670 | 1712 | 1674 | 1570 | 1419 | 1242 | 1055 | 0872 | 0703 | 0554 | 44 |
| 7 | 1297 | 1467 | 1572 | 1606 | 1575 | 1487 | 1358 | 1203 | 1037 | 0870 | 43 |
| 8 | 0862 | 1075 | 1262 | 1406 | 1493 | 1523 | 1495 | 1420 | 1307 | 1169 | 42 |
| 9 | 0497 | 0684 | 0880 | 1068 | 1230 | 1353 | 1429 | 1454 | 1431 | 1364 | 41 |
| 10 | 0252 | 0383 | 0539 | 0713 | 0890 | 1057 | 1200 | 1309 | 1376 | 1398 | 40 |
| 11 | 0113 | 0190 | 0293 | 0422 | 0571 | 0732 | 0894 | 1045 | 1174 | 1271 | 39 |
| 12 | 0045 | 0084 | 0142 | 0223 | 0328 | 0453 | 0595 | 0745 | 0895 | 1033 | 38 |
| 13 | 0016 | 0034 | 0062 | 0106 | 0169 | 0252 | 0356 | 0478 | 0613 | 0755 | 37 |
| 14 | 0005 | 0012 | 0025 | 0046 | 0079 | 0127 | 0193 | 0277 | 0380 | 0499 | 36 |
| 15 | 0002 | 0004 | 0009 | 0018 | 0033 | 0058 | 0095 | 0146 | 0214 | 0299 | 35 |
| 16 | 0000 | 0001 | 0003 | 0006 | 0013 | 0024 | 0042 | 0070 | 0110 | 0164 | 34 |
| 17 | 0000 | 0000 | 0001 | 0002 | 0005 | 0009 | 0017 | 0031 | 0052 | 0082 | 33 |
| 18 | 0000 | 0000 | 0000 | 0001 | 0001 | 0003 | 0007 | 0012 | 0022 | 0037 | 32 |
| 19 | 0000 | 0000 | 0000 | 0000 | 0000 | 0001 | 0002 | 0005 | 0009 | 0016 | 31 |
| 20 | 0000 | 0000 | 0000 | 0000 | 0000 | 0000 | 0001 | 0002 | 0003 | 0006 | 30 |
| 21 | 0000 | 0000 | 0000 | 0000 | 0000 | 0000 | 0000 | 0000 | 0001 | 0002 | 29 |
| 22 | 0000 | 0000 | 0000 | 0000 | 0000 | 0000 | 0000 | 0000 | 0000 | 0001 | 28 |
| | 89 | 88 | 87 | 86 | 85 | 84 | 83 | 82 | 81 | 80 | π  x |

# Binomial Distribution (cont.)

n = 50

| x \ π | 21 | 22 | 23 | 24 | 25 | 26 | 27 | 28 | 29 | 30 | |
|---|---|---|---|---|---|---|---|---|---|---|---|
| 1 | 0001 | 0001 | 0000 | 0000 | 0000 | 0000 | 0000 | 0000 | 0000 | 0000 | 49 |
| 2 | 0007 | 0004 | 0002 | 0001 | 0001 | 0000 | 0000 | 0000 | 0000 | 0000 | 48 |
| 3 | 0028 | 0018 | 0011 | 0007 | 0004 | 0002 | 0001 | 0001 | 0000 | 0000 | 47 |
| 4 | 0088 | 0059 | 0039 | 0025 | 0016 | 0010 | 0006 | 0004 | 0002 | 0001 | 46 |
| 5 | 0214 | 0152 | 0106 | 0073 | 0049 | 0033 | 0021 | 0014 | 0009 | 0006 | 45 |
| 6 | 0427 | 0322 | 0238 | 0173 | 0123 | 0087 | 0060 | 0040 | 0027 | 0018 | 44 |
| 7 | 0713 | 0571 | 0447 | 0344 | 0259 | 0191 | 0139 | 0099 | 0069 | 0048 | 43 |
| 8 | 1019 | 0865 | 0718 | 0583 | 0463 | 0361 | 0276 | 0207 | 0152 | 0110 | 42 |
| 9 | 1263 | 1139 | 1001 | 0859 | 0721 | 0592 | 0476 | 0375 | 0290 | 0220 | 41 |
| 10 | 1377 | 1317 | 1226 | 1113 | 0985 | 0852 | 0721 | 0598 | 0485 | 0386 | 40 |
| 11 | 1331 | 1351 | 1332 | 1278 | 1194 | 1089 | 0970 | 0845 | 0721 | 0602 | 39 |
| 12 | 1150 | 1238 | 1293 | 1311 | 1294 | 1244 | 1166 | 1068 | 0957 | 0838 | 38 |
| 13 | 0894 | 1021 | 1129 | 1210 | 1261 | 1277 | 1261 | 1215 | 1142 | 1050 | 37 |
| 14 | 0628 | 0761 | 0891 | 1010 | 1110 | 1186 | 1233 | 1248 | 1233 | 1189 | 36 |
| 15 | 0400 | 0515 | 0639 | 0766 | 0888 | 1000 | 1094 | 1165 | 1209 | 1223 | 35 |
| 16 | 0233 | 0318 | 0417 | 0529 | 0648 | 0769 | 0885 | 0991 | 1080 | 1147 | 34 |
| 17 | 0124 | 0179 | 0249 | 0334 | 0432 | 0540 | 0655 | 0771 | 0882 | 0983 | 33 |
| 18 | 0060 | 0093 | 0137 | 0193 | 0264 | 0348 | 0444 | 0550 | 0661 | 0772 | 32 |
| 19 | 0027 | 0044 | 0069 | 0103 | 0148 | 0206 | 0277 | 0360 | 0454 | 0558 | 31 |
| 20 | 0011 | 0019 | 0032 | 0050 | 0077 | 0112 | 0159 | 0217 | 0288 | 0370 | 30 |
| 21 | 0004 | 0008 | 0014 | 0023 | 0036 | 0056 | 0084 | 0121 | 0168 | 0227 | 29 |
| 22 | 0001 | 0003 | 0005 | 0009 | 0016 | 0026 | 0041 | 0062 | 0090 | 0128 | 28 |
| 23 | 0000 | 0001 | 0002 | 0004 | 0006 | 0011 | 0018 | 0029 | 0045 | 0067 | 27 |
| 24 | 0000 | 0000 | 0001 | 0001 | 0002 | 0004 | 0008 | 0013 | 0021 | 0032 | 26 |
| 25 | 0000 | 0000 | 0000 | 0000 | 0001 | 0002 | 0003 | 0005 | 0009 | 0014 | 25 |
| 26 | 0000 | 0000 | 0000 | 0000 | 0000 | 0001 | 0001 | 0002 | 0003 | 0006 | 24 |
| 27 | 0000 | 0000 | 0000 | 0000 | 0000 | 0000 | 0000 | 0001 | 0001 | 0002 | 23 |
| 28 | 0000 | 0000 | 0000 | 0000 | 0000 | 0000 | 0000 | 0000 | 0000 | 0001 | 22 |
| | 79 | 78 | 77 | 76 | 75 | 74 | 73 | 72 | 71 | 70 | π  x |

# Binomial Distribution (cont.)

### n = 50

| x \ π | 31 | 32 | 33 | 34 | 35 | 36 | 37 | 38 | 39 | 40 | |
|---|---|---|---|---|---|---|---|---|---|---|---|
| 4 | 0001 | 0000 | 0000 | 0000 | 0000 | 0000 | 0000 | 0000 | 0000 | 0000 | 46 |
| 5 | 0003 | 0002 | 0001 | 0001 | 0000 | 0000 | 0000 | 0000 | 0000 | 0000 | 45 |
| 6 | 0011 | 0007 | 0005 | 0003 | 0002 | 0001 | 0001 | 0000 | 0000 | 0000 | 44 |
| 7 | 0032 | 0022 | 0014 | 0009 | 0006 | 0004 | 0002 | 0001 | 0001 | 0000 | 43 |
| 8 | 0078 | 0055 | 0037 | 0025 | 0017 | 0011 | 0007 | 0004 | 0003 | 0002 | 42 |
| 9 | 0164 | 0120 | 0086 | 0061 | 0042 | 0029 | 0019 | 0013 | 0008 | 0005 | 41 |
| 10 | 0301 | 0231 | 0174 | 0128 | 0093 | 0066 | 0046 | 0032 | 0022 | 0014 | 40 |
| 11 | 0493 | 0395 | 0311 | 0240 | 0182 | 0136 | 0099 | 0071 | 0050 | 0035 | 39 |
| 12 | 0719 | 0604 | 0498 | 0402 | 0319 | 0248 | 0189 | 0142 | 0105 | 0076 | 38 |
| 13 | 0944 | 0831 | 0717 | 0606 | 0502 | 0408 | 0325 | 0255 | 0195 | 0147 | 37 |
| 14 | 1121 | 1034 | 0933 | 0825 | 0714 | 0607 | 0505 | 0412 | 0330 | 0260 | 36 |
| 15 | 1209 | 1168 | 1103 | 1020 | 0923 | 0819 | 0712 | 0606 | 0507 | 0415 | 35 |
| 16 | 1188 | 1202 | 1189 | 1149 | 1088 | 1008 | 0914 | 0813 | 0709 | 0606 | 34 |
| 17 | 1068 | 1132 | 1171 | 1184 | 1171 | 1133 | 1074 | 0997 | 0906 | 0808 | 33 |
| 18 | 0880 | 0976 | 1057 | 1118 | 1156 | 1169 | 1156 | 1120 | 1062 | 0987 | 32 |
| 19 | 0666 | 0774 | 0877 | 0970 | 1048 | 1107 | 1144 | 1156 | 1144 | 1109 | 31 |
| 20 | 0463 | 0564 | 0670 | 0775 | 0875 | 0956 | 1041 | 1098 | 1134 | 1146 | 30 |
| 21 | 0297 | 0379 | 0471 | 0570 | 0673 | 0776 | 0874 | 0962 | 1035 | 1091 | 29 |
| 22 | 0176 | 0235 | 0306 | 0387 | 0478 | 0575 | 0676 | 0777 | 0873 | 0959 | 28 |
| 23 | 0096 | 0135 | 0183 | 0243 | 0313 | 0394 | 0484 | 0580 | 0679 | 0778 | 27 |
| 24 | 0049 | 0071 | 0102 | 0141 | 0190 | 0249 | 0319 | 0400 | 0489 | 0584 | 26 |
| 25 | 0023 | 0035 | 0052 | 0075 | 0106 | 0146 | 0195 | 0255 | 0325 | 0405 | 25 |
| 26 | 0010 | 0016 | 0025 | 0037 | 0055 | 0079 | 0110 | 0150 | 0200 | 0259 | 24 |
| 27 | 0004 | 0007 | 0011 | 0017 | 0026 | 0039 | 0058 | 0082 | 0113 | 0154 | 23 |
| 28 | 0001 | 0003 | 0004 | 0007 | 0012 | 0018 | 0028 | 0041 | 0060 | 0084 | 22 |
| 29 | 0000 | 0001 | 0002 | 0003 | 0005 | 0008 | 0012 | 0019 | 0029 | 0043 | 21 |
| 30 | 0000 | 0000 | 0001 | 0001 | 0002 | 0003 | 0005 | 0008 | 0013 | 0020 | 20 |
| 31 | 0000 | 0000 | 0000 | 0000 | 0001 | 0001 | 0002 | 0003 | 0005 | 0009 | 19 |
| 32 | 0000 | 0000 | 0000 | 0000 | 0000 | 0000 | 0001 | 0001 | 0002 | 0003 | 18 |
| 33 | 0000 | 0000 | 0000 | 0000 | 0000 | 0000 | 0000 | 0000 | 0001 | 0001 | 17 |
| | 69 | 68 | 67 | 66 | 65 | 64 | 63 | 62 | 61 | 60 | π x |

$$n = 50$$

| $x$ \ $\pi$ | 41 | 42 | 43 | 44 | 45 | 46 | 47 | 48 | 49 | 50 | |
|---|---|---|---|---|---|---|---|---|---|---|---|
| 8 | 0001 | 0001 | 0000 | 0000 | 0000 | 0000 | 0000 | 0000 | 0000 | 0000 | 42 |
| 9 | 0003 | 0002 | 0001 | 0001 | 0000 | 0000 | 0000 | 0000 | 0000 | 0000 | 41 |
| 10 | 0009 | 0006 | 0004 | 0002 | 0001 | 0001 | 0001 | 0000 | 0000 | 0000 | 40 |
| 11 | 0024 | 0016 | 0010 | 0007 | 0004 | 0003 | 0002 | 0001 | 0001 | 0000 | 39 |
| 12 | 0054 | 0037 | 0026 | 0017 | 0011 | 0007 | 0005 | 0003 | 0002 | 0001 | 38 |
| 13 | 0109 | 0079 | 0057 | 0040 | 0027 | 0018 | 0012 | 0008 | 0005 | 0003 | 37 |
| 14 | 0200 | 0152 | 0113 | 0082 | 0059 | 0041 | 0029 | 0019 | 0013 | 0008 | 36 |
| 15 | 0334 | 0264 | 0204 | 0155 | 0116 | 0085 | 0061 | 0043 | 0030 | 0020 | 35 |
| 16 | 0508 | 0418 | 0337 | 0267 | 0207 | 0158 | 0118 | 0086 | 0062 | 0044 | 34 |
| 17 | 0706 | 0605 | 0508 | 0419 | 0339 | 0269 | 0209 | 0159 | 0119 | 0087 | 33 |
| 18 | 0899 | 0803 | 0703 | 0604 | 0508 | 0420 | 0340 | 0270 | 0210 | 0160 | 32 |
| 19 | 1053 | 0979 | 0893 | 0799 | 0700 | 0602 | 0507 | 0419 | 0340 | 0270 | 31 |
| 20 | 1134 | 1099 | 1044 | 0973 | 0588 | 0795 | 0697 | 0600 | 0506 | 0419 | 30 |
| 21 | 1126 | 1137 | 1126 | 1092 | 1030 | 0967 | 0884 | 0791 | 0695 | 0598 | 29 |
| 22 | 1031 | 1086 | 1119 | 1131 | 1119 | 1086 | 1033 | 0963 | 0880 | 0788 | 28 |
| 23 | 0872 | 0957 | 1028 | 1082 | 1115 | 1126 | 1115 | 1082 | 1029 | 0960 | 27 |
| 24 | 0682 | 0780 | 0872 | 0956 | 1026 | 1079 | 1112 | 1124 | 1112 | 1080 | 26 |
| 25 | 0493 | 0587 | 0684 | 0781 | 0873 | 0956 | 1026 | 1079 | 1112 | 1123 | 25 |
| 26 | 0329 | 0409 | 0497 | 0590 | 0687 | 0783 | 0875 | 0957 | 1027 | 1080 | 24 |
| 27 | 0203 | 0263 | 0333 | 0412 | 0500 | 0593 | 0690 | 0786 | 0877 | 0960 | 23 |
| 28 | 0116 | 0157 | 0206 | 0266 | 0336 | 0415 | 0502 | 0596 | 0692 | 0788 | 22 |
| 29 | 0061 | 0086 | 0118 | 0159 | 0208 | 0268 | 0338 | 0417 | 0504 | 0598 | 21 |
| 30 | 0030 | 0044 | 0062 | 0087 | 0119 | 0160 | 0210 | 0270 | 0339 | 0419 | 20 |
| 31 | 0013 | 0020 | 0030 | 0044 | 0063 | 0088 | 0120 | 0161 | 0210 | 0270 | 19 |
| 32 | 0006 | 0009 | 0014 | 0021 | 0031 | 0044 | 0063 | 0088 | 0120 | 0160 | 18 |
| 33 | 0002 | 0003 | 0006 | 0009 | 0014 | 0021 | 0031 | 0044 | 0063 | 0087 | 17 |
| 34 | 0001 | 0001 | 0002 | 0003 | 0006 | 0009 | 0014 | 0020 | 0030 | 0044 | 16 |
| 35 | 0000 | 0000 | 0001 | 0001 | 0002 | 0003 | 0005 | 0009 | 0013 | 0020 | 15 |
| 36 | 0000 | 0000 | 0000 | 0000 | 0001 | 0001 | 0002 | 0003 | 0005 | 0006 | 14 |
| 37 | 0000 | 0000 | 0000 | 0000 | 0000 | 0000 | 0001 | 0001 | 0002 | 0003 | 13 |
| 38 | 0000 | 0000 | 0000 | 0000 | 0000 | 0000 | 0000 | 0000 | 0001 | 0001 | 12 |
| | 59 | 58 | 57 | 56 | 55 | 54 | 53 | 52 | 51 | 50 $\pi$ | $x$ |

The Poisson mass function is defined by

$$P(x) = \frac{e^{-\lambda} \lambda^x}{x!}$$

The probability of $x$ successes, for various values of $\lambda$, are defined by the corresponding values in the body of the table.

**EXAMPLES**   If $\lambda = 1.6$, then $P(1) = 0.3230$, $P(5) = 0.0176$

This table gives the Poisson distribution for $\lambda = 0.1$ through $\lambda = 10$.

**Table B.3**                                    **Poisson Distribution**

| | | | | | $\lambda$ | | | | | |
|---|---|---|---|---|---|---|---|---|---|---|
| x | 0.1 | 0.2 | 0.3 | 0.4 | 0.5 | 0.6 | 0.7 | 0.8 | 0.9 | 1.0 |
| 0 | .9048 | .8187 | .7408 | .6703 | .6065 | .5488 | .4966 | .4493 | .4066 | .3679 |
| 1 | .0905 | .1637 | .2222 | .2681 | .3033 | .3293 | .3476 | .3595 | .3659 | .3679 |
| 2 | .0045 | .0164 | .0333 | .0536 | .0758 | .0988 | .1217 | .1438 | .1647 | .1839 |
| 3 | .0002 | .0011 | .0033 | .0072 | .0126 | .0198 | .0284 | .0383 | .0494 | .0613 |
| 4 | .0000 | .0001 | .0002 | .0007 | .0016 | .0030 | .0050 | .0077 | .0111 | .0153 |
| 5 | .0000 | .0000 | .0000 | .0001 | .0002 | .0004 | .0007 | .0012 | .0020 | .0031 |
| 6 | .0000 | .0000 | .0000 | .0000 | .0000 | .0000 | .0001 | .0002 | .0003 | .0005 |
| 7 | .0000 | .0000 | .0000 | .0000 | .0000 | .0000 | .0000 | .0000 | .0000 | .0001 |

| | | | | | $\lambda$ | | | | | |
|---|---|---|---|---|---|---|---|---|---|---|
| x | 1.1 | 1.2 | 1.3 | 1.4 | 1.5 | 1.6 | 1.7 | 1.8 | 1.9 | 2.0 |
| 0 | .3329 | .3012 | .2725 | .2466 | .2231 | .2019 | .1827 | .1653 | .1496 | .1353 |
| 1 | .3662 | .3614 | .3543 | .3452 | .3347 | .3230 | .3106 | .2975 | .2842 | .2707 |
| 2 | .2014 | .2169 | .2303 | .2417 | .2510 | .2584 | .2640 | .2678 | .2700 | .2707 |
| 3 | .0738 | .0867 | .0998 | .1128 | .1255 | .1378 | .1496 | .1607 | .1710 | .1804 |
| 4 | .0203 | .0260 | .0324 | .0395 | .0471 | .0551 | .0636 | .0723 | .0812 | .0902 |
| 5 | .0045 | .0062 | .0084 | .0111 | .0141 | .0176 | .0216 | .0260 | .0309 | .0361 |
| 6 | .0008 | .0012 | .0018 | .0026 | .0035 | .0047 | .0061 | .0078 | .0098 | .0120 |
| 7 | .0001 | .0002 | .0003 | .0005 | .0008 | .0011 | .0015 | .0020 | .0027 | .0034 |
| 8 | .0000 | .0000 | .0001 | .0001 | .0001 | .0002 | .0003 | .0005 | .0006 | .0009 |
| 9 | .0000 | .0000 | .0000 | .0000 | .0000 | .0000 | .0001 | .0001 | .0001 | .0002 |

From *Handbook of Probability and Statistics* by R. S. Burington and D. C. May, Jr. Copyright 1953 by McGraw-Hill, Inc. Used with permission of McGraw-Hill Book Company.

# Poisson Distribution (cont.)

| | λ | | | | | | | | | |
|---|---|---|---|---|---|---|---|---|---|---|
| x | 2.1 | 2.2 | 2.3 | 2.4 | 2.5 | 2.6 | 2.7 | 2.8 | 2.9 | 3.0 |
| 0 | .1225 | .1108 | .1003 | .0907 | .0821 | .0743 | .0672 | .0608 | .0550 | .0498 |
| 1 | .2572 | .2438 | .2306 | .2177 | .2052 | .1931 | .1815 | .1703 | .1596 | .1494 |
| 2 | .2700 | .2681 | .2652 | .2613 | .2565 | .2510 | .2450 | .2384 | .2314 | .2240 |
| 3 | .1890 | .1966 | .2033 | .2090 | .2138 | .2176 | .2205 | .2225 | .2237 | .2240 |
| 4 | .0992 | .1082 | .1169 | .1254 | .1336 | .1414 | .1488 | .1557 | .1622 | .1680 |
| 5 | .0417 | .0476 | .0538 | .0602 | .0668 | .0735 | .0804 | .0872 | .0940 | .1008 |
| 6 | .0146 | .0174 | .0206 | .0241 | .0278 | .0319 | .0362 | .0407 | .0455 | .0504 |
| 7 | .0044 | .0055 | .0068 | .0083 | .0099 | .0118 | .0139 | .0163 | .0188 | .0216 |
| 8 | .0011 | .0015 | .0019 | .0025 | .0031 | .0038 | .0047 | .0057 | .0068 | .0081 |
| 9 | .0003 | .0004 | .0005 | .0007 | .0009 | .0011 | .0014 | .0018 | .0022 | .0027 |
| 10 | .0001 | .0001 | .0001 | .0002 | .0002 | .0003 | .0004 | .0005 | .0006 | .0008 |
| 11 | .0000 | .0000 | .0000 | .0000 | .0000 | .0001 | .0001 | .0001 | .0002 | .0002 |
| 12 | .0000 | .0000 | .0000 | .0000 | .0000 | .0000 | .0000 | .0000 | .0000 | .0001 |

| | λ | | | | | | | | | |
|---|---|---|---|---|---|---|---|---|---|---|
| x | 3.1 | 3.2 | 3.3 | 3.4 | 3.5 | 3.6 | 3.7 | 3.8 | 3.9 | 4.0 |
| 0 | .0450 | .0408 | .0369 | .0334 | .0302 | .0273 | .0247 | .0224 | .0202 | .0183 |
| 1 | .1397 | .1304 | .1217 | .1135 | .1057 | .0984 | .0915 | .0850 | .0789 | .0733 |
| 2 | .2165 | .2087 | .2008 | .1929 | .1850 | .1771 | .1692 | .1615 | .1539 | .1465 |
| 3 | .2237 | .2226 | .2209 | .2186 | .2158 | .2125 | .2087 | .2046 | .2001 | .1954 |
| 4 | .1734 | .1781 | .1823 | .1858 | .1888 | .1912 | .1931 | .1944 | .1951 | .1954 |
| 5 | .1075 | .1140 | .1203 | .1264 | .1322 | .1377 | .1429 | .1477 | .1522 | .1563 |
| 6 | .0555 | .0608 | .0662 | .0716 | .0771 | .0826 | .0881 | .0936 | .0989 | .1042 |
| 7 | .0246 | .0278 | .0312 | .0348 | .0385 | .0425 | .0466 | .0508 | .0551 | .0595 |
| 8 | .0095 | .0111 | .0129 | .0148 | .0169 | .0191 | .0215 | .0241 | .0269 | .0298 |
| 9 | .0033 | .0040 | .0047 | .0056 | .0066 | .0076 | .0089 | .0102 | .0116 | .0132 |
| 10 | .0010 | .0013 | .0016 | .0019 | .0023 | .0028 | .0033 | .0039 | .0045 | .0053 |
| 11 | .0003 | .0004 | .0005 | .0006 | .0007 | .0009 | .0011 | .0013 | .0016 | .0019 |
| 12 | .0001 | .0001 | .0001 | .0002 | .0002 | .0003 | .0003 | .0004 | .0005 | .0006 |
| 13 | .0000 | .0000 | .0000 | .0000 | .0001 | .0001 | .0001 | .0001 | .0002 | .0002 |
| 14 | .0000 | .0000 | .0000 | .0000 | .0000 | .0000 | .0000 | .0000 | .0000 | .0001 |

λ

| x | 4.1 | 4.2 | 4.3 | 4.4 | 4.5 | 4.6 | 4.7 | 4.8 | 4.9 | 5.0 |
|---|------|------|------|------|------|------|------|------|------|------|
| 0 | .0166 | .0150 | .0136 | .0123 | .0111 | .0101 | .0091 | .0082 | .0074 | .0067 |
| 1 | .0679 | .0630 | .0583 | .0540 | .0500 | .0462 | .0427 | .0395 | .0365 | .0337 |
| 2 | .1393 | .1323 | .1254 | .1188 | .1125 | .1063 | .1005 | .0948 | .0894 | .0842 |
| 3 | .1904 | .1852 | .1798 | .1743 | .1687 | .1631 | .1574 | .1517 | .1460 | .1404 |
| 4 | .1951 | .1944 | .1933 | .1917 | .1898 | .1875 | .1849 | .1820 | .1789 | .1755 |
| 5 | .1600 | .1633 | .1662 | .1687 | .1708 | .1725 | .1738 | .1747 | .1753 | .1755 |
| 6 | .1093 | .1143 | .1191 | .1237 | .1281 | .1323 | .1362 | .1398 | .1432 | .1462 |
| 7 | .0640 | .0686 | .0732 | .0778 | .0824 | .0869 | .0914 | .0959 | .1002 | .1044 |
| 8 | .0328 | .0360 | .0393 | .0428 | .0463 | .0500 | .0537 | .0575 | .0614 | .0653 |
| 9 | .0150 | .0168 | .0188 | .0209 | .0232 | .0255 | .0280 | .0307 | .0334 | .0363 |
| 10 | .0061 | .0071 | .0081 | .0092 | .0104 | .0118 | .0132 | .0147 | .0164 | .0181 |
| 11 | .0023 | .0027 | .0032 | .0037 | .0043 | .0049 | .0056 | .0064 | .0073 | .0082 |
| 12 | .0008 | .0009 | .0011 | .0014 | .0016 | .0019 | .0022 | .0026 | .0030 | .0034 |
| 13 | .0002 | .0003 | .0004 | .0005 | .0006 | .0007 | .0008 | .0009 | .0011 | .0013 |
| 14 | .0001 | .0001 | .0001 | .0001 | .0002 | .0002 | .0003 | .0003 | .0004 | .0005 |
| 15 | .0000 | .0000 | .0000 | .0000 | .0001 | .0001 | .0001 | .0001 | .0001 | .0002 |

λ

| x | 5.1 | 5.2 | 5.3 | 5.4 | 5.5 | 5.6 | 5.7 | 5.8 | 5.9 | 6.0 |
|---|------|------|------|------|------|------|------|------|------|------|
| 0 | .0061 | .0055 | .0050 | .0045 | .0041 | .0037 | .0033 | .0030 | .0027 | .0025 |
| 1 | .0311 | .0287 | .0265 | .0244 | .0225 | .0207 | .0191 | .0176 | .0162 | .0149 |
| 2 | .0793 | .0746 | .0701 | .0659 | .0618 | .0580 | .0544 | .0509 | .0477 | .0446 |
| 3 | .1348 | .1293 | .1239 | .1185 | .1133 | .1082 | .1033 | .0985 | .0938 | .0892 |
| 4 | .1719 | .1681 | .1641 | .1600 | .1558 | .1515 | .1472 | .1428 | .1383 | .1339 |
| 5 | .1753 | .1748 | .1740 | .1728 | .1714 | .1697 | .1678 | .1620 | .1632 | .1606 |
| 6 | .1490 | .1515 | .1537 | .1555 | .1571 | .1584 | .1594 | .1656 | .1605 | .1606 |
| 7 | .1086 | .1125 | .1163 | .1200 | .1234 | .1267 | .1298 | .1301 | .1353 | .1377 |
| 8 | .0692 | .0731 | .0771 | .0810 | .0849 | .0887 | .0925 | .0926 | .0998 | .1033 |
| 9 | .0392 | .0423 | .0454 | .0486 | .0519 | .0552 | .0586 | .0662 | .0654 | .0688 |
| 10 | .0200 | .0220 | .0241 | .0262 | .0285 | .0309 | .0334 | .0359 | .0386 | .0413 |
| 11 | .0093 | .0104 | .0116 | .0129 | .0143 | .0157 | .0173 | .0190 | .0207 | .0225 |
| 12 | .0039 | .0045 | .0051 | .0058 | .0065 | .0073 | .0082 | .0092 | .0102 | .0113 |
| 13 | .0015 | .0018 | .0021 | .0024 | .0028 | .0032 | .0036 | .0041 | .0046 | .0052 |
| 14 | .0006 | .0007 | .0008 | .0009 | .0011 | .0013 | .0015 | .0017 | .0019 | .0022 |
| 15 | .0002 | .0002 | .0003 | .0003 | .0004 | .0005 | .0006 | .0007 | .0008 | .0009 |
| 16 | .0001 | .0001 | .0001 | .0001 | .0001 | .0002 | .0002 | .0002 | .0003 | .0003 |
| 17 | .0000 | .0000 | .0000 | .0000 | .0000 | .0001 | .0001 | .0001 | .0001 | .0001 |

## Binomial Distribution (cont.)

| x | λ | | | | | | | | | |
|---|------|------|------|------|------|------|------|------|------|------|
| | 6.1 | 6.2 | 6.3 | 6.4 | 6.5 | 6.6 | 6.7 | 6.8 | 6.9 | 7.0 |
| 0 | .0022 | .0020 | .0018 | .0017 | .0015 | .0014 | .0012 | .0011 | .0010 | .0009 |
| 1 | .0137 | .0126 | .0116 | .0106 | .0098 | .0090 | .0082 | .0076 | .0070 | .0064 |
| 2 | .0417 | .0390 | .0364 | .0340 | .0318 | .0296 | .0276 | .0258 | .0240 | .0223 |
| 3 | .0848 | .0806 | .0765 | .0726 | .0688 | .0652 | .0617 | .0584 | .0552 | .0521 |
| 4 | .1294 | .1249 | .1205 | .1162 | .1118 | .1076 | .1034 | .0992 | .0952 | .0912 |
| 5 | .1579 | .1549 | .1519 | .1487 | .1454 | .1420 | .1385 | .1349 | .1314 | .1277 |
| 6 | .1605 | .1601 | .1595 | .1586 | .1575 | .1562 | .1546 | .1529 | .1511 | .1490 |
| 7 | .1399 | .1418 | .1435 | .1450 | .1462 | .1472 | .1480 | .1486 | .1489 | .1490 |
| 8 | .1066 | .1099 | .1130 | .1160 | .1188 | .1215 | .1240 | .1263 | .1284 | .1304 |
| 9 | .0723 | .0757 | .0791 | .0825 | .0858 | .0891 | .0923 | .0954 | .0985 | .1014 |
| 10 | .0441 | .0469 | .0498 | .0528 | .0558 | .0588 | .0618 | .0649 | .0679 | .0710 |
| 11 | .0245 | .0265 | .0285 | .0307 | .0330 | .0353 | .0377 | .0401 | .0426 | .0452 |
| 12 | .0124 | .0137 | .0150 | .0164 | .0179 | .0194 | .0210 | .0227 | .0245 | .0264 |
| 13 | .0058 | .0065 | .0073 | .0081 | .0089 | .0098 | .0108 | .0119 | .0130 | .0142 |
| 14 | .0025 | .0029 | .0033 | .0037 | .0041 | .0046 | .0052 | .0058 | .0064 | .0071 |
| 15 | .0010 | .0012 | .0014 | .0016 | .0018 | .0020 | .0023 | .0026 | .0029 | .0033 |
| 16 | .0004 | .0005 | .0005 | .0006 | .0007 | .0008 | .0010 | .0011 | .0013 | .0014 |
| 17 | .0001 | .0002 | .0002 | .0002 | .0003 | .0003 | .0004 | .0004 | .0005 | .0006 |
| 18 | .0000 | .0001 | .0001 | .0001 | .0001 | .0001 | .0001 | .0002 | .0002 | .0002 |
| 19 | .0000 | .0000 | .0000 | .0000 | .0000 | .0000 | .0000 | .0001 | .0001 | .0001 |

# Poisson Distribution (cont.)

|  | $\lambda$ | | | | | | | | | |
|---|---|---|---|---|---|---|---|---|---|---|
| x | 7.1 | 7.2 | 7.3 | 7.4 | 7.5 | 7.6 | 7.7 | 7.8 | 7.9 | 8.0 |
| 0 | .0008 | .0007 | .0007 | .0006 | .0006 | .0005 | .0005 | .0004 | .0004 | .0003 |
| 1 | .0059 | .0054 | .0049 | .0045 | .0041 | .0038 | .0035 | .0032 | .0029 | .0027 |
| 2 | .0208 | .0194 | .0180 | .0167 | .0156 | .0145 | .0134 | .0125 | .0116 | .0107 |
| 3 | .0492 | .0464 | .0438 | .0413 | .0389 | .0366 | .0345 | .0324 | .0305 | .0286 |
| 4 | .0874 | .0836 | .0799 | .0764 | .0729 | .0696 | .0663 | .0632 | .0602 | .0573 |
| 5 | .1241 | .1204 | .1167 | .1130 | .1094 | .1057 | .1021 | .0986 | .0951 | .0916 |
| 6 | .1468 | .1445 | .1420 | .1394 | .1367 | .1339 | .1311 | .1282 | .1252 | .1221 |
| 7 | .1489 | .1486 | .1481 | .1474 | .1465 | .1454 | .1442 | .1428 | .1413 | .1396 |
| 8 | .1321 | .1337 | .1351 | .1363 | .1373 | .1382 | .1388 | .1392 | .1395 | .1396 |
| 9 | .1042 | .1070 | .1096 | .1121 | .1144 | .1167 | .1187 | .1207 | .1224 | .1241 |
| 10 | .0740 | .0770 | .0800 | .0829 | .0858 | .0887 | .0914 | .0941 | .0967 | .0993 |
| 11 | .0478 | .0504 | .0531 | .0558 | .0585 | .0613 | .0640 | .0667 | .0695 | .0722 |
| 12 | 0.283 | .0303 | .0323 | .0344 | .0366 | .0388 | .0411 | .0434 | .0457 | .0481 |
| 13 | .0154 | .0168 | .0181 | .0196 | .0211 | .0227 | .0243 | .0260 | .0278 | .0296 |
| 14 | .0078 | .0086 | .0095 | .0104 | .0113 | .0123 | .0134 | .0145 | .0157 | .0169 |
| 15 | .0037 | .0041 | .0046 | .0051 | .0057 | .0062 | .0069 | .0075 | .0083 | .0090 |
| 16 | .0016 | .0019 | .0021 | .0024 | .0026 | .0030 | .0033 | .0037 | .0041 | .0045 |
| 17 | .0007 | .0008 | .0009 | .0010 | .0012 | .0013 | .0015 | .0017 | .0119 | .0021 |
| 18 | .0003 | .0003 | .0004 | .0004 | .0005 | .0006 | .0006 | .0007 | .0008 | .0009 |
| 19 | .0001 | .0001 | .0001 | .0002 | .0002 | .0002 | .0003 | .0003 | .0003 | .0004 |
| 20 | .0000 | .0000 | .0001 | .0001 | .0001 | .0001 | .0001 | .0001 | .0001 | .0002 |
| 21 | .0000 | .0000 | .0000 | .0000 | .0000 | .0000 | .0000 | .0000 | .0001 | .0001 |

**Table B.3** Poisson Distribution (cont.)

| | λ | | | | | | | | | |
|---|---|---|---|---|---|---|---|---|---|---|
| x | 8.1 | 8.2 | 8.3 | 8.4 | 8.5 | 8.6 | 8.7 | 8.8 | 8.9 | 9.0 |
| 0 | .0003 | .0003 | .0002 | .0002 | .0002 | .0002 | .0002 | .0002 | .0001 | .0001 |
| 1 | .0025 | .0023 | .0021 | .0019 | .0017 | .0016 | .0014 | .0013 | .0012 | .0011 |
| 2 | .0100 | .0092 | .0086 | .0079 | .0074 | .0068 | .0063 | .0058 | .0054 | .0050 |
| 3 | .0269 | .0252 | .0237 | .0222 | .0208 | .0195 | .0183 | .0171 | .0160 | .0150 |
| 4 | .0544 | .0517 | .0491 | .0466 | .0443 | .0420 | .0398 | .0377 | .0357 | .0337 |
| 5 | .0882 | .0849 | .0816 | .0784 | .0752 | .0722 | .0692 | .0663 | .0635 | .0607 |
| 6 | .1191 | .1160 | .1128 | .1097 | .1066 | .1034 | .1003 | .0972 | .0941 | .0911 |
| 7 | .1378 | .1358 | .1338 | .1317 | .1294 | .1271 | .1247 | .1222 | .1197 | .1171 |
| 8 | .1395 | .1392 | .1388 | .1382 | .1375 | .1366 | .1356 | .1344 | .1332 | .1318 |
| 9 | .1256 | .1269 | .1280 | .1290 | .1299 | .1306 | .1311 | .1315 | .1317 | .1318 |
| 10 | .1017 | .1040 | .1063 | .1084 | .1104 | .1123 | .1140 | .1157 | .1172 | .1186 |
| 11 | .0749 | .0776 | .0802 | .0828 | .0853 | .0878 | .0902 | .0925 | .0948 | .0970 |
| 12 | .0505 | .0530 | .0555 | .0579 | .0604 | .0629 | .0654 | .0679 | .0703 | .0728 |
| 13 | .0315 | .0334 | .0354 | .0374 | .0395 | .0416 | .0438 | .0459 | .0481 | .0504 |
| 14 | .0182 | .0196 | .0210 | .0225 | .0240 | .0256 | .0272 | .0289 | .0306 | .0324 |
| 15 | .0098 | .0107 | .0116 | .0126 | .0136 | .0147 | .0158 | .0169 | .0182 | .0194 |
| 16 | .0050 | .0055 | .0060 | .0066 | .0072 | .0079 | .0086 | .0093 | .0101 | .0109 |
| 17 | .0024 | .0026 | .0029 | .0033 | .0036 | .0040 | .0044 | .0048 | .0053 | .0058 |
| 18 | .0011 | .0012 | .0014 | .0015 | .0017 | .0019 | .0021 | .0024 | .0026 | .0029 |
| 19 | .0005 | .0005 | .0006 | .0007 | .0008 | .0009 | .0010 | .0011 | .0012 | .0014 |
| 20 | .0002 | .0002 | .0002 | .0003 | .0003 | .0004 | .0004 | .0005 | .0005 | .0006 |
| 21 | .0001 | .0001 | .0001 | .0001 | .0001 | .0002 | .0002 | .0002 | .0002 | .0003 |
| 22 | .0000 | .0000 | .0000 | .0000 | .0001 | .0001 | .0001 | .0001 | .0001 | .0001 |

# Poisson Distribution (cont.)

| | | | | | λ | | | | | |
|---|---|---|---|---|---|---|---|---|---|---|
| x | 9.1 | 9.2 | 9.3 | 9.4 | 9.5 | 9.6 | 9.7 | 9.8 | 9.9 | 10 |
| 0 | .0001 | .0001 | .0001 | .0001 | .0001 | .0001 | .0001 | .0001 | .0001 | .0000 |
| 1 | .0010 | .0009 | .0009 | .0008 | .0007 | .0007 | .0006 | .0005 | .0005 | .0005 |
| 2 | .0046 | .0043 | .0040 | .0037 | .0034 | .0031 | .0029 | .0027 | .0025 | .0023 |
| 3 | .0140 | .0131 | .0123 | .0115 | .0107 | .0100 | .0093 | .0087 | .0081 | .0076 |
| 4 | .0319 | .0302 | .0285 | .0269 | .0254 | .0240 | .0226 | .0213 | .0201 | .0189 |
| 5 | .0581 | .0555 | .0530 | .0506 | .0483 | .0460 | .0439 | .0418 | .0398 | .0378 |
| 6 | .0881 | .0851 | .0822 | .0793 | .0764 | .0736 | .0709 | .0682 | .0656 | .0631 |
| 7 | .1145 | .1118 | .1091 | .1064 | .1037 | .1010 | .0982 | .0955 | .0928 | .0901 |
| 8 | .1302 | .1286 | .1269 | .1251 | .1232 | .1212 | .1191 | .1170 | .1148 | .1126 |
| 9 | .1317 | .1315 | .1311 | .1306 | .1300 | .1293 | .1284 | .1274 | .1263 | .1251 |
| 10 | .1198 | .1210 | .1219 | .1228 | .1235 | .1241 | .1245 | .1249 | .1250 | .1251 |
| 11 | .0991 | .1012 | .1031 | .1049 | .1067 | .1083 | .1098 | .1112 | .1125 | .1137 |
| 12 | .0752 | .0776 | .0799 | .0822 | .0844 | .0866 | .0888 | .0908 | .0928 | .0948 |
| 13 | .0526 | .0549 | .0572 | .0594 | .0617 | .0640 | .0662 | .0685 | .0707 | .0729 |
| 14 | .0342 | .0361 | .0380 | .0399 | .0419 | .0439 | .0459 | .0479 | .0500 | .0521 |
| 15 | .0208 | .0221 | .0235 | .0250 | .0265 | .0281 | .0297 | .0313 | .0330 | .0347 |
| 16 | .0118 | .0127 | .0137 | .0147 | .0157 | .0168 | .0180 | .0192 | .0204 | .0217 |
| 17 | .0063 | .0069 | .0075 | .0081 | .0088 | .0095 | .0103 | .0111 | .0119 | .0128 |
| 18 | .0032 | .0035 | .0039 | .0042 | .0046 | .0051 | .0055 | .0060 | .0065 | .0071 |
| 19 | .0015 | .0017 | .0019 | .0021 | .0023 | .0026 | .0028 | .0031 | .0034 | .0037 |
| 20 | .0007 | .0008 | .0009 | .0010 | .0011 | .0012 | .0014 | .0015 | .0017 | .0019 |
| 21 | .0003 | .0003 | .0004 | .0004 | .0005 | .0006 | .0006 | .0007 | .0008 | .0009 |
| 22 | .0001 | .0001 | .0002 | .0002 | .0002 | .0002 | .0003 | .0003 | .0004 | .0004 |
| 23 | .0000 | .0001 | .0001 | .0001 | .0001 | .0001 | .0001 | .0001 | .0002 | .0002 |
| 24 | .0000 | .0000 | .0000 | .0000 | .0000 | .0000 | .0000 | .0001 | .0001 | .0001 |

### Table B.4    Standard Normal Distribution

The cumulative standardized normal distribution $F(x)$ is defined by

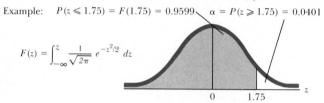

Example:    $P(z \leqslant 1.75) = F(1.75) = 0.9599$    $\alpha = P(z \geqslant 1.75) = 0.0401$

$$F(z) = \int_{-\infty}^{z} \frac{1}{\sqrt{2\pi}}\, e^{-z^2/2}\, dz$$

| z | .00 | .01 | .02 | .03 | .04 | .05 | .06 | .07 | .08 | .09 |
|---|---|---|---|---|---|---|---|---|---|---|
| .0 | .5000 | .5040 | .5080 | .5120 | .5160 | .5199 | .5239 | .5279 | .5319 | .5359 |
| .1 | .5398 | .5438 | .5478 | .5517 | .5557 | .5596 | .5636 | .5675 | .5714 | .5753 |
| .2 | .5793 | .5832 | .5871 | .5910 | .5948 | .5987 | .6026 | .6064 | .6103 | .6141 |
| .3 | .6179 | .6217 | .6255 | .6293 | .6331 | .6368 | .6406 | .6443 | .6480 | .6517 |
| .4 | .6554 | .6591 | .6628 | .6664 | .6700 | .6736 | .6772 | .6808 | .6844 | .6879 |
| .5 | .6915 | .6950 | .6985 | .7019 | .7054 | .7088 | .7123 | .7157 | .7190 | .7224 |
| .6 | .7257 | .7291 | .7324 | .7357 | .7389 | .7422 | .7454 | .7486 | .7517 | .7549 |
| .7 | .7580 | .7611 | .7642 | .7673 | .7704 | .7734 | .7764 | .7794 | .7823 | .7852 |
| .8 | .7881 | .7910 | .7939 | .7967 | .7995 | .8023 | .8051 | .8078 | .8106 | .8133 |
| .9 | .8159 | .8186 | .8212 | .8238 | .8264 | .8289 | .8315 | .8340 | .8365 | .8389 |
| 1.0 | .8413 | .8438 | .8461 | .8485 | .8508 | .8531 | .8554 | .8577 | .8599 | .8621 |
| 1.1 | .8643 | .8665 | .8686 | .8708 | .8729 | .8749 | .8770 | .8790 | .8810 | .8830 |
| 1.2 | .8849 | .8869 | .8888 | .8907 | .8925 | .8944 | .8962 | .8980 | .8997 | .9015 |
| 1.3 | .9032 | .9049 | .9066 | .9082 | .9099 | .9115 | .9131 | .9147 | .9162 | .9177 |
| 1.4 | .9192 | .9207 | .9222 | .9236 | .9251 | .9265 | .9279 | .9292 | .9306 | .9319 |
| 1.5 | .9332 | .9345 | .9357 | .9370 | .9382 | .9394 | .9406 | .9418 | .9429 | .9441 |
| 1.6 | .9452 | .9463 | .9474 | .9484 | .9495 | .9505 | .9515 | .9525 | .9535 | .9545 |
| 1.7 | .9554 | .9564 | .9573 | .9582 | .9591 | .9599 | .9608 | .9616 | .9625 | .9633 |
| 1.8 | .9641 | .9649 | .9656 | .9664 | .9671 | .9678 | .9686 | .9693 | .9699 | .9706 |
| 1.9 | .9713 | .9719 | .9726 | .9732 | .9738 | .9744 | .9750 | .9756 | .9761 | .9767 |
| 2.0 | .9772 | .9778 | .9783 | .9788 | .9793 | .9798 | .9803 | .9808 | .9812 | .9817 |
| 2.1 | .9821 | .9826 | .9830 | .9834 | .9838 | .9842 | .9846 | .9850 | .9854 | .9857 |
| 2.2 | .9861 | .9864 | .9868 | .9871 | .9875 | .9878 | .9881 | .9884 | .9887 | .9890 |
| 2.3 | .9893 | .9896 | .9898 | .9901 | .9904 | .9906 | .9909 | .9911 | .9913 | .9916 |
| 2.4 | .9918 | .9920 | .9922 | .9925 | .9927 | .9929 | .9931 | .9932 | .9934 | .9936 |
| 2.5 | .9938 | .9940 | .9941 | .9943 | .9945 | .9946 | .9948 | .9949 | .9951 | .9952 |
| 2.6 | .9953 | .9955 | .9956 | .9957 | .9959 | .9960 | .9961 | .9962 | .9963 | .9964 |
| 2.7 | .9965 | .9966 | .9967 | .9968 | .9969 | .9970 | .9971 | .9972 | .9973 | .9974 |
| 2.8 | .9974 | .9975 | .9976 | .9977 | .9977 | .9978 | .9979 | .9979 | .9980 | .9981 |
| 2.9 | .9981 | .9982 | .9982 | .9983 | .9984 | .9984 | .9985 | .9985 | .9986 | .9986 |
| 3.0 | .9987 | .9987 | .9987 | .9988 | .9988 | .9989 | .9989 | .9989 | .9990 | .9990 |
| 3.1 | .9990 | .9991 | .9991 | .9991 | .9992 | .9992 | .9992 | .9992 | .9993 | .9993 |
| 3.2 | .9993 | .9993 | .9994 | .9994 | .9994 | .9994 | .9994 | .9995 | .9995 | .9995 |
| 3.3 | .9995 | .9995 | .9995 | .9996 | .9996 | .9996 | .9996 | .9996 | .9996 | .9997 |
| 3.4 | .9997 | .9997 | .9997 | .9997 | .9997 | .9997 | .9997 | .9997 | .9997 | .9998 |

## Table B.5      _t_ Distribution*

The cumulative _t_ distribution is defined by

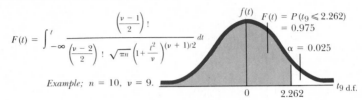

$$F(t) = \int_{-\infty}^{t} \frac{\left(\frac{\nu-1}{2}\right)!}{\left(\frac{\nu-2}{2}\right)! \; \sqrt{\pi n}\left(1+\frac{t^2}{\nu}\right)^{(\nu+1)/2}}\,dt$$

$F(t) = P(t_9 \leqslant 2.262)$
$= 0.975$

$\alpha = 0.025$

_Example; n = 10, ν = 9._

$t_9$ d.f.

0      2.262

| F(t) | .75 | .90 | .95 | .975 | .99 | .995 | .9995 |
|---|---|---|---|---|---|---|---|
| ν (α) | (.25) | (.10) | (.05) | (.025) | (.01) | (.005) | (.0005) |
| 1 | 1.000 | 3.078 | 6.314 | 12.706 | 31.821 | 63.657 | 636.619 |
| 2 | .816 | 1.886 | 2.920 | 4.303 | 6.965 | 9.925 | 31.598 |
| 3 | .765 | 1.638 | 2.353 | 3.182 | 4.541 | 5.841 | 12.941 |
| 4 | .741 | 1.533 | 2.132 | 2.776 | 3.747 | 4.604 | 8.610 |
| 5 | .727 | 1.476 | 2.015 | 2.571 | 3.365 | 4.032 | 6.859 |
| 6 | .718 | 1.440 | 1.943 | 2.447 | 3.143 | 3.707 | 5.959 |
| 7 | .711 | 1.415 | 1.895 | 2.365 | 2.998 | 3.499 | 5.405 |
| 8 | .706 | 1.397 | 1.860 | 2.306 | 2.896 | 3.355 | 5.041 |
| 9 | .703 | 1.383 | 1.833 | 2.262 | 2.821 | 3.250 | 4.781 |
| 10 | .700 | 1.372 | 1.812 | 2.228 | 2.764 | 3.169 | 4.587 |
| 11 | .697 | 1.363 | 1.796 | 2.201 | 2.718 | 3.106 | 4.437 |
| 12 | .695 | 1.356 | 1.782 | 2.179 | 2.681 | 3.055 | 4.318 |
| 13 | .694 | 1.350 | 1.771 | 2.160 | 2.650 | 3.012 | 4.221 |
| 14 | .692 | 1.345 | 1.761 | 2.145 | 2.624 | 2.977 | 4.140 |
| 15 | .691 | 1.341 | 1.753 | 2.131 | 2.602 | 2.947 | 4.073 |
| 16 | .690 | 1.337 | 1.746 | 2.120 | 2.583 | 2.921 | 4.015 |
| 17 | .689 | 1.333 | 1.740 | 2.110 | 2.567 | 2.898 | 3.965 |
| 18 | .688 | 1.330 | 1.734 | 2.101 | 2.552 | 2.878 | 3.922 |
| 19 | .688 | 1.328 | 1.729 | 2.093 | 2.539 | 2.861 | 3.883 |
| 20 | .687 | 1.325 | 1.725 | 2.086 | 2.528 | 2.845 | 3.850 |
| 21 | .686 | 1.323 | 1.721 | 2.080 | 2.518 | 2.831 | 3.819 |
| 22 | .686 | 1.321 | 1.717 | 2.074 | 2.508 | 2.819 | 3.792 |
| 23 | .685 | 1.319 | 1.714 | 2.069 | 2.500 | 2.807 | 3.767 |
| 24 | .685 | 1.318 | 1.711 | 2.064 | 2.492 | 2.797 | 3.745 |
| 25 | .684 | 1.316 | 1.708 | 2.060 | 2.485 | 2.787 | 3.725 |
| 26 | .684 | 1.315 | 1.706 | 2.056 | 2.479 | 2.779 | 3.707 |
| 27 | .684 | 1.314 | 1.703 | 2.052 | 2.473 | 2.771 | 3.690 |
| 28 | .683 | 1.313 | 1.701 | 2.048 | 2.467 | 2.763 | 3.674 |
| 29 | .683 | 1.311 | 1.699 | 2.045 | 2.462 | 2.756 | 3.659 |
| 30 | .683 | 1.310 | 1.697 | 2.042 | 2.457 | 2.750 | 3.646 |
| 40 | .681 | 1.303 | 1.684 | 2.021 | 2.423 | 2.704 | 3.551 |
| 60 | .679 | 1.296 | 1.671 | 2.000 | 2.390 | 2.660 | 3.460 |
| 120 | .677 | 1.289 | 1.658 | 1.980 | 2.358 | 2.617 | 3.373 |
| $\infty(z_a)$ | .674 | 1.282 | 1.645 | 1.960 | 2.326 | 2.576 | 3.291 |

* This table is abridged from the "Statistical Tables" of R. A. Fisher and Frank Yates published by Oliver & Boyd, Ltd., Edinburgh and London. 1938. It is here published with the kind permission of the authors and their publishers.

## Table B.6　　　　　F **Distribution**

The cumulative $F$ distribution at 0.95 ($\alpha = 0.05$) is defined by the figure at right. The critical values of the $F$ distribution for a cumulative probability of 0.95 ($\alpha = 0.05$) are given below. The probability ($\alpha$) represents the area exceeding the value of $F_{0.05,\nu_1,\nu_2}$, as shown by the shaded area in the figure.

**EXAMPLE**　If $\nu_1 = 15$ (d.f. for the numerator) and $\nu_2 = 20$, then the critical value cutting off 0.05 is 2.20. $P(F \geq 2.20) = 0.05$, $P(F \leq 2.20) = 0.95$.

| | | $\nu_1 =$ Degrees of freedom for numerator | | | | | | | |
|---|---|---|---|---|---|---|---|---|---|
| | 1 | 2 | 3 | 4 | 5 | 6 | 7 | 8 | 9 |
| 1 | 161 | 200 | 216 | 225 | 230 | 234 | 237 | 239 | 241 |
| 2 | 18.5 | 19.0 | 19.2 | 19.2 | 19.3 | 19.3 | 19.4 | 19.4 | 19.4 |
| 3 | 10.1 | 9.55 | 9.28 | 9.12 | 9.01 | 8.94 | 8.89 | 8.85 | 8.81 |
| 4 | 7.71 | 6.94 | 6.59 | 6.39 | 6.26 | 6.16 | 6.09 | 6.04 | 6.00 |
| 5 | 6.61 | 5.79 | 5.41 | 5.19 | 5.05 | 4.95 | 4.88 | 4.82 | 4.77 |
| 6 | 5.99 | 5.14 | 4.76 | 4.53 | 4.39 | 4.28 | 4.21 | 4.15 | 4.10 |
| 7 | 5.59 | 4.74 | 4.35 | 4.12 | 3.97 | 3.87 | 3.79 | 3.73 | 3.68 |
| 8 | 5.32 | 4.46 | 4.07 | 3.84 | 3.69 | 3.58 | 3.50 | 3.44 | 3.39 |
| 9 | 5.12 | 4.26 | 3.86 | 3.63 | 3.48 | 3.37 | 3.29 | 3.23 | 3.18 |
| 10 | 4.96 | 4.10 | 3.71 | 3.48 | 3.33 | 3.22 | 3.14 | 3.07 | 3.02 |
| 11 | 4.84 | 3.98 | 3.59 | 3.36 | 3.20 | 3.09 | 3.01 | 2.95 | 2.90 |
| 12 | 4.75 | 3.89 | 3.49 | 3.26 | 3.11 | 3.00 | 2.91 | 2.85 | 2.80 |
| 13 | 4.67 | 3.81 | 3.41 | 3.18 | 3.03 | 2.92 | 2.83 | 2.77 | 2.71 |
| 14 | 4.60 | 3.74 | 3.34 | 3.11 | 2.96 | 2.85 | 2.76 | 2.70 | 2.65 |
| 15 | 4.54 | 3.68 | 3.29 | 3.06 | 2.90 | 2.79 | 2.71 | 2.64 | 2.59 |
| 16 | 4.49 | 3.63 | 3.24 | 3.01 | 2.85 | 2.74 | 2.66 | 2.59 | 2.54 |
| 17 | 4.45 | 3.59 | 3.20 | 2.96 | 2.81 | 2.70 | 2.61 | 2.55 | 2.49 |
| 18 | 4.41 | 3.55 | 3.16 | 2.93 | 2.77 | 2.66 | 2.58 | 2.51 | 2.46 |
| 19 | 4.38 | 3.52 | 3.13 | 2.90 | 2.74 | 2.63 | 2.54 | 2.48 | 2.42 |
| 20 | 4.35 | 3.49 | 3.10 | 2.87 | 2.71 | 2.60 | 2.51 | 2.45 | 2.39 |
| 21 | 4.32 | 3.47 | 3.07 | 2.84 | 2.68 | 2.57 | 2.49 | 2.42 | 2.37 |
| 22 | 4.30 | 3.44 | 3.05 | 2.82 | 2.66 | 2.55 | 2.46 | 2.40 | 2.34 |
| 23 | 4.28 | 3.42 | 3.03 | 2.80 | 2.64 | 2.53 | 2.44 | 2.37 | 2.32 |
| 24 | 4.26 | 3.40 | 3.01 | 2.78 | 2.62 | 2.51 | 2.42 | 2.36 | 2.30 |
| 25 | 4.24 | 3.39 | 2.99 | 2.76 | 2.60 | 2.49 | 2.40 | 2.34 | 2.28 |
| 30 | 4.17 | 3.32 | 2.92 | 2.69 | 2.53 | 2.42 | 2.33 | 2.27 | 2.21 |
| 40 | 4.08 | 3.23 | 2.84 | 2.61 | 2.45 | 2.34 | 2.25 | 2.18 | 2.12 |
| 60 | 4.00 | 3.15 | 2.76 | 2.53 | 2.37 | 2.25 | 2.17 | 2.10 | 2.04 |
| 120 | 3.92 | 3.07 | 2.68 | 2.45 | 2.29 | 2.18 | 2.09 | 2.02 | 1.96 |
| $\infty$ | 3.84 | 3.00 | 2.60 | 2.37 | 2.21 | 2.10 | 2.01 | 1.94 | 1.88 |

$\nu_2 =$ Degrees of freedom for denominator

# Table B.6     $F$ Distribution (cont.)

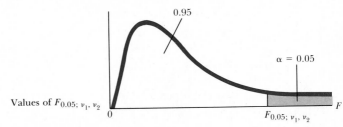

Values of $F_{0.05;\ \nu_1,\ \nu_2}$

$\nu_1 = $ Degrees of freedom for numerator

| $\nu_2$ | 10 | 12 | 15 | 20 | 24 | 30 | 40 | 60 | 120 | $\infty$ |
|---|---|---|---|---|---|---|---|---|---|---|
| 1 | 242 | 244 | 246 | 248 | 249 | 250 | 251 | 252 | 253 | 254 |
| 2 | 19.4 | 19.4 | 19.4 | 19.4 | 19.5 | 19.5 | 19.5 | 19.5 | 19.5 | 19.5 |
| 3 | 8.79 | 8.74 | 8.70 | 8.66 | 8.64 | 8.62 | 8.59 | 8.57 | 8.55 | 8.53 |
| 4 | 5.96 | 5.91 | 5.86 | 5.80 | 5.77 | 5.75 | 5.72 | 5.69 | 5.66 | 5.63 |
| 5 | 4.74 | 4.68 | 4.62 | 4.56 | 4.53 | 4.50 | 4.46 | 4.43 | 4.40 | 4.37 |
| 6 | 4.06 | 4.00 | 3.94 | 3.87 | 3.84 | 3.81 | 3.77 | 3.74 | 3.70 | 3.67 |
| 7 | 3.64 | 3.57 | 3.51 | 3.44 | 3.41 | 3.38 | 3.34 | 3.30 | 3.27 | 3.23 |
| 8 | 3.35 | 3.28 | 3.22 | 3.15 | 3.12 | 3.08 | 3.04 | 3.01 | 2.97 | 2.93 |
| 9 | 3.14 | 3.07 | 3.01 | 2.94 | 2.90 | 2.86 | 2.83 | 2.79 | 2.75 | 2.71 |
| 10 | 2.98 | 2.91 | 2.85 | 2.77 | 2.74 | 2.70 | 2.66 | 2.62 | 2.58 | 2.54 |
| 11 | 2.85 | 2.79 | 2.72 | 2.65 | 2.61 | 2.57 | 2.53 | 2.49 | 2.45 | 2.40 |
| 12 | 2.75 | 2.69 | 2.62 | 2.54 | 2.51 | 2.47 | 2.43 | 2.38 | 2.34 | 2.30 |
| 13 | 2.67 | 2.60 | 2.53 | 2.46 | 2.42 | 2.38 | 2.34 | 2.30 | 2.25 | 2.21 |
| 14 | 2.60 | 2.53 | 2.46 | 2.39 | 2.35 | 2.31 | 2.27 | 2.22 | 2.18 | 2.13 |
| 15 | 2.54 | 2.48 | 2.40 | 2.33 | 2.29 | 2.25 | 2.20 | 2.16 | 2.11 | 2.07 |
| 16 | 2.49 | 2.42 | 2.35 | 2.28 | 2.24 | 2.19 | 2.15 | 2.11 | 2.06 | 2.01 |
| 17 | 2.45 | 2.38 | 2.31 | 2.23 | 2.19 | 2.15 | 2.10 | 2.06 | 2.01 | 1.96 |
| 18 | 2.41 | 2.34 | 2.27 | 2.19 | 2.15 | 2.11 | 2.06 | 2.02 | 1.97 | 1.92 |
| 19 | 2.38 | 2.31 | 2.23 | 2.16 | 2.11 | 2.07 | 2.03 | 1.98 | 1.93 | 1.88 |
| 20 | 2.35 | 2.28 | 2.20 | 2.12 | 2.08 | 2.04 | 1.99 | 1.95 | 1.90 | 1.84 |
| 21 | 2.32 | 2.25 | 2.18 | 2.10 | 2.05 | 2.01 | 1.96 | 1.92 | 1.87 | 1.81 |
| 22 | 2.30 | 2.23 | 2.15 | 2.07 | 2.03 | 1.98 | 1.94 | 1.89 | 1.84 | 1.78 |
| 23 | 2.27 | 2.20 | 2.13 | 2.05 | 2.01 | 1.96 | 1.91 | 1.86 | 1.81 | 1.76 |
| 24 | 2.25 | 2.18 | 2.11 | 2.03 | 1.98 | 1.94 | 1.89 | 1.84 | 1.79 | 1.73 |
| 25 | 2.24 | 2.16 | 2.09 | 2.01 | 1.96 | 1.92 | 1.87 | 1.82 | 1.77 | 1.71 |
| 30 | 2.16 | 2.09 | 2.01 | 1.93 | 1.89 | 1.84 | 1.79 | 1.74 | 1.68 | 1.62 |
| 40 | 2.08 | 2.00 | 1.92 | 1.84 | 1.79 | 1.74 | 1.69 | 1.64 | 1.58 | 1.51 |
| 60 | 1.99 | 1.92 | 1.84 | 1.75 | 1.70 | 1.65 | 1.59 | 1.53 | 1.47 | 1.39 |
| 120 | 1.91 | 1.83 | 1.75 | 1.66 | 1.61 | 1.55 | 1.50 | 1.43 | 1.35 | 1.25 |
| $\infty$ | 1.83 | 1.75 | 1.67 | 1.57 | 1.52 | 1.46 | 1.39 | 1.32 | 1.22 | 1.00 |

$\nu_2 = $ Degrees of freedom for denominator

## Table B.7 Chi-Square Distribution

The cumulative chi-square distribution is defined by

$$F(\chi^2) = \int_0^{\chi^2} \frac{\chi^{(\nu-2)/2} e^{-\chi/2} d\chi}{2^{\nu/2}[(\nu-2)/2]!}$$

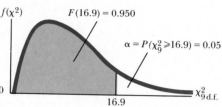

$f(\chi^2)$   $F(16.9) = 0.950$

$\alpha = P(\chi_9^2 \geqslant 16.9) = 0.05$

16.9    $\chi_{9\,d.f.}^2$

Example: $P(\chi_9^2 \leqslant 16.9$ for d.f. = 9
$P(\chi^2 \leqslant 30.1) = F(16.9) = 0.950$

| $F(\chi^2)$ | .005 | .010 | .025 | .050 | .100 | .900 | .950 | .975 | .990 | .995 |
|---|---|---|---|---|---|---|---|---|---|---|
| $\nu$ (α) | (.995) | (.990) | (.975) | (.950) | (.900) | (.100) | (.050) | (.025) | (.010) | (.005) |
| 1 | .0⁴393 | .0³157 | .0³982 | .0²393 | 0.158 | 2.71 | 3.84 | 5.02 | 6.63 | 7.88 |
| 2 | .0100 | .0201 | .0506 | .103 | .211 | 4.61 | 5.99 | 7.38 | 9.21 | 10.6 |
| 3 | .0717 | .115 | .216 | .352 | .584 | 6.25 | 7.81 | 9.35 | 11.3 | 12.8 |
| 4 | .207 | .297 | .484 | .711 | 1.06 | 7.78 | 9.49 | 11.1 | 13.3 | 14.9 |
| 5 | .412 | .554 | .831 | 1.15 | 1.61 | 9.24 | 11.1 | 12.8 | 15.1 | 16.7 |
| 6 | .676 | .872 | 1.24 | 1.64 | 2.20 | 10.6 | 12.6 | 14.4 | 16.8 | 18.5 |
| 7 | .989 | 1.24 | 1.69 | 2.17 | 2.83 | 12.0 | 14.1 | 16.0 | 18.5 | 20.3 |
| 8 | 1.34 | 1.65 | 2.18 | 2.73 | 3.49 | 13.4 | 15.5 | 17.5 | 20.1 | 22.0 |
| 9 | 1.73 | 2.09 | 2.70 | 3.33 | 4.17 | 14.7 | 16.9 | 19.0 | 21.7 | 23.6 |
| 10 | 2.16 | 2.56 | 3.25 | 3.94 | 4.87 | 16.0 | 18.3 | 20.5 | 23.2 | 25.2 |
| 11 | 2.60 | 3.05 | 3.82 | 4.57 | 5.58 | 17.3 | 19.7 | 21.9 | 24.7 | 26.8 |
| 12 | 3.07 | 3.57 | 4.40 | 5.23 | 6.30 | 18.5 | 21.0 | 23.3 | 26.2 | 28.3 |
| 13 | 3.57 | 4.11 | 5.01 | 5.89 | 7.04 | 19.8 | 22.4 | 24.7 | 27.7 | 29.8 |
| 14 | 4.07 | 4.66 | 5.63 | 6.57 | 7.79 | 21.1 | 23.7 | 26.1 | 29.1 | 31.3 |
| 15 | 4.60 | 5.23 | 6.26 | 7.26 | 8.55 | 22.3 | 25.0 | 27.5 | 30.6 | 32.8 |
| 16 | 5.14 | 5.81 | 6.91 | 7.96 | 9.31 | 23.5 | 26.3 | 28.8 | 32.0 | 34.3 |
| 17 | 5.70 | 6.41 | 7.56 | 8.67 | 10.1 | 24.8 | 27.6 | 30.2 | 33.4 | 35.7 |
| 18 | 6.26 | 7.01 | 8.23 | 9.39 | 10.9 | 26.0 | 28.9 | 31.5 | 34.8 | 37.2 |
| 19 | 6.84 | 7.63 | 8.91 | 10.1 | 11.7 | 27.2 | 30.1 | 32.9 | 36.2 | 38.6 |
| 20 | 7.43 | 8.26 | 9.59 | 10.9 | 12.4 | 28.4 | 31.4 | 34.2 | 37.6 | 40.0 |
| 21 | 8.03 | 8.90 | 10.3 | 11.6 | 13.2 | 29.6 | 32.7 | 35.5 | 38.9 | 41.4 |
| 22 | 8.64 | 9.54 | 11.0 | 12.3 | 14.0 | 30.8 | 33.9 | 36.8 | 40.3 | 42.8 |
| 23 | 9.26 | 10.2 | 11.7 | 13.1 | 14.8 | 32.0 | 35.2 | 38.1 | 41.6 | 44.2 |
| 24 | 9.89 | 10.9 | 12.4 | 13.8 | 15.7 | 33.2 | 36.4 | 39.4 | 43.0 | 45.6 |
| 25 | 10.5 | 11.5 | 13.1 | 14.6 | 16.5 | 34.4 | 37.7 | 40.6 | 44.3 | 46.9 |
| 26 | 11.2 | 12.2 | 13.8 | 15.4 | 17.3 | 35.6 | 38.9 | 41.9 | 45.6 | 48.3 |
| 27 | 11.8 | 12.9 | 14.6 | 16.2 | 18.1 | 36.7 | 40.1 | 43.2 | 47.0 | 49.6 |
| 28 | 12.5 | 13.6 | 15.3 | 16.9 | 18.9 | 37.9 | 41.3 | 44.5 | 48.3 | 51.0 |
| 29 | 13.1 | 14.3 | 16.0 | 17.7 | 19.8 | 39.1 | 42.6 | 45.7 | 49.6 | 52.3 |
| 30 | 13.8 | 15.0 | 16.8 | 18.5 | 20.6 | 40.3 | 43.8 | 47.0 | 50.9 | 53.7 |
| $z_\alpha$ | −2.576 | −2.326 | −1.960 | −1.645 | −1.282 | +1.282 | +1.645 | +1.960 | +2.326 | +2.576 |

NOTE: For $\nu > 30$ (i.e., for more than 30 degrees of freedom) take

$$\chi^2 = \nu\left[1 - \frac{2}{9\nu} + z_x\sqrt{\frac{2}{9\nu}}\right]^2 \quad \text{or} \quad \chi^2 = \tfrac{1}{2}[z_x + \sqrt{(2\nu-1)}]^2$$

according to the degree of accuracy required. $z_\alpha$ is the standardized normal deviate corresponding to the α level of significance, and is shown in the bottom line of the table.
This table is abridged from "Tables of percentage points of the incomplete beta function and of the chi-square distribution," *Biometrika*. Vol. 32 (1941). Reprinted with permission of its author, Catherine M. Thompson, and the editor of *Biometrika*.

## Table B.8 Critical Value of r in the Runs Test

This table gives various critical values of $r$ for various values of $n_1$ and $n_2$. For the Wald-Wolfowitz two-sample runs test, any value of $r$ that is equal to or smaller than that shown is significant at the 0.05 level.

| $n_1$ \ $n_2$ | 2 | 3 | 4 | 5 | 6 | 7 | 8 | 9 | 10 | 11 | 12 | 13 | 14 | 15 | 16 | 17 | 18 | 19 | 20 |
|---|---|---|---|---|---|---|---|---|---|---|---|---|---|---|---|---|---|---|---|
| 2 |  |  |  |  |  |  |  |  |  |  | 2 | 2 | 2 | 2 | 2 | 2 | 2 | 2 | 2 |
| 3 |  |  |  |  | 2 | 2 | 2 | 2 | 2 | 2 | 2 | 2 | 2 | 3 | 3 | 3 | 3 | 3 | 3 |
| 4 |  |  |  | 2 | 2 | 2 | 3 | 3 | 3 | 3 | 3 | 3 | 3 | 3 | 4 | 4 | 4 | 4 | 4 |
| 5 |  |  | 2 | 2 | 3 | 3 | 3 | 3 | 3 | 4 | 4 | 4 | 4 | 4 | 4 | 4 | 5 | 5 | 5 |
| 6 |  | 2 | 2 | 3 | 3 | 3 | 3 | 4 | 4 | 4 | 4 | 5 | 5 | 5 | 5 | 5 | 5 | 6 | 6 |
| 7 |  | 2 | 2 | 3 | 3 | 3 | 4 | 4 | 5 | 5 | 5 | 5 | 5 | 6 | 6 | 6 | 6 | 6 | 6 |
| 8 |  | 2 | 3 | 3 | 3 | 4 | 4 | 5 | 5 | 5 | 6 | 6 | 6 | 6 | 6 | 7 | 7 | 7 | 7 |
| 9 |  | 2 | 3 | 3 | 4 | 4 | 5 | 5 | 5 | 6 | 6 | 6 | 7 | 7 | 7 | 7 | 8 | 8 | 8 |
| 10 |  | 2 | 3 | 3 | 4 | 5 | 5 | 5 | 6 | 6 | 7 | 7 | 7 | 7 | 8 | 8 | 8 | 8 | 9 |
| 11 |  | 2 | 3 | 4 | 4 | 5 | 5 | 6 | 6 | 7 | 7 | 7 | 8 | 8 | 8 | 9 | 9 | 9 | 9 |
| 12 | 2 | 2 | 3 | 4 | 4 | 5 | 6 | 6 | 7 | 7 | 7 | 8 | 8 | 8 | 9 | 9 | 9 | 10 | 10 |
| 13 | 2 | 2 | 3 | 4 | 5 | 5 | 6 | 6 | 7 | 7 | 8 | 8 | 9 | 9 | 9 | 10 | 10 | 10 | 10 |
| 14 | 2 | 2 | 3 | 4 | 5 | 5 | 6 | 7 | 7 | 8 | 8 | 9 | 9 | 9 | 10 | 10 | 10 | 11 | 11 |
| 15 | 2 | 3 | 3 | 4 | 5 | 6 | 6 | 7 | 7 | 8 | 8 | 9 | 9 | 10 | 10 | 11 | 11 | 11 | 12 |
| 16 | 2 | 3 | 4 | 4 | 5 | 6 | 6 | 7 | 8 | 8 | 9 | 9 | 10 | 10 | 11 | 11 | 11 | 12 | 12 |
| 17 | 2 | 3 | 4 | 4 | 5 | 6 | 7 | 7 | 8 | 9 | 9 | 10 | 10 | 11 | 11 | 11 | 12 | 12 | 13 |
| 18 | 2 | 3 | 4 | 5 | 5 | 6 | 7 | 8 | 8 | 9 | 9 | 10 | 10 | 11 | 11 | 12 | 12 | 13 | 13 |
| 19 | 2 | 3 | 4 | 5 | 6 | 6 | 7 | 8 | 8 | 9 | 10 | 10 | 11 | 11 | 12 | 12 | 13 | 13 | 13 |
| 20 | 2 | 3 | 4 | 5 | 6 | 6 | 7 | 8 | 9 | 9 | 10 | 10 | 11 | 12 | 12 | 13 | 13 | 13 | 14 |

Adapted from Frieda S. Swed and C. Eisenhart, "Tables for testing randomness of grouping in a sequence of alternatives." *Ann. Math. Statist.*, Vol. 14 (1943), pp. 83–86, with the kind permission of the authors and publisher.

# ANSWERS TO SELECTED EXERCISES

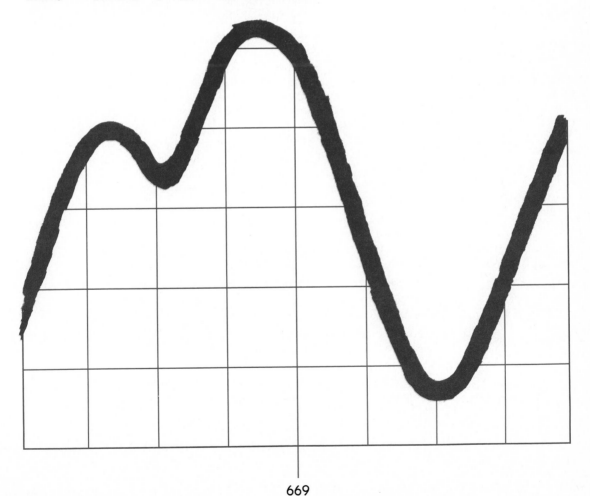

# CHAPTER ONE

**1.2** One example of a situation for which a sample must be drawn because it is impossible to examine an entire population would be the case of testing the durability of batteries. Since testing the batteries drains their power and renders them useless, only a small number can be tested.

**1.4**
a) U.S. Bureau of Labor Statistics, *Employment and Earnings.*

b) U.S. Bureau of Labor Statistics, *Employment and Earnings.*

c) U.S. Bureau of Labor Statistics, *Monthly Labor Review.*

d) U.S. Department of Commerce, Bureau of the Census, *Statistical Abstract of the United States: 1985*, see pp. 515 and 519.

e) *Statistical Abstract*, p. 517; and U.S. Internal Revenue Service, *Statistics of Income for Corporation Income Tax Returns.*

**1.6** There is no such thing as a perfectly controlled experiment in which subjects are identical or randomly assigned to a control and experimental group to obtain perfect representation of the population. Furthermore, unless all the characteristics of a population are known, there is no way to know if a given sample is or is not representative of the population. Random assignment does not ensure that each possible sample represents the characteristics of the population.

**1.8** Talking to a sample of all union members should generate a good picture of the opinions of the union as a whole. However, if voting behavior (i.e., voting or not voting) is consistent over time, then a sample of those members who voted the previous year might give a more accurate picture of the possible election outcome.

**1.10**
a) These differences could be caused by sampling error. Measurement error also is possible here because the people questioned may or may not have enough knowledge of the question to give a meaningful answer.

b) This situation might cause a bias because of the low response rate. Measurement error could also be a problem because the term *head of household* may be ambiguous.

c) This is a measurement error.

**1.12** Stratification can reduce costs by allowing for a smaller sample for national polls. Because strata are represented in the sample in the same proportions as in the population, the sample can be small and highly representative at the same time.

**1.14** In a truly random sample each member of the population has an equal chance to be chosen each time a choice is made. If a researcher does not want to draw the same name twice, he or she does not replace name cards once drawn from a hat. Not replacing names once drawn, however, implies a change in the probability of selecting any remaining name on each subsequent draw.

**1.16** Sample data used are in business and economics because population data usually are too large and would be too costly, difficult, or time consuming to obtain. If samples are taken carefully, they should provide reasonably accurate representations of the population.

**1.18** a) If no list of customers is available, first determine the approximate number of people who visit the store on a representative day. Then, using systematic sampling, sample every $n$th customer, where

$$n = \frac{\text{Number of customers per day}}{150}$$

b) If a list of regular customers is available, number the names on the list. Then, using a random number table or a computer program, randomly select 150 names. These people could be telephoned.

**1.20** a) A copy machine retailer wants to know what types of businesses or institutions used his or her company most over the past year. The retailer could take a chronological list of purchasers over the past year and, depending on the size of the population and sample desired, choose, e.g., every tenth, fifteenth, or twentieth customer.

b) Block sequence sampling might be used by a quality control analyst who suspects that lower-quality products are being put out in a factory at the end of worker shifts. Items produced in equally spaced time periods throughout the day might be drawn and checked for quality.

c) Stratified sampling might be used by a toothpaste manufacturer who wishes to determine which flavors of toothpaste are more appealing and to which age groups. The strata used would be age groups.

d) Cluster sampling would be used by a national manufacturer who wanted to test a new product's appeal—e.g., paper towels. Rather than randomly choose households from all over the country, a few areas around the country that are representative of the entire population might be selected. From these few areas random samples could be drawn by interviewers.

**1.22** The average age of each person in the statistics class is a population value if we are interested only in the ages of persons in this class. If we are interested in a larger group—say, the entire student body or the residents of the city—then it is a sample value. If it is a sample value, this class might be considered a cluster sample. This sample might not be representative of the population. For example, if the population is the student body and if persons in the statistics class consist of all seniors, then this class would tend to be older than the representative class.

**1.24** a) Benderly is warning about nonsampling error because the sample used may not just contain the trend. It may reflect other variables such as seasonality. December is the month of the year that usually has the strongest business activity because of the holiday season. It is difficult to tell if positive signs in December are seasonal only or indicators also of economic improvement.

b) The change could have been as high as a 13–20% increase and as low as a 3–10% decrease.

1.26 a) From a list of actual voters, a simple random sample should be chosen, by random numbers, and telephone interviews conducted. The position of the subject and the strength of that opinion (i.e., strongly in favor, somewhat in favor, etc.) should be recorded. Subjects also should be asked whether or not they plan to vote on the referendum. Telephone interviews would be used because they would be fast and relatively inexpensive. Only a few simple questions would be asked. Return-by-mail questionnaires would be too time consuming and might not produce a good response rate. It might be difficult to cover the entire city evenly with door-to-door interviews because of probable time constraints.

b) The market researcher might choose to use cluster sampling to select stores to pilot test the paper. Based on sales of the new paper towels relative to the sales of all other paper towels sold by the stores in a fixed period of time, the researcher can estimate the potential market share of the new towels.

c) If the delinquent accounts receivable are alphabetically ordered, then a systematic random sample might be drawn. Accounts receivable should be chosen out of the total at specific intervals, choosing as high a percentage as possible with the number still remaining workable. A simple random sample could also be used, but the systematic random sample might take a bit less time. Working with the entire population would be too cumbersome, requiring too much work. The amount of the total delinquent accounts receivable may be estimated from the average size of these accounts determined from the sample.

d) The most efficient sampling method might involve a stratified sample, by industry, with random sampling within industry. Written questionnaires could be given to randomly chosen graduates of the training program and employers of graduates. Trainees would be questioned about whether they feel the program adequately prepared them and whether the self-paced aspect was appropriate. Employers would be questioned about the relative level of preparation of these trainees and asked to compare them to others who had undergone other types of training. Written questionnaires would allow the participants time to think about their responses carefully and give meaningful evaluations.

1.28 Example:

| Randomly Chosen List | | Name | 12-Mo Earnings ($ Per Share) |
|---|---|---|---|
| No. | No. | | |
| 1 | 4 | Apollo Computer | 0.75 |
| 2 | 20 | Duplex Products | 2.61 |
| 3 | 37 | Tandon | 0.11 |

| Randomly Chosen List | | Name | 12-Mo Earnings ($ Per Share) |
|---|---|---|---|
| No. | No. | | |
| 4 | 48 | AMP | 1.87 |
| 5 | 59 | Burndy | 1.07 |
| 6 | 77 | Kolimorgen | 1.06 |
| 7 | 80 | M/A-Com | 0.94 |
| 8 | 112 | BankAmerica | 1.77 |
| 9 | 126 | First Interstate Bancorp | 6.16 |
| 10 | 132 | Marine Midland Bank | 4.17 |
| 11 | 147 | Southeast Banking | 3.30 |
| 12 | 170 | Avnel | 2.21 |
| 13 | 200 | Ducommun | 3.38 |
| 14 | 217 | Genuine Parts | 2.20 |
| 15 | 222 | Handleman | 2.83 |
| 16 | 238 | Kay | 0.66 |
| 17 | 246 | Mass Merchandisers | 0.81 |
| 18 | 247 | Maxicare Health Plans | 0.65 |
| 19 | 282 | SYSCO | 2.27 |
| 20 | 283 | TDC | 1.12 |

**1.30** Plaintiffs would argue for the preselection pool to be the entire working population because women and minorities are typically underrepresented in many types of jobs, especially the high-paying, prestigious jobs. The defendants would argue for a pre-selection pool of perhaps only those in the local community with a specific educational level because this may be the pool from which they draw their employees. Thus the percentages within the population considered would change significantly depending on which group was chosen as the benchmark.

**1.32** The population for this study would be the faculty, staff, and students of the university as well as residents of the area in which the university is located. A stratified random sample would be appropriate to ensure the proper proportions of each group in the sample. A written questionnaire, which could be returned via campus mail, would be good for all those connected with the university. The nonuniversity people could be contacted either through the mail or by telephone, whichever is less expensive. Within the student body, care should be taken to get appropriate proportions by class in the sample. When the data have been collected, it should be analyzed as a whole, but it might also be informative to analyze the data for only those connected with the university (i.e., minus area residents). The importance of analyzing each group separately would depend on the purpose of the questionnaire.

# CHAPTER TWO

**2.2** Absolute frequencies for sample data give counts on the number of times each different observation value occurs in the sample. By definition, the total number of observations in the sample ($n$) is less than that in the population ($N$). To make inferences about the number of times a certain value might be observed in the population, the absolute frequencies of this value in the sample must be translated into a relative frequency; then this sample relative frequency can be multiplied by the population size.

**2.4** To make the classes of equal width throughout and to ensure that there are between 5 and 15 classes, the intervals of $300, $400, and $600 could be used. These would result in distributions with 12, 9, and 6 classes respectively. The final choice for interval width would depend on the appearance of the distributions.

**2.6** a)

| $i$ | Typing Speed | $f_i$ | $f_i/N$ | Cum. Rel. Freq. for Part (c) |
|---|---|---|---|---|
| 1 | 30–39 wpm | 2 | 2/25 = 0.08 | |
| 2 | 40–49 | 4 | 4/25 = 0.16 | 0.24 |
| 3 | 50–59 | 5 | 5/25 = 0.20 | 0.44 |
| 4 | 60–69 | 7 | 7/25 = 0.28 | 0.72 |
| 5 | 70–79 | 4 | 4/25 = 0.16 | 0.88 |
| 6 | 80–89 | 2 | 2/25 = 0.08 | 0.96 |
| 7 | 90–100 | 1 | 1/25 = 0.04 | 1.00 |

b) Relative Frequency Histogram for Typing Speed

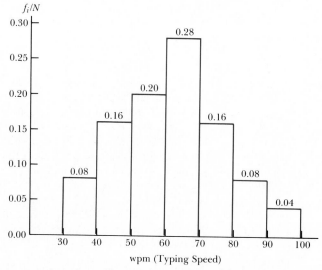

c) Cumulative Frequency and Ogive for Typing Speed

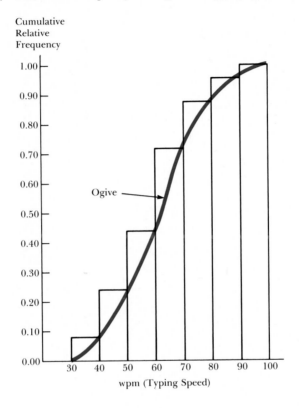

Cumulative
Relative
Frequency

Ogive

wpm (Typing Speed)

**2.8 a)**

| Stem | Leaf | $f$ |
|------|------|-----|
| 1 | 4 7 4 4 7 8 | 6 |
| 2 | 9 9 6 4 6 3 7 7 9 5 7 8 | 12 |
| 3 | 3 7 7 4 0 9 6 7 6 | 9 |
| 4 | 2 7 6 2 2 9 6 7 2 8 2 | 11 |
| 5 | 9 1 3 6 0 6 | 6 |
| 6 | 1 1 5 | 3 |
| 7 | 2 2 | 2 |
| 8 | | 0 |
| 9 | 2 | 1 |

**2.8** a)

| Stem | Leaf | $f$ |
|------|------|-----|
| 1L | 4 4 4 | 3 |
| 1U | 7 7 8 | 3 |
| 2L | 4 3 | 2 |
| 2U | 9 9 6 6 7 7 9 5 7 8 | 10 |
| 3L | 3 4 0 | 3 |
| 3U | 7 7 9 6 7 6 | 6 |
| 4L | 2 2 2 2 2 | 5 |
| 4U | 7 6 9 6 7 8 | 6 |
| 5L | 1 3 0 | 3 |
| 5U | 9 9 6 | 3 |
| 6L | 1 1 | 2 |
| 6U | 5 | 1 |
| 7L | 2 2 | 2 |
| 7U | | 0 |
| 8L | | 0 |
| 8U | | 0 |
| 9L | 2 | 1 |
| 9U | | 0 |

Intervals of width 10 are perhaps most appropriate since, for this interval width, there are between 5 and 15 classes (9) and there is only one class that has no observations (8).

| $i$ | $f_i$ | $f_i/N$ | Cum. Rel. Freq. for Part (c) |
|-----|-------|---------|------------------------------|
| 1 | 6 | $6/50 = 0.12$ | 0.12 |
| 2 | 12 | $12/50 = 0.24$ | 0.36 |
| 3 | 9 | $9/50 = 0.18$ | 0.54 |
| 4 | 11 | $11/50 = 0.22$ | 0.76 |
| 5 | 6 | $6/50 = 0.12$ | 0.88 |
| 6 | 3 | $3/50 = 0.06$ | 0.94 |
| 7 | 2 | $2/50 = 0.04$ | 0.98 |
| 8 | 0 | $0/50 = 0.00$ | 0.98 |
| 9 | 1 | $1/50 = 0.02$ | 1.00 |

Answers to Selected Exercises

b) Relative Frequency Histogram for Book Value

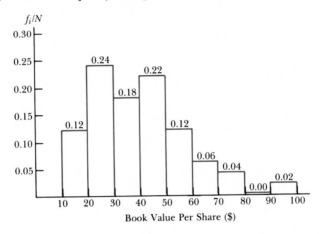

c) Cumulative Relative Frequency and Ogive for Book Value

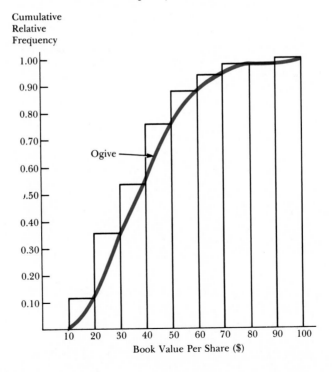

**2.10** a)

| $i$ | Classes | $f_i$ | $f_i/N$ | Cum. Rel. Freq. for Part (c) |
|---|---|---|---|---|
| 1 | 200–399 | 4 | $4/30 = 0.13$ | |
| 2 | 400–599 | 7 | $7/30 = 0.23$ | 0.36 |
| 3 | 600–799 | 8 | $8/30 = 0.27$ | 0.63 |
| 4 | 800–999 | 6 | $6/30 = 0.20$ | 0.83 |
| 5 | 1000–1199 | 2 | $2/30 = 0.07$ | 0.90 |
| 6 | 1200–1399 | 1 | $1/30 = 0.03$ | 0.93 |
| 7 | 1400–1599 | 2 | $2/30 = 0.07$ | 1.00 |

b) Relative Frequency Histogram for CEO Compensation

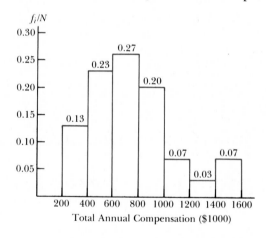

c) Cumulative Relative Frequency and Ogive for CEO Compensation

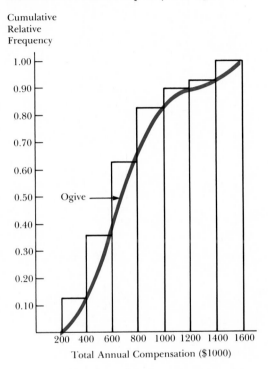

2.12 From 1980 to 1981 VW's market share rose approximately 3 percentage points to reach a high of approximately 25% of the West German market. Ford's share also rose by 3 percentage points but still held less than 12% of the market. From 1981 to 1982 VW lost a fraction of a percent. Ford also lost, but Opel jumped approximately 2 percentage points. In 1983, VW fell to its 1980 level, while both its competitors, Opel and Ford, registered increased market shares over the previous year. For the 4-yr period, VW managed only to maintain its 1980 share of the market, while Ford and Opel each gained approximately 3 percentage points of the West German market for autos.

| 2.14 | | $n$ | $f_i/n$ | $f_i/n \times 360°$ | % |
|---|---|---|---|---|---|
| | Yes | 485 | 0.808 | 290.88 | 80.8 |
| | No | 73 | 0.122 | 43.92 | 12.2 |
| | DK | 42 | 0.070 | 25.20 | 7.0 |
| | Total = | 600 | 1.000 | 360.00 | 100.0 |

a) Pie Chart of 600 Telephone Poll Responses

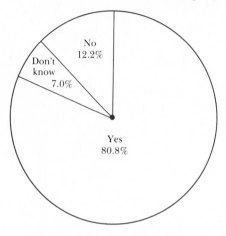

b) Bar Chart of Telephone Poll Responses

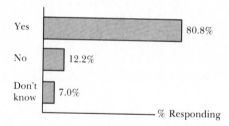

c) Probably the bar chart should be used in the annual report. It seems to give the clearer picture of the data.

2.16 Such economic quantities are represented in line charts because line charts present data as a continuous series. Sales, income, and production are quantities that are generated continuously over time. Thus they should be presented as continuous flows.

2.18 The placement office at Indiana University (IU) has data from the College Scholastic Service, although it has none for the graduating IU class in particular. These data are presented in the form of a chart. The level of degree and the type of curriculum of the student are listed vertically. Types of employment are listed horizontally. Average starting salaries are also presented in the chart, but this chart is not a frequency distribution since the number receiving these salaries is not given. This chart simply allows a lot of information, which varies widely, to be presented in a clear and easy to read fashion.

2.20 The 1983 price ($2500) relative to the 1981 price ($3800) is 0.6579 (2500/3800). This represents a 34.21% fall in prices [i.e., $-0.3421 = (2500 - 3800)/3800$].

680

**2.22**  The Laspeyers price index in 1983 for the data in Ex. 2.21 was 101.5, which implies that for this bundle of goods the general price rise from the base year 1982–1983 was 1.5%.

**2.24**  The absolute values of the index numbers would be changed, but the relative values would be unchanged. The rate of inflation is thus unaffected by reindexing since yearly percentage changes in each index would be the same.

**2.26**

1970:  $\dfrac{213,387}{116.3} \times 100 = \$183,479.79$

1971:  $\dfrac{205,523}{112.3} \times 100 = \$183,012.47$

1972:  $\dfrac{431,033}{125.3} \times 100 = \$344,000.80$

1973:  $\dfrac{438,762}{116.3} \times 100 = \$329,648.38$

1974:  $\dfrac{387,671}{147.7} \times 100 = \$262,471.90$

1975:  $\dfrac{272,043}{161.2} \times 100 = \$168,761.17$

1976:  $\dfrac{442,432}{170.5} \times 100 = \$259,490.91$

1977:  $\dfrac{577,245}{181.5} \times 100 = \$318,041.32$

1978:  $\dfrac{780,987}{195.4} \times 100 = \$399,686.28$

1979:  $\dfrac{1,015,262}{217.4} \times 100 = \$467,001.84$

**2.32**  a)

|  | 1990 | | 2000 | |
|---|---|---|---|---|
| **Ages** | $f_i$ | $f_i/N$ | $f_i$ | $f_i/N$ |
| under 5 yr. | 19 | 0.082 | 18 | 0.069 |
| 5–13 | 29 | 0.124 | 35 | 0.135 |
| 14–17 | 14 | 0.060 | 16 | 0.062 |
| 18–24 | 28 | 0.120 | 25 | 0.096 |
| 25–34 | 40 | 0.172 | 34 | 0.131 |
| 35–44 | 31 | 0.133 | 41 | 0.158 |
| 45–54 | 23 | 0.099 | 36 | 0.138 |
| 55–64 | 22 | 0.094 | 23 | 0.088 |
| 65+ | 27 | 0.116 | 32 | 0.123 |

b) Relative Frequency Histogram for Population Data

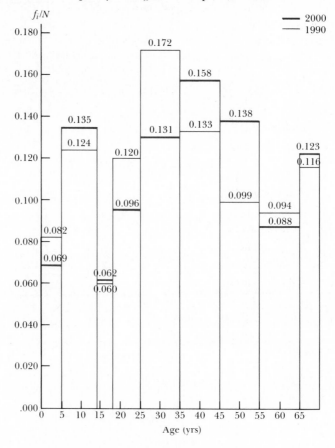

c) The percentage of the population age 5 yr and under is expected to drop from 1990–2000 by 1.3% from 8.2 to 6.9 percentage points. Those age 5–13 yr will rise from 12.4% to 13.5%. The age group 14–17 yr will rise a small amount, from 6% to 6.2%. The age group 18–24 yr will drop from 12% to 9.6%. Those 25–34 will drop from 17.2% of the population to 13.1%. The age group 35–44 yr will rise from 13.3% to 15.8% of the population. The percentage of people age 45–54 will rise from 9.9% to 13.8%. Those 55–64 will decrease from 9.4% to 8.8% of the population. Finally, those age 65 and over will constitute 12.3% of the population in 2000 as opposed to 11.6% in 1990. The most dramatic changes predicted are thus the decrease for ages 18 yr to 34 yr and the increase for ages 35–54.

d) Relative frequency data are used because what is important here is not the absolute size of the population or of the age groups but the makeup of the population by these age groups.

**2.34** a) Bar Chart for Projected Earnings

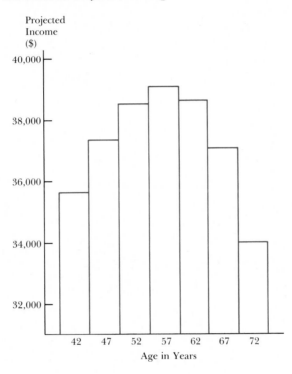

b) Line Chart for Projected Earnings

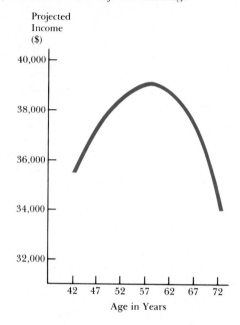

c) The line chart should be used because the data depict a continuous flow over time.

**2.36** Price-Earnings Frequency Distribution (answer will depend on class widths selected)

| Classes | $f_i$ |
|---------|-------|
| 8–10 | 9 |
| 11–13 | 15 |
| 14–16 | 14 |
| 17–19 | 12 |
| 20–22 | 4 |
| 23–25 | 2 |
| 26–28 | 2 |
| 29–31 | 0 |
| 32–34 | 1 |

**2.38** These two firms appear to have the same or close to the same profit trends. The graphs simply look different because the values are placed on the axes at different intervals.

**2.40** In 1973, Appliance Components constituted 33% of sales, or $396,000,000 in sales, for Emerson. In 1982, Appliance Components constituted 20% of sales, bringing in revenue of $700,000,000. Thus Appliance Component sales fell by 43.4%.

**2.42**  a) The chart is a bar chart, not a histogram, because the vertical axis shows a quantitative value but not a frequency.

     b) On July 29, the average value was 1200. On August 1, the average had dropped to 1194. August 2, the Dow Jones Average dropped again to 1190. August 3, it rose again to 1198, almost to its value of July 29. On August 4, the average dropped again to 1184 and rose slightly the next day to 1185. After the weekend, on Monday, August 8, the average dropped sharply to 1166. The total decrease from July 29–August 8 was 34 points.

     c) $\dfrac{1194}{1200} = \dfrac{x}{\$64.25}$    Thus $x = \$63.93$

     d) The prediction in part (c) was wrong because one cannot take an average value, such as the Dow Jones Average, and expect it to reflect the changes in any one of the many stocks that make up the average.

**2.44** The line graphs cover the same time period for each of five computer firms. It is the vertical axes, showing dollars/share, that differ greatly. The values are of course different, and the range of values also is different. Although the charts look the same from high point to low point, the percentage of dollars/share lost was quite different for the companies:

IBM Stock lost $\approx 9.49\%$ of its value.
Data General lost $\approx 43.24\%$ of its value.
DEC lost $\approx 19.35\%$ of its value.
Wang lost $\approx 34.48\%$ of its value.
Apple lost $\approx 33.33\%$ of its value.

**2.46** Yearly Assets of Workingmans Federal
The chart indicates that yearly assets grew continuously throughout the period. During the 1970s assets grew at rather rapid rates. In the 1980s asset growth leveled off somewhat, although there was a considerable gain (more than $500,000) between 1982 and 1983.

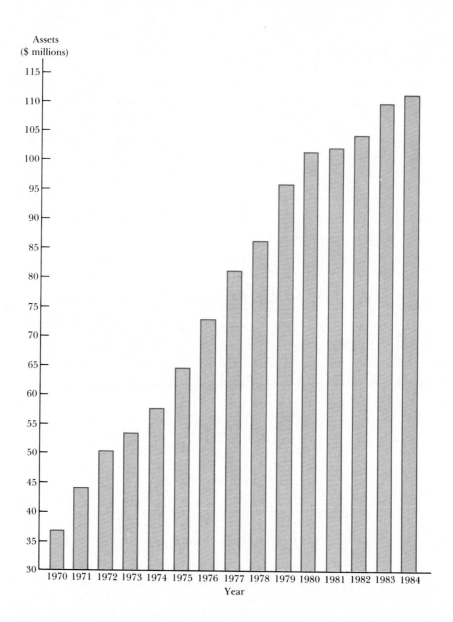

Assets
($ millions)

Year

**2.48**  Assets represent a stock or a given amount accumulated as of a specific date, while net income represents a flow or the continuous stream generated by ongoing business activity.

# CHAPTER THREE

**3.2** To calculate a mean or median from group data, it is necessary to assume that observations are evenly distributed throughout a class.

**3.4** The median is emphasized over the mean or mode as a measure of central location because it is less affected by extreme values. For income data, there are often a few extremely high values that cause the distribution to be positively skewed. If one wants a measure of the average value, however, then the median is inappropriate.

**3.6** No, one cannot make such a conclusion. No information is given for what proportion of MBAs received nontechnical or technical undergraduate degrees.

**3.8** a) Mean change $= 27.7\%$

    b) Median change $= 24.3\%$

    c) The mean has been pulled up by a couple of extremely high changes in the DJIA. The two biggest changes occurred prior to World War II. Considering the mean and median data and the more recent trends, the median might be the best value to predict in the case of a future slump. However, the data cover a fairly wide range, so any prediction would be associated with great uncertainty.

**3.10** a) $(9 \times 300) + (9.5 \times 500) + (10 \times 400) + (10.5 \times 300) + (11 \times 200) + (11.5 \times 100) + (12 \times 100) = 19{,}150$.

$$\text{Mean} = \frac{19{,}150}{1{,}900} = 10.08\% \qquad \text{Approximate median} = 9.95\%$$

    b) The distribution is positively skewed.

**3.12** a) $\dfrac{60 + 50 + 30 + 20 + 30 + 70 + 80 + 90 + 80}{9} = 56.67 = \text{mean}$

    b) 20 30 30 50 *60* 70 80 80 90,     median $= 60$

    c) Modes $= 30$ and $80$

**3.14** The participant did not necessarily do better on the second exam, although he or she may have. Although the mean on both tests was 50 points, the proportion of scores above and below the mean on each test could be different. If the distribution of the first exam scores was positively skewed while the scores on the second were negatively skewed, then the letter grade on the second exam could be lower than on the first.

**3.16** The mean percentage is 33.85%. This mean may be of little value in predicting future percentages because the data appear to be trended upward. If this trend continues, the mean would always be less than the next observed value.

**3.18** The following is one randomly drawn sample of return on common equity, after ordering. Other random samples would yield different values. Thus answers depend on the sample selected.

a)  Sample values: $-170.7$, 9.7, 9.9, 11.2, 11.2, 11.6, 13.6, 13.8, 14.1, 14.8, 14.9, 15.2, 15.7, 16.9, and 17.7%

Sample mean $= 1.31\%$     Sample median $= 13.8\%$     Sample mode $= 11.2\%$

b)  Population mean $= 7.74\%$     Population median $= 12.7\%$     Population mode $= 14.9\%$

The sample mean is very far off the population mean because the extreme value of $-170.7$ was randomly included in this sample. The sample median is quite close to the population median because it is not as affected by extreme values. The two mode values are not the same because only one of the three values of the population mode was chosen for the sample. The sample mode has a frequency of 2 in both the sample and the population.

c)  12/15, or 80%, of the sample had a return $\geq 10\%$. 37/50, or 74%, of the population had a return $\geq 10\%$. These two values are only 6% apart, which is fairly close.

**3.20**  $\mu = \$11.43$.

$$\sigma^2 = 1/7[(14 - 11.43)^2 + (10 - 11.43)^2 + (11 - 11.43)^2$$
$$+ (13 - 11.43)^2 + (10 - 11.43)^2 + (12 - 11.43)^2 + (10 - 11.43)^2]$$
$$= 1/7(6.60 + 2.04 + 0.18 + 2.46 + 2.04 + 0.32 + 2.04)$$
$$= \frac{15.68}{7} = 2.24 \ (\$ \ \text{squared})$$

**3.22**

| $m_i$ | $f_i$ | $f_i m_i$ |
|-------|-------|-----------|
| 35 | 1 | 35 |
| 45 | 7 | 315 |
| 55 | 12 | 660 |
| 65 | 11 | 715 |
| 75 | 6 | 450 |
| 85 | 0 | 0 |
| 95 | 3 | 285 |
| 105 | 1 | 105 |
| | $N = 41$ | 2565 |

$\mu = 2565/41 = 62.56$

$$\sigma^2 = \frac{1}{41}[(35 - 62.56)^2 + 7(45 - 62.56)^2 + 12 (55 - 62.56)^2 + 11(65 - 62.56)^2$$
$$+ 6(75 - 62.56)^2 + 3(95 - 62.56)^2 + (105 - 62.56)^2]$$
$$= \frac{1}{41}(759.55 + 2158.48 + 685.84 + 65.49 + 928.52 + 3157.06 + 2801.15)$$
$$= \frac{9556.09}{41} = 233.08$$

**3.24**   Using the rule of normality, approximately 16% are above $890, and approximately 2.5% are below $620.

**3.26**   a)   $\bar{x} = 31.22 =$ sample mean

$$s^2 = (1/4)[(31.1 - 31.22)^2 + (31.2 - 31.22)^2 + (31.3 - 31.22)^2 \\ + (31.1 - 31.22)^2 + (31.3 - 31.22)^2]$$

$$= (1/4)(0.0144 + 0.0004 + 0.0064 + 0.0144 + 0.0064)$$

$$= (1/4)(0.042)$$

$$= 0.0105 = \text{sample variance}$$

$$s = 0.1025 = \text{sample standard deviation}$$

b)   $\bar{x} = 0.22$, $s^2 = 0.0105$, and $s = 0.1025$

c)   Since the sample values have all been reduced by the same amount, the shape of the distribution remains the same and only its central location is shifted. The measures of dispersion remain the same.

**3.28**   Since $\bar{x} = 27.75$ and $s = 7.48$, if $k = 3$, then at least $1 - (1/3)^2 = 1 - 1/9 = 8/9 = 0.8889$, or 88.89% of the distribution should be between 5.31 and 50.19. Since all the data fall between these limits, the data are consistent with Tchebysheff's Theorem.

**3.30**   The rule of normality is specific to bell-shaped distributions, while Tchebysheff's Theorem applies to any distribution no matter what its shape.

**3.32**

| $m_i$ | $f_i$ | $f_i m_i$ | $(f_i/N)(m_i - \mu)^2$ |
|---|---|---|---|
| 22,500 | 76 | 1,710,000 | 2,014,996,617 |
| 15,000 | 928 | 13,920,000 | 25,493,050,543 |
| 62,500 | 2,708 | 169,250,000 | 58,740,994,946 |
| 450,000 | 2,593 | 1,166,850,000 | 28,868,745 |
| 5,000,000 | 314 | 1,570,000,000 | 985,819,178,683 |
| | $N = 6,619$ | 2,921,730,000 | $1,072,097,089,534 = \sigma^2$ |
| | | $\mu = \$441,416$ | $\$1,035,422 = \sigma$ |

**3.34**

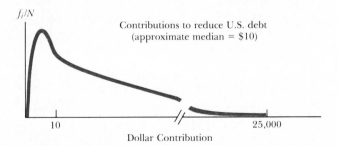

$f_i/N$

Contributions to reduce U.S. debt
(approximate median = $10)

10        25,000

Dollar Contribution

**3.36** a)  14.29% responded for Instructor A.
83.33% responded for Instructor B.

b)  Instructor A could have been as high as 7.3.
Instructor B could have been as high as 4.7.
Instructor A could have been as low as 0.43.
Instructor B could have been as low as 3.33.

c)  Instructor A's distribution is skewed. By Tchebysheff's Theorem,

$$1 - \left(\frac{1}{1.3}\right)^2 = 0.41,$$

so at least 41% gave A between 1 and 5.

Instructor B's distribution is symmetric. Using the rule of normality, approximately 50% are between 1 and 4—i.e., 3 standard deviations.
Approximately 34% are between 4 and 5—i.e., 1 standard deviation.
Thus, about 84% rated instructor B between 1 and 5.

d)  The cutoff point for the majority is the median. The median is higher for instructor A than for B.

Variability, as measured by the standard deviation, does not depend on skewness.

Instructor B's distribution of scores is symmetric.

The truth of a statement is not necessarily determined by the majority or any other measure of central location.

We may not be able to conclude anything from these data because the question may not measure teaching ability (i.e., it is not a valid instrument), the response rate for A is quite low, and there is no reason to believe that this sample information is in any way representative of the population (the sampling method was not random).

**3.38** a)  The average is the best of the worst when the average is also the median value, dividing the distribution into two equal parts. The assumption is that the distribution is symmetric.

b)  It is possible to be average and among the best, if the average value is higher than the median value. This is the case with positively skewed distributions.

c)  The governor does not understand that all distributions are not symmetric. Nor does he understand the difference between the mean and the median and their relationship.

**3.40** a)  $\bar{x} = 51.95$ for $n = 20$

$$s^2 = \frac{1}{19}[(6.05)^2 + (-10.95)^2 + (-31.95)^2 + (-27.95)^2$$

$$+ (-21.95)^2 + (12.95)^2 + (16.05)^2 + (-6.95)^2$$
$$+ (17.05)^2 + (39.05)^2 + (3.05)^2 + (8.05)^2$$
$$+ (-4.95)^2 + (19.05)^2 + (14.05)^2 + (-18.95)^2$$
$$+ (-0.95)^2 + (-9.95)^2 + (-14.95)^2 + (30.05)^2]$$

$$= \frac{1}{19}(7395).\ \text{Sample variance} = 389\ (\text{days squared})$$

$s = 19.73$ days, the sample standard deviation

b) $\bar{x} \pm s$: 32.2 to 71.7 days (14/20 or 70%)
$\bar{x} \pm 2s$: 12.5 to 91.4 days (20/20 or 100%)

For the interval $\bar{x} \pm s$, the rule of normality may be applied. According to this rule approximately 68% of the distribution should fall within this interval. Seventy percent is very close, so the rule gives a good approximation.

For the interval $\bar{x} \pm 2s$, the rule of normality states that approximately 95% should fall within the limits. Actually 100% is within this interval for this distribution so the rule of normality does not appear to apply here.

Tchebysheff's Theorem states that at least 75% of the distribution should fall within the interval of $\bar{x} \pm 2s$. Since 100% are contained within the interval, the data are consistent with this theorem.

**3.44** a) $\bar{x} = (1.5)(0.05) + (3.5)(0.25) + (5.5)(0.30) + (7.5)(0.30) + (9.5)(0.10)$

$= 0.075 + 0.875 + 1.65 + 2.25 + 0.95$

$= 5.8$

$s^2 = \frac{1}{19}[(18.49) + 5(5.29) + 6(0.09) + 6(2.89) + 2(13.69)] = 4.74$

b) The assumption had to be made that the observations were evenly distributed within classes so that the midpoint would be representative of the average of the class.

**3.46** a) $\bar{x} = 595.9$

$s^2 = \frac{1}{9}(50{,}670.01 + 12{,}122.01 + 3{,}612.01 + 3{,}492.81 + 967.21 + 16.81$

$+ 3{,}831.61 + 19{,}293.21 + 20{,}420.41 + 21{,}286.81)$

$= (1/9)(135{,}712.9) = 15{,}079.211$

$s = 122.797$

b) $\bar{x} \pm 1s$: 473.10 $-$ 718.70
$\bar{x} \pm 2s$: 350.31 $-$ 1314.60

$\bar{x} \pm 1s$: 6/10 = 60%
$\bar{x} \pm 2s$: 10/10 = 100%

For the interval $\bar{x} \pm 1s$, the rule of normality estimates 68%. The preceding data show 60% within the interval. The two percentages are not close. The difference indicates that the distribution is not symmetric. For the interval $\bar{x} \pm 2s$ the rule of normality estimates 95%. One hundred percent are contained in the interval, which is not close. (Once again, the distribution is not symmetric.) Tchebysheff's Theorem states that at least 75% of the distribution would be contained within two standard deviations of the mean. Therefore, the results are consistent with this theorem.

**3.48**   The mean for 1990 is 25.89, while the median for 1990 is 27.

The mean for 2000 is 28.89, while the median for 2000 is 32.

The difference in means is due to the fact that overall the population is expected to grow in size between 1990 and 2000 because more people would be living longer. The median values are also not the same because relative proportions within the population are expected to shift.

**3.50**   59 months − 2(3.3 months) = 52.4 months

# CHAPTER FOUR

**4.2**   a)  Experiment: A situation in which factors other than chance are controlled so that the situation is at least theoretically capable of being replicated.

For example, an experiment could be a retail store offering a product at various different prices to establish the effect on the volume of sales where the characteristics and conditions in the store are held constant.

b)  Outcome: The result of an experiment.

For example, outcomes for the experiment in (a) would be the results of each customer's decision over equal time periods for the product offered at different prices.

c)  Event: One or more outcomes treated as a group.

For example, an event of interest might be "first and second customers buy product at lowest price."

d)  Mutually exclusive events: Events that cannot occur together. They do not share outcomes.

For example, for a case of predicting the weather, mutually exclusive events could be that on a particular day there would be rain or no rain.

e)  Exhaustive events: A set of events that leaves no other event possible.

For example, the preceding example of mutually exclusive events also illustrates exhaustive events.

f)  Independent events: The occurrence of one does not depend on the occurrence of the other, or the reverse. The probability of either event cannot be affected by the occurrence of the other event.

For example, a 9-year-old and a 20-year-old are shown an ad. The 9-year-old's ability to understand the ad could be independent of the 20-year-old's ability if the two are unrelated and do not talk to each other.

**4.4**   $P(\$1 \text{ or } \$5) = P(\$1) + P(\$5)$ (these are mutually exclusive)
$P(\$1 \text{ or } \$5) = (0.30) + (0.10) = 0.40$

**4.6**   a)   $(A, B)\ (B, D)\ (A, C)\ (B, E)\ (A, D)\ (C, D)\ (A, E)\ (C, E)\ (B, C)\ (D, E)$

   b)   $P(A) = 4/10 = 0.40$

   c)   $P(A \text{ or } B) = P(A) + P(B) - P(A \text{ and } B)$
   $P(A \text{ or } B) = 0.40 + 0.40 - 0.10$
   $P(A \text{ or } B) = 0.70$

**4.8**   a)   $1/366 = 0.0027 = P(\text{November } 21)$

   b)   $30/366 = 0.082 = P(\text{November})$

   c)   $P(\text{Nov}_2|\text{Nov}_1) = \dfrac{P(\text{Nov}_2 \text{ and } \text{Nov}_1)}{P(\text{Nov})} = 29/366 = 0.079$

**4.10**   a)   $P(50) = 1/100 = 0.01$

   b)   $P(50 < x < 80) = 29/100 = 0.29$

   c)   The actual occurrence of numbers between 50 and 80 is a random occurrence and will depend on the sample selected. In any given sample there is no reason to get 29% between 50 and 80.

**4.12**   Frequency Table

|  | ≤ $10,000 Short Form | ≤ $10,000 Long Form | $10,000–25,000 Short Form | $10,000–25,000 Long Form | $25,000 –50,000 | $50,000 or More | Sum |
|---|---|---|---|---|---|---|---|
| Audited | 0.081 | 0.09 | 0.126 | 0.275 | 0.522 | 0.228 | 1.322 |
| Not Audited | 26.919 | 8.91 | 20.874 | 10.725 | 17.478 | 3.772 | 88.678 |
| Sum | 27 | 9 | 21 | 11 | 18 | 4 | 90 |

Joint Probability Table

|  | ≤ $10,000 Short Form | ≤ $10,000 Long Form | $10,000–25,000 Short Form | $10,000–25,000 Long Form | $25,000 –50,000 | $50,000 or More | Sum |
|---|---|---|---|---|---|---|---|
| Audited | 0.0009 | 0.001 | 0.0014 | 0.0031 | 0.0058 | 0.0025 | 0.0147 |
| Not Audited | 0.2991 | 0.2991 | 0.2319 | 0.1192 | 0.1942 | 0.0419 | 0.9853 |
| Sum | 0.300 | 0.100 | 0.2333 | 0.1223 | 0.2000 | 0.0444 | 1.00 |

a)  $1.322/90 = 0.0147$

b)  $P(\$50,000|\text{audited}) = 0.228/1.322 = 0.172$

c)  $0.0025 = P(\$50,000 \text{ and audited})$

**4.14**  $P(\text{Lee}|\text{Display A}) = 30/70 = 0.429$ and $P(\text{Lee}) = 78/182 = 0.429$ are equal probabilities. Or $P(\text{Lee and Display A}) = 30/182 = 0.165$ and $P(\text{Lee})P(\text{Display A}) = 5,460/33,124 = 0.165$; again, equal probabilities. Either condition gives independence.

**4.16**  a)  No. An exhaustive list would include win A, win B, lose A, lose B (and any combination of A and B events). The mutually exclusive events could be win A and lose A.

b)  $P(\text{win A and win B}) = P(\text{win A})\, P(\text{win B}|\text{win A}) = 0.40 \times 0.09$
$$= 0.036$$

c)  $P(\text{win A or win B}) = P(\text{win A}) + P(\text{win B}) - P(\text{win A and win B})$
$$= 0.40 + 0.24 - 0.036$$
$$= 0.604$$

d)  $P(\text{win A and win B}) = 0.36$ and $P(\text{win A})P(\text{win B}) = 0.096$ are not equal. Therefore the events win A and win B are dependent.

**4.18**  a)  The event RH+ is not independent of the event Type A. This is because the proportion RH+ blood is affected by what type of blood a patient has. Eighty percent of Type As have RH+ and only 60% of Type ABs have RH+ blood.

b)  $P(\text{RH}+|\text{Type A}) = 0.80$ and $P(\text{RH}-|\text{Type AB}) = 0.40$

c)  Since we do not know and cannot find the proportion of patients who are Type A or the proportion who are Type AB, we cannot determine the exact proportion who have RH+ blood. If types and RH factors were independent, we could determine intersections, but they are not. We do know the following relationships, however: $0.8P(A) + 0.6P(AB) = P(\text{RH}+)$ and $P(A) + P(B) = 1$. Thus $P(\text{RH}+)$ must be between 0.6 and 0.8.

**4.20**  a)  Marginal probabilities:
$B_1$: 0.25      $B_2$: 0.40      $B_3$: 0.35
$A_1$: 0.40      $A_2$: 0.20      $A_3$: 0.40

b)  $P(A_1 \text{ and } B_1) = 0.10$
$P(A_1|B_1) = 0.10/0.25 = 0.40$

c)  $P(A_1 \text{ or } B_2) = 0.40 + 0.40 - 0.20 = 0.60$

d)  $P(A_1 \text{ and } B_2) = 0.20$
$P(A_1)P(B_2) = 0.40 \times 0.40 = 0.16$
These two values are not equal so $A_1$ and $B_2$ are dependent.

**4.22**  a)  True.

b)  False. If $A_1$ and $A_2$ are independent, then $P(A_1|A_2) = P(A_1)$.

c)  True.

d) False. Independent does not mean that two events have equal probabilities.

**4.24**  a)  $x$ = rates of interest opted for where the outcomes are $x = 6\%$, $x = 7\%$, and $x = 9\%$.

b)  PMF for Interest Rates

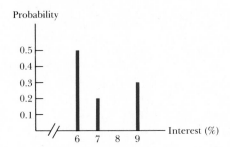

c)  $\mu_x = 0.50(6) + 0.20(7) + 0.30(9)$
$= 3 + 1.4 + 2.7$
$= 7.1\%$

d)  $\sigma_x^2 = (6 - 7.1)^2(0.50) + (7 - 7.1)^2(0.20) + (9 - 7.1)^2(0.30)$
$= 0.605 + 0.002 + 1.083 = 1.69$

**4.26**  a)

| $x$ | 4 | 3 | 2 | 1 | 0 | |
|---|---|---|---|---|---|---|
| | A | B | C | D | F | |
| $P(x)$ | 0.20 | 0.40 | 0.30 | 0.05 | 0.05 | $=1.00$ |

b)  $\mu_x = 4(0.20) + 3(0.40) + 2(0.30) + 1(0.05) + 0(0.05)$
$= 0.80 + 1.20 + 0.60 + 0.05 = 2.65$

c)  $\sigma_x^2 = (4 - 2.65)^2(0.20) + (3 - 2.65)^2(0.40) + (2 - 2.65)^2(0.30)$
$+ (1 - 2.65)^2(0.05) + (2.65)^2(0.05)$

$= 0.3645 + 0.049 + 0.12675 + 0.136125 + 0.351125 = 1.0275$

$\sigma_x = \sqrt{1.0275} = 1.014$

$2.65 \pm 1.014$

$P(1.636 \le x \le 3.664) = P(2 \le x \le 3) = 0.70 = 70\%$
This value is quite close to the 68% predicted.

$x \pm 2\sigma$

$P(0.622 \le x \le 4.678) = P(1 \le x \le 4) = 0.95 = 95\%$
This is exactly the percentage predicted.

$x \pm 3\sigma$

$P(-0.392 \le x \le 5.692) = P(0 \le x \le 4) = 1 = 100\%$
This is approximately the percentage predicted.

**4.28** $x = 1$ through 12 for each month of the year; i.e., January $= 1$, February $= 2 \ldots$ December $= 12$.

| $x$ | 1 | 2 | 3 | 4 | 5 | 6 | 7 | 8 | 9 | 10 | 11 | 12 |
|---|---|---|---|---|---|---|---|---|---|---|---|---|
| $P(x)$ | 0.083 | 0.083 | 0.083 | 0.083 | 0.083 | 0.083 | 0.083 | 0.083 | 0.083 | 0.083 | 0.083 | 0.083 |

$$\mu_x = 0.083 + 2(0.083) + 3(0.083) + 4(0.083) + 5(0.083) + 6(0.083)$$
$$+ \; 7(0.083) + 8(0.083) + 9(0.083) + 10(0.83) + 11(0.083) + 12(0.083)$$
$$= 78(0.083) = 6.474$$

**4.30** $x = $ Number of days of treasury note
$x = 30$, $x = 90$, or $x = 120$

| $x$ | 30 | 90 | 120 |
|---|---|---|---|
| $P(x)$ | 0.20 | 0.50 | 0.30 |

$$\mu_x = 30(0.20) + 90(0.50) + 120(0.30) = 6 + 45 + 36 = 87 \text{ days}$$
$$\sigma_x^2 = (30 - 87)^2(0.20) + (90 - 87)^2(0.50) + (120 - 87)^2(0.30)$$
$$= 649.8 + 4.5 + 326.7 = 981 \text{ days}^2$$

**4.32**  a)  Additive

b)  Conditional

c)  Additive

d)  Conditional

e)  Joint

**4.34**  a)  $0.50 + 0.15 = 0.65$

b)  0.20 (this is a conditional probability)

c)  1.  The events (works fewer than 50 hr/wk) and (works 50 or more hr/wk) are mutually exclusive and exhaustive.
2.  The events large and medium are mutually exclusive but not exhaustive.
3.  The events works fewer than 60 hr/wk and works at least 50 hr/wk are exhaustive but not mutually exclusive.

d)  $P$(fewer than 50 hr and small firm) $= 0.004$

**4.36**  a)  $200/2,000,000 = 0.0001 = P$(winner)

b)  $1/5 \times 200,000 = 40,000$ yes responses
$100/40,000 = 0.0025 = P$(winner|yes);     conditional

c)  $100/160,000 = 0.000625 = P$(winner|No) This answer is different from (b) because the same number of winners would be chosen from two groups of very different size. Thus the probability of winning if one responded no is far less than if one responded yes.

d)  $200/200,000 = 0.001 = P$(winner|responded)

**4.38**   $P$(victimized) $= 0.002$ and $P$(not victimized) $= 0.998$

Expected value $= (0.002)(50,000) - \$210 = -\$110$

Because the expected value is negative, it would seem that the policy is not worth buying to a risk-neutral person. A risk-averse person might want the policy, however.

To use the probability value of 0.002 in the calculations, one must assume that the rate of violent crimes will be the same in the future as it has been in the past and that this rate applies to the situations faced in daily life.

**4.40**   a)   PMF for Farm Machinery

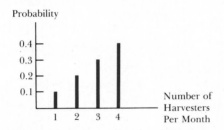

b)   $\mu_x = (0.10)(1) + (0.20)(2) + (0.30)(3) + (0.40)(4)$
$= 0.10 + 0.40 + 0.90 + 1.6 = 3$

c)   $\sigma_x^2 = (1 - 3)^2(0.10) + (2 - 3)^2(0.20) + (3 - 3)^2(0.30) + (4 - 3)^2(0.40)$

$= 0.4 + 0.2 + 0 + 0.4 = 1.0$

$\sigma_x = 1.0$

**4.42**

|         | White Male | White Female | Nonwhite Male | Nonwhite Female | Total |
|---------|------------|--------------|---------------|-----------------|-------|
| Adult   | 0.36       | 0.25         | 0.10          | 0.08            | 0.79  |
| Teenage | 0.09       | 0.08         | 0.02          | 0.02            | 0.21  |
| Total   | 0.45       | 0.33         | 0.12          | 0.10            | 1     |

$P$(teenage or nonwhite) $= 0.21 + 0.22 - 0.04 = 0.39$

**4.44**

| $x$    | 1     | 2     | 3     |
|--------|-------|-------|-------|
| $P(x)$ | 0.167 | 0.333 | 0.500 |

$\mu_x = 0.167 + 0.666 + 1.5 = 2.333$

$\sigma_x^2 = (1 - 2.333)^2(0.167) + (2 - 2.333)^2(0.333)\ (3 - 2.333)^2(0.5)$

$= 0.297 + 0.037 + 0.222 = 0.556$

**4.46**   $P(E_2|E_1) = \dfrac{P(E_1|E_2)[1 - P(E_1)]}{P(E_1)}$

**4.48**   a)   $\mu_x$ = mean value owed to bank (regardless of cash advance or no cash advance) (also using midpoint formula)

$$= \frac{2{,}952(\$100) + 2{,}378(\$300) + 1{,}640(\$500) + 738(\$700) + 492(\$900)}{8{,}200}$$

$$= \frac{\$295{,}200 + \$713{,}400 + \$820{,}000 + \$516{,}600 + \$442{,}800}{8{,}200}$$

$$= \$340$$

$\sigma_x^2 = (100 - 340)^2(0.36) + (300 - 340)^2(0.29) + (500 - 340)^2(0.20)$

$\quad\quad + (700 - 340)^2(0.09) + (900 - 340)^2(0.06)$

$\quad\quad = 20{,}736 + 464 + 5{,}120 + 11{,}664 + 18{,}816 = 56{,}800$ (\$ squared)

$\sigma_x = \$238.30 \qquad \mu_x \pm 2\sigma_x: \$0 \le x \le \$816.60 \qquad 7749/8200 = 0.94 = 94\%$

Ninety-four percent of the population falls within 2 standard deviations of the mean. This is in line with Tchebysheff's Theorem, which says that at least 75% of the distribution will fall within $\pm 2$ standard deviations of the mean.

b)   $\mu_x \pm 3\sigma_x: 0 \le x \le 1000$

The entire distribution of the population falls within $\pm 3$ standard deviations of the mean.

This satisifes Tchebysheff's Theorem, which states that $1 - (1/K)^2$, or 88.9%, of the population (at least) must fall within $\mu_x \pm 3\sigma_x$.

# CHAPTER FIVE

**5.4**   a)   $P(x)$

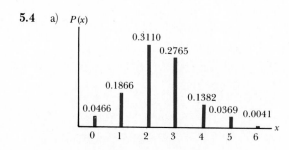

b) $\mu = \Sigma x P(x) = 0(0.0466) + 1(0.1866) + \ldots + 6(0.0041) = 2.40 = n\pi = 6(0.40) = 2.40; \sigma^2 = n\pi(1 - \pi) = (6)(.4)(.6) = 1.44$

c) $P(x \geq 3 | n = 6, \pi = 0.40) = 0.45568$

d) $P(x < 2 | n = 6, \pi = 0.40) = 0.23328$

**5.6** a) $\mu = n\pi = 100(0.02) = 2,\qquad \sigma^2 = n\pi(1 - \pi) = 100(0.02)(0.98) = 1.96$

b) $P(x > 5 | n = 100, \pi = 0.02) = 0.01548$

c) $\sigma = \sqrt{1.96} = 1.44 \qquad P[2 - 2(1.44) \leq x \leq 2 + 2(1.44)]$,
or $P(0 \leq x \leq 4) = 0.94917$

**5.8** $P(x \leq 12 | n = 100, \pi = 0.20) = 0.02533$
Might conclude discrimination since 0.02533 is quite low.

**5.10** If $\pi < 0.50$, skewed right
If $\pi > 0.50$, skewed left $\quad\Big\}\quad$ Holds for any $n$ or $\pi$
If $\pi = 0.50$, symmetrical

**5.12** a) $P(x = 4 | n = 6, \pi = 0.90) = \dfrac{6!}{4!2!}(0.90)^4(0.10)^2 = 0.098415$

$P(x = 6) = 0.5314$

b)

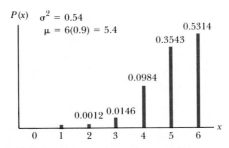

**5.14** $P(x \geq 18 | n = 100, \pi = 0.12) = 0.0510$
Might advertise because of the possibility of higher incomes.

**5.16** $P(x > 50 | n = 100, \pi = 0.40) = 0.0270$

**5.18** $P(x \leq 1 | n = 20, \pi = 0.15) = 0.17556$
Conclude not enough evidence to indicate discrimination.

**5.20** $P(x \leq 25 | n = 50, \pi = 0.60) = 0.09781$

**5.22** a) $P(x \geq 26 | n = 50, \pi = 0.50) = 0.44386$

b) Select a number, $c$, so that $P(x > c | n = 50, \pi = 0.50)$ is low enough to convince you. For example, if $c = 33$ is picked, $P(x > 33 | n = 50, \pi = 0.50) = 0.01642$ is quite low.

**5.24** $P(x \leq 128 | n = 200, \pi = 0.75) = 0.00035$

**5.26** a) $P[x \geq (.65)(120)|n = 120, \pi = 0.50] = 0.00065$

b) Select a number, $c$, so that $P(x > c|n = 120, \pi = 0.50)$ is low enough to convince you. For example, if $c = 71$ is picked, $P(x > 71|n = 120, \pi = 0.50) = 0.02722$ is quite low.

**5.28** a) $n = 5, N = 9, N_1 = 5, N_2 = 4; P(x_1 = 3) = 0.47619$

b) $P(x_1 \geq 3) = 0.64286$

d) $E(x) = 2.77778$

**5.30** a) $n = 2, N = 15, N_1 = 5, N_2 = 10$
$P(x_1 = 2, x_2 = 0) = 0.09524$

b) $n = 4, P(x_1 \geq 2) = P(x = 2) + P(x = 3) + P(x = 4)$
$$= 0.32967 + 0.07326 + 0.00366 = 0.40659$$

c) $P(x_1 = 3, x_2 = 0) = 0.02198$

This probability is quite small, which might lead one to suspect more than five betas.

**5.32** $N = 12, N_1 = 7, N_2 = 5, n = 6$
$P(x_1 \geq 5) = P(x_1 = 5) + P(x_2 = 6) = 0.12121$

**5.34** a) $\mu = (7/10)(0.20) + (3/10)(0.50) = 0.29$

b) $N = 10, N_1 = 7, N_2 = 3, n = 3; P(x_1 = 2) = 0.5250$

c) $P(2 \leq x \leq 3|n = 5, \pi = 0.20) = 0.256$

**5.36** $N = 100, N_1 = 45, N_2 = 55, n = 10$
$P(x_1 \geq 7) = P(x = 7) + \cdots + P(x = 10) = 0.09027$

**5.38** a) $N = 300, N_1 = 180, N_2 = 120, n = 208$
$P(x \geq 15) = 0.11731$

**5.40** $P(x = 0) = 0.048169$

**5.44** a) $\mu = \Sigma x P(x) = 0(0.7408) + 1(0.2222) + \ldots + 5P(0.00004) = 3$

b) $P(x > 3) = 0.0003 + 0.0001 = 0.0004$

c) Not symmetrical—skewed right; 96.3%

**5.46** a) Poisson since we are dealing with periods of time. Assume misdialed calls are independent of one another.

b) Binomial since we are dealing with the number of successes over trials. Assume incorrect guesses are independent and occur with constant probability.

c) Hypergeometric since we are sampling without replacement from a finite population. Assume occurrences are independent.

**5.48** a) $\mu = n\pi = 8.8(2.64) = 23.23$ no shows or $88 - 23.23 = 64.77$ expected.

b) $\mu \pm 2\sigma$, where $\mu = 64.77$ and $\sigma = \sqrt{n\pi(1 - \pi)} = \sqrt{4.14}$
$64.77 \pm 2(4.14)$ is $(56.49$–$73.05)$

c) $P(50 \leq x \leq 79|n = 88, \pi = 0.736) = 0.99974$

**5.52**  a)  $P(10) = \dfrac{9!}{4!5!}(0.4)^5(0.6)^5 = 0.1003$

b)  $E(n) = r/p = 5/0.40 = 12.5$

c)  $\sigma^2 = r(1-p)^2/p = 5(1-0.4)^2/0.4 = 4.5$

**5.54**  $P(5, 3, 2, 0) = \dfrac{10!}{5!3!2!0!}(0.50)^5(0.20)^3(0.15)^2(0.15)^0 = 0.014175$

# CHAPTER SIX

**6.2**  Symmetrical, bell-shaped curve with a single mode, where the mean = median = mode.

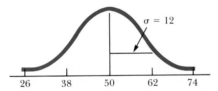

**6.4**  The three statements are rounded-off versions of the normal distribution probabilities, that is, 0.68 is the rounded equivalent of 0.6826; 0.95 is the rounded equivalent of 0.9544; and 1 is the rounded equivalent of 0.9974.

**6.6**  a)    1.53

b)  $-2.45$

c)    2.37

d)  $-2.17$

e)    0.97

f)    0.51

**6.8**  a)  51.6

b)  16.6

c)  52.9

d)  28.3

e)  29.2

f)    6.7

**6.10**  143.3

**6.12**   0.0475

**6.14**   a)

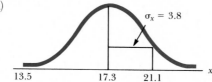

b)

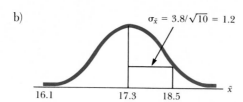

c)   $\bar{x} = 18.95,$   $P\left(\bar{x} \geq \dfrac{18.95 - 17.30}{3.8}\right) = P(z \geq 0.957)$

$\quad\quad = 1 - 0.8289 = 0.1711$

d)   $17.3 \pm 1.96(3.8)$ is 9.85 to 24.75

e)   $17.3 \pm 1.96(3.8/\sqrt{10})$ is 15.44 to 19.16

**6.16**   $\bar{x}$ is normally distributed if $x$ is normal or if the sample size is large.

**6.18**   a)   $P(\bar{c} \geq 115) = P\left(z \geq \dfrac{115 - 103}{12/2}\right) = P(z \geq 2) = 0.0228$

b)   $P(\bar{x} \geq 115) = P\left(z \geq \dfrac{115 - 103}{12/\sqrt{10}}\right) = P(z \geq 4) = 0.0000$

c)   The standard deviation decreases by one-half, from 6 to 3.

d)   It decreased from 0.0228 to 0.0000

**6.20**   a)   $P(x \geq 70,000) = P(z \geq 2.25) = 0.0122$

b)   $P(\bar{x} \geq 70,000) = P(z \geq 15.75) = 0.0000$

c)   The probability of exceeding 15,000 is much smaller with the larger sample size.

**6.22**   Since $n = 16$ is not very large, we need to assume $x$ is (approximately) normally distributed.

**6.24**   a)   0.95

b)   0.005

c)   0.975

d)   0.040

e)   0.005

f)   0.925

**6.26**  a)  $P(\overline{w} > 22.90) = P(t > 1.64|df = 3) = 0.10$

b)  $P(\overline{w} > 22.77) = P(t > 1.395|df = 8) = 0.10$

c)  The $t$-distribution is less spread out for $n = 9$, so a smaller $t$-value cuts off 10% when $n = 9$.

**6.28**  a)  $\overline{x} = \$548.75, \quad s_x = \sqrt{9637.22} = 98.169$

$P(\overline{x} \geq 548.75|\mu_x = 375) = P(t \geq 3.540|df = 3) = 0.0192$

**6.30**  a)  1.534

b)  $-1.032$

c)  1.476

d)  $-1.036$

e)  0.969

f)  0.511

**6.32**  a)  $\overline{x} = 3.000098, \quad s = 0.00014436$

b)  $P(\overline{x} \geq 3.000098) = P(t \geq 2.149|df = 9) = 0.0301$

c)  This low probability suggests it is very unlikely the machine is working properly.

**6.34**  Both are symmetrical bell-shaped curves with a mean of zero. The $t$-distribution is more spread out than the $z$, and the $t$ depends on the sample size while the $z$ does not. The $z$ assumes the population variance is known, while the $t$ assumes the variance is unknown.

**6.36**  a)  $z$

b)  $t$

c)  Neither $t$ nor $z$

d)  $z$

e)  $t$ is most appropriate since the variance is unknown; since $x$ is large, the $z$ can be used to approximate the $t$.

# CHAPTER SEVEN

**7.2**  a)  False. While $\overline{x}$ is an unbiased estimator of $\mu$, this does not imply that any single value of $\overline{x}$ will equal $\mu$.

b)  False. The mean of all the sample means is equal to the population mean, which is unknown. Just one possible sample mean is $438.12. It is not the population mean.

c)  False. The fact that $\bar{x}$ is an unbiased estimator of $\mu$ says nothing about how close an individual value of $\bar{x}$ is to $\mu$.

d)  True.

7.4  a)  $\alpha = 0.06$     $z_{\alpha/2} = z_{0.03} = 1.88$

b)  $\alpha = 0.001$     $z_{0.0005} = 3.27$

c)  $\alpha = 0.03$     $z_{0.015} = 2.17$

d)  $\alpha = 0.01$     $z_{0.005} = 2.58$

7.6  a)  False. Prior to sampling there was a 98% chance that the interval constructed would contain the true population income. This implies nothing about the proportion of Buick owners with income between \$30,388 and \$42,162.

b)  False. Ninety-eight percent of all intervals that could be constructed would contain the true population mean income of new Buick owners. This says nothing about the endpoints for those intervals.

c)  False. The proportion of people with given incomes who buy Buicks was not estimated.

d)  True.

7.8  a)  $\bar{x} = 6.166$, the point estimate of $\mu_x$

b)  The margin for sample error is
$$z_{\alpha/2}(\sigma/\sqrt{n}) = 1.64\,(1.4/\sqrt{6}) = 1.64(1.4/2.449) = 0.937$$
The confidence interval is
$\bar{x} \pm z_{\alpha/2}(\sigma/\sqrt{n})$, which upon substitution gives
$6.166 - 0.937 < \mu_x < 6.166 + 0.937$, or $5.229 < \mu_x < 7.103$

c)

| $x$ | $x - \bar{x}$ | $(x - \bar{x})^2$ | |
|---|---|---|---|
| 7 | 0.834 | 0.695 | |
| 4 | −2.166 | 4.691 | $\bar{x} = 6.166$ |
| 9 | 2.834 | 8.031 | |
| 2 | −4.166 | 17.355 | $s_x^2 = 34.830/(6 - 1) = 6.766$ |
| 8 | 1.834 | 3.363 | |
| 7 | 0.834 | 0.695 | $s_x = 2.639$, the point estimate of $\sigma_x$ |
| | | 34.830 | |

7.10  a)  The margin for sampling error is 13.

b)  $150 = 163 - 1.96\sigma/\sqrt{n}$,     if $n = 52$, $\sigma = 47.8$

7.12  Point estimate for $\mu$ is the sample mean $\bar{x} = 64.425$. The 95% confidence interval is
$64.425 - 1.96(20/\sqrt{40}) < \mu_x < 64.425 + 1.96(20/\sqrt{40})$ $58.227 < \mu_x < 70.623$

7.14  Answer will depend on sample selected.

**7.16** No. Prior to sampling there was a 95% probability that the interval constructed by the accountant would contain the true population mean. After the sample is taken and the interval is constructed, however, no probability statement can be made.

**7.18** a) $0.04 - 2.02(0.00078) < \mu_x < 0.04 + 2.02(0.00078)$

$$0.04 - 0.0016 < \mu_x < 0.04 + 0.0016$$

$$0.0384 < \mu_x < 0.0416$$

b) $0.04 - 1.96(0.005/6.4) < \mu_x < 0.04 + 1.96(0.005/6.4)$

$$0.04 - 0.0015 < \mu_x < 0.04 + 0.0015$$

$$0.0385 < \mu_x < 0.0415$$

c) The answer in (a) is more appropriate because the $t$-distribution is based on two random variables, $\bar{x}$ and $s_x$. The $z$-distribution is based on only one random variable, $\bar{x}$.

**7.20** Sample 44 accounts—i.e.,

$$n = \left| \frac{z_{\alpha/2}\sigma_x}{D} \right|^2 = \left| \frac{(1.645)(200)}{50} \right|^2 = (6.58)^2 = 43.29$$

**7.22** $$p - z_{\alpha/2}\sqrt{p(1-p)/n} < \pi < p + z_{\alpha/2}\sqrt{p(1-p)/n}$$

$$0.21 - (2.57)\sqrt{\frac{0.21(1-0.21)}{200}} < \pi < 0.21 + (2.57)\sqrt{\frac{0.21(1-0.21)}{200}}$$

$$0.21 - (2.57)(0.0288) < \pi < 0.21 + (2.57)(0.0288)$$

$$0.21 - 0.0740 < \pi < 0.21 + 0.0740$$

$$0.136 < \pi < 0.284$$

**7.24** a) $n = 426$ $\quad n = \left| \frac{z_{\alpha/2}\sigma_x}{D} \right|^2 = \left| \frac{1.96(3980)}{378.09} \right|^2 = 425.88$

$\bar{x} = 32,000$

$s_x = 3,980$

$D = \$378.09$

b) $n = 299$ $\quad n = \left| \frac{1.64(3980)}{378.09} \right|^2 = (17.267)^2 = 298.032$

$z_{\alpha/2} = z_{0.05} = 1.64$

or

$$\left| \frac{z_{\alpha/2}\text{ (new)}}{z_{\alpha/2}\text{ (old)}} \right|^2 = \left| \frac{1.64}{1.96} \right|^2 = 0.700$$

$n = (0.700)(425.88) = 298.116$

c) The old sample size is 1/4 of the new sample size.

$D = 1/2$ old $\quad \left| \frac{378}{189} \right|^2 = 4 \quad n = (4)(425.88) = 1703$

**7.26** a) Use the sample standard deviation as an approximate of the population standard deviation. Using the minimum and maximum values is a very crude estimator that has no known statistical properties. It is simply based on a rule of thumb.

b) $n = 99$

$$n = \left|\frac{z_{\alpha/2}\sigma_x}{D}\right|^2 = \left|\frac{(1.645)(12.0726)}{2}\right|^2 = 98.6$$

**7.28** Answer will depend on sample selected.

**7.30** a) No.

b) Yes, because both economists are going to use the same standard deviation and the same $n$.

c) No, because each economist will use the standard deviation calculated on the basis of the sample selected, and these samples need not have the same values or the same means.

**7.32** a) $135/300 = 0.45 = x/n = p$

b) 95% confidence interval for $\pi$ is

$$0.45 - 1.96\sqrt{\frac{0.45(1 - 0.45)}{300}} < \pi < 0.45 + 1.96\sqrt{\frac{0.45(1 - 0.45)}{300}}$$

$$0.394 < \pi < 0.506$$

**7.34** a) $n_{old} = 400$
$\alpha_{old} = 0.10$
$\alpha_{new} = 0.05$

$$\frac{n\,(\text{new})}{n\,(\text{old})} = \left|\frac{z_{\alpha/2}\,(\text{new})}{z_{\alpha/2}\,(\text{old})}\right|^2 = \left|\frac{1.96}{1.645}\right|^2 = 1.4196$$

$$(1.42)(400) = 568 = n_{new}$$

b) $D_{new} = 200$
$D_{old} = 100$

$$\frac{n\,(\text{new})}{n\,(\text{old})} = \left|\frac{D\,(\text{old})}{D\,(\text{new})}\right|^2 = \left|\frac{100}{200}\right|^2 = 0.25$$

$$(0.25)(400) = 100 = n_{new}$$

c) If the value of $\sigma_x$ is 1/2 of what it was, the new desired sample size is 1/4 of the old.

**7.36** Answer will depend on sample selected.

**7.38** a) Sample descriptive statistics

| $n$ | Mean | Standard Deviation | Minimum | Maximum |
|---|---|---|---|---|
| 50 | 3.0248 | 0.3190 | 2.2400 | 3.7800 |

b) Approximate 99% confidence interval for $\mu$:

$3.0248 \pm (2.58)(0.3190/7.07)$

$2.91 < \mu < 3.14$

c) $p = 29/50 = 0.58$ so the 95% confidence interval for $\pi$ is

$0.58 \pm (1.96)\sqrt{0.58(0.42)/50}$

$0.44 < \pi < 0.72$

**7.40** The sample median can be used as an estimate of the population median, but it is a biased estimate of the population mean unless the population is symmetrical.

**7.42** This is a false statement because we cannot attach a probability statement to the resulting values for one confidence interval calculation. A 95% confidence interval can be interpreted only in terms of probability prior to sampling.

# CHAPTER EIGHT

**8.2** A low $p$-value implies that the null hypothesis should be rejected because it implies a low probability that the sample data could have occurred if the null hypothesis was correct. There is always a chance, however, that this conclusion to reject the null hypothesis is wrong (equal to the $p$-value), since nonrepresentative samples can occur by random sampling.

**8.4** a) $H_0: \mu_x \geq 18$  $\sigma_x = 6$  $n = 81$
$H_A: \mu_x < 18$  $\bar{x} = 16$

$$Z_c = \frac{\bar{x} - \mu_x}{\sigma_x/\sqrt{n}} = \frac{16 - 18}{6/\sqrt{81}} = -\frac{2}{6/9} = -3$$

$p$-value $= P(z \leq -3) = 1 - 0.9987 = 0.0013$
The $p$-value is very low; therefore reject the null hypothesis.

b) There is no test because $\bar{x} = 20$ fulfills the null hypothesis. Thus, the null hypothesis cannot be rejected.

c) $z_c = -0.5/0.6667 = -0.75$, and the $p$-value $= 0.226$. This relatively large $p$-value suggests that the null hypothesis should not be rejected.

**8.6** a) Two-sided:

$H_0: \mu_x = 23.4$ and $H_A: \mu_x \neq 23.4$

b) One-sided:

$H_0: \mu_x \leq \$34,603.80$ and $H_A: \mu_x > \$34,603.80$

c) One-sided:

$H_0: \pi \leq 0.08$ and $H_A: \pi > 0.08$

d) One-sided:

$H_0: \mu_x \leq 3,000 \text{ lb/ft}^2$ and $H_A: \mu_x > 3,000 \text{ lb/ft}^2$

**8.8** a) A Type I error would occur if a sample suggested a large change in the number of applicants so that the null hypothesis was rejected, when actually the sample simply was a poor representation of the population and the true population mean was still 23.4.

A Type II error occurs if a sample had a mean at or near 23.4, allowing the null hypothesis to be accepted, when actually the population mean had changed significantly.

b) If a sample of salaries was taken that showed a large increase, when the overall increase was actually 7%, then a rejection of the null hypothesis would be a Type I error.

A Type II error would occur if a sample suggested that the increase was 7% when actually the population increase was far higher.

c) A Type I error would occur if the null hypothesis was rejected because a non-representative sample showed a defective rate higher than 8% when the population proportion was actually 8%.

A Type II error would occur if the null hypothesis was accepted on the basis of a sample indicating an 8% proportion of defective gaskets when actually the population rate is much higher.

d) A Type I error would occur if the null hypothesis was rejected due to a sample that suggested that the new plastic had an average breaking point of well over 3000 lb/ft$^2$ when actually the population mean breaking point was the same as the old plastic.

A Type II error would occur if the null hypothesis was accepted due to a sample indicating a mean breaking point close to the 3000 lb/ft$^2$ mark when actually the new plastic was far stronger.

**8.10** a) One rule of thumb that can be used to determine the null hypothesis is that if a current or established theory exists, it should be chosen as the null hypothesis. Also, the null hypothesis should contain the theory that implies the greatest cost if it is erroneously rejected.

**8.12** a) $H_0: \mu_x \geq 4.1$ yr and $H_A: \mu_x < 4.1$ yr

b) A Type I error would be to reject $H_0$ erroneously based on a sample that was not representative of the population (i.e., one that suggested that the average work experience was less than the national average when indeed it was the same or higher).

A Type II error would occur if $H_0$ were accepted erroneously because a sample suggested that the average was 4.1 yr or greater when actually it was less.

c) A Type I error would lead them to believe that their personnel are underexperienced and that perhaps more-experienced people should be hired. This could cost more money for salaries.

A Type II error might cause the personnel director to assume erroneously that personnel had sufficient experience when indeed experience was lacking.

**8.14** Both $\alpha$ and $\beta$ are probabilities of error that cannot be avoided in hypotheses testing. $\alpha$ is defined as the probability of Type I error, incorrectly rejecting $H_0$. $\beta$ is the probability of a Type II error, incorrectly accepting $H_0$. Because the null hypothesis contains the theory that, if incorrectly rejected, would produce the greater cost, it is desirable to limit the size of $\alpha$. Since $\alpha$ and $\beta$ have an inverse relationship, however, one cannot always make $\alpha$ as small as one would like because $\beta$ might become unacceptably large. The focus has traditionally been on $\alpha$ because a level of $\alpha$ may be specified, while calculating $\beta$ requires knowledge of the true parameter value and the reason for testing is to find this value.

**8.16**  a)  $H_0$: $\mu_x \le \$232.10$ and $H_A$: $\mu_x > \$232.10$

      b)  A Type I error would be to reject erroneously the null hypothesis and mistakenly believe the average balance in the bank is higher than it actually is.

          A Type II error would be to accept erroneously the null hypothesis and mistakenly believe that the average balance in the bank is lower than it actually is.

          It would appear that in this case a Type I error would be more serious because the bank would be overestimating its deposits. Since loans are made on the basis of deposits, it may make excessive loans if $H_A$ is accepted when $H_0$ is true.

      c)  $H_0$ rejection region is $z > 1.645$

      d)  $n = 100,$    $\bar{x} = \$248.95,$    $\sigma_x = \$150.00$

$$z_c = \frac{248.95 - 232.10}{150/\sqrt{100}} = 1.12$$

      e)  $p\text{-value} = P(z_c > 1.12) = 1 - 0.8686 = 0.1314$

      f)  $p\text{-value of } 0.1314 > \alpha = 0.05$ implies acceptance of $H_0$.

**8.18**  a)  $\alpha = 0.05$    $z_{\alpha/2} = z_{0.025} = 1.96$

$$1.96 = \frac{\bar{x} - 17.5}{2.3/\sqrt{100}} = \frac{\bar{x} - 17.5}{0.23}$$

$\bar{x} - 17.5 = 0.4508$; Upper critical $\bar{x} = 17.9508$

$$-1.96 = \frac{\bar{x} - 17.5}{0.23}$$

$\bar{x} - 17.5 = -0.4508$; Lower critical $\bar{x} = 17.0492$

      b)  $\alpha = 0.04$    $z_{0.04} = 1.75$

$$z = \frac{\bar{x} - \mu_x}{\sigma_x/\sqrt{n}}$$

$$1.75 = \frac{\bar{x} - 1078}{12.7/\sqrt{100}} = \frac{\bar{x} - 1078}{1.27}$$

$\bar{x} - 1078 = 2.2225$; Critical $\bar{x} = 1080.2$

**8.20**  a)  $t$

      b)  $z$

c) $t$, but $z$ may be used if $n$ is extremely large

d) Neither

e) $t$, but $z$ may be used if $n$ is extremely large

**8.22**  a) Accept $H_0$.

b) Accept $H_0$.

c) Reject $H_0$.

d) Accept $H_0$.

**8.24**  Step 1: $H_0$: $\mu_x \leq 58.7$ million shares/day

$H_A$: $\mu_x > 58.7$ million shares/day

Step 2: $\alpha = 0.05$

Step 3: The hypotheses are about a population mean, and the sample size is greater than 30. If $\sigma$ is fixed at 14.3, the $z$ distribution is appropriate.

$$z_c = \frac{\bar{x} - \mu_0}{\sigma/\sqrt{n}} = \frac{61.3 - 58.7}{14.3/\sqrt{50}} = 1.29$$

Step 4: $p$-value $= P(z \geq 1.29) = 1 - 0.9015 = 0.0985$

Step 5: If the $\alpha$ value is 0.05, then $H_0$ would be accepted. The $p$ value of 0.0985 is higher than 0.05. (If $\alpha = 0.10$, then $H_0$ would be rejected.)

**8.26**  $H_0$: $\mu_x \geq 3.32$

$H_A$: $\mu_x < 3.32$

$n = 145 \qquad \bar{x} = 3.25 \qquad \sigma_x = 0.19 \qquad \alpha = 0.04$

$$z_c = \frac{\bar{x} - \mu_0}{\sigma/\sqrt{n}} = \frac{3.25 - 3.32}{0.19/\sqrt{145}} = \frac{-0.07}{0.01578} = -4.44$$

$p$-value $= P(z \leq -4.44)$ is approximately 0.

The probability that an $\bar{x}$ of 3.25 or less could occur if the mean were actually 3.32 is approximately zero. Therefore $H_0$ is rejected.

No, a lower average GPA does not mean that the quality of students has necessarily decreased. It could be that professors are grading harder.

**8.28**  Step 1: $H_0$: $\mu_x \geq 2$ cents/bushel

$H_A$: $\mu_x < 2$ cents/bushel

$n = 100 \qquad \bar{x} = 1.9 \qquad s_x = 0.2$

Step 2: $\alpha = 0.05$

Step 3: Use $t$-distribution:

$$t_c = \frac{\bar{x} - \sigma_0}{s_x/\sqrt{n}} = \frac{1.9 - 2}{0.2/\sqrt{100}} = \frac{-0.1}{0.02} = -5$$

Step 4: $p$-value $= P(t \leq -5)$ is approximately 0.

Step 5: $H_0$ is rejected.

**8.30** Step 1: $H_0 = \pi \leq 0.50$
$H_A = \pi > 0.50$

Step 2: $\alpha = 0.01$

Step 3: We use a $z$-test statistic for testing population proportions, when $n \geq 30$:

$$z = \frac{(x/n) - \pi_0}{\sqrt{\pi_0(1 - \pi_0)/n}} = \frac{0.59 - 0.50}{\sqrt{0.50(0.50)/2465}} = 8.94$$

Step 4: $p$-value $= P(z \geq 8.94)$ is approximately 0.
$p$-value is less than $\alpha$-value.

Step 5: We must reject the null hypothesis and conclude that greater than 50% of voters thought they were better off in 1984 than in 1980.

**8.32** Step 1: $H_0\colon \mu_1 - \mu_2 \leq 0$
$H_A\colon \mu_1 - \mu_2 > 0$

Step 2: $\alpha = 0.10$

Step 3: The $t$-test statistic is appropriate because the population standard deviations are not known. We assume that the populations are normal and they have equal variances.

$$t_c = \frac{\bar{x}_1 - \bar{x}_2 - 0}{\sqrt{\left[\dfrac{s_1^2(n_1 - 1) + s_2^2(n_2 - 1)}{n_1 + n_2 - 2}\right]\left[\dfrac{n_1 + n_2}{n_1(n_2)}\right]}}$$

$$= \frac{55 - 52}{\sqrt{\left[\dfrac{(5)^2(14) + (7)^2(13)}{15 + 14 - 2}\right]\left[\dfrac{15 + 14}{15(14)}\right]}} = 1.335$$

Step 4: $p$-value $= P(t \geq 1.335 | \mathrm{df} = 27)$ is slightly less than 0.1.
$P(t \geq 1.314 | \mathrm{df} = 27) = 1 - 0.90 = 0.10$

Step 5: The $p$-value is less than $\alpha$, so reject $H_0$.

**8.34** Step 1: $H_0\colon \pi = 0.67$
$H_A\colon \pi \neq 0.67$

Step 2: $\alpha = 0.05$

Step 3: Use a $z$-test statistic for testing population proportions when $n \geq 30$.

$$z = \frac{(x/n) - \pi_0}{\sqrt{\pi_0(1 - \pi_0)/n}} = \frac{30/50 - 0.67}{\sqrt{0.67(0.33)/50}} = \frac{-0.07}{0.0665} = -1.05$$

Step 4: $p$-value $= 2P(z \geq 1.05) = 2(1 - 0.8531) = 0.2938$

Step 5: The $p$-value is far greater than the $\alpha = 0.05$, so $H_0$ must be accepted.

**8.36** Step 1: $H_0\colon \mu_x = \$45.00$
$H_A\colon \mu_x \neq \$45.00$

Step 2: $\alpha = 0.05$

Step 3: Use $t$-test statistic because the population standard deviation is unknown

$$\bar{x} = 52.07 \qquad s_x = 8.2$$

$$t_c = \frac{\bar{x} - \mu_0}{s_x/\sqrt{n}} = \frac{52.07 - 45.00}{8.2/\sqrt{26}} = 4.4$$

Step 4: $p$-value $= 2P(t \geq 4|df = 25)$ is approximately zero

Step 5: The $p$-value is lower than $\alpha = 0.05$, so $H_0$ is rejected.

**8.38** Step 1: $H_0$: $\mu_x = 90$ (units/hr)
$H_A$: $\mu_x \neq 90$ (units/hr)

Step 2: $\alpha = 0.05$

Step 3: Use $t$-test statistic because the population standard deviation is not known and $n \geq 30$

$$t_c = \frac{\bar{x} - \mu_0}{s_x/\sqrt{n}} = \frac{86 - 90}{20/\sqrt{36}} = \frac{-4}{20/6} = -1.2$$

Step 4: $p$-value $= 2P(t \geq 1.2|df = 35) > 0.05$

Step 5: The approximate $p$-value is much higher than the $\alpha = 0.05$, so $H_0$ is accepted.

**8.40** Step 1: $H_0$: $\pi \geq .33$
$H_A$: $\pi < .33$

Step 2: $\alpha = 0.04$

Step 3: Use a $z$-test statistic for a population proportion test ($n \geq 30$):

$$z = \frac{(x/n) - \pi_0}{\sqrt{\dfrac{\pi_0(1 - \pi_0)}{n}}} = \frac{0.36 - 0.33}{\sqrt{\dfrac{0.33(0.67)}{200}}} = 0.90$$

Step 4: $p$-value $= P(z \geq 0.90) = (1 - 0.8159) = 0.1841$

Step 5: The $p$-value is higher than $\alpha = 0.04$, so $H_0$ is accepted.

**8.42** Step 1: $H_0$: $\pi = 0.60$
$H_A$: $\pi \neq 0.60$

Step 2: $\alpha = 0.05$

Step 3: Use a $z$-test statistic for a population proportion test ($n \geq 30$)

$$z = \frac{(x/n) - \pi_0}{\sqrt{\pi_0(1 - \pi_0)/n}} = \frac{0.50 - 0.60}{\sqrt{0.60(0.40)/30}} = -1.12$$

Step 4: $p$-value $= 2P(z \leq -1.12) = 2(1 - 0.8686) = 0.2628$

Step 5: The $p$-value is much higher than the $\alpha = 0.05$, so $H_0$ must be accepted.

**8.44** Step 1: $H_0$: $\mu_x \leq \$12{,}983$
$H_A$: $\mu_x > \$12{,}983$

Step 2: $\alpha = 0.04$

Step 3: Use a $t$-test statistic because the population standard deviation is unknown

$$t_c = \frac{\bar{x} - \mu_0}{s_x/\sqrt{n}} = \frac{14{,}039 - 12{,}983}{2{,}129/\sqrt{200}} = \frac{1{,}056}{2{,}129/\sqrt{200}} = 7.015$$

Step 4: $p$-value $= P(t \geq 7.015 | \mathrm{df} = 199)$ is approximately zero.

Step 5: Because the $p$-value is approximately zero, and thus far below $\alpha = 0.04$, the null hypothesis must be rejected.

**8.46** Step 1: $H_0: \mu_1 - \mu_2 = 0$
$H_A: \mu_1 - \mu_2 \neq 0$

Step 2: $\alpha = 0.05$

Step 3: Use the $t$-test statistic because the population variances are unknown, and each $n$ is less than 30

$\bar{x}_1 = 52.07 \qquad \bar{x}_2 = 50.65$
$s_1 = 8.2 \qquad s_2 = 6.8$
$n_1 = 26 \qquad n_2 = 26$
$t_c = 0.68$

Step 4: $p$-value $= P(t \geq 0.68 | \mathrm{df} = 50)$ is approximately $0.25$

Step 5: The $p$-value is much higher than the $\alpha = 0.05$, so $H_0$ cannot be rejected. The two sample means do not differ significantly using $\alpha = 0.05$.

**8.48** The company's 80 new accountants might be considered a random sample if it is assumed that each time one was chosen, all of those available had an equal chance of being chosen; that is, each hiring was identical so that the 80 persons could be viewed as all being hired at the same time.

# CHAPTER NINE

**9.2** a) Positive relationship between $x$ and $y$

b) Least Squares Regression, $\hat{y} = -15 + 3.2x$

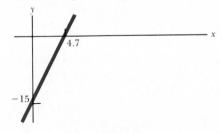

c) $\hat{y} = 145$, if $x = 50$.

**9.4** The method of least squares implies nothing about the number of points above or below the regression line. For example, see Fig. 9.3.

**9.6** a) $\hat{y} = 12 - 2x$

b) The five residuals are 0, 0, 2, $-2$, 0, which sum to zero.
SSE $= 8$
The sum of squared errors is minimized by the method of least squares.

c) Regression Line and Errors

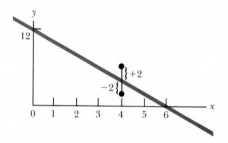

**9.8** a) $b = 52.57$ and $a = 46.49$ so $\hat{y} = 46.49 + 52.57x$.

b) Regression Line

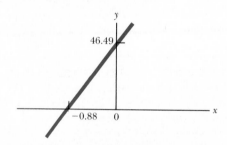

c) Predicted sales are $990,600 if 10,000 people see the billboard.

**9.10** a) The sign of $r$ indicates a positive or negative relationship between $x$ and $y$. It is the same sign as the direction of the slope of the regression line.

b) The coefficient of determination ($r^2$) is the percentage of variability in $y$ around $\bar{y}$ explained by the regression line.

**9.12** The nearer $r$ and $r^2$ are to 1, the more likely the sample points will be near the regression line. However, it is not necessary that any of the sample points lies exactly on the regression line unless $r$ and $r^2$ are equal to 1. The magnitude of $r$ and $r^2$ has nothing to do with the side of the regression line on which the sample points tend to lie.

Answers to Selected Exercises

**9.14** There is a negative relationship between $x$ and $y$, where 81% of the variability in $y$ around its mean $\bar{y}$ is explained by $x$.

**9.16** a) $\hat{y} = 0.93 + 0.90x$

b) SST = 198.59    SSE = 105.35    SSR = 93.24

c) $r = 0.69$    $r^2 = 0.47$

d) MSE = 5.27, MSR = 93.24, and standard error of estimate = 2.30
If $x = 5$, $\hat{y} \pm 2$ (standard error) is 0.8 to 10.

**9.18** If $x = 3$, $\hat{y} = 6$; standard error of estimate = 1.633; and $\hat{y} \pm 2$ (standard error) = $6 \pm 3.266$.

**9.20** If $b$ is an unbiased estimator of $\beta$, then on average $b$ equals $\beta$.

**9.22** a) No, not linear.

b) No, not linear.

c) Yes.

d) No, errors are not randomly distributed.

e) Yes.

f) No, size of error seems to be a function of $x$.

**9.24** $H_0$: $\beta \geq 0$ and $H_A$: $\beta < 0$
$P(t < -4.899) = 0.0081 < 0.05$; thus $H_0$ is rejected.

**9.26** a) $\hat{y} = 177.263 - 0.289x$. If $x = 490$, $\hat{y} = 35.65$

b) SST = 200, SSE = 8.95, SST = 191.05, $r^2 = 0.955$, and $r = -0.977$

c) $P(t < -8) = 0.002$. Thus reject $\beta = 0$ and accept $\beta \neq 0$.

**9.28** a) $\hat{y} = 4.4448 + 0.2986x$

b) $P(t > 3.07) = 0.0065$. Thus reject the null hypothesis of no linear relationship, and accept the alternative hypothesis of a linear relationship.

c) SST = 410.14, SSE = 200.65, and SSR = 209.49
Coefficient of determination = 0.5108
Correlation coefficient = 0.7147
The regression line explains 51.08% of the variance
The correlation between $x$ and $y$ is fairly strong and positive.

**9.30** a) The information given does not suggest which variable depends on the other.

b) $\hat{y} = 5.07 - .1195x$, where $\hat{y}$ is predicted unemployment rate and $x$ is inflation rate. The line shifts for the data after 1972.

c) The residuals tend to clump together over several years' time before swinging to the other side.

**9.32** a) $y = \alpha + \beta x + \epsilon$

b) $\hat{y} = 578.66 + 17.21x$; this line explains 37% of the variability.

c) There is a strong relationship between scores and raises even though $r^2$ is relatively low because the $t$ coefficient for $b$ is relatively large ($t = 4.62$).

**9.34** The distribution of residuals does not appear to be random. Negative values tend to be extreme, while positive values cluster near the mean. A nonlinear relationship may be more appropriate.

**9.36**
a) False. $\epsilon$ is a random variable and random variables are not estimated. Only parameters are estimated.

b) True. This is the definition of the least squares method.

c) True. If there are no errors in predicting, SSE $= 0$.

d) False. If SSE $=$ SSR, 50% of the variability in $y$ is explained.

e) False. The sum of errors around the least squares regression line is always zero regardless of the expected value of $\epsilon$.

**9.38**
a) Before 1981, demand was inelastic. Therefore $Q = 40$. After 1981, demand became somewhat sensitive to price. Thus $P = 8 - 0.025Q$ might be the post-1981 demand curve.

b) 1. $P = 8 + 0.025$

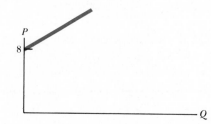

3. $P = 8 - 0.025Q$

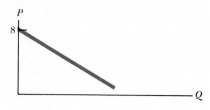

2. $P = 7$

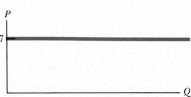

4. $Q = 40$

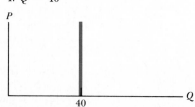

c) As can be seen in Fig. b.3, if quantity demanded is price sensitive, the quantity demanded falls as the price is increased.

d) When the demand curve is price sensitive, fixed forecasts do not work. The demand curve can be estimated using regression methods.

**9.40**
a) A negative deficit means the government revenues exceeded expenditures.

b) $\hat{y} = 26.06 + 0.5543x$

c) $\hat{y} = 76.78$, given $x = 91.5$. The regression line only loosely reflects the sample data in this case.

d) $s_e = 26.03$, $\hat{y} \pm 2s_e = 50.71$–$102.77$

**9.42** a) Predicted sales $= -153.3 + 20.4$ (Expense)

b) If Expense $= 60$, Predicted sales $= 1673.71$, or $1,673,710$.
Average error $= 199.50$, or $199,500$.

c) If Expense $= 100$, Predicted sales $= 1891.65$, or $1,891,650$.
This number is dubious because $100,000 is outside the range of expenses sampled. $\hat{y} \pm z(s_e) = \$1,592,644$–$2,190,656$.

d) Only 52.7% of the deviation of $y$ from its mean is explained by advertising expense.

**9.44** a) Let $x$ = time in seconds for response, and let $y = 1Q$. Then the sample regression line is $\hat{y} = 150 - 750x$, and the population equation is $y = \alpha + \beta x + \epsilon$.

b) Implied Regression Line

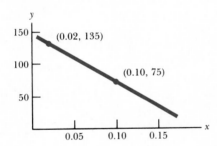

# CHAPTER TEN

**10.2** The computer $p$-value can be checked by comparing it with the value from the appropriate table in Appendix B. For example, if the $p$-value is one-sided, it will agree with the $p$-value given in Appendix Table B.4.

**10.4**

REGRESSION

| VAR. | COEFFICIENT | STD. ERROR | T(DF = 5) | PROB. |
|------|-------------|------------|-----------|-------|
| FL | -10.8853 | 34.1220 | -0.319 | 0.76261 |
| RM | 12.3465 | 5.3621 | 2.303 | 0.06955 |
| CONSTANT | 44.2727 | | | |

Predicted price $= 44.2727 + 12.3465(9) - 10.8853(2.8) = 124.912$, or $124,912

**10.6** Multiplie regression permits using more than one variable in an attempt to explain the dependent variable. The hope is that the additional variables will improve the predictive ability.

**10.8** Two separate simple regressions do not take into account any interrelationship between prices and unemployment. Multiple regression will find the best fit considering both variables simultaneously.

**10.10**
a) $\hat{y} = -3.8428 + 1.456x + 0.3787z$

b) No, as $z$ is not significant ($p = 0.20146$). However, $x$ is significant ($p = 0.00544$).

c) Using both $x$ and $z$, $\hat{y} = -3.8428 + 1.4564(6) + 0.3787(7)$
$$= 7.5465$$

d)

| $y$ | $y - \hat{y}$ | $e$ | $e^2$ |
|-----|---------------|---------|---------|
| 1 | $1 - 0.9635$ | $0.0365$ | $0.0013$ |
| 3 | $3 - 3.9347$ | $-0.9347$ | $0.8736$ |
| 6 | $6 - 5.0124$ | $0.9876$ | $0.9754$ |
| 9 | $9 - 9.3232$ | $-0.3232$ | $0.1045$ |
| 11 | $11 - 10.4009$ | $0.5991$ | $0.3589$ |
| 12 | $12 - 12.3670$ | $-0.3670$ | $0.1349$ |
| | | | $2.4484$ |

$$s_e = \sqrt{2.4484/3} = 0.9034$$

e) Since $r^2 = 0.9750$, the fit is good (97.50% of the variability in $y$ is explained by $x$ and $z$).

f) From the correlation matrix, $(-0.83582)^2 = 0.6986 \Rightarrow 69.86\%$ of $z$ is explained by $x$. Similarly, 95.29% of $y$ is explained by $x$.

**10.12** $r^2_{\text{rate, index}} = (0.68977)^2 \Rightarrow 47.58\%$ of one variable is explained by the other. Index is much more highly correlated with wage (0.99242).

**10.14** The $F$-test is used to test the overall fit (all independent variables taken together), while the $t$-test is used to test the significance of individual variables.

**10.16**
a) $\hat{y} = -26.5690 + 12.7857 \text{ (labor)} + 0.0107 \text{ (horsepower)}$
$$= -26.5690 + 12.7857(5) + 0.0107(4000) = 80.1595$$

b) Since $p = 0$ for both independent variables, both $b$s are significantly different from zero. The overall $p$-value is also 0, so the overall fit is significant as well.

c) $r^2 = 0.85 \Rightarrow 85\%$ of the variability in output is explained by the two independent variables. $s_e = 14.9641$ is the average variability.

**10.18** Multiple regression is not the sum of simple regressions. For multiple regression the least squares procedure minimizes the SSE by simultaneously taking into account all the independent variables. Thus the executive's procedure is incorrect.

**10.22**  Trend

**10.24**  0.0954

**10.26**  Predicted sales (January 1986) = 124.2629

**10.28**  a)  When $x_2 = 1$, $\hat{y} = a + b_1x_1 + b_2 = a + b_2 + b_1x_1$. Thus the intercept is $(a + b_2)$.

   b)  When $x_2 = 0$, $\hat{y} = a + b_1x_1$, and the intercept is $a$.

   c)

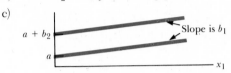

**10.30**  The coefficient $-1.05$ indicates that $y$ will decrease by 1.05 when $x_2$ increases by one unit, with $x_1$ held constant.

**10.32**  a)  False. $x_2$ is held constant but not necessarily at its mean.

   b)  True.

   c)  True.

   d)  False. Multicollinearity occurs when two or more independent variables are highly correlated.

   e)  True.

   f)  False. The assignment of 0 or 1 is arbitrary.

**10.34**  a)  $R^2 = 0.7957$ indicates a fairly good fit.

   b)  The overall $p$-value ($p = 0.00007263$) indicates a good fit, supporting the theory.

   c)  Productivity is certainly highly related to price ($p = 0.00191$), while profit is much less related ($p = 0.21248$).

   d)  A list of the residuals would be most helpful.

   e)  $\hat{y} = -498.745883 + 77.876707(1) + 465.096072(0) = -420.869$

   f)  The prediction in (e) has little meaning (a negative price) because an unreasonable value (zero) was selected for profits.

**10.36**  DEPENDENT VARIABLE: money

| VAR. | REGRESSION COEFFICIENT | STD. ERROR | T(DF = 15) | PROB. |
|---|---|---|---|---|
| YEAR | 18.6083 | 1.8003 | 10.336 | 0.00000 |
| DUMMY | -11.5861 | 18.6802 | -0.620 | 0.54441 |
| CONSTANT | -1073.3083 | | | |

The large $p$-value for the dummy variable, $p = 0.54441$, suggests that there is not a significant difference in the slopes.

**10.38**  $\hat{y} = -7808.9240 + 1175.0043x - 10.5243x^2$
$= -7808.9240 + 1175.0043(40) - 10.5243(40)^2$
$= 22352.368$

**10.40**  b) Only the population variable is significant because the other $p$-values are quite large.

**10.42**  a) DEPENDENT VARIABLE: sales

| VAR. | REGRESSION COEFFICIENT | STD. ERROR | T(DF = 61) | PROB. |
|---|---|---|---|---|
| TREND | 101.7449 | 4.6468 | 21.896 | 0.00000 |
| ADV | 8.1279 | 0.3468 | 23.439 | 0.00000 |
| CONSTANT | 2922.7453 | | | |

STD. ERROR OF EST. = 598.0658
R SQUARED = 0.9708
MULTIPLE R = 0.9853

The residuals (not given here) show two patterns: (1) a tendency to increase in variability over time (might be caused by increasing prices) and (2) similar groups of four (probably caused by seasonality).

b) DEPENDENT VARIABLE: lnsales

| VAR. | REGRESSION COEFFICIENT | STD. ERROR | T(DF = 61) | PROB. |
|---|---|---|---|---|
| TREND | 0.0117 | 4.77556E-04 | 24.518 | 0.00000 |
| ADV | 7.61162E-04 | 3.56014E-05 | 21.380 | 0.00000 |
| CONSTANT | 8.4086 | | | |

STD. ERROR OF EST. = 0.0614
R SQUARED = 0.9715
MULTIPLE R = 0.9857

This transformation seems to have taken care of much of the problems in the residuals in part (a). The overall fit has improved only very slightly.

c) DEPENDENT VARIABLE: lnsales

First quarter: D1=1, D2=D3=0, . . . , fourth quarter: D1=D2=D3=0

| VAR. | REGRESSION COEFFICIENT | STD. ERROR | T(DF = 58) | PROB. |
|---|---|---|---|---|
| D3 | -0.2656 | 0.0405 | -6.558 | 0.00000 |
| D2 | -0.3836 | 0.0553 | -6.932 | 0.00000 |
| D1 | -0.4328 | 0.0560 | -7.732 | 0.00000 |
| TREND | 0.0161 | 6.89826E-04 | 23.403 | 0.00000 |
| ADV | 1.2047E-05 | 1.04315E-04 | 0.115 | 0.00000 |
| CONSTANT | 8.8311 | | | |

STD. ERROR OF EST. = 0.0431
       R SQUARED = 0.9867
     MULTIPLE R = 0.9933

The dummy variables are all significantly different from zero. The standard error of the estimate has decreased, indicating an improved fit.

d) DEPENDENT VARIABLE: lnsales

```
                REGRESSION
VAR.       COEFFICIENT  STD. ERROR  T(DF = 53)   PROB.
ADV        -7.5198E-06  1.01253E-04   -0.074    0.94108
TREND       0.0128       0.0021        5.989     0.00000
D1         -0.3415       0.0775       -4.405     0.00005
D2         -0.3010       0.0732       -4.113     0.00014
D3         -0.2085       0.0522       -3.993     0.00020
LAGSALES    0.2352       0.1237        1.901     0.06276
CONSTANT    6.7614
```

STD. ERROR OF EST. = 0.0397
       R SQUARED = 0.9883
       MULTIPLE = 0.9941

Again, $s_e$ has decreased, indicating an improved fit.

f) Ln(12730) = 9.45

$\hat{y}$ = 6.7614 − 0.0000075198ADV + 0.0128TREND − 0.3415D1 − 0.3010D2
     − 0.2085D3 + 0.2352LAGSALES

   = 6.7614 − 0.0000075198(350) + 0.0128(65) − 0.3415(0) − 0.3010(1) − 0.2085(0)
     + 0.2352(9.45)

   = 9.512    Taking antilogs: estimated sales = 13,251

In this case it probably would be better to have omitted the ADV variable since its $p$-value is very large. The difference in the resulting forecast, however, is very small.

**10.44** DEPENDENT VARIABLE: sales

```
                REGRESSION
VAR.       COEFFICIENT  STD. ERROR  T(DF = 16)   PROB.
D1          5.6800       4.7939        1.185     0.25338
D2          2.9000       4.7939        0.605     0.55371
D3          1.5000       4.7939        0.313     0.75840
CONSTANT  116.1000
```

STD. ERROR OF EST. = 7.5799
       R SQUARED = 0.0870
     MULTIPLE R = 0.2950

This fit is clearly much worse, by comparing $R^2$s and $s_e$s. Table 10.14 is better because the upward trend in sales is taken into account by using the lag of sales.

**10.46** DEPENDENT VARIABLE: netinc

```
                   REGRESSION
VAR.              COEFFICIENT    STD. ERROR    T(DF = 16)    PROB.
ASSETS                0.0025        0.0079        0.322      0.75199
D1             -18989.3605    103652.3769        -0.183      0.85694
D2             -47749.9629    109506.9085        -0.436      0.66863
D3             -68068.4544    108446.6902        -0.628      0.53908
CONSTANT      -270097.1589
```

```
STD. ERROR OF EST. = 171070.0018
        R SQUARED = 0.0378
       MULTIPLE R = 0.1945
```

The high $p$-values indicate none of the four independent variables is related to net income.

# CHAPTER ELEVEN

**11.2** The computer ANOVA table is:

```
              GROUP          MEAN        n
            Fert. 1        40.167        6
            Fert. 2        36.833        6
            Fert. 3        36.833        6

            GRAND MEAN     37.944       18
```

| SOURCE | SUM OF SQUARES | DF | MEAN SQUARE | F RATIO | PROB. |
|--------|----------------|----|----|----|----|
| BETWEEN | 44.444 | 2 | 22.222 | 1.375 | 0.2830 |
| WITHIN | 242.500 | 15 | 16.167 | | |
| TOTAL | 286.944 | 17 | | | |

a) The means are 40.167, 36.833, and 36.833 respectively.

b) $s_1^2 = \dfrac{1}{5}[(44 - 37.944)^2 + (38 - 37.944)^2 + \ldots + (36 - 37.944)^2]$

$\qquad = 30.567$

$\quad s_2^2 = 8.567$

$\quad s_3^2 = 9.367$

c) $F = 22.222/16.167 = 1.375$

d) Difference is not significant since $p = 0.2830 > \alpha = 0.05$.

e) est. $\tau_1 = 40.167 - 37.944 = 2.223$
est. $\tau_2 = 36.833 - 37.944 = -1.111$
est. $\tau_3 = 36.833 - 37.944 = -1.111$

**11.4** The signs had to be reversed in one of the two series to make the rally and the crash percentages comparable. A 10% increase is offset by a 10% decrease, not a $-10\%$ decrease.

**11.6** We might expect that the errors in the returns do not have the same variance for the three firms (assumption 1); that is, the firms may be more or less conservative and thus have a different variance in their errors. Also, the errors may not be independent over time, resulting from periods of varying prosperity in the economy.

**11.8** The computer ANOVA output is:

| SOURCE | SUM OF SQUARES | DF | MEAN SQUARE | F RATIO | PROB. |
|--------|----------------|-----|-------------|---------|-------|
| BETWEEN | 2.2500E-04 | 1 | 2.2500E-04 | 1.340 | 0.2663 |
| WITHIN | 2.3500E-03 | 14 | 1.6786E-04 | | |
| TOTAL | 2.5750E-03 | 15 | | | |

Because $p = 0.2663 > \alpha = 0.05$, $H_0$ should be accepted and the conclusion reached that there is not a significant difference in tire wear.

**11.10** The computer ANOVA output is:

| GROUP | MEAN | N |
|-------|------|---|
| 1 | 25.825 | 4 |
| 2 | 23.100 | 4 |
| 3 | 25.325 | 4 |
| 4 | 24.875 | 4 |
| GRAND MEAN | 24.781 | 16 |

| SOURCE | SUM OF SQUARES | DF | MEAN SQUARE | F RATIO | PROB. |
|--------|----------------|-----|-------------|---------|-------|
| BETWEEN | 16.882 | 3 | 5.627 | 1.453 | 0.2764 |
| WITHIN | 46.463 | 12 | 3.872 | | |
| TOTAL | 63.344 | 15 | | | |

a) $y_{4,2} = 23.6$

b) Est. $\mu = 24.781$, est. $\tau_2 = 23.100 - 24.781 = -1.681$
Est. $\epsilon_{4,2} = 24.1 - 23.6 = 0.5$
$23.6 = $ est. $\mu + $ est. $\tau_2 + $ est. $\epsilon_{4,2} = 24.781 - 1.681 + 0.5$

**11.12** a) $(61.070 + 53.035)/2 = 57.053$ (rounded)

b) MSC $= 645.612$, MSE $= 142.519$

c) The $p$-value is $p = 0.0398$. Thus if $\alpha > 0.0398$, conclude the difference is significant. If $\alpha < 0.0398$, conclude the difference is not significant.

**11.14** The computer ANOVA output is:

| SOURCE | SUM OF SQUARES | DF | MEAN SQUARE | F RATIO | PROB. |
|---|---|---|---|---|---|
| COLS | 44.444 | 2 | 22.222 | 1.262 | 0.3181 |
| ROWS | 2.722 | 1 | 2.722 | 0.155 | 0.7011 |
| INTERACTION | 28.444 | 2 | 14.222 | 0.808 | 0.4688 |
| ERROR | 211.333 | 12 | 17.611 | | |
| TOTAL | 286.944 | 17 | | | |

**11.16** The computer ANOVA output is:

| SOURCE | SUM OF SQUARES | DF | MEAN SQUARE | F RATIO | PROB. |
|---|---|---|---|---|---|
| COLS | 2.2500E-04 | 1 | 2.2500E-04 | 1.174 | 0.2999 |
| ROWS | 2.5000E-05 | 1 | 2.5000E-05 | 0.130 | 0.7243 |
| INTERACTION | 2.5000E-05 | 1 | 2.5000E-05 | 0.130 | 0.7243 |
| ERROR | 2.3000E-03 | 12 | 1.9167E-04 | | |
| TOTAL | 2.5750E-03 | 15 | | | |

Main effect: Tires
$H_0$: $\tau_1 - \tau_2 = 0$
$H_A$: $\tau_1 - \tau_2 \neq 0$

Main effect: Drivers
$H_0$: $\lambda_1 - \lambda_2 = 0$
$H_A$: $\lambda_1 - \lambda_2 \neq 0$

Interaction effect
$H_0$: $(\tau\lambda)_{1,1} = (\tau\lambda)_{1,2} = (\tau\lambda)_{2,1} = (\tau\lambda)_{2,2} = 0$
$H_A$ = At least one of the preceding interaction terms is not equal to zero.

The computer output indicated that none of the effects is significant ($H_0$ cannot be rejected). Thus conclude no difference in tires or drivers.

**11.18** The column/row means are:

| COL | MEAN | N | ROW | MEAN | N |
|---|---|---|---|---|---|
| 1 | 5.963 | 8 | 1 | 6.133 | 12 |
| 2 | 5.154 | 8 | 2 | 5.714 | 12 |
| 3 | 6.655 | 8 | | | |

CELL MEANS

| ROW | COL | MEAN | N | | | |
|---|---|---|---|---|---|---|
| 1 | 3 | 7.360 | 4 | GRAND MEAN: 5.924 | $n = 24$ |
| 2 | 3 | 5.950 | 4 | | |

Treatment effects:
Col 1: 5.963 − 5.924 = 0.039
Col 2: 5.154 − 5.924 = −0.770
Col 3: 6.655 − 5.924 = 0.731
Row 1: 6.133 − 5.924 = 0.209
Row 2: 5.714 − 5.924 = −0.210

Est. $\epsilon_{3,1,2} = 4.68 - 5.795 = -1.115$
Est. $(\tau\lambda)_{2,1} = 4.910 - 5.963 - 5.74 + 5.924 = 0.869$
$$y_{3,1,2} = \mu + \tau_1 + \lambda_2 + (\tau\lambda)_{1,2} + \epsilon_{3,1,2}$$
$$4.68 = 5.924 + 0.039 - 0.210 + 0.042 - 1.115$$

**11.20** a) Since $n - 1 = 59$, $n = 60$.

b) MSR/MSE $= 1503.001/14.613 = 102.854$
df (rows) $= 1,54$
$p$-value $= 0.000000001$ indicates there is a very small probability that $H_0: \tau_1 - \tau_2 = 0$ is true.

c) Column, row, and interaction effects are all highly significant.

**11.22** There are 3 column treatments, 2 row treatments, and 12 replications per cell.

**11.24** Both indicate the relationship between variables, using explained and unexplained variability. Both use comparable assumptions about the population. Regression analysis uses quantitative variables, while some of the variables in ANOVA are qualitative.

**11.26** In a two-factor ANOVA model, two variables are available for explaining variability. Thus SSE may be smaller for the two-factor model than for the one-factor model, which could lead to a significant column effect for the two-factor model and a nonsignificant column effect for the comparable one-factor model.

**11.28**

| GROUP | MEAN | N |
|-------|------|---|
| 1 | 34.600 | 5 |
| 2 | 39.000 | 5 |
| 3 | 28.600 | 5 |

GRAND MEAN: 34.067   $n = 15$

Estimated Column Effects:
Col 1: $34.600 - 34.067 = 0.533$
Col 2: $39.000 - 34.067 = 4.933$
Col 3: $28.600 - 34.067 = -5.467$

Est. $\epsilon_{4,3} = 19.00 - 28.60 = -9.60$
Est. $\tau_3 = 28.600 - 34.067 = -5.467$
$$y_{4,3} = \mu + \tau_3 + \epsilon_{4,3}$$
$$19 = 34.067 + (-5.467) + (-9.60)$$

**11.30** The two-factor computer output for the data in 11.29 is:

| SOURCE | SUM OF SQUARES | DF | MEAN SQUARE | F RATIO | PROB. |
|--------|----------------|-----|-------------|---------|-------|
| COLS | 0.094 | 2 | 0.047 | 0.229 | 0.7988 |
| ROWS | 0.423 | 1 | 0.423 | 2.058 | 0.1770 |
| INTERACTION | 0.065 | 2 | 0.033 | 0.160 | 0.8547 |
| ERROR | 2.468 | 12 | 0.206 | | |
| TOTAL | 3.051 | 17 | | | |

These $p$-values do not indicate a significant main effect for either cars or drivers.

**11.32**  a)  $H_0$: $\mu_{before} - \mu_{after} = 0$
$H_A$: $\mu_{before} - \mu_{after} \neq 0$

b)  Since $p = 0.0001851$, reject $H_0$.

c)  Not sensitive because the $p$-value is much smaller than typical $\alpha$-values.

**11.34**  a)  Three columns and two rows.

b)  $n = 90$

c)  The $p$-values indicate significant column, row, and interaction effects.

**11.36**  $H_0$: Each A treatment effect equals zero.
$H_0$: Each B treatment effect equals zero.
$H_0$: Two-way interaction effects all equal zero.
$H_0$: Three-way interaction effects all equal zero.
$H_0$: Four-way interaction effects all equal zero.

**11.38**  If the confidence interval overlaps zero, then the probability the two treatment means are equal is greater than $\alpha$, which implies that the treatments being compared are not significantly different from zero.

**11.40**  To test each of the three factors (A, B, and C) would require $3 \times 3 \times 3 = 27$ different combinations. The Latin square design requires only 9. Notice that all three types of wheat are tested with each level of the two factors. The pattern is a diagonal (notice that C1 runs down the main diagonal).

# CHAPTER TWELVE

**12.2**  Yes, the states might differ among people, such as sunny, cloudy, partly cloudy, rainy, snowy, hot, humid, mild, etc. This may make specifying the actions a difficult subjective task.

**12.4**  This means picking the action with the highest average payoff. One weakness is that the variability in payoffs is not considered.

**12.6**

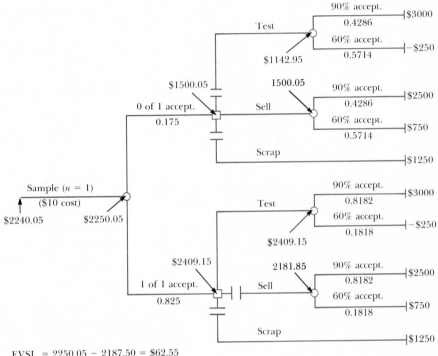

$$EVSI = 2250.05 - 2187.50 = \$62.55$$
$$ENGS = \phantom{00}62.55 - \phantom{0}10.00 = \$52.55$$

**12.8**

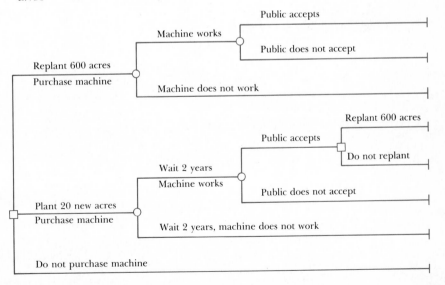

**12.10** a)

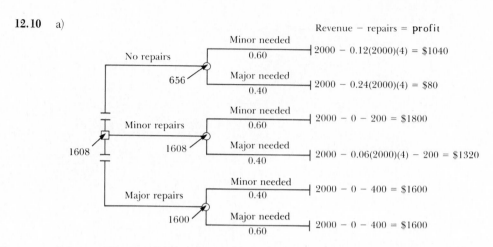

Revenue − repairs = profit

The tree can be simplified from now on by noting that no repairs can never be optimal and that major repairs always results in a payoff of $1600. A table for the calculations for $n = 1$ and $n = 2$ is given:

b)

| S. of N. | Prior | Likelihood | (Prior)(Likelihood) | Posterior |
|---|---|---|---|---|
| **$n = 1$, one defective** | | | | |
| Minor needed | 0.60 | 0.12 | 0.072 | 0.4286 |
| Major needed | 0.40 | 0.24 | 0.096 | 0.5714 |
| | | | 0.168 | 1.0000 |
| **$n = 1$, one good** | | | | |
| Minor needed | 0.60 | 0.88 | 0.528 | 0.6346 |
| Major needed | 0.40 | 0.76 | 0.304 | 0.3654 |
| | | | 0.832 | 1.0000 |
| **$n = 2$, two defectives** | | | | |
| Minor needed | 0.60 | 0.0144 | 0.00864 | 0.27273 |
| Major needed | 0.40 | 0.0576 | 0.02304 | 0.72727 |
| | | | 0.03168 | 1.00000 |
| **$n = 2$, one defective, one good** | | | | |
| Minor needed | 0.60 | 0.2112 | 0.12672 | 0.46479 |
| Major needed | 0.40 | 0.3648 | 0.14592 | 0.53521 |
| | | | 0.27264 | 1.00000 |
| **$n = 2$, two good** | | | | |
| Minor needed | 0.60 | 0.7744 | 0.46464 | 0.66789 |
| Major needed | 0.40 | 0.5776 | 0.23104 | 0.33211 |
| | | | 0.69568 | 1.00000 |

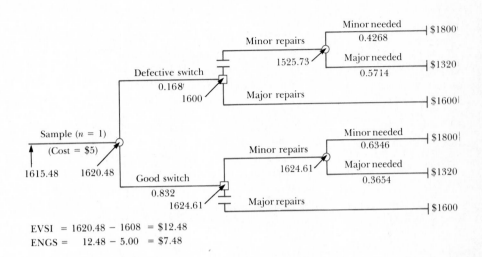

EVSI = 1620.48 − 1608 = $12.48
ENGS =    12.48 − 5.00 = $7.48

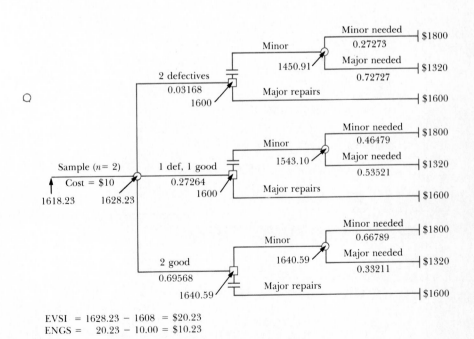

EVSI = 1628.23 − 1608 = $20.23
ENGS =    20.23 − 10.00 = $10.23

12.14    No, utilities must be substituted at the right-hand margin. Otherwise, expected values would replace payoffs, and some element of risk would be ignored.

12.16    a)   $EU = 0.50(400) + 0.50(-100) = 150$
No, $U(\$0) = \$0$, so gamble has a higher utility.

        b)   $EU = 0.50(400) + 0.50(820) = 610$
Yes, $U(\$200) = 650$, so guarantee has a higher utility.

        c)   $EU = 0.50(-100) + 0.50(900) = 400$

        d)   $EU = 0.50(900) + 0.50(400) = 650$
Utility of 650 equals about \$200.

12.18    Only three actions are viable because the monitors only action can never be optimal; it will always result in the same or a smaller payoff than the neither action.

12.20    The minimums, which occur when both suits are lost, are 425, 800, 850, and 875. The maximum of these is 875, which means the neither action maximizes the minimum payoff.

12.22    a)   EMV(50) = 275, EMV(100) = 315, EMV(150) = 308.75, EMV(200) = 281.25, EMV(250) = 215

        b)   Order 100 to maximize EMV.

12.24    A risk avoider might order 10,000 copies because the EMV of 10,000 is only slightly less than the EMV of 5,000, but it has more risk.

12.26    EMV(train) = 4040, EMV(truck) = 4192. Pick the train.

12.30    $U(\$20) = 0.50U(\$50) + 0.50U(\$10) = 0.50(100) + 0.50(50) = 75$

12.32    Yes, a person who purchases insurance and buys a lottery ticket is both risk avoiding (the insurance) and risk taking (the lottery ticket).

12.34    $U(\$0) = 0.3(0) - 0.002(0)^2 = 0$

        $U(\$80) = 0.3(80) - 0.002(80)^2 = 11.20$

        $U(\text{gamble}) = 0.50(0) + 0.50(11.2) = 5.6$

        $U(\$20) = 0.3(20) - 0.002(20)^2 = 5.20$

        The gamble has the higher utility and is thus preferred.

# CHAPTER THIRTEEN

13.2    a)   26.2

        b)   18.3

        c)    2.71

**13.4** Expected frequencies are:

| 1 | 2 | |
|---|---|---|
| 12.98 | 9.72 | |
| 17.67 | 13.23 | |
| 7.78 | 5.82 | |
| 1.77 | 1.33 | $\chi^2 = 15.873$ with 5 df |
| 8.06 | 6.04 | $p = 0.007216$ |
| 11.44 | 8.56 | |

Conclude sex and occupation are related (not independent).

**13.6** Expected frequencies are:

| | 1 | 2 | 3 | 4 |
|---|---|---|---|---|
| 1 | 25.67 | 17.05 | 29.05 | 20.24 |
| 2 | 13.39 | 8.90 | 15.15 | 10.56 |
| 3 | 69.75 | 46.33 | 78.92 | 54.99 |
| 4 | 16.74 | 11.12 | 18.94 | 13.20 |
| 5 | 11.44 | 7.60 | 12.94 | 9.02 |

$\chi^2 = 20.517$ with 12 df, $p = 0.0579$

**13.8** Use Spearman's rho for ranked data. Change to ranked data if the original variables are not normally distributed and the sample size is small.

**13.10** a) $\Sigma d_1^2 = 350$

$$r_s = 1 - \frac{6(350)}{5814} = 0.6388$$

b) $t_c = 0.6388\sqrt{(18 - 2)/(1 - 0.9348^2)} = 3.32$

Since $t_c$ exceeds the critical value of 2.120 (for 16 df), conclude there is a relationship.

**13.12** a) $\Sigma d_1^2 = 184$, $r_s = 1 - \frac{6(184)}{2184} = 0.4945$

b) $t_c = 0.4945\sqrt{(13 - 2)/(1 - 0.484^2)} = 1.8869$
$p = 0.0288$; they are significantly related if $\alpha = 0.0288$ or higher.

c) Spearman's rho uses only the rank data and makes no assumptions (e.g., normality) about the parent population.

**13.14**

| A | A | A | A | B | B | A | A | B | B | A | B | B | B |
|---|---|---|---|---|---|---|---|---|---|---|---|---|---|
| 50 | 51 | 52 | 61 | 63 | 68 | 72 | 74 | 77 | 80 | 81 | 82 | 86 | 92 |
| | | 1 | | | 2 | | 3 | | 4 | 5 | | 6 | |

The critical value for $n_1 = n_2 = 7$ is three runs. With $r = 6$, we cannot reject the null hypothesis of randomness.

**13.16**  a)  There are 11 runs to these data. Because the critical value for $n_1 = n_2 = 10$, the null hypothesis of randomness cannot be rejected.

       b)  The official might want to determine if accidents are related to one another at the intersection and then find out why.

**13.18**  There are 13 + signs and 11 − signs, with 16 runs. With $n_1 = 13$, $n_2 = 11$, the critical value is 7. Do not reject the null hypothesis of randomness.

**13.20**

| B | A | A | B | A | A | A | A | B | B | B | B | B |
|---|---|---|---|---|---|---|---|---|---|---|---|---|
| 8 | 9 | 9 | 10 | 12 | 13 | 14 | 15 | 16 | 16 | 17 | 19 | 20 |

$r_A = 31$, $r_B = 59$
$T_A = 32$, $T_B = 10$, $U = \min\{32, 10\} = 10$

The $p$-value for $n_1 = 6$, $n_2 = 7$, and $U = 10$ is 0.069 (from a table not in the text). Thus if $\alpha = 0.05$, do not reject the null hypothesis of randomness. A large $U$-value indicates the two samples were drawn from comparable populations.

**13.22**  $$t = \frac{13.92 - 11.08}{\sqrt{\dfrac{35.29(11) + 64.80(11)}{12 + 12 - 2}}} = \frac{2.84}{7.07} = 0.402$$

Do not reject $H_0$.

**13.24**  a)  The nonparametric tests do not require the assumption that the population is normally distributed.

       b)  $r_A = 143$, $r_B = 157$, $T_A = 60$, $T_B = 44$, $U = \min\{60, 44\} = 44$
          The critical value for $n_1 = n_2 = 12$ is 37. Do not reject $H_0$.

$$t = \frac{11.92 - 13.08}{\sqrt{\dfrac{56.99(11) + 46.81(11)}{12 + 12 - 2}}} = \frac{-1.16}{7.2042} = -0.1610$$

Do not reject $H_0$.

**13.26**  There are 12 + signs ($>$ 2 min) and 6 − signs ($<$ 2 min)
$P(x \le 6 | n = 18, \pi = 0.50) = 0.11894$
Do not reject the 2-min assumption.

**13.28**  $P(x \le 31 | n = 100, \pi = 0.50) = 0.0009$
Claim is not reasonable.

**13.30**  There are 6 + signs (friendliness $>$ response time) and 8 − signs.
$P(x \le 6 | n = 14, \pi = 0.50) = 0.39526$
Not significantly different.

**13.32**  There are 6 + signs and 2 − signs.
$P(x \le 2 | n = 8, \pi = 0.50) = 0.14453$

**13.34** Expected frequencies:

| 51.92 | 23.08 | 75 | |
|-------|-------|-----|---|
| 79.62 | 35.38 | 115 | $\chi^2 = 50.65$ with 2 df |
| 48.46 | 21.54 | 70 | $p = 0$ |
| 180 | 80 | 260 | |

**13.36** a)

| Ranks | 1960 | 1970 | $d^2$ |
|-------|------|------|-------|
| M + M | 4 | 4 | 0 |
| Wholesale | 2 | 1 | 1 |
| Retail | 5 | 5 | 0 |
| Construction | 3 | 3 | 0 |
| Com Service | 1 | 2 | $\frac{1}{2}$ |

$$r_s = 1 - \frac{6(2)}{5^3 - 5} = 1 - \frac{12}{120} = 0.9$$

**13.38** $r_s = 1 - \dfrac{6(12.25)}{15^3 - 15} = 0.978$

The measures differ because one $(r)$ is based on the original data, while the other $(r_s)$ is based on the ranked data.

**13.40** a) Because the sample size is small and the data highly skewed, a nonparametric test is more appropriate.

b) For the Mann-Whitney $U$ test, $r_M = 84$, $r_W = 87$, $T_M = 51$, $T_W = 29$. $U = \min\{51,29\} = 29$. The critical value for $n_1 = 10$, $n_2 = 8$ is 17; hence the null hypothesis of no difference is not rejected. There are $r = 8$ runs in these data, and the critical value is 5 runs, so again $H_0$ is accepted.

**13.42** Could use the sign test, with $\pi = 0.50$, the Mann-Whitney $U$ test, or perhaps the runs test.

**13.44** There are 7 positive signs and 8 negative signs, with 7 runs. Therefore, do not reject the null hypothesis. The residuals appear random.

**13.46** There are ten changes, six have + signs (increasing) and four have − signs. There are five runs. The critical value for $n_1 = 6$, $n_2 = 4$ is 3. Thus the null hypothesis of randomness cannot be rejected.

# INDEX

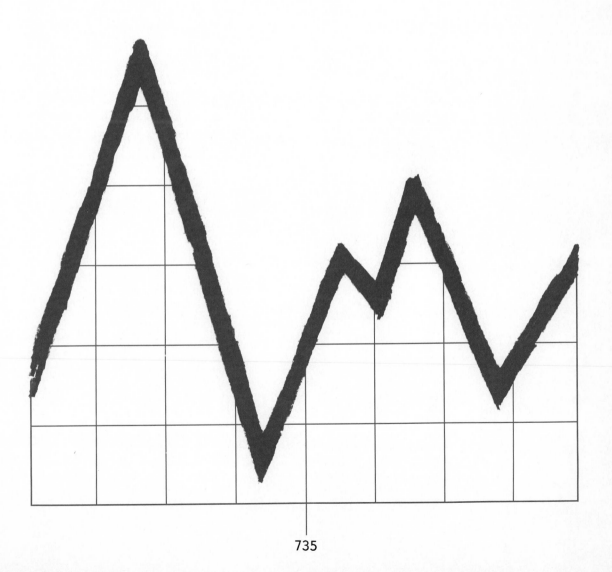

735